Frommer's®

Chicago

2004

by Elizabeth Canning Blackwell

Here's what the critics say about Frommer's:

"Amazingly easy to use. Very portable, very complete."

—*Booklist*

"Detailed, accurate, and easy-to-read information for all price ranges."
—*Glamour Magazine*

"Hotel information is close to encyclopedic."

—*Des Moines Sunday Register*

"Frommer's Guides have a way of giving you a real feel for a place."
—*Knight Ridder Newspapers*

WILEY
Wiley Publishing, Inc.

About the Author

Elizabeth Canning Blackwell began life on the East Coast, but 4 years at North-western University transformed her into a Midwesterner. She has worked as a writer and editor at *Encyclopedia Britannica,* Northwestern University Medical School, the *Chicago Tribune,* and *North Shore,* a lifestyle magazine for the Chicago suburbs. She also has written for national magazines on everything from planning the perfect wedding to fighting a duel. She lives just outside the city with her husband, daughter, and an extensive collection of long underwear.

Published by:

Wiley Publishing, Inc.

111 River St.
Hoboken, NJ 07030

ISBN 0-7645-3903-5
ISSN 1040-936X

Editor: Kendra L. Falkenstein
Production Editor: Bethany André
Cartographer: Elizabeth Puhl
Photo Editor: Richard Fox
Chapter 2 illustrations by Rashell Smith
Production by Wiley Indianapolis Composition Services

For information on our other products and services or to obtain technical support, please contact our Customer Care Department within the U.S. at 800-762-2974, outside the U.S. at 317-572-3993 or fax 317-572-4002.

Wiley also publishes its books in a variety of electronic formats. Some content that appears in print may not be available in electronic formats.

Manufactured in the United States of America

5 4 3 2 1

Contents

9 Shopping   221

10 Chicago After Dark   247

Appendix: Chicago in Depth   288

Index   300

List of Maps

An Invitation to the Reader

In researching this book, we discovered many wonderful places—hotels, restaurants, shops, and more. We're sure you'll find others. Please tell us about them, so we can share the information with your fellow travelers in upcoming editions. If you were disappointed with a recommendation, we'd love to know that, too. Please write to:

Frommer's Chicago 2004
Wiley Publishing, Inc. • 111 River St. • Hoboken, NJ 07030

An Additional Note

Please be advised that travel information is subject to change at any time—and this is especially true of prices. We therefore suggest that you write or call ahead for confirmation when making your travel plans. The authors, editors, and publisher cannot be held responsible for the experiences of readers while traveling. Your safety is important to us, however, so we encourage you to stay alert and be aware of your surroundings. Keep a close eye on cameras, purses, and wallets, all favorite targets of thieves and pickpockets.

Other Great Guides for Your Trip:

Frommer's Memorable Walks in Chicago

Frommer's Chicago with Kids

Chicago For Dummies

The Unofficial Guide to Chicago

The Irreverent Guide to Chicago

Frommer's Portable Chicago

Frommer's USA

Frommer's Star Ratings, Icons & Abbreviations

Every hotel, restaurant, and attraction listing in this guide has been ranked for quality, value, service, amenities, and special features using a **star-rating system.** In country, state, and regional guides, we also rate towns and regions to help you narrow down your choices and budget your time accordingly. Hotels and restaurants are rated on a scale of zero (recommended) to three stars (exceptional). Attractions, shopping, nightlife, towns, and regions are rated according to the following scale: zero stars (recommended), one star (highly recommended), two stars (very highly recommended), and three stars (must-see).

In addition to the star-rating system, we also use **seven feature icons** that point you to the great deals, in-the-know advice, and unique experiences that separate travelers from tourists. Throughout the book, look for:

Finds	Special finds—those places only insiders know about
Fun Fact	Fun facts—details that make travelers more informed and their trips more fun
Kids	Best bets for kids and advice for the whole family
Moments	Special moments—those experiences that memories are made of
Overrated	Places or experiences not worth your time or money
Tips	Insider tips—great ways to save time and money
Value	Great values—where to get the best deals

The following **abbreviations** are used for credit cards:

AE	American Express	DISC	Discover	V	Visa
DC	Diners Club	MC	MasterCard		

Frommers.com

Now that you have the guidebook to a great trip, visit our website at **www.frommers.com** for travel information on more than 3,000 destinations. With features updated regularly, we give you instant access to the most current trip-planning information available. At Frommers.com, you'll also find the best prices on airfares, accommodations, and car rentals—and you can even book travel online through our travel booking partners. At Frommers.com, you'll also find the following:

- Online updates to our most popular guidebooks
- Vacation sweepstakes and contest giveaways
- Newsletter highlighting the hottest travel trends
- Online travel message boards with featured travel discussions

What's New in Chicago

PLANNING YOUR TRIP TO CHICAGO Good news for budget travelers: The new **Midway International Airport** building (© 773/838-0600) has added more gates for the discount airlines that fly here, which means more flight options for visitors. Should you be stuck here waiting for a delayed flight, the attractive food court now has outposts of independently owned Chicago restaurants, including Pegasus (Greek), Lalo's (Mexican), and Gold Coast Dogs (hot dogs).

For more details on planning your trip, see chapter 3.

WHERE TO STAY Average hotel prices have dropped somewhat in Chicago as of late, thanks to the economic climate and subsequent slowdown in business travel. Now more than ever, it pays to shop around to find the best deal.

The newest hotel on the scene is **Hotel 71,** at 71 E. Wacker Drive (© 800/621-4005 or 312/346-7100). A complete rehab of a bland 1950s high-rise, it has the soul of a boutique hotel (although with more than 400 rooms, it's far from intimate). It's a good midpriced option in the Loop, with wonderful views of the Chicago River and larger-than-average rooms.

Winter 2004 should also see the debut of the **Hard Rock Hotel** (68 E. Wacker Dr.; © 312/345-1000), just a few blocks from Hotel 71, near Michigan Avenue south of the river.

For more hotel information, see chapter 6.

WHERE TO DINE Asian fusion cuisine continues to be all the rage in Chicago.

At his namesake restaurant, **Kevin,** 9 W. Hubbard St. (© 312/595-0055), chef Kevin Shikami specializes in Asian-inspired seafood creations (his appetizer version of tuna tartare is considered one of the best in the city).

In the South Loop, Asian goes dramatic at **Opera,** 1301 S. Wabash Ave. (© 312/461-0161). Although the restaurant's upscale take on Chinese cuisine has gotten raves, the bold red-and-gold decor makes this place a feast for the eyes as well as the palate.

You'll find the city's only upscale, modern twist on Indian cuisine at **Monsoon,** 2813 N. Broadway (© 773/665-9463), in Lincoln Park. The combination of fine-dining ingredients (lobster, Cornish hen) and Indian flavors should spice up even the most jaded taste buds.

If your tastes run more traditional, try **South Water Kitchen,** 225 N. Wabash Ave. (© 888/306-3507). This Loop newcomer serves up an all-American mix of comfort foods in a setting that recalls an old-fashioned city saloon. One of the most family-friendly downtown spots, South Water Kitchen even has a kids' menu.

See chapter 7 for more on Chicago restaurants.

EXPLORING CHICAGO So what if it's been 4 years since we celebrated the arrival of the new millennium— the much-delayed **Millennium Park** has finally taken shape at the north end of Grant Park along Michigan Avenue. The dramatic centerpiece of the park is a Frank Gehry–designed music pavilion, the home of free summer music concerts by the Grant Park Symphony Orchestra.

The **Shedd Aquarium** has opened a major new exhibit, **Wild Reef—Sharks at Shedd** (1200 S. Lake Shore Dr.; © **312/939-2438**), which is made up of 26 interconnected habitats that bring visitors up close and personal with these toothy predators and other sea creatures.

Animal lovers should also check out the **Lincoln Park Zoo** (2200 N. Cannon Dr., at Fullerton Pkwy.; © **312/742-2000**), home to the recently opened **Regenstein African Journey,** where visitors can stroll through the habitats of elephants, giraffes, hippos, and other large mammals, and kids can test their gross-out tolerance at an exhibit of hissing cockroaches.

For more details on Chicago's attractions, see chapter 8.

SHOPPING Despite gloomy economic forecasts, shoppers continue to throng the designer boutiques and bustling high-rise malls along Michigan Avenue, the city's prime shopping district. The street's newest luxury-shopping destination is **Louis Vuitton,** 919 N. Michigan Ave. (© **312/944-2010**). Yes, you can find pricey shoes and clothes here, but most shoppers go straight for the handbags and iconic gold-and-brown luggage.

If Louis Vuitton is out of your price range, you'll want to walk a few blocks south to the new **H&M,** 840 N. Michigan Ave. (© **312/867-7587**), the first Midwest outpost of the Swedish department store chain specializing in "cheap chic," with trendy looks at affordable prices.

With its sleek white decor, **Lille,** 1923 W. North Ave. (© **773/342-0563**), could be mistaken for an art gallery, but this Wicker Park home accessories store is actually a lot less intimidating than it seems at first sight. The store's mix of high style and quirky charm has attracted Chicago trendsetters. This is the place to find pieces by internationally known designers whose work is not widely available in Chicago (Lulu de Kwiatkowski handbags, Christian Tortu vases), but you'll also find plenty of inexpensive, fun objects.

For more information on shopping in Chicago, see chapter 9.

CHICAGO AFTER DARK The **Lookingglass Theatre Company,** one of the city's most creative acting troupes, has moved to a high-profile location at the Water Tower Pumping Station, 821 N. Michigan Ave. (© **312/337-0665**). Its original adaptations of great literary works are now more accessible than ever to out-of-town visitors—and well worth checking out.

To make the scene after dinner, laid-back lounges are drawing the crowds more than nightclubs. At **Domaine,** 1045 N. Rush St. (© **312/397-1045**), the over-the-top baroque decor attracts a sophisticated clientele. A small dance floor here heats up later in the evening, but reserve a table if you want to spend the evening indulging in Domaine's prime activity: people-watching.

To satisfy a sweet tooth, make your way to the "dessert bar" **Sugar,** 108 W. Kinzie St. (© **312/822-9999**). Decorated in bright, candy-inspired colors, this combination pastry shop/cocktail bar serves up elaborate dessert combinations and creative mixed drinks. If you're in a romantic mood, reserve one of the booths that can be closed off with a privacy curtain.

For more on Chicago's after-dark options, see chapter 10.

1

The Best of Chicago

Has Chicago finally gotten over its "Second City" inferiority complex? Sure looks like it. The city is booming, bursting with restaurants, hotels, and shops in every price range. The heart of downtown, formed by the "Loop" of elevated train tracks, was on life support a decade ago; now it beats with a new energy, invigorated by the renovation of some grand old theaters and nightlife options that keep office workers out well past sundown. In Grant Park, the massive Millennium Park complex—Chicago's largest public-works project in decades—has taken shape. Loft condos and trendy bistros have sprung up in formerly deserted industrial areas, creating brand-new residential neighborhoods. Walk around Chicago these days, and you'll feel an undeniable energy, a sense that the town is on a roll.

This isn't the first time Chicago has reinvented itself. From the ashes of the Great Chicago Fire in 1871, Chicagoans not only rebuilt—they reached for the heavens with the first steel-frame skyscrapers. Before too long, a frontier trading town was transformed into a center of international business, and Chicago proudly showed off its new muscle by hosting the World's Columbian Exposition in 1893, a massive fair that celebrated the 400th anniversary of Columbus's arrival in the New World. Legendary Chicago architect and urban planner Daniel Burnham summed up the city's attitude at the turn of the 19th century: "Make no little plans. They have no magic to stir men's blood."

Today Chicago continues to think big, creating such attractions as an easy-to-navigate Museum Campus; lively Navy Pier; a resurrected North Loop theater district; and a "who's who" of luxury shopping destinations along the city's fabled Magnificent Mile. A busy convention trade has sparked hotel construction, and the city's eclectic mix of restaurants has gained an international reputation, with star chefs such as Charlie Trotter and Rick Bayless showing that Chicago cuisine goes far beyond deep-dish pizza and bratwurst (although you find plenty of that too).

But the Second City complex still lurks just beneath the surface. Chicago still feels that it has something to prove. Visitors find that Chicagoans like myself will readily brag about our hometown. Get us talking, and we'll keep going, full of suggestions about what you should do and eager to help you enjoy your visit. (Remember, it's called the "Windy City" after our bombastic politicians, not our much-maligned weather.) So without further ado, let me tell you what we locals consider the quintessential Chicago experiences.

1 Frommer's Favorite Chicago Experiences

- **Studying the Skyline:** The birthplace of the modern skyscraper, Chicago is the perfect place to learn about—and appreciate— these dramatic buildings that reach for the sky. A good way to ground yourself in the city's history is to take an architectural

Chicago & Vicinity

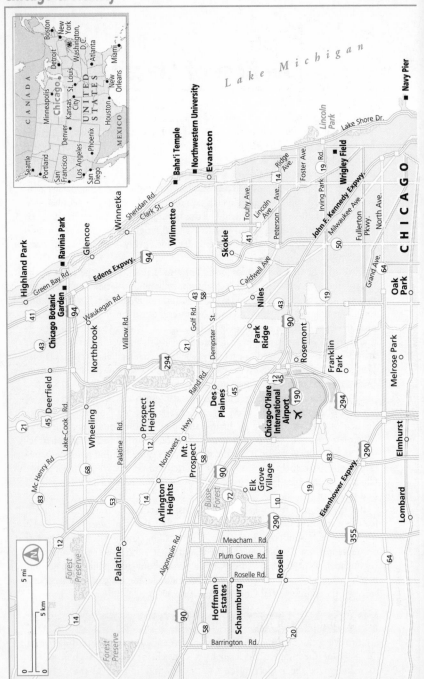

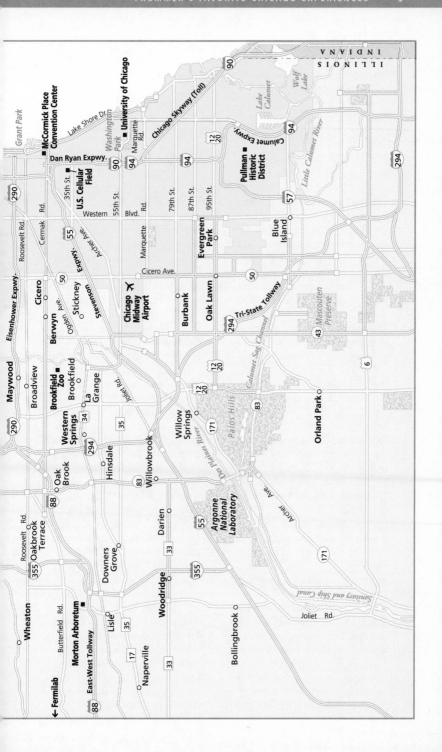

Impressions

Hog butcher for the world,
Tool maker, stacker of wheat,
Player with railroads and the nation's freight handler;
Stormy, husky, brawling,
City of the big shoulders.
                    —Carl Sandburg, "Chicago," from *Chicago Poems* (1916)

tour—by foot, bus, bike, or boat. See "Sightseeing Tours," beginning on p. 209.

- **Getting Lost at the Art Institute:** This vast art museum offers myriad places for private meditation. Internationally known for its French Impressionist collection, the Art Institute can also transport you to Renaissance Italy, ancient China, or any number of other worlds. See p. 165.

- **Chilling Out on the Lakefront:** It really is cooler by the lake—meteorologically and metaphorically. There are 29 miles of lakefront for biking, 'blading, or simply being, so get out there and contemplate Chicago's very own ocean. To experience Chicago to its fullest, don't just sit on the shore; get out on the water for a fresh look at the city. Navy Pier is the place to board a boat that's just your speed, from a powerboat to a tall-masted schooner. Or, if you feel like putting your own wind in some sails, rent one of the boats from the Chicago Sailing Club in Belmont Harbor. See the "Staying Active," section in chapter 8, beginning on p. 215.

- **Listening to Music Under the Stars:** Pack a picnic and take the train (or drive) to the Ravinia Festival in Highland Park, summer home of the Chicago Symphony, or stay in town to enjoy the free concerts presented in the city's front yard, Grant Park. See p. 205 and 249.

- **Getting the Blues:** Here in the world capital of the blues, you've got your pick of places to feel them, from the collegiate atmosphere of Kingston Mines in Lincoln Park, where musicians perform continuously on two stages, to the earthy roadhouse New Checkerboard Lounge on the South Side, where neighborhood locals mingle with the tourists, blues lovers all. See "The Music Scene," beginning on p. 262.

- **Walking the Walk:** You notice the most interesting things when you lace up your sneakers and let your curiosity power you. Explore Chicago's diversity with a neighborhood walkabout; it's one of the best ways to get a feeling for how the people here actually live, from Hispanic families in Pilsen to gay couples on Halsted Street. See "Neighborhoods in Brief," beginning on p. 66.

- **Taking in a Show:** The stage lights rarely go dark on one of the country's most bustling theater scenes, home to a downtown Broadway-style district anchored by some beautifully restored historic theaters, the nationally known Goodman Theatre company, and the city's resident Shakespeare troupe. But beyond downtown you'll also find a number of innovative independent theater companies, where future stars get their big breaks and the pure love of theater practically leaps off the stage. See "The Performing Arts," beginning on p. 247.

- **Riding the Rails:** Find out why the Loop is so named by hopping a southbound Brown Line elevated train (or "the El," for short), and watch the city unfold as the train crosses the Chicago River and screeches through downtown canyons. See "Getting Around" on p. 69 and "Sightseeing Tours" on p. 209.

- **Shopping the Town:** Chicago may have two baseball teams, but shopping is the national pastime when you're browsing and buying your way up Michigan Avenue or discovering the one-of-a-kind boutiques in Wicker Park, along Armitage Avenue, or in one of the city's other trendy enclaves. See chapter 9.

- **Taking in Some Cool Jazz at the Green Mill:** This atmospheric Uptown jazz club is the place to go to soak up some smooth sounds from some of the hottest up-and-coming performers on the jazz scene today. But don't just go for the tunes—the club, a living

museum of 1930s Chicago, is an attraction in itself. See p. 263.

- **Bonding with the Animals at Lincoln Park Zoo:** You have no excuse not to visit: The Lincoln Park Zoo is open 365 days a year and—astonishingly—remains completely free, despite many recent upgrades. Occupying a prime spot of Lincoln Park close to the lakefront, the zoo is small enough to explore in an afternoon, and varied enough to make you feel like you've traveled around the world. Most of the exhibits have been renovated in the past few years, making the place look better than ever. For families, this is a don't-miss stop. See p. 186.

- **Soaking Up Sun at Wrigley Field:** It's a Chicago tradition to play hooky for an afternoon to sit in the bleachers at this historic baseball park and watch the Cubbies try to hit 'em onto Waveland Avenue. Should the perennial losers actually win, you can celebrate at one of the neighborhood's many

The Best Chicago Websites

The **World Wide Web** makes vacation planning a snap—or should I say "click." These Chicago-based sites provide up-to-date listings on everything from restaurants to blues clubs, as well as valuable links to other sites:

- **www.metromix.com** is the *Chicago Tribune*'s entertainment-oriented site.
- **www.ci.chi.il.us/landmarks** is a city website that includes definitions of Chicago architectural styles, tour information, and maps.
- **www.chireader.com** is the site of the *Chicago Reader*, the city's alternative weekly paper.
- **www.chicago.citysearch.com** offers reviews of restaurants, bars, shows, and shops.
- **www.centerstage.net** provides entertainment reviews.
- Many of the city's performing arts groups sell tickets online through **www.ticketweb.com**, so you can reserve seats before leaving home.
- Two good general sites are **www.ci.chi.il.us/tourism** (Chicago Office of Tourism) and **www.enjoyillinois.com** (Illinois Bureau of Tourism).

watering holes. See "In the Grandstand" beginning on p. 218.

- **Getting Jurassic:** The newest resident of the Field Museum is mighty Sue, the largest T-rex skeleton ever uncovered. Standing majestically in the museum's grand entrance hall, she greets gawkers with a pointy-toothed snarl—or is it a grin? See p. 178.
- **Playing in the Sand at Oak Street Beach:** If you're staying at a North Michigan Avenue hotel, you can hit the sands of this unique urban beach about as fast as your elevator gets you to the lobby. Of course, you might not want to venture very far into the chilly waters (even in summer), but the scene offers enough peoplewatching to while away a sunny afternoon. See p. 215.
- **Exploring the Wright Stuff in Oak Park:** Seeing the earliest examples of Frank Lloyd Wright's Prairie-style homes side by side with rambling Victorian villas is an eye-opening lesson in architectural history. The town of Oak Park—with its funky shops and vibrant community spirit—makes a great side trip. See "Exploring the 'Burbs," beginning on p. 199.

2 Best Hotel Bets

Gone are the days when Chicago hotels catered mainly to a conservative, convention-going crowd. Today, the city has a hotel to suit every taste and budget, from small-but-hip North Side hideaways to luxe grandes dames (although you'll still see plenty of conventioneers at most of these places). The biggest growth has been at the luxury end of the market, with the first Chicago outposts of the Peninsula and Sofitel chains now tempting wellheeled travelers. Room rates have been on the rise—but with the recent economic slowdown, many properties seem more willing to offer special deals. For details on these and other Chicago hotels, see chapter 6.

- **Best Historic Hotel: The Drake,** 140 E. Walton Place (© **800/ 55-DRAKE**), is a master at combining the decorous charm of yesteryear with every modern convenience. See p. 93.
- **Best Rehab of Historic Structure:** The Loop's revered Reliance Building, one of the world's first glasswalled skyscrapers, has regained its dignity, thanks to a thrilling reincarnation as the tony **Hotel Burnham,** 1 W. Washington St. (© **877/294-9712**). See p. 84.
- **Best for Business Travelers:** Virtually every hotel in Chicago qualifies. The **Swissôtel Chicago,** 323 E. Wacker Dr. (© **888/737- 9477**), combines extensive business services with stunning city views from all rooms—when you need a mental break from endless paperwork. See p. 86.
- **Best Hotel Dining Experience:** Almost every luxury hotel in town has a first-class restaurant—usually with eye-popping prices. Atwood Cafe at the **Hotel Burnham,** 1 W. Washington St. (© **877/294- 9712**), offers more affordable meals in a dining room with real character. See p. 84. Looking to hang with beautiful people? Strike a pose at Wave, the Mediterraneanthemed spot in the **W Chicago Lakeshore,** 644 N. Lake Shore Dr. (© **877/W-HOTELS**). See p. 96.
- **Best Service:** The attention to detail, regal pampering, and wellconnected concierges at both the ultraluxe **Ritz-Carlton,** 160 E. Pearson St. (© **800/621-6906**),

and the **Four Seasons,** 120 E. Delaware Place (© **800/332-3442**), make them the hotels of choice for travelers who want to feel like royalty while in town. See p. 92 and 89, respectively.

- **Best for a Romantic Getaway:** For a splurge, **The Peninsula,** 108 E. Superior St. (© **866/288-8889**), or the **Park Hyatt,** 800 N. Michigan Ave. (© **800/233-1234**), will pamper you with luxurious rooms and top-notch amenities. For a cozier getaway, try the European-styled **Le Méridien,** 521 N. Rush St. (© **800/543-4300**), which is centrally located but tucked away from the crowds. See p. 90, 89, and 94, respectively.
- **Best Trendy Hotel:** The **W Chicago Lakeshore,** 644 N. Lake Shore Dr. (© **877/W-HOTELS**), brings the hip W sensibility to a can't-miss location overlooking Lake Michigan. For a theatrical hotel experience, the **House of Blues Hotel,** 333 N. Dearborn St. (© **877/569-3742**), can't be beat, with its riotous mix of colors and playful attitude. See p. 96 and 100, respectively.
- **Best Views:** This isn't an easy call. Consider several hotels for their mix of lake and city views: the **Swissôtel;** the **Four Seasons; The Drake;** the **Ritz-Carlton;** the **Park Hyatt Chicago;** and the **Holiday Inn–Chicago City Centre** (p. 86, 89, 93, 92, 89, and 98, respectively). Peering over the elevated tracks, the **Crowne Plaza**

Chicago—**The Silversmith,** 10 S. Wabash Ave. (© **800/2CROWNE**), in the Loop, offers a distinctly urban vista. See p. 81.

- **Best for Families:** With every room a suite, the **Embassy Suites,** 600 N. State St. (© **800/362-2779**), is ideal for families looking for a little more space than the typical hotel room provides. The in-room Nintendo, indoor pool, and location near two popular kid-friendly venues—ESPN Zone and the Hard Rock Cafe—should keep junior happy, too. See p. 99.
- **Best Value:** Alas, Chicago hotel prices keep surging. For the best combination of decent rates and excellent location, try the **Red Roof Inn,** 162 E. Ontario St. (© **800/733-7663**), or the **Hampton Inn & Suites,** 33 W. Illinois St. (© **800/HAMPTON**)—the latter getting bonus points for having a pool. See p. 99 and 101, respectively.
- **Best Off-the-Beaten-Path Hotels:** The **City Suites Hotel,** 933 W. Belmont Ave. (© **800/248-9108**), and the **Majestic Hotel,** 528 W. Brompton St. (© **800/727-5108**), located in residential North Side neighborhoods, are uniquely designed, cheap, and convenient to public transportation. See p. 103
- **Best Location:** Most visitors will be more than happy with the location of any hotel on the Magnificent Mile of North Michigan Avenue. See "Near North & the

---

Impressions

We were on one of the most glamorous corners of Chicago. I dwelt on the setting. The lakeshore view was stupendous. I couldn't see it but I knew it well and felt its effect—the shining road beside the shining gold vacancy of Lake Michigan. Man had overcome the emptiness of this land. But the emptiness had given him a few good licks in return.
—Saul Bellow, *Humboldt's Gift* (1975)

Impressions

By its padlocked poolrooms and its nightshade neon, by its carbon Christs punching transfers all night long; by its nuns studying gin-fizz ads in the Englewood Local, you shall know Chicago.

By nights when the yellow salamanders of the El bend all one way and the cold rain runs with the red-lit rain. By the way the city's million wires are burdened only by lightest snow; and the old year yet lighter upon them. When chairs are stacked and glasses are turned and arc-lamps all are dimmed. By days when the wind bangs alley gates ajar and the sun goes by on the wind. By nights when the moon is an only child above the measured thunder of the cars, you may know Chicago's heart at last:

You'll know it's the place built out of Man's ceaseless failure to overcome himself. Out of Man's endless war against himself we build our successes as well as our failures. Making the city of all cities most like Man himself—loneliest creation of all this very old poor earth.

—Nelson Algren, City on the Make (1951)

Magnificent Mile," beginning on p. 89.

- **Best Health Club:** The fitness center and spa at **The Peninsula,** 108 E. Superior St. (© **866/288-8889**), offer the latest workouts and skin treatments in a sparkling new setting; afterwards, you can relax on the outdoor sun deck or take a dip in the pool with stunning city views. See p. 90.

- **Best Hotel Pool:** With its dazzling all-tile junior Olympic-size pool constructed in 1929, the **Hotel Inter-Continental Chicago,** 505 N. Michigan Ave. (© **800/327-0200**), takes this award easily. See p. 94.

- **Best for Travelers with Disabilities:** The **Omni Ambassador East,** 1301 N. State Pkwy. (© 800/843-6664); **Omni Chicago Hotel,** 676 N. Michigan Ave. (© 800/843-6664); the **Four Seasons Hotel,** 120 E. Delaware Place (© 800/332-3442); and **Fairmont Hotel,** 200 N. Columbus Dr. (© **800/526-2008**, go the extra distance for guests with special needs, also providing high-tech accessories for those who are hearing- and vision-impaired. See p. 102, 95, 89, and 81, respectively.

3 Best Dining Bets

Yes, we Chicagoans do eat plenty of deep-dish pizza, but we don't stop there. Chicago is home to an ever-expanding galaxy of sophisticated restaurants whose kitchens are energized by culinary stars. The average dinner price has risen accordingly, but if you're willing to splurge, you can experience one-of-a-kind meals from some of the top chefs in the country.

Budget-minded diners can take refuge at a variety of fine ethnic restaurants, where a satisfying meal won't break the bank. For details on these and other terrific restaurants, see chapter 7.

- **Best Spot for a Romantic Dinner:** Few activities are more intimate than dipping lobster tails in fondue by candlelight at **Geja's Cafe,** 340 W. Armitage Ave.

(© 773/281-9101), with a classical guitarist playing softly in the background. See p. 145. A strong challenge is being mounted by the **North Pond,** 2610 N. Cannon Dr. (© 773/477-5845), an Arts and Crafts–styled, Midwestern-flavored restaurant with a postcard-perfect setting in Lincoln Park. Not only does it boast a dramatic vista of the Gold Coast skyline, but the restaurant's out-of-the-way locale also requires diners to begin and end their meal with an idyllic stroll through the park. See p. 145.

- **Best Spot for a Business Lunch:** A millennial take on the classic American steakhouse, stylish **Nine,** 440 W. Randolph St. (© 312/575-9900), offers super-slick environs, prime steaks, fresh seafood, a champagne-and-caviar bar, and—most importantly—tiny TV sets above the men's-room urinals for those who can't bear to miss the latest from CNBC. See p. 114.

- **Best Spot for a Celebration:** Not only does **Nacional 27,** 325 W. Huron St. (© 312/664-2727), offer a grand setting and a menu of creative Latin American dishes, it also turns into a party on Friday and Saturday nights, when a DJ spins salsa tunes and center tables are cleared for dancing. See p. 136.

- **Best Scene:** The Gold Coast's rich and beautiful flock to the bar at **Gibsons Bar & Steakhouse,** 1028 N. Rush St. (© 312/266-8999), to gossip while sipping on massive martinis. Hang out with a drink (and maybe spot a visiting celeb) while working up an appetite for a super-sized steak. See p. 125.

- **Best View:** Forty stories above Chicago, **Everest,** 440 S. LaSalle St. (© 312/663-8920), astounds with a spectacular view—and food

to match. See p. 110. Another dazzler, day or night, is the view from the **Signature Lounge** atop the 100-story John Hancock Building, 875 N. Michigan Ave. (© 312/787-7230). Though this is really a bar, not a restaurant, the Signature Lounge is a good place to perch for a drink before or after your dinner. See p. 278. Closer to earth, diners on the rooftop terrace at Greektown's **Pegasus,** 130 S. Halsted St. (© 312/226-3377), get a panoramic view of the city skyline. See p. 297.

- **Best Value:** At longtime city favorite **Carson's,** 612 N. Wells St. (© 312/280-9200), $20 gets you a full slab of incredible baby-back ribs, accompanied by a bowl of Carson's almost-as-famous coleslaw and a choice of potatoes. See p. 138. Lincoln Park residents swarm to **RoseAngelis,** 1314 W. Wrightwood Ave. (© 773/296-0081), where $20 buys a glass of wine, a massive plate of pasta, and a generous slice of possibly the city's best bread pudding. See p. 151.

- **Best for Kids:** A meal at **ESPN Zone,** 43 E. Ohio St. (© 312/475-0263). Yes, you'll find a kids' menu here, but the main attraction is the enormous Sports Arena, where kids can work off some excess energy playing the interactive games. See p. 128.

- **Best American Cuisine:** Tucked away at the edge of Randolph Street's trendy Restaurant Row, **one sixtyblue,** 1400 W. Randolph St. (© 312/850-0303), consistently delivers a refined menu that mixes American flavors and preparations with touches of practically every world cuisine. See p. 120.

- **Best French Cuisine:** For fine French dining, **Tru,** 676 N. St.

Clair St. (© **312/202-0001**), represents the perfect convergence of artful cuisine and elegant ambience. See p. 126. For a more casual Parisian cafe experience, few places delight quite like Bucktown's charming **Le Bouchon,** 1958 N. Damen Ave. (© **773/862-6600**), with its cozy atmosphere and delectable bistro fare. See p. 160.

- **Best Italian Cuisine:** Even without the glamorous view of the Magnificent Mile, **Spiaggia,** 980 N. Michigan Ave. (© **312/280-2750**), would draw diners in droves with its gourmet takes on classic Italian cuisine. See p. 126. For a more casual, old-world experience, it's hard to beat **Rosebud on Taylor,** 1500 W. Taylor St. (© **312/942-1117**), which has reigned supreme in Chicago's Little Italy neighborhood for as long as anyone can remember. See p. 296.

- **Best Steak House:** Legendary Chicago restaurateur Arnie Morton no longer prowls the dining room, but **Morton's,** 1050 N. State St. (© **312/266-4820**), remains the king of the city's old-guard steakhouses, serving up gargantuan wet-aged steaks and baked potatoes. See p. 125.

- **Best Pizza:** In the town where deep-dish pies were born, Chicagoans take their out-of-town relatives to either **Gino's East,** 633 N. Wells St. (© **312/943-1124**), or **Lou Malnati's,** 439 N. Wells St. (© **312/828-9800**), to taste the real thing: mouthwatering slabs of pizza loaded with fresh ingredients atop delectably sweet crusts. See p. 141 and 131.

- **Best Pretheater Dinner:** A local favorite, the **Italian Village,** 71 W. Monroe St. (© **312/332-7005**)—actually three restaurants run by one family under one roof—knows how to get its clientele seated and (well) fed in time for a show. See p. 117. For Chicago Symphony Orchestra audiences, **Rhapsody,** 65 E. Adams St. (© **312/786-9911**), is conveniently located in the Symphony Center building. See p. 115. If you're seeing a play in Lincoln Park, go for tasty tapas at **Café Ba-Ba-Reeba!,** 2024 N. Halsted St. (© **773/935-5000**). See p. 149.

- **Best Wine List:** Two spots take their food-drink pairings especially seriously: Try **Zealous,** 419 W. Superior St. (© **312/475-9112**), if money is no object, and **Bin 36,** 339 N. Dearborn St. (© **312/755-9463**), if you're looking for a more casual vibe. See p. 134.

- **Best Fast Food:** A few steps above the standard food court, **foodlife** in Water Tower Place, 835 N. Michigan Ave. (© **312/335-3663**), offers everything from Asian noodles and vegetarian fare to pizza and burgers. See p. 130.

- **Best Brunch:** The luxury hotels along Michigan Avenue offer all-you-can-eat gourmet spreads, but the locals prefer the funky Southern-inspired combinations at **Soul Kitchen,** 1576 N. Milwaukee Ave. (© **773/342-9742**), and the sinfully rich cinnamon rolls at **Ann Sather,** 929 W. Belmont Ave. (© **773/348-2378**). See p. 159 and 154, respectively.

4 Most Overrated Bets

- **Most Overrated Hotel:** The **Palmer House Hilton** was once the grande dame of elegant

Chicago hotels, but its glittering lobby is the only remnant of that past. Now it's basically a gathering

Impressions

He glances at the new Civic Center, a tower of russet steel and glass, fronted by a gracious plaza with a fountain and a genuine Picasso-designed metalwork sculpture almost fifty feet high. He put it all there, the Civic Center, the plaza, the Picasso. And the judges and county officials who work in the Civic Center, he put most of them there, too.

Wherever he looks as he marches, there are new skyscrapers up or going up. The city has become an architect's delight, except when the architects see the great Louis Sullivan's landmark buildings being ripped down for parking garages or allowed to degenerate into slums.

—Mike Royko, *Boss: Richard J. Daley of Chicago* (1971)

place for conventioneers. Stay here only if you get a good rate—but don't expect anything special. See p. 85.

- **Most Overrated Restaurants:** The **Cape Cod Room** and the **Pump Room** are two venerable old restaurants in venerable old hotels (The Drake and the Omni Ambassador East, respectively). Chicagoans who have been dining there for years have a soft spot for these places—understandably—but they don't offer visitors any dishes that can't be found at dozens of other places—for much more reasonable prices. See p. 124 and 125, respectively.

- **Most Overrated Entertainment:** **Steppenwolf Theatre Company** deserves much of the credit for making Chicago a thriving theater town. Its in-your-face performances in the 1970s and 1980s—featuring future stars such as John Malkovich and Gary Sinise—were truly revolutionary. Going to see a Steppenwolf show meant a guaranteed thrill ride on an emotional roller coaster. Alas, the actors that gave Steppenwolf its edge are now focusing on their movie careers.

Although names such as Sinise, Malkovich, Joan Allen, and John Mahoney are still listed as part of the Steppenwolf "company," they hardly ever appear on stage. Steppenwolf's productions are now a combination of new works and imports from New York, some impressive, some so-so. But hardly revolutionary. See p. 259.

- **Most Overrated Attraction:** The view is stunning from the **Sears Tower Skydeck**—once you finally get there. But long lines and crushed-together crowds can make you feel as if you're ready to hit the road by the time you finally reach the top. You'll enjoy the same vistas from the top of the John Hancock Building, which is usually less crowded and in a more tourist-friendly location. See p. 168.

- **Most Overrated Store:** When it opened, **Niketown** was something new, a sports-as-entertainment retail complex. Now it no longer feels so fresh; it's really just another sporting goods store with a more limited selection than most—a fact that doesn't stop the crowds from streaming in. See p. 244.

2

A Traveler's Guide to Chicago's Architecture

by Lisa Torrance

Although the Great Chicago Fire leveled almost 3 square miles of the downtown area in 1871, destroying lives and property, it did clear the stage for Chicago's emergence as the country's second city. Because the industrial base was left intact, local businessmen could afford to finance the massive rebuilding that ensued. Architects and engineers from around the nation addressed the city's need for immediate and generous office space by creating the first skyscrapers. Building innovations continued in Chicago through the turn of the 20th century and well into the next 100 years, as architects sought to follow in the footsteps of these pioneers. This chapter guides you to the best of the early buildings and the many that followed.

See the map "Chicago's Best Architecture" on p. 16 for the locations of the buildings mentioned in this chapter.

1 Richardsonian Romanesque (1870–1900)

Boston-based architect **Henry Hobson Richardson** (1838–86) explored designs and forms based on the Romanesque (a style distinguished by rounded arches, thick walls, and small windows). His structures, ranging from university and civic buildings to railroad stations and homes, were marked by a simplification of form and the elimination of extraneous ornament and historical detail—features that set his buildings apart from others of the period. The overall effect depended on mass, volume, and scale. Richardson's 1872 design for Boston's Trinity Church propelled him to national attention. In the 1880s, he completed two commissions in Chicago, the Marshall Field Wholesale Store and the John J. Glessner House, which both had a strong influence on Chicago architects, notably Louis Sullivan. For more information on Sullivan, see the box "Master Builders: Sullivan, Wright & Mies" on p. 20.

Richardsonian Romanesque buildings share the following characteristics:

- A massive quality
- Arched entrances
- Squat towers
- Deeply recessed porches and doorways
- Heavy masonry exteriors
- Use of rough-hewn stone

Richardson's **John J. Glessner House** (see illustration), 1800 S. Prairie Ave. (1885–87), an elegant urban residence, still stands on Chicago's near South Side. The influence of this structure can be seen in the **Carl C. Heisen House,** 1250 N. Lake Shore Dr. (Frank B. Abbott, 1890), and the **Mason Brayman Starring**

> ⌐ **Fun Fact** **Rival Revivals: Architectural Styles in the Late 19th Century**
>
> During the latter half of the 19th century, several architectural styles—including Romanesque Revival, Gothic Revival, Italianate, Renaissance Revival, Second Empire, and even the exotic Moorish and Egyptian Revivals—existed in Chicago. What these styles share is a certain eclecticism and picturesqueness. Mid-century architects reasoned that no age had produced the perfect architectural expression, so why not borrow freely from the best of the past and even mix different styles on the same building?
>
> Although some of these styles were popular, none became dominant. In the 1870s, technological advancements and imaginative design came together in Chicago to create the world's first skyscrapers—*the* style that would one day dominate America's downtowns.

House, 1254 N. Lake Shore Dr. (L. Gustav Hallberg, 1889), two side-by-side residences on the city's North Side, and in **Excalibur,** 632 N. Dearborn St. (formerly the Chicago Historical Society; Henry Ives Cobb, 1892). The most celebrated example of Richardson's influence is the **Auditorium Building,** 430 S. Michigan Ave. (Adler & Sullivan, 1887–89), based on the now-demolished Marshall Field Wholesale Store and an important early example of the emerging Chicago skyscraper.

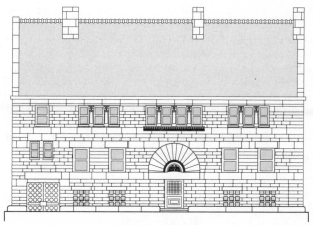

John J. Glessner House

2 Early Skyscrapers (1880–1920)

The invention of the skyscraper can be traced directly to the use of cast iron in the 1840s for storefronts, particularly in New York and later in cities such as Chicago. Experimentation with cast and wrought iron in the construction of interior skeletons eventually allowed buildings to rise higher. (Previously, buildings were restricted by the height supportable by their load-bearing walls.) Following the Great Chicago Fire of 1871, important technical innovations—involving safety elevators, electricity, fireproofing, foundations, plumbing, and

Chicago's Best Architecture

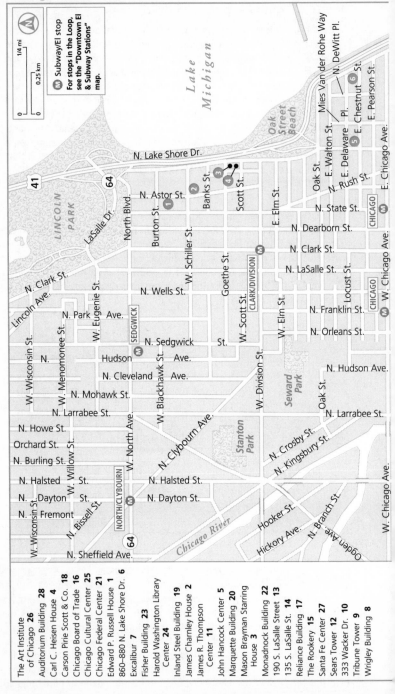

Ⓜ Subway/El stop
For stops in the Loop,
see the "Downtown El
& Subway Stations"
map.

1/4 mi

0.25 km

Lake Michigan

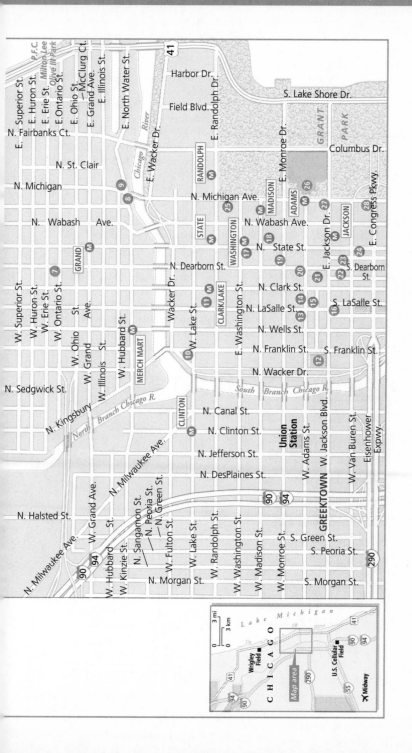

telecommunications—combined with advances in skeletal construction to create a new building type, the skyscraper. These buildings were spacious, cost-effective, efficient, and quickly erected—in short, the perfect architectural solution for Chicago's growing downtown.

Solving the technical problems of the skyscraper did not resolve how the building should look. Most solutions relied on historical precedents, including decoration reminiscent of the Romanesque, with its rounded arches; Gothic, with its spires, pointy arches, and even buttresses; or beaux arts, with its exuberant classical details. **Louis Sullivan** (1865–1924) was the first to formalize a vision of a tall building based on the parts of a classical column. His theories inspired the **Chicago school of architecture,** examples of which still fill the city's downtown.

Features of the Chicago school include:

- A rectangular shape with a flat roof
- Tripartite divisions of the facade similar to that of a classical column (see illustration) with a *base* (usually of two stories), *shaft* (midsection with a repetitive window pattern), and *capital* (typically an elaborate, terra-cotta cornice)
- Exterior expression of the building's interior skeleton through an emphasis on horizontal and vertical elements
- Large windows made possible by the development of load-bearing interior skeletons; particularly popular are *Chicago windows* (large windows flanked by two narrow ones with double-hung sashes)

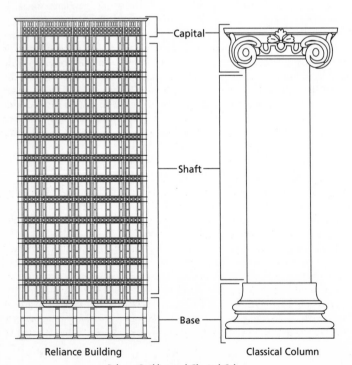

Capital

Shaft

Base

Reliance Building   Classical Column

Reliance Building and Classical Column

- Use of terra cotta, a light and fireproof material that could be cast in any shape and attached to the exterior, often for decoration

A good example of the development of the skyscraper is the **Monadnock Building,** 53 W. Jackson Blvd. (Holabird & Root, 1889–91; Holabird & Roche, 1893). Built in two parts, the northern section has masonry load-bearing walls, while the southern half has a steel frame clad in terra cotta. To support its 17 stories, the northern section has 6-foot-thick walls at its base. The entire building is notable for its clean, contemporary lines.

Three Chicago school examples are the recently restored **Reliance Building** (see illustration), now Hotel Burnham (p. 84), 1 W. Washington. (Burnham & Root and Burnham & Co., 1891–95), outstanding for its use of glass and decorative *spandrels* (the horizontal panel below a window); the **Fisher Building,** 343 S. Dearborn St. (D.H. Burnham & Co., 1896), similar in its use of glass, but with the addition of Gothic and aquatic-inspired details; and the **Marquette Building,** 140 S. Dearborn St. (Holabird & Roche, 1893–95), which exhibits all the style's features, although the terra-cotta cornice has been removed.

A good later example (taller and more technically sophisticated than their earlier incarnations) that most visitors will pass at some point during their visit is the **Tribune Tower,** 435 N. Michigan Ave. (Howells & Hood, 1923–25). The winning entry of a major design competition, this 36-story tower has the neo-Gothic detailing (flying buttresses, spires, and a tower) popularized by New York's 1913 Woolworth Building and clearly shows the characteristics mentioned above.

3 Second Renaissance Revival (1890–1920)

Buildings in this style show a definite studied formalism. A relative faithfulness to Renaissance precedents of window and doorway treatments distinguish it from the much looser adaptations of the Italianate, a mid-19th-century style that took its inspiration from Italian architecture. Scale and size, in turn, set the Second Renaissance Revival apart from the first, which occurred from about 1840 to 1890. The grand buildings of the Second Renaissance Revival, with their textural richness, well suited the tastes of the wealthy Gilded Age. The style was used primarily on the East Coast but also in Chicago for swank town houses, government buildings, and private clubs.

Typical features include:

- A cubelike structure with a massive, imposing quality
- Symmetrical arrangement of the facade, including distinct horizontal divisions
- A different stylistic treatment for each floor, with different column capitals, finishes, and window treatments on each level
- Use of *rustification* (masonry cut in massive blocks and separated from each other by deep joints) on the lowest floor
- The mixing of Greek and Roman styles on the same facade (Roman arches and arcades may appear with Greek-style windows with straight-heads or *pediments,* a low-pitched triangular feature above a window, door, or pavilion.)
- A *cornice* (a projecting feature along the roofline) supported by large brackets
- A balustrade (a railing supported by a series of short posts) above the cornice

A fine example of this style is the **Chicago Cultural Center** (see illustration), 78 E. Washington St. (Shepley, Rutan & Coolidge, 1897), originally built as a public library. This tasteful edifice, with its sumptuous decor, was constructed in part to help secure Chicago's reputation as a culture-conscious city.

Master Builders: Sullivan, Wright & Mies

Visitors from around the world flock to Chicago to see the ground-breaking work of three major architects: Sullivan, Wright, and Mies. They all lived and worked in the Windy City, leaving behind a legacy of innovative structures that still inspire architects today. Here's the rundown on each of them:

Louis Sullivan (1865–1924)

- **Quote:** "Form ever follows function."
- **Chicago buildings:** Auditorium Building, 430 S. Michigan Ave. (Adler & Sullivan, 1887–89); James Charnley House, 1365 Astor St. (Adler & Sullivan, with Frank Lloyd Wright, 1892); and Carson Pirie Scott & Co., 1 S. State St. (1899, 1903, with later additions).
- **Innovations:** Father of the Chicago school, Sullivan was perhaps at his most original in the creation of his intricate, nature-inspired ornamentation, examples of which cover the entrance to Carson Pirie Scott & Co.

Frank Lloyd Wright (1867–1959)

- **Quote:** "Nature is my manifestation of God."
- **Chicago buildings:** Frank Lloyd Wright Home & Studio, 951 Chicago Ave., Oak Park (1889–1911); Unity Temple, 875 Lake St., Oak Park (1905–08); The Rookery, 209 S. LaSalle St. (interior renovation, 1907); and Frederick C. Robie House, 5757 S. Woodlawn Ave., Hyde Park (1909).
- **Innovations:** While in Chicago, Wright developed the architecture of the Prairie School, a largely residential style combining natural materials, an intercommunication between interior and exterior spaces, and the sweeping horizontals of the Midwestern landscape. (For tours of Wright's home and studio, see "Exploring the 'Burbs," beginning on p. 199.)

Ludwig Mies van der Rohe (1886–1969)

- **Quote:** "Less is more."
- **Chicago buildings:** 860–880 N. Lake Shore Dr. (1949–51); S.R. Crown Hall, 3360 S. State St. (1956); and Chicago Federal Center, Dearborn St. between Adams St. and Jackson Blvd. (1959–74).
- **Innovations:** Mies van der Rohe brought the office tower of steel and glass to the United States. His stark facades don't immediately reveal his careful attention to details and materials. (For more on Mies van der Rohe, see this chapter's section 6, "International Style.")

Chicago Cultural Center

4 Beaux Arts (1890–1920)

This style takes its name from the Ecole des Beaux-Arts in Paris, where a number of prominent American architects (including H. H. Richardson [see section 1, "Richardsonian Romanesque (1870–1900)"] and Louis Sullivan) received their training, beginning around the mid-19th century. These architects adopted the academic principles of the Ecole, which emphasized the study of Greek and Roman structures, composition, and symmetry, and the creation of elaborate presentation drawings. Because of the idealized origins and grandiose use of classical forms, the beaux arts in America was seen as the ideal style for expressing civic pride.

In 1893, Chicago hosted the **World's Columbian Exposition,** attended by 21 million people at a time when Chicago's population was just over 1 million. Overseen by Chicagoan **Daniel H. Burnham** (1846–1912), the fairgrounds in Hyde Park were laid out in beaux-arts style with broad boulevards, fountains, and temporary ornate, white buildings, mostly by New York–based architects. (One of the few permanent structures is now the Museum of Science and Industry, p. 191.) The style created somewhat of a classical revival in Chicago and led to Burnham's spearheading of a movement to beautify America's urban areas. (In 1909, he created a plan for Chicago that forever ensured lakefront access by the public.)

Grandiose compositions, an exuberance of detail, and a variety of stone finishes typify most beaux-arts structures. Particular features include:

- A pronounced cornice topped by a *parapet* (a low wall), balustrade, or attic story
- Projecting pavilions, often with colossal columns grouped in pairs
- Windows framed by freestanding columns, a sill with a balustrade, and pediments or decorative *keystones* (the central stone of an arch)
- Grand staircases
- Grand arched openings
- Classical decoration: freestanding statuary, ornamental panels, swags, and medallions

Chicago has several beaux-arts buildings, exhibiting the style's main features. The oldest part of the **Art Institute of Chicago,** Michigan Avenue at Adams Street (Shepley, Rutan & Collidge, 1893), was built for the World's Columbian Exposition. The **Santa Fe Center,** 80 E. Jackson Blvd. (D.H. Burnham & Co., 1904), across the street from the museum, is an example of a Chicago school skyscraper with beaux-arts ornamentation (the lobby also has a very grand staircase). A later example of yet another skyscraper is the gleaming white **Wrigley Building,** 400–410 N. Michigan Ave. (Graham, Anderson, Probst & White, 1919–24), which serves as a gateway to North Michigan Avenue.

5 Art Deco (1925–33)

Art Deco is a decorative style that took its name from the Exposition Interna-
tionale des Arts Décoratif, held in Paris in 1925. One of the first widely accepted
styles not based on historic precedents (the jazzy style embodied the idea of
modernity), it influenced all areas of design, from jewelry and household goods
to cars, trains, and ocean liners.

Chevron

Art Deco buildings are characterized by a linear, hard edge or angular composition, often with
a vertical emphasis and highlighted with stylized
decoration. The Chicago zoning ordinance of
1923, which required setbacks in buildings above
a certain height to ensure that light and air could
reach the street, gave Art Deco skyscrapers their
distinctive profile. Other important features include:

- An emphasis on geometric form
- Strips of windows with decorated spandrels, adding to
  the sense of verticality
- Use of hard-edged, low-relief ornamentation around
  doors and windows
- Frequent use of marble and black and silver tones
- Decorative motifs of parallel straight lines, zigzags,
  chevrons (see illustration), and stylized florals

Chicago Board of Trade

The **Chicago Board of Trade** (see illustration), 141
W. Jackson Blvd. (Holabird & Root, 1930), punctuates
LaSalle Street with its dramatic Art Deco facade. High
atop the pyramidal roof, an aluminum statue of Ceres,
the Roman goddess of agriculture, gazes down over the
building's setbacks. **135 S. LaSalle St.** (originally the
Field Building; Graham, Anderson, Probst & White,
1934), the last major construction project in Chicago
before the Great Depression deepened, has a magnificent Art Deco lobby. A fine example of an Art Deco
town house is the **Edward P. Russell House,** 1444
N. Astor St. (Holabird & Root, 1929), in the city's
Gold Coast.

6 International Style (1932–45)

In 1932, the Museum of Modern Art in New York hosted its first architecture
exhibit, simply titled "Modern Architecture." Displays included images of International Style buildings from around the world, many designed by architects
from Germany's Bauhaus, a progressive design school. The structures all shared
a stark simplicity and vigorous functionalism, a definite break from historically
based, decorative styles.

The International Style was popularized in the United States through the
teachings and designs of **Ludwig Mies van der Rohe** (1886–1969), a German
émigré who taught and practiced architecture in Chicago after leaving the
Bauhaus school of design. Interpretations of the "Miesian" International Style
were built in most U.S. cities as late as 1980. In the 1950s, erecting an office
building in this mode made companies appear progressive. In later decades, after

the International Style was a corporate mainstay, the style took on conservative connotations.

Features of the International Style as popularized by Mies van der Rohe include:

- A rectangular shape
- Frequent use of glass
- Balance and regularity, but not symmetry
- Horizontal bands of windows
- Windows meeting at corners
- Absence of ornamentation
- Clear expression of the building's form and function (The interior structure of stacked office floors is clearly visible, as are the locations of mechanical systems, such as elevator shafts and air-conditioning units.)
- Placement, or cantilevering, of building on tall piers

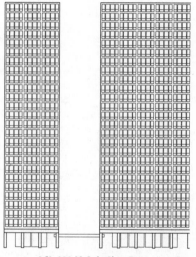

860–880 N. Lake Shore Dr.

Some famous Mies van der Rohe designs are the **Chicago Federal Center,** Dearborn Street between Adams Street and Jackson Boulevard (1959–74), and **860–880 N. Lake Shore Dr.** (1949–51; see illustration). Interesting interpretations of the style by Skidmore, Owings & Merrill, a Chicago firm that helped make the International Style a corporate staple, are the **Inland Steel Building** (1954–58), the **Sears Tower** (1968–74), and the **John Hancock Center** (1969)—the latter two impressive engineering feats rising to 110 and 100 stories, respectively.

7 Postmodern (1975–90)

After years of steel-and-glass office towers in the International Style, postmodernism burst on the scene in the 1970s with the reintroduction of historical precedents in architecture. With many feeling that the office towers of the previous style were too cold, postmodernists began to incorporate classical details and recognizable forms into their designs—often applied in outrageous proportions.

Tips Field Study

To learn more about Chicago's architecture, take a tour by foot, boat, or bus with the **Chicago Architecture Foundation.** (See "Sightseeing Tours," beginning on p. 209, for details.)

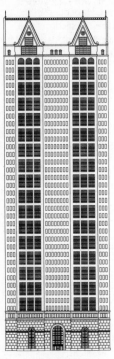

190 S. LaSalle Street

Postmodern skyscrapers tend to include:

- An overall shape (or incorporation) of a recognizable object not necessarily associated with architecture
- Classical details, such as columns, domes, or vaults, often oversized and used in inventive ways
- A distinctive profile in the skyline
- Use of stone rather than glass

190 S. LaSalle Street (John Burgee Architects with Philip Johnson, 1987; see illustration) brings the shape of a famous Chicago building back to the skyline. The overall design is that of the 1892 Masonic Temple (now razed), complete with the tripartite divisions of the Chicago school. Another amalgam of historical precedents is the **Harold Washington Library Center,** 400 S. State St. (Hammond, Beeby & Babka, 1991). An extremely modern interpretation of a three-part skyscraper—but you have to look for the divisions to find them—is **333 Wacker Dr.** (Kohn Pedersen Fox, 1979–83), an elegant, green-glass structure that curves along a bend in the Chicago River. Unlike this harmonious juxtaposition, the **James R. Thompson Center,** 100 W. Randolph St. (Murphy/Jahn, 1979–85), inventively clashes with everything around it.

3

Planning Your Trip to Chicago

After choosing a destination, most prospective travelers have two fundamental questions: "What will it cost?" and "How will I get there?" This chapter answers both of these questions and resolves other important issues—such as when to go and where to obtain more information about Chicago before you leave home and once you get there.

1 Visitor Information

The **Chicago Office of Tourism,** Chicago Cultural Center, 78 E. Washington St., Chicago, IL 60602 (℃ **312/ 744-2400** or TTY 312/744-2947; www.ci.chi.il.us/tourism), will mail you a packet of materials with information on upcoming events and attractions. The **Illinois Bureau of Tourism** (℃ **800/2CONNECT** or TTY 800/406-6418; www.enjoy illinois.com) will also send you a packet of information about Chicago and other Illinois destinations.

In addition to the above websites, which offer visitors a good deal of information, see chapter 1 for a list of the best Chicago websites.

2 Money

ATMS

The easiest and best way to get cash away from home is from an ATM (automated teller machine). The **Cirrus** (℃ **800/424-7787;** www.master card.com) and **PLUS** (℃ **800/843-7587;** www.visa.com) networks span the globe; look at the back of your bank card to see which network you're on, then call or check online for ATM locations in Chicago (they're all over the city, so you shouldn't have trouble finding one). Be sure you know your personal identification number (PIN) before you leave home and be sure to find out your daily withdrawal limit before you depart. Also keep in mind that many banks impose a fee every time a card is used at a different bank's ATM, and that fee can be higher for international transactions (up to $5 or more) than for domestic ones (where

they're rarely more than $1.50). On top of this, the bank from which you withdraw cash may charge its own fee. To compare banks' ATM fees within the U.S., use www.bankrate.com.

You can also get cash advances on your credit card at an ATM. Keep in mind that credit card companies try to protect themselves from theft by limiting the funds someone can withdraw outside their home country, so call your credit card company before you leave home.

TRAVELER'S CHECKS

Traveler's checks are something of an anachronism from the days before the ATM made cash accessible at any time. Most downtown restaurants, hotels, and shops in Chicago accept traveler's checks, and banks generally exchange them for cash (for a small fee). When you get away from downtown and the more affluent neighborhoods, however, smaller restaurants and shops may be reluctant to accept traveler's checks.

You can get traveler's checks at almost any bank. **American Express** offers denominations of $20, $50, $100, $500, and (for cardholders only) $1,000. You'll pay a service charge ranging from 1% to 4%. You can also get American Express traveler's checks over the phone by calling ☏ **800/221-7282;** Amex gold and platinum cardholders who use this number are exempt from the 1% fee.

Visa offers traveler's checks at Citibank locations nationwide, as well as at several other banks. The service charge ranges between 1.5% and 2%; checks come in denominations of $20, $50, $100, $500, and $1,000. Call ☏ **800/732-1322** for information. AAA members can obtain Visa checks without a fee at most AAA offices or by calling ☏ **866/339-3378. MasterCard** also offers traveler's

checks. Call ☏ **800/223-9920** for a location near you.

If you choose to carry traveler's checks, be sure to keep a record of their serial numbers separate from your checks in the event that they are stolen or lost. You'll get a refund faster if you know the numbers.

CREDIT CARDS
Credit cards are safe way to carry money, they provide a convenient record of all your expenses, and they generally offer good exchange rates. You can also withdraw cash advances from your credit cards at banks or ATMs, provided you know your PIN. If you've forgotten yours, or didn't even know you had one, call the number on the back of your credit card and ask the bank to send it to you. It usually takes 5 to 7 business days, though some banks will provide the number over the phone if you tell them your mother's maiden name or some other personal information.

3 When to Go

THE CLIMATE
When I tell people from more temperate climates that I live in Chicago, without fail they ask me how I handle the winters. In reality, the winters here are no worse than other northern cities, but it still isn't exactly prime tourist season. The ideal time to visit is summer or fall. Summer offers a nonstop selection of special events and outdoor activities, but you will be contending with the biggest crowds and periods of hot, muggy weather. Autumn days are generally sunny, and the crowds at major tourist attractions grow thinner—you don't have to worry about snow until late November at the earliest. Spring here is extremely unpredictable, with dramatic fluctuations of cold and warm weather, and usually lots of rain. If your top priority is indoor cultural

sights, winter's not such a bad time to visit: no lines at museums, the cheapest rates at hotels, and the pride that comes in slogging through the slush with the natives (after all, we don't hibernate at the first sign of snow).

Chicagoans like to joke that if you don't like the weather, just wait an hour—and it will change (in spring and autumn, I've been known to use my car's heat in the morning and the air-conditioning in the afternoon). The key is to be prepared for a wide range of weather with clothing that can take you from a sunny morning to a chilly, drizzly evening. As close to your departure as possible, check the local weather forecast at the websites of the Chicago Office of Tourism (www.ci.chi.il.us/tourism/weather) or the *Chicago Tribune* newspaper (www.chicagotribune.com).

Chicago's Average Temperatures & Precipitation

	Jan	Feb	Mar	Apr	May	June	July	Aug	Sept	Oct	Nov	Dec
High °F	20	34	44	59	70	79	85	82	76	64	48	35
Low °F	14	18	28	39	48	58	63	62	54	42	31	20
High °C	-7	1	7	15	21	26	29	28	24	18	9	2
Low °C	-10	-8	-2	4	9	14	17	17	12	6	-1	-7
Rainfall (in.)	1.60	1.31	2.59	3.66	3.15	4.08	3.63	3.53	3.35	2.28	2.06	2.10

CHICAGO CALENDAR OF EVENTS

The best way to stay on top of the city's current crop of special events is to ask the **Chicago Office of Tourism** (✆ **312/744-2400**; www.ci.chi.il.us/tourism) or the **Illinois Bureau of Tourism** (✆ **800/2 CONNECT**; www.enjoyillinois.com) to mail you a copy of *Chicago Calendar of Events,* an excellent quarterly publication that surveys special events, including parades and street festivals, concerts and theatrical productions, and museum exhibitions. Also ask to be sent the latest materials produced by the **Mayor's Office of Special Events** (✆ 312/744-3315, or call the Special Events Hot Line at ✆ 312/744-3370, TTY 312/744-2964; www.cityofchicago.org/specialevents), which keeps current with citywide and neighborhood festivals. The one thing you can count on, whether or not you research the topic in advance, is that you'll be able to choose from a slew of happenings, regardless of what month you visit Chicago.

Of the annual events, the most lively and unpredictable tend to revolve around the national parades and the street celebrations staged by many of Chicago's numerous ethnic groups. In addition, food, music, art, and flower fairs have their special niches in the city's yearly schedule.

Remember that new events might be added every year, and occasionally special events are discontinued or rescheduled. So, to avoid disappointment, be sure to telephone in advance to the sponsoring organization or check out the Mayor's Office of Special Events website to verify dates, times, and locations.

January

Chicago Boat, RV & Outdoor Show, McCormick Place, 23rd Street and Lake Shore Drive (✆ **312/946-6200**). All the latest boats and recreational vehicles are on display, plus trout fishing, a climbing wall, boating safety seminars, and big-time entertainment. January 21 to 25.

February

Chinese New Year Parade, Wentworth and Cermak streets (✆ **312/326-5320**). Join in as the sacred dragon whirls down the boulevard and restaurateurs pass out small envelopes of money to their regular customers. Call to verify the date, which varies from year to year.

Chicago Auto Show, McCormick Place, 23rd Street and Lake Shore Drive (✆ **630/495-2282**). More than a thousand cars and trucks, domestic and foreign, current and futuristic, are on display. The event draws nearly a million visitors. Look for special weekend packages at area hotels that include show tickets. February 6 to 15.

March

St. Patrick's Day Parade. In a city with a strong Irish heritage (and a mayor of Irish descent), this holiday is a big deal. The Chicago River is even dyed green for the occasion. The parade route is along Dearborn Street from Wacker Drive to Van Buren; the best place to view it is around Wacker and Dearborn. Saturday closest to March 17. A second, more neighborhoodlike parade is held on the South Side on the Sunday immediately following the Saturday parade, on Western Avenue from 103rd to 115th streets.

April

Opening Day. For the Cubs, call ℭ 773/404-CUBS; for the White Sox, call ℭ 312/674-1000. Make your plans early to get tickets for this eagerly awaited day. The calendar may say spring, but be warned: Opening Day is usually freezing in Chi-town (in 2003, the first home game was postponed because of snow).

May

Buckingham Fountain Color Light Show, in Grant Park, at Congress Parkway and Lake Shore Drive. The water and the ever-changing colored lights put on their show in the landmark fountain daily from May 1 to October 1, until 11pm nightly.

The Ferris Wheel and Carousel begin spinning again at Navy Pier, 600 E. Grand Ave. (ℭ 312/595-PIER). The rides operate through October. Another seasonal event along the water is the Pier Walk, a temporary installation of more than 150 large-scale sculptures displayed along the pier's South Dock. The sculptures remain on display through mid-October.

Art 2004 Chicago, one of the country's largest international contemporary art fairs, at Navy Pier's Festival Hall, 600 E. Grand Ave. (ℭ 312/587-3300 or 312/595-PIER). More than 200 art galleries and 2,000 artists participate. May 7 to 10 (Mother's Day weekend).

Wright Plus Tour (Frank Lloyd Wright Home and Studio; ℭ 708/848-1976). An annual tour of 10 buildings in Oak Park, including Frank Lloyd Wright's home and studio, the Unity Temple, and several other notable Oak Park buildings in both Prairie and Victorian styles. Tickets go on sale March 1 and can sell out within 6 weeks. Third Saturday in May.

June

Chicago Blues Festival, Petrillo Music Shell, at Jackson Drive and Columbus Drive in Grant Park (ℭ 312/744-3315). Muddy Waters would scratch his noggin over the sea of suburbanites who flood into Grant Park every summer to quaff Budweisers and accompany local legends Buddy Guy and Lonnie Brooks on air guitar. Truth be told, you can hear the same great jams and wails virtually any night of the week in one of the city's many blues clubs. Still, a thousand-voice chorus of "Sweet Home Chicago" under the stars has a rousing appeal. Blues Fest is free, with dozens of acts performing over 4 days, but get there in the afternoon to get a good spot on the lawn for the evening show. June 2 through 6.

Printers Row Book Fair, on Dearborn Street from Congress Parkway to Polk Street (ℭ 312/987-9896). One of the largest free outdoor book fairs in the country, this weekend-long event celebrates the written word with everything from readings and book signings by big-name authors to panel discussions on penning your first novel. Located within easy walking distance of the Loop, the fair also features more than 150 booksellers displaying new, used, and antiquarian books for sale; a poetry tent; and special activities for children. First weekend in June.

Ravinia Festival, Ravinia Park, in suburban Highland Park (ℭ 847/266-5100 for tickets), is the open-air summer home of the Chicago Symphony Orchestra and the venue of many first-rate visiting orchestras, chamber ensembles, pop artists, dance companies, and so forth. See also "Exploring the 'Burbs," in chapter 8. June through September.

Chicago Gospel Festival, Petrillo Music Shell, at Jackson Drive and Columbus Drive in Grant Park (© **312/744-3315**). Blues may be the city's more famous musical export, but Chicago is also the birthplace of gospel music: Thomas Dorsey, the "father of gospel music," and the greatest gospel singer ever, Mahalia Jackson, were Southsiders. This 3-day festival—the largest outdoor, free-admission event of its kind— offers music on three stages with more than 40 performances. June 11 through 13.

Boulevard Lakefront Bike Tour (Chicagoland Bicycle Federation © **312/42-PEDAL**). This 35-mile leisurely bicycle excursion is a great way to explore the city, from the neighborhoods and the lakefront to Chicago's historic link of parks and boulevards. There's also a 10-mile tour for children and families. It starts and ends at the University of Chicago in Hyde Park, which hosts the annual Bike Expo, with vendors and entertainment, on that day. A Sunday morning in mid-June.

Puerto Rican Fest, Humboldt Park, Division Street and Sacramento Boulevard (© **773/276-0200**). One of Chicago's animated Latino street celebrations, this festival includes 5 days of live music, theater, games, food, and beverages. It peaks with a parade that winds its way from Wacker Drive and Dearborn Street to the West Side Puerto Rican enclave of Humboldt Park. Mid-June.

Old Town Art Fair, historic Old Town neighborhood, at Lincoln Park West and Wisconsin Street (© **312/337-1938;** www.oldtown triangle.com). This juried fine arts fair has been drawing crowds for more than 50 years with the work of more than 200 painters, sculptors, and jewelry designers from the Midwest and around the country. It also features an art auction, a garden walk, food and drink, and children's art activities. Second full weekend in June.

Wells Street Art Festival, Wells Street from North Avenue to Division Street (© **312/951-6106**). Held on the same weekend as the more prestigious Old Town Art Fair, this arts fest is still lots of fun, with 200 arts and crafts vendors, food, music, and carnival rides. Second full weekend in June.

Summer Solstice Celebration, Museum of Contemporary Art, 220 E. Chicago Ave. (© **312/280-2660**). Party with Andy Warhol and Jackson Pollock until the sun comes up. For 24 hours straight, the MCA transforms into a madcap festival of art, dance, music, and performance activities. General admission is $5; children 12 and under are admitted free—although you may want to consider how your kids will react to a shuffling mass of bedraggled, bleary-eyed celebrants at 4 in the morning. June 18 to 19.

Jammin' at the Zoo, Lincoln Park Zoo, 2200 N. Cannon Dr., at Fullerton Parkway (© **773/742-2000**). The lovely lawn south of the zoo's Park Place Café is certainly one of the more unusual outdoor venues for rock, zydeco, and reggae music fans, who can be animals themselves at times—though, in this case, the emphasis is on family fun. The first of three summer concerts is held in late June. Ticket prices vary.

Grant Park Music Festival, Millennium Park Music Pavilion, at Randolph Street and Columbus Drive in Grant Park (© **312/742-4763**). The free outdoor musical concerts in the park begin the last week in June and continue through August.

Chicago Country Music Festival, Petrillo Music Shell, at Jackson Drive and Columbus Drive in Grant Park (☎ 312/744-3315). Y'all might not think fans of Garth Brooks and Trisha Yearwood would thrive in these northern urban climes. Think again, partner. This free event features big-name entertainers of the country-and-western genre. June 25 and 26, concurrent with the first weekend of the Taste of Chicago (see below).

Taste of Chicago, Grant Park (☎ 312/744-3315). The city claims that this is the largest free outdoor food fest in the nation. Three-and-a-half million rib and pizza lovers feeding at this colossal alfresco trough say they're right. Over 10 days of feasting in the streets, scores of Chicago restaurants cart their fare to food stands set up throughout the park. To avoid the heaviest crowds at this event, try going weekdays earlier in the day. Claustrophobics, take note: If you're here the evening of July 3, when Chicago launches its Independence Day fireworks, pick out a vantage point farther north on the lakefront—unless dodging sweaty limbs, spilled beer, and the occasional bottle rocket sounds adventurous to you. Admission is free; you pay for the sampling, of course. June 25 through July 4.

Gay and Lesbian Pride Parade, Halsted Street, from Belmont Avenue to Broadway, south to Diversey Parkway, and east to Lincoln Park, where a rally and music festival are held (☎ 773/348-8243). The floats and marching units have to be seen to be believed at this colorful culmination of a month of activities by Chicago's gay and lesbian community. Halsted Street is usually mobbed; take up a spot on Broadway for a better and less claustrophobic view. Last Sunday in June.

July

Independence Day Celebration (☎ 312/744-3315). The holiday is celebrated in Chicago on the third of July, concurrent with the Taste of Chicago. Concerts and fireworks are the highlights of the festivities in Grant Park. Expect huge crowds. July 3.

Sheffield Garden Walk, starting at Sheffield and Webster avenues (☎ 773/929-WALK). Here's your chance to snoop into the lush backyards of Lincoln Park homeowners. The walk isn't just for garden nuts; the bands, children's activities, and food and drink tents attract lots of swinging singles and young families. Mid-July.

Dearborn Garden Walk & Heritage Festival, North Dearborn and Astor streets (☎ 312/632-1241). A more upscale event than the Sheffield Garden Walk, this event allows regular folks to peer into private gardens on the Gold Coast, one of the most expensive and exclusive neighborhoods in the city. As you'd expect, many of yards are done up by the best landscape architects, designers, and art-world luminaries that old money can buy. There's also live music, a marketplace, and a few architectural tours on tap. Mid-July.

Old St. Patrick's World's Largest Block Party, 700 W. Adams St. at Des Plaines Avenue (☎ 312/648-1021). This annual, hugely popular blowout is hosted by the city's oldest church, an Irish Catholic landmark in the west Loop area. It can get pretty crowded, but Old St. Pat's always lands some major acts, who are presumably doing penance for skipping their Hail Marys. Six bands perform over 2 nights on two stages and attract a young, lively crowd. July 17 to 18.

Chicago SummerDance, east side of South Michigan Avenue between Balbo and Harrison streets (© **312/ 744-6630**). From July to early September, the city's Department of Cultural Affairs transforms a patch of Grant Park into a lighted outdoor dance venue on Thursday, Friday, and Saturday evenings from 6 to 9:30pm, and Sunday from 4 to 7pm; ethnic dance lessons for kids are offered Saturday from 4 to 5pm. The 3,500-square-foot dance floor provides ample room for throwing down moves while live bands play music from ballroom, jazz, klezmer, and country and western to samba, zydeco, blues, and soul. One-hour lessons are offered from 6 to 7pm. Free admission.

Chicago Yacht Club's Race to Mackinac Island has a starting line at the Monroe Street Harbor (© **312/861-7777**). The grandest of the inland water races, this 3-day competition is scheduled toward the middle of July. The public is welcome at a Friday-night party. On Saturday jockey for a good place to watch the boats set sail.

Venetian Night, from Monroe Harbor to the Adler Planetarium (© **312/744-3315**). This carnival of illuminated boats on the lake is complete with fireworks and synchronized music by the Grant Park Symphony Orchestra. Shoreline viewing is fine, but the best way to take it in is from another boat nearby, if you can swing it. Consider this a fine time to woo your sweetie with a dinner cruise. (See "Sightseeing Tours," in chapter 8.) July 24.

Taste of Lincoln Avenue, Lincoln Park, between Fullerton Avenue and Wellington Street (© **773/ 348-6784**). This is one of the largest and most popular of Chicago's many neighborhood street fairs; it features 50 bands performing music on five stages. Neighborhood restaurants man the food stands, and there's also a kids' carnival. Third weekend in July.

Newberry Library Book Fair and Bughouse Square Debates, 69 W. Walton St. and Washington Square Park (© **312/255-3501**). Over 4 days, the esteemed Newberry Library invites the masses to rifle through bins stuffed with tens of thousands of used books, most of which go for less than $2 a pop. Better than the book fair is what happens across the street in Washington Square Park: Soapbox orators re-create the days when left-wing agitators came here, with Pulitzer Prize–winning author Studs Terkel, oral historian nonpareil, emceeing the spirited chaos. Late July.

August

Oz Festival, Lincoln Park (© **773/ 929-8686**). This popular summer event celebrates "the magical spirit of Frank Baum's book *The Wizard of Oz*," with plenty for kids to enjoy (Baum lived in the Lincoln Park neighborhood). The festival takes over a grassy area along Cannon Drive on the east side of the Lincoln Park Zoo. First weekend of August.

Northalsted Market Days, on Halsted Street between Belmont Avenue and Addison Street (© **773/ 868-3010**). The largest of the city's street festivals, held in the heart of this gay neighborhood, Northalsted Market Days offers music on three stages, lots of food and offbeat merchandise, and the best people-watching of the summer. Early August.

Bud Billiken Parade and Picnic starting at 39th Street and King Drive and ending at 55th Street and Washington Park (© **312/ 225-2400**). This annual African-American celebration, which celebrates its 75th anniversary in 2004, is one of the oldest parades of its kind in the nation. It's named for the mythical figure Bud Billiken, reputedly the patron saint of "the little guy," and features the standard floats, bands, marching and military units, drill teams, and glad-handing politicians. Second Saturday in August.

Chicago Air & Water Show, North Avenue Beach (© **312/744-3315**). The U.S. Air Force Thunderbirds and Navy Seals usually make an appearance at this hugely popular, perennial aquatic and aerial spectacular. (Even if you don't plan to watch it, you can't help but experience it with jets screaming overhead all weekend.) Free admission. Because the crowds are intense, an alternative viewing spot is Oak Street Beach, along the Gold Coast. August 14 to 15.

Viva! Chicago Latin Music Festival, Petrillo Music Shell, at Jackson Drive and Columbus Drive in Grant Park (© **312/744-3370**). This musical celebration runs the gamut from salsa to mambo to the hottest Latin rock outfits. Free admission. August 21 to 22.

Chicago Jazz Festival, Petrillo Music Shell, Jackson Drive and Columbus Drive in Grant Park (© **312/744-3315**). Several national headliners are always on hand at this steamy gathering, which provides a swell end-of-summer bookend opposite the gospel and blues fests in June. The event is free; come early and stay late. August 26 to 29.

September

The art season, in conjunction with the annual Absolut Visions series of art gallery programs for the general public, begins with galleries holding their season openers in the Loop, River North, River West, and Wicker Park/Bucktown gallery districts. Call the River North Gallery District at © **312/649-0064** for details. First Friday after Labor Day.

Berghoff's Oktoberfest, Adams Street between Dearborn and State streets (© **312/427-3170**). Oktoberfest in September makes sense in Chicago, where the mercury plummets at the end of autumn. A popular 4-day beer fest with live music is sponsored by one of Chicago's oldest and best-loved restaurants, right down in the Loop at Federal Plaza. Mid-September.

Mexican Independence Day Parade, along Dearborn Street between Wacker Drive and Van Buren Street (© **312/744-3315**). Saturday in mid-September. Another parade is held the next day on 26th Street in the Little Village neighborhood (© **773/521-5387**).

World Music Festival Chicago, various locations around the city (© **312/744-6630**). The new World Music Festival is a major undertaking by the city's Department of Cultural Affairs. Held at venues around town—notably, the Chicago Cultural Center, Museum of Contemporary Art, Old Town School of Folk Music, and Hot House—the festival brings in top performers from Hungary to Sri Lanka to Zimbabwe, performing traditional, contemporary, and fusion music. Shows are a mix of free and ticketed ($10 or less) events. Call for information and to receive updates on scheduled performances. Late September.

Celtic Fest Chicago, Petrillo Music Shell, Jackson Drive and Columbus Drive in Grant Park (✆ **312/744-3315**). The city's newest music festival celebrates the music and dance of global Celtic traditions. September 11 and 12.

October

Chicago International Film Festival (✆ **312/425-9400,** or 312/332-FILM for a film schedule). The oldest U.S. festival of its kind screens films from around the world at various theaters over 2 weeks beginning the first Thursday in October.

Chicago Marathon (✆ **312/904-9800**). Sponsored by LaSalle Banks, Chicago's marathon is a major event on the international long-distance running circuit. It begins and ends in Grant Park, but obviously can be viewed from any number of vantage points along the race route. Late Sunday in October.

November

Chicago Humanities Festival takes over locations throughout downtown, from libraries to concert halls (✆ **312/661-1028;** www.chfestival.org). Over a period of 11 days, the festival presents cultural performances, readings, and symposiums tied to an annual theme (recent themes included "Brains & Beauty" and "Crime & Punishment"). Expect appearances by major authors, scholars, and

policymakers, all at a very reasonable cost ($5 per event). Early November.

Magnificent Mile Lights Festival (✆ **312/642-3570**). Beginning at dusk, a colorful parade of Disney characters makes its way south along Michigan Avenue, from Oak Street to the Chicago River, with lights being illuminated block by block as the procession passes. Carolers, elves, and minstrels appear with Santa along the avenue throughout the day and into the evening, and many of the retailers offer hot chocolate and other treats. Saturday before Thanksgiving.

Christmas Tree Lighting, Daley Center Plaza, in the Loop (✆ **312/744-3315**). The switch is flipped the day after Thanksgiving, around dusk.

December

A Christmas Carol, Goodman Theatre, 170 N. Dearborn St. (✆ **312/443-3800**). This seasonal favorite, performed for more than 2 decades, runs from about Thanksgiving to the end of December.

The *Nutcracker* ballet, Joffrey Ballet of Chicago, Auditorium Theatre, 50 E. Congress Pkwy. For tickets, call ✆ **312/559-1212** (Ticketmaster) or 312/739-0120 (Joffrey office). The esteemed company performs its Victorian-American twist on the holiday classic. The production runs 3 weeks from late Thanksgiving to mid-December.

4 Travel Insurance

Check your existing insurance policies and credit-card coverage before you buy travel insurance. You may already be covered for lost luggage, cancelled tickets, or medical expenses. The cost of travel insurance varies widely, depending on the cost and length of your trip, your age, health, and the type of trip you're taking.

TRIP-CANCELLATION INSURANCE Trip-cancellation insurance helps you get your money back if you have to back out of a trip, if you have to go home early, or if your travel supplier goes bankrupt. Allowed reasons for cancellation can range from sickness to natural disasters to the State Department declaring your destination unsafe for travel. (Insurers usually won't cover vague fears, though, as many travelers discovered who tried to cancel their trips in Oct 2001 because they were wary of flying.) In this unstable world, trip-cancellation insurance is a good buy if you're getting tickets well in advance—who knows what the state of the world, or of your airline, will be in 9 months? Insurance policy details vary, so read the fine print—and especially make sure that your airline or cruise line is on the list of carriers covered in case of bankruptcy. For information, contact one of the following insurers: **Access America** (✆ 866/807-3982; www.access america.com); **Travel Guard International** (✆ 800/826-4919; www.travel guard.com); **Travel Insured International** (✆ 800/243-3174; www.travel insured.com); and **Travelex Insurance Services** (✆ 888/457-4602; www.travelex-insurance.com).

MEDICAL INSURANCE Most health insurance policies cover you if you get sick away from home—but check, particularly if you're insured by an HMO.

LOST-LUGGAGE INSURANCE On domestic flights, checked baggage is covered up to $2,500 per ticketed passenger. On international flights (including U.S. portions of international trips), baggage is limited to approximately $9.07 per pound, up to approximately $635 per checked bag. If you plan to check items more valuable than the standard liability, see if your valuables are covered by your homeowner's policy, get baggage insurance as part of your comprehensive travel-insurance package, or buy Travel Guard's "BagTrak" product. Don't buy insurance at the airport, as it's usually overpriced. Be sure to take any valuables or irreplaceable items with you in your carry-on luggage, as many valuables (including books, money, and electronics) aren't covered by airline policies.

If your luggage is lost, immediately file a lost-luggage claim at the airport, detailing the luggage contents. For most airlines, you must report delayed, damaged, or lost baggage within 4 hours of arrival. The airlines are required to deliver luggage, once found, directly to your house or destination free of charge.

5 Health & Safety

If you get sick, consider asking your hotel concierge to recommend a local doctor—even his or her own. You can also try the emergency room at a local hospital; many have walk-in clinics for emergency cases that are not life threatening. You may not get immediate attention, but you won't pay the high price of an emergency room visit (usually a minimum of $300 just for signing your name).

If you suffer from a chronic illness, consult your doctor before your departure. For conditions like epilepsy, diabetes, or heart problems, wear a **Medic Alert Identification Tag** (✆ 800/825-3785; www.medicalert. org), which will immediately alert doctors to your condition and give them access to your records through Medic Alert's 24-hour hotline.

Pack **prescription medications** in your carry-on luggage, and carry prescription medications in their original containers, with pharmacy labels—otherwise they won't make it through airport security. Also bring along copies of your prescriptions in case you lose your pills or run out. Don't forget an extra pair of contact lenses or prescription glasses.

STAYING SAFE
Although Chicago's crime rate rivals that of any other American big city, the neighborhoods covered in this

guidebook are quite safe. Use the same precautions you would in any other major urban area: Beware of pickpockets in crowds and on the subway; don't wander through dark parks late at night; and take a taxi if you're traveling late in the evening and are unsure of how to get to your destination.

6 Specialized Travel Resources

TRAVELERS WITH DISABILITIES

Most of Chicago's sidewalks, as well as major museums and tourist attractions, are fitted with wheelchair ramps. Many hotels provide special accommodations for visitors in wheelchairs, such as ramps and large bathrooms, as well as telecommunications devices for visitors with hearing impairments; inquire when you make your reservation.

Several of the **Chicago Transit Authority**'s (CTA's) El stations on each line are fitted with elevators. Call the CTA at ℂ **312/836-7000** for a list of those that are accessible. All city buses are equipped to accommodate wheelchairs. For other questions about CTA special services, call ℂ **312/432-7025.**

For specific information on facilities for people with disabilities, call or write the **Mayor's Office for People with Disabilities,** 121 N. LaSalle St., Room 1104, Chicago, IL 60602 (ℂ **312/744-6673** for voice; 312/744-4780 for TTY). The office is staffed from 8:30am to 4:30pm Monday through Friday.

Horizons for the Blind, 16A Meadowdale Center, Carpentersville, IL 60110 (ℂ **847/836-1400**), is a social-service agency that can provide information about local hotels equipped with Braille signage and cultural attractions that offer Braille signage and special tours. The **Illinois Relay Center** enables hearing- and speech-impaired TTY callers to call individuals or businesses without TTYs 24 hours a day. Calls are confidential and billed at regular phone rates. Call TTY at ℂ **800/526-0844**

or voice 800/526-0857. The city of Chicago operates a 24-hour information service for hearing-impaired callers with TTY equipment; call ℂ **312/744-8599.**

Many travel agencies offer customized tours and itineraries for travelers with disabilities. **Flying Wheels Travel** (ℂ **507/451-5005;** www.flyingwheelstravel.com) offers escorted tours and cruises that emphasize sports and private tours in minivans with lifts. **Accessible Journeys** (ℂ **800/846-4537** or 610/521-0339; www.disabilitytravel.com) caters specifically to slow walkers and wheelchair travelers and their families and friends.

Organizations that offer assistance to disabled travelers include the **Moss-Rehab Hospital** (www.mossresourcenet.org), which provides a library of accessible-travel resources online; the **Society for Accessible Travel and Hospitality** (ℂ **212/447-7284;** www.sath.org; annual membership fees: $45 adults, $30 seniors and students), which offers a wealth of travel resources for all types of disabilities; and the **American Foundation for the Blind** (ℂ **800/232-5463;** www.afb.org), which provides information on traveling with Seeing Eye dogs.

For more information specifically targeted to travelers with disabilities, the community website **iCan** (www.icanonline.net/channels/travel/index.cfm) has destination guides and several regular columns on accessible travel. Also check out the quarterly magazine **Emerging Horizons** ($15 per year, $20 outside the U.S.; www.emerginghorizons.com); **Twin Peaks**

Press (℡ 360/694-2462; http://
disabilitybookshop.virtualave.net/blist
84.htm), offering travel-related books
for travelers with special needs; and
Open World Magazine, published by
the Society for Accessible Travel and
Hospitality (see above; subscription:
$18 per year, $35 outside the U.S.).

GAY & LESBIAN TRAVELERS

While it's not quite San Francisco,
Chicago is a very gay-friendly city.
The neighborhood commonly referred
to as "Boys Town" (roughly from
Belmont Ave. north to Irving Park
Ave., and from Halsted St. east to the
lakefront) is the center of gay nightlife
(and plenty of daytime action, too).
Gay and Lesbian Pride Week (℡ 773/
348-8243), highlighted by a lively
parade on the North Side, is a major
event on the Chicago calendar each
June. You also might want to stop by
Unabridged Books, 3251 N. Broadway (℡ 773/883-9119), an excellent
independent bookseller with a large
lesbian and gay selection. Here and
elsewhere in the Lakeview neighborhood, you can pick up several gay
publications, including the news-
weekly *Windy City Times* (www.windy
citymediagroup.com/index.html),
which publishes a useful calendar of
events, and *Gay Chicago* (www.gay
chicagomag.com), a weekly entertainment magazine. A helpful website,
with lists of community and social
groups, nightlife options, and an
events calendar, is **www.outchicago.
org. Horizon Community Services**
(℡ 773/929-HELP), a gay social-
service agency with counseling services,
support groups, and an antiviolence
project, provides referrals daily from
6pm to 10pm; you can also call the
main switchboard at ℡ 773/472-
6469 during the day.

The **International Gay & Lesbian
Travel Association (IGLTA)** (℡ 800/
448-8550 or 954/776-2626; www.
iglta.org) is the trade association for
the gay and lesbian travel industry,
and offers an online directory of gay-
and lesbian-friendly travel businesses;
go to their website and click on
"Members."

Many agencies offer tours and
travel itineraries specifically for gay
and lesbian travelers. **Above and
Beyond Tours** (℡ 800/397-2681;
www.abovebeyondtours.com) is the
exclusive gay and lesbian tour operator
for United Airlines. **Now, Voyager**
(℡ 800/255-6951; www.nowvoyager.
com) is a well-known San Francisco–
based gay-owned and -operated travel
service.

The following travel guides are
available at most travel bookstores and
gay and lesbian bookstores, or you can
order them from **Giovanni's Room**
bookstore, 1145 Pine St., Philadelphia,
PA 19107 (℡ 215/923-2960; www.
giovannisroom.com): *Out and About*
(℡ 800/929-2268 or 415/644-8044;
www.outandabout.com), which offers
guidebooks and a newsletter 10 times
a year packed with solid information
on the global gay and lesbian scene;
Spartacus International Gay Guide
(Bruno   Gmunder   Verlag)   and
*Odysseus: The International Gay
Travel Planner* (Odysseus Enterprises
Ltd.), both good annual English-
language guidebooks focused on gay
men; the *Damron* guides (Damron
Company), with separate annual
books for gay men and lesbians; and
*Gay Travel A to Z: The World of
Gay & Lesbian Travel Options at
Your Fingertips,* by Marianne Ferrari
(Ferrari Publications; Box 35575,
Phoenix, AZ 85069), a very good gay
and lesbian guidebook series.

MULTICULTURAL TRAVELERS

Chicago is a very cosmopolitan city,
with a population that is about 36%
African American, 30% white, and
26% Latino (Chicago now has the
second-largest Mexican population in
the U.S., after Los Angeles). Visitors
of all racial and ethnic groups shouldn't

expect to encounter any discrimination, especially in the downtown area. We're used to welcoming tourists and businesspeople from around the world. That said, Chicago is still extremely divided residentially along racial lines. The South Side is overwhelmingly African American, the North Side is mostly white, and Latino residents tend to settle in neighborhoods such as Pilsen, just southwest of downtown.

Travelers can explore the city's rich black heritage with a specialized tour (see "Chicago & The Great Black Migration" on p. 294, and "Neighborhood Tours" on p. 214). Visitors with an interest in Latin-American art might want to stop by the vibrant Mexican Fine Arts Center Museum in Pilsen (p. 197).

SENIOR TRAVEL

Mention the fact that you're a senior citizen when you make your travel reservations. Although all of the major U.S. airlines except America West have cancelled their senior-discount and coupon-book programs, many hotels still offer discounts for seniors. In Chicago, people over the age of 60 qualify for reduced admission to theaters, museums, and other attractions, as well as discounted fares on public transportation.

Members of **AARP** (formerly known as the American Association of Retired Persons), 601 E St. NW, Washington, DC 20049 (C **800/ 424-3410** or 202/434-2277; www. aarp.org), get discounts on hotels, airfares, and car rentals. AARP offers members a wide range of benefits, including AARP: The Magazine and a monthly newsletter. Anyone over 50 can join.

Many reliable agencies and organizations target the 50-plus market. **Elderhostel** (C **877/426-8056;** www. elderhostel.org) arranges study programs for those aged 55 and over (and a spouse or companion of any age).

Most courses last 5 to 7 days in the U.S. and many include airfare, accommodations in university dormitories or modest inns, meals, and tuition.

Recommended publications offering travel resources and discounts for seniors include: the quarterly magazine *Travel 50 & Beyond* (www.travel 50andbeyond.com); *Travel Unlimited: Uncommon Adventures for the Mature Traveler* (Avalon); *101 Tips for Mature Travelers,* available from Grand Circle Travel (C **800/221- 2610** or 617/350-7500; www.gct. com); *The 50+ Traveler's Guidebook* (St. Martin's Press); and *Unbelievably Good Deals and Great Adventures That You Absolutely Can't Get Unless You're Over 50* (McGraw-Hill).

FAMILY TRAVEL

If you have enough trouble getting your kids out of the house in the morning, dragging them thousands of miles away may seem like an insurmountable challenge. But family travel can be immensely rewarding, giving you new ways of seeing the world through smaller pairs of eyes.

Chicago is full of sightseeing opportunities and special activities geared toward children. See "Kid Stuff," in chapter 8, for information and ideas for families. Chapter 6 includes a list of the best hotel deals for families, and chapter 7 lists kid-friendly restaurants. For information on finding a babysitter, see "Fast Facts: Chicago," in chapter 5. The guidebook *Frommer's Chicago with Kids* (Wiley Publishing, Inc.) highlights the many family-friendly activities available in the city.

Familyhostel (C **800/733-9753;** www.learn.unh.edu/familyhostel) takes the whole family, including kids ages 8 to 15, on moderately priced domestic and international learning vacations. Lectures, field trips, and sightseeing tours are guided by a team of academics.

You can find good family-oriented vacation advice on the Internet from sites like the **Family Travel Network** (www.familytravelnetwork.com); **Traveling Internationally with Your Kids** (www.travelwithyourkids.com), a comprehensive site offering sound advice for long-distance and international travel with children; and **Family Travel Files** (www.thefamily travelfiles.com), which offers an online magazine and a directory of off-the-beaten-path tours and tour operators for families.

How to Take Great Trips with Your Kids (The Harvard Common Press) is full of good general advice that can apply to travel anywhere.

STUDENT TRAVEL

The best resource for students in Chicago is **STA Travel,** one of the biggest student-travel agencies in the world, which can set you up with an ID card and get you discounts on plane tickets and rail travel. You can contact the STA office in Chicago at 1160 N. State St., Chicago, IL 60610

(ⓒ 312/951-0585; fax 312/951-7437; www.sta-travel.com).

Chicago also has several hostels offering students and other travelers inexpensive, no-frills lodging. The newest is the **J. Ira & Nicki Harris Family Hostel,** 24 E. Congress Pkwy., in the Loop (ⓒ 312/360-0300; fax 312/360-0313; www.hichicago.org). Opened in 2000, it features many amenities and can help set up activities throughout the city. Other hostels open year-round include **Arlington House International Hostel,** 616 W. Arlington Place, Chicago, IL 60614 (ⓒ 800/HOSTEL-5 or 773/929-5380; fax 773/665-5485), in Lincoln Park; **Chicago International Hostel,** 6318 N. Winthrop Ave., Chicago, IL 60660 (ⓒ 773/262-1011; fax 773/262-3632), on the North Side of the city; and **International House of Chicago,** 1414 E. 59th St., Chicago, IL 60637 (ⓒ 773/753-2270; fax 773/753-1227; www2.uchicago.edu/adm-ihouse), on the University of Chicago campus in Hyde Park.

7 Planning Your Trip Online

SURFING FOR AIRFARES

The "big three" online travel agencies, **Expedia.com, Travelocity.com,** and **Orbitz.com,** sell most of the air tickets bought on the Internet. (Canadian travelers should try expedia.ca and Travelocity.ca; U.K. residents can go for expedia.co.uk and opodo.co.uk.) Each has different business deals with the airlines and may offer different fares on the same flights, so it's wise to shop around. Expedia and Travelocity will also send you **e-mail notification** when a cheap fare becomes available to your favorite destination. Of the smaller travel agency websites, **Side-Step** (www.sidestep.com) has gotten the best reviews from Frommer's authors. It's a browser add-on that purports to "search 140 sites at once,"

but in reality only beats competitors' fares as often as other sites do.

Also remember to check **airline websites,** especially those for low-fare carriers such as AirTran, ATA, and Southwest, whose fares are often misreported or simply missing from travel agency websites. Even with major airlines, you can often shave a few bucks from a fare by booking directly through the airline and avoiding a travel agency's transaction fee. But you'll get these discounts only by **booking online:** Most airlines now offer online-only fares that even their phone agents know nothing about. For the websites of airlines that fly to and from your destination, go to "Getting There," later in this chapter.

Great **last-minute deals** are available through free weekly e-mail services provided directly by the airlines. Most of these are announced on Tuesday or Wednesday and must be purchased online. Most are only valid for travel that weekend, but some (such as Southwest's) can be booked weeks or months in advance. Sign up for weekly e-mail alerts at airline websites or check megasites that compile comprehensive lists of last-minute specials, such as **Smarter Living** (smarterliving. com). For last-minute trips, **site59. com** in the U.S. and **lastminute.com** in Europe often have better deals than the major-label sites.

If you're willing to give up some control over your flight details, use an **opaque fare service** like **Priceline** (www.priceline.com; www.priceline. co.uk for Europeans) or **Hotwire** (www.hotwire.com). Both offer rock-bottom prices in exchange for travel on a "mystery airline" at a mysterious time of day, often with a mysterious change of planes en route. The mystery airlines are all major, well-known carriers—and the possibility of being sent from Philadelphia to Chicago via Tampa is remote; the airlines' routing computers have gotten a lot better than they used to be. But your chances of getting a 6am or 11pm flight are pretty high. Hotwire tells you flight prices before you buy; Priceline usually has better deals than Hotwire, but you have to play their "name our price" game. If you're new at this, the helpful folks at **BiddingForTravel** (www.biddingfortravel.com) do a good job of demystifying Priceline's prices. Priceline and Hotwire are great for flights within North America and between the U.S. and Europe. But for flights to other parts of the world, consolidators will almost always beat their fares.

For much more about airfares and savvy air-travel tips and advice, pick up a copy of *Frommer's Fly Safe, Fly Smart* (Wiley Publishing, Inc.).

SURFING FOR HOTELS

Of the "big three" sites, **Expedia** may be the best choice, thanks to its long list of special deals. **Travelocity** runs a close second. Hotel specialist sites **hotels.com** and **hoteldiscounts.com** are also reliable. An excellent free program, **TravelAxe** (www.travelaxe.net), can help you search multiple hotel

Frommers.com: The Complete Travel Resource

For an excellent travel-planning resource, we highly recommend Frommers.com (www.frommers.com). We're a little biased, of course, but we guarantee that you'll find the travel tips, reviews, monthly vacation giveaways, and online-booking capabilities thoroughly indispensable. Among the special features are our popular Message Boards, where Frommer's readers post queries and share advice (sometimes even our authors show up to answer questions); Frommers.com Newsletter, for the latest travel bargains and insider travel secrets; and Frommer's Destinations Section, where you'll get expert travel tips, hotel and dining recommendations, and advice on the sights to see for more than 3,000 destinations around the globe. When your research is done, the Online Reservations System (www.frommers.com/book_ a_trip) takes you to Frommer's preferred online partners for booking your vacation at affordable prices.

sites at once, even ones you may never have heard of.

Priceline and Hotwire are even better for hotels than for airfares; with both, you're allowed to pick the neighborhood and quality level of your hotel before offering up your money. Priceline seems to be much better at getting five-star lodging for three-star prices than at finding anything at the bottom of the scale. *Note:* Hotwire overrates its hotels by one star—what Hotwire calls a four-star is a three-star anywhere else.

SURFING FOR RENTAL CARS

For booking rental cars online, the best deals are usually found at rental-car company websites, although all the major online travel agencies also offer rental-car reservations services. Priceline and Hotwire work well for rental cars, too; the only "mystery" is which major rental company you get, and for most travelers the difference between Hertz, Avis, and Budget is negligible.

8 The 21st-Century Traveler

INTERNET ACCESS AWAY FROM HOME

Travelers have any number of ways to check their e-mail and access the Internet on the road. Of course, using your own laptop—or even a PDA (personal digital assistant) or electronic organizer with a modem—gives you the most flexibility. But even if you don't have a computer, you can still access your e-mail and even your office computer from cybercafes.

WITHOUT YOUR OWN COMPUTER

It's hard nowadays to find a city that *doesn't* have a few cybercafes. Although there's no definitive directory for cybercafes—these are independent businesses, after all—three places to start looking are at www.cybercaptive. com, www.netcafeguide.com, and www.cybercafe.com.

Aside from formal cybercafes, most youth hostels nowadays have at least one computer you can get to the Internet on. In Chicago, the public libraries offer Internet access free of charge. Avoid hotel business centers, which often charge exorbitant rates.

Most major airports now have Internet kiosks scattered throughout their gates. These kiosks, which you'll also see in shopping malls, hotel lobbies, and tourist information offices around the world, give you basic Web access for a per-minute fee that's usually higher than cybercafe prices. The kiosks' clunkiness and high price means they should be avoided whenever possible.

To retrieve your e-mail, ask your Internet Service Provider (ISP) if it has a Web-based interface tied to your existing e-mail account. If your ISP doesn't have such an interface, you can use the free mail2web service (www. mail2web.com) to view and reply to your home e-mail. For more flexibility, you may want to open a free, Web-based e-mail account with Yahoo! Mail (http://mail.yahoo.com). (Microsoft's Hotmail is another popular option, but Hotmail has severe spam problems.) Your home ISP may be able to forward your e-mail to the Web-based account automatically.

If you need to access files on your office computer, look into a service called GoToMyPC (www.gotomypc. com). The service provides a Web-based interface for you to access and manipulate a distant PC from anywhere—even a cybercafe—provided your "target" PC is on and has an always-on connection to the Internet (such as with Road Runner cable). The service offers top-quality security, but if you're worried about hackers, use your own laptop rather than a cybercafe to access the GoToMyPC system.

WITH YOUR OWN COMPUTER

Major Internet Service Providers (ISP) have **local access numbers** around the world, allowing you to go online by simply placing a local call. Check your ISP's website or call its toll-free number and ask how you can use your current account away from home, and how much it will cost.

Wherever you go, bring a **connection kit** of the right power and phone adapters, a spare phone cord, and a spare Ethernet network cable.

Most business-class hotels in Chicago offer dataports for laptop modems, and some now offer high-speed Internet access using an Ethernet network cable. You'll have to bring your own cables either way, so **call your hotel in advance** to find out what the options are.

Many business-class hotels in the U.S. also offer a form of computer-free Web browsing through the room TV set. We've successfully checked Yahoo! Mail and Hotmail on these systems.

If you have an 802.11b/**Wi-fi** card for your computer, several commercial companies have made wireless service available in airports, hotel lobbies, and coffee shops, primarily in the U.S. **T-Mobile Hotspot** (www.t-mobile.com/hotspot) serves up wireless connections at more than 1,000 Starbucks coffee shops nationwide. **Boingo** (www.boingo.com) and **Wayport** (www.wayport.com) have set up networks in airports and high-class hotel lobbies. Best of all, you don't need to be staying at the Four Seasons to use the hotel's network; just set yourself up on a nice couch in the lobby. Unfortunately, the companies' pricing policies are byzantine, with a variety of monthly, per-connection, and per-minute plans.

Community-minded individuals have also set up **free wireless networks** in major cities around the world. These networks are spotty, but you get what you (don't) pay for. Each network has a home page explaining how to set up your computer for their particular system; start your explorations at www.personaltelco.net/ index.cgi/ WirelessCommunities.

USING A CELLPHONE ACROSS THE U.S.

Just because your cellphone works at home doesn't mean it'll work elsewhere in the country (thanks to our nation's fragmented cellphone system). It's a good bet that your phone will work in a major city like Chicago, but take a look at your wireless company's coverage map on its website before heading out. If you need to stay in touch at a destination where you know your phone won't work, **rent** a phone that does from **InTouch USA** (☎ **800/872-7626;** www.intouch global.com) or a rental car location, but beware that you'll pay $1 a minute or more for airtime.

If you're not from the U.S., you'll be appalled at the poor reach of our **GSM (Global System for Mobiles) wireless network,** which is used by much of the rest of the world (see below). Your phone will probably work in Chicago; it definitely won't work in many rural areas. (To see where GSM phones work in the U.S., check out www.t-mobile.com/ coverage/national_popup.asp) And you may or may not be able to send SMS (text messaging) home—something Americans tend not to do anyway, for various cultural and technological reasons. (International budget travelers like to send text messages home because it's much cheaper than making international calls.) Assume nothing—call your wireless provider and get the full scoop. In a worst-case scenario, you can always rent a phone; InTouch USA delivers to hotels.

9 Getting There

BY PLANE

Chicago's **O'Hare International Airport** (ⓒ **773/686-2200**) has long battled with Atlanta's Hartsfield for the title of the world's busiest airport. O'Hare is located northwest of the city proper; depending on traffic, the drive to/from downtown can take anywhere from 30 minutes to more than an hour.

O'Hare has information booths in all five terminals; most are located on the baggage level. The multilingual personnel, who are outfitted in red jackets, can assist travelers with everything from arranging ground transportation to getting information about local hotels. The booths also offer a plethora of useful tourism brochures. The booths, labeled "Airport Information," are open daily from 9am to 8pm.

On the opposite end of the city, the Southwest Side, is Chicago's other major airport, **Midway International Airport** (ⓒ **773/838-0600**). A new terminal, which opened in 2001, has eased considerable crowding problems and expanded the selection of restaurants and shops. Although it's smaller than O'Hare and fewer airlines have routes here, Midway is closer to the Loop and you may be able to get a cheaper fare flying into here. (Always check fares to both airports if you want to find the best deal.) You can find the latest information on both airports at the city's Department of Aviation website: www.chicago airports.com.

Domestic carriers that fly regularly to O'Hare include **America West** (ⓒ 800/235-9292; www.americawest. com), **American** (ⓒ 800/433-7300; www.aa.com), **Continental** (ⓒ 800/ 525-0280; www.continental.com), **Delta** (ⓒ 800/221-1212; www.delta. com), **Northwest** (ⓒ 800/225-2525; www.nwa.com), **United** (ⓒ 800/241-6522; www.united.com), and **US Airways** (ⓒ 800/428-4322; www.usair ways.com). Commuter service is also provided by several regional airlines. Airlines that fly to Chicago's Midway International Airport are **AirTran** (ⓒ 800/247-8726; www.airtran. com), **ATA** (ⓒ 800/435-9282; www. ata. com), **Continental** (ⓒ 800/525-0280; www.continental.com), **Frontier** (ⓒ 800/432-1359; www.frontier airlines.com), **Northwest** (ⓒ 800/ 225-2525; www.nwa.com), and **Southwest** (ⓒ 800/435-9792; www. southwest.com). The toll-free numbers listed are for use in the United States and Canada.

GETTING INTO TOWN FROM THE AIRPORT

Taxis are plentiful at both O'Hare and Midway, but both are quite easily accessible by public transportation as well. A cab ride into the city will cost about $30 to $35 from O'Hare, and $25 to $30 from Midway.

If you're not carting enormous amounts of luggage, I would highly recommend taking public transportation, which is convenient from both airports. For $1.50, you can take the El (vernacular for the elevated train)

Fun Fact O'Hare, Oh My

Chicago's O'Hare International Airport handles more passengers and aircraft operations than any other airport in the world. Approximately 200,000 travelers pass through O'Hare each day, generating about 500,000 jobs for the region. O'Hare is completely self-supporting, requiring no local taxpayer dollars to keep it going.

straight into downtown. O'Hare is located on the Blue Line; a trip to downtown takes about 40 minutes. Trains leave every 6 to 10 minutes during the day, and every half-hour in the evening and overnight. Getting downtown from Midway is even faster; the ride on the Orange Line takes 20 to 30 minutes. (The Orange Line stops operating each night at about 11:30pm and resumes service by 5am.) Trains leave the station every 6 to 15 minutes. Both airports also have outposts for every major car-rental company (see "Getting Around," in chapter 5, for details).

Continental Airport Express (© **888/2-THEVAN** or 312/454-800; www.airportexpress.com) services most first-class hotels in Chicago with its blue-and-white vans; ticket counters are located at both airports near the baggage claim (outside Customs at the international terminal at O'Hare). For transportation to the airport, reserve a spot from one of the hotels (check with the bell captain). The cost is $20 one-way ($36 round-trip) to or from O'Hare and $15 one-way ($28 round-trip) to or from Midway. The shuttles operate from 6am to 11:30pm. For limo service from either O'Hare or Midway, call **Carey Limousine of Chicago** (© 773/763-0009), or **Chicago Limousine Services** (© 312/726-1035). Depending on the number of passengers and whether you opt for a sedan or stretch limo, the service will cost about $75 to $130, including gratuity and tax.

With 1 week's notice, **CTA paratransit** offers door-to-door lift services to and from O'Hare for travelers with disabilities. Visitors must be registered with a similar program in their home city. For information, call © **312/432-7025,** or TTY 312/917-1338.

GETTING THROUGH THE AIRPORT

With the federalization of airport security, security procedures at U.S. airports are more stable and consistent than ever. Generally, you'll be fine if you arrive at the airport **1 hour** before a domestic flight and **2 hours** before an international flight; if you show up late, tell an airline employee and he or she will probably whisk you to the front of the line.

Bring a **current, government-issued photo ID** such as a driver's license or passport, and if you've got an e-ticket, print out the **official confirmation page;** you'll need to show your confirmation at the security checkpoint, and your ID at the ticket counter or the gate. (Children under 18 do not need photo IDs for domestic flights, but the adults checking in with them need them.)

Security lines are getting shorter than they were during 2001 and 2002, but some doozies remain. If you have trouble standing for long periods of time, tell an airline employee; the airline will provide a wheelchair. Speed up security by **not wearing metal objects** such as big belt buckles or clanky earrings. If you've got metallic body parts, a note from your doctor can prevent a long chat with the security screeners. Keep in mind that only **ticketed passengers** are allowed past security, except for folks escorting disabled passengers or children.

Federalization has stabilized **what you can carry on** and **what you can't.** The general rule is that sharp things are out, nail clippers are okay, and food and beverages must be passed through the X-ray machine—but that security screeners can't make you drink from your coffee cup. Bring food in your carry-on rather than checking it, as explosive-detection machines used on checked luggage have been known to mistake food (especially chocolate, for some reason) for bombs. Travelers in the U.S. are allowed one carry-on bag, plus a "personal item" such as a purse, briefcase, or laptop bag. Carry-on hoarders can stuff all sorts of things into a laptop bag; as long as it has a laptop in it, it's still considered a personal item. The Transportation Security Administration (TSA) has issued a list of restricted items; check its website (www.tsa.gov/public/index.jsp) for details.

In 2003, the TSA will be phasing out **gate check-in** at all U.S. airports. Passengers with e-tickets and without checked bags can still beat the ticket-counter lines by using **electronic kiosks** or even **online check-in.** Ask your airline which alternatives are available, and if you're using a kiosk, bring the credit card you used to book the ticket. If you're checking bags, you will still be able to use most airlines' kiosks; again call your airline for up-to-date information. **Curbside check-in** is also a good way to avoid lines, although a few airlines still ban curbside check-in entirely; call before you go.

At press time, the TSA is also recommending that you **not lock your checked luggage** so screeners can search it by hand if necessary. The agency says to use plastic "zip ties" instead, which can be bought at hardware stores and can be easily cut off.

FLYING FOR LESS: TIPS FOR GETTING THE BEST AIRFARE

Passengers sharing the same airplane cabin rarely pay the same fare. Travelers who need to purchase tickets at the last minute, change their itinerary at a moment's notice, or fly one-way often get stuck paying the premium rate. Here are some ways to keep your airfare costs down.

- Passengers who can book their ticket **long in advance,** who can **stay over Saturday night,** or who **fly midweek** or **at less-trafficked hours** will pay a fraction of the full fare. If your schedule is flexible, say so, and ask if you can secure a cheaper fare by changing your flight plans.
- You can also save on airfares by keeping an eye out in local newspapers for **promotional specials** or **fare wars,** when airlines lower prices on their most popular routes. You rarely see fare wars offered for peak travel times, but if you can travel in the off-months, you may snag a bargain.
- Search **the Internet** for cheap fares (see "Planning Your Trip Online," earlier in this chapter).
- Join **frequent-flier clubs.** Accrue enough miles, and you'll be rewarded with free flights and elite status. It's free, and you'll get the best choice of seats, faster response to phone inquiries, and prompter service if your luggage is stolen, your flight is canceled or delayed, or if you want to change your seat. You don't need to fly to build frequent-flier miles—**frequent-flier credit cards** can provide thousands of miles for doing your everyday shopping.
- For many more tips about air travel, including a rundown of the major frequent-flier credit cards, pick up a copy of *Frommer's Fly Safe, Fly Smart* (Wiley Publishing, Inc.).

BY CAR

Interstate highways from all major points on the compass service Chicago. I-80 and I-90 approach from the east, crossing the northern sector of Illinois, with I-90 splitting off and emptying into Chicago via the Skyway and the Dan Ryan Expressway. From here, I-90 runs through Wisconsin, following a northern route to Seattle. I-55 snakes up the Mississippi Valley from the vicinity of New Orleans and enters Chicago from the west along the Stevenson Expressway, and in the opposite direction it provides an outlet to the Southwest. I-57 originates in southern Illinois and forms part of the interstate linkage to Florida and the South, connecting within Chicago on the west leg of the Dan Ryan. I-94 links Detroit with Chicago, arriving on the Calumet Expressway and leaving the city via the Kennedy Expressway en route to the Northwest.

Here are a few approximate driving distances in miles to Chicago: from **Milwaukee,** 92; from **St. Louis,** 297; from **Detroit,** 286; from **Denver,** 1,011; from **Atlanta,** 716; from **Washington, D.C.,** 715; from **New York City,** 821; and from **Los Angeles,** 2,034.

BY TRAIN

Rail passenger service has made enormous advances in service, comfort, and efficiency since the creation of Amtrak in 1971. Still, traveling great distances by train is certainly not the quickest way to go, nor always the most convenient. But many travelers still prefer it to flying or driving.

For tickets, consult your travel agent or call **Amtrak** (© **800/USA-RAIL;** www.amtrak.com). Ask the reservations agent to send you Amtrak's useful travel planner, with information on train accommodations and package tours.

When you arrive in Chicago, the train will pull into **Union Station** at 210 S. Canal St. between Adams and Jackson streets (© **312/655-2385**). Bus nos. 1, 60, 125, 151, and 156 all stop at the station, which is just west across the river from the Loop. The nearest El stop is at Clinton Street and Congress Parkway (on the Blue Line), which is a fair walk away, especially when you're carrying luggage.

10 Packages for the Independent Traveler

Before you start your search for the lowest airfare, you may want to consider booking your flight as part of a travel package. Package tours are not the same thing as escorted tours. Package tours are simply a way to buy the airfare, accommodations, and other elements of your trip (such as car rentals, airport transfers, and sometimes even activities) at the same time and often at discounted prices—kind of like one-stop shopping. Packages are sold in bulk to tour operators—who resell them to the public at a cost that usually undercuts standard rates.

One good source of package deals is the airlines themselves. Most major airlines offer air/land packages, including **American Airlines Vacations** (© 800/321-2121; www.aavacations. com), **Delta Vacations** (© 800/221-6666; www.deltavacations.com),

Continental Airlines Vacations (© 800/301-3800; www.coolvacations. com), and **United Vacations** (© 888/854-3899; www.unitedvacations.com). Several big **online travel agencies**—Expedia, Travelocity, Orbitz, Site59, and Lastminute.com—also do a brisk business in packages. If you're unsure about the pedigree of a smaller packager, check with the Better Business Bureau in the city where the company is based, or go online at www.bbb.org. If a packager won't tell you where it's based, don't fly with them.

Travel packages are also listed in the travel section of your local Sunday newspaper. Or check ads in the national travel magazines such as *Arthur Frommer's Budget Travel Magazine, Travel & Leisure, National Geographic Traveler,* and *Condé Nast Traveler.*

Package tours can vary by leaps and bounds. Some offer a better class of hotels than others. Some offer the same hotels for lower prices. Some offer flights on scheduled airlines, while others book charters. Some limit your choice of accommodations and travel days. You are often required to make a large payment up front. On the plus side, packages can save you money, offering group prices but allowing for independent travel. Some even let you add on a few guided excursions or escorted day trips (also at prices lower than if you booked them yourself) without booking an entirely escorted tour.

Before you invest in a package tour, get some answers. Ask about the **accommodations choices** and prices for each. Then look up the hotels' reviews in a Frommer's guide and check their rates for your specific dates of travel online. You'll also want to find out what **type of room** you get. If you need a certain type of room, ask for it; don't take whatever is thrown your way. Request a nonsmoking room, a quiet room, a room with a view, or whatever you fancy.

Finally, look for **hidden expenses.** Ask whether airport departure fees and taxes, for example, are included in the total cost.

11 Tips on Accommodations

SAVING ON YOUR HOTEL ROOM

The **rack rate** is the maximum rate that a hotel charges for a room. Hardly anybody pays this price, however. To lower the cost of your room:

- **Ask about special rates or other discounts.** Always ask whether a room less expensive than the first one quoted is available, or whether any special rates apply to you. You may qualify for corporate, student, military, senior, or other discounts. Mention membership in AAA, AARP, frequent-flier programs, or trade unions, which may entitle you to special deals as well. Find out the hotel policy on children—do kids stay free in the room or is there a special rate?

- **Dial direct.** When booking a room in a chain hotel, you'll often get a better deal by calling the individual hotel's reservation desk than at the chain's main number.

- **Book online.** Many hotels offer Internet-only discounts, or supply rooms to Priceline, Hotwire, or Expedia at rates much lower than the ones you can get through the hotel itself.

- **Remember the law of supply and demand.** Resort hotels are most crowded and therefore most expensive on weekends, so discounts are usually available for midweek stays. Business hotels in downtown locations are busiest during the week, so you can expect big discounts over the weekend. Many hotels have high-season and low-season prices, and booking the day after high season ends can mean big discounts.

- **Look into group or long-stay discounts.** If you come as part of a large group, you should be able to negotiate a bargain rate, since the hotel can then guarantee occupancy in a number of rooms. Likewise, if you're planning a long stay (at least 5 days), you might qualify for a discount. As a general rule, expect 1 night free after a 7-night stay.

- **Avoid excess charges and hidden costs.** When you book a room, ask whether the hotel charges for parking. Use your own cellphone, pay phones, or prepaid phone cards instead of dialing direct from hotel phones, which usually have exorbitant rates. And don't be tempted by the room's minibar offerings: Most hotels charge through the nose for water, soda, and snacks. Finally, ask about local taxes and service charges, which can increase the cost of a room by 15% or more. If a hotel insists upon tacking on a surprise "energy surcharge" that wasn't mentioned at check-in or a "resort fee" for amenities you didn't use, you can often make a case for getting it removed.

- **Book an efficiency.** A room with a kitchenette allows you to shop for groceries and cook your own meals. This is a big money saver, especially for families on long stays.
- **What's the view like?** Cost-conscious travelers may be willing to pay less for a back room facing the parking lot, especially if they don't plan to spend much time in their room.

LANDING THE BEST ROOM

Somebody has to get the best room in the house. It might as well be you. You can start by joining the hotel's frequent-guest program, which may make you eligible for upgrades. A hotel-branded credit card usually gives it owner "silver" or "gold" status in frequent-guest programs for free. Always ask about a corner room. They're often larger and quieter, with more windows and light, and they often cost the same as standard rooms. When you make your reservation, ask if the hotel is renovating; if it is, request a room away from the construction. Ask about nonsmoking rooms, rooms with views, rooms with twin, queen- or king-size beds. If you're a light sleeper, request a quiet room away from vending machines, elevators, restaurants, bars, and discos. Ask for one of the rooms that have been most recently renovated or redecorated.

If you aren't happy with your room when you arrive, say so. If another room is available, most lodgings will be willing to accommodate you.

12 Recommended Reading & Films

So many great American writers have come from Chicago, lived here during their productive years, or set their work within the city's confines that it is impossible to recommend a single book that says all there is to say about Chicago. However, here are a few suggestions to get you started.

Upton Sinclair's *The Jungle* tells the tale of a young immigrant encountering the filthy, brutal city. Its 1906 publication caused an uproar that led to the passage of the Pure Food and Drug Act. James T. Farrell's trilogy *Studs Lonigan,* published in the 1930s, explores the power of ethnic and neighborhood identity in Chicago. Other novels set in Chicago include Saul Bellow's *The Adventures of Augie March* and *Humboldt's Gift,* and Richard Wright's *Native Son.*

For an engrossing overview of the city's history, read *City of the Century* by Donald Miller (an excellent PBS special based on the book is also available on video and DVD). For a contemporary look at life in Chicago, take a look at two books that give a human face to the city's shameful public-housing history: Daniel Coyle's *Hardball: A Season in the Projects,* the true story of youngsters on a Little League baseball team from Cabrini Green; and Alex Kotlowitz's *There Are No Children Here,* a portrait of children growing up in the Robert Taylor homes.

And, of course, no one has given a voice to the people of Chicago as have the estimable Studs Terkel, whose books *Division Street: America, Working* and *Chicago* are based on interviews with Chicagoans from every neighborhood and income level; and the late newspaper columnist Mike Royko, author of perhaps the definitive account of Chicago machine politics, *Boss*. His columns have been collected in *One More Time: The Best of Mike Royko* and *For The Love of Mike: More of the Best of Mike Royko*.

Chicago became a popular setting for feature films in the 1980s and '90s. For a look at Chicago on the silver screen, check out *Ferris Bueller's Day Off* (1985), the ultimate teenage wish-fulfillment fantasy; *The Fugitive* (1993), which used the city's El trains as an effective backdrop; and *My Best Friend's Wedding* (1996). For many Chicagoans, though, the quintessential hometown movie scene is the finale to *The Blues Brothers* (1979), which features a multicar pileup in the center of downtown Daley Plaza.

4

For International Visitors

Whether it's your first visit or your tenth, a trip to the United States may require an additional degree of planning. This chapter will provide you with essential information, helpful tips, and advice for the more common problems that some visitors encounter.

1 Preparing for Your Trip

ENTRY REQUIREMENTS
Check at any U.S. embassy or consulate for current information and requirements. You can also obtain a visa application and other information online at the **U.S. State Department**'s website, at **www.travel.state.gov**.

VISAS The U.S. State Department has a **Visa Waiver Program** allowing citizens of certain countries to enter the United States without a visa for stays of up to 90 days. At press time these included Andorra, Australia, Austria, Belgium, Brunei, Denmark, Finland, France, Germany, Iceland, Ireland, Italy, Japan, Liechtenstein, Luxembourg, Monaco, the Netherlands, New Zealand, Norway, Portugal, San Marino, Singapore, Slovenia, Spain, Sweden, Switzerland, and the United Kingdom. Citizens of these countries need only a valid passport and a round-trip air or cruise ticket in their possession upon arrival. If they first enter the United States, they may also visit Mexico, Canada, Bermuda, and/or the Caribbean islands and return to the United States without a visa. Further information is available from any U.S. embassy or consulate. Canadian citizens may enter the United States without visas; they need only proof of residence.

Citizens of all other countries must have (1) a valid passport that expires at least 6 months later than the scheduled end of their visit to the United States, and (2) a tourist visa, which may be obtained without charge from any U.S. consulate.

To obtain a visa, the traveler must submit a completed application form (either in person or by mail) with a 1½-inch-square photo, and must demonstrate binding ties to a residence abroad. Usually you can obtain a visa at once or within 24 hours, but it may take longer during the summer rush from June through August. If you cannot go in person, contact the nearest U.S. embassy or consulate for directions on applying by mail. Your travel agent or airline office may also be able to provide you with visa applications and instructions. The U.S. consulate or embassy that issues your visa will determine whether you will be issued a multiple- or single-entry visa and any restrictions regarding the length of your stay.

British subjects can obtain up-to-date visa information by calling the **U.S. Embassy Visa Information Line** (© **0891/200-290**) or by visiting the "Consular Services" section of the American Embassy London's website at www.usembassy.org.uk.

Irish citizens can obtain up-to-date visa information through the **Embassy of the USA Dublin,** 42 Elgin Rd.,

Dublin 4, Ireland (℡ **353/1-668-8777;** or by checking the "Consular Services" section of the website at www.usembassy.ie.

Australian citizens can obtain up-to-date visa information by contacting the **U.S. Embassy Canberra,** Moonah Place, Yarralumla, ACT 2600 (℡ **02/6214-5600**) or by checking the U.S. Diplomatic Mission's website at http://usembassy-australia.state.gov/consular.

Citizens of **New Zealand** can obtain up-to-date visa information by contacting the **U.S. Embassy New Zealand,** 29 Fitzherbert Terrace, Thorndon, Wellington (℡ **644/472-2068**), or get the information directly from the "Services to New Zealanders" section of the website at http://usembassy.org.nz.

MEDICAL   REQUIREMENTS
Unless you're arriving from an area known to be suffering from an epidemic (particularly cholera or yellow fever), inoculations or vaccinations are not required for entry into the United States. If you have a medical condition that requires **syringe-administered medications,** carry a valid signed prescription from your physician—the Federal Aviation Administration (FAA) no longer allows airline passengers to pack syringes in their carry-on baggage without documented proof of medical need. If you have a disease that requires treatment with **narcotics,** you should also carry documented proof with you—smuggling narcotics aboard a plane is a serious offense that carries severe penalties in the U.S.

For **HIV-positive visitors,** requirements for entering the United States are somewhat vague and change frequently. According to the latest publication of *HIV and Immigrants: A Manual for AIDS Service Providers,* the Immigration and Naturalization Service (INS) doesn't require a medical exam for entry into the United States, but INS officials may stop individuals because they look sick or because they are carrying AIDS/HIV medicine.

If an HIV-positive noncitizen applies for a nonimmigrant visa, the question on the application regarding communicable diseases is tricky no matter which way it's answered. If the applicant checks "no," INS may deny the visa on the grounds that the applicant committed fraud. If the applicant checks "yes" or if INS suspects the person is HIV-positive, it will deny the visa unless the applicant asks for a special waiver for visitors. This waiver is for people visiting the United States for a short time (to attend a conference, for instance), to visit close relatives, or to receive medical treatment. It can be a confusing situation. For up-to-the-minute information, contact **AIDSinfo** (℡ **800/448-0440** or 301/519-6616 outside the U.S.; www.aidsinfo.nih.gov) or the **Gay Men's Health Crisis** (℡ **212/367-1000;** www.gmhc.org).

DRIVER'S   LICENSES
Foreign driver's licenses are mostly recognized in the U.S., although you may want to get an international driver's license if your home license is not written in English.

PASSPORT INFORMATION
Safeguard your passport in an inconspicuous, inaccessible place like a money belt. Make a copy of the critical pages, including the passport number, and store it in a safe place, separate from the passport itself. If you lose your passport, visit the nearest consulate of your native country as soon as possible for a replacement. Passport applications are downloadable from the websites listed below.

Note that the International Civil Aviation Organization (ICAO) has recommended a policy requiring that *every* individual who travels by air have his or her own passport. In response, many countries are now requiring that children must be issued their own passport to travel internationally, where before those under 16 or so may have been allowed to travel on a parent or guardian's passport.

FOR RESIDENTS OF CANADA

You can pick up a passport application at one of 28 regional passport offices or most travel agencies. Canadian children who travel must have their own passport. However, if you hold a valid Canadian passport issued before December 11, 2001, that bears the name of your child, the passport remains valid for you and your child until it expires. Passports cost C$85 for those 16 years and older (valid 5 years), C$35 for children 3 to 15 (valid 5 years), and C$20 for children under 3 (valid for 3 years). Applications, which must be accompanied by two identical passport-sized photographs and proof of Canadian citizenship, are available at travel agencies throughout Canada or from the central **Passport Office,** Department of Foreign Affairs and International Trade, Ottawa, ON K1A 0G3 (© **800/567-6868;** www.ppt.gc.ca). Processing takes 5 to 10 days if you apply in person, or about 3 weeks by mail.

FOR RESIDENTS OF THE UNITED KINGDOM

As a member of the European Union, you need a passport to travel to the United States. To pick up an application for a standard 10-year passport (5-year passport for children under 16), visit the nearest passport office, major post office, or travel agency. You can also contact the **United Kingdom Passport Service** at © **0870/571-0410** or visit its website at www.passport.gov.uk. Passports are £33 for adults and £19 for children under 16, with an additional £30 fee if you apply in person at a passport office. Processing takes about 2 weeks (1 week if you apply at a passport office).

FOR RESIDENTS OF IRELAND

You can apply for a 10-year passport, costing €57, at the **Passport Office,** Setanta Centre, Molesworth Street, Dublin 2 (© **01/671-1633;** www.irlgov.ie/iveagh). Those under age 18 and over 65 must apply for a €12 3-year passport. You can also apply at 1A South Mall, Cork (© **021/272-525**) or over the counter at most main post offices.

FOR RESIDENTS OF AUSTRALIA

You can pick up an application from your local post office or any branch of Passports Australia, but you must schedule an interview to present your application materials. Call the **Australian Passport Information Service** at © **131-232,** or visit the government website at www.passports.gov.au. Passports for adults are A$144 and for those under 18 are A$72.

FOR RESIDENTS OF NEW ZEALAND

You can pick up a passport application at any New Zealand Passports Office or download it from their website. Contact the **Passports Office** at © **0800/225-050** in New Zealand or 04/474-8100, or log on to www.passports.govt.nz. Passports for adults are NZ$80 and for children under 16, NZ$40.

CUSTOMS
WHAT YOU CAN BRING IN

Every visitor more than 21 years of age may bring in, free of duty, the following: (1) 1 liter of wine or hard liquor; (2) 200 cigarettes, 100 cigars (but not from Cuba), or 3 pounds of smoking tobacco; and (3) $100 worth of gifts. These exemptions are offered to travelers who spend at least 72 hours in the United States and who have not claimed them within the preceding 6 months. It is altogether forbidden to bring into the country foodstuffs (particularly fruit, cooked meats, and canned goods) and plants (vegetables, seeds, tropical plants, and the like). Foreign tourists may bring in or take out up to $10,000 in U.S. or foreign currency with no formalities; larger sums must be declared to U.S. Customs on entering or leaving, which includes filing form CM 4790. For more specific information regarding U.S. Customs, contact your nearest U.S. embassy or consulate, or the **U.S. Customs** office (℡ **202/927-1770** or www.customs.ustreas.gov).

WHAT YOU CAN TAKE HOME

U.K. citizens returning from a non-EU country have a customs allowance of: 200 cigarettes; 50 cigars; 250g of smoking tobacco; 2 liters of still table wine; 1 liter of spirits or strong liqueurs (over 22% volume); 2 liters of fortified wine, sparkling wine or other liqueurs; 60cc (ml) perfume; 250cc (ml) of toilet water; and £145 worth of all other goods, including gifts and souvenirs. People under 17 cannot have the tobacco or alcohol allowance. For more information, contact HM Customs & Excise at ℡ **0845/010-9000** (from outside the U.K., 020/8929-0152), or consult their website at www.hmce.gov.uk.

For a clear summary of **Canadian** rules, request the booklet *I Declare,* issued by the **Canada Customs and Revenue Agency** (℡ **800/461-9999** in Canada, or 204/983-3500; www.ccra-adrc.gc.ca). Canada allows its citizens a C$750 exemption, and you're allowed to bring back duty-free one carton of cigarettes, one can of tobacco, 40 imperial ounces of liquor, and 50 cigars. In addition, you're allowed to mail gifts to Canada valued at less than C$60 each day, provided they're unsolicited and don't contain alcohol or tobacco (write on the package "Unsolicited gift, under $60 value"). All valuables should be declared on the Y-38 form before departure from Canada, including serial numbers of valuables you already own, such as expensive foreign cameras. *Note:* The $750 exemption can only be used once a year and only after an absence of 7 days.

The duty-free allowance in **Australia** is A$400 or, for those under 18, A$200. Citizens age 18 and over can bring in 250 cigarettes or 250 grams of loose tobacco, and 1,125 milliliters of alcohol. If you're returning with valuables you already own, such as foreign-made cameras, you should file form B263. A helpful brochure available from Australian consulates or Customs offices is *Know Before You Go.* For more information, call the **Australian Customs Service** at ℡ **1300/363-263,** or log on to www.customs.gov.au.

The duty-free allowance for **New Zealand** is NZ$700. Citizens over 17 can bring in 200 cigarettes, 50 cigars, or 250 grams of tobacco (or a mixture of all three if their combined weight doesn't exceed 250g); plus 4.5 liters of wine and beer, or 1.125 liters of liquor. New Zealand currency does not carry import or export restrictions. Fill out a certificate of export, listing the valuables you are taking out of the country; that way, you can bring them back without paying duty. Most questions are answered in a free pamphlet available at New Zealand consulates and Customs offices: *New Zealand Customs Guide for Travellers, Notice no. 4.* For more information, contact **New Zealand Customs,** The Customhouse, 17–21 Whitmore St., Box 2218, Wellington (℡ **0800/428-786** or 04/473-6099; www.customs.govt.nz).

HEALTH INSURANCE

Although it's not required of travelers, health insurance is highly recommended. Unlike many European countries, the United States does not usually offer free or low-cost medical care to its citizens or visitors. Doctors and hospitals are expensive, and in most cases will require advance payment or proof of coverage before they render their services. Policies can cover everything from the loss or theft of your baggage and trip cancellation to the guarantee of bail in case you're arrested. Good policies will also cover the costs of an accident, repatriation, or death. See "Travel Insurance" in chapter 3 for more information. Packages such as **Europ Assistance's "Worldwide Healthcare Plan"** are sold by European automobile clubs and travel agencies at attractive rates. **Worldwide Assistance Services, Inc.** (✆ **800/821-2828;** www.worldwide assistance.com) is the agent for Europ Assistance in the United States.

Though lack of health insurance may prevent you from being admitted to a hospital in nonemergencies, don't worry about being left on a street corner to die: The American way is to fix you now and bill the living daylights out of you later.

INSURANCE FOR BRITISH TRAVELERS Most big travel agents offer their own insurance and will probably try to sell you their package when you book a holiday. Think before you sign. **Britain's Consumers' Association** recommends that you insist on seeing the policy and reading the fine print before buying travel insurance. **The Association of British Insurers** (✆ **020/7600-3333;** www. abi.org.uk) gives advice by phone and publishes *Holiday Insurance,* a free guide to policy provisions and prices. You might also shop around for better deals: Try **Columbus Direct** (✆ **020/7375-0011;** www.columbus direct.net).

INSURANCE FOR CANADIAN TRAVELERS Canadians should check with their provincial health plan offices or call **Health Canada** (✆ **613/957-2991;** www.hc-sc.gc.ca) to find out the extent of their coverage and what documentation and receipts they must take home in case they are treated in the United States.

MONEY

CURRENCY The U.S. monetary system is very simple: The most common **bills** are the $1 (colloquially, a "buck"), $5, $10, and $20 denominations. There are also $2 bills (seldom encountered), $50 bills, and $100 bills (the last two are usually not welcome as payment for small purchases). All the paper money was recently redesigned, making the famous faces adorning them disproportionately large. The old-style bills are still legal tender.

There are seven denominations of coins: 1¢ (1 cent, or a penny); 5¢ (5 cents, or a nickel); 10¢ (10 cents, or a dime); 25¢ (25 cents, or a quarter); 50¢ (50 cents, or a half dollar); the new gold-colored "Sacagawea" coin worth $1; and, prized by collectors, the rare, older silver dollar.

Note: The "foreign-exchange bureaus" so common in Europe are rare even at airports in the United States, and nonexistent outside major cities. It's best not to change foreign money (or traveler's checks denominated in a currency other than U.S. dollars) at a small-town bank, or even a branch in a big city; in fact, leave any currency other than U.S. dollars at home—it may prove a greater nuisance to you than it's worth.

TRAVELER'S CHECKS Though traveler's checks are widely accepted, make sure that they're denominated in U.S. dollars, as foreign-currency checks are often difficult to exchange. The three traveler's checks that are most widely recognized—and least likely to be denied—are **Visa, American Express,** and **Thomas Cook.** Be sure to record the numbers of the checks, and keep that information in a separate place in case they get lost or stolen. Most businesses are pretty good about taking traveler's checks, but you're better off cashing them in at a bank (in small amounts, of course) and paying in cash. Remember: You'll need identification, such as a driver's

> **Tips   A Travel Tip**
>
> Be sure to keep a copy of all your travel papers separate from your wallet or purse, and leave a copy with someone at home in case you need it faxed in an emergency.

license or passport, to change a traveler's check.

CREDIT CARDS & ATMs   Credit cards are the most widely used form of payment in the United States: **Visa** (Barclaycard in Britain), **MasterCard** (EuroCard in Europe, Access in Britain, and Chargex in Canada), **American Express, Diners Club,** and **Discover.** There are, however, a handful of stores and restaurants that do not take credit cards, so be sure to ask in advance. Most businesses display a sticker near their entrance to let you know which cards they accept. *Note:* Businesses may require a minimum purchase, usually around $10, to use a credit card.

It is strongly recommended that you bring at least one major credit card. You must have a credit or charge card to rent a car. Hotels and airlines usually require a credit-card imprint as a deposit against expenses, and in an emergency, a credit card can be priceless.

You'll find **automated teller machines (ATMs)** on just about every block—at least in almost every town—across the country. Some ATMs will allow you to draw U.S. currency against your bank and credit cards. Check with your bank before leaving home, and remember that you will need your personal identification number (PIN) to do so. Most accept Visa, MasterCard, and American Express, as well as ATM cards from other U.S. banks. Expect to be charged up to $3 per transaction, however, if you're not using your own bank's ATM.

One way around these fees is to ask for cash back at grocery stores that accept ATM cards and don't charge usage fees. Of course, you'll have to purchase something first.

ATM cards with major-credit-card backing, known as "debit cards," are now a commonly acceptable form of payment in most stores and restaurants. Debit cards draw money directly from your checking account. Some stores enable you to receive cash back on your debit-card purchases as well.

SAFETY

GENERAL SAFETY SUGGESTIONS   Although Chicago's tourist areas are quite safe, you should always stay alert. Asking hotel front-desk staff or the local tourist office about the safety of a particular neighborhood is a good idea.

Avoid deserted areas, especially at night, and don't go into public parks after dark unless there's a concert or similar occasion that will attract a crowd.

Avoid carrying valuables with you on the street, and keep expensive cameras or electronic equipment bagged up or covered when not in use. If you're using a map, try to consult it inconspicuously—or better yet, study it before you leave your room. Hold onto your pocketbook, and place your billfold in an inside pocket. In theaters, restaurants, and other public places, keep your possessions in sight.

Always lock your room door—don't assume that once you're inside the hotel you are automatically safe and no longer need to be aware of your surroundings. Hotels are open to the public, and in a large hotel, security may not be able to screen everyone who enters. For more about personal safety in Chicago, see "Safety" under "Fast Facts: Chicago," in chapter 5.

DRIVING SAFETY Driving safety is important too, and carjacking is not unprecedented. Question your rental agency about personal safety and ask for a traveler-safety brochure when you pick up your car. Obtain written directions—or a map with the route clearly marked—from the agency showing how to get to your destination. (Many agencies now offer the option of renting a cellphone for the duration of your car rental; check with the rental agent when you pick up the car.) And, if possible, arrive and depart during daylight hours.

If you drive off a highway and end up in a dodgy-looking neighborhood, leave the area as quickly as possible. If you have an accident, even on the highway, stay in your car with the doors locked until you assess the situation or until the police arrive. If you're bumped from behind on the street or are involved in a minor accident with no injuries, and the situation appears to be suspicious, motion to the other driver to follow you. Never get out of your car in such situations. Go directly to the nearest police precinct, well-lit service station, or 24-hour store.

You may want to look into renting a cellphone on a short-term basis. One recommended wireless rental company is **InTouch USA** (© **800/872-7626**; www.intouchusa.com).

Park in well-lit and well-traveled areas whenever possible. Always keep your car doors locked, whether the vehicle is attended or unattended. Never leave any packages or valuables in sight in your vehicle. If someone attempts to rob you or steal your car, don't try to resist the thief/carjacker. Report the incident to the police department immediately by calling © **911.**

2 Getting to the United States

AIRLINE DISCOUNTS The smart traveler can find numerous ways to reduce the price of a plane ticket simply by taking time to shop around. For example, overseas visitors can take advantage of the APEX (Advance Purchase Excursion) reductions offered by all major U.S. and European carriers. For more money-saving airline advice, see "Getting There," in chapter 3. For the best rates, compare fares and be flexible with the dates and times of travel.

British Airways (© 800/247-9297 in the U.S., 03/4522-2111 in the UK; www.british-airways.com) offers direct flights from London's Heathrow Airport to Chicago. Some of the other major international carriers that service Chicago are **Aer Lingus** (© 800/474-7424 in the U.S., 01/886-8888 in Ireland; www.aerlingus.com), **Air Canada** (© 888/247-2262 in the U.S. and Canada; www.aircanada.ca), **Qantas** (© 800/227-4500 in the U.S., 612/9691-3636 in Australia; www.qantas.com), and **Air New Zealand** (© 800/262-1234 in the U.S., 0800/737-767 in New Zealand; www.airnewzealand.com).

IMMIGRATION AND CUSTOMS CLEARANCE Visitors arriving by air, no matter what the port of entry, should cultivate patience and resignation before setting foot on U.S. soil. Getting through immigration control can take as long as 2 hours on some days, especially on summer weekends, so be sure to carry this guidebook or something else to read. This is especially true in the aftermath of the September 11, 2001 terrorist attacks, when security clearances were considerably beefed up at U.S. airports.

People traveling by air from Canada, Bermuda, and certain

countries in the Caribbean can sometimes clear Customs and Immigration
at the point of departure, which is
much quicker.

3 Getting Around the United States

BY PLANE   Some large airlines (for
example, Northwest and Delta) offer
travelers on their transatlantic or
transpacific flights special discount
tickets under the name **Visit USA,**
allowing mostly one-way travel from
one U.S. destination to another at
very low prices. These discount tickets
are not on sale in the United States
and must be purchased abroad in conjunction with your international
ticket. This system is the best, easiest,
and fastest way to see the United
States at low cost. You should obtain
information well in advance from
your travel agent or the office of the
airline concerned, since the conditions
attached to these discount tickets can
be changed without advance notice.

BY TRAIN   International visitors
(excluding Canada) can also buy a
USA Rail Pass, good for 15 or 30
days of unlimited travel on Amtrak
(© **800/USA-RAIL;** www.amtrak.
com). The pass is available through
many overseas travel agents. Prices in
2003 for a 15-day pass were $295 off-
peak, $440 peak; a 30-day pass costs
$385 off-peak, $550 peak. With a foreign passport, you can also buy passes
at some Amtrak offices in the United
States, including locations in San
Francisco, Los Angeles, Chicago, New
York, Miami, Boston, and Washington, D.C. Reservations are generally
required and should be made for each
part of your trip as early as possible.
Regional rail passes are also available.

BY BUS   Although bus travel is
often the most economical form of
public transit for short hops between
U.S. cities, it can also be slow and
uncomfortable—certainly not an
option for everyone (particularly when
Amtrak, which is far more luxurious,
offers similar rates). **Greyhound/**
Trailways (© **800/231-2222;** www.
greyhound.com), the sole nationwide
bus line, offers an **International**
Ameripass that must be purchased
before coming to the United States, or
by phone through the Greyhound
International Office at the Port
Authority Bus Terminal in New York
City (© **212/971-0492**). The pass
can be obtained from foreign travel
agents or through Greyhound's website (order at least 21 days before your
departure to the U.S.) and costs less
than the domestic version. 2003
passes were available in the following
units: 4 days ($160), 7 days ($219),
10 days ($269), 15 days ($329), 21
days ($379), 30 days ($439), 45 days
($489), or 60 days ($599). You can get
more info on the pass at the website,
or by calling © **402/330-8552.** In
addition, special rates are available for
seniors and students.

BY CAR   Outside of Chicago, the
most cost-effective, convenient, and
comfortable way to travel around the
United States is by car. The interstate
highway system connects cities and
towns all over the country; in addition
to these high-speed, limited-access
roadways, there's an extensive network
of federal, state, and local highways
and roads. Some of the national car-
rental companies include **Alamo**
(© 800/462-5266; www.alamo.com),
Avis (© 800/230-4898; www.avis.
com), **Budget** (© 800/527-0700;
https://rent.drivebudget.com/Home.
jsp), Dollar (© 800/800-3665; www.
dollar.com), Hertz (© 800/654-3131;
www.hertz.com), **National** (© 800/
227-7368; www.nationalcar.com), and
Thrifty (© 800/847-4389; www.
thrifty.com).

   If you plan to rent a car in the
United States, you probably won't

need the services of an additional automobile organization. If you're planning to buy or borrow a car, automobile-association membership is recommended. The **American Automobile Association (AAA)** (© 800/222-4357) is the country's largest auto club and supplies its members with maps, insurance, and, most important, emergency road service. The cost of joining runs from $63 for singles to $87 for two members, but if you're a member of a foreign auto club with reciprocal arrangements, you can enjoy free AAA service in America. See "Getting There," in chapter 3, for more information.

FAST FACTS: **For the International Traveler**

Automobile Organizations Auto clubs will supply maps, suggested routes, guidebooks, accident and bail-bond insurance, and emergency road service. The **American Automobile Association (AAA)** is the major auto club in the United States. If you belong to an auto club in your home country, inquire about AAA reciprocity before you leave. You may be able to join AAA even if you're not a member of a reciprocal club; to inquire, call AAA (© **800/222-4357**). AAA is actually an organization of regional auto clubs, so look under "AAA Automobile Club" in the White Pages of the telephone directory. AAA has a nationwide emergency road service telephone number (© 800/AAA-HELP).

Business Hours Offices are usually open weekdays from 9am to 5pm. Banks are open weekdays from 9am to 5pm or later and sometimes Saturday mornings. Stores typically open between 9 and 10am and close between 5 and 6pm Monday through Saturday. Stores in shopping complexes or malls tend to stay open late, until about 9pm on weekdays and weekends, and many malls and larger department stores are open on Sundays.

Currency & Currency Exchange Currency-exchange bureaus are relatively rare in Chicago, so plan accordingly. When arriving in Chicago, you can exchange international currency in **Terminal 5** (the international terminal) at O'Hare Airport. In the city, there are **American Express** offices at 55 W. Monroe St. (© **312/541-5440**) and 605 N. Michigan Ave. (© **312/943-7840**). Most banks will not exchange foreign currency. If you find yourself in need of a foreign-exchange service while in Chicago, the Chicago consumer Yellow Pages lists names and numbers of foreign-exchange services under the heading "Foreign Exchange Brokers." In the Loop, try **World's Money Exchange, Inc.,** 203 N. LaSalle St. (© **312/641-2151**). Also see "Money" under "Preparing for Your Trip," earlier in this chapter.

Drinking Laws The legal age for purchase and consumption of alcoholic beverages is 21; proof of age is required and often requested at bars, nightclubs, and restaurants, so it's always a good idea to bring ID when you go out. Beer and wine often can be purchased in supermarkets, but liquor laws vary from state to state.

Do not carry open containers of alcohol in your car or any public area that isn't zoned for alcohol consumption. The police can fine you on the spot. And nothing will ruin your trip faster than getting a citation for DUI ("driving under the influence"), so don't even think about driving while intoxicated.

Electricity Like Canada, the United States uses 110 to 120 volts AC (60 cycles), compared to 220 to 240 volts AC (50 cycles) in most of Europe, Australia, and New Zealand. If your small appliances use 220 to 240 volts, you'll need a 110-volt transformer and a plug adapter with two flat parallel pins to operate them here. Downward converters that change 220–240 volts to 110–120 volts are difficult to find in the United States, so bring one with you.

Embassies & Consulates All embassies are located in the nation's capital, Washington, D.C. Some consulates are located in major U.S. cities, and most nations have a mission to the United Nations in New York City. If your country isn't listed below, call for directory information in Washington, D.C. (© 202/555-1212) or log on to **www.embassy.org/embassies**.

The embassy of **Australia** is at 1601 Massachusetts Ave. NW, Washington, DC 20036 (© 202/797-3000; www.austemb.org). There are consulates in New York, Honolulu, Houston, Los Angeles, and San Francisco.

The embassy of **Canada** is at 501 Pennsylvania Ave. NW, Washington, DC 20001 (© 202/682-1740; www.canadianembassy.org). Other Canadian consulates are in Buffalo (NY), Detroit, Los Angeles, New York, and Seattle.

The embassy of **Ireland** is at 2234 Massachusetts Ave. NW, Washington, DC 20008 (© 202/462-3939; www.irelandemb.org). Irish consulates are in Boston, Chicago, New York, and San Francisco.

The embassy of **Japan** is at 2520 Massachusetts Ave. NW, Washington, DC 20008 (© 202/238-6700; www.embjapan.org). Japanese consulates are located in many cities including Atlanta, Boston, Detroit, New York, San Francisco, and Seattle.

The embassy of **New Zealand** is at 37 Observatory Circle NW, Washington, DC 20008 (© 202/328-4800; www.nzemb.org). New Zealand consulates are in Los Angeles, Salt Lake City, San Francisco, and Seattle.

The embassy of the **United Kingdom** is at 3100 Massachusetts Ave. NW, Washington, DC 20008 (© 202/462-1340; www.britainusa.com). Other British consulates are in Atlanta, Boston, Chicago, Cleveland, Houston, Los Angeles, New York, San Francisco, and Seattle.

Emergencies Call © 911 to report a fire, contact the police, or get an ambulance anywhere in the United States. This is a toll-free call. (No coins are required at public telephones.)

If you encounter serious problems, contact the **Traveler's Aid International** (© 202/546-1127; www.travelersaid.org) to help direct you to a local branch. This nationwide, nonprofit, social-service organization geared to helping travelers in difficult straits offers services that might include reuniting families separated while traveling, providing food and/or shelter to people stranded without cash, or even emotional counseling. If you're in trouble, seek them out.

Gasoline (Petrol) Petrol is known as gasoline (or simply gas) in the United States, and petrol stations are known as both gas stations and service stations. Gasoline costs about half as much here as it does in Europe (about $1.70 per gallon in Chicago at press time), and taxes are already included in the printed price. One U.S. gallon equals 3.8 liters or .85 imperial gallons.

Holidays Banks, government offices, post offices, and many stores, restaurants, and museums are closed on the following legal national holidays: January 1 (New Year's Day), the third Monday in January (Martin Luther King, Jr. Day), the third Monday in February (Presidents' Day), the last Monday in May (Memorial Day), July 4 (Independence Day), the first Monday in September (Labor Day), the second Monday in October (Columbus Day), November 11 (Veterans' Day), the fourth Thursday in November (Thanksgiving Day), and December 25 (Christmas). Also, the Tuesday following the first Monday in November is Election Day and is a federal government holiday in presidential-election years (held every four years, and next in 2004).

Legal Aid If you are "pulled over" for a minor infraction (such as speeding), never attempt to pay the fine directly to a police officer; this could be construed as attempted bribery, a much more serious crime. Pay fines by mail, or directly into the hands of the clerk of the court. If accused of a more serious offense, say and do nothing before consulting a lawyer. Here the burden is on the state to prove a person's guilt beyond a reasonable doubt, and everyone has the right to remain silent, whether he or she is suspected of a crime or actually arrested. Once arrested, a person can make one telephone call to a party of his or her choice. Call your embassy or consulate.

Mail If you aren't sure what your address will be in the United States, mail can be sent to you, in your name, c/o General Delivery at the main post office of the city or region where you expect to be. (Call ✆ **800/275-8777** for information on the nearest post office.) The addressee must pick up mail in person and must produce proof of identity (driver's license, passport, etc.). Most post offices will hold your mail for up to one month, and are open Monday to Friday from 8am to 6pm, and Saturday from 9am to 3pm.

Generally found at intersections, mailboxes are blue with a red-and-white stripe and carry the inscription U.S. Mail. If your mail is addressed to a U.S. destination, don't forget to add the five-digit postal code (or zip code), after the two-letter abbreviation of the state to which the mail is addressed. This is essential for prompt delivery.

At press time, domestic postage rates were 23¢ for a postcard and 37¢ for a letter. For international mail, a first-class letter of up to one-half ounce costs 80¢ (60¢ to Canada and Mexico); a first-class postcard costs 70¢ (50¢ to Canada and Mexico); and a preprinted postal aerogramme costs 70¢.

Measurements See the chart on the inside front cover of this book for details on converting metric measurements to U.S. equivalents.

Taxes The United States has no value-added tax (VAT) or other indirect tax at the national level. Every state, county, and city has the right to levy its own local tax on all purchases, including hotel and restaurant checks, airline tickets, and so on.

Telephone, Telegraph, Telex, & Fax The telephone system in the United States is run by private corporations, so rates, especially for long-distance service and operator-assisted calls, can vary widely. Generally, hotel surcharges on long-distance and local calls are astronomical, so you're usually better off using a **public pay telephone,** which you'll find clearly marked in most public buildings and private establishments as well as on the street. Convenience grocery stores and gas stations always have them. Many convenience groceries and packaging services sell **prepaid calling cards** in denominations up to $50; these can be the least expensive way to call home. Many public phones at airports now accept American Express, MasterCard, and Visa credit cards. **Local calls** made from public pay phones in most locales cost either 25¢ or 35¢. Pay phones do not accept pennies, and few will take anything larger than a quarter.

You may want to look into leasing a cell phone for the duration of your trip.

Most long-distance and international calls can be dialed directly from any phone. **For calls within the United States and to Canada,** dial 1 followed by the area code and the seven-digit number. **For other international calls,** dial 011 followed by the country code, city code, and the telephone number of the person you are calling.

Calls to area codes **800, 888, 877,** and **866** are toll-free. However, calls to numbers in area codes **700** and **900** (chat lines, bulletin boards, "dating" services, and so on) can be very expensive—usually a charge of 95¢ to $3 or more per minute, and they sometimes have minimum charges that can run as high as $15 or more.

For **reversed-charge or collect calls,** and for person-to-person calls, dial 0 (zero, not the letter O) followed by the area code and number you want; an operator will then come on the line, and you should specify that you are calling collect, or person-to-person, or both. If your operator-assisted call is international, ask for the overseas operator.

For **local directory assistance** ("information"), dial 411; for long-distance information, dial 1, then the appropriate area code and 555-1212.

Telegraph and telex services are provided primarily by Western Union. You can bring your telegram into the nearest Western Union office (there are hundreds across the country) or dictate it over the phone (© **800/325-6000**). You can also telegraph money, or have it telegraphed to you, very quickly over the Western Union system, but this service can cost as much as 15 to 20 percent of the amount sent.

Most hotels have **fax machines** available for guest use (be sure to ask about the charge to use it). Many hotel rooms are even wired for guests' fax machines. A less expensive way to send and receive faxes may be at stores such as **The UPS Store** (formerly Mail Boxes Etc.), a national chain of retail packing service shops. (Look in the Yellow Pages directory under "Packing Services.")

There are two kinds of telephone directories in the United States. The so-called **White Pages** list private households and business subscribers in alphabetical order. The inside front cover lists emergency numbers for police, fire, ambulance, the Coast Guard, poison-control center, crime-victims' hotline, and so on. The first few pages will tell you how to make long-distance and international calls, complete with country codes and area codes. Government numbers are usually printed on blue paper, or blue-edged paper within the White Pages. Printed on yellow paper, the so-called **Yellow Pages** list all local services, businesses, industries, and houses of worship according to activity with an index at the front or back.

(Drugstores/pharmacies and restaurants are also listed by geographic location.) The Yellow Pages also include city plans or detailed area maps, postal zip codes, and public transportation routes.

Time The continental United States is divided into **four time zones:** Eastern Standard Time (EST), Central Standard Time (CST), Mountain Standard Time (MST), and Pacific Standard Time (PST). Alaska and Hawaii have their own zones. For example, noon in New York City (EST) is 11am in Chicago (CST), 10am in Denver (MST), 9am in Los Angeles (PST), 8am in Anchorage (AST), and 7am in Honolulu (HST).

Daylight savings time is in effect from 1am on the first Sunday in April through 1am on the last Sunday in October, except in Arizona, Hawaii, most of Indiana, and Puerto Rico. Daylight savings time moves the clock 1 hour ahead of standard time.

Tipping Tips are a very important part of certain workers' income, and gratuities are the standard way of showing appreciation for services provided. (Tipping is certainly not compulsory if the service is poor!) In hotels, tip **bellhops** at least $1 per bag ($2–$3 if you have a lot of luggage) and tip the **chamber staff** $1 to $2 per day (more if you've left a disaster area for him or her to clean up). Tip the **doorman** or **concierge** only if he or she has provided you with some specific service (for example, calling a cab for you or obtaining difficult-to-get theater tickets). Tip the **valet-parking attendant** $1 every time you get your car.

In restaurants, bars, and nightclubs, tip **service staff** 15% to 20% of the check, tip **bartenders** 10% to 15%, tip **checkroom attendants** $1 per garment, and tip **valet-parking attendants** $1 per vehicle.

As for other service personnel, tip **cab drivers** 15% of the fare; tip **skycaps** at airports at least $1 per bag ($2–$3 if you have a lot of luggage); and tip **hairdressers** and **barbers** 15% to 20%.

Toilets You won't find public toilets or "restrooms" on the streets in most U.S. cities, but they can be found in hotel lobbies, bars, restaurants, museums, department stores, railway and bus stations, and service stations. Large hotels and fast-food restaurants are probably the best bet for good, clean facilities. If possible, avoid the toilets at parks and beaches, which tend to be dirty; some may be unsafe. Restaurants and bars in resorts or heavily visited areas may reserve their restrooms for patrons. Some establishments display a notice indicating this. You can ignore this sign or, better yet, avoid arguments by paying for a cup of coffee or a soft drink, which will qualify you as a patron.

5

Getting to Know
the Windy City

The orderly configuration of Chicago's streets and the excellent public transportation system make the city quite accessible—once you identify and locate a few basic landmarks.

This chapter provides an overview of the city's design, as well as some suggestions for how to maneuver within it. The chapter also lists some resources that travelers frequently require, from babysitters to all-night pharmacies.

1 Orientation

VISITOR INFORMATION

The **Chicago Office of Tourism** runs a toll-free visitor hot line (© 877/ CHICAGO or 312/744-2400; TTY 312/744-2947; www.cityofchicago.org/ specialevents) and operates three visitor information centers staffed with people who can answer questions and stocked with plenty of brochures on area attractions, including materials on everything from museums and city landmarks to lakefront biking maps and even fishing spots. The main visitor center, located in the Loop and convenient to many places that you'll likely be visiting, is on the first floor of the **Chicago Cultural Center,** 78 E. Washington St. (at Michigan Ave.). The center has a phone that you can use to make hotel reservations, and several couches and a cafe where you can study maps and plan your itinerary. The center is open Monday through Friday from 10am to 6pm, Saturday from 10am to 5pm, and Sunday from 11am to 5pm; it's closed on holidays.

A second, smaller center is located in the heart of the city's shopping district, in the old pumping station at Michigan and Chicago avenues. Recently renamed the **Chicago Water Works Visitor Center,** its entrance is on the Pearson Street side of the building, across from the Water Tower Place mall. It's open daily from 7:30am to 7pm. This location has the added draw of housing a location of Hot Tix, which offers both half-price day-of-performance and full-price tickets to many theater productions around the city, as well as a gift shop. Part of the building has been converted into a theater, including a small cabaret space for tourist-oriented shows and a larger playhouse for the acclaimed Lookingglass Theatre Company.

A third visitor outpost is located at **Navy Pier** in the Illinois Market Place gift shop; it's open Sunday through Thursday from 10am to 9pm, and Friday and Saturday from 10am to midnight.

The **Illinois Bureau of Tourism** (© 800/2CONNECT or TTY 800/406-6418; www.enjoyillinois.com) can provide general and specific information 24 hours a day. The agency also has staff at the information desk in the lobby of the **James R. Thompson Center,** 100 W. Randolph St., in the Helmut Jahn–designed

Chicago Neighborhood Map Index

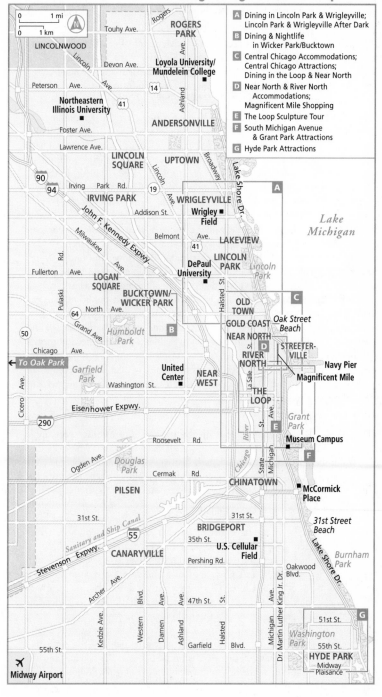

A Dining in Lincoln Park & Wrigleyville;
Lincoln Park & Wrigleyville After Dark
B Dining & Nightlife
in Wicker Park/Bucktown
C Central Chicago Accommodations;
Central Chicago Attractions;
Dining in the Loop & Near North
D Near North & River North
Accommodations;
Magnificent Mile Shopping
E The Loop Sculpture Tour
F South Michigan Avenue
& Grant Park Attractions
G Hyde Park Attractions

ROGERS PARK
Touhy Ave.
LINCOLNWOOD
Devon Ave.
Loyola University/
Mundelein College
Peterson Ave.
Northeastern
Illinois University
Foster Ave.
ANDERSONVILLE
Lawrence Ave.
LINCOLN SQUARE
UPTOWN
Irving Park Rd.
IRVING PARK
WRIGLEYVILLE
Addison St.
Wrigley Field
John F. Kennedy Expwy.
Belmont Ave.
LAKEVIEW
LINCOLN PARK
DePaul University
Lincoln Park
Fullerton Ave.
LOGAN SQUARE
Lake Michigan
OLD TOWN
GOLD COAST
Oak Street Beach
NEAR NORTH
RIVER NORTH
STREETER-VILLE
Navy Pier
Magnificent Mile
BUCKTOWN/
WICKER PARK
North Ave.
Humboldt Park
Grand Ave.
Chicago Ave.
To Oak Park
Garfield Park
United Center
NEAR WEST
Washington St.
THE LOOP
Eisenhower Expwy.
Grant Park
Roosevelt Rd.
Museum Campus
Ogden Ave.
Douglas Park
Cermak Rd.
CHINATOWN
McCormick Place
PILSEN
31st St.
31st St.
31st Street Beach
BRIDGEPORT
35th St.
U.S. Cellular Field
Burnham Park
Sanitary and Ship Canal
Stevenson Expwy.
CANARYVILLE
Pershing Rd.
Oakwood Blvd.
Archer Ave.
47th St.
51st St.
Kedzie Ave.
Western Ave.
Damen Ave.
Ashland Ave.
Garfield Blvd.
Halsted St.
Michigan Ave.
Dr. Martin Luther King Jr. Dr.
Washington Park
HYDE PARK
Midway Plaisance
55th St.
Midway Airport

building at LaSalle and Randolph streets in the Loop. The desk is open from 8:30am to 4:30pm Monday through Friday.

INFORMATION BY TELEPHONE The **Mayor's Office of Special Events** operates a recorded hot line (© **312/744-3370;** www.ci.chi.il.us/SpecialEvents) listing current special events, festivals, and parades occurring throughout the city. The city of Chicago also maintains a 24-hour information line for those with hearing impairments; call © **312/744-8599.**

PUBLICATIONS Chicago's major daily newspapers are the *Tribune* and the *Sun-Times.* Both have cultural listings, including movies, theaters, and live music, not to mention reviews of the very latest restaurants that are sure to have appeared in the city since this guidebook went to press. The Friday edition of both papers contains a special pullout section with more detailed, up-to-date information on special events happening over the weekend. *Chicago* magazine is an upscale monthly with good restaurant listings.

In a class by itself is the *Chicago Reader,* a free weekly that is an invaluable source of entertainment listings, classifieds, and well-written articles on contemporary issues of interest in Chicago. Published every Thursday (except the last week of Dec), the weekly has a wide distribution downtown and on the North Side; it is available in many retail stores, in building lobbies, and at the paper's offices, 11 E. Illinois St. (© **312/828-0350**), by about noon on Thursday.

Another free weekly, *New City* (© **312/243-8786**), also publishes excellent comprehensive listings of entertainment options. Appealing to a slightly younger audience than the *Reader,* its editorial tone tends toward the edgy and irreverent. Published every Wednesday, it's available in the same neighborhoods and locations as the *Reader.*

Most Chicago hotels stock their rooms or lobbies with at least one informational magazine, such as *Where Chicago,* that lists some of the city's entertainment, shopping, and dining locales.

CITY LAYOUT

The **Chicago River** forms a Y that divides the city into its three geographic zones: North Side, South Side, and West Side (Lake Michigan is where the East Side would be). The downtown financial district is called **the Loop.** The city's key shopping street is **North Michigan Avenue,** also known as the **Magnificent Mile.** In addition to department stores and vertical malls, this stretch of property north of the river houses many of the city's most elegant hotels. North and south of this downtown zone, Chicago stretches along 29 miles of Lake Michigan shoreline that is, by and large, free of commercial development, reserved for public use as green space and parkland from one end of town to the other.

Today Chicago proper has about 3 million inhabitants living in an area about two-thirds the size of New York City; another 5 million make the suburbs their home. The towns north of Chicago now stretch in an unbroken mass nearly to the Wisconsin border; the city's western suburbs extend 30 miles to Naperville, one of the fastest-growing towns in the nation over the past 2 decades. (Lake Michigan, a resort area, is to the city's east, while, a few miles to the south, you've got economically-depressed former steel towns such as Gary, Indiana.) The real signature of Chicago, however, is found between the suburbs and the Loop, where a colorful patchwork quilt of residential neighborhoods gives the city a character all its own.

FINDING AN ADDRESS Having been a part of the Northwest Territory, Chicago is laid out in a **grid system,** with the streets neatly lined up as if on a

Fun Fact **A River Runs Through It**

The Chicago River remains one of the most visible of the city's major physical features. It's spanned by more movable bridges (52 at last count) than any city in the world. An almost-mystical moment occurs downtown when all the bridges spanning the main and south branches—connecting the Loop to both the Near West Side and the Near North Side—are raised, allowing for the passage of some ship or barge or contingent of high-masted sailboats. The Chicago River has long outlived the critical commercial function that it once performed. Most of the remaining millworks that still occupy its banks no longer depend on the river alone for the transport of their materials, raw and finished. The river's main function today is to serve as a fluvial conduit for sewage, which, owing to an engineering feat that reversed its flow inland in 1900, no longer pollutes the waters of Lake Michigan. Recently, Chicagoans have begun to discover another role for the river, that of leisure resource, providing short cruises on its water, park areas, cafes, and public art installations on its banks, and the beginnings of a river-side bike path that connects to the lakefront route near Wacker Drive. Actually, today's developers aren't the first to wonder why the river couldn't be Chicago's Seine. A look at the early-20th-century beaux arts balustrades lining the river along Wacker Drive, complete with comfortably spaced benches—as well as Parisian-style bridge houses—shows that Daniel Burnham knew full well what a treasure the city had.

giant piece of graph paper. Because the city itself isn't rectangular (it's rather elongated), the shape is a bit irregular, but the perpendicular pattern remains. Easing movement through the city are a half-dozen or so major diagonal thoroughfares.

Point zero is located at the downtown intersection of State and Madison streets. **State Street** divides east and west addresses, and **Madison Street** divides north and south addresses. From here, Chicago's highly predictable addressing system begins. Making use of this grid, it is relatively easy to plot the distance in miles between any two points in the city.

Virtually all of Chicago's principal north-south and east-west arteries are spaced by increments of 400 in the addressing system—regardless of the number of smaller streets nestled between them. And each addition or subtraction of 400 numbers to an address is equivalent to a half mile. Thus, starting at point zero on Madison Street and traveling north along State Street for 1 mile, you will come to 800 N. State St., which intersects Chicago Avenue. Continue uptown for another half mile and you arrive at the 1200 block of North State Street at Division Street. And so it goes, right to the city line, with suburban Evanston located at the 7600 block north, 9½ miles from point zero.

The same rule applies when you're traveling south, or east to west. Thus, heading west from State Street along Madison Street, Halsted Street—at 800 W. Madison St.—is a mile's distance, while Racine Avenue, at the 1200 block of West Madison Street, is 1½ miles from the center. Madison Street then continues westward to Chicago's boundary with the nearby suburb of Oak Park along

Austin Avenue, which, at 6000 W. Madison, is approximately 7½ miles from point zero.

The key to understanding the grid is that the side of any square formed by the principal avenues (noted in dark or red ink on most maps) represents a distance of half a mile in any direction. Understanding how Chicago's grid system works is of particular importance to those visitors who want to do a lot of walking in the city's many neighborhoods and who want to plot in advance the distances involved in trekking from one locale to another.

The other convenient aspect of the grid is that every major road uses the same numerical system. In other words, the cross street (Division St.) at 1200 N. Lake Shore Dr. is the same as at 1200 N. Clark St. and 1200 N. LaSalle St.

STREET MAPS   A suitably detailed map of Chicago is published by **Rand McNally** (p. 240), available at many newsstands and bookstores for less than $5 (the smaller, more manageable laminated versions cost $6.95). Rand McNally operates a thoroughly stocked retail store at 444 N. Michigan Ave. (© **312/ 321-1751**), just north of the Wrigley Building.

NEIGHBORHOODS IN BRIEF
The Loop & Vicinity

Downtown   In the case of Chicago, downtown means the Loop. The Loop refers literally to a core of primarily commercial, governmental, and cultural buildings contained within a corral of elevated train tracks, but greater downtown Chicago overflows these confines and is bounded by the Chicago River to the north and west, by Michigan Avenue to the east, and by Roosevelt Avenue to the south.

The North Side

Near North/Magnificent Mile North Michigan Avenue is known as the Magnificent Mile, from the bridge spanning the Chicago River to its northern tip at Oak Street. Many of the city's best hotels, shops, and restaurants are to be found on and around elegant North Michigan Avenue. The area stretching east of Michigan Avenue to the lake is sometimes referred to as "Streeterville"—the legacy of George Wellington "Cap" Streeter, an eccentric, bankrupt showman who staked out 200 acres of self-created landfill here about a century ago after his steamship ran aground, and then declared himself "governor" of the "District of Lake Michigan." True story.

River North   Just to the west of the Mag Mile's zone of high life and sophistication is an old warehouse district called River North. Over the past 20 years, the area has experienced a rebirth as one of the city's most vital commercial districts, and today it holds many of the city's hottest restaurants, nightspots, art galleries, and loft dwellings. Several large-scale residential loft-conversion developments have lately been sprouting on its western and southwestern fringes.

The Gold Coast   Some of Chicago's most desirable real estate and historic architecture are found along Lake Shore Drive, between Oak Street and North Avenue and along the adjacent side streets. Despite trendy little pockets of real estate popping up elsewhere, the moneyed class still prefers to live by the lake. On the neighborhood's southwestern edge, around Division and Rush streets, a string of raucous bars and late-night eateries contrasts sharply with the rest of the area's sedate quality.

Old Town West of LaSalle Street, principally on North Wells Street between Division Street and North Avenue, is the residential district of Old Town, which boasts some of the city's best-preserved historic homes. This area was a hippie haven in the 1960s and 1970s, but in recent years its residential areas have begun to become rapidly gentrified as Cabrini Green, a notorious housing project, has been gradually falling to the wrecking ball. Old Town's biggest claim to fame, the legendary Second City comedy club, has served up the lighter side of life to Chicagoans for more than 30 years.

Lincoln Park Chicago's most popular residential neighborhood is fashionable Lincoln Park. Stretching from North Avenue to Diversey Parkway, it's bordered on the east by the huge park of the same name, which is home to two major museums and one of the nation's oldest zoos (established in 1868). The trapezoid formed by Clark Street, Armitage Avenue, Halsted Street, and Diversey Parkway also contains many of Chicago's most happening bars, restaurants, retail stores, music clubs, and off-Loop theaters—including the nationally acclaimed Steppenwolf Theatre Company.

Lakeview & Wrigleyville Midway up the city's North Side is a one-time blue-collar, now mainstream middle-class and bohemian quarter called Lakeview. It has become the neighborhood of choice for many gays and lesbians, recent college graduates, and a growing number of residents priced out of Lincoln Park. The main thoroughfare is Belmont Avenue, between Broadway and Sheffield Avenue. Wrigleyville is the name given to the neighborhood in the vicinity of Wrigley Field—home of the Chicago Cubs—at Sheffield Avenue and

Addison Street. Many homesteaders have moved into these areas in recent years, and a slew of nightclubs and restaurants have followed in their wake.

Uptown & Andersonville Uptown, along the lake and about as far north as Foster Avenue, has traditionally attracted waves of immigrants; while crime was a major problem a decade ago, the area has stabilized recently, with formerly decrepit buildings being converted into—you guessed it—condominiums. Vietnamese and Chinese immigrants have transformed Argyle Street between Broadway and Sheridan Road into a teeming market for fresh meat, fish, and all kinds of exotic vegetables. Slightly to the north and west is the old Scandinavian neighborhood of Andersonville, whose main drag is Clark Street, between Foster and Bryn Mawr avenues. The area has the feel of a small Midwestern village, albeit one with an eclectic mix of Middle Eastern restaurants, a distinct cluster of women-owned businesses, and a burgeoning colony of gays and lesbians.

Lincoln Square West of Andersonville and slightly to the south, where Lincoln, Western, and Lawrence avenues intersect, is Lincoln Square, the only identifiable remains of Chicago's once-vast German-American community. The surrounding leafy residential streets are now experiencing an influx of white middle-class families, who flock to the Old Town School of Folk Music's theater and education center, a beautiful restoration of a former library building.

Rogers Park Rogers Park, which begins at Devon Avenue, is located on the northern fringes of the city bordering suburban Evanston. Its western half has been a Jewish neighborhood for decades. The eastern half, dominated by Loyola University's lakefront campus, has become the most cosmopolitan enclave in the entire city: African Americans, Asians, East Indians, German Americans, and Russian Jews live side by side with the ethnically mixed student population drawn to the Catholic university. Much of Rogers Park has a neohippie ambience, but the western stretch of Devon Avenue is a Midwestern slice of Calcutta, colonized by Indians who've transformed the street into a veritable restaurant row serving tandoori chicken and curry-flavored dishes.

The West Side

Near West On the Near West Side, just across the Chicago River from the Loop, on Halsted Street between Adams and Monroe streets, is Chicago's old Greektown, still the Greek culinary center of the city. Much of the old Italian neighborhood in this vicinity was the victim of urban renewal, but remnants still survive on Taylor Street; the same is true for a few old delis and shops on Maxwell Street, dating from the turn of the 20th century when a large Jewish community lived in the area.

Bucktown/Wicker Park Centered near the confluence of North, Damen, and Milwaukee avenues, where the Art Deco Northwest Tower is the tallest thing for miles, this resurgent area is said to be home to the third-largest concentration of artists in the country. Over the past century, the area has hosted waves of German, Polish, and, most recently, Spanish-speaking immigrants (not to mention writer Nelson Algren). In recent years, it has morphed into a bastion of hot new restaurants, alternative culture, and loft-dwelling yuppies surfing the gentrification wave that's washing over this still-somewhat-gritty neighborhood.

The South Side

South Loop The generically rechristened South Loop area was Chicago's original "Gold Coast" in the late 19th century, with Prairie Avenue (now a historic district) as its most exclusive address. But in the wake of the 1893 World's Columbian Exposition in Hyde Park, and continuing through the Prohibition era of the 1920s, the area was infamous for its Levee vice district, home to gambling and prostitution, some of the most corrupt politicians in Chicago history, and Al Capone's headquarters at the old Lexington Hotel. However, in recent years, its prospects have turned around. The South Loop—stretching from Harrison Street's historic Printers Row south to Cermak Road (where Chinatown begins), and from Lake Shore Drive west to the south branch of the Chicago River—is one of the fast-growing residential neighborhoods in the city.

Pilsen Originally home to the nation's largest settlement of Bohemian-Americans, Pilsen (which derives its name from a city in Bohemia, the Czech Republic) was for decades the principal entry point in Chicago for immigrants of every ethnic background. Centered at Halsted and 18th streets just southwest of the Loop, Pilsen now contains the second-largest Mexican-American community in the United States. This vibrant and colorful neighborhood, which was happily invaded by the outdoor mural movement launched years earlier in Mexico, boasts a profusion of authentic taquerias and bakeries. The neighborhood's annual Day of the Dead celebration, which begins in September, is an elaborate festival that runs for 8 weeks. The artistic spirit that permeates the

community isn't confined to Latin-American art. In recent years, artists of every stripe, drawn partly by the availability of loft space in Pilsen, have nurtured a small but thriving artists' colony.

Bridgeport & Canaryville Bridgeport, whose main intersection is 35th and Halsted streets, has been the neighborhood of two Mayor Daleys, father and son (although the son now lives in the South Loop). After the old Comiskey Park was torn down, the Chicago White Sox stayed in Bridgeport, inaugurating their new stadium there. Nearby Canaryville, just south and west, is typical of the "back of the yard" blue-collar neighborhoods that once surrounded the Chicago Stockyards. Neither area offers much to the typical visitor; in fact, "outsiders" aren't all that welcome.

Hyde Park Hyde Park is like an independent village within the confines of Chicago, right off Lake Michigan and roughly a 30-minute train ride from the Loop. Fifty-seventh Street is the main drag, and the University of Chicago—with all its attendant shops and restaurants—is the neighborhood's principal tenant. The most successful racially integrated community in the city, Hyde Park is an oasis of furious intellectual activity and liberalism that, ironically, is hemmed in on all sides by neighborhoods suffering some of the highest crime rates in Chicago. Its main attraction is the world-famous Museum of Science and Industry.

2 Getting Around

The best way to savor Chicago is by walking its streets. Walking is not always practical, however, particularly when moving between distant neighborhoods and on harsh winter days. In those situations, Chicago's public train and bus systems are efficient modes of transportation.

BY PUBLIC TRANSPORTATION

The **Chicago Transit Authority (CTA)** operates an extensive system of trains and buses throughout the city of Chicago. The sturdy system carries about 1.5 million passengers a day. Recently, the CTA has been trying to reverse declining ridership by sprucing up some of the grittier stations and introducing more efficient operating procedures, such as timetables and fare cards. Subways and elevated trains (known as the El) are generally safe and reliable, although it's advisable to avoid long rides through unfamiliar neighborhoods late at night.

Tips **Free Ride**

During the summer, the city of Chicago operates free trolleys daily between Michigan Avenue and the Museum Campus (site of the Adler Planetarium, the Field Museum of Natural History, and the Shedd Aquarium); the trolleys run only on weekends in the fall and spring. Free trolleys also run year-round between Navy Pier and the Grand/State El station on the Red Line (you can check out the routes and get details on schedules at www.cityofchicago.org/Transportation/trolleys). While the trolleys are supposed to make stops every 30 minutes, waits can be far longer during peak tourist season—and the trolleys aren't air-conditioned. If you get tired of waiting, remember that CTA public buses travel the same routes for only $1.50 per person.

Fares for the bus, subway, and El are $1.50, with an additional 30¢ for a transfer that allows CTA riders to make two transfers on the bus or El within 2 hours of receipt. Children under 7 ride free, and those between the ages of 7 and 11 pay 75¢ (15¢ for transfers). Seniors can also receive the reduced fare if they have the appropriate reduced-fare permit (call ☎ **312/836-7000** for details on how to obtain one, although this is probably not a realistic option for a short-term visitor).

Adopting a system used by other urban transit agencies, the CTA uses credit-card-size fare cards that automatically deduct the exact fare each time you take a ride. The reusable cards can be purchased with a preset value already stored ($14 for 10 rides, or $17 for 10 rides and 10 transfers), or riders can obtain cards at vending machines located at all CTA train stations and charge them with whatever amount they choose (a minimum of $3 and up to $100). If within 2 hours of your first ride you transfer to a bus or the El, the turnstiles at the El stations and the fare boxes on buses will automatically deduct from your card just the cost of a transfer (30¢). If you make a second transfer within 2 hours, it's free. The same card can be recharged continuously.

Fare cards can be used on buses, but you can't buy a card on the bus. If you get on the bus without a fare card, you'll have to pay $1.50 cash (either in coins or in dollar bills); the bus drivers cannot make change, so make sure that you've got the right amount before hopping on board.

CTA INFORMATION   The CTA operates a useful telephone information service (☎ **836-7000** or TTY 836-4949 from any area code in the city and suburbs) that functions daily from 5am to 1am. When you want to know how to get from where you are to where you want to go, call the CTA. Make sure that you specify any conditions you might require—the fastest route, for example, or the simplest (the route with the fewest transfers or the least amount of walking), and so forth. You can also check out the CTA's website at **www.transitchicago.com**. Excellent CTA comprehensive maps, which include both El and bus routes, are usually available at subway or El stations, or by calling the CTA. The CTA also has added a toll-free customer service hot line (☎ **888/YOUR-CTA** or TTY 888/CTA-TTY1 Mon–Fri 7am–8pm, with voice mail operating after hours) to field questions and feedback. While the new fare-box system has eliminated the need for ticket agents, agents are still available at some El stations to offer customer assistance.

Tips **Ticket to Ride**

Visitors may consider buying a **Visitor Pass,** which works like a fare card and allows individual users unlimited rides on the El and CTA buses over a 24-hour period. The cards cost $5 and are sold at airports, hotels, museums, Hot Tix outlets, transportation hubs, and Chicago Office of Tourism visitor information centers (you can also buy them in advance online at www.transitchicago.com or by calling ☎ 888/YOUR-CTA). Also available now are 2-, 3-, and 5-day passes. While the passes save you the trouble of feeding the fare machines yourself, remember that they're economical only if you plan to make at least three distinct trips at least 2 or more hours apart (remember that you get two additional transfers for an additional 30¢ on a regular fare).

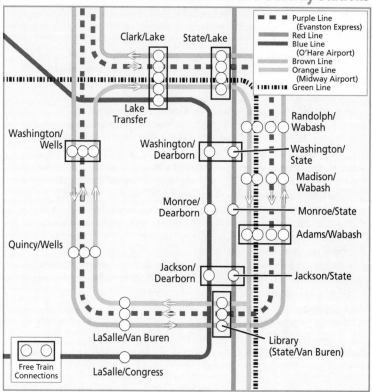

Purple Line
(Evanston Express)
Red Line
Blue Line
(O'Hare Airport)
Brown Line
Orange Line
(Midway Airport)
Green Line

Clark/Lake   State/Lake

Lake
Transfer

Randolph/
Wabash

Washington/
Wells

Washington/
Dearborn

Washington/
State

Madison/
Wabash

Monroe/
Dearborn

Monroe/State

Adams/Wabash

Quincy/Wells

Jackson/
Dearborn

Jackson/State

LaSalle/Van Buren

Library
(State/Van Buren)

Free Train
Connections

LaSalle/Congress

BY THE EL & THE SUBWAY   The rapid transit system operates five major
lines, which the CTA identifies by color: The **Red Line** runs north-south; the
Green Line runs west-south; the **Blue Line** runs through Wicker Park/Buck-
town west-northwest to O'Hare Airport; the **Brown Line** runs in a northern
zigzag route; and the **Orange Line** runs southwest, serving Midway airport.

A separate express line, the **Purple Line,** services Evanston, while a smaller,
local line in Skokie (the **Yellow Line**) is linked to the north-south Red Line.
Skokie and Evanston are adjacent suburbs on Chicago's northern boundary.

I highly recommend taking at least one El ride while you're here—you'll get
a whole different perspective on the city (not to mention fascinating views inside
downtown office buildings and North Side homes as you whiz past their windows). While the Red Line is the most efficient for traveling between the Magnificent Mile and points south, your only views along this underground stretch
will be of dingy stations. For sightseers, I recommend taking the aboveground
Brown Line, which runs around the downtown Loop and then north through
residential neighborhoods. You can ride all the way to the end of the line at Kimball (about a 45-min. ride from downtown) or hop off at Belmont to wander the
Lakeview neighborhood. Avoid this scenic ride during rush hour (before about
9am and between 3:30 and 6:30pm), when your only view will be of weary,
sweaty commuters.

Study your CTA map carefully (there's one printed on the inside back cover
of this guide) before boarding any train. While most trains run every 5 to 20

> *Fun Fact* **Sky Train: Chicago's El**
>
> Watch any Hollywood film or TV series set in Chicago, and chances are they'll feature at least one scene set against our screeching elevated train system, more commonly known as the **"El"** (witness *The Fugitive*, *ER*, and others). The trains symbolize Chicago's gritty, "city-that-works" attitude, but they actually began as a cutting-edge technology.
>
> After the Great Fire of 1871, Chicago made a remarkable recovery; within 20 years, the downtown district was swarming with people, streetcars, and horses (but no stoplights). To help relieve congestion, the city took to the sky, building a system of elevated trains 15 feet above all the madness. The first El trains were steam-powered, but by the end of the century all the lines—run by separate companies—used electricity. In 1895, the three El companies collaborated to build a set of tracks into and around the central business district that all the lines would then share. By 1897, the "Loop" was up and running, but it would take almost 100 years before the "El" would connect the whole city.
>
> Chicago's El wasn't the nation's first. That honor belongs to New York City, which started running its elevated trains in 1867, 25 years before Chicago. But the New York El has almost disappeared, moving underground and turning into a subway early last century. With 289 miles of track, Chicago has the biggest El in the country, and the second-largest public transportation system.

minutes, decreasing in frequency in the off-peak and overnight hours, some stations close after work hours (as early as 8:30pm) and remain closed on Saturday, Sunday, and holidays. The Orange Line train does not operate from about 11:30pm to 5am, the Brown Line operates only north of Belmont after about 9:30pm, the Blue Line's Cermak branch has ceased operating overnight and on weekends, and the Purple Line does not run overnight.

The CTA recently posted timetables on the El platforms so that you can determine when the next train should arrive.

BY BUS   Add to Chicago's gridlike layout a comprehensive system of public buses, and virtually every place in the city is within close walking distance of a bus stop. Other than on foot or bicycle, the best way to get around Chicago's warren of neighborhoods—the best way to actually see what's around you—is by riding a public bus, especially if you're staying near the lakefront, where the trains don't run. Look for the **blue-and-white signs to locate bus stops,** which are spaced about 1 or 2 blocks apart.

A few buses that are particularly handy for many visitors are the **no. 146 Marine/Michigan,** an express bus from Belmont Avenue on the North Side that cruises down North Lake Shore Drive (and through Lincoln Park during non-peak times) to North Michigan Avenue, State Street, and the Grant Park museum campus; the **no. 151 Sheridan,** which passes through Lincoln Park en route to inner Lake Shore Drive and then travels along Michigan Avenue as far south as Adams Street, where it turns west into the Loop (and stops at Union Station); and the **no. 156 LaSalle,** which goes through Lincoln Park and then into the Loop's financial district on LaSalle Street.

PACE buses (✆ **836-7000** from any Chicago area code, or 847/364-7223, Mon–Fri 8am–5pm; www.pacebus.com) cover the suburban zones that surround Chicago. They run every 20 to 30 minutes during rush hour, operating until midevening Monday through Friday and early evening on weekends. Suburban bus routes are marked no. 208 and above, and vehicles may be flagged down at intersections where stops aren't marked.

BY COMMUTER TRAIN

The **Metra** commuter railroad (✆ **312/322-6777** or TTY 312/322-6774 Mon–Fri 8am–5pm; at other times, call Regional Transportation Authority [RTA] at ✆ 312/836-7000 or TTY 312/836-4949; www.metrarail.com) serves the six-county suburban area around Chicago with 12 train lines. Several terminals are located downtown, including **Union Station** at Adams and Canal streets, **LaSalle Street Station** at LaSalle and Van Buren streets, **North Western Station** at Madison and Canal streets, and **Randolph Street Station** at Randolph Street and Michigan Avenue.

To view the leafy streets of Chicago's northern suburbs, take the **Union Pacific North Line** (previously known as the North Western train), which departs at the North Western Station, and select from among the following destinations: Kenilworth, Winnetka, Glencoe, Highland Park, and Lake Forest.

The **Metra Electric** (once known as the Illinois Central–Gulf Railroad, or the IC), running close to Lake Michigan on a track that occupies some of the most valuable real estate in Chicago, will take you to Hyde Park (see "Exploring Hyde Park: The Museum of Science & Industry & More," in chapter 8). You can catch the Metra Electric in the Loop at the Randolph Street Station and at the Van Buren Street Station at Van Buren Street and Michigan Avenue.

Commuter trains have graduated fare schedules based on the distance you ride. On weekends and holidays and during the summer, Metra offers a family discount that allows up to three children under age 12 to ride free when accompanying a paid adult. The commuter railroad also offers a $5 weekend pass for unlimited rides on Saturday and Sunday.

BY TAXI

Taxis are a pretty affordable way to get around the Loop and to get to the dining, shopping, and entertainment options found beyond downtown, such as on the Near North Side, in Old Town and Lincoln Park, and on the Near West Side. But for longer distances, the fares will add up.

Taxis are easy to hail in the Loop, on the Magnificent Mile and the Gold Coast, in River North, and in Lincoln Park, but if you go much beyond these key areas, you might need to call. Cab companies include **Flash Cab** (✆ 773/561-1444), **Yellow Cab** (✆ 312/TAXI-CAB or 312/829-4222), and **Checker Cab** (✆ **312/CHECKER** or 312/243-2537).

The meter in Chicago cabs currently starts at $1.90 for the first mile and $1.60 for each additional mile, with a 50¢ surcharge for each additional rider age 12 to 65.

BY CAR

Chicago is laid out so logically that it's relatively easy for visitors to get around the city by car. Although rush-hour traffic jams are just as frustrating as they are in other large U.S. cities, traffic runs fairly smoothly at most times of the day. The combination of wide streets and strategically spaced expressways makes for generally easy riding. But Chicagoans have learned to be prepared for unexpected delays; it seems that at least one major highway and several downtown streets are under repair throughout the spring and summer months (some say we have two seasons: winter and construction).

Great diagonal corridors—such as Lincoln Avenue, Clark Street, and Milwaukee Avenue—slice through the grid pattern at key points in the city and shorten many a trip that would otherwise be tedious on the checkerboard surface of the Chicago streets. On scenic **Lake Shore Drive** (also known as the Outer Dr.) you can travel the length of the city (and beyond), never far from the great lake that is Chicago's most awesome natural feature.

DRIVING RULES   One bizarre anomaly in the organization of Chicago's traffic is the occasional absence of signal lights off the principal avenues, notably in the River North and Streeterville neighborhoods. A block east or west of the Magnificent Mile (North Michigan Ave.)—one of the most traveled streets in the city—you will in some cases encounter only stop signs to control the flow of traffic. Once you've become accustomed to the system, it works very smoothly, with everyone—pedestrians and motorists alike—advancing in their proper turn.

Unless otherwise posted, a right turn on red is allowed after stopping and signaling.

PARKING   Parking regulations are vigorously enforced throughout the city. Read signs carefully: The streets around Michigan Avenue have no-parking restrictions during rush hour—and I know from firsthand experience that your car will be towed immediately. Many neighborhoods have adopted resident-only parking that prohibits others from parking on their streets, usually after 6pm each day (even all day in a few areas, such as Old Town). The neighborhood around Wrigley Field is off-limits during Cubs night games, so look for yellow sidewalk signs alerting drivers about the dozen-and-a-half times the Cubs play under lights. You can park in permit zones if you're visiting a friend, who can provide you with a pass to stick on your windshield. Beware of tow zones, and, if visiting in winter, make note of curbside warnings regarding snow plowing.

A safe bet is valet parking, which most restaurants provide for $6 to $9. Downtown you might also opt for a public garage, but you'll have to pay premium prices. (Several garages connected with malls or other major attractions offer discounted parking with a validated ticket.)

The very best parking deal in the Loop is the city-run Millennium Park garage, which charges $10 for 12 hours or less (enter on Columbus Dr., 1 block east of Michigan Ave., between Monroe and Randolph sts.). Also relatively affordable are two lots underneath **Grant Park,** with entrances at Michigan Avenue and Van Buren Street (✆ **312/745-2862**) and Michigan Avenue and Madison Street (✆ **312/742-7530**). Parking costs $9 for the first hour, $12 for 1 to 2 hours, $15 for 2 to 10 hours, and $18 for 24 hours. You'll find higher prices at most other downtown lots, including **McCormick Place Parking,** 2301 S. Lake Shore Dr. (✆ 312/747-7194); **Midcontinental Plaza Garage,** 55 E. Monroe St. (✆ 312/986-6821); and **Navy Pier Parking,** 600 E. Grand Ave. (✆ 312/595-7437).

CAR RENTAL   **Hertz** (✆ 800/654-3131), **Avis** (✆ 800/831-2847), **National** (✆ 800/227-7368), and **Budget** (✆ 800/527-0700) all have offices at O'Hare Airport and at Midway Airport. Each company also has at least one office downtown: Hertz at 401 N. State St., Avis at 214 N. Clark St., National at 203 N. LaSalle St., and Budget at 65 E. Lake St.

How to Get to McCormick Place Conference Center

BY PUBLIC TRANSPORTATION Although many trade shows at McCormick Place, 23rd Street and Lake Shore Drive (*©* **312/791-7000;** www.mccormickplace.com), arrange transportation from hotels downtown and along North Michigan Avenue, you can also get there from Michigan Avenue by taking either the **no. 3 King Drive bus** or the **no. 4 Cottage Grove bus.** Both buses deposit passengers at the foot of McCormick Place's new South Building, at 23rd Street and Martin Luther King Jr. Drive. The no. 3 runs from early morning to about 11pm, and the no. 4 runs around the clock.

You can also take a **Metra Electric** commuter train directly to McCormick Place North. Catch the train in the Loop at the Randolph Street Station at Randolph Street and Michigan Avenue. For more information, call the RTA/CTA Travel Information hotline at *©* **312/ 836-7000.**

BY CAR From the Loop and North Michigan Avenue Take Lake Shore Drive South and follow the signs to McCormick Place.

From O'Hare Airport Take the Northwest Tollway (I-90) to the Kennedy/Dan Ryan Expressway (I-94) to the Stevenson Expressway North (I-55). Take the Stevenson Expressway north to Lake Shore Drive, and follow the signs to McCormick Place.

From Midway Airport Take the Stevenson Expressway (I-55) north to Lake Shore Drive South. Follow the signs to McCormick Place.

PARKING There are two main parking lots, one at 31st Street and Lake Shore Drive, and the other across the street from the new South Building, at 2215 S. Prairie Ave.

BY BOAT

During the summer, boat traffic booms along the Lake Michigan shoreline and the Chicago River. The water taxi service offered by **Shoreline Sightseeing** (*©* 312/222-9328) ferries passengers on the lake between Navy Pier and the Shedd Aquarium, and on the Chicago River between Navy Pier and the Sears Tower (Adams St. and the river). The boats run daily from Memorial Day to Labor Day every half-hour from 10am to 6pm and cost $6 for adults, $5 for seniors, and $3 for children.

The "RiverBus" operated by **Wendella Commuter Boats** (*©* 312/337-1446) floats daily April through October between a dock below the Wrigley Building (the northwest side of the Michigan Ave. bridge) and North Western Station, a commuter train station across the river from the Loop (near the Sears Tower). The ride, which costs $2 each way (or $3 round-trip) and takes about 8 minutes, is popular with both visitors and commuters. The service operates every 10 minutes from 7am to 7pm.

BY BICYCLE

The city of Chicago has earned kudos for its efforts to improve conditions for bicycling (designated bike lanes have been installed on stretches of Wells St., Roosevelt Rd., Elston Ave., and Halsted St.), but it can still be a tough prospect trying to compete with cars and their drivers, who aren't always so willing to share the road. Make sure that you wear a helmet at all times and stick to the lakefront path or area parks if you're nervous about veering into traffic.

The **Chicagoland Bicycle Federation** (✆ **312/42-PEDAL;** www.chibikefed. org), a nonprofit advocacy group, is a good resource for bicyclists. The group publishes several bicycling maps with tips on recommended on-street routes and parkland routes as well as a guide to safe cycling in the city.

Bike and Roll rents all sorts of bikes, including tandems and four-seater "quadcycles," as well as in-line skates, from two locations: at Navy Pier (✆ **312/ 595-9600**) and North Avenue Beach (✆ **773/327-2706**). Bikes rent for $9.75 an hour or $34 a day. Helmets, pads, and locks are free. The shops are open daily from 9am to 7pm, weather permitting.

FAST FACTS: Chicago

American Express Travel-service offices are located in the Loop at 55 W. Monroe St. (✆ **312/541-5440**) and across from the Virgin Megastore, at 605 N. Michigan Ave. (✆ **312/943-7840**).

Area Codes The 312 area code applies to the Loop and the neighborhoods closest to it, including River North, North Michigan Avenue, and the Gold Coast. The code for the rest of the city is 773. Suburban area codes are 847 (north), 708 (west and southwest), and 630 (far west). You must dial "1" plus the area code for all telephone numbers, even if you are making a call within the same area code.

Babysitters Check with the concierge or desk staff at your hotel, who are likely to maintain a list of reliable sitters with whom they have worked in the past. Many of the top hotels work with **American ChildCare Service** (✆ **312/644-7300**), a state-licensed and insured babysitting service that can match you with a sitter. The sitters are required to pass background checks, provide multiple child-care references, and be trained in infant and child CPR. It's best to make a reservation 24 hours in advance; the office is open from 9am to 5pm. Rates are $17 per hour, with a 4-hour minimum.

Business Hours Shops generally keep normal business hours, 10am to 6pm Monday through Saturday. Most stores generally stay open late at least 1 evening a week. And certain businesses, such as bookstores, are almost always open during the evening hours all week. Most shops (other than in the Loop) are now open on Sunday as well, usually from noon to 5pm. Malls are generally open to 7pm and on Sunday as well. Banking hours in Chicago are normally from 9am (8am, in some cases) to 5pm Monday through Friday, with select banks remaining open later on specified afternoons and evenings.

Car Rentals See "Getting Around," earlier in this chapter.

Dentists The 24-hour **Dental Referral Service** (✆ **630/978-5745**) can refer you to an area dentist. Your hotel concierge or desk staff may also keep a list of dentists.

Doctors In the event of a medical emergency, your best bet—unless you have friends who can recommend a doctor—is to rely on your hotel physician or go to the nearest hospital emergency room. **Northwestern**

Memorial Hospital also has a **Physician Referral Service** (☏ 877/926-4664). See also "Hospitals" below.

Driving Rules See "Getting Around," earlier in this chapter.

Embassies & Consulates See "Fast Facts: For the International Traveler," in chapter 4.

Emergencies For fire or police emergencies, call ☏ **911**. This is a free call. The nonemergency phone number for the Chicago Police Department is ☏ **311**. The city of Chicago proclaims the following policy: "In emergency, dial 911 and a city ambulance will respond free of charge to the patient. The ambulance will take the patient to the nearest emergency room according to geographic location." If you desire a specific, nonpublic ambulance, call **Chicago Ambulance** (☏ 773/521-7777).

Hospitals The best hospital emergency room in Chicago is, by consensus, at **Northwestern Memorial Hospital,** 251 E. Huron St. (☏ **312/926-2000;** www.nmh.org), which opened a state-of-the-art medical center right off North Michigan Avenue in the spring of 1999. The emergency department (☏ 312/926-5188 or 312/944-2358 for TDD access) is located at 251 E. Erie St. near Fairbanks Court. For an ambulance, dial ☏ **911.**

Internet Access Many Chicago **hotels** have business centers with computers available for guests' use. Computers with Internet access are also available to the public at the **Harold Washington Library Center,** 400 S. State St. (☏ 312/747-4300) and at the Internet cafe inside the **Apple** computer store, 679 N. Michigan Ave. (☏ 312/981-4104).

Liquor Laws Most bars and taverns have a 2am license, allowing them to stay open until 3am on Sunday (Sat night); some have a 4am license and may remain open until 5am on Sunday.

Maps See "City Layout," earlier in this chapter.

Newspapers & Magazines The *Chicago Tribune* (☏ 312/222-3232; www.chicagotribune.com) and the *Chicago Sun-Times* (☏ 312/321-3000; www.suntimes.com) are the two major dailies. The *Chicago Reader* (☏ 312/828-0350; www.chireader.com) is a free weekly that appears each Thursday, with all the current entertainment and cultural listings. *Chicago Magazine* (www.chicagomag.com) is a monthly that is widely read for its restaurant reviews. *CS* is a free lifestyle monthly that covers nightlife, dining, fashion, shopping, and other cultural pursuits. The *Chicago Defender* covers local and national news of interest to the African-American community. The Spanish-language *La Raza* (www.laraza.com) reports on stories from a Latino point of view. *Windy City Times* (www.outlineschicago.com) publishes both news and feature articles about gay and lesbian issues.

Pharmacies **Walgreens,** 757 N. Michigan Ave. (☏ 312/664-4000), is open 24 hours. The other big pharmacy chain in town, **Osco Drugs,** has a toll-free number (☏ 800/654-6726) that you can call to locate the 24-hour pharmacy nearest you.

Police For emergencies, call ☏ **911**. This is a free call (no coins required). For nonemergencies, call ☏ **311**.

Post Office The main post office is at 433 W. Harrison St. (☏ 312/983-8182); free parking is available. You also find convenient branches in the Sears Tower, the Federal Center Plaza at 211 S. Clark St., the James R.

Thompson Center at 100 W. Randolph St., and a couple of blocks off the Magnificent Mile at 227 E. Ontario St.

Radio **WBEZ** (91.5 FM) is the local National Public Radio station, which plays jazz in the evenings. **WFMT** (98.7 FM) specializes in fine arts and classical music. **WXRT** (93.1 FM) is a progressive rock station whose DJs mix things up with shots of blues, jazz, and local music. On the AM side of the dial, you'll find talk radio on **WGN** (720) and **WLS** (890). News junkies should tune to **WBBM** (780) for nonstop news, traffic, and weather reports, and sports fans will find company on the talk station **WSCR** (1160).

Safety Chicago has all the crime problems of any urban center, so use your common sense and stay cautious and alert. Everyone has a different comfort level in unfamiliar terrain, so you'll have to decide for yourself where and when you want to venture. At night you might want to stick to well-lighted streets along the Magnificent Mile, River North, Gold Coast, and Lincoln Park (stay out of the park proper after dark, though), which are all high-traffic areas late into the night. Don't walk alone at night, and avoid wandering down dark residential streets, even those that seem perfectly safe. Muggings can—and do—happen anywhere.

After dark, you might want to avoid the Loop's interior, which gets deserted after business hours, as well as neighborhoods such as Hyde Park, Wicker Park (beyond the busy intersection of Milwaukee, Damen, and North aves.), and Pilsen, which border areas with more troublesome reputations. You can also ask your hotel concierge or an agent at the tourist visitor center about the safety of a particular area.

If you're traveling alone, avoid riding the El after the rush-hour crowds thin out. Of course, it's always smarter to ride with a group. Many of the El stations can be eerily deserted at night, when you'll have to wait around for 15 minutes or longer for the next train. In that case, it's a good idea to spring for a taxi. Buses are a safe option, too, especially nos. 146 and 151, which pick up along North Michigan Avenue and State Street and connect to the North Side via Lincoln Park.

Blue-and-white police cars are a common sight, and officers also patrol by bicycle downtown and along the lakefront and by horseback at special events and parades. There are police stations in busy nightlife areas, such as the 18th District station at Chicago Avenue and LaSalle Street in River North and the 24th District station (known as Town Hall) at Addison and Halsted streets.

Taxes The local sales tax is 8.75%. Restaurants in the central part of the city, roughly the 312 area code, are taxed an additional 1%, for a total of 9.75%. The hotel room tax is a steep 14.9%.

Time Zone All of Illinois, including Chicago, is located in the central time zone.

Transit Info The **CTA** has a useful number to find out which bus or El train will get you to your destination: ✆ **836-7000** (from any area code in the city or suburbs) or TTY 836-4949.

Weather For the **National Weather Service**'s current conditions and forecast, dial ✆ **312/976-1212** (for a fee), or check the weather on the Web at www.ci.chi.il.us/Tourism/Weather/.

6

Where to Stay

Downtown Chicago is packed with hotels, thanks to the city's booming convention trade. The competition among luxury hotels is especially intense, with the Ritz-Carlton and Four Seasons winning international awards even as newer properties (such as the Peninsula Chicago and Sofitel Chicago Water Tower) get in on the action. In recent years, that meant steadily rising prices, with budget lodgings becoming harder to find. But since the September 11, 2001, terrorist attacks and the subsequent stock market woes, both business and tourist traffic has slowed—which means more and more hotels are willing to make a deal. In the past year, average room rates have dipped significantly.

Most Chicago hotels offer a quintessential urban experience: Rooms come with views of surrounding skyscrapers, and the bustle of city life hits you as soon as you step outside the lobby doors. Although every property listed here caters to business travelers, Chicago attracts lots of tourists as well, and you won't have a problem finding plenty of midrange, family-friendly hotels in the most convenient neighborhoods; this is not a city where luxury hotels have dibs on all the prime real estate.

Although Chicago now has a few places that tout themselves as "boutique" hotels (Hotel Burnham, Hotel Monaco, W Chicago Lakeshore), these aren't quite the same as their New York, Miami, or Los Angeles counterparts—the so-called beautiful people who frequent these spots on the coasts don't tend to stop off in Chicago. No matter where you stay, you'll likely find that your fellow guests are business travelers or vacationing families.

The rates given in this chapter are per night and do not include taxes, which are quite steep at 14.9%, nor do they take into account corporate or other discounts. Prices are always subject to availability and vary according to the time of week and season.

Note: For information on getting good room rates and the best rooms in hotels, see "Tips on Accommodations," beginning on p. 46.

Because Chicago's hospitality industry caters first and foremost to the business traveler, rates tend to be higher during the week. The city's slow season is from January to March, when outsiders tend to shy away from the cold and the threat of being snowed in at O'Hare. (If you'd like to watch your pennies but don't want to sightsee in a heavy down coat, another option is to stay in an outlying neighborhood during the week and then move into downtown for the weekend.)

You never know when some huge convention will gobble up all the desirable rooms in the city (even on the weekends), so you're wise to book a room well in advance at any time of year. To find out if an upcoming convention coincides with your visit, contact the **Chicago Convention & Tourism Bureau** (© 312/567-8500; www.choosechicago.com—click on "Convention Calendar").

RESERVATIONS   Whenever you visit, making reservations well in advance will help you get the best room at the best rate. While our listings give the national toll-free numbers for most of the hotels in this book, you may obtain better rates by calling hotels directly. You may also want to check hotel websites, which often advertise special deals.

Most hotels have check-in times somewhere between 3 and 6pm; if you are going to be delayed, call ahead and reconfirm your reservation to prevent cancellation.

CORPORATE DISCOUNTS   Most hotels offer discounts of roughly 10% to individuals who are visiting Chicago on business. To qualify for this rate, your company usually must have an account on file at the hotel; in some cases, however, you may be required only to present some perfunctory proof of your commercial status, such as a business card or an official letterhead, to receive the discount. It never hurts to ask.

RESERVATION SERVICES   You can check on the latest rates and availability, as well as book a room, by calling the **Illinois Reservation Service** (© **800/491-1800**). The 24-hour service is free. Another reservation service is **Hot Rooms** (© **800/468-3500** or 773/468-7666; www.hotrooms.com), which offers discounts at selected downtown hotels (my parents have used this service, and they were quite happy with the results—a night at a downtown hotel at half the regular price). The 24-hour service is free, but if you cancel a reservation, you're

assessed a $25 fee. For a copy of the annual *Illinois Hotel-Motel Directory,* which also provides information about weekend packages, call the **Illinois Bureau of Tourism** at © **800/2CONNECT.**

BED & BREAKFAST RESERVATIONS   A centralized reservations service called **Bed & Breakfast/Chicago Inc.,** P.O. Box 14088, Chicago, IL 60614 (© **800/375-7084** or 773/394-2000; fax 773/394-2002; www.chicago-bed-breakfast.com), lists more than 70 accommodations in Chicago. Options range from high-rise and loft apartments to guest rooms carved from a former private club on the 40th floor of a Loop office building. Most lie within 3 miles of downtown (many are located in the Gold Coast, Old Town, and Lincoln Park) and will run you $135 to $300 for apartments, and as low as $85 for guest rooms in private homes. Most require a minimum stay of 2 or 3 nights.

ACCESSIBILITY   Most hotels are prepared to accommodate travelers with physical disabilities, but you should always inquire when you make reservations to make sure that the hotel can meet your particular needs. Older properties, in particular, may not meet current requirements or may only have limited numbers of specially equipped rooms.

A WORD ABOUT SMOKING   Most hotels offer rooms or entire floors for nonsmokers. If it's important to you, be sure to specify whether you want a smoking or nonsmoking room when you make your reservation.

1 The Loop

Strictly speaking, "downtown" in Chicago means the Loop—the central business district, a 6-by-8-block rectangle enveloped by elevated tracks on all four sides. Within these confines are the city's financial institutions, trading markets, and municipal government buildings, making for a lot of hustle and bustle Monday through Friday. The Art Institute of Chicago sits on the Loop's edge and the Museum Campus, home to the Field Museum of Natural History and

John G. Shedd Aquarium, is an easy walk to the south on a nice day. For visitors who want a real "city" experience, the Loop offers dramatic urban vistas of skyscrapers and the feeling that you're at the heart of the action—on weekdays. Come Saturday and Sunday, however, the Loop is pretty dead; on Sundays, almost all the stores are closed. If nightlife is a priority, you won't find much here, but you do have some very good dining options.

VERY EXPENSIVE

Fairmont Hotel ★★   The Fairmont is easily one of the city's most luxurious hotels, offering an array of deluxe amenities and services and regularly hosting high-level politicians and high-profile fundraisers. The overall effect is chic but a bit impersonal. The entrance faces anonymous office towers, and you're likely to wander the circular lobby before finding the check-in desk. Still, the rooms are large and decorated in a comfortable, upscale style (ask for one with a lake view, although city-view rooms aren't bad either). The posh bathrooms feature extra-large tubs, separate vanity areas, and swivel TVs. The windows open (a rarity in high-rise hotels), so you can enjoy the breeze drifting off Lake Michigan. Suites have one or two bedrooms, a living room, a dining area, and a built-in bar—and all come with lake views. The hotel is connected to the city's underground "pedway" system, through which you can walk all the way to Marshall Field's on State Street—a bonus on inclement days (a florist, pharmacy, and salon are conveniently located in an adjoining building).

200 N. Columbus Dr. (at Lake St.), Chicago, IL 60601. ✆ **800/526-2008** or 312/565-8000. Fax 312/856-1032. www.fairmont.com. 692 units. $189–$354 double. AE, DC, DISC, MC, V. Valet parking $34 with in/out privileges. Subway/El: Red, Green, Orange, Brown, or Blue line to State/Lake. Small pets accepted. **Amenities:** Restaurant (American/eclectic); lounge; access to Lakeshore Athletic Club, one of the top health clubs in the city (with full-court basketball, climbing wall, pool, and spa); concierge; business center; 24-hr. room service; babysitting; laundry service; 24-hr. dry cleaning. *In room:* A/C, TV w/pay movies, high-speed Internet access, minibar, hair dryer, iron.

EXPENSIVE

Crowne Plaza Chicago—The Silversmith ★★ *Finds*   You might call The Silversmith a hidden gem. The landmark building, designed by the celebrated firm of D. H. Burnham and Company, was built in 1897 to serve the jewelry and silver trade on Wabash Avenue, still known as Jeweler's Row. Rooms come in varying configurations, with 12-foot-high ceilings, 10-foot picture windows, Frank Lloyd Wright–inspired wrought-iron fixtures, armoires, and homey bedding; bathrooms are generously sized. Because buildings surround this very urban hotel, natural light is limited in the rooms; those along the hotel's main corridor tend to be dark. Rooms at the front on the fifth floor or higher have a quintessentially Chicago view: hard-working Wabash Avenue and the El tracks. Yes, the windows are extra-thick to muffle the noise of the rumbling trains, but you'll want to avoid the lower-level floors if you like things quiet. For the best combination of natural light and views, request a Wabash Avenue room on the 9th or 10th floor.

Word about The Silversmith has been slow getting out (even Loop office workers who pass by it daily don't know it's there), so rooms don't book up as quickly as other, hotter spots. That's good news for thrifty travelers looking for deals (I hear the suites often get discounted). You may also be able to find a room here during the busy convention season. Guest-friendly touches include an evening wine-and-cheese reception and complimentary desserts available at night in the lobby (including Eli's cheesecake, one of the city's signature sweet treats).

Central Chicago Accommodations

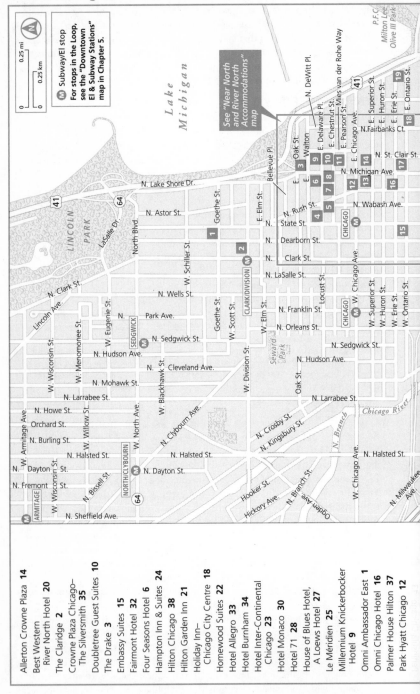

Allerton Crowne Plaza **14**
Best Western
River North Hotel **20**
The Claridge **2**
Crowne Plaza Chicago—
The Silversmith **35**
Doubletree Guest Suites **10**
The Drake **3**
Embassy Suites **15**
Fairmont Hotel **32**
Four Seasons Hotel **6**
Hampton Inn & Suites **24**
Hilton Chicago **38**
Hilton Garden Inn **21**
Holiday Inn—
Chicago City Centre **18**
Homewood Suites **22**
Hotel Allegro **33**
Hotel Burnham **34**
Hotel Inter-Continental
Chicago **23**
Hotel Monaco **30**
Hotel 71 **28**
House of Blues Hotel,
A Loews Hotel **27**
Le Méridien **25**
Millennium Knickerbocker
Hotel **9**
Omni Ambassador East **1**
Omni Chicago Hotel **16**
Palmer House Hilton **37**
Park Hyatt Chicago **12**

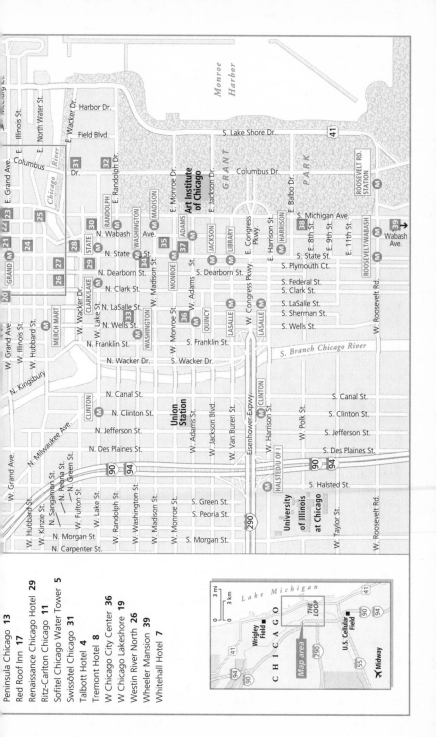

Peninsula Chicago **13**
Red Roof Inn **17**
Renaissance Chicago Hotel **29**
Ritz-Carlton Chicago **11**
Sofitel Chicago Water Tower **5**
Swissôtel Chicago **31**
Talbott Hotel **4**
Tremont Hotel **8**
W Chicago City Center **36**
W Chicago Lakeshore **19**
Westin River North **26**
Wheeler Mansion **39**
Whitehall Hotel **7**

10 S. Wabash Ave. (at Madison St.), Chicago, IL 60603. ☎ **800/2CROWNE** or 312/372-7696. Fax 312/372-7320. www.ichotelsgroup.com. 143 units. $149–$279 double; from $289 suite; weekend rates available. AE, DC, DISC, MC, V. Valet parking $28 with in/out privileges. Subway/El: Brown, Green, or Orange line to Madison/Wabash, or Red Line to Washington/State. **Amenities:** Restaurant (deli); lounge; tiny fitness room (with access to nearby health club at a charge); concierge; business center and secretarial services; limited room service; laundry service; dry cleaning; club-level rooms. *In room:* A/C, TV w/pay movies, dataport, minibar, coffeemaker, hair dryer, iron, safe.

Hotel Burnham ★★★   If you're looking for a spot with a sense of history, this is it. A brilliant $30 million restoration in 1999 of the historic Reliance Building—one of the first skyscrapers ever built and a highly significant architectural treasure—resulted in this intimate boutique hotel named for Daniel Burnham, whose firm designed the building in 1895. The prime State Street location is across from Marshall Field's and 1 block south of the hopping North Loop theater district. The Burnham is a must for architecture buffs: Wherever possible, the restoration retained period elements—most obviously in the hallways, which recall the original office corridors with terrazzo tile floors, white marble wainscoting, mahogany door and window frames, and room numbers painted on the translucent glass doors. Rooms are clubby but glamorous, with plush beds, mahogany writing desks, and chaise lounges. The hotel's 19 suites feature a separate living-room area and CD stereo systems. Don't come to the Burnham if you're looking for extensive amenities—the lobby is tiny, as is the exercise room. But the Burnham is one of Chicago's most distinctive hotels, and it's highly recommended for visitors who want a historic location jazzed up with a dash of colorful modern style. Ask for a room on a high floor in the northeast corner—the views north and east are dazzling. The on-site Atwood Café (p. 111) serves creative comfort food against a Gilded Age backdrop.

1 W. Washington St. (at State St.), Chicago, IL 60602. ☎ **877/294-9712** or 312/782-1111. Fax 312/782-0899. www.burnhamhotel.com. 122 units. $149–$299 double; $199–$349 suite. AE, DC, DISC, MC, V. Valet parking $29 with in/out privileges. Subway: Red or Blue line to Washington/State. **Amenities:** Restaurant (contemporary American); small fitness room (and access to nearby health club); concierge; business services; 24-hr. room service; laundry service; dry cleaning. *In room:* A/C, TV, fax, dataport, minibar, hair dryer, iron.

Hotel Monaco ★★★   This 14-story boutique hotel may try a little too hard to be "fun": Guests are greeted by derby-hatted doormen, funky house music plays in the lobby, and a goldfish with its own name swims about a fishbowl in your room. But it offers an upbeat alternative to the many cookie-cutter business hotels in the city. The plush, jewel-toned, 1930s-inspired decor makes the sizeable rooms resemble theatrical set pieces. The eclectic furnishings include armoires, mahogany writing desks, and marshmallow-soft beds; suites come with a two-person whirlpool spa and CD player. (For wannabe Mick Jaggers there's a "Party Like a Rock Star" suite with a Sony 52-disc CD player, rock costume replicas, an electric guitar and amplifier, concert photographs of rock icons, and a 19-inch TV set that appears to have been thrown through the window.) Rooms on the top three floors have views of the Chicago River and surrounding skyscrapers. The cozy lobby is the spot for free morning coffee and an evening wine reception. Given the hotel's playful spirit, it attracts a younger clientele, with an overall vibe that is laid-back and friendly rather than so-hip-it-hurts (this is Chicago, after all, not New York).

225 N. Wabash Ave. (at Wacker Dr.), Chicago, IL 60601. ☎ **800/397-7661** or 312/960-8500. Fax 312/960-8538. www.monaco-chicago.com. 192 units. $139–$299 double; $279–$429 suite. AE, DC, DISC, MC, V. Valet parking $28 with in/out privileges. Subway: Brown, Green, or Orange line to Randolph/Wabash, or Red Line to Washington/State. Small pets allowed. **Amenities:** Restaurant (American); fitness room (and access to

nearby health club); concierge; business center; 24-hr. room service; in-room massage; babysitting; laundry service; dry cleaning. *In room:* A/C, TV w/pay movies, fax, dataport, minibar, coffeemaker, hair dryer, iron.

Hotel 71 ★★   The city's newest hotel is actually a complete renovation of a rather drab 1950-era high-rise. Don't let the boring exterior fool you. Hotel 71 is too big to be considered a "boutique hotel" (with more than 400 rooms spread over 30-plus stories), but it is filled with unique touches that reflect the boutique sensibility. The rather-cramped lobby feels like a nightclub, with black curtains covering the walls and atmospheric trance music wafting from the stereo system. The rooms, by contrast, are bright and cheery—and much larger than average. Everything is brand new, from the yellow-checked linens and curtains, to the spotless white bathrooms. Every room has a well-lit work desk and a minibar stocked with gourmet treats from Dean & DeLuca. Rooms on the north side of the hotel (overlooking the Chicago River) have the best views; if you can, snag one of the rooms on the west end of the building, which have views in two directions. Suites come with either a living room or meeting room and a bedroom down the hall (but the bathrooms are actually smaller than those in the regular rooms). The hotel's gift shop is well worth a look; a step above the usual aspirin-and-candy store, it features upscale bath products and unique travel accessories. But the real draw at Hotel 71 is the spacious rooms—especially those with a view.

71 E. Wacker Dr. (at Wabash Ave.), Chicago, IL 60601. © **800/621-4005** or 312/346-7100. Fax 312/346-1721. www.hotel71.com. 454 units. $149–$249 double. AE, DC, DISC, MC, V. Valet parking $32 with in/out privileges. Subway: Brown, Green, or Orange line to Randolph/Wabash, or Red Line to Washington/State. **Amenities:** Restaurant (contemporary American); fitness room; concierge; business services; 24-hr. room service; laundry service; dry cleaning. *In room:* A/C, TV, high-speed Internet access, minibar, hair dryer, iron, CD player.

Palmer House Hilton *(Overrated*   Chicago's oldest hotel, the namesake of legendary State Street merchant prince Potter Palmer, is decidedly from another era—and the massive complex feels somewhat lost in time. The elegance of the grand lobby isn't matched in the rooms (decorated in an anonymous midlevel hotel style) or the clientele (which tends heavily toward conventioneers). And don't expect grand views of surrounding skyscrapers, because most rooms look out into offices across the street. All the rooms are in the process of being renovated, but upgrades at the palatial Palmer House take place, understandably, on a staggered basis; be sure to ask for a refurbished room when making reservations. Bathrooms are on the smallish size (some rooms come with two bathrooms, a plus for families). Kids might appreciate the sheer size of the place, with plenty of room to wander, and the location is good for access to the

---

Fun Fact   Did You Know?

Merriel Abbott, the dance choreographer who booked all the acts at the Palmer House's famed Empire Room—one of the nation's leading supper clubs from the 1930s to the 1950s—gave Liberace and Bob Fosse their first breaks. Liberace, a cocktail pianist at the club, was "discovered" in Milwaukee by Abbott, who is credited with dressing up the flamboyant entertainer's piano with a candelabra to lend his act some pizzazz. Fosse, a native Chicagoan, made his debut at 18 as part of a dance team. He and his partner made $500 a month in 1947; Liberace was paid a miserly $1,100 for 5 weeks in 1946.

Museum Campus, but the Palmer House's days as one of Chicago's top hotels are gone.

17 E. Monroe St. (at State St.), Chicago, IL 60603. (℃) **800/HILTONS** or 312/726-7500. Fax 312/917-1797. www.hilton.com. 1,640 units. $129–$350 double; $450–$1,500 suite. AE, DC, DISC, MC, V. Valet parking $31 with in/out privileges; self-parking across the street $21. Subway/El: Red Line to Monroe/State. **Amenities:** 4 restaurants (including the legendary but dated Trader Vic's, a Cajun restaurant, and 2 American bar and grills); 2 lounges; indoor pool; health club; Jacuzzi; sauna; children's programs; concierge; business center; shopping arcade; room service until 2am; babysitting referrals; laundry service; overnight dry cleaning; executive rooms. In room: A/C, TV w/pay movies, minibar, coffeemaker, hair dryer, iron.

Renaissance Chicago Hotel ★★ A hotel in search of a personality, the Renaissance Chicago is tasteful and understated—perfectly suited to the business travelers who are the hotel's bread and butter. This large operation offers all your standard high-end amenities but is indistinguishable from any number of executive-style hotels elsewhere in the country. Still, this is a good bet for high-end service if you want a Loop location, and the hotel's bay windows provide stunning views of the Chicago River and the towers of North Michigan Avenue. Standard double rooms include a small sitting area with a couch and smallish bathrooms; deluxe doubles have much bigger bathrooms (some with separate showers and bathtubs) and two couches. Club-level rooms, located on the top four floors, are half a room larger and have their own concierge in a private lounge, where complimentary continental breakfast and evening hors d'oeuvres are served. Request a room on the 20th floor or higher on the east side for views of both the Chicago River and Lake Michigan. Another good bet are rooms on the hotel's north side, all of which have river views.

1 W. Wacker Dr. (at State St.), Chicago, IL 60601. (℃) **800/HOTELS-1** or 312/372-7200. Fax 312/372-0093. www.renaissancehotels.com. 553 units. $159–$259 double; $189–$289 club-level double; $500–$2,500 suite. AE, DC, DISC, MC, V. Valet parking $34 with in/out privileges. Subway/El: Brown Line to State/Lake or Red Line to Washington/State. Small pets accepted. **Amenities:** Restaurant (American); lounge; indoor pool w/skylights; health club w/sauna and whirlpool; concierge; 24-hr. Kinko's business center; salon; 24-hr. room service; babysitting; laundry service; club-level rooms. In room: A/C, TV w/pay movies, high-speed Internet access, minibar, coffeemaker, hair dryer, iron, wet bar in some rooms.

Swissôtel Chicago ★★ This sleek, modern hotel is all business, and may therefore feel a bit icy to some visitors. Panoramic vistas from every room—of Lake Michigan, Grant Park, the Chicago River, or the nine-hole, par-three FamilyGolf Center next door—are the hotel's best features. The spacious rooms have separate sitting areas and warm contemporary furnishings. Business travelers will appreciate the oversize desks (convertible to dining tables), ergonomic chairs, and—in upgraded executive-level rooms—CD players. Executive suites, with wonderful, 180-degree views, have separate sleeping areas. All executive-level guests also receive complimentary breakfast and hors d'oeuvres and have access to a lounge with Internet connections, library, and personal concierge.

The Swissôtel has a slick, professional aura that's not particularly family-friendly, which makes it especially attractive to business travelers in search of tranquility. Active travelers will want to break a sweat in the lofty environs of the Penthouse Health Spa, perched on the 42nd floor. And those who just want to indulge themselves can enjoy the ultimate steak-and-lobster expense-account restaurant: the on-site outpost of New York's The Palm.

323 E. Wacker Dr., Chicago, IL 60601. (℃) **888/737-9477** or 312/565-0565. Fax 312/565-0540. www.swissotel. com. 632 units. $159–$409 double; $395–$2,500 suite. AE, DC, DISC, MC, V. Valet parking $35 with in/out privileges. Subway/El: Red, Brown, Orange, or Green line to Randolph. **Amenities:** 3 restaurants (steakhouse, American); lounge; penthouse fitness center with indoor pool, spa, Jacuzzi, and sauna; concierge; business center with extensive meeting services; 24-hr. room service; massage; babysitting; laundry service; 24-hr. dry

cleaning; executive-level rooms. *In room:* A/C, TV w/pay movies, dataport, minibar, coffeemaker, hair dryer, iron.

W Chicago City Center 🐾 One of two Chicago properties in the hip W hotel chain (the other is the W Chicago Lakeshore, below), this is an oasis of cool in the button-down Loop. Unfortunately, the rooms tend toward the small and dark (most look out into a central courtyard). The W color scheme—dark purple and gray—doesn't do much to brighten the spaces; don't stay here if you crave lots of natural light. All W properties pride themselves on their "whatever, whenever" service: whatever you want, whenever you want it (the modern version of a 24-hr. on-call concierge). The bar, designed by nightlife wunderkind Rande Gerber (Mr. Cindy Crawford), gives hotel guests a stylish spot to sit and pose amid dance music and cocktail waitresses who look like models. Given its location, this W is foremost a business hotel—although one that's definitely geared toward younger workers rather than crusty old executives.

172 W. Adams St. (at LaSalle St.), Chicago, IL 60603. ℂ **877/W-HOTELS** or 312/332-1200. Fax 312/332-5909. www.whotels.com. 390 units. $199–$329 double; from $369 suite. AE, DC, DISC, MC, V. Valet parking $30 with in/out privileges. Subway/El: Brown Line to Quincy. Pets allowed. **Amenities:** Restaurant (European); bar; exercise room; concierge; business services; 24-hr. room service; in-room massage; babysitting; same-day laundry service; dry cleaning. *In room:* A/C, TV w/VCR and pay movies, fax, high-speed Internet access, minibar, coffeemaker, hair dryer, iron, safe, CD player.

MODERATE

Hotel Allegro Chicago 🐾 *Value* Owned by the same company as the Hotel Monaco and the Hotel Burnham (both listed above), the Allegro is the best choice in the Loop for families in search of a fun vibe. Although its published rates are about the same as those of its sister properties, the Allegro is far larger than the Monaco or the Burnham, and consequently is more likely to offer special rates to fill space (especially on weekends and in the winter). Guests enter a lobby with plush, eclectic, and boldly colorful furnishings: This whimsical first impression segues into the rooms, which vary wildly in size and configuration, so be sure to request the biggest available room when making your reservation. Suites have robes, VCRs, and two-person Jacuzzi tubs.

Befitting a place where the concierge wears a stylish leather jacket and the doorman hums along to the tunes playing on speakers out front, the Allegro appeals to younger travelers. There's plenty of opportunity for socializing at Encore, the Jetsons-esque cafe that hosts DJs at night, or at the complimentary evening wine reception in the lobby. The hotel's restaurant, 312 Chicago (p. 117), attracts nonguests in search of excellent Italian cuisine.

171 W. Randolph St. (at LaSalle St.), Chicago, IL 60601. ℂ **800/643-1500** or 312/236-0123. Fax 312/236-0917. www.allegrochicago.com. 483 units. $149–$299 double; $225–$399 suite. AE, DC, DISC, MC, V. Valet parking $30 with in/out privileges. Subway/El: All lines to Washington. **Amenities:** Restaurant (northern Italian); lounge; exercise room (and access to nearby health club w/indoor pool); concierge; business services; salon; limited room service; same-day laundry service; dry cleaning. *In room:* A/C, TV w/pay movies, high-speed Internet access (upon request), minibar, hair dryer, iron.

2 South Loop

The South Loop is less about glamour and more about old Chicago. Running the length of Grant Park, South Michigan Avenue is ideal for a long city stroll, passing grand museums, imposing architecture, and the park's greenery and statuary. But the overall feel is stately rather than lively. Over the last decade, however, the surrounding neighborhood has revitalized itself with the conversion of industrial buildings into loft apartments. Old-timers might complain about

> ⌒ **Kids   Family-Friendly Hotels**
>
> Chicago has plenty of options for families on the go. The **Hampton Inn & Suites** (p. 101) keeps the kids in a good mood with a pool, Nintendo, and proximity to the Hard Rock Cafe and the Rainforest Cafe. Children under 18 stay free. Kiddies also stay free at the **Holiday Inn–Chicago City Centre** (p. 98), which has a large outdoor pool and is near Navy Pier and the beach.
>
> When you want a little extra room to spread out, both **Homewood Suites** (p. 98) and **Embassy Suites** (p. 99) offer affordable ways to travel en masse (and keep your sanity).
>
> Of course, luxury hotels can afford to be friendly to all of their guests. At the **Four Seasons** (p. 89), kids are indulged with little robes, balloon animals, Nintendo, and milk and cookies; the hotel also has a wonderful pool. The concierge at the **Ritz-Carlton** (p. 92) keeps a stash of toys and games for younger guests to borrow, and kids' menu items are available 24 hours; the hotel even provides a special gift pack just for teenage guests. The upscale **Westin River North** (p. 100), the **Omni Chicago Hotel** (p. 95), and the **Omni Ambassador East** (p. 102) also cater to families with baby accessories and programs for older kids, respectively.

gentrification, but it's good news for visitors who can now find more restaurant options and a more active street life.

EXPENSIVE

Hilton Chicago ★★   When it opened in 1927, this massive brick-and-stone edifice billed itself as the largest hotel in the world. Today, the Hilton still runs like a small city, with numerous restaurants and shops and a steady stream of conventioneers. Its colorful history includes visits by Queen Elizabeth, Emperor Hirohito, and every president since FDR—and riots outside its front door during the 1968 Democratic Convention. The classical-rococo public spaces—including the Versailles-inspired Grand Ballroom and Grand Stair Lobby—are magnificent, but the rest of the hotel is firmly entrenched in the present.

Some rooms are on the small side, but all are comfortable and warm, and many of the standard rooms have two bathrooms (great for families). High rooms facing Michigan Avenue offer sweeping views of Grant Park and the lake. The hotel's Tower section has a separate registration area, upgraded amenities (including robes, fax machines, and VCRs), and a lounge open from 6am to 11pm, serving complimentary continental breakfast and evening hors d'oeuvres and cocktails (you'll pay about $50 above the standard rate for these rooms).

The Hilton is a great choice for families, thanks to its vast public spaces, proximity to major museums and Grant Park (where kids can run around), and policy of children under 18 staying free in their parents' room. Because the Hilton depends heavily on convention traffic, those seeking a cozy, romantic getaway should go elsewhere.

720 S. Michigan Ave. (at Balbo Dr.), Chicago, IL 60605. © **800/HILTONS** or 312/922-4400. Fax 312/922-5240. www.chicagohilton.com. 1,544 units. $124–$324 double; $139–$339 junior suite. AE, DC, DISC, MC, V. Valet parking $32; self-parking $29. Subway/El: Red Line to Harrison/State. **Amenities:** 4 restaurants

(Continental, Irish, American); 2 lounges; indoor pool; health club w/indoor track, hot tubs, sauna, and steam room; concierge; business center; 24-hr. room service; massage; babysitting; laundry service; 24-hr. dry cleaning; tower rooms. *In room:* A/C, TV w/pay movies, dataport, minibar, coffeemaker, hair dryer, iron.

Wheeler Mansion ★★ *Finds*   This grand Italianate building had fallen on hard times—until Debra and Scott Seger saw its potential as a bed-and-breakfast. Today, completely restored and refurbished, the Wheeler Mansion is one of the city's most charming small hotels. The Segers kept intact whatever was salvageable, including the mosaic tile floor in the vestibule and some of the dark walnut woodwork and fixtures. But they added good-size private bathrooms to each room (some have only shower stalls rather than bathtubs). The rooms—which are spacious enough to include armoires and armchairs—feel even larger, thanks to the high ceilings. Antique furniture that the Segers found in Europe fills the house, and guests dine on bone china and sleep on goose-down feather beds. A continental breakfast by the resident chef is served weekdays. On weekends, the buffet features a more elaborate array of dishes.

2020 S. Calumet Ave., Chicago, IL 60616. © **312/945-2020.** Fax 312/945-2021. www.wheelermansion.com. 11 units. $230–$285 double; $265–$365 suite. Prices include taxes. AE, DC, DISC, MC, V. Free parking. Bus: No. 62 from State Street downtown. **Amenities:** Laundry service; computer rental available. *In room:* A/C, cable TV, fax machine, dataport, hair dryer, iron.

3 Near North & the Magnificent Mile

Along the Magnificent Mile—a stretch of Michigan Avenue running north of the Chicago River to Oak Street—you'll find most of the city's premium hotels. The location, near some of the city's best shopping and dining, can't be beat.

VERY EXPENSIVE

Four Seasons Hotel ★★★ *Kids*   Consistently voted one of the top hotels in the world by frequent travelers, the Four Seasons offers an understated luxury that appeals to publicity-shy Hollywood stars and wealthy families. Although the hotel has every conceivable luxury amenity, the overall look is that of an English country manor rather than a glitzy getaway. The real attraction here is the service, not the decor.

The city's tallest hotel, the Four Seasons occupies a rarefied aerie between the 30th and 46th floors above the Mag Mile's most upscale vertical mall. The beautiful rooms have English furnishings, custom-woven carpets and tapestries, and dark-wood armoires. Each has windows that open to let in the fresh air. Bathrooms boast such indulgences as a lighted makeup mirror, oversize towels and robes, scales, and Bulgari toiletries. Kid-friendly services include little robes, balloon animals, Nintendo, a special room-service menu, and milk and cookies. The hotel's elegant fitness center and spa exude the same upscale, old-money feel as the rest of the public areas. An 18-foot-high white marble fountain marks the entrance to the opulent Seasons Restaurant.

120 E. Delaware Place (at Michigan Ave.), Chicago, IL 60611. © **800/332-3442** or 312/280-8800. Fax 312/280-1748. www.fourseasons.com. 343 units. $420–$515 double; $555–$3,500 suite; weekend rates from $305. AE, DC, DISC, MC, V. Valet parking $35 with in/out privileges; self-parking $25. Subway/El: Red Line to Chicago/State. Pets accepted. **Amenities:** 2 restaurants (New American, cafe); lounge; indoor pool; fitness center and spa; concierge; business center; 24-hr. room service; babysitting; laundry service; 24-hr. dry cleaning. *In room:* A/C, TV w/VCR and pay movies, high-speed Internet access, minibar, coffeemaker, hair dryer, iron.

Park Hyatt Chicago ★★★   For those in search of chic modern luxury, the Park Hyatt is the coolest hotel in town (as long as money is no object). The building occupies one of the most desirable spots on North Michigan Avenue and the best rooms are those that face east, overlooking the bustle of the Mag Mile and the lake in the distance.

Luxury might be the watchword here, but the look is anything but stuffy: The lobby feels like a sleek modern art gallery. German painter Gerhard Richter's *Piazza del Duomo Milan* masterpiece is the visual centerpiece of the space, providing ample evidence of what visual treats lie in store for guests. Rooms feature Eames and Mies van der Rohe reproduction furniture and window banquettes with stunning city views (the windows actually open). The comfortable beds are well appointed with several plush pillows. While most hotels might provide a TV and VCR, this is the kind of place where you get a DVD player and flat-screen TV. The bathrooms are especially wonderful: Slide back the cherrywood wall for views of the city while you soak in the tub.

NoMI, a restaurant nestled on the seventh floor overlooking Water Tower Square and the Museum of Contemporary Art, serves French-inspired cuisine and features an *Architectural Digest*–worthy interior by New York–based designer Tony Chi; the place has gotten stellar reviews, but be prepared for fairly small portions at expense-account prices.

800 N. Michigan Ave., Chicago, IL 60611. (C) **800/233-1234** or 312/335-1234. Fax 312/239-4000. www. hyatt.com. 203 units. $375–$425 double; $695–$3,000 suite. AE, DC, DISC, MC, V. Valet parking $36 with in/out privileges. Subway/El: Red Line to Chicago/State. **Amenities:** Restaurant (French/American); lounge; indoor pool; health club with Jacuzzi and spa; concierge; business center with computer technical support; 24-hr. room service; massage; babysitting; laundry service; 24-hr. dry cleaning. *In room:* A/C, TV w/DVD player and pay movies, dataport, minibar, coffeemaker, hair dryer, iron, CD player.

The Peninsula Chicago ★★★   Do believe the hype. The first Midwest location from the luxury Peninsula hotel group promised to wow us, and it does not disappoint. Taking design cues from the chain's flagship Hong Kong hotel, the Peninsula Chicago mixes an Art Deco sensibility with modern, top-of-the-line amenities. Service is practically a religion; every staff member I passed here made a point of greeting me, and the well-equipped business center can provide administrative assistants to handle everything from Internet searches to dictation.

Rooms are average in size (the "junior suites" are fairly small, with living rooms that can comfortably seat only about four people). But the hotel's in-room technology is cutting edge: A small silver "command station" by every bed allows guests to control all the lights, curtains, and room temperature without getting out from under the covers. The marble-filled bathrooms have separate shower stalls and tubs, vanities with plenty of room to sit, and another "command station" by the bathtub. Add in the flat-screen TVs and you have a classic hotel that's very much attuned to the present.

The sultry hotel bar is already one of the city's top spots for romantic assignations (or confidential late-night business negotiations). The hotel's four full-service restaurants include Shanghai Terrace, with cuisine reflecting the Peninsula Group's Asian properties (if you're here in nice weather, snag a table on the outdoor terrace overlooking Michigan Ave., but be prepared to get dizzy when you see the bill). The bright, airy spa and fitness center fill the top two floors and make a lovely retreat (especially the outdoor deck).

108 E. Superior St. (at Michigan Ave.), Chicago, IL 60611. (C) **866/288-8889** or 312/337-2888. Fax 312/932-9529. www.peninsula.com. 339 units. $445–$455 double; $500–$4,500 suite. AE, DC, DISC, MC, V. Valet parking $36 with in/out privileges. Subway/El: Red Line to Chicago/State. Pets accepted. **Amenities:** 4 restaurants (seafood, Asian, Continental, and European bakery); bar; indoor pool with outdoor deck; free fitness center; spa; hot tub; sauna; children's amenities; concierge; business center; 24-hr. room service; in-room massage; babysitting; laundry service; same-day dry cleaning. *In room:* A/C, TV w/pay movies (VCRs and DVD players upon request), fax, dataport, minibar, fridge (upon request), hair dryer, safe.

Near North & River North Accommodations

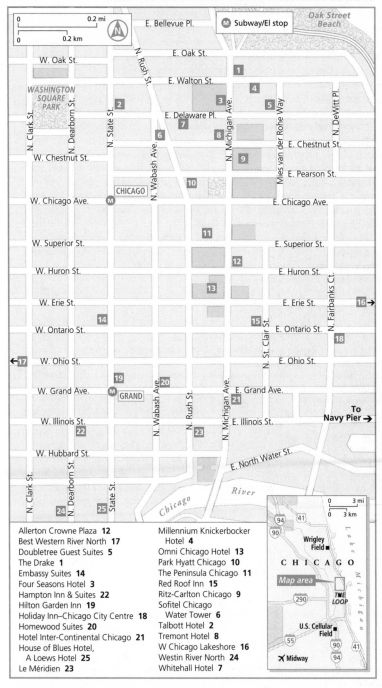

0 0.2 mi
0 0.2 km

Ⓜ Subway/El stop

E. Bellevue Pl.
Oak Street Beach
E. Oak St.
W. Oak St.
N. Rush St.
E. Walton St.
WASHINGTON SQUARE PARK
N. Clark St.
N. Dearborn St.
N. State St.
E. Delaware Pl.
N. Michigan Ave.
Mies van der Rohe Way
N. DeWitt Pl.
E. Chestnut St.
W. Chestnut St.
N. Wabash Ave.
E. Pearson St.
CHICAGO Ⓜ
W. Chicago Ave.
E. Chicago Ave.
W. Superior St.
E. Superior St.
W. Huron St.
E. Huron St.
W. Erie St.
E. Erie St.
N. Fairbanks Ct.
W. Ontario St.
St. Clair St.
E. Ontario St.
W. Ohio St.
E. Ohio St.
W. Grand Ave.
GRAND Ⓜ
N. Wabash Ave.
N. Rush St.
N. Michigan Ave.
E. Grand Ave.
To Navy Pier →
W. Illinois St.
E. Illinois St.
W. Hubbard St.
E. North Water St.
N. Clark St.
N. Dearborn St.
State St.
Chicago River

1 4 3 5 2 7 6 8 9 10 11 12 13 14 15 16 17 18 19 20 21 22 23 24 25

Allerton Crowne Plaza **12**
Best Western River North **17**
Doubletree Guest Suites **5**
The Drake **1**
Embassy Suites **14**
Four Seasons Hotel **3**
Hampton Inn & Suites **22**
Hilton Garden Inn **19**
Holiday Inn–Chicago City Centre **18**
Homewood Suites **20**
Hotel Inter-Continental Chicago **21**
House of Blues Hotel,
  A Loews Hotel **25**
Le Méridien **23**

Millennium Knickerbocker
  Hotel **4**
Omni Chicago Hotel **13**
Park Hyatt Chicago **10**
The Peninsula Chicago **11**
Red Roof Inn **15**
Ritz-Carlton Chicago **9**
Sofitel Chicago
  Water Tower **6**
Talbott Hotel **2**
Tremont Hotel **8**
W Chicago Lakeshore **16**
Westin River North **24**
Whitehall Hotel **7**

CHICAGO
Wrigley Field ■
THE LOOP
Map area
U.S. Cellular Field ■
✈ Midway
Lake Michigan
0 3 mi
0 3 km
94 41 90 290 55 90 41

Ritz-Carlton Chicago ★★★ *Kids*   Top-notch service and an open, airy setting make this one of Chicago's most welcoming hotels. Perched high atop the
Water Tower Place mall, the Ritz-Carlton's lobby is on the 12th floor, with a
large bank of windows to admire the city below. Not surprisingly, the quality of
the accommodations is of the highest caliber, although the standard rooms aren't
very large. Doubles have space for a loveseat and desk but not much more; the
bathrooms are elegant but not huge (for extra-large, lavish bathrooms, request a
"Premier" room or suite on the 30th floor). Guests staying in any of the hotel's
suites (premier or not) are treated to a gratis wardrobe pressing upon arrival, personalized stationery, Bulgari toiletries, and fresh flowers. Service is the Ritz-
Carlton's selling point, whether it's the "compcierge" who helps guests with
computer problems, or the "allergy-sensitive" rooms that are cleaned with special nonirritating products and come stocked with nonfeather duvets and pillows and hypoallergenic bath products on request. Lake views cost more but are
spectacular (although in all the rooms, you're up high enough that you're not
staring into surrounding apartment buildings).

Families will find this luxury crash pad quite welcoming. Every child receives
a gift and can borrow toys and games from a stash kept by the concierge.
PlayStation and Nintendo are also available, and kids' food is available from
room service 24 hours a day.

Whether or not you stay here, the Ritz-Carlton is an elegant place for afternoon tea, served at 2:30 and 4:30pm in the lobby. The hotel's excellent Sunday
brunch in The Dining Room includes a special buffet for children replete with
M&Ms, macaroni and cheese, and pizza.

160 E. Pearson St., Chicago, IL 60611. ✆ 800/621-6906 or 312/266-1000. Fax 312/266-1194. www.four
seasons.com. 430 units. $380–$485 double; $515–$3,500 suite; weekend rates from $305. Valet parking $36
with in/out privileges; self-parking $25 with no in/out privileges. Subway/El: Red Line to Chicago/State. Pets
accepted. **Amenities:** 4 restaurants (French, American); 2 lounges; indoor pool; health club with spa, Jacuzzi,
and sauna; children's programs; concierge; business center; 24-hr. room service; in-room massage; babysitting; laundry service; same-day dry cleaning; premier suites. *In room:* A/C, TV w/VCR and pay movies, fax, dataport, minibar, hair dryer.

Sofitel Chicago Water Tower ★★   The latest addition to Chicago's already-
crowded luxury hotel scene, the Sofitel aims to impress by drawing on the city's
tradition of great architecture. French architect Jean-Paul Viguier created a
building that's impossible to pass without taking a second look: a soaring, triangular white tower that sparkles in the sun. But the place doesn't take itself too
seriously, as you'll see when you walk in the airy lobby and check out the lumi-
nescent floor tiles that change color in a never-ending light show. The overall
feel of the hotel is European modern; you'll hear French accents from the front-
desk staff, and foreign-language magazines are scattered on tables throughout
the lobby. The bright, stylish Café des Architects has become a favorite business
lunch spot for locals.

The guest rooms feature contemporary decor with natural beechwood walls
and chrome hardware for a modern touch. All the rooms enjoy good views of
the city (but the privacy-conscious will want to stay on the upper floors, where
they won't be on display to surrounding apartment buildings). The standard
doubles are fairly compact—but thanks to large picture windows, the spaces
don't feel cramped. The luxurious marble bathrooms (with separate tub and
shower stall) are quite spacious. The amenities are topnotch. Recognizing that
business travelers are the bread and butter of Chicago hotel profits, ample support services exist for working visitors. But this doesn't mean that Sofitel doesn't

welcome families; in fact, up to two children can stay in a room for no extra charge (they'll even roll in a portable bed for the kids).

20 E. Chestnut St. (at Wabash St.), Chicago, IL 60611. © 800/SOFITEL or 312/324-4000. Fax 312/324-4026. www.sofitel.com. 415 units. $199–$459 double; $499–$599 suite. AE, DC, DISC, MC, V. Valet parking $35. Subway/El: Red Line to Chicago/State. Small pets accepted. **Amenities:** Restaurant (French cafe); bar; fitness center; concierge; business center; 24-hr. room service; babysitting; laundry service; same-day dry cleaning. *In room:* A/C, TV w/pay movies, high-speed Internet access, minibar, coffeemaker, hair dryer, iron.

EXPENSIVE

Doubletree Guest Suites ★ This full-service all-suites hotel is a good choice for families and business travelers seeking something with a little less starch. Best of all is its location, just off the Mag Mile and next door to the Hancock Building and Water Tower Place.

Suites might not be huge, but they're warm, inviting, and immaculate. All feature a separate living room (with pullout sofa) and bedroom. The price depends on bed size, floor (some have spectacular lake views), and furnishings. The hotel doesn't feel that different from other Doubletree properties, but that consistency might be just what some people are looking for.

The homespun service and little touches are what count here: fresh flowers in the lobby and two freshly baked chocolate-chip cookies presented to guests on check-in. The hotel's high spot—literally—is the fitness center on the 30th floor; stop by on summer Wednesday and Saturday evenings for a great view of the fireworks at Navy Pier.

198 E. Delaware Place, Chicago, IL 60611. © 800/222-TREE or 312/664-1100. Fax 312/664-9881. www. doubletree.com. 345 units. $109–$309 double suite. Children under 18 stay free in parent's room. AE, DC, DISC, MC, V. Valet parking $34 with in/out privileges. Subway/El: Red Line to Chicago/State. **Amenities:** Restaurant (American); lounge; indoor pool; health club; Jacuzzi; sauna; concierge; business center; 24-hr. room service; babysitting; laundry room; dry cleaning. *In room:* A/C, TV w/pay movies, dataport, minibar, fridge, coffeemaker, hair dryer, iron.

The Drake ★★★ If ever the term "grande dame" fit a hotel, it's The Drake, which opened in 1920. Fronting East Lake Shore Drive, this landmark building is Chicago's version of New York's Plaza or Paris's Ritz. Despite a massive renovation in the 1990s, the Drake still feels lost in time compared to places like the glitzy new Peninsula. But for many, that is part of The Drake's charm.

The Drake's public spaces still maintain the regal grandeur of days gone by, but the guest rooms have been modernized with new furniture and linens. Most rooms include a small sitting area with couch and chairs; some have two bathrooms. The lake-view rooms are lovely, and—no surprise—you'll pay more for them. Be forewarned that "city view" rooms on the lower floors look out onto another building, so you'll probably be keeping your drapes shut. Rooms and suites on the "executive floors" provide such additional amenities as disposable cameras, a generous continental breakfast in a private lounge, and free cocktails and hors d'oeuvres, plus a daily newspaper and valet assistance for polishing shoes, packing and unpacking, and securing theater tickets.

The hotel's restaurants include the Oak Terrace, a large dining room serving up American fare and some great views of the lake and Michigan Avenue; the Cape Cod Room (p. 124), an old-timey seafood spot; and the Coq d'Or (p. 271), one of Chicago's most atmospheric piano bars.

140 E. Walton Place (at Michigan Ave.), Chicago, IL 60611. © 800/55-DRAKE or 312/787-2200. Fax 312/787-1431. www.hilton.com. 537 units. $255–$295 double; $335–$430 executive floor; from $600 suite; weekend rates start at $289 with continental breakfast. AE, DC, DISC, MC, V. Valet parking $32 with in/out privileges. Subway/El: Red Line to Chicago/State. **Amenities:** 3 restaurants (American, seafood); 2 lounges; fitness center; concierge; business center; shopping arcade (including a Chanel boutique); barbershop; 24-hr.

room service; in-room massage; laundry service; 24-hr. dry cleaning; executive-level rooms. *In room:* A/C, TV w/pay movies, dataport, minibar, coffeemaker, hair dryer, iron.

Hilton Garden Inn ★   This hotel doesn't have much personality—the lobby is strictly business and feels cold—but it does offer a high-rise experience that will appeal to anyone looking for an urban fix (despite its name, there's nothing garden-related here). Perched between North Michigan Avenue and the River North neighborhood, it's every inch a big-city player. The hotel caters to business types, but families certainly won't feel out of place here: The building is adjacent to ESPN Zone, a Virgin Megastore, and The Shops at North Bridge mall. The ample rooms are located between the 13th and the 23rd floors. Views higher up, especially on the east side and from corner suites facing north and south, afford dramatic vistas of the cityscape and skyline. The hotel's six suites include a parlor area, wet bar, and dining table, with possible connections to adjacent rooms.

10 E. Grand Ave. (at State St.), Chicago, IL 60611. © **800/HILTONS** or 312/595-0000. Fax 312/595-0955. www.hiltongardeninn.com. 357 units. $129–$269 double; $400–$700 suite. AE, DC, DISC, MC, V. Valet parking $32 with in/out privileges; self-parking $20 with no in/out privileges. Subway/El: Red Line to Grand/State. **Amenities:** Restaurant (American); lounge; indoor pool; fitness center with whirlpool and sauna; concierge; business center; room service; laundry service; same-day dry cleaning. *In room:* A/C, TV w/pay movies, high-speed Internet access, fridge, microwave, coffeemaker, hair dryer, iron.

Hotel Inter-Continental Chicago ★★   The newer hotels might be getting all the attention, but the Hotel Inter-Continental remains a sentimental favorite for many Chicagoans (ranking right up there with The Drake in our affections). A recent renovation removed some of the building's quirky originality, but it has definitely brought the guest rooms up several notches. Built as an athletic club in 1929, the building's original lobby features truly grand details: marble columns, hand-stenciled ceilings, and historic tapestries (for a peek, go in the southern entrance, on the corner of Illinois St.).

Rooms are located in the original club building (the South Tower) and in a 1960s addition (the North Tower). Although all the rooms have new furnishings and fabrics, the North Tower rooms have a more generic, sterile feel; I'd recommend the South Tower for a more distinctive experience—but be prepared for smaller bathrooms. South Tower rooms don't cost more, but they do vary widely in size; the concierge here suggests making your reservation through the toll-free phone line, then calling the front desk to request the biggest room available during your stay.

The hotel's restaurant, Amber, is the only street-level restaurant on Michigan Avenue (try to grab a table by the front windows to enjoy the never-ending street scene), and the Salon is a cozy spot for afternoon tea. The Inter-Continental's main claim to fame is the junior Olympic-size pool on the top floor, a beautiful 1920s gem surrounded by elegant mosaics.

505 N. Michigan Ave. (at Grand Ave.), Chicago, IL 60611. © **800/327-0200** or 312/944-4100. Fax 312/944-1320. www.chicago.interconti.com. 807 units. $249–$350 double; $500–$3,000 suite; weekend and promotional rates from $145. AE, DC, DISC, MC, V. Valet parking $27–$34 with in/out privileges. Subway/El: Red Line to Grand/State. **Amenities:** Restaurant (American); 2 lounges; indoor pool; fitness center with sauna; concierge; business center; 24-hr. room service; massage; babysitting; laundry service; same-day dry cleaning; executive rooms. *In room:* A/C, TV w/pay movies, dataport, minibar, coffeemaker, hair dryer, iron.

Le Méridien ★★   Tucked into the back of The Shops at North Bridge mall, Le Méridien is a recent addition to the competitive high-end Chicago hotel market, and it seems that the general public has yet to discover it. Le Méridien touts its design philosophy as "European with a French accent," which, in this case, means marble floors, vaguely 18th-century-inspired furniture, and some whimsical artwork (a large painting of a Napoleonic figure with the head of a dog hangs in the lobby). A terrace offers outdoor seating, and a casual bistro is hidden away in the back of the lobby (depending on your perspective, it's either pleasantly secluded or isolated). Rooms are a bit small (especially the least expensive ones on the north side), but the amenities are top of the line: The safes come with chargers for cellphones and laptop computers, and the in-room phones are cordless. High rollers will want to book one of the suites overlooking Michigan Avenue; a few even come with private terraces, something few hotels in this city offer. Le Méridien can't quite compete with the Park Hyatt or the Peninsula in the glamour department, but its cozy style should appeal to travelers looking for some place a little more personal. It also makes a good base for anyone visiting during frigid winter weather; with a whole mall just a few steps away, you can get out without even putting on your coat.

521 N. Rush St. (at Grand St.), Chicago, IL 60611. ℂ 800/543-4300 or 312/645-1500. Fax 312/645-1550. www.lemeridien-chicago.com. 311 units. $129–$425 double; $375–$3,500 suite. AE, DC, DISC, MC, V. Valet parking $33 with in/out privileges. Subway/El: Red Line to Chicago/State. Pets accepted. **Amenities:** Restaurant (European bistro); bar; health club with spa, Jacuzzi, and steam room; concierge; business center; 24-hr. room service; in-room massage; babysitting; laundry service; same-day dry cleaning. *In room:* A/C, TV w/pay movies and video games, dataport, minibar, fridge, coffeemaker, hair dryer, iron, safe, CD player.

Millennium Knickerbocker Hotel ⭐

Another historic hotel that has undergone a major face-lift, the Knickerbocker looks spiffy from the lobby but still retains a shabby-chic feel on the guest floors. The epitome of Jazz Age indulgence when built in 1927, the hotel was rumored to have shady underworld connections during the Capone era. In the 1970s, Hugh Hefner turned it into the gaudy Playboy Towers and invited the leisure-suit set to a perpetual disco inferno on the hotel's famed illuminated ballroom floor. By the time the 1980s rolled around, the Knickerbocker had been through the ringer.

But thanks to a $20 million renovation a couple of years ago, the Knickerbocker once more exudes vintage charm. It has a superb location, a block from Oak Street Beach and across the street from The Drake. While the rooms aren't especially spacious, they are warm and comfortable (with new, comfy beds). Bathrooms are small but nicely done. One caveat: Views are often rather dismal, but you can catch a glimpse of the lake in all rooms ending in 18, and corner rooms (ending in 17, 28, or 35) look onto Michigan Avenue. Club-level guests are served complimentary breakfast, coffee, and munchies in a second-floor lounge.

163 E. Walton Place (½ block east of Michigan Ave.), Chicago, IL 60611. ℂ 800/621-8140 or 312/751-8100. Fax 312/751-9663. www.millenniumhotels.com. 305 units. $129–$269 double; $285–$1,000 suite. AE, DC, DISC, MC, V. Valet parking $30 with in/out privileges; self-parking $24 with in/out privileges. Subway/El: Red Line to Chicago/State. **Amenities:** Restaurant (fusion); bar; exercise room; concierge; business center; 24-hr. room service; babysitting; laundry service; dry cleaning; club-level rooms. *In room:* A/C, TV w/pay movies, fax, dataport, minibar, coffeemaker, hair dryer, iron.

Omni Chicago Hotel ⭐ *Kids*

The tranquil interior of this business hotel is a welcome retreat from the frenetic shopping activity on Michigan Avenue. No less a Chicago luminary than Oprah Winfrey has given the Omni her stamp of approval, designating it the official crash pad for guests appearing on her show.

All the units are suites with one king-size or two double beds. Each unit has a living room with a sitting area, a dining table, a wet bar, and a refrigerator, all of which are divided from the bedroom by a set of French doors. About a third of the suites have pullout sofas. You can request a corner suite, with lots of light and views looking down Michigan Avenue, for $20 extra.

While the hotel's hushed tones exude a feeling of business rather than pleasure, the Omni Kids Program makes younger guests feel welcome. All children receive a bag of games and ideas for Chicago activities and Nintendo in their rooms, as well as kids' menus.

676 N. Michigan Ave. (at Huron St.), Chicago, IL 60611. ✆ **800/843-6664** or 312/944-6664. Fax 312 /266-3015. www.omnihotels.com. 347 units. $259–$329 suite; weekend rates $179–$209. AE, DC, DISC, MC, V. Valet parking $32 with in/out privileges. Subway/El: Red Line to Grand/State. **Amenities:** Restaurant (American/Mediterranean); lounge; lap pool; health club; Jacuzzi; courtesy car available for trips within the downtown area; business services; 24-hr. room service; babysitting; laundry service; 24-hr. dry cleaning; executive-level rooms. *In room:* A/C, TV w/pay movies, fax, dataport, minibar, coffeemaker, hair dryer, iron, safe.

Talbott Hotel ★★ *(Finds)*   The Talbott is not for anyone who needs extensive hotel facilities, but the cozy atmosphere and personal level of service appeal to visitors looking for the feeling of a bed-and-breakfast rather than a sprawling, corporate hotel. Constructed in the 1920s as an apartment building, the Talbott was converted to a hotel in 1989. Proprietors Basil and Laurie Ann Kromelow take a keen personal interest in the hotel's decor: Most of the gorgeous antiques strewn throughout are purchases from Basil's European shopping trips. The wood-paneled lobby, decorated with leather sofas and velvety armchairs, two working fireplaces, tapestries, and numerous French horns used for fox hunts, is intimate and inviting—all the better in which to enjoy your complimentary continental breakfast.

Although comfortable, the rooms aren't quite as distinctive; they also vary in size, so ask when making reservations. Suites and the hotel's "executive king" rooms entice with Jacuzzi tubs; suites have separate sitting areas with sofa beds and dining tables.

20 E. Delaware Place (between Rush and State sts.), Chicago, IL 60611. ✆ **800/TALBOTT** or 312/944-4970. Fax 312/944-7241. www.talbotthotel.com. 149 units. $149–$289 double; $319–$449 suite. AE, DC, DISC, MC, V. Self-parking $21. Subway/El: Red Line to Chicago/State. **Amenities:** Lounge; access to nearby health club; concierge; business services; 24-hr. room service; laundry service; dry cleaning; executive rooms. *In room:* A/C, TV, minibar, hair dryer, iron, safe.

Tremont Hotel ★★   The Tremont won't dazzle you with style or amenities, but it fits the bill for anyone looking for a small, European-style hotel. The cozy lobby (complete with fireplace) makes a fine space to hang out and plan your itinerary for the day. The guest rooms aren't too big—there's space for a bed, a desk, and either a sofa or two chairs—but they are cheery, with yellow walls and large windows. Ask for a room facing Delaware Street if you crave natural light (rooms in other parts of the hotel look into neighboring buildings). The furniture shows signs of wear, and the bathrooms are fairly basic, but the Tremont will appeal to anyone who likes their hotels homey rather than slick.

The steak-and-chops restaurant off the lobby, the memorabilia-filled Mike Ditka's Restaurant (p. 127), is co-owned by legendary former Chicago Bears football coach Mike Ditka.

100 E. Chestnut St. (1 block west of Michigan Ave.), Chicago, IL 60611. ✆ **800/621-8133** or 312/751-1900. Fax 312/751-8650. www.tremontchicago.com. 130 units. $119–$279 double; $199–$299 suite. AE, DC, DISC, MC, V. Valet parking $34. Subway/El: Red Line to Chicago/State. **Amenities:** Restaurant (American); small exercise room (and access to nearby health club); concierge; business services; massage; babysitting; dry cleaning. *In room:* A/C, TV w/VCR, minibar, hair dryer, iron, safe, CD player.

W Chicago Lakeshore ★★   The only hotel in Chicago with a location on the lake, this property prides itself on being a hip boutique hotel—but sophisticated travelers may feel like it's trying way too hard with dance music playing in the lobby and the black-clad staff members doing their best to be eye candy.

The compact rooms are decorated in deep red, black, and gray—a scheme that might strike some travelers as gloomy. And although the Asian-inspired bathrooms are stylish, the wooden shades that separate them from the bedroom don't make for much privacy. In W-speak, rooms and suites are designated "wonderful" (meaning standard, with a city view) or "spectacular" (meaning a lake view, for which you'll pay more). Because looking out over the lake means staring at a big expanse of blue, I recommend the "wonderful" rooms with their dramatic city views. Of the few boutique hotels in Chicago, the W Lakeshore has the best location, within easy reach of outdoor activities (the beach, bike paths, and Navy Pier), restaurants, and nightlife—just don't take the place too seriously.

The W Lakeshore boasts Wave, a signature restaurant and bar by noted restaurateur David Zadikoff (p. 128), and Whiskey Sky, the hotel's see-and-be-seen spot designed by Rande Gerber.

644 N. Lake Shore Dr. (at Ontario St.), Chicago, IL 60611. (C) 877/W-HOTELS or 312/943-9200. Fax 312/255-4411. www.whotels.com. 556 units. $229–$429 double; from $369 suite. AE, DC, DISC, MC, V. Valet parking $36 with in/out privileges. Subway/El: Red Line to Grand/State. Pets allowed. **Amenities:** Restaurant (Mediterranean); bar; pool; exercise room; concierge; business services; 24-hr. room service; in-room massage; babysitting; same-day laundry service; dry cleaning. In room: A/C, TV w/VCR and pay movies, dataport, minibar, coffeemaker, hair dryer, iron, safe, CD player.

Whitehall Hotel ★★   Staying here is like visiting a wealthy, sophisticated aunt's town house: elegant but understated, welcoming but not effusive. Before the Four Seasons and Ritz-Carlton entered the picture, the patrician Whitehall reigned as Chicago's most exclusive luxury hotel, with rock stars and Hollywood royalty dropping by when in town. Although those glory days have passed, the independently owned Whitehall still attracts a devoted clientele who relish its subdued ambience and highly personalized service.

Since this is an older property, the hallways are quite narrow and the bathrooms are small. But the rooms are quite spacious and bright, with new furniture. Rooms on the north side of the building come with a wonderful straight-on view of the Hancock Building, with Lake Michigan sparkling in the background. "Pinnacle Level" rooms are the same size as standard rooms, but come with extra amenities, including four-poster beds (with luxury linens), irons and ironing boards, fax machines and umbrellas; Pinnacle guests also receive complimentary breakfast.

The hotel's restaurant, Molive, offers an eclectic American menu with Californian, Mediterranean, and Asian accents. (The warm chocolate cake was picked by the *Chicago Tribune*'s restaurant critic as one of the top chocolate desserts in the city.) The covered, heated sun porch attracts outdoor diners all year round. And don't miss the hotel's dimly lit, clubby bar, which hasn't changed since the hotel opened in 1928 (ask the staff to point out Katharine Hepburn's favorite seat).

105 E. Delaware Place (west of Michigan Ave.), Chicago, IL 60611. (C) 800/948-4295 or 312/944-6300. Fax 312/944-8552. www.slh.com/whitehall. 221 units. $179–$279 double; from $500 suite; weekend packages from $199. AE, DC, DISC, MC, V. Valet parking $31 with in/out privileges. Subway/El: Red Line to Chicago/State. **Amenities:** Restaurant (American); lounge; exercise room (and access to nearby health club for an extra charge); concierge; business center (for upper floors); 24-hr. room service; babysitting; laundry service; dry cleaning; club floors. In room: A/C, TV w/pay movies, dataport, minibar, hair dryer, safe.

MODERATE

Allerton Crowne Plaza ★   A historic hotel that received a fairly bland makeover, the Allerton will appeal to travelers who like their lodgings to be brand spanking new. Built in 1924 as a "club hotel," providing permanent residences for single men and women, the Allerton was recently converted into the flagship hotel of the Crowne Plaza chain. The Italian Renaissance–inspired exterior has been painstakingly restored to its original dark-red brickwork and stone carvings and limestone base. Too bad the distinctive exterior style wasn't replicated inside. The rooms have a generic chain-hotel feel, and because the hotel originally was built for single men and women, the rooms are fairly small (even the suites). Still, all the rooms and public areas have a warm and homey feel. Snag one overlooking Michigan Avenue to get the best views (or at least stop by the hotel's Renaissance Ballroom for a peek at the Mag Mile).

701 N. Michigan Ave. (at Huron St.), Chicago, IL 60611. ℂ 800/621-8311 outside Illinois, or 312/440-1500. Fax 312/440-1819. www.allertonchi.crowneplaza.com. 443 units. $109–$299 double; $159–$359 suite. AE, DC, DISC, MC, V. Valet parking $34 with in/out privileges. Subway/El: Red Line to Chicago/State. **Amenities:** Restaurant (American); lounge; fitness center (w/excellent city views); sauna; concierge; business center; 24-hr. room service; laundry service; same-day dry cleaning. *In room:* A/C, TV w/pay movies, dataport, minibar, coffeemaker, hair dryer, iron.

Holiday Inn–Chicago City Centre ★★ *Kids* *Value*   Enter the soaring modern atrium, with its vases of blooming fresh flowers, and you won't believe that this place is kin to Holiday Inn's assembly-line roadside staples. Its location is a nice surprise as well: east of the Magnificent Mile and close to the Ohio Street Beach and Navy Pier. Although the rooms are pretty basic, the amenities make this one of the best values in the city.

Fitness devotees will rejoice because the Holiday Inn is located next door to the McClurg Court Sports Complex, where guests may enjoy the extensive facilities free of charge. The hotel also has its own spacious outdoor pool and sun deck. The views are excellent, especially looking north toward the Hancock Building and Monroe Harbor. You might want to splurge on one of the master suites, which boast large living-room areas with wet bars, along with a Jacuzzistyle tub and sauna in the bathroom.

The Holiday Inn is a good bet for the budget-conscious family: Kids under 18 stay free in their parents' room, and those 12 and under eat free in the hotel's restaurants. Leave the pay-per-view movies one night and head to the massive new AMC theaters next door, where all 21 screens offer stadium seating.

300 E. Ohio St. (at Fairbanks Court), Chicago, IL 60611. ℂ 800/HOLIDAY or 312/787-6100. Fax 312/787-6259. www.chicc.com. 500 units. $128–$270 double; weekend and promotional rates $99–$119. AE, DC, DISC, MC, V. Valet parking $19. Subway/El: Red Line to Grand/State. **Amenities:** 2 restaurants (American, cafe); bar; outdoor and indoor pools; access to nearby health club; whirlpool; sauna; children's programs; concierge; business services; limited room service; babysitting; laundry room; dry cleaning. *In room:* A/C, TV w/pay movies, dataport, coffeemaker, hair dryer, iron.

Homewood Suites ★ *Kids*   An excellent choice for families, this hotel offers both fresh, clean rooms and some nice little extras. Because all of the rooms are suites with full kitchens, you can prepare your own meals (a real money saver) and there's plenty of room for everyone to spread out at the end of the day. Housed just off the Mag Mile in a sleek tower above retail shops, offices, and a health club—and adjacent to ESPN Zone—the hotel is "Italian Renaissance meets Crate & Barrel." Distressed-leather sofas, Mediterranean stone tile, wrought-iron chandeliers, and beaded lampshades adorn its sixth-floor lobby. Rooms—one- and two-bedroom suites and a handful of double-double suites, which can connect to king suites—feature velvet sofas that are all sleepers, and the beds have big, thick mattresses. Each comes with a full kitchen, a dining-room table that doubles as a workspace, and decent-size bathrooms. The hotel provides a complimentary hot breakfast buffet as well as beverages and hors d'oeuvres every evening; there is also a free grocery-shopping service and free access to an excellent health club next door.

40 E. Grand Ave. (at Wabash Ave.), Chicago, IL 60611. © **800/CALL-HOME** or 312/644-2222. Fax 312/644-7777. www.homewoodsuiteschicago.com. $99–$249 2-room suite. AE, DC, DISC, MC, V. Valet parking $32 with in/out privileges. Subway/El: Red Line to Grand/State. **Amenities:** Fitness room w/small pool and nice views of the city; concierge; business services; babysitting; laundry machines on all floors; dry cleaning. *In room:* A/C, TV w/pay movies, fully equipped kitchen, coffeemaker, hair dryer, iron.

INEXPENSIVE

Red Roof Inn *(Value)*   This is your best bet for the lowest-priced lodgings in downtown Chicago. The location is the main selling point: right off the Magnificent Mile (and within blocks of the Ritz-Carlton and Peninsula, where rooms will cost you at least three times as much). The guest rooms are stark and small (much like the off-the-highway Red Roof Inns), but all have new linens and carpeting. Ask for a room facing Ontario Street, where at least you'll get western exposure and some natural light (rooms in other parts of the hotel look right into neighboring office buildings). The bathrooms are tiny but newly renovated (and spotless). You're not going to find much in the way of style or amenities here—but then you don't stay at a place like this to hang out in the lobby.

162 E. Ontario St. (½ block east of Michigan Ave.), Chicago, IL 60611. © **800/733-7663** or 312/787-3580. Fax 312/787-1299. www.redroof.com. 195 units. $86–$102 double. AE, DC, DISC, MC, V. Valet parking $18 with no in/out privileges. Subway/El: Red Line to Grand/State. **Amenities:** Business services; free morning coffee available in the lobby. *In room:* A/C, TV w/pay movies, dataport, hair dryer, iron.

4 River North

The name *River North* designates a vast area parallel to the Magnificent Mile. The zone is bounded by the river to the west and south, and roughly by Clark Street to the east and by Chicago Avenue to the north. The earthy redbrick buildings that characterize the area were once warehouses of various kinds and today hold Chicago's art-gallery district and some very trendy restaurants.

EXPENSIVE

Embassy Suites *(★★) (Kids)*   Although this hotel does a healthy convention business, its vaguely Floridian ambience—with a gushing waterfall and palm-lined ponds at the bottom of a huge central atrium—makes the place very family-friendly (there's plenty of room for the kids to run around). The accommodations are spacious enough for both parents and kids: All suites have two rooms, consisting of a living room with a sleeper sofa, a round table, and four chairs; and a bedroom with either a king-size bed or two double beds. Guests staying on the VIP floor get nightly turndown service and in-room fax machines and robes. At one end of the atrium, the hotel serves a complimentary cooked-to-order breakfast in the morning and, in the other end, supplies complimentary cocktails and snacks in the evening.

Off the lobby is an excellent restaurant, Papagus Greek Taverna, and next door is a Starbucks outlet with outdoor seating.

600 N. State St. (at West Ohio St.), Chicago, IL 60610. © **800/362-2779** or 312/943-3800. Fax 312/943-7629. www.embassy-suites.com. 358 units. $199–$259 king suite; $269–$299 double suite. AE, DC, DISC, MC, V. Valet parking $34 with in/out privileges. Subway/El: Red Line to Grand/State. **Amenities:** Restaurant (Greek); coffee bar; indoor pool; exercise room with whirlpool and sauna; concierge; business center; limited room service; babysitting; laundry machines; dry cleaning; VIP rooms. *In room:* A/C, TV w/pay movies and video games, dataport, kitchenette, coffeemaker, hair dryer, iron.

House of Blues Hotel, a Loews Hotel ★★★   The funky vibe here makes this a great choice for teenagers and anyone who wants a hotel to be an experience—not just a place to sleep. Blending Gothic, Moroccan, East Indian, and New Orleans influences, the House of Blues lobby is a riot of crimsons and deep blues (stop by to check it out even if you're not staying here). Banquettes and couches heaped with pillows invite lounging—grab a drink at the Kaz Bar and soak it all in.

You can catch your breath in the lighter, whimsical rooms, which feature some of the most exciting Southern folk art you'll ever come across. The casually dressed, friendly staff invents creative nightly turndowns for guests—such as fragrant mood crystals or a written thought for the day left on your pillow. One of the hotel's biggest selling points is its location in the entertainment-packed Marina Towers complex. Within steps of the hotel you've got the AMF Bowling Center (with billiards), a marina with boat rentals, the riverside Smith & Wollensky steakhouse (an outpost of the New York restaurant), the innovative Bin 36 wine bar and restaurant (p. 134), and, of course, the House of Blues Music Hall and Restaurant (don't miss the Sunday gospel brunch).

333 N. Dearborn St. (at the river), Chicago, IL 60610. © 877/569-3742 or 312/245-0333. Fax 312/923-2458. www.loewshotels.com. 365 units. $139–$349 double; $500–$1,200 suite; weekend and promotional rates available. AE, DC, DISC, MC, V. Valet parking $28 with in/out privileges. Subway/El: Brown Line to Clark/Lake or Red Line to Grand/State. Pets accepted. **Amenities:** Lounge; access to the very hip Crunch Health & Fitness Center for $15; concierge; business center; 24-hr. room service; babysitting; laundry service; same-day dry cleaning. *In room:* A/C, TV w/VCR, pay movies and video games, dataport, minibar, coffeemaker (upon request), hair dryer, iron, CD player.

Westin Chicago River North ★★ *Kids*   Geared to upscale business travelers, the Westin Chicago River North has an understated, modern feel that will appeal to those looking for a quiet retreat. On the northern bank of the Chicago River, the hotel has continued to evolve since it ceased being the Hotel Nikko a couple of years ago. Traces of the hotel's Japanese sensibility linger in the small rock garden at the rear of the lobby and the bamboo growing beside one of the lobby's staircases; the lobby's Hana Lounge also offers a sushi menu.

Rooms are handsome, with furniture and artwork that give them a residential feel. New beds were added in 2000. For the best view, get a room facing south, overlooking the river. For those who feel like splurging, a suite on the 19th floor more than satisfies, with three enormous rooms, including a huge bathroom and a large window offering a side view of the river.

Although the Westin River North has the personality of a business hotel, it has made an effort to be family-friendly; especially notable are the many baby and toddler accessories available to guests, from bottle warmers and cribs to night lights and electrical outlet covers. Older kids can while away the hours with in-room Sony PlayStation.

320 N. Dearborn St. (on the river), Chicago, IL 60610. © 800/WESTIN1 or 312/744-1900. Fax 312/527-9761. www.westinchicago.com. 424 units. $199–$498 double; $419–$2,800 suite; weekend rates $199–$249. AE, DC, DISC, MC, V. Valet parking $34 with in/out privileges; self-parking $16. Subway/El: Brown, Orange, or Green line to State/Lake. **Amenities:** Restaurant (contemporary American); lounge; fitness center; concierge; business center; 24-hr. room service; babysitting; laundry service, same-day dry cleaning. *In room:* A/C, TV w/pay movies and video games, fax, dataport, minibar, coffeemaker, hair dryer, iron.

MODERATE

Best Western River North Hotel *Value*   This former motor lodge and cold storage structure conceals a very attractive, sharply designed interior that scarcely resembles any Best Western in which you're likely to have spent the night. One of the few hotels located right in the midst of one of the busiest nightlife and restaurant zones in the city, the Best Western lies within easy walking distance of interesting boutiques and Chicago's art-gallery district. Rooms are spacious, and the bathrooms, though no-frills, are spotless. One-room suites have a sitting area, while other suites have a separate bedroom; all suites come with a sleeper sofa. The Best Western's reasonable rates and rooftop pool (with sweeping views) will appeal to families on a budget—and the almost unheard-of free parking can add up to significant savings for anyone planning to stay a week or more.

125 W. Ohio St. (at LaSalle St.), Chicago, IL 60610. ✆ 800/528-1234 or 312/467-0800. Fax 312/467-1665. www.rivernorthhotel.com. 150 units. $105–$149 double; $250 suite. AE, DC, DISC, MC, V. Free parking for guests (1 car per room). Subway/El: Red Line to Grand/State. **Amenities:** Restaurant (American); lounge; indoor pool with sun deck; exercise room; business services; limited room service; laundry service. *In room:* AC, TV w/pay movies and video games, dataport, coffeemaker, hair dryer, iron, safe.

Hampton Inn & Suites Chicago Downtown ★ *Kids* *Value*   While the Hampton Inn does attract some business travelers on a budget, it is mainly a family hotel. You can book a room, a two-room suite, or a studio; most don't have much in the way of views, but request one overlooking Illinois Street if you crave natural light. Rooms are residential and warm, with framed collages of vintage Chicago postcards on the walls. The apartment-style suites feature galley kitchens with fridges, microwaves, dishwashers, and cooking utensils. An American diner is located off the lobby, and a second-floor skywalk connects to Ruth's Chris Steak House next door. Guests with children will appreciate the indoor pool (the suites have VCRs, for when the little ones need to chill out after a busy day). Children under 18 stay free, and there is a complimentary buffet breakfast each morning.

33 W. Illinois St. (at Dearborn St.), Chicago, IL 60610. ✆ 800/HAMPTON or 312/832-0330. Fax 312/832-0333. www.hamptoninn-suites.com. 230 units. $129–$179 double; $189–$229 suite. AE, DC, DISC, MC, V. Valet parking $32 with in/out privileges; self-parking $14 with no in/out privileges. Subway/El: Red Line to Grand/State. **Amenities:** Restaurant (American diner); indoor pool with sun deck; exercise room with sauna; business services; room service; laundry machines. *In room:* A/C, TV, dataport, coffeemaker, hair dryer, iron, safe.

5 The Gold Coast

The Gold Coast begins approximately at Division Street and extends north to North Avenue, bounded on the west by Clark Street and on the east by the lake. The area encompasses a short strip of some of the city's priciest real estate along Lake Shore Drive. From the standpoint of social status, the streets clustered here are among the finest addresses in Chicago. It's a lovely neighborhood for a stroll among the graceful town houses and the several lavish mansions that remain, relics from a glitzier past. The hotels here tend to be upscale, but don't offer amenities as lavish as the top Michigan Avenue hotels.

EXPENSIVE

The Claridge ★ *Finds*   If a modest, cost-effective option in a lovely setting within walking distance of Michigan Avenue, Division Street, Old Town's nightlife, and Lincoln Park's many attractions sounds pretty good to you, don't dismiss The Claridge. Ask for a room above the eighth floor that overlooks the tree-lined street (kings and double-doubles are spacious and sunny); avoid at all cost the dark "king superior" rooms, which look onto the fire escape. Some deluxe accommodations have sitting areas, and three executive suites on the 14th floor have working fireplaces.

The Claridge won't overwhelm you with facilities; the hotel's restaurant and bar are both quite small. Where this small hotel really wins its Brownie points is for the very pleasant staff and nice touches such as freshly baked cookies at turndown. In the lobby, there's a small sitting area where you can linger over your complimentary continental breakfast. The surrounding neighborhood of elegant town houses makes a great place for a stroll—without the traffic and noise of other downtown neighborhoods.

1244 N. Dearborn St. (1 block north of Division St.), Chicago, IL 60610. © **800/245-1258** or 312/787-4980. Fax 312/266-0978. www.claridgehotel.com. 163 units. $175–$250 double; $475–$750 suite. AE, DC, DISC, MC, V. Valet parking $34 with in/out privileges. Subway/El: Red Line to Clark/Division. Pets accepted. **Amenities:** Restaurant (Continental); lounge; exercise room; concierge; business services; limited room service; laundry service; same-day dry cleaning. *In room:* A/C, TV w/pay movies, dataport, minibar, coffeemaker, hair dryer, iron.

Omni Ambassador East ★★ *Kids*   The ring-a-ding glory days of the Ambassador East, when stars including Frank Sinatra, Humphrey Bogart, and Liza Minnelli shacked up here during layovers or touring stops in Chicago, are ancient history. But even though big-name celebs tend to ensconce themselves at the Ritz-Carlton or Four Seasons these days, the Ambassador name still evokes images of high glamour in these parts. For the past 50 years, celebrities who have come to town to mingle with Chicago's Gold Coast society have done so most publicly from Booth One in the ritzy Pump Room restaurant (p. 125).

The Ambassador suffered a slow decline in the 1960s and 1970s, which didn't turn around until 1986, when Omni bought and renovated the property. Today, after a recent second face-lift, the Ambassador East has reclaimed its strut and splendor. Rooms here have been spruced up and bathrooms feature the usual higher-end amenities. Executive suites have separate sitting areas; celebrity suites (named for the stars who've crashed in them) come with a separate bedroom, two bathrooms, a small kitchen, and a dining room. Most extravagant is the Presidential Suite, which boasts a canopied terrace and marble fireplace.

The Ambassador East has the same kids' program as the Omni Chicago (p. 95), and both Omnis make an extra effort for guests with disabilities, offering equipment such as TDD telephones and strobe fire alarms for deaf guests.

1301 N. State Pkwy. (1 block north of Division St.), Chicago, IL 60610. © **800/843-6664** or 312/787-7200. Fax 312/787-4760. www.omnihotels.com. 285 units. $160–$200 double; $259–$799 suite. AE, DC, DISC, MC, V. Valet parking $34 with in/out privileges. Subway/El: Red Line to Clark/Division. **Amenities:** Restaurant (contemporary American); small fitness room (and access to nearby health club); concierge; business services; 24-hr. room service; babysitting; 24-hr. laundry service; dry cleaning. *In room:* A/C, TV w/pay movies, dataport, minibar, coffeemaker, hair dryer, iron.

6 Lincoln Park & the North Side

If you prefer the feel of living amid real Chicagoans in a residential neighborhood, several options await you in Lincoln Park and farther north. Although these hotels aren't necessarily more affordable than those downtown, they do provide a different vantage point from which to view Chicago. If you stay at the Majestic Hotel or the City Suites Hotel, for example, you can join the locals on a pedestrian pilgrimage to Wrigley Field for a Cubs game. The area is flush with restaurants, and public transportation via the El or buses is a snap.

EXPENSIVE

Windy City Urban Inn ★★ *Finds*   This grand 1886 home is located on a tranquil side street just blocks from busy Clark Street and Lincoln Avenue—both chock-full of shops, restaurants, and bars. While the inn is charming enough, the true selling point is hosts Andy and Mary Shaw. He's a well-known political reporter, while she has 20 years of experience in the Chicago bed-and-breakfast business. Together, they are excellent resources for anyone who wants to get beyond the usual tourist sites. Plus, their subtle touches give guests a distinctive, Chicago experience: Blues and jazz play during the buffet breakfast, and local food favorites offered to guests include the famous cinnamon buns from Ann Sather's restaurant and beer from Goose Island Brewery.

The more-open-than-typical remodeled Victorian home has five rooms in the main house and three apartment suites in a coach house; all are named after Chicago writers. Lovebirds should request the Nelson Algren and Simone De Beauvoir Suite, which has a large bathroom with a Jacuzzi tub and a view of the Sears Tower. Two of the coach house apartments can sleep four: two in an upstairs bedroom and two on a bed that folds up against the wall (custom-made for the Shaws, these feature top-quality mattresses, making them much more comfortable than the Murphy beds of old). In good weather, guests are invited to eat breakfast on the back porch or in the garden between the main house and the coach house.

607 W. Deming Place, Chicago, IL 60614. © 877/897-7091 or 773/248-7091. Fax 773/248-7090. www. chicago-inn.com. 8 units. $115–$185 double; $225–$325 suite. Rates include buffet breakfast. AE, DC, DISC, MC, V. Parking $6 in nearby lot with in/out privileges. Subway/El: Red Line to Fullerton. **Amenities:** Laundry machines, kitchenettes, coffeemaker, hair dryer, and iron available for guest use upon request. *In room:* A/C, TV.

MODERATE

City Suites Hotel *(Value)*   A few doors down from the elevated train stop on Belmont Avenue, this former transient dive has been transformed into a charming small hotel, something along the lines of an urban bed-and-breakfast. Most rooms are suites, with separate sitting rooms and bedrooms, all furnished with first-rate pieces and decorated in a homey and comfortable style. The amenities are excellent for a hotel in this price range, including local limousine service, plush robes, and complimentary continental breakfast. A bonus—or drawback, depending on your point of view—is the hotel's neighborhood setting. Most rooms can be fairly noisy; those facing north overlook Belmont Avenue, where the nightlife continues into the early morning hours, and those facing west look right out over the rumbling El tracks. On your way in and out of the hotel you'll mingle with plenty of locals, everybody from young professional families to gay couples to punks in full regalia. Blues bars, nightclubs, and restaurants abound hereabouts, making the City Suites a find for the bargain-minded and adventuresome. Suites have fridges and microwaves on request. Room service is available from Ann Sather, a Swedish diner and neighborhood institution (p. 154).

933 W. Belmont Ave. (at Sheffield Ave.), Chicago, IL 60657. © 800/248-9108 or 773/404-3400. Fax 773/ 404-3405. www.cityinns.com. 45 units. $99–$169. Rates include continental breakfast. AE, DC, DISC, MC, V. Parking $17 in nearby lot with in/out privileges. Subway/El: Red Line to Belmont. **Amenities:** Exercise room; business services; concierge; limited room service; laundry service; same-day dry cleaning. *In room:* A/C, TV w/pay movies, dataport, minibar, coffeemaker, hair dryer, iron.

Majestic Hotel *★★ (Finds)*   Owned by the same group as the City Suites Hotel, the Majestic blends seamlessly into its residential neighborhood. Located on a charming tree-lined street (but convenient to the many restaurants and shops of Lincoln Park), this is a good choice for anyone who wants a quiet bed-and-breakfast type hotel stay. Guests receive a complimentary continental breakfast and afternoon tea in the lobby. Some of the larger suites—the most appealing are those with sun porches—offer butler's pantries with a fridge, microwave, and wet bar. Most of the other rooms are fairly dark (since you're surrounded by apartment buildings on almost all sides), and you should avoid the claustrophobic single rooms with alley views, even if you are traveling alone. Ideally suited for enjoying the North Side, the Majestic is only a short walk from both Wrigley Field and the lake.

528 W. Brompton St. (at Lake Shore Dr.), Chicago, IL 60657. ℂ **800/727-5108** or 773/404-3499. Fax 773/404-3495. www.cityinns.com. 52 units. $99–$179. Rates include continental breakfast. AE, DC, DISC, MC, V. Self-parking $19 in nearby garage with no in/out privileges. Subway/El: Red Line to Addison; walk several blocks east to Lake Shore Dr. and then 1 block south. **Amenities:** Exercise room; business services; limited room service; laundry service; same-day dry cleaning. *In room:* A/C, TV w/pay movies, dataport, minibar, coffeemaker, hair dryer, iron.

7 Near McCormick Place

MODERATE

Hyatt Regency McCormick Place ✪   The Hyatt Regency rises 33 stories from Chicago's ever-sprawling convention center. While the hotel is often solidly booked during trade shows and meetings, it has plenty of rooms to spare during winter and late summer, so vacationers might find bargains if they're willing to sacrifice the convenience of staying downtown. Although the hotel is only minutes from the Museum Campus, the lakefront, and the Loop, getting around is a little tricky without a car or a cab, although the hotel does off a complimentary shuttle to downtown shopping areas, the main museums, and Navy Pier. The average-size rooms are freshened up with upbeat, contemporary furnishings. Bathrooms are smallish, with the sink and vanity outside the bathroom. Business-plan rooms ($20 extra) include a workstation with a fax/copier/printer machine and complimentary continental breakfast. Most north-facing rooms feature scenic views of the city skyline and lakefront.

2233 S. Martin Luther King Dr. (at 22nd St.), Chicago, IL 60616. ℂ **800/233-1234** or 312/567-1234. Fax 312/528-4000. www.mccormickplace.hyatt.com. 800 units. $129–$339 double; $350–$1,190 suites; weekend rates from $99. AE, DC, DISC, MC, V. Valet parking $27 with in/out privileges; self-parking $23. Bus: No. 3 or 4. **Amenities:** Restaurant (American); bar; indoor lap pool; exercise room; sauna; concierge; business center; 24-hr. room service; laundry service; same-day dry cleaning; business-plan rooms. *In room:* A/C, TV w/pay movies, dataport, coffeemaker, hair dryer, iron.

7

Where to Dine

Joke all you want about bratwurst and deep-dish pizza—Chicago has come into its own as a culinary hotspot. Our top local chefs win national cooking awards and show up regularly on the Food Network, while we locals have had a hard time keeping up with all the new restaurant openings. What makes eating out in Chicago fun is the variety: We've got it all, such as stylish see-and-be-seen spots, an amazing array of steakhouses, chef-owned temples to fine dining, and every kind of ethnic cuisine you could possibly crave.

It's no easy task to narrow down the very impressive list of restaurants in this city. The competition at the high end is especially intense. A few well-regarded chefs—Jean Joho at Everest, Arun Sampanthavivat at Arun's, Charlie Trotter at his namesake place—still reign supreme at restaurants that have been long-time favorites of local epicures. But relative newcomers, including Tru, one sixtyblue, mk, and Zealous, have upped the stakes (and the average check price) considerably.

Ethnic cuisine continues to get an upscale makeover, from the sophisticated Mexican dishes at Chilpancingo and Don Juan on Halsted to the trendy maki at Mirai Sushi and Sushi Wabi. But (attitude-free) restaurants still thrive in the city's original immigrant neighborhoods—Greektown, Little Italy, and Chinatown. For more on ethnic food, please see the "Ethnic Dining Near the Loop" box on p. 296.

Unfortunately, Chicago is no longer the budget-dining destination it once was. (Hipness doesn't come cheap.) But just because the prices have risen doesn't mean that the attitude has. Restaurants in Chicago might have gotten trendy, but they're still friendly.

I've divided restaurants into four price categories in this chapter: "Very Expensive" means that entrees cost $20 to $30 (and sometimes more); "Expensive" means that most entrees run from $15 to $25; "Moderate" means that entrees cost between $10 and $20; and, at an "Inexpensive" place, they cost $15 or less.

Whether you're looking for a restaurant to impress a business colleague or simply a no-frills spot to dig in, these are the places the locals go when they want to eat well. To find out more about restaurants that have opened since this book went to press, check out the *Chicago Tribune*'s entertainment website at **www.metromix.com**, the website for *Chicago* magazine at **www.chicagomag.com**, or the entertainment/nightlife website **www.chicago.citysearch.com**.

1 Restaurants by Cuisine

ALSATIAN
Brasserie Jo ★ (River North, $$, p. 137)

Everest ★★★ (the Loop, $$$$, p. 110)

AMERICAN
Ann Sather ★★ (Wrigleyville/ North Side, $, p. 154)

Atwood Café ★★ (the Loop, $$$, p. 111)

Key to Abbreviations: $$$$ = Very Expensive $$$ = Expensive $$ = Moderate $ = Inexpensive

The Berghoff ✪ (the Loop, $$, p. 116)

Bin 36 ✪✪ (River North, $$$, p. 134)

Blackbird ✪✪✪ (Randolph St. Market District, $$$, p. 121)

Bongo Room (Wicker Park/ Bucktown, $, p. 139)

Carson's ✪ (River North, $$, p. 138)

Charlie's Ale House (Lincoln Park, $, p. 143)

Charlie's Ale House at Navy Pier (Magnificent Mile/Gold Coast, $, p. 142)

Crofton on Wells ✪✪ (River North, $$$, p. 135)

Dave & Buster's (Magnificent Mile/Gold Coast, $, p. 119)

d. kelly ✪ (Randolph St. Market District, $$$$, p. 120)

ESPN Zone (Magnificent Mile/Gold Coast, $$, p. 128)

Goose Island Brewing Company (Lincoln Park, $, p. 150)

Harry Caray's (River North, $$, p. 140)

John Barleycorn Memorial Pub (Lincoln Park, $, p. 143)

Lou Mitchell's (the Loop, $, p. 138)

Meritage Café and Wine Bar ✪✪ (Wicker Park/Bucktown, $$$, p. 156)

Mike Ditka's Restaurant ✪ (Magnificent Mile/Gold Coast, $$$, p. 127)

mk ✪✪✪ (River North, $$$$, p. 133)

Mr. Beef ✪ (River North, $, p. 144)

MOD ✪✪✪ (Wicker Park/ Bucktown, $$$, p. 158)

Moody's (Far North Side, $, p. 143)

Naha ✪✪ (River North, $$$$, p. 133)

Nine ✪✪✪ (the Loop, $$$, p. 114)

North Pond ✪✪✪ (Lincoln Park, $$$$, p. 145)

Northside Café (Wicker Park/ Bucktown, $, p. 161)

Oak Street Beachstro (Magnificent Mile/Gold Coast, $$, p. 142)

Oak Tree ✪ (Magnificent Mile/Gold Coast, $, p. 130)

O'Brien's Restaurant (Lincoln Park, $, p. 143)

one sixtyblue ✪✪✪ (Randolph St. Market District, $$$$, p. 120)

Orange (Lincoln Park, $, p. 139)

Petterino's ✪✪ (the Loop, $$$, p. 115)

Piece ✪ (Wicker Park/Bucktown, $, p. 161)

Pump Room (Magnificent Mile/ Gold Coast, $$$$, p. 125)

Rainforest Cafe (River North, $$, p. 119)

Rhapsody ✪✪ (the Loop, $$$, p. 115)

Silver Cloud ✪✪ (Wicker Park/ Bucktown, $, p. 162)

South Water Kitchen ✪ (the Loop, $$, p. 116)

Spring ✪✪✪ (Wicker Park/ Bucktown, $$$, p. 159)

312 Chicago ✪ (the Loop, $$, p. 117)

Thyme (River North, $$, p. 142)

Toast (Lincoln Park, $, p. 139)

Zealous ✪✪✪ (River North, $$$$, p. 134)

ASIAN

Hi Ricky Asia Noodle Shop & Satay Bar ✪ (Wrigleyville/ North Side, $, p. 155)

Kevin ✪✪ (River North, $$$$, p. 133)

Opera ✪✪ (the Loop, $$$, p. 114)

Penny's Noodle Shop ✪ (Wrigleyville/North Side, $, p. 155)

Red Light ✪ (Randolph St. Market District, $$$, p. 122)

Saigon Vietnamese Restaurant (near the Loop, $, p. 296)

Vong's Thai Kitchen ✪ (River North, $$, p. 140)

BARBECUE

Carson's ⭐ (River North, $$, p. 138)

Twin Anchors ⭐ (Lincoln Park, $, p. 153)

BISTRO

Bistrot Margot ⭐⭐ (Lincoln Park, $$, p. 149)

Cyrano's Bistrot & Wine Bar ⭐ (River North, $$, p. 139)

La Sardine ⭐ (Randolph St. Market District, $$, p. 123)

Le Bouchon ⭐⭐ (Wicker Park/ Bucktown, $$, p. 160)

Marché ⭐ (Randolph St. Market District, $$$, p. 122)

Mon Ami Gabi ⭐ (Lincoln Park, $$$, p. 148)

Yoshi's Café (Wrigleyville/ North Side, $$$, p. 153)

BREAKFAST & BRUNCH

Ann Sather ⭐⭐ (Wrigleyville/ North Side, $, p. 154)

Bic's Hardware Café (Pilsen, $, p. 297)

Billy Goat Tavern ⭐ (Magnificent Mile/Gold Coast, $, p. 129)

Bongo Room (Wicker Park/ Bucktown, $, p. 139)

The Café, Four Seasons Hotel (Magnificent Mile/Gold Coast, $$$, p. 138)

The Café, The Drake hotel (Magnificent Mile/Gold Coast, $$$, p. 138)

Heaven on Seven ⭐⭐ (the Loop, $, p. 118)

House of Blues (River North, $$, p. 138)

Lou Mitchell's (the Loop, $, p. 138)

Nookies (Lincoln Park, $, p. 139)

Orange (Lincoln Park, $, p. 139)

Toast (Lincoln Park, $, p. 139)

Wishbone ⭐⭐ (Randolph St. Market District, $, p. 124)

BURGERS

Billy Goat Tavern ⭐ (Magnificent Mile/Gold Coast, $, p. 129)

Northside Café (Wicker Park/ Bucktown, $, p. 161)

CAJUN/CREOLE

Heaven on Seven ⭐⭐ (the Loop, $, p. 118)

House of Blues (River North, $$, p. 138)

Soul Kitchen ⭐ (Wicker Park/ Bucktown, $$$, p. 159)

Wishbone ⭐⭐ (Randolph St. Market District, $, p. 124)

CALIFORNIAN

Puck's at the MCA (Magnificent Mile/Gold Coast, $, p. 142)

Spago ⭐⭐ (River North, $$$, p. 136)

CARIBBEAN

Soul Kitchen ⭐ (Wicker Park/ Bucktown, $$, p. 159)

CHINESE

Hong Min (near the Loop, $, p. 296)

Phoenix (near the Loop, $$, p. 296)

Won Kow (Chinatown, $, p. 296)

CONTINENTAL

Bistro 110 (Magnificent Mile/ Gold Coast, $$, p. 128)

DINER

Ed Debevic's (River North, $, p. 119)

Heaven on Seven ⭐⭐ (the Loop, $, p. 118)

Lou Mitchell's (the Loop, $, p. 138)

Nookies (Lincoln Park, $, p. 139)

ECLECTIC

Cafe Absinthe ⭐⭐ (Wicker Park/ Bucktown, $$$, p. 156)

foodlife ⭐⭐ (Magnificent Mile/Gold Coast, $, p. 130)

Jane's ⭐ (Wicker Park/Bucktown, $$, p. 160)

Spago ⭐⭐ (River North, $$$, p. 136)

FONDUE

Geja's Cafe ⭐ (Lincoln Park, $$$$, p. 145)

FRENCH

Ambria ⭐⭐ (Lincoln Park, $$$$, p. 144)

Bistrot Margot ✦✦ (Lincoln Park, $$, p. 149)

Brasserie Jo ✦ (River North, $$, p. 137)

Cyrano's Bistrot & Wine Bar ✦ (River North, $$, p. 139)

Escargot ✦✦ (Lincoln Park, $$, p. 150)

Everest ✦✦✦ (the Loop, $$$$, p. 110

La Creperie ✦✦ (Lincoln Park, $, p. 151)

La Sardine ✦ (Randolph St. Market District, $$, p. 123)

Le Bouchon ✦✦ (Wicker Park/ Bucktown, $$, p. 160)

Le Colonial ✦✦ (Magnificent Mile/Gold Coast, $$, p. 129)

Marché ✦ (Randolph St. Market District, $$$, p. 122)

Mon Ami Gabi ✦ (Lincoln Park, $$$, p. 148)

Pump Room (Magnificent Mile/ Gold Coast, $$$$, p. 125)

Tizi Melloul ✦✦ (River North, $$$, p. 137)

Tru ✦✦✦ (Magnificent Mile/ Gold Coast, $$$$, p. 126)

Yoshi's Café (Wrigleyville/ North Side, $$, p. 153)

FUSION

Kevin ✦✦ (River North, $$$$, p. 133)

GERMAN

The Berghoff ✦ (the Loop, $$, p. 116)

GREEK

Artopolis (Greektown, $, p. 297)

Athena (Greektown, $$, p. 142)

Costas (Greektown, $$, p. 297)

Greek Islands (Greektown, $$, p. 297)

Parthenon (Greektown, $$, p. 297)

Pegasus (Greektown, $$, p. 297)

Santorini (Greektown, $$, p. 297)

HOT DOGS

Fluky's (Magnificent Mile/ Gold Coast, $, p. 131)

Gold Coast Dogs (Magnificent Mile/Gold Coast, $, p. 131)

Murphy's Red Hots (Wrigleyville, $, p. 131)

Portillo's (River North, $, p. 131)

The Wieners Circle (Lincoln Park, $, p. 131)

INDIAN

Monsoon ✦ (Lincoln Park, $$$, p. 148)

ITALIAN

Buca di Beppo (Lincoln Park, $$, p. 119)

Club Lucky ✦ (Wicker Park/ Bucktown, $$, p. 159)

Francesca's on Taylor (near the Loop, $$, p. 154)

Gene & Georgetti ✦ (River North, $$$, p. 136)

Gioco ✦ (the Loop, $$$, p. 114)

Harry Caray's (River North, $$, p. 140)

La Cantina Enoteca (the Loop, $$, p. 118)

Maggiano's (River North, $, p. 119)

Mia Francesca (Wrigleyville/ North Side, $$, p. 154)

Ranalli's Pizzeria, Libations & Collectibles (Lincoln Park, $, p. 131)

RoseAngelis ✦✦ (Lincoln Park, $, p. 151)

Rosebud on Taylor (near the Loop, $$, p. 296)

Spiaggia ✦✦✦ (Magnificent Mile/ Gold Coast, $$$$, p. 126)

312 Chicago ✦ (the Loop, $$, p. 117)

Trattoria No. 10 (the Loop, $$, p. 117)

Tuscany (near the Loop, $$, p. 297)

The Village ✦ (the Loop, $$, p. 118)

Vivere ✦ (the Loop, $$, p. 118)

Vivo (Randolph St. Market District, $$$, p. 123)

JAPANESE

Mirai Sushi ✦✦ (Wicker Park/ Bucktown, $$$, p. 158)

Sai Café ✦ (Lincoln Park, $, p. 152)

Sushi Wabi ✿ (Randolph St. Market District, $$$, p. 122)

KOREAN

Soju (Wicker Park/Bucktown, $$, p. 161)

LATIN AMERICAN

Mas ✿✿ (Wicker Park/Bucktown, $$$, p. 156)

Nacional 27 ✿✿ (River North, $$$, p. 136)

Soul Kitchen ✿ (Wicker Park/Bucktown, $$, p. 159)

MALAYSIAN

Penang (near the Loop, $$, p. 296)

MEDITERRANEAN

Wave ✿ (Magnificent Mile/Gold Coast, $$$, p. 128)

MEXICAN

Adobo Grill (Lincoln Park, $$, p. 148)

Café Jumping Bean (Pilsen, $, p. 297)

Chilpancingo ✿✿ (River North, $$$, p. 134)

Don Juan on Halsted ✿✿ (Lincoln Park, $$, p. 149)

Frontera Grill & Topolobampo ✿✿✿ (River North, $$$, p. 135)

Nuevo Leon (Pilsen, $, p. 297)

Playa Azul (Pilsen, $, p. 297)

MIDDLE EASTERN

Reza's ✿✿ (River North, $$, p. 140)

Tizi Melloul ✿✿ (River North, $$$, p. 137)

NOUVELLE

Charlie Trotter's ✿✿✿ (Lincoln Park, $$$$, p. 145)

Yoshi's Café (Wrigleyville/North Side, $$, p. 153)

PIZZA

Chicago Pizza & Oven Grinder (Lincoln Park, $, p. 131)

Edwardo's (Magnificent Mile/Gold Coast, South Loop, and Lincoln Park; $; p. 131)

Gino's East ✿✿ (River North, $, p. 141)

Leona's Pizzeria (Wrigleyville, $, p. 131)

Lou Malnati's Pizzeria (River North, $, p. 131)

Pat's Pizzeria (Wrigleyville, $, p. 131)

Piece ✿ (Wicker Park/Bucktown, $, p. 161)

Pizzeria Due (River North, $, p. 144)

Pizzeria Uno ✿ (River North, $, p. 144)

Ranalli's Pizzeria, Libations & Collectibles (Lincoln Park, $, p. 131)

RUSSIAN

Russian Tea Time ✿✿ (the Loop, $$$, p. 116)

SANDWICHES

Potbelly Sandwich Works (Lincoln Park, $, p. 151)

SEAFOOD

Bluepoint Oyster Bar ✿✿ (Randolph St. Market District, $$$, p. 121)

Cape Cod Room (Magnificent Mile/Gold Coast, $$$$, p. 124)

La Cantina Enoteca (the Loop, $$, p. 118)

Nick's Fishmarket ✿✿ (the Loop, $$$$, p. 111)

Shaw's Crab House and Blue Crab Lounge ✿ (Magnificent Mile/Gold Coast, $$, p. 129)

SOUTHERN

House of Blues (River North, $$, p. 138)

Soul Kitchen ✿ (Wicker Park/Bucktown, $$, p. 159)

Wishbone ✿✿ (Randolph St. Market District, $, p. 124)

SPANISH/TAPAS

Arco de Cuchilleros ✿ (Wrigleyville, $$, p. 143)

Café Ba-Ba-Reeba! ✿ (Lincoln Park, $$, p. 149)

Cafe Iberico ✿✿ (River North, $, p. 141)

STEAK/CHOPS

Eli's, the Place for Steak ⭐ (Magnificent Mile/Gold Coast, $$$, p. 127)

Gene & Georgetti ⭐ (River North, $$$, p. 136)

Gibsons Bar & Steakhouse ⭐⭐ (Magnificent Mile/Gold Coast, $$$$, p. 125)

Mike Ditka's Restaurant ⭐ (Magnificent Mile/Gold Coast, $$$, p. 127)

Morton's ⭐⭐⭐ (Magnificent Mile/Gold Coast, $$$$, p. 125)

Petterino's ⭐⭐ (the Loop, $$$, p. 115)

SUSHI

Mirai Sushi ⭐⭐ (Wicker Park/ Bucktown, $$$, p. 158)

Sai Café ⭐ (Lincoln Park, $, p. 152)

Sushi Wabi ⭐ (Randolph St. Market District, $$$, p. 122)

SWEDISH

Ann Sather ⭐⭐ (Wrigleyville/ North Side, $, p. 154)

TEA

The Greenhouse, Ritz-Carlton Hotel (Magnificent Mile/Gold Coast, $$$, p. 127)

Palm Court, The Drake hotel (Magnificent Mile/Gold Coast, $$$, p. 127)

Seasons Lounge, Four Seasons Hotel (Magnificent Mile/Gold Coast, $$$, p. 127)

THAI

Arun's ⭐⭐⭐ (Wrigleyville/North Side, $$$$, p. 153)

Amarit (Magnificent Mile/Gold Coast, $, p. 152)

Bamee Noodle Shop (Wrigleyville, $, p. 152)

Erawan ⭐ (River North, $$$$, p. 132)

Hi Ricky Asia Noodle Shop & Satay Bar ⭐ (Wrigleyville/North Side, $, p. 155)

Penny's Noodle Shop ⭐ (Wrigleyville/North Side, $, p. 155)

Star of Siam (Magnificent Mile/ Gold Coast, $, p. 152)

Thai Classic (Wrigleyville, $, p. 152)

VIETNAMESE

Le Colonial ⭐⭐ (Magnificent Mile/Gold Coast, $$, p. 129)

Saigon Vietnamese Restaurant (near the Loop, $, p. 296)

2 The Loop

In keeping with their proximity to the towers of power, many of the restaurants in the Loop and its environs—namely, the emerging South Loop and the trendy Randolph Street Market District—feature expense-account-style prices. But it's still possible to dine here for less than the cost of your hotel room. *Note:* Keep in mind that several of the best downtown spots are closed on Sunday.

VERY EXPENSIVE

Everest ⭐⭐⭐ ALSATIAN/FRENCH Towering high above the Chicago Stock Exchange, Everest is an oasis of four-star fine-dining civility, a place where you can taste the creations of one of Chicago's top chefs while enjoying one of the city's top views. The dining room is nothing dramatic (it looks like a high-end corporate dining room), because diners are meant to focus on the food—and the sparkling lights of surrounding skyscrapers. Chef Jean Joho, who draws inspiration from the earthy cookery of his native Alsace, enjoys mixing what he calls "noble" and "simple" ingredients (caviar or foie gras with potatoes or turnips) for unique flavor combinations. While the menu changes frequently, the salmon soufflé or cream-of-Alsace-cabbage soup with smoked sturgeon and caviar are popular choices as appetizers; signature entrees include roasted Maine lobster in Alsace Gewürztraminer butter and ginger, and poached tenderloin of beef cooked *pot-au-feu* style and served with horseradish cream. Desserts are suitably sumptuous. This is the sort of restaurant where the clairvoyant service team seamlessly anticipates your every need, and the wine list offers some wonderful American and Alsatian selections.

440 S. LaSalle St., 40th Floor (at Congress Pkwy.). © 312/663-8920. www.leye.com. Reservations required. Main courses $27–$33; menu degustation $79; 3-course pretheater dinner $44. AE, DC, DISC, MC, V. Tues–Thurs 5:30–9:30pm; Fri–Sat 5:30–10pm. Complimentary valet parking. Subway/El: Brown Line to LaSalle/Van Buren.

Nick's Fishmarket ★★ SEAFOOD   Taking the elevator down below street level to Nick's feels a little like plunging underwater in a submarine. Once submerged, you'll find yourself in one of the best seafood restaurants in the city. This is definitely special-occasion dining which attracts an older, power-elite crowd, as well as a fair amount of business travelers with generous expense accounts.

The dining room is a spacious, open affair overlooking an outdoor plaza with an illuminated fountain and Chagall mosaic. Plush booths and loveseats (with individual light dimmers, no less) attract cuddly couples, while the generous space between tables allows for quiet conversation. Fresh seafood is the focus of the menu, which highlights specials flown in daily. Most of the preparations are straightforward, although some dishes include French or Asian accents (such as the seared ahi tuna served with a wasabi soy sauce). The menu also offers a fair selection for nonseafood lovers, including steak, veal chop with Barolo wine–truffle sauce, and lamb chops with mint sauce.

The street level Nick's Grill serves more casual fare, including sandwiches and flatbread pizzas. It's an appealing option for a late-afternoon light meal or for theater patrons in a hurry to catch a show.

Bank One Plaza at Monroe and Clark sts. © 312/621-0200. Reservations recommended. Main courses $25–$47; fixed-price lunch $21. AE, DC, DISC, MC, V. Mon–Thurs 11:30am–3pm and 5:30–11:30pm; Fri 11:30am–3pm and 5:30pm–midnight; Sat 5:30pm–midnight. Subway/El: Blue or Red line to Monroe.

EXPENSIVE

Atwood Café ★★ *Finds* AMERICAN   If you're tired of the exotic menus of trendy restaurants, Atwood Café will come as a welcome relief. Located in the historic Hotel Burnham, this place combines a gracious, 1900-era feel with a fresh take on American comfort food. The dining room—one of my favorites in the city—mixes elegance and humor with soaring ceilings, lush velvet curtains, and whimsical china and silverware.

Executive chef Heather Terhune plays around with global influences (most notably Asian and Southwestern). Appetizers include smoked salmon piled on sweet-corn cakes in a spicy chipotle chile dressing, chunky clam chowder, and duck quesadillas. Entrees include grilled rack of lamb in a mint-infused port-wine sauce; hoisin-glazed duck breast with snow peas and ginger basmati rice; and fusilli pasta in a roasted-garlic cream sauce with smoked ham, broccoli, and tomatoes. In the winter, try one of the signature potpies. Terhune began as a pastry chef, so desserts are a high point of Atwood Café's menu. Seasonal fruit is the basis for cobblers, trifles, and pies; for a decadently rich experience, tackle the banana-and-white-chocolate bread pudding.

Open for every meal, Atwood Café also serves a lovely afternoon tea.

1 W. Washington St. (at State St.). © 312/368-1900. Reservations accepted. Main courses $16–$24; 3-course prix fixe $39. AE, DC, DISC, MC, V. Mon–Fri 7am–10pm; Sat–Sun 8am–10pm. Formal tea service daily. Subway/El: Red Line to Randolph/Washington.

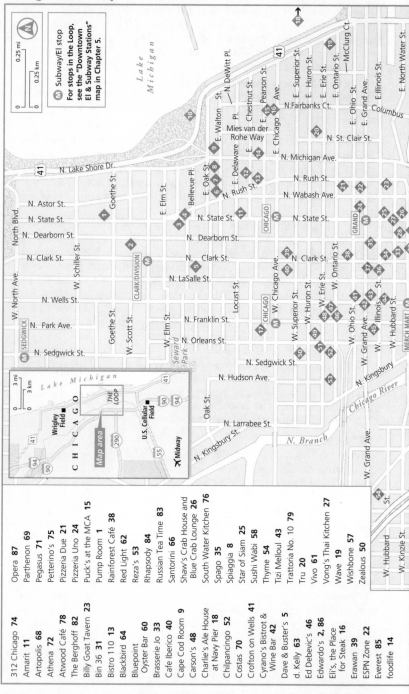

Gioco ⭐ NORTHERN ITALIAN   The South Loop was officially gentrified with the opening of this funky Italian restaurant. The cozy, convivial ambience—with exposed brick, mahogany accents, an open kitchen, stacks of wine bottles, and hip music—is par for the course in other restaurant-rich neighborhoods, but it's a welcome oasis of good food in this area. While Gioco's nouveau Italian dishes include many standard appetizers (fried calamari, pizza with prosciutto, Caesar salad, and so forth), you'll also find some creative new options: octopus carpaccio, confit of rabbit with fava-bean purée, and steamed mussels with white wine. The fine selection of pastas includes eggplant ravioli with pesto sauce, pappardelle in a duck sauce, and gnocchi *ai frutti di mare* (with mixed seafood). Seafood shows up in various preparations on the menu as well, along with heartier dishes such as filet of beef in Barolo wine sauce or the massive Bistecca all Fiorentina (served in a portion for two). Even if you're loath to order tiramisu for the umpteenth time, try this heavenly version—light as air and easy on the rum. The lunch menu adds a few panini and more pasta selections. The wine list is well balanced but limited.

1312 S. Wabash St. ✆ 312/939-3870. Reservations recommended. Main courses $12–$30. AE, DC, MC, V. Mon–Wed 11:30am–2:30pm and 5–10pm; Thurs 11:30am–2:30pm and 5–11pm; Fri 11:30am–2:30pm and 5pm–midnight; Sat 5pm–midnight; Sun 5–10pm. Subway/El: Red Line to Roosevelt/State.

Nine ★★★ CONTEMPORARY AMERICAN   The sizzle isn't all on the grill at this contemporary Chicago steakhouse–meets–Vegas dining palace. You'll feel like you're making a grand entrance from the moment you walk in the front door and step down an open staircase into the high-ceilinged, white-and-silver dining room where the dramatic central champagne-and-caviar bar and glittering crowd all vie for your immediate attention. Nine is all about the beautiful people, so dress the part (that is, leave the khaki shorts at home).

Begin with something from the caviar appetizers or "crustacea" station (clams and oysters, crab, shrimp, and crawfish). The signature starter is the "two cones" appetizer, one overflowing with tuna tartare, another with chunks of lobster and avocado. The prime, dry-aged steaks, particularly the 24-ounce bone-in rib eye and 22-ounce porterhouse, are the main attraction, but the menu wisely accommodates a variety of tastes. Non-red-meat options include a generous veggie chop salad, roast chicken with chipotle marinade, and a daily pasta selection. For dessert, grill your own high-style s'mores on a hibachi grill at your table. The lunch menu adds some burgers, flatbread pizzas, sandwiches, and entree salads.

If you want to keep hanging with the beautiful people after dinner, head upstairs to the sleek, futuristic **Ghost Bar.**

440 W. Randolph St. ✆ 312/575-9900. Reservations recommended. Lunch $9–$15; main courses $14–$32. AE, DC, MC, V. Sun–Wed 11:30am–2pm and 5:30–10pm; Thurs 11:30am–2pm and 5:30–11pm; Fri 11:30am–2pm and 5pm–midnight; Sat 5pm–midnight. Subway/El: Blue, Orange, Brown, or Green line to Clark/Lake.

Opera ★★ ASIAN   This place has nothing to do with *Aida* or *La Boheme,* but the mood is certainly theatrical at the South Loop's most happening spot. The newest concept from the folks behind Red Light (p. 122), Opera takes classic Chinese dishes to the next level. You'll know you're in for something far beyond Chinatown when you walk past the dramatic velvet curtains and take in the bold red-and-orange decor, not to mention the grand staircase leading up to the private dining room. Signature East-meets-West dishes include a spicy crab cake served with "chopsticks" (skinny crab-stuffed spring rolls), and peppered filet mignon served over a brandied buerre blanc with a side of broccoli in black-bean sauce. Even egg foo young gets an upscale makeover with the addition of lobster and fresh peas. Do make sure to save room for dessert, whether it's one of the light homemade sorbets, or the more decadent Tao of Chocolate (a liquid-center flourless chocolate cake with sticks of frozen chocolate mousse). The building used to house a film warehouse, and the storage vaults in the back have been converted into cozy dining nooks—the best tables in the house for romantic couples.

1301 S. Wabash Ave. (at 13th St.). ℭ **312/461-0161.** Reservations recommended. Main courses $15–$25; degustation menu $60. AE, DC, MC, V. Sun–Wed 5–10pm; Thurs 5–11pm; Fri–Sat 5pm–midnight. Subway: Red Line to Roosevelt/State.

Petterino's ★★ STEAK/AMERICAN   Named for Arturo Petterino, maitre d' at the Pump Room in the days when it swarmed with celebrities, Chicago's newest steakhouse re-creates the feeling of downtown dining in the 1940s and 1950s. Located in the new Goodman Theatre building, Petterino's is a popular pretheater option, so book early if you have to catch a show. The dimly lit dining room is decorated in dark wood with red leather booths, and the overall feel is relaxed rather than hyped-up. The menu is straightforward and filled with classic American big-night-out favorites: veal chops, New York strip steak, slow-cooked beef brisket, and some fresh fish selections. Pastas include baked ravioli and fettucine Alberto (a version of Alfredo with peas and prosciutto). Among the old-time appetizers, you'll find shrimp *de jonghe,* coated with garlic and breadcrumbs, and an excellent tomato bisque soup. In keeping with the restaurant's entertainment connection, some dishes are named after local celebrities; a nicely done salad of chopped mixed lettuces and blue cheese is named for long-time *Sun-Times* columnist Irv Kupcinet (who has been known to dine here). The lunch menu offers smaller versions of the dinner entrees, along with a good mix of salads and sandwiches.

150 N. Dearborn St. (at Randolph St.). ℭ **312/422-0150.** Reservations recommended. Main courses $13–$36 dinner. AE, DC, DISC, MC, V. Mon–Thurs 11am–10pm; Fri 11am–11pm; Sat 5pm–11pm. Subway/El: Red Line to Randolph/Washington or Brown Line to State/Lake.

Rhapsody ★★ CONTEMPORARY AMERICAN   The fine-dining restaurant inside Symphony Center (with floor-to-ceiling windows overlooking an outdoor dining area and a small park) is a hit with the concert-going crowd, as much for the setting as for the food. Rhapsody has, however, experienced a revolving door of chefs in the past few years, so the menu and service have suffered from a lack of consistency.

The current menu emphasizes contemporary American dining with a strong French influence. Foie gras and warm goat cheese show up on the appetizer list, but so do crab cakes and seasonal soups (asparagus in the spring, mushroom in the fall). Entrees include an all-American free-range chicken breast with homemade pumpkin gnocchi and apple-cider sauce; Dover sole with mascarpone polenta, wild mushrooms, and sherry sauce; and beef tenderloin with portobello mushroom timbale, potato purée, and bordelaise sauce. There is always at least one vegetarian option, in addition to the chef's daily risotto, which is often meat-free. The lunch menu features mostly salads, pastas, and sandwiches, such as brie, tomato, and pesto served on a baguette. For dessert, the Chocolate Symphony is a signature dish: a chocolate brownie with a gooey, molten center, topped with chocolate sorbet and a treble clef chocolate leaf.

65 E. Adams St. (at Wabash Ave.). ℭ **312/786-9911.** Reservations recommended. Main courses $15–$27. AE, DC, DISC, MC, V. Mon–Wed 11:30am–2pm and 5–9pm; Thurs–Fri 11:30am–2pm and 5–10pm; Sat 5–10pm; Sun 5–9pm. Subway/El: Brown Line to Adams.

Russian Tea Time ★★ *Finds* RUSSIAN   Another spot very popular with Chicago Symphony Orchestra patrons and musicians, this is far from being the simple tea cafe that its name implies. The menu offers classic dishes of czarist Russia and the former Soviet republics (for Russian neophytes, all the dishes are well described, sometimes with charming background stories). The atmosphere is old-world and cozy, with lots of woodwork and a friendly staff. Start off a meal with potato pancakes, blini with Russian caviar, or chilled smoked sturgeon; if you can't decide, there are a number of mixed appetizer platters to share. My top entree picks are the beef stroganoff; *kulebiaka* (meat pie with ground beef, cabbage, and onions); and roast pheasant served with a brandy, walnut, and pomegranate sauce and brandied prunes. Nonmeat eaters will also feel very welcome here; both the appetizer and entree listings include vegetarian dishes.

77 E. Adams St. (between Michigan and Wabash aves.). ℂ 312/360-0000. Reservations recommended. Main courses $15–$27. AE, DC, DISC, MC, V. Sun–Mon 11am–9pm; Tues–Thurs 11am–11pm; Fri–Sat 11am–midnight. Subway/El: Brown, Purple, Green, or Orange line to Adams, or Red Line to Monroe/State or Jackson/State.

MODERATE

The Berghoff ℱ GERMAN/AMERICAN   Having celebrated its centennial in 1998, The Berghoff is a Chicago landmark and its 20-foot ceilings, checked linoleum floor, and sepia photos of old Chicago make you feel like you've stepped back in time. The Berghoff holds Chicago liquor license no. 1, issued at the close of Prohibition, and it still serves its own brand of beer. This is old-school dining—some of the dark-jacketed waiters seem almost as old as the building.

While the menu rotates seasonally, classic German favorites are always available and promise the most dependable dining experience (when I asked the waiter if he recommended one Mexican-inspired dish on the daily specials menu, he shook his head disapprovingly, then cheered up when I said we'd take Wiener schnitzel instead). The Berghoff serves hundreds of orders of Wiener schnitzel every day, plus bratwurst, sauerbraten, corned beef, and the like. Because some of us have arteries to worry about, the third and fourth generations of family management have added some lighter fare in the form of salads, broiled fish, and vegetarian dishes. The Berghoff also holds a popular Oktoberfest celebration each year in mid-September that spills from the restaurant out into the street.

17 W. Adams St. (between State and Dearborn sts.). ℂ 312/427-3170. www.berghoff.com. Reservations recommended. Main courses $7.95–$12 lunch, $11–$17 dinner. AE, MC, V. Mon–Thurs 11am–9pm; Fri 11am–9:30pm; Sat 11:30am–10pm. Subway/El: Red or Blue line to Jackson/State or Monroe/State.

South Water Kitchen ℱ *Kids* AMERICAN   Loop restaurants cater to office workers and business travelers; there aren't a lot of family-friendly options other than fast food. So while South Water Kitchen isn't breaking any new culinary ground, it deserves a mention as one of the few places in the area that welcomes kids—while featuring food sophisticated enough for discerning moms and dads. The dining room evokes the spirit of an old-fashioned city saloon, and the menu goes the retro route as well. Entrees include modern twists on familiar favorites, including a pork chop with sage bread pudding; free-range chicken fricassee with herb dumplings, and a different "blue plate special" every night (at $14, it's an excellent deal for the neighborhood). The restaurant provides not only kids' menus but also games to keep the little ones occupied. Best of all, half the proceeds of all children's meals go to the Chicago Coalition for the Homeless.

In the Hotel Monaco, 225 N. Wabash Ave. (at Wacker Dr.). ℂ **888/306-3507**. www.swk.citysearch.com. Reservations accepted. Main courses $8–$17 lunch, $14–$22 dinner. AE, DC, MC, V. Mon–Fri 11:30am–2:30pm and 5–9pm; Sat–Sun 5–9pm. Subway: Red Line to State/Lake.

312 Chicago ✭ ITALIAN/AMERICAN   The in-house restaurant of the flashy Hotel Allegro, 312 Chicago has proved itself by relying on the Italian-inspired specialties of chef Dean Zanella. The restaurant has a clubby Jazz Age feel, with mahogany, antiques, and an earthy coloring. Because this is a hotel restaurant, the hours are more extensive than those of other dining spots in the area (including breakfast and lunch every day of the week) and the crowd is as eclectic as the guests who patronize the Allegro. 312 Chicago isn't the sort of place that sends food critics into a frenzy, but it serves consistently dependable meals at prices that are quite reasonable for downtown.

The seared day-boat scallops appetizer with wild mushrooms and truffle oil is a signature dish. The entree list is filled with familiar pasta and meat favorites, but most dishes have subtly creative touches (ravioli filled with shrimp, or grilled lamb chops served with a goat-cheese-and-spinach pie and artichoke sauce); there are always at least a couple seafood dishes. Zanella draws on his family heritage for dishes such as Grandma Anna's veal meatballs, topped with tomato sauce and ricotta. On weekends, the restaurant has simple brunch offerings distinguished by home-baked breads.

136 N. LaSalle St. (at Randolph St.). ℂ **312/696-2420**. Reservations recommended. Main courses $13–$23. AE, DC, DISC, MC, V. Mon–Thurs 7–10am, 11am–3pm, and 5–10pm; Fri 7–10am, 11am–3pm, and 5–11pm; Sat 7am–noon and 5–11pm; Sun 8am–3pm and 5–10pm. Subway/El: Red Line to Washington/State.

Trattoria No. 10 NORTHERN ITALIAN   Elegant but not pretentious, Trattoria No. 10 is a favorite with Chicagoans who work in the Loop. A professional restaurant designer once told me he considers this one of the best-designed restaurants in the city: the burnt-orange tones, ceramic floor tiles, and gracefully arched ceilings set a dining-in-Italy mood. The house specialty is ravioli, which can be ordered as an appetizer or as a main course (recent fillings included butternut and acorn squash, topped with walnut sauce, and homemade Italian sausage and mozzarella, served with spicy Arrabbiatta sauce). If you're not in the mood for ravioli, there are plenty of other interesting pasta dishes to choose from, such as farfalle with duck confit, asparagus, caramelized onions, and pine nuts, or the linguine with roasted eggplant, grilled tomatoes, and smoked mozzarella; there's also a daily risotto special. While Trattoria No. 10 serves beef, veal, and a decent variety of seafood dishes, the restaurant's strength is clearly pasta. For a lighter (and cheaper) meal, stop by after work for the all-you-can-eat buffet at the bar; $10 (with a $5 drink minimum) gets you tastes of beef tenderloin, shrimp, and various pasta specials.

10 N. Dearborn St. (between Madison and Washington sts.). ℂ **312/984-1718**. Reservations recommended. Main courses $14–$27. AE, DC, DISC, MC, V. Mon–Thurs 11:30am–2pm and 5:30–9pm; Fri 11:30am–2pm and 5:30–10pm; Sat 5:30–10pm. Subway/El: Red or Blue line to Dearborn.

THE ITALIAN VILLAGE

Along with The Berghoff (see listing above), the Italian Village ranks as a downtown dining landmark. Open since 1927, the building houses three separate Italian restaurants, each with its own menu and unique ambience, and all three are popular for pre- and posttheater meals. They also share an exemplary wine cellar and fresh produce grown in a family garden. Since each restaurant in the Italian Village is distinct, I have reviewed them separately below.

La Cantina Enoteca *Value* ITALIAN/SEAFOOD La Cantina, the most moderately priced of the three restaurants in the Italian Village, makes the most of its basement location by creating the feel of a wine cellar. Focusing on seafood, La Cantina offers at least five fresh varieties every day. Specialties include a fish soup appetizer, macaroni with scallops and shrimp in a garlic pesto cream sauce, and seafood-filled ravioli. There's also a small selection of non-seafood items (your basic pasta favorites and some beef and veal dishes). The dinner menu offers a big-time bargain: A la carte dishes (most under $20) include a salad, and for $2 more you also get soup, dessert, and coffee.

71 W. Monroe St. (between Clark and Dearborn sts.). ℂ 312/332-7005. Reservations recommended. Main courses (including soup, salad, dessert, and coffee) $12–$23; salads $9.95–$12; sandwiches $7.50–$7.95. Lunch prices slightly lower. AE, DC, DISC, MC, V. Mon–Thurs 11:30am–11pm; Fri 11:30am–midnight; Sat 5pm–midnight; closed most Sun, except a few in the summer; call to check. Subway/El: Red or Blue line to Monroe.

The Village *Finds* SOUTHERN ITALIAN Upstairs in the Italian Village is The Village, with its charming interpretation of alfresco dining in a small Italian town, complete with a midnight-blue ceiling, twinkling "stars," and banquettes tucked into private, cavelike little rooms. It's the kind of pan-Chicago place where you might see one man in a tux and another in shorts. The massive menu includes some time-warp appetizers (oysters Rockefeller, shrimp *de jonghe*) and all the old-time, hearty southern Italian standards. This is old-school Italian: eggplant parmigiana, a heavy spaghetti *alla carbonara* that would send your cardiologist into fits, veal scaloppine, and even calves' liver. The food is good rather than great, but what sets The Village apart is the bordering-on-corny faux-Italian atmosphere. The service, too, is outstanding, from the Italian maitre d' who flirts with all the ladies, to the ancient waiters who manage somehow to keep up with the nonstop flow. The staff are pros at handling pretheater dining.

71 W. Monroe St. (between Clark and Dearborn sts.). ℂ 312/332-7005. Reservations recommended (accepted for parties of 3 or more). Main courses (including salad) $11–$27; salads $5.50–$10; pizza $11–$14; sandwiches $7.95–$15; lunch prices slightly lower. AE, DISC, MC, V. Mon–Thurs 11am–1am; Fri–Sat 11am–2am; Sun noon–midnight. Subway/El: Red or Blue line to Monroe.

Vivere *REGIONAL ITALIAN On the main floor of the Italian Village is Vivere, the Italian Village's take on gourmet cooking—and eye-catching design. The bold interior, with rich burgundies, textured walls, spiraling bronze sculptures, and fragmented mosaic floors, makes dinner a theatrical experience. No fettucine Alfredo here; the pasta dishes feature upscale ingredients, from the *pappardelle* with braised duck to the *agnolottini* filled with pheasant. Fresh fish is always on the menu (a recent entree selection was salmon with spiced carrot broth), along with a good selection of meats and game. Grilled venison medallions are served with foie gras ravioli, while roasted duck is accompanied by a potato terrine and sautéed spinach. If you just can't decide, go for the five-course chef's tasting menu ($65).

71 W. Monroe St. (between Clark and Dearborn sts.). ℂ 312/332-4040. Reservations recommended. Main courses $14–$29. AE, DC, DISC, MC, V. Mon–Thurs 11:30am–2:30pm and 5–10pm; Fri 11:30am–2:30pm and 5–11pm; Sat 5–11pm. Subway/El: Red or Blue line to Monroe.

INEXPENSIVE

Heaven on Seven *Finds* CAJUN/DINER Heaven on Seven is loud and crowded, and serves a mean bowl of gumbo. This is truly a Chicago insider's spot. Hidden on the seventh floor of an office building opposite Marshall

Kids Family-Friendly Restaurants

One of the city's first "theme" restaurant's, **Ed Debevic's,** 640 N. Wells St. at Ontario St. (© **312/664-1707**), is a temple to America's home-town lunch-counter culture. The burgers-and-milkshakes menu is kid-friendly, but it's the staff schtick that makes this place memorable. The waitresses play the parts of gum-chewing toughies who make wise-cracks, toss out good-natured insults, and even sit right down at your table. It's all a performance—but it works.

Down the street is the kiddie fave **Rainforest Cafe,** 605 N. Clark St. at Ohio St. (© **312/787-1501**), the Chicago outpost of a Minnesota-based chain that bills itself as "a wild place to shop and eat." The restaurant strives to create the feel of a rainforest with the sounds of waterfalls, thunder and lightning, and wild animals echoing through-out the place. The menu features salads, sandwiches, and a range of entrees that will please a family of picky eaters.

One of the best all-around options, and a homegrown place as well, the Southern-style restaurant **Wishbone** (p. 124) has much to recom-mend it. Children can be kept busy looking at the large and surrealis-tic farm-life paintings on the walls or reading a picture book, *Floop the Fly,* loaned to diners (written and illustrated by the parents of the own-ers). The food is diverse enough that both adults and kids can find something to their liking, but there's also a menu geared just toward children. Another all-American choice in the Loop is **South Water Kitchen** (p. 116), which offers a kids' menu and coloring books.

A fun breakfast and lunch spot in Lincoln Park, **Toast,** 746 W. Web-ster St. at Halsted St. (© **773/935-5600**), serves up all-American favorites (pancakes, eggs, sandwiches) and employs an age-old restau-rateur's device for keeping idle hands and minds occupied: Tables at this neighborhoody spot are covered with blank canvases of butcher-block paper on which kids of all ages can doodle away with crayons.

Of course, the same goes at **Gino's East** (p. 141), the famous Chicago pizzeria, except patrons are invited to scrawl all over the graffiti-strewn walls and furniture. Another good pizza spot for older kids, who will find its loft-like space cool, is **Piece** in Wicker Park (p. 161). For fun and games of the coin-operated and basement rec-room variety, seek out **Dave & Buster's,** 1024 N. Clark St. (© **312/943-5151**), the Chicago location of the Dallas-based mega entertainment/dining chain. Another spot for sports-minded families is **ESPN Zone** (p. 128).

With its heaping plates of pasta served up family style, **Maggiano's,** 516 N. Clark St. (© **312/644-7700**), in River North is a good choice for a budget-conscious family. Even better is **Buca di Beppo,** 521 N. Rush St., right off Michigan Ave. (© **312/396-0001**). This Italian-American restaurant (part of a national chain) serves humongous family-style dishes in a catacomblike setting of cozy rooms. Each room is plastered from floor to ceiling with mementos and memorabilia gathered from basements, garages, and attics by the owners on periodic trips to Italy. Request the Pope Room, which features pontiff memorabilia and one special thronelike chair at its round table for your own VIP.

Field's, this isn't the kind of place you stumble on by accident, but you'll find it by following the office workers who line up for lunch during the week. Chef/owner Jimmy Bannos's Cajun and Creole specialties come with a cup of soup, and include such Louisiana staples as red beans and rice, a catfish po' boy sandwich, and jambalaya. If you don't have a taste for Tabasco, the enormous coffee shop–style menu covers all the traditional essentials: grilled-cheese sandwiches, omelets, tuna—the works. Indulge in chocolate pecan pie or chicory coffee crème brûlée for dessert. Although Heaven on Seven is usually open only for breakfast and lunch, they do serve dinner on the first and third Friday of the month from 5:30 to 9pm.

Although the Loop original has the most character, Heaven also has locations along the Mag Mile at **600 N. Michigan Ave.** (℃ **312/280-7774**), adjacent to a cineplex, and in Wrigleyville at **3478 N. Clark St.** (℃ **773/477-7818**); unlike the original location, both accept reservations and credit cards.

111 N. Wabash Ave. (at Washington St.), 7th floor. ℃ **312/263-6443**. Reservations not accepted. Menu items $3.95–$13. No credit cards. Mon–Fri 8:30am–5pm; Sat 10am–3pm. 1st and 3rd Fri of month 5:30–9pm. Subway/El: Red Line to Washington/State.

3 The Randolph Street Market District

The Market District used to be filled with warehouses and produce trucks that shut down tight after nightfall. But when a few bold restaurant pioneers moved in—and brought their super-hip clientele with them—this short stretch of Randolph Street, west of the Loop, got red hot. These days, the Market District is home to some of the city's best dining spots and swarms with luxury cars and scenemakers after dark. There's nothing much to do here besides eat—but if you have a few days in Chicago, try to make it here for at least one meal.

Transportation to the Market District is easy—it's about a $5 cab ride from Michigan Avenue or a slightly longer trek by bus (no. 8 or 9) or El, with stops at Halsted and Lake, a block from the restaurants. The walk from the Loop is pleasant and secure in the daytime, but at night, save your stroll for Michigan Avenue.

VERY EXPENSIVE

d. kelly ☆ AMERICAN   Sure, not many Chicagoans knew who Daniel Kelly was when he opened his namesake restaurant in 2002 (he'd spent the previous 10 years cooking at various Hyatt hotels). But his lineup of creative American dishes has won him a solid reputation in town among diners more interested in quality than buzz. The dining room here is simple (exposed brick walls, maple floor) and the crowd similarly understated. Kelly shines when it comes to putting a fresh spin on some neglected foods. One highlight of the menu, believe it or not, is the Brussels sprouts in garlic sauce. Puréed parsnips are spiced up with horseradish and served with ruby trout. Even relatively simple dishes (pan-roasted pork tenderloin with apple ragout) feature top-notch ingredients. The place is rather pricey for "simple" American cuisine, but Kelly is definitely one of Chicago's chefs to watch.

623 W. Randolph St. (at Jefferson St.). ℃ **312/628-0755**. Reservations accepted. Main courses $25–$30. AE, DC, MC, V. Mon–Thurs 11:30am–2pm and 5:30–10pm; Fri 11:30am–2pm and 5:30–11pm; Sat 5:30–11pm; closed Sun. Subway: Blue Line to Damen.

one sixtyblue ☆☆☆ CONTEMPORARY AMERICAN   Anchoring the western border of Randolph Street's restaurant row, one sixtyblue has lived down

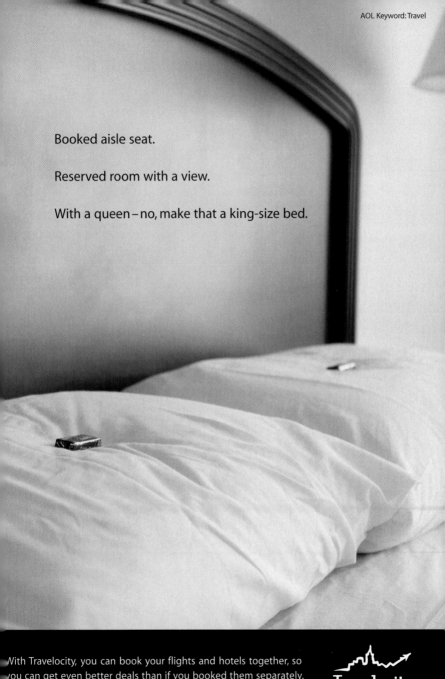

Booked aisle seat.

Reserved room with a view.

With a queen – no, make that a king-size bed.

the hype over its not-so-secret silent partner Michael Jordan (yes, he does eat here when he's in town, but usually only in the restaurant's private dining room). Some Chicago foodies consider this the best contemporary American restaurant in town.

The menu changes seasonally; dishes are artfully composed and perfectly satisfying. Chef Martial Noguier brings a French influence to the preparation of the contemporary dishes, but he draws on practically every world cuisine for inspiration. Appetizers run the gamut from ravioli with lobster-tarragon sauce to Thai lobster soup to a modern version of moussaka (made in this case with eggplant puree, braised lamb shoulder, lemon confit, and dried tomatoes). Entrees include thinly sliced loin of lamb with a casserole of fresh vegetables, venison with dried-plum bread pudding, and a rich honey-glazed salmon topped with an emulsion of chestnuts and walnuts. There is also a daily vegetarian entree selection. Designed by Adam Tihany (Le Cirque 2000, Jean Georges), the setting is quietly sophisticated. Begin or end your meal with a drink in the stylish lounge.

1400 W. Randolph St. (at Ogden Ave.). ✆ 312/850-0303. Reservations recommended. Main courses $21–$30. AE, DC, MC, V. Mon–Thurs 5–10pm; Fri–Sat 5–11pm; Sun 5–9pm.

EXPENSIVE

Blackbird ★★★ CONTEMPORARY AMERICAN   On the eastern boundary of the Randolph Street Market District's "restaurant row," ultrachic Blackbird draws a hip power crowd. Stylishly spare, Blackbird exudes a smart urban chic that could blend into the dining scene of any major city. The narrow room is dense with close-packed tables, and everyone pretends not to be looking around too much. As in many newer restaurants, the noise level can get high, but it's fun for people who like to make the scene.

Chef Paul Kahan's seasonal menu features creative but uncontrived fare, from a charcuterie plate to a modern take on the "soup and sandwich" concept (celery-root bisque garnished with small trout, cucumber, and red-onion sandwiches). An appetizer for more adventurous diners is the sautéed scallop carpaccio accompanied by blood orange, candied ginger, and mint. Familiar comfort foods in new guises make up the entree list: rack of lamb with figs, leeks and honey, and rosemary-infused mashed potatoes; and grilled sturgeon with caramelized carrots and curried cauliflower. Desserts might include lavender crème caramel with pine nuts, tangerines, and caramel sauce; chocolate mousse tower with grapefruit-vanilla salad; and various other enticements.

619 W. Randolph St. ✆ 312/715-0708. www.blackbirdrestaurant.com. Reservations recommended. Main courses $8–$20 lunch, $16–$29 dinner. AE, DC, DISC, MC, V. Mon–Thurs 11:30am–2pm and 5:30–10:30pm; Fri 11:30am–2pm and 5:30–11:30pm; Sat 5:30–11:30pm.

Bluepoint Oyster Bar ★★ SEAFOOD   Bluepoint has the stylings of an Art Deco 1940s fish house; the expansive, handsome dining room has huge, comfy booths and tufted banquettes, maroon-and-black marble floors, and ceiling fans spinning overhead. Oyster lovers will be delighted by the selection of more than a dozen varieties at the raw bar. Other appetizers include clams, sushi and sashimi, seafood cocktails, cold salads, and several specialty items such as baked and stuffed cherrystone clams and steamed Prince Edward Island mussels. The extensive list of entrees includes a range of fresh fish and seafood items prepared to your liking (broiled, grilled, blackened, and sautéed), and there are some big-ticket items such as Maine lobsters, Alaskan king crab legs, and stone crab dinners (Oct–May). Some of the house specialties are spicy, braised catfish shanks;

scallion-crusted marlin; grilled tuna bordelaise; and Bluepoint oyster and wild-mushroom ragout. There are a few steak and chicken alternatives, too.

741 W. Randolph St. ℂ 312/207-1222. Reservations recommended. Main courses $15–$23 (lobster and crab market prices higher). AE, DC, DISC, MC, V. Mon–Thurs 11:30am–10pm; Fri 11:30am–11pm; Sat 5–11pm; Sun 5–10pm.

Marché ⭐ FRENCH/BISTRO   If you've ever longed to run away and join the Cirque du Soleil, spend an evening at Marché. An Americanized, oversized take on the French bistro, Marché offers a convivial (noisy) dining experience, enhanced by the phantasmagoric decor and bustling bar scene that blends into the dining room. Multilevel seating, brightly colored umbrellas that hang from the ceiling, and velvet seats in shades of red and yellow add to the circus atmosphere, as does the clang of the open kitchen and enticing scents from the rotisserie. The food—a mix of bistro favorites—is fine, but the decor is the real draw here. The spit-roasted chicken is quite popular, and you can't miss with the New York strip au poivre partnered with a mound of shoestring frites. Chops and creative seafood entrees round out the menu. Simple, classic desserts and a cheese plate provide a refreshingly light finale to the meal.

833 W. Randolph St. (1 block west of Halsted St.). ℂ **312/226-8399.** Reservations recommended. Main courses $12–$18 lunch, $16–$31 dinner; chef's tasting menu Sun–Thurs 4-course $50, 5-course $65. AE, DC, MC, V. Mon–Wed 11:30am–2pm and 5:30–10pm; Thurs 11:30am–2pm and 5:30–11pm; Fri 11:30am–2pm and 5:30pm–midnight; Sat 5:30pm–midnight; Sun 5:30pm–10pm.

Red Light ⭐ ASIAN   One of the "theatrical" restaurants (along with Marché, Nine, and others) that wowed Chicago when they opened in the late 1990s, Red Light has only recently gotten its menu on track after much tweaking. With input from noted Thai chef Arun Sampanthavivat (see listing for Arun's on p. 153), dishes are now more focused and balanced, incorporating seasonal American, French, Thai, and other Asian ingredients and cooking techniques. But let's be honest—the main reason to go to Red Light is the setting: two dramatic dining rooms with deep red walls, colorful lanterns, gently waving palm fronds, sensuously curved windows and ceilings, and chairs that could be mistaken for metal sculptures. (Okay, they're not very comfortable, but they do look cool.)

The menu focuses on vegetarian and seafood entrees, including pan-seared Atlantic salmon with smoked salmon–chive rangoons, sweet Chinese mustard, and chile sauce; and seared sesame sea scallops with Thai chile corn pudding and sweet corn–lemon grass cream. You can also dig in to traditional dishes such as pad thai or a modern version of mu shu pork. And as befits a restaurant that's big on style, there's a fine selection of (expensive) specialty cocktails.

820 W. Randolph St. ℂ **312/733-8880.** www.redlight-chicago.com. Reservations recommended on weekends. Main courses $14–$24. AE, DC, DISC, MC, V. Mon–Wed 11:30am–2pm and 5:30–10pm; Thurs 11:30am–2pm and 5:30–11pm; Fri 11:30am–2pm and 5:30pm–midnight; Sat 5:30pm–midnight; Sun 5:30pm–10pm.

Sushi Wabi ⭐ JAPANESE/SUSHI   Artfully presented sushi and chic crowds are the order of the day at Sushi Wabi, Randolph Street's Japanese jewel. Choose from dozens of nigiri sushi (fish and various eggs perched on vinegared rice), maki (cone-shaped rolls of seafood, veggies, and rice in seaweed), a chef's selection sashimi plate, and a smattering of appetizers, entrees, and sides.

Sushi highlights include the sea scallop roll with smelt roe, mayonnaise, avocado, and sesame seeds; the dragon roll of shrimp tempura, eel, and avocado; and the spiky, crunchy spider roll of soft-shell crab, smelt roe, mayonnaise, and pepper-vinegar sauce. Simple entrees such as seared tuna, grilled salmon, teriyaki beef, and sesame-crusted chicken breast will satisfy landlubbers who are accommodating their sushi-loving companions. An intriguing side is the Japanese whipped potato salad with ginger, cucumber, carrots, and scallions. The minimal-chic decor is industrial and raw, and the lighting is dark and seductive. Make a reservation or expect quite a wait, even on school nights. Weekend DJ music adds to the clubby feel. Lunch offers a limited entree selection. A selection of teas in cast-iron pots and chilled sakes is offered; try a martini with a ginger-stuffed olive.

842 W. Randolph St. ℂ 312/563-1224. www.sushiwabi.com. Reservations recommended. Main courses $9.25–$21. AE, DC, DISC, MC, V. Mon–Fri 11:30am–2pm and 5pm–midnight; Sat 5pm–midnight; Sun 5–11pm.

Vivo NORTHERN ITALIAN   Back in 1991, everyone thought the owners of Vivo were crazy to locate this pioneering restaurant amid the gritty Randolph Street wholesale vegetable markets. But charming, cellar-chic Vivo caught on from the start. And today this pioneering restaurant is still a hip, not-too-flashy, and never dull destination. Cleverly angled ceiling lights pinpoint each table with its own glow, creating an intimacy that counteracts the loft-like feel of the room. The best table in the house, perched in a converted elevator shaft, overlooks the whole restaurant—but be prepared to book a month in advance to snag it.

The menu selections might not dazzle, but they remain fairly consistent. Vivo serves up a great carpaccio, tasty salads and pastas (try the black linguine with crabmeat or the daily homemade ravioli selection), and simple meat and fish entrees (grilled salmon or swordfish, a grilled filet mignon with Gorgonzola, and roasted leek purée). Lunch selections include a nice Caprese salad of fresh mozzarella, tomatoes, and basil; a few panini; and pastas such as fusilli with chicken, sun-dried tomatoes, and mozzarella. For dessert, try the wicked double-chocolate cake with espresso sauce.

838 W. Randolph St. (1 block west of Halsted St.). ℂ 312/733-3379. www.vivo-chicago.com. Main courses $13–$26. AE, DC, MC, V. Mon–Wed 11:30am–2:30pm and 5:30–10pm; Thurs 11:30am–2:30pm and 5:30–11pm; Fri 11:30am–2:30pm and 5:30pm–midnight; Sat 5:30pm–midnight; Sun 5:30–10pm.

MODERATE

La Sardine ✸ *Finds* FRENCH/BISTRO   Sister to Jean-Claude Poilevey's popular Le Bouchon (and named after a critic's description of that tiny Bucktown bistro), this more spacious and gracious destination is bathed in a honeyed glow and sensual aromas wafting from the open kitchen and rotisserie. La Sardine has the classic bistro look as well as warm, friendly service that makes this the Randolph Street version of a neighborhood restaurant.

Well-prepared versions of bistro standards include the delicate bouillabaisse in a lobster-saffron broth; ragout of super-tender rabbit, onions, and mashed potatoes; steak frites; sensational escargots bourguignon; onion soup; and salade Lyonnaise (greens, bacon lardons, croutons, and poached egg). The dessert menu boasts a frozen Grand Marnier soufflé with strawberry coulis and a warm passion-fruit soufflé with crème anglaise. At lunch, choose from an abbreviated menu of appetizers and salads, soups, sandwiches, and entrees, or opt for a hearty *plat du jour,* perhaps tuna niçoise on Monday, or duck legs braised in red wine with mushrooms and potato purée on Thursday. There's also a daily $16 three-course lunch featuring soup or salad and your choice of entree and dessert.

111 N. Carpenter St. ℂ 312/421-2800. Reservations recommended. Main courses $13–$19. AE, DC, DISC, MC, V. Mon–Thurs 11:30am–2:30pm and 5–10pm; Fri 11:30am–2:30pm and 5–11pm; Sat 5–11pm.

INEXPENSIVE

Wishbone ★★ *Kids* SOUTHERN/CAJUN/BREAKFAST   One of my best friends—a transplanted Chicagoan who now lives in New York—always has one request when she comes back to town: dinner at Wishbone. It's that kind of place, a down-home, casual spot that inspires intense loyalty (even if the food is only good rather than outstanding).

Known for Southern food and big-appetite breakfasts, Wishbone's extensive, reasonably priced menu blends hearty, home-style choices with healthful and vegetarian items. Brunch is the 'Bone's claim to fame, when an eclectic crowd of bedheads pack in for the plump and tasty salmon cakes, omelets, and red eggs (a lovely mess of tortillas, black beans, cheese, scallions, chile ancho sauce, salsa, and sour cream). However, brunch at Wishbone can be a mob scene, so I suggest lunch or dinner; offerings run from "yardbird" (charbroiled chicken with sweet red-pepper sauce) and blackened catfish to hoppin' John or Jack (vegetarian variations on the black-eyed pea classic). The tart Key lime pie is one of my favorite desserts in the city. The casual ambience is a good bet for families (a children's menu is available).

There's a newer location at 3300 N. Lincoln Ave. (© **773/549-2663**), but the original location has more character.

1001 Washington St. (at Morgan St.). © **312/850-2663**. Reservations accepted for parties of 6 or more (no reservations on Sun). Main courses $3.25–$8.75 breakfast and lunch, $5.75–$14 dinner. AE, DC, DISC, MC, V. Mon 7am–3pm; Tues–Fri 7am–3pm and 5–10pm; Sat–Sun 8am–3pm and 5–11pm.

4 The Magnificent Mile & the Gold Coast

A great many tourists who visit Chicago never stray far from the Magnificent Mile and the adjoining Gold Coast area. From the array of restaurants, shops, and pretty streets in the area, it's not hard to see why. The Gold Coast is home to some of the city's wealthiest, most tradition-bound families, people who have been frequenting the same restaurants for years. But newer places like Tru are also carving out new culinary niches. Restaurants here are some of the best in the city—and their prices are right in line with Michigan Avenue's designer boutiques.

VERY EXPENSIVE

Cape Cod Room *Overrated* SEAFOOD   A venerable old restaurant in a venerable old hotel, the Cape Cod Room is usually filled to capacity even during the middle of the week, underscoring its perennial popularity, even though I think it's overrated. This is the kind of place where waiters debone the Dover sole tableside, while businessmen work out their next deal. There's nothing nouvelle about the Cape Cod Room, which is part of the draw for old-timers; the restaurant, located on the lower level of The Drake hotel, is dimly lit and hasn't changed much since it opened in the 1930s. Although the food is fine, plenty of other restaurants offer similar dishes at much lower prices.

For starters, the hearty Bookbinder red snapper soup is a signature dish; it's flavored to taste with dry sherry brought to the table. Or, you might order a mixed seafood appetizer of shrimp, crab fingers, clams, and oysters. Main course offerings include sautéed striped bass served with a potato champagne sauce, New England scrod, red snapper, or Atlantic salmon baked with a potato horseradish crust. You'll also find a small selection of prime meat cuts, steaks, and chops. I wouldn't call the Cape Cod Room a good value, but the people-watching can be priceless.

In The Drake hotel, 140 E. Walton Place (at Michigan Ave.). ℂ 312/787-2200. Reservations recommended. Main courses $24–$40. AE, DC, DISC, MC, V. Daily noon–11pm. Closed Dec 25. Subway/El: Red Line to Chicago/State.

Gibsons Bar & Steakhouse ★★ STEAK   Popular with its Gold Coast neighbors, Gibsons is the steakhouse you visit when you want to make the scene. There are sporty cars idling at the valet stand, photos of celebs and near-celebs who've appeared here, and overdressed denizens mingling and noshing in the bar, which has a life all its own. The dining rooms evoke a more romantic time, from the sleek Art Deco decor to the bow-tied bartenders. The portions are notoriously enormous, so Gibson's is best for groups who are happy to share dishes (I wouldn't recommend it for a romantic dinner *a deux*). The namesake martinis are served in 10-ounce glasses, and the entrees are outlandishly scaled, from the six-piece shrimp cocktail, so huge you swore you downed a dozen, to the turtle pie that comes with a steak knife (and could easily serve 8 people). Yes, Gibsons has a clubby atmosphere, but the food also deserves some credit for the crowds who show up every night. You can also order from the bar menu.

1028 N. Rush St. (at Bellevue Place). ℂ 312/266-8999. Reservations strongly recommended. Main courses $22–$30. AE, DC, DISC, MC, V. Daily 3pm–midnight (bar open later). Subway/El: Red Line to Clark/Division.

Morton's ★★★ STEAK   Morton's is a well-known chain with a couple dozen locations nationwide; but it's Chicago born and bred, and many people still consider it the king of the Chicago-style steakhouses. Named for its founding father, renowned Chicago restaurateur Arnie Morton, Morton's holds its own against an onslaught of steakhouse competition with gargantuan portions of prime, wet-aged steaks, football-size baking potatoes, and trees of broccoli rolled out on a presentation cart. The restaurant is somewhat hidden in an undistinguished high-rise, and the decor hasn't changed in years. Neither has the menu: starters include lobster bisque, Caesar salad, shrimp, or jumbo lump crabmeat cocktail, but meat is the main event. House specialties include the double filet mignon with sauce béarnaise, and classic cuts of porterhouse, New York strip, and rib eye. A la carte sides include baked or mashed potatoes, hash browns, potato skins, or potatoes Lyonnaise.

This is a great place for a slice of carnivorous Chicago power dining—and a slice of Key lime pie or New York cheesecake.

1050 N. State St. ℂ 312/266-4820. www.mortons.com. Reservations recommended. Main courses $20–$33. AE, DC, DISC, MC, V. Mon–Sat 5:30–11pm; Sun 5–10pm. Subway/El: Red Line to State/Chicago.

Pump Room *Overrated* AMERICAN/FRENCH   Come here for the nostalgia, not the food. Back when celebrities journeyed by train between Hollywood and New York and stopped in Chicago to court the press, they always had a meal at the Pump Room. Diners at Booth One inevitably showed up in the morning papers. Today, the only celebrities you're likely to see at the Pump Room are the photographs of movie stars lining the walls. It's the kind of place that's thought of fondly as a local institution, but a recent turnover of chefs has made the cuisine inconsistent.

Like the interior, the menu has had a few makeovers over the years; today, the focus is on classic American dishes with a sophisticated twist. Appetizers run the range from simple escargot in garlic butter to foie gras served with hibiscus nectar or sea scallops with mushrooms and caviar. For entrees, try the three preparations of lamb served together (seared rack, oven roasted, and braised shank), or veal chop stuffed with prosciutto and asiago cheese. A more exotic choice is the roasted Muscovy duck breast with seaweed salad and mango sauce.

In the Omni Ambassador East Hotel, 1301 N. State Pkwy. (at Goethe St.). (C) **312/266-0360.** Reservations required. Jackets required. Main courses $23–$36. AE, DC, DISC, MC, V. Mon–Thurs 7am–2:30pm and 6–10pm; Fri–Sat 7am–2:30pm and 5pm–midnight; Sun 11am–2:30pm and 5–10pm. Subway/El: Red Line to Clark/Division.

Spiaggia ★★★ ITALIAN   *Spiaggia* means "beach" in Italian, and the restaurant's name is a tribute to its spectacular view of Lake Michigan and the Oak Street Beach. But this is no casual beach cafe. Spiaggia is widely acknowledged as the best fine-dining Italian restaurant in the city. The dining room is bright, airy, and sophisticated, an atmosphere far removed from your neighborhood trattoria (wear your jackets, gentlemen).

You can order a la carte or from two different degustation menus. The menu changes often and emphasizes seasonal ingredients. For starters, consider carpaccio of smoked Sicilian swordfish or pork loin wrapped in pancetta, served with sautéed artichoke hearts in a balsamic vinegar dressing. This ain't your Mama's pasta, either: Recent offerings have included pheasant-stuffed ravioli, pumpkin risotto, and gnocchi with wild mushrooms. Entree examples include classic *zuppa di pesce* and products of the restaurant's wood-burning oven, including monkfish; salmon; duck breast with Ligurian black olives, tomatoes, fennel, and baby artichokes; and grilled squab over lentils with foie gras. The classic Spiaggia dessert is the *baba all'arancia,* a cake soaked in orange liqueur and served with orange cream; the chilled mascarpone-cheese torte with rich chocolate gelato and espresso sauce is another high point.

Adjacent to the restaurant in a narrow, window-lined space is the informal, lower-priced **Café Spiaggia** ((C) **312/280-2764**), which has the same hours but also (unlike the main restaurant) serves Sunday brunch.

980 N. Michigan Ave. (at Oak St.). (C) **312/280-2750.** www.levyrestaurants.com. Reservations required on weekends. Main courses $17–$25 lunch, $29–$38 dinner; menu degustation $95–$135; fixed-price 3-course lunch $35. AE, DC, DISC, MC, V. Tues–Thurs 5:30–9:30pm; Fri–Sat 11:30am–2pm and 5:30–10:30pm; Sun 5:30–9pm. Subway/El: Red Line to Chicago/State.

Tru ★★★ PROGRESSIVE FRENCH   The sense of humor of chefs Rick Tramonto and Gale Gand shines through this menu (which recently included Insane Black Truffle Soup and Nut 'n Honey Foie Gras), making Tru an approachable fine-dining experience. The menu is divided into a series of prix-fixe options; if your wallet and stomach permits, shell out the big bucks for the 7-course Grand Collection or 8-course Tramonto's Collection. Appetizers include a visually sensational caviar staircase (caviars and fixin's climbing a glass spiral staircase), black-truffle risotto with rabbit confit and chanterelles, or venison carpaccio with sweet-potato compote and cherry sauce. For entrees, Surf, Turf, and Turf combines roasted lobster with sweetbreads and foie gras; also, a grilled beef tenderloin is paired with gratin of artichoke and marrow sauce. The latest additions to the menu are dishes that are prepared and served tableside, such as roasted duck with duck consommé and duck foie gras ravioli.

Gand's desserts perfectly echo Tramonto's savory menus; sate your sweet tooth with her roasted pineapple carpaccio, "soup and sandwich" (hot chocolate soup with marshmallows, peanut butter, and banana bread pudding), or chocolate and blood orange soufflés. Service is generally polished but not pompous; the expansive wine list is a treat for oenophiles, with 1,200 selections. The restaurant is nonsmoking.

676 N. St. Clair St. (at Huron St.). (C) **312/202-0001.** www.trurestaurant.com. Reservations required. Dinner 3-course prix-fixe menu $75; 7- or 8-course menu $75–$125. AE, DC, DISC, MC, V. Mon–Thurs 5:30–10pm; Fri–Sat 5:30–11pm. Subway/El: Red Line to Chicago/State.

> *Tips* **A Spot of Tea**
>
> If you're shopping on the Magnificent Mile and feel like having an elegant afternoon tea complete with finger sandwiches, scones, and pastry, go to the Palm Court at **The Drake,** 140 E. Walton Place (© **312/ 787-2200**), or the sunny Seasons Lounge of the **Four Seasons Hotel,** 120 E. Delaware Place (© **312/280-8800**). A fine afternoon tea is also served at The Greenhouse in the **Ritz-Carlton,** 160 E. Pearson St. (© **312/266-1000**), in the 12th-floor lobby above the Water Tower Place mall.

EXPENSIVE

Eli's, the Place for Steak ☆ STEAK   Every big town has its short list of restaurant institutions—Eli's is definitely on Chicago's. But although Eli's is now mostly known for its dense cheesecake (one of our mayor's favorite desserts), the restaurant has some deep roots of its own. The potato pancakes and the sautéed liver and onions served here are variations on the central European comfort foods that found their way to Chicago by way of a neighborhood delicatessen where the late Eli Schulman got his start in Chicago 50 years ago (a stained-glass portrait of Schulman overlooks the somewhat dated dining room).

This is definitely old-school dining, with a piano bar in front and some vintage waiters, but it will appeal to visitors who value tradition over trendiness. Meals begin with a scoop of delicate chopped liver, accompanied by diced eggs and onions, colorful crudités of fresh vegetables, and a basket of various breads and rolls. The restaurant's signature appetizer is the shrimp *de jonghe,* baked to succulent perfection with garlic and breadcrumbs. The steaks are among the menu's highlights, and liver connoisseurs will appreciate the calves' liver Eli, a truly delicate and palate-pleasing selection. Be sure to save some room for a slice of that famous cheesecake—which homesick former Chicagoans have shipped to them across the country.

215 E. Chicago Ave. (at Fairbanks Court). © **312/642-1393.** Reservations recommended. Main courses $20–$33. AE, DC, DISC, MC, V. Mon–Fri 11am–3pm and 5–11pm; Sat–Sun 5–11pm. Subway/El: Red Line to Chicago/State.

Mike Ditka's Restaurant ☆ AMERICAN/STEAK   In this city, nobody refers to him by name. He is simply "Da Coach." Immortalized as such in the classic "Super Fans" sketch on *Saturday Night Live,* "Iron" Mike Ditka remains the quintessential cigar-chomping, hard-nosed Chicagoan—despite the fact that it's been almost two decades since he led the Chicago Bears to victory in Super Bowl XX in 1985. Flooded with dim, amber light and filled with dark wood, leather banquettes, and walls lined with Ditka memorabilia and artful tributes to the coach's own sports heroes, this is real-man country—and the food is a good step up from your average sports bar. Appetizers here are called "Kickoffs" and include a "Duck Cigar," a hand-rolled pastry with a hearty duck-and-mushroom filling, and a "Souper Bowl" of corn chowder ("the Coach's favorite"). There are lots of salads, pastas, and seafood dishes to choose from, but why be a wimp? Go for the "Fullback Size" filet mignon, with spinach and homemade onion rings, or "Da Pork Chop," surrounded by warm cinnamon apples and a green-peppercorn sauce. When you're finished, light up a stogie in the second-floor cigar lounge.

100 E. Chestnut St. (in the Tremont Hotel, between Michigan Ave. and Rush St.). © **312/587-8989.** Reservations accepted. Main courses $14–$29 (less at breakfast and lunch). AE, DC, DISC, MC, V. Mon–Thurs 7am–11pm; Fri–Sat 7am–midnight; Sun 7am–10pm. Subway/El: Red Line to Chicago.

Wave ★ MEDITERRANEAN   Dinner is theater at this restaurant in the W Chicago Lakeshore hotel. A large, red, undulating canopy simulates—you guessed it—a wave overhead. The prime tables are the booths lined along one wall, unless you're social and want to pull up a chair at the 18-seat communal table. While the setting is the main draw for the hip young things that dine here, the food is refreshingly simple with an emphasis on seafood and hearty Mediterranean flavors. Instead of the usual fried calamari, Wave offers up grilled baby octopus with an olive tapenade and sautéed jumbo sea scallops with couscous, arugula, and carrot-cumin sauce. There's a whole-fish dinner special that changes daily; other recommended entrees include lamb shank served on a bed of orzo flavored with preserved lemon; or the perfectly roasted chicken which owes its flavor to a rub of thyme, garlic, paprika, and cayenne pepper. Desserts tend toward the trendy (chocolate soufflé with a hot, melted center), but the banana napoleon is a fine way to end a meal. The lunch menu offers "taverna" favorites such as kebabs, Greek-style salads, and a variety of pizzas.

644 N. Lake Shore Drive (at Ontario St.). © **312/255-4460.** Reservations accepted. Main courses $16–$26. AE, DC, DISC, MC, V. Mon–Thurs 6:30am–2pm and 5–10pm; Fri–Sat 6:30am–2pm and 5–11pm; Sun 6:30am–2pm and 5–9pm. Subway/El: Red Line to Chicago/State.

MODERATE

Bistro 110 CONTINENTAL   Bistro 110 enjoys a prime location just a half block west of North Michigan Avenue. Although a harbinger of the now-booming bistro trend, it's really too large and pricey to be considered an authentic bistro. The menu does cover a broad price range and several bistro classics such as escargots in puff pastry, mussels in white-wine sauce, French onion soup, cassoulet, and steak au poivre. More ambitious items include a spice-rubbed lamb, roasted and braised for 20 hours, and wood-roasted Maine sea scallops over spinach and basmati rice. Chicago holds Bistro 110 dear for the roasted heads of garlic served with crusty bread, and an early commitment to wood-roasting of meats and vegetables (the wood-roasted items, including a delicious, savory half chicken and a bountiful roast vegetable plate, are among your best bets—some of the other items can be inconsistent). Although the menu touts "la fameuse" crème brûlée, there's nothing that really distinguishes it from its many cousins. Other desserts include chocolate mousse, lemon and apple tarts, and a Gâteau Paradis au Chocolat, another "famous" dessert layering chocolate cake with caramel and toffee. On Sundays the restaurant hosts a popular brunch with live jazz music.

110 E. Pearson St. (just west of Michigan Ave.). © **312/266-3110.** www.bistro110restaurant.com. Main courses $13–$28. AE, DC, DISC, MC, V. Mon–Sat 11:30am–1am; Sun 11am–1am. Subway/El: Red Line to Chicago/State.

ESPN Zone *Kids* AMERICAN   Forget about catching the big game on the pint-size TV at the neighborhood tavern. Sports fans, welcome to nirvana. This massive 35,000-square-foot sports-themed dining and entertainment complex features three components: the Studio Grill, designed with replicas of studio sets from the cable networks' shows (including *SportsCenter*); the Screening Room, a sports pub featuring a 16-foot screen and an armada of TV monitors and radio sets carrying live broadcasts of games; and the Sports Arena, a gaming area with interactive and competitive attractions. The food here is better-than-average tavern fare, including quite a few salads and upscale items such as a salmon filet baked on cedar and served with steamed rice and grilled vegetables. There's also a special kids' menu.

43 E. Ohio St. (at Wabash Ave.). ✆ 312/644-3776. Main courses $7.25–$20. Sun–Thurs 11:30am–11:30pm; Fri–Sat 11:30am–midnight. Subway/El: Red Line to Grand.

Le Colonial ★★ *Finds* VIETNAMESE/FRENCH   Le Colonial is an escapist's paradise, a cleverly crafted re-creation of the civilized yet exotic world of French Indochina. Here in its tony Oak Street environs, Le Colonial has one of the loveliest dining rooms in the city—and the second-floor lounge is a sultry, seductive cocktail destination.

The restaurant evokes 1920s Saigon, with bamboo shutters, rattan chairs, potted palms and banana trees, fringed lampshades and ceiling fans, and evocative period photography. While the ambience certainly merits a visit, the flavorful cuisine is a draw on its own. Start with the hearty oxtail soup or the light and refreshing beef-and-watercress salad. Entrées include grilled lime-glazed sea scallops with garlic noodle salad; sautéed jumbo shrimp in curried coconut sauce; and roasted chicken with lemon grass–and-lime dipping sauce. Refresh with the orange-mint iced tea, and finish with banana tapioca pudding or gooey Le Colonial macaroon—or an after-dinner drink upstairs. Le Colonial offers outdoor seating in warm weather; try to reserve one of the coveted, romantic mezzanine terrace tables.

937 N. Rush St. (just south of Oak St.). ✆ 312/255-0088. Reservations recommended. Main courses $14–$19. AE, DC, MC, V. Mon–Fri noon–2:30pm and 5–11pm; Sat noon–2:30pm and 5pm–midnight; Sun 5–10pm. Subway/El: Red Line to Chicago/State.

Shaw's Crab House and Blue Crab Lounge ★ SEAFOOD   Shaw's has become a local institution; if you asked average Chicagoans where to go for seafood, chances are they'd point you here. The bright, busy dining room has a lively vibe, and the extensive menu should suit all tastes (the appetizers, for example, run the gamut from popcorn shrimp and fried calamari to exotic sushi combinations). And lest you wonder about ordering seafood when you're so far from an ocean, Shaw's does fly in seasonal seafood daily. You can even order fresh oysters according to their provenance (Nova Scotia, British Columbia, and so on). Main courses include sautéed scallops, Texas stone-crab claws, crab cakes, and french-fried shrimp; you can also take advantage of various (expensive) surf-and-turf combinations. Shaw's trademark dessert, Key lime pie, suggests the restaurant's subtle Key West/Papa Hemingway theme, as do the suave strains of such 1930s tunes as "Begin the Beguine" playing in the background. On Sunday, Tuesday, and Thursday nights, there's live jazz and blues in the lounge.

21 E. Hubbard St. (between State St. and Wabash Ave.). ✆ 312/527-2722. www.shawscrabhouse.com. Reservations accepted only for the main dining room. Main courses $14–$31. AE, DC, DISC, MC, V. Mon–Thurs 11:30am–2pm and 5:30–10pm; Fri 11:30am–2pm and 5–11pm; Sat 5–11pm; Sun 5–10pm. Subway/El: Red Line to Grand.

INEXPENSIVE

Billy Goat Tavern ★ *Value* BURGERS/BREAKFAST   "Cheezeborger, Cheezeborger—No Coke . . . Pepsi." Viewers of the original *Saturday Night Live* will certainly remember the classic John Belushi routine, a moment in the life of a crabby Greek short-order cook. The comic got his material from the Billy Goat Tavern, located under North Michigan Avenue near the bridge that crosses to

---

Tips Kitchens Up Close

Serious food fans can get a firsthand look at how some of the city's culinary stars work by booking a seat at a chef's table. You'll get a personal tour of the kitchen, a special selection of dishes and—best of all—a front-row seat for dinner-hour drama. At **Tru** (© **312/202-0001**), four to six people can sit in a glass-enclosed room off the kitchen, where they can check out the scene without feeling the heat. The chef's table at **Charlie Trotter's** (© **773/248-6228**) seats four to six right in the kitchen, so diners can catch Trotter's legendary perfectionism up close. The chef's table at **Zealous** (© **312/475-9112**) is in the main dining room—but bamboo trees surround it, so other diners won't get jealous when chef Michael Taus stops by for some one-on-one taste tests.

Chef's tables don't come cheap ($100–$150 per person), but they're a special splurge for die-hard foodies. Just remember to reserve well in advance because these tables book fast.

---

the Loop (you'll find it by walking down the steps across the street from the Chicago Tribune building). Just BUTT IN ANYTIME says the sign on the red door. The tavern is a classic dive: dark, seedy, and no-frills. But unlike the *Saturday Night Live* skit, the guys behind the counter are friendly ("Double cheezeborger is the best!" one shouted out cheerfully to me when I couldn't make up my mind what to order recently). The Billy Goat is a hangout for the newspaper workers and writers who occupy the nearby Tribune Tower and Sun-Times Building, so you might overhear the latest media buzz. After work, this is a good place to watch a game, chitchat at the bar, and down a few beers.

430 N. Michigan Ave. © **312/222-1525.** Reservations not accepted. Menu items $4–$8. No credit cards. Mon–Fri 7am–2am; Sat 10am–2am; Sun 11am–2am. Subway/El: Red Line to Chicago/State.

foodlife ★★ *Finds* ECLECTIC Taking the standard food court up a few notches, foodlife consists of a dozen or so kiosks offering both ordinary and exotic specialties on the mezzanine of Water Tower Place mall. Seats are spread out cafe-style in a very pleasant environment under realistic boughs of artificial trees festooned with strings of lights. A hostess will seat you, give you an electronic card, and then it's up to you to stroll around and get whatever food strikes your fancy (each purchase is recorded on your card, then you pay on the way out).

The beauty of a food court, of course, is that it offers something for everybody. At foodlife, diners can choose from burgers and pizza, south-of-the-border dishes, an assortment of Asian fare, and veggie-oriented, low-fat offerings. A lunch or a snack is basically inexpensive, but the payment method makes it easy to build up a big tab while holding a personal taste-testing session at each kiosk.

In Water Tower Place, 835 N. Michigan Ave. © **312/335-3663.** Reservations not accepted. Most items $5–$10. AE, DC, DISC, MC, V. Juice, espresso, and corner bakery Sun–Thurs 7:30am–9pm; Fri–Sat 7:30am–10pm. All other kiosks Sun–Thurs 11am–9pm; Fri–Sat 11am–10pm. Subway/El: Red Line to Chicago/State.

Oak Tree ★ AMERICAN Tucked away on the sixth floor of the ritzy 900 N. Michigan indoor mall (home of Bloomingdale's, Gucci, and more), Oak Tree isn't exactly high-profile. But it's popular with the younger ladies-who-lunch crowd—in fact, it's one of my favorite places for a meal during a day of

Only in Chicago

PIZZA

We have three pizza styles in Chicago: Chicago style, also known as deep-dish, which is thick-crusted and often demands a knife and fork; stuffed, which is similar to a pie, with a crust on both top and bottom; and thin crust. Many pizzerias serve both thick and thin, and some make all three kinds.

Three of Chicago's best gourmet deep-dish restaurants are **Pizzeria Uno** (p. 144), **Pizzeria Due** (p. 144), and **Gino's East** (p. 141). In River North, **Lou Malnati's Pizzeria,** at 439 N. Wells St. (✆ **312/828-9800**), bakes both deep-dish and thin-crust pizza and even has a low-fat cheese option. **Edwardo's** is a local pizza chain that serves all three varieties, but with a wheat crust and all-natural ingredients (spinach pizza is the specialty here); locations are in the Gold Coast, at 1212 N. Dearborn St. at Division Street (✆ **312/337-4490**); in the South Loop, at 521 S. Dearborn St. (✆ **312/939-3366**); and in Lincoln Park, at 2662 N. Halsted St. (✆ **773/871-3400**). Not far from Lincoln Park Zoo is **Ranalli's Pizzeria, Libations & Collectibles,** 1925 N. Lincoln Ave. (✆ **312/642-4700**), with its terrific open-air patio and extensive selection of beers.

In Wrigleyville, just off Belmont Avenue, are **Leona's Pizzeria,** 3215 N. Sheffield Ave. (✆ **773/327-8861**), and **Pat's Pizzeria,** 3114 N. Sheffield Ave. (✆ **773/248-0168**), both of which serve all three kinds of pizza. Leona's also has a location in Little Italy, at 1419 W. Taylor St. (✆ **312/ 850-2222**), and Pat's has one downtown in the Athletic Club Illinois Center, at 211 N. Stetson Ave. (✆ **312/946-0220**).

For a unique take on the deep-dish phenomenon, try the "pizza pot-pie" at **Chicago Pizza & Oven Grinder,** 2121 N. Clark St., steps from Lincoln Park Zoo (✆ **773/248-2570**); the pizzas are baked in a bowl and then turned over when served, for a distinctive upside-down pizza experience.

HOT DOGS

The classic Chicago hot dog includes a frankfurter by Vienna Beef (a local food processor and hallowed institution), heaps of chopped onions and green relish, a slather of yellow mustard, pickle spears, fresh tomato wedges, a dash of celery salt, and, for good measure, two or three "sport" peppers, those thumb-shaped holy terrors that turn your mouth into its own bonfire.

Chicago is home to many standout hot-dog spots such as **Gold Coast Dogs,** 418 N. State St., at Hubbard Street (✆ **312/527-1222**), two blocks off North Michigan Avenue. **Fluky's,** in The Shops at North Bridge mall at 520 N. Michigan Ave. (✆ **312/245-0702**), is part of a local chain that has been serving great hot dogs since the Depression (Dan Aykroyd and Jay Leno are fans). **Portillo's,** at 100 W. Ontario St. (✆ **312/587-8930**), is another local chain that specializes in hot dogs but also serves excellent pastas and salads. **Murphy's Red Hots,** 1211 W. Belmont Ave. (✆ **773/935-2882**), is a neighborhoody spot not too far from Wrigley Field, while **The Wieners Circle,** in Lincoln Park at 2622 N. Clark St. (✆ **773/477-7444**), is a late-night favorite where rude order-takers are part of the shtick.

downtown shopping. The cafe decor is bright and cheery (with nature-inspired murals to help you momentarily forget that you're inside a mall). If you can, get a table along the windows that look down on Michigan Avenue—but be aware that everyone else coming to eat here wants those tables, too. Oak Tree's real draw is the enormous, varied menu. You'll find something to suit every taste: a large salad selection, Asian noodles, sandwiches that range from trendy (duck breast with mango chutney) to manly (meatball with roasted bell peppers), Mexican quesadillas, even blue-plate specials such as turkey hash or a patty melt. The breakfast menu is just as extensive. Oak Tree can get crowded during prime weekend lunch hours, but it's relatively calm by mid-afternoon—just about the time you've power-shopped all your energy away and need a break.

900 N. Michigan Ave., 6th floor ℂ 312/751-1988. Reservations not accepted. Main courses $7.95–$12. AE, DC, DISC, MC, V. Sun–Thurs 7:30am–8:30pm; Fri–Sat 7:30am–9:30pm. Subway/El: Red Line to Chicago/State.

5 River North

River North, the area north of the Loop and west of Michigan Avenue, is home to the city's most concentrated cluster of art galleries and to a something-for-everyone array of restaurants—from fast food to theme and chain restaurants, to some of our trendiest dining destinations. Whether you seek a quick dog or burger, contemporary American fine dining or more exotic Moroccan or world-class Mexican fare, River North has it all.

VERY EXPENSIVE

Erawan ✦ THAI A joint venture by three veterans of the local Asian dining scene, Erawan offers a sleek, serene setting to enjoy Thai with a fusion twist, using many Western ingredients and techniques. Presentation is Erawan's strong point. The modern, high-ceilinged dining room is accented with Asian artwork and carved wood columns; you can even sit Thai-style on floor pillows in one room. Plates come garnished with colorful flowers or cleverly carved vegetables; the "snowbird" chicken dumplings, for example, look like tiny ducklings, with sliced carrots for beaks and black sesame seeds for eyes. East-meets-West appetizers include the venison tenderloin satay and a light salmon-and–lemon grass salad. Familiar Thai noodle and curry dishes get a boost from top-quality ingredients (the rich lamb *mussaman* curry is a highlight), while whole red snapper is lightly fried, with thinly sliced tomatoes arranged on top to simulate gills and "fins" made of carrots. The relatively high prices are Erawan's main drawback—you may not want to pay more than $20 for a dish you can get far cheaper at a local Thai takeout place. But if you like to be pampered and presented with visually stunning dishes, Erawan is worth a splurge.

729 N. Clark St. (at Chicago Ave.). ℂ 312/642-6888. Reservations accepted. Main courses $18–$38. AE, DC, DISC, MC, V. Sun–Thurs 5–10pm; Fri–Sat 5–10:30pm. Subway: Brown or Red line to Chicago.

⌒ Fun Fact Chicago Treats

Deep-dish pizza may be Chicago's culinary claim to fame, but the city has also added to the national waistline in other ways. Twinkies and Wonder Bread were invented here; Chicago businessman James L. Kraft created the first processed cheese; and Oscar Mayer got his start as a butcher in the Old Town neighborhood.

Kevin ★★ ASIAN/FUSION Chef Kevin Shikami had been cooking up fusion dishes for years in various restaurants around town; since opening his own place in 2002, he has finally been able to let loose. The overall mood is Zen calm (dark wood tables, chairs, and floor; recessed lights that illuminate textured paper covers). The menu emphasizes Japanese and Thai preparations and flavors; almost half the entrees are seafood. Shikami's signature dish is his tuna tartare, widely acknowledged as one of the city's best versions of this now-trendy appetizer (here, it's livened up with spicy wasabi and paired with a seasonal salad). Lobster and scallops get a kick from mandarin-orange sauce, while grilled salmon is glazed with a spicy mango sauce and served with Thai red curry. The uneven service means that Kevin hasn't quite reached the high standards of other restaurants in this price range, but if you crave creative takes on Asian cuisine, Kevin comes through.

9 W. Hubbard St. (at State St.). © 312/595-0055. Reservations accepted. Main courses $23–$30. AE, DC, MC, V. Mon–Thurs 11:30am–2pm and 5:30–10pm; Fri 11:30am–2pm and 5:30–11pm; Sat 5:30–11pm. Subway: Red Line to Merchandise Mart.

mk ★★★ CONTEMPORARY AMERICAN Considered by foodies to be one of the top American restaurants in the city, mk doesn't flaunt its pedigree. The loftlike dining room is as understated as the lowercase initials that give the restaurant its name. Chef Michael Kornick specializes in creative combinations, such as sautéed whitefish and Maine lobster with sweet corn, mushrooms, and a light cream sauce; a nouvelle surf and turf of grilled filet mignon and lobster with truffle aioli, red-wine sauce, and potato purée; and a New York sirloin steak with veal porterhouse. The presentations are tasteful rather than dazzling; Kornick wants you to concentrate on the food, and that's just what the chic, mixed-age crowd does. Service is disciplined yet agreeable, and fine table appointments signal this restaurant's commitment to quality. Pastry chef Mindy Segal is mk's not-so-secret weapon: her sweet seasonal masterpieces, from intriguing home-made ice creams to playful adaptations of classic fruit desserts, shouldn't be missed. The One Banana, Two Banana plate (banana brioche bread pudding, banana sherbet, and banana coffee cake topped with butterscotch and hot fudge) is worth the calories.

868 N. Franklin St. (1 block north of Chicago Ave.). © 312/482-9179. www.mkchicago.com. Reservations recommended. Main courses $19–$34; menu degustation $55. AE, DC, MC, V. Mon–Thurs 11:30am–2pm and 5:30–10pm; Fri 11:30am–2pm and 5:30–11pm; Sat 5:30–11pm; Sun 5:30–10pm. Subway/El: Brown Line to Chicago/Franklin.

Naha ★★ CONTEMPORARY AMERICAN Chef Carrie Nahabedian (who named the place from her nickname) did time at four-star hotels in California before returning to her hometown, and a West Coast influence is clear in Naha's wine list and use of seasonal ingredients. But she adds Mediterranean flavors into the mix, including dishes that reflect her Armenian heritage.

Dishes at Naha combine diverse flavors without getting fussy. The duck liver with roasted preserved quince is a delightfully rich starter, and tartare of ahi tuna topped with caviar comes garnished with a colorful mix of diced vegetables. Entrees are hearty: veal rib-eye with oven-cured tomatoes and cipollini onions; sirloin steak with a gratin of goat cheese; and hot smoked salmon with lentils, cabbage, and caramelized onions. The dessert menu leans toward fruit; a highlight is the warm pear cake topped with almond ice cream, served with a red Bartlett pear sorbet and pear compote on the side (as my waiter described it, "Naughty, but not too naughty.").

A front lounge offers a special menu of *meze,* Mediterranean "small dishes," including flatbread with tomatoes, goat cheese, and artichokes; lamb kebabs; and feta cheese phyllo triangles made from the chef's mother's recipe.

500 N. Clark St. (at Illinois St.). ⓒ 312/321-6242. Reservations recommended. Main courses $15–$20 lunch, $20–$32 dinner. AE, DC, DISC, MC, V. Mon–Thurs 11:30am–2pm and 5:30–10pm; Fri 11:30am–2pm and 5:30–10:30pm; Sat 5:30–10:30pm. Subway/El: Red Line to Grand.

Zealous ★★★ CONTEMPORARY AMERICAN   One of the most stylish contemporary restaurants in town, Zealous also has one of the most eclectic menus. Chef Michael Taus's cooking combines American ingredients with the subtle complexity of Chinese, Vietnamese, Korean, and Indian cuisines. Diners order from the a la carte menu or from one of three degustation menus; there is always a vegetarian menu, and Taus welcomes vegan diners as well. Recent entrees have ranged from Asian-inspired (sesame-crusted Chilean sea bass with red coconut curry sauce) to heartland hearty (roasted pork rack stuffed with dried peaches and served with carrot pierogi). The lunch menu features mostly pastas, along with some upscale sandwiches (all quite reasonably priced for a restaurant of this quality). The dining room is bright and airy (thanks to a central skylight); the purple chairs, green banquettes, and silver accents make the space feel trendy but not intimidating. The 6,000-bottle wine collection and glass-enclosed wine cellar show that Zealous takes its libations just as seriously as it takes its food (450 label selections appear on the wine list).

419 W. Superior St. ⓒ 312/475-9112. www.zealousrestaurant.com. Reservations recommended. Main courses $12–$19 lunch, $15–$32 dinner; menu degustation $75–$105. AE, DISC, MC, V. Tues–Fri 11:30am–2:30pm and 5:30–11pm; Sat 5:30–11pm. Subway/El: Brown Line to Chicago.

EXPENSIVE

Bin 36 ★★ CONTEMPORARY AMERICAN   In one lofty, airy space, this River North hot spot combines wine bar, restaurant, and retail in a successful, wine-centric concept. In the Tavern wine bar, you can swirl, sniff, and snack, and then move on to a table in the Cellar for a full meal of American bistro fare (where a list of higher-end wines by the bottle is available).

Bin 36 manages to be both upscale and relaxed. The restaurant is certainly serious about wine, but you're not expected to be an expert—this is a place where you're encouraged to experiment. The menu includes two or three suggested wines for every dish, all of which are available by the glass—and you won't go wrong by following the menu's suggestions. "Small plates" available at the Tavern include shiitake spring rolls, steamed mussels, and a selection of homemade patés, along with a few basic full-portion entrees (hamburgers, roast chicken, ahi tuna); you can also have fun ordering creative "wine flights," small glasses organized around a theme (Italian, Australian, and so on). The Cellar menu focuses on upscale American dishes, including a variety of seafood, seared venison, and braised pork shank. The food-wine pairings continue on the dessert menu—I'm no after-dinner drink fan, but when I tried a recommended sherry along with a slice of gingerbread-pear cake here one evening, I was converted.

339 N. Dearborn St. ⓒ 312/755-9463. www.bin36.com. Reservations recommended. Main courses $9–$15 lunch, $18–$26 dinner. AE, DC, DISC, MC, V. Sun–Thurs 6:30am–midnight; Fri–Sat 6:30am–1:30am. Subway/El: Red Line to Grand.

Chilpancingo ★★ MEXICAN   Here, chef Geno Bahena provides further evidence why Chicago is a center of modern Mexican cooking. The understated, dark wood of the loftlike interior is livened up with colorful Mexican folk art and masks, making this a very cheerful place to enjoy a meal. The name comes from the capital of Mexico's Guerrero state, a town where (according to the menu) "everything goes." The same could be said for the restaurant's menu, which includes a range of upscale Latin American cuisine. Starters include ceviche on crispy tortilla triangles, *sopa de ajo* (roasted garlic soup), and jalapeño peppers stuffed with pork and served with black-bean sauce. Bahena has built up a reputation with his mole sauces; the version to try here mixes 25 ingredients in a dark, complex sauce served over chicken. Salmon, rack of lamb, and tuna with squid also take adventurous diners far beyond enchiladas and tacos. Whatever you have for dessert—crepes, pecan bars, flan—don't miss the Café Maya Xtabentun, coffee flavored with Kahlua and a Mayan liquor, delivered by servers who light the Kahlua before pouring it into your glass. For a mix of flavors, try the five-course tasting menu ($45).

358 W. Ontario St. (at Orleans St.). ⓒ 312/266-9525. Reservations recommended. Main courses $7.50–$13 lunch, $15–$25 dinner. AE, DC, DISC, MC, V. Mon–Thurs 11:30am–2:30pm and 5–10pm; Fri–Sat 11:30am–2:30pm and 5–11pm; Sun 10:30am–3pm. Subway/El: Red Line to Grand.

Crofton on Wells ★★ *Finds* CONTEMPORARY AMERICAN   Chef-owner Suzy Crofton has devoted herself to this contemporary American restaurant, a 70-seat River North storefront with a loyal following and plenty of critical acclaim to its credit. Crofton's food is simply sophisticated and decidedly American, and the relatively spare dining room fits in with her no-attitude, Midwestern aesthetic.

Crofton's menu is based on seasonally available ingredients: You might start with a chilled cucumber-and–Vidalia onion soup in the summer, or a roasted squash soup in colder weather. Entree selections always include a vegan choice and run the gamut from a simple ginger-miso broth with soba noodles and seasonal vegetables to more complex creations (such as grilled venison medallions, soaked in a red-wine sauce with cabbage, huckleberries, and arugula pesto). Crofton's signature dish is the barbecue pork tenderloin garnished with apple chutney. Close with a Granny Smith apple tart or bittersweet chocolate cake with espresso ice cream and black peppercorn–caramel sauce. Other chefs may wow the food critics with their spectacular presentations, but Crofton has built her reputation with accessible dishes that attract a low-key crowd of satisfied regulars.

535 N. Wells St. (between Grand Ave. and Ohio St.). ⓒ 312/755-1790. www.croftononwells.com. Reservations recommended. Main courses $7.75–$14 lunch, $18–$29 dinner. AE, DC, MC, V. Mon–Thurs 11:30am–2:30pm and 5–10pm; Fri 11:30am–2:30pm and 5–11pm; Sat 5–11pm. Subway/El: Brown Line to Merchandise Mart.

Frontera Grill & Topolobampo ★★★ MEXICAN   Forget all your notions of burritos and chalupas. Owners Rick and Deann Groen Bayless, authors of the popular *Authentic Mexican: Regional Cooking from the Heart of Mexico,* are widely credited with bringing authentic Mexican regional cuisine to a wider audience. The building actually houses two restaurants: the casual Frontera Grill (plain wood tables, terra-cotta tile floor) and the fine-dining Topolobampo (white linen tablecloths, a more hushed environment).

At Frontera, the signature appetizer is the *sopes surtidos,* corn tortilla "boats" with a sampler of fillings (chicken in red mole, black beans with homemade chorizo, and so on). The ever-changing entree list features fresh, organic ingredients: pork loin in a green mole sauce; smoked chicken breast smothered in a sauce of chiles, pumpkin seeds, and roasted garlic; or a classic *sopa de pan* ("bread soup" spiced up with almonds, raisins, grilled green onions, and zucchini). Yes, you can also get tacos (with fillings such as portobello mushrooms, duck, and catfish). The Baylesses up the ante at the adjacent Topolobampo, where both the ingredients and presentation are more upscale.

It can be tough to snag a table at Frontera during prime dining hours, so do what the locals do: Put your name on the list and order a few margaritas in the lively, large bar area.

445 N. Clark St. (between Illinois and Hubbard sts.). © 312/661-1434. Reservations accepted at Frontera Grill only for parties of 5–10; accepted at Topolobampo for parties of 1–8. Main courses Frontera Grill $15–$21; Topolobampo $20–$29 (chef's 5-course tasting menu $70). AE, DC, DISC, MC, V. Frontera Grill Tues 11:30am–2:30pm and 5:30–10pm; Wed–Thurs 11:30am–2:30pm and 5–10pm; Fri 11:30am–2:30pm and 5–11pm; Sat 10:30am–2:30pm and 5–11pm. Topolobampo Tues 11:45am–2pm and 5:30–9:30pm; Wed–Thurs 11:30am–2pm and 5:30–9:30pm; Fri 11:30am–2pm and 5:30–10:30pm; Sat 5:30–10:30pm. Subway/El: Red Line to Grand.

Gene & Georgetti ⚘ STEAK/ITALIAN   Another vestige of old Chicago, Gene & Georgetti is a family-run steakhouse that has been serving up steak and Italian fare in a wood-frame house in the shadow of the El since 1941. The restaurant is dark and clubby, and the (exclusively male) waiters seem to have worked here for decades—and they no doubt have been serving some of the same patrons all that time. Gene & Georgetti has a popular following, so expect to wait in the bar area. The first floor is smoker-friendly; nonsmokers get tables upstairs. Although the place is best known for steaks, pasta and Italian specialties are also an essential part of the menu. This is not a place where you come to make the scene, but fans of old-time restaurants will find plenty of local character.

500 N. Franklin St. (at Illinois St.). © 312/527-3718. Reservations recommended. Main courses $15–$37. AE, DC, MC, V. Mon–Sat 11am–midnight (open Sun during major conventions). Subway/El: Brown Line to Merchandise Mart.

Nacional 27 ⚘⚘ *Finds* CONTEMPORARY LATIN   Part sleek supper club, part sultry nightclub, Nacional 27 showcases the cuisine of 27 Latin American nations, including Venezuela, Argentina, Costa Rica, and Brazil. Rich walnut and bamboo woods and gauzy curtains lend a tropical air to the grand dining room, which has cozy booth seating and tables arranged around a central dance floor. Steaks and seafood, along with exotic fruits and vegetables, are the stars of the menu (and all seem to call for one of the innovative Latin cocktails on the drink menu). For starters there are a variety of skewers, ceviches, and empanadas. Good choices are coconut-crusted shrimp and scallop-and-shrimp ceviche with avocado. For entrees, house specialties include chimichurri churrasco steak, a pounded sirloin with black-bean salsa, roasted peppers, and *papas fritas* (fried potatoes); and Chilean sea bass *en zarzuela en cazuela* (poached in shellfish and spicy tomato broth and served over annatto rice). The food can tend toward the spicy, so ask before you order if you've got sensitive taste buds. Nacional 27 heats up on Friday and Saturday nights after 10pm, when a DJ starts spinning fiery Latin tunes and couples take to the dance floor.

325 W. Huron St. (between Franklin and Orleans sts.). © 312/664-2727. Reservations recommended. Main courses $14–$25. AE, DC, DISC, MC, V. Dining room Mon–Thurs 5:30–9:30pm; Fri–Sat 5:30–11pm. Bar Mon–Thurs 5–10pm; Fri–Sat 5pm–2am. Subway/El: Brown Line to Chicago.

Spago ⚘⚘ CALIFORNIAN/ECLECTIC   Celebrity chef Wolfgang Puck, who pioneered the Californian-Asian style of cooking, brought the high-powered Spago brand here a few years ago, with a few menu adaptations for the city's cold-weather climate. The menu and decor have been tweaked over the past few years; in many ways, Spago still seems to be finding its identity. The plus for visitors? It's easier to get a table here (and taste Puck's legendary cuisine) than you might think.

Starters include the pizzas that made Puck famous (although they feature ingredients that are commonplace these days: goat cheese, fresh mozzarella, prosciutto, sun-dried tomatoes). The main courses are a mix of pastas (risotto with scallops and shrimp in a tomato-tarragon broth; angel hair with scallops, shrimp, and calamari) and fairly straightforward meat preparations (veal scaloppine; almond-crusted salmon with celery-root purée; grilled pork chop with blue cheese–potato gratin). Spago Chicago doesn't have the same celebrity caché as Spago in Los Angeles, but you may catch a glimpse of Puck himself, who makes regular visits to town.

520 N. Dearborn St. (at Grand Ave.). © 312/527-3700. Reservations recommended. Main courses $16–$32; 6-course tasting menu $65. AE, DC, DISC, MC, V. Mon–Thurs 11:30am–2pm and 5:30–10pm; Fri 11:30am–2pm and 5:30–11pm; Sat 5:30–11pm. Subway/El: Red Line to Grand.

Tizi Melloul ★★ FRENCH/MIDDLE EASTERN   An exotic haven in a neighborhood rife with raucous theme restaurants, Tizi Melloul creates an Arabian Nights fantasy world of rich reds, deep blues, and sparkling metallics. The food is good rather than spectacular—the real draw here is the decor. In the vibrantly colored, circular Crescent Room, you'll be seated on low banquettes and floor pillows—and you're encouraged to eat with your hands (although they'll bring silverware if you request it). The sultry, red-hued main dining room offers more traditional service, while the stark white Lounge is a hangout for the hipster set.

For the full experience, order the five-course Crescent Room menu, a bargain at $30, which can include French-influenced dishes such as mussels and bouillabaisse, along with tabbouleh and other familiar Mediterranean fare (to begin your meal, servers materialize to bathe your hands with rose water). *Tagines* (traditional Moroccan stews) are a specialty of the house and are served in their glazed earthenware crocks, with choices of lamb shank, a seafood medley, or *poussin* (a small chicken). Other eclectic entrees include braised lamb shank with feta and basil; pan-roasted cod with grilled calamari and salsa verde; and crispy roast duck flavored with cardamom.

531 N. Wells St. © 312/670-4338. www.tizimelloul.com. Reservations recommended. Main courses $11–$14 lunch, $16–$26 dinner. AE, MC, V. Sun–Wed 5:30–10pm; Thurs–Sat 5–11pm. Subway/El: Brown Line to Merchandise Mart or Red Line to Grand.

MODERATE

Brasserie Jo ★ ALSATIAN/FRENCH   Brasserie Jo showcases the casual side of chef Jean Joho (whose upscale Everest is one of the city's long-time gourmet destinations; see listing on p. 110). The high-ceilinged dining room here is open and spacious (as compared to a cozy bistro); you'll feel as if you're dining in an Art Deco Parisian cafe. Following in the tradition of the classic Alsatian *brasserie* (meaning "brewery"), Brasserie Jo makes a malty house brew, and diners are welcome for a quick stop-in snack with a glass of wine or a full five-course meal. Since the restaurant is open relatively late on weekends, this also makes a good stop for dessert (grab a seat at the pressed-metal bar).

You can order a hearty Alsatian choucroute here, but the menu focuses more on casual French classics: Entrees are divided into fruits *de mer* (including mussels and oysters), seafood dishes, and a variety of bistro-style steaks. One house specialty that's worth a try is the "shrimp bag," a phyllo pastry filled with shrimp, peas, and herb rice garnished with lobster sauce. Save room for dessert:

Breakfast & Brunch

NEAR THE LOOP & MAGNIFICENT MILE

You can get a good (and upscale) breakfast at one of the hotels near the Loop or Magnificent Mile. Favorites include the restaurants (both named The Café) at the **Four Seasons Hotel**, 120 E. Delaware Place (© **312/280-8800**), and **The Drake**, 140 E. Walton Place at Michigan Avenue (© **312/787-2200**).

A more informal choice in the Loop, just across from Marshall Field's, is **Heaven on Seven** (p. 118), where the Cajun and Creole specialties supplement an enormous diner-style menu that has anything you could possibly desire.

For brunch with some soul, head to **House of Blues**, 329 N. Dearborn St., at Kinzie Street (© **312/527-2583**), for its popular Sunday gospel brunch. To guarantee seating, it's a good idea to book a spot 2 weeks in advance.

A favorite for breakfast among Chicagoans since 1923 is **Lou Mitchell's**, 565 W. Jackson Blvd. (© **312/939-3111**), across the south branch of the Chicago River from the Loop, a block farther west than Union Station. You're greeted at the door with a basket of doughnut holes and milk duds so that you can nibble while waiting for a table.

For a Southern-style breakfast of spicy red eggs, cheese grits, or biscuits and gravy, head over to **Wishbone** (p. 124), a homespun dining hall in a warehouse district west of the Loop.

LINCOLN PARK & THE NORTH SIDE

A perfect breakfast or brunch spot if you're heading up to Wrigleyville for a Cubs game or for a day of antiquing on Belmont Avenue is **Ann Sather** (p. 154), famous for the homemade cinnamon rolls.

The delightfully decadent "crepes magnifique" live up to their name with an amazing alchemy of thin crepes, bananas, and chocolate. I also love the rich chocolate mousse, which is served tableside from a massive silver bowl, then topped with fresh cream and shaved chocolate—just like in Paris.

59 W. Hubbard St. (between Dearborn and Clark sts.). © 312/595-0800. www.leye.com. Reservations recommended. Main courses $12–$26. AE, DC, DISC, MC, V. Mon–Fri 5:30–10:30pm; Sat 5–11pm; Sun 5–10pm. Subway/El: Brown Line to Merchandise Mart or Red Line to Grand.

Carson's ⓐ AMERICAN/BARBECUE   A true Chicago institution, Carson's calls itself "The Place for Ribs," and, boy, is it ever. The barbecue sauce is sweet and tangy, and the ribs are meaty. Included in the $20 price for a full slab of baby backs are coleslaw and one of four types of potatoes (the most decadent are au gratin), plus right-out-of-the-oven rolls.

For dinner there's often a wait, but don't despair: In the bar area, you'll find a heaping mound of some of the best chopped liver around and plenty of cocktail rye to go with it. When you're seated at your table, tie on your plastic bib—and indulge. In case you don't eat ribs, Carson's also barbecues chicken, pork chops, and (in a nod to health-consciousness) even salmon. But let's be honest: You don't come to a place like this for the seafood. The waitstaff will be shocked if no one in your group orders the famous ribs. If by some remarkable feat you have room left after dinner, the candy-bar sundaes are a scrumptious finale to

The **Nookies** restaurants are also Chicago favorites for all the standard morning fare. Locations include Lincoln Park, 2114 N. Halsted St. (© **773/327-1400**); Old Town, 1748 N. Wells St. (© **312/337-2454**); and Lakeview, 3334 N. Halsted St. (© **773/248-9888**).

Come to **Orange**, 3231 N. Clark St., at Belmont (© **773/549-4400**), for a fun twist on breakfast foods. Try the Green Eggs and Ham—eggs scrambled with pesto, tomatoes, mozzarella, and pancetta. There's a kids' menu, too, making this a popular choice for families. But a warning to all those with hungry kids (and parents): come early or late; the line for a table winds outside during prime weekend brunch hours.

Lincoln Park's **Toast**, 746 W. Webster St., at Halsted Street (© **773/935-5600**), is homey yet slightly funky. The crayons and butcher-block table coverings will keep kids busy. Breakfast includes a twist on the usual diner fare. Pancakes come in all sorts of tempting varieties, from lemon/poppy seed drizzled with honey to the "pancake orgy" of a strawberry, mango, and banana-pecan pancake topped with granola, yogurt, and honey.

WICKER PARK/BUCKTOWN

The brightly colored **Bongo Room**, 1470 N. Milwaukee Ave. (© **773/489-0690**), is a neighborhood gathering place for the hipsters of Wicker Park/Bucktown, but the restaurant's tasty, creative breakfasts have drawn partisans from all over the city who feel right at home stretching out the morning with a late breakfast.

the meal. Carson's popularity has led to something of a factory mentality among management, which evidently feels the need to herd 'em in and out, but the servers are responsive to requests not to be hurried through the meal.

612 N. Wells St. (at Ontario St.). © 312/280-9200. Reservations not accepted. Main courses $8.95–$30. AE, DC, DISC, MC, V. Mon–Thurs 11am–11pm; Fri 11am–12:30am; Sat noon–12:30am; Sun noon–11pm. Subway/El: Red Line to Grand.

Cyrano's Bistrot & Wine Bar ★ *Value* FRENCH/BISTRO   Warm and welcoming, Cyrano's represents a haven of authentic bistro charm in the congested River North restaurant scene, due in no small part to the friendly presence of chef Didier Durand and his wife, Jamie. The cheery blue-and-red wood exterior, eclectic artwork, and charming personal asides on the menu ("Use of cellular phones may interfere with the stability of our whipped cream") all signal the owner's personal touch. The dining room is cozy but not overly noisy; still, Cyrano's works best for smaller groups (or romantic couples). The house specialties are the rotisserie duck and chicken served with your choice of sauce and stick-to-your-ribs classics: steak frites, roasted rabbit with mustard sauce, and cassoulet. There are also a variety of salads to choose from (and some vegetarian options), but overall this is a place to eat hearty. Be sure to start with one of Durand's sensationally flavorful soups (the lobster bisque is a highlight) or the pomme frites, served with three condiments (Dijon mustard, homemade ketchup, and mayonnaise). Service is knowledgeable and friendly; on a recent visit, my group said we were too full for dessert, but the waiter brought us a plate of sorbet on the house. "You can't eat at a French restaurant and not have *some* kind of dessert," he admonished (good philosophy, I think). In warmer months, a sidewalk cafe is open all day.

546 N. Wells St. (between Ohio St. and Grand Ave.). *©* **312/467-0546.** Main courses $14–$23; 3-course prix-fixe dinner $25. AE, DC, DISC, MC, V. Mon–Thurs 11:30am–2:30pm and 5:30–10pm; Fri 11:30am–2:30pm and 5–10:30pm; Sat 5–11pm. Subway/El: Brown Line to Merchandise Mart.

Harry Caray's AMERICAN/ITALIAN   A shrine to the legendary Cubs play-by-play announcer, this landmark building is a repository for Harry's staggering collection of baseball memorabilia. But you don't have to be a baseball lover to appreciate Harry's.

The dining rooms have an old-Chicago feel that is comfortable and familiar, with high tin ceilings, exposed brick walls, and red-checked tablecloths. It would be easy to lump Harry's with other celebrity restaurants, but as one reviewer pointed out, the food is better than it has to be. The portions are enormous; you'll have enough left over to eat for days. Main-course offerings run from traditional items such as pastas with red sauce to chicken Vesuvio, veal, and a variety of seafood choices. Harry's is also a good place to order big plates of meat: dry-aged steaks, lamb, veal, and pork chops. From the list of side dishes, be sure to order the signature Vesuvio potatoes. The restaurant also has a (surprisingly) extensive and well-chosen wine list. If you don't want a full-service meal, the bar is a lively place for watching a game and grabbing some munchies—and, incidentally, the bar is 60 feet, 6 inches long, the same distance from the pitcher's mound to home plate.

33 W. Kinzie St. (at Dearborn St.). *©* **312/828-0966.** Main courses $11–$33. AE, DC, DISC, MC, V. Mon–Thurs 11:30am–3pm and 5–10:30pm; Fri–Sat 11:30am–3pm and 5–11pm; Sun noon–4pm (lunch bar only) and 4–10pm. Subway/El: Brown Line to Merchandise Mart or Red Line to Grand.

Reza's ★★ *Value* MIDDLE EASTERN   Reza's doesn't look like the typical Middle Eastern restaurant; housed in a former microbrewery, it has high ceilings and expansive, loftlike dining rooms. But the Persian-inspired menu will soon make you forget all about pints of ale. Specialties include a deliciously rich chicken in pomegranate sauce and a variety of kebabs (make sure you ask for the dill rice). Despite the menu's meat-heavy emphasis, there's a full selection of vegetarian options too. Can't decide what to order? Go for an appetizer combo, a generous sampler of Middle Eastern dishes (including hummus, stuffed grape leaves, tabbouleh, and other standbys, nicely presented in a red lacquer bento box). Reza's has another location in Andersonville, at 5255 N. Clark St. (*©* **773/561-1898**), but the River North spot is the most convenient for visitors staying downtown.

432 W. Ontario St (at Orleans St.). *©* **312/664-4500.** Main courses $9.95–$17. AE, DC, DISC, MC, V. Daily 11am–midnight. Subway/El: Red Line to Grand.

Vong's Thai Kitchen ★ PAN-ASIAN   Chef Jean-Georges Vongerichten's Vong concept was a huge hit in New York and London, so hopes were high when the trendy Thai/French restaurant hit Chicago a few years ago. But it didn't take long for the buzz to die down. Recently, both the decor and the menu were completely overhauled; the result is a new name and more Chicago-friendly atmosphere—and no menu item is over $20.

Though it bills itself as a Thai kitchen, the menu offers a broad range of Asian and fusion dishes (tuna wasabi pizza, anyone?). There are a few holdovers from the original Vong menu, including the signature Black Plate of appetizers (shrimp satay, tuna sashimi roll, chicken-scallion satay, Peking duck roll, and crab roll). Traditional Thai curry dishes get a kick from nontraditional ingredients (halibut, duck), and there's always at least one seafood dish that's been wok-seared for extra flavor and texture. The wine list is adequate, but the emphasis is on specialty cocktails, including the best-selling Red Passion (raspberry-flavored vodka, cranberry, champagne, and pineapple). The lunch menu offers an appealing selection of Asian-inspired salads and sandwiches, as well as various combination plates that let you sample two or three different dishes.

6 W. Hubbard St. (at State St.). © **312/644-8664**. Reservations accepted. Main courses $7.95–$14 lunch, $14–$20 dinner. AE, DC, DISC, MC, V. Mon–Thurs 11:30am–2pm and 5:30–9:30pm; Fri 11:30am–2pm and 5–11pm; Sat 5–11pm; Sun 5–9pm. Subway/El: Red Line to Grand.

INEXPENSIVE

Cafe Iberico ★★ SPANISH/TAPAS   This no-frills tapas spot won't win any points for style, but the consistently good food and festive atmosphere makes it a long-time local favorite for singles in their 20s and 30s. Cafe Iberico gets very loud, especially on weekends, so it makes for a fun group destination—but plan your romantic tête-à-tête elsewhere. Crowds begin pouring in at the end of the workday, so you'll probably have to wait for a table. Not to worry: Order a pitcher of fruit-filled sangria at the bar along with everyone else. Put a dent in your appetite with a plate of *queso de cabra* (baked goat cheese with fresh tomato-basil sauce), and when your waiter returns with the first dish, put in a second order for a round of both hot and cold tapas. (The waiters may take some effort to flag down.) Then continue to order as your hunger demands. A few standout dishes are the vegetarian Spanish omelet, spicy potatoes with tomato sauce, chicken brochette with caramelized onions and rice, and grilled octopus with potatoes and olive oil. There are a handful of entrees on the menu, and a few desserts if you're still not sated.

739 N. LaSalle St. (between Chicago Ave. and Superior St.). © **312/573-1510**. Reservations accepted during the week for parties of 6 or more. Tapas $3.50–$4.95; main courses $7.95–$13. DC, DISC, MC, V. Mon–Thurs 11am–11pm; Fri 11am–1:30am; Sat noon–1:30am; Sun noon–11pm. Subway/El: Red Line to Chicago/State or Brown Line to Chicago.

Gino's East ★★ (Kids) PIZZA   It was a Chicago tourist rite of passage: waiting in the frigid cold (or sweltering heat) to get into Gino's, a warren of tiny rooms and dark wood booths covered with a few generations' worth of carved graffiti. Now that the restaurant has moved into the vast space formerly occupied by Planet Hollywood, there are no more lines out front (but the graffiti-covered booths were brought along to keep the "authentic" flavor). Gino's does a ton of business with families, but it might be best for older kids since they don't have highchairs or booster seats.

Many Chicagoans consider Gino's the quintessential deep-dish Chicago-style pizza (I know transplanted Midwesterners who come here for their cheesy fix whenever they're back in town). True to its reputation, the pizza is heavy (a small cheese pizza is enough for two), so work up an appetite before chowing down. Specialty pizzas include the supreme, with layers of cheese, sausage, onions, green pepper, and mushrooms; and the vegetarian, with cheese, onions, peppers, asparagus, summer squash, zucchini, and eggplant. Gino's also offers salads, sandwiches, and pastas—but I've never seen anyone order them. If you want to take a pizza home on the plane, call a day in advance and Gino's will pack a special frozen pie for the trip.

633 N. Wells St. (at Ontario St.). © **312/943-1124**. Reservations no accepted. Pizza $8.25–$17. AE, DC, DISC, MC, V. Mon–Thurs 11am–11pm; Fri–Sat 11am–midnight; Sun noon–10pm. Subway/El: Red Line to Chicago/State.

Dining Alfresco

Cocooned for 6 months of the year, with furnaces and electric blankets blazing, Chicagoans revel in the warm months of late spring, summer, and early autumn. For locals and visitors alike, dining alfresco is an ideal way to experience the sights, sounds, smells, and social fabric of this multifaceted city. Just remember to be prepared to wait on a nice night, because you'll be fighting a lot of other diners for a coveted outdoor table.

LOOP & VICINITY

Athena   This Greektown mainstay offers a stunning three-level outdoor seating area. It's paved with brick and landscaped with 30-foot trees, flower gardens, and even a waterfall. Best of all: an incredible view of the downtown skyline with the Sears Tower right in the middle. 212 S. Halsted St.; ☎ 312/655-0000.

Charlie's Ale House at Navy Pier   One of several outdoor dining options along Navy Pier, this outpost of the Lincoln Park restaurant wins for lip-smacking pub fare and a great location on the southern promenade overlooking the lakefront and Loop skyline. 700 E. Grand Ave.; ☎ 312/595-1440.

Chicago Riverwalk   The outdoor cafes along the banks of the Chicago River's main branch, between Wabash Avenue and Wells Street, are run by restaurants that change from year to year, so I don't recommend any place or anything specific. But food is almost an afterthought on days when schooners and speedboats glide by en route to Lake Michigan harbors.

MAGNIFICENT MILE & GOLD COAST

Le Colonial   This lovely French-Vietnamese restaurant, located in a vintage Gold Coast town house and evocative of 1920s Saigon, has a sidewalk cafe. But you'd do better to reserve a table on the tiny second-floor porch, overlooking the street and close to Le Colonial's atmospheric cocktail lounge. For a full review, see p. 129. 937 N. Rush St.; ☎ 312/255-0088.

Oak Street Beachstro   Suit up and head for this warm-weather-only beachfront cafe—literally on the sands of popular Oak Street Beach—which serves inventive cafe fare (fresh seafood, sandwiches, and pastas). Beer and wine are available. 1000 N. Lake Shore Dr. at Oak Street Beach; ☎ 312/915-4100.

Puck's at the MCA   This offshoot of celebrity chef Wolfgang Puck's Spago is tucked in the back of the Museum of Contemporary Art. From the terrace you've got a view of the museum's sculpture garden. Take in the art, the fresh air, and a shrimp club sandwich, Chinois salad, or wood-grilled pizza. (Restaurant-only patrons can bypass museum admission.) 220 E. Chicago Ave.; ☎ 312/397-4034.

RIVER NORTH

Thyme   One of the most beautiful alfresco spots in the city belongs to this contemporary American restaurant on the western fringe of River

North. Thyme's garden is full of plants and light-illuminated trees. **464 N. Halsted St.** (at Grand Ave.); ✆ **312/226-4300.**

LINCOLN PARK

Charlie's Ale House Déjà vu? Nope, Charlie's triumphs again with its wonderful beer garden in Lincoln Park. It's spacious, surrounded by tall ivy-covered brick walls, and buzzing with activity and good vibes. **1224 W. Webster Ave.;** ✆ **773/871-1440.**

John Barleycorn Memorial Pub Tapping kegs since the 1960s, this popular neighborhood pub, situated in an 19th-century building, is long on authenticity and short on pretension. Relax with a cold one and a thick, juicy burger in the outdoor patio. **658 W. Belden Ave.;** ✆ **773/348-8899.**

North Pond Set on the banks of one of Lincoln Park's beautiful lagoons, the excellent North Pond serves American cuisine in a romantic and sylvan setting. One caveat: Alcohol is not permitted on the outdoor patio. See also p. 145. **2610 N. Cannon Dr.;** ✆ **773/477-5845.**

O'Brien's Restaurant Wells Street in Old Town is lined with several alfresco options, but the best belongs to O'Brien's, the unofficial nucleus of neighborhood life. The outdoor patio has teakwood furniture, a gazebo bar, and a mural of the owners' country club on a brick wall. Order the dressed-up chips, a house specialty. **1528 N. Wells St.** (2 blocks south of North Ave.); ✆ **312/787-3131.**

WRIGLEYVILLE & VICINITY

Arco de Cuchilleros Savvy Spanish tapas aficionados thumb their noses at trendy Cafe Iberico and Café Ba-Ba-Reeba!; the tapas and sangria at this lesser-known Wrigleyville restaurant can compete with the best of them. The intimate, leafy terrace out back glows with lantern light. **3445 N. Halsted St.;** ✆ **773/296-6046.**

Moody's For 30 years, Moody's has been grilling some of the best burgers in Chicago. It's ideal in winter for its dark, cozy dining room warmed by a fireplace, but it's better still in summer for its awesome outdoor patio, a real hidden treasure. **5910 N. Broadway Ave.;** ✆ **773/275-2696.**

WICKER PARK/BUCKTOWN

Meritage Café and Wine Bar Meritage wins my vote for most romantic outdoor nighttime seating. The food (American cuisine with Pacific Northwest influences) is top-notch, but it's the outdoor patio, twinkling with overhead lights, that makes for a magical experience. Best of all, the patio is covered and heated in the winter, so you can enjoy the illusion of outdoor dining even in February. For a full review, see p. 156. **2118 N. Damen Ave.;** ✆ **773/235-6434.**

Northside Café On a sunny summer day, Northside seems like Wicker Park's town square, packed with an eclectic mixture of locals catching up and checking out the scene. The entire front of the restaurant opens onto the street, making it relatively easy to get an "outdoor" table. For more info, see p. 161. **1635 N. Damen Ave.** ✆ **773/384-3555.**

Mr. Beef ★ *Finds* AMERICAN   Mr. Beef doesn't have much atmosphere or seating room, but it's a much-loved Chicago institution. Its claim to fame is the classic Italian beef sandwich, the Chicago version of a Philly cheese steak. The Mr. Beef variety is made of sliced beef dipped in jus, piled high on a chewy bun, and topped with sweet or hot peppers. Heavy, filling, and *very* Chicago, Mr. Beef really hops during lunchtime, when dusty construction workers and suit-wearing businessmen crowd in for their meaty fix. While you're chowing, check out the celebrity photos and newspaper clippings covering the walls, and you'll see why this place is considered a local monument.

666 N. Orleans St. (at Erie St.). ☎ **312/337-8500.** Sandwiches $5.95–$8.50. No credit cards. Mon–Fri 7am–4:45pm; Sat 10am–2pm. Subway/El: Red Line to Grand.

Pizzeria Uno ★ *Value* PIZZA   Pizzeria Uno invented Chicago-style pizza, and many deep-dish aficionados still refuse to accept any imitations. Uno's is now a chain of restaurants throughout the country, but this location is the original. You may eat in the restaurant itself on the basement level or, weather permitting, on the outdoor patio right off the sidewalk. Salads, sandwiches, and a house mine-strone are also available, but, hey—the only reason to come here is for the pizza.

Uno was so successful that the owners opened **Pizzeria Due** in a lovely gray-brick Victorian town house nearby at 619 N. Wabash Ave. at Ontario Street (☎ **312/943-2400**).

29 E. Ohio St. (at Wabash Ave.). ☎ **312/321-1000.** Lunch reservations accepted Mon–Fri. Pizza $7–$18. AE, DC, DISC, MC, V. Mon–Fri 11:30am–1am; Sat 11:30am–2am; Sun 11:30am–11pm. Subway/El: Red Line to Grand.

6 Lincoln Park

Singles and upwardly mobile young families inhabit Lincoln Park, the neigh-borhood roughly defined by North Avenue on the south, Diversey Parkway on the north, the park on the east, and Clybourn Avenue on the west. No surprise, then, that the neighborhood has spawned a dense concentration of some of the city's best restaurants.

VERY EXPENSIVE

Ambria ★★ FRENCH   Across the street from the Lincoln Park Zoo and housed in the impressive former Belden-Stratford Hotel, Ambria is ensconced in several large rooms off the old lobby. It has enjoyed an enviable 20-year run as one of Chicago's finest restaurants, one of the places Chicagoans choose when they want to celebrate a special occasion. The dimly lit, wood-paneled interior is intimate, almost clublike, and eminently civilized.

The menu, masterfully orchestrated by Chef Gabino Sotelino, changes fre-quently but always features beautifully prepared French-influenced dishes. Appetizers might include lobster medallions in a caviar beurre blanc, or a pastry stuffed with escargot and seasonal vegetables. Main courses run the gamut from roasted rack of lamb with stuffed baby eggplant, couscous, and artichoke chips to roasted medallions of New Zealand venison with wild-rice pancakes, caramelized rhubarb, and root vegetables. You can order a la carte or from a selection of fixed-price menus (including a five-course shellfish degustation and the "Ambria Classic Menu" of tried-and-true favorites). The wine list is exten-sive; take advantage of the top-notch sommelier if you need guidance.

2300 N. Lincoln Park West (at Belden Ave.). ☎ **773/472-0076.** Reservations recommended. Main courses $24–$36; fixed-price meals $60–$75. AE, DC, DISC, MC, V. Mon–Fri 6–10pm; Sat 5–10:30pm. Bus: No. 151.

Charlie Trotter's ★★★ NOUVELLE   Foodies flock to the namesake restaurant of chef Charlie Trotter, Chicago's first celebrity chef. Yes, he's done TV shows and authored a series of cookbooks (with almost impossible-to-follow recipes), but Trotter's focus is this restaurant, a shrine to creative fine dining.

There is no a la carte menu, so this is not the place to come if you're a picky eater. Decide at the outset if you would like the vegetable ($90) or grand ($110) degustation menu. Trotter delights in presenting diners with unfamiliar ingredients and presentations, and prides himself on using only organic or free-range products (so you can feel good about indulging). The very long entree descriptions signal Trotter's attention to detail; sample dishes from a recent menu include ragout of leek confit, braised carrots, salsify, and cauliflower with Perigord black-truffle emulsion; and black buck venison with Japanese *kumai* (jasmine rice cake and red-wine Kalamata olive emulsion). Be prepared to linger; dinner here can take up to 3 hours. The dining room may be formal, but the staff are not intimidating. The wine list is extensive, and a sommelier is on hand to help match wines with each course. The entire restaurant is nonsmoking.

For a taste of Trotter's gourmet fare without the high price tag, check out **Trotter's to Go,** his new gourmet food store in Lincoln Park at 1337 W. Fullerton Ave. (✆ **773/868-6510**).

816 W. Armitage Ave. (at Halsted St.). ✆ **773/248-6228**. www.charlietrotters.com. Reservations required. Jackets required, ties requested. Fixed-price menus $90 and $110. AE, DC, DISC, MC, V. Tues–Sat 6–10pm. Subway/El: Brown Line to Armitage.

Geja's Cafe ★ FONDUE   A dark, subterranean hideaway, Geja's (pronounced gay-*haz*) regularly shows up on lists of the most romantic restaurants in Chicago (cozy couples should request a booth off the main dining room). If there are at least two in your party (all main courses are served for two or more), choose the connoisseur fondue dinner, the best Geja's has to offer. The meal begins with a Gruyère cheese fondue appetizer with apple wedges and chunks of dark bread. Next, a huge platter arrives, brimming with squares of beef tenderloin, lobster tails, and jumbo shrimp—all raw—and a caldron of boiling oil to cook them in. These delicacies are accompanied by a variety of raw vegetables, and eight different dipping sauces. When the flaming chocolate fondue arrives for dessert, with fresh fruit and pound cake for dipping and marshmallows for roasting, you'll want to beg for mercy. One word of caution: You have to work for your fondue—keeping track of how long each piece of meat has been cooking—so Geja's is not the best choice if you just want to sit back and be pampered.

340 W. Armitage Ave. (between Lincoln Ave. and Clark St.). ✆ **773/281-9101**. Reservations accepted every day except late Fri–Sat. Main courses $20–$37. AE, DC, DISC, MC, V. Mon–Thurs 5–10:30pm; Fri 5pm–midnight; Sat 5pm–12:30am; Sun 4:30–10pm. Subway/El: Brown Line to Armitage. Bus: No. 22.

North Pond ★★★ *Finds* AMERICAN   Tucked away in Lincoln Park, North Pond is a hidden treasure. There are no roads leading here—you must follow a path to reach the restaurant, which was formerly a warming hut for ice skaters. The building's Arts and Crafts–inspired interior blends perfectly with the park outside, and a recently added glass-enclosed addition lets you dine "outside" all year long.

In keeping with the natural setting, chef Bruce Sherman emphasizes organic, locally grown ingredients and favors simple preparations—although the overall result is definitely upscale (at these prices, it better be). Examples of seasonal menu items include herbed Parmesan gnocchi with braised rabbit, fava beans, asparagus, Wisconsin ramps, and lovage (a celerylike green); poached farm-fresh

Dining in Lincoln Park & Wrigleyville

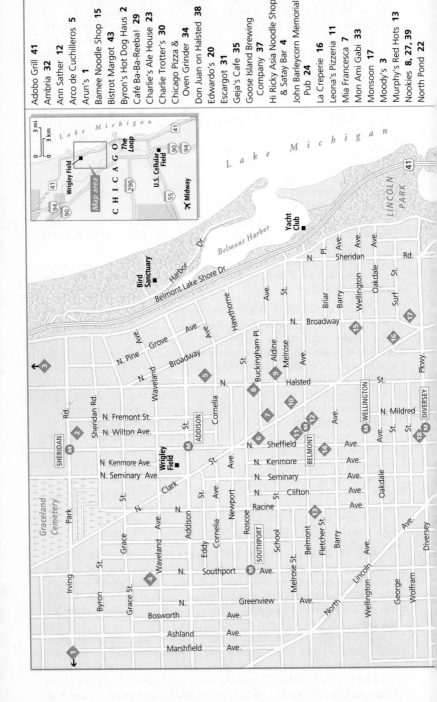

Adobo Grill **41**
Ambria **32**
Ann Sather **12**
Arco de Cuchilleros **5**
Arun's **1**
Bamee Noodle Shop **15**
Bistrot Margot **43**
Byron's Hot Dog Haus **2**
Café Ba-Ba-Reeba! **29**
Charlie's Ale House **23**
Charlie Trotter's **30**
Chicago Pizza & Oven Grinder **34**
Don Juan on Halsted **38**
Edwardo's **20**
Escargot **31**
Geja's Cafe **35**
Goose Island Brewing Company **37**
Hi Ricky Asia Noodle Shop & Satay Bar **4**
John Barleycorn Memorial Pub **24**
La Creperie **16**
Leona's Pizzeria **11**
Mia Francesca **7**
Mon Ami Gabi **33**
Monsoon **17**
Moody's **3**
Murphy's Red Hots **13**
Nookies **8, 27, 39**
North Pond **22**

146

O'Brien's Restaurant **42**
Orange **10**
Pat's Pizzeria **14**
Penny's Noodle Shop **18**
Potbelly Sandwich
Works **25**
Ranalli's Pizzeria, Libations
& Collectibles **36**
RoseAngelis **19**
Sai Café **28**
Thai Classic **6**
Toast **26**
Twin Anchors **40**
The Wieners Circle **21**
Yoshi's Café **9**

M Subway/El stop

0   0.25 mi
0   0.25 km

*North Avenue
Beach*

LINCOLN
PARK

Chicago
Historical
Society

Burton Pl.

N. State St.
N. Dearborn St.
N. Clark St.
N. La Salle St.

Lake   Shore   Dr.

John   Cannon   Dr.

Diversey Harbor

Lincoln
Park
Zoo

Stockton

West

Park

St.

*South
Pond*

Dr.

North
Pond

Clark

Lincoln

Ave.

Schiller

SEDGWICK

N. Park   Eugenie   Ave.

N.   Sedgwick   St.

Wisconsin   St.
Menomonee

N. Cleveland   Ave.
N. Mohawk   St.
N. Larrabee   St.

Wrightwood

Deming

Pl.

N.

Arlington Pl.

OZ
PARK

N. Orchard

N. Burling St.

N.   Halsted   St.

Ave.

Ave.

North

Ave.

Armitage

N.   Orchard   St.
N.   Burling   St.

N.   Halsted   St.

Avenue

North

NORTH/CLYBOURN

Weed St.

N.   Dayton   St.

N.   Fremont   St.

N.   Bissell   St.

N.   Sheffield   Ave.

Wisconsin St.

Willow

Ave.

North

DePaul
University

FULLERTON

ARMITAGE

Webster

Belden

Dickens

Clifton   St.

Wrightwood

St.

Montana

N. Racine   Ave.

Lakewood

Wayne

N.   Southport   Ave.

N.   Greenview

N.   Ashland

Schubert Ave.

Fullerton

TREBES
PARK

Clybourn

North

Kingsbury

Chicago River

North Branch

Cortland

Elston

Kennedy   Expwy.

North   Ave.

*Turning
Basin*

Noble

N. Greenview
N. Bosworth
N. Ashland

N.   Wood

West   St.

egg with wilted baby spinach and lemon-caviar butter sauce; and grilled sea scallops with orange-Parmesan grain salad, glazed organic baby carrots, and spiced lobster sauce. For dessert, try mango "soup" with banana mousse and candied hazelnuts. To enjoy the restaurant's setting with a slightly lower price tag, try the fixed-price Sunday brunch ($28). The all-American wine list of 100 or so selections focuses on boutique vintners.

2610 N. Cannon Dr. (south of Diversey Pkwy.). © **773/477-5845.** www.northpondrestaurant.com. Reservations recommended. Main courses $24–$30. AE, DC, MC, V. Tues–Sat 5:30–10pm; Sun 11am–2pm and 5:30–10pm. Bus: No. 151.

EXPENSIVE

Mon Ami Gabi ⭐ FRENCH/BISTRO   This "French steakhouse" concept from Gabino Sotelino (whose upscale Ambria is right next door) seduces with its aromatic atmosphere, tasty steak preparations, and one of the best tarte Tatins in town. Gabi's decor is like a movie set of a cozy, boisterous bistro. There are numerous classic bistro starters and hot seafood appetizers, and the chilled fruits *de mer* selection is impressive (if you can bear to bypass your favorites, I suggest the coquilles Gabi, a cold dish of just barely poached and artfully dressed sea scallops). Exquisitely simple entrees include chicken paillard (a crusty, pounded chicken breast in lemon butter) and trout Grenobloise (perfectly pan-seared trout in caper butter with a sprinkle of croutons). Steak frites can be had with maître d'hotel butter, au poivre, Roquefort, or bordelaise (with caramelized onions in mushroom-and-red-wine sauce). Numerous seafood entrees, a section of seasonal specialties, and sides along the lines of parsnip purée and ratatouille round out the menu. Did I mention the fantastic tarte Tatin (inverted apple tart)? You can also get a chocolate soufflé served with vanilla sauce, as well as various familiar bistro dessert offerings.

2300 N. Lincoln Park West. © **773/348-8886.** www.leye.com. Reservations recommended. Main courses $13–$28. AE, DC, DISC, MC, V. Mon–Thurs 5:30–10pm; Fri–Sat 5–11pm; Sun 5–10pm. Bus: No. 151.

Monsoon ⭐ INDIAN   You won't find any tandoori chicken on this *nouveau* Indian menu. Pappadams—that Indian-restaurant appetizer staple—are transformed here into eggroll-like wrappers for prawns, and corn chowder takes an exotic turn with the addition of saffron. This is the only place in Chicago—for now—that mixes traditional Indian spices with trendy ingredients and French techniques. Cornish hen is smoked with Darjeeling tea and served on a mix of rice, cashews, pistachios, and golden raisins, while lobster is poached in ghee and treated to a five-spice rub. A word of warning to those with delicate taste buds: Even some of the innocent-sounding dishes can be quite hot, so ask before ordering. Dessert isn't usually the highlight of an Indian meal, but the creative sweets here are worth a try (mocha spice cake with cardamom ice cream; saffron cheesecake). Monsoon is definitely an upscale restaurant, with an elegant look (deep red velvet drapes, upholstered banquettes) and prices that are quite high for the area. But this is the only place in town to taste-test these kinds of treats.

2813 N. Broadway (at Diversey Ave.). © **773/665-9463.** Reservations recommended. Main courses $13–$32. AE, DC, MC, V. Tues–Sun 5–10pm; bar open until 12am. Subway: Brown Line to Diversey.

MODERATE

Adobo Grill MEXICAN   Although lacking the authenticity and character of some of our finer Mexican establishments (Topolobampo/Frontera Grill, Chilpancingo), Adobo Grill is definitely a cut above your average neighborhood Mexican restaurant. If you don't mind noisy crowds, join the action on the first floor. Otherwise, request the smoke-free second floor.

Adobo Grill's claim to fame is the fresh guacamole prepared tableside (you choose the spice level, but be warned that even the "medium" will give your tongue quite a jolt). Less spicy starters include a refreshing jicama and mango salad, or grilled baby octopus with *guajillo* salsa and a few roasted pumpkin seeds. Flavorful roast quail is marinated in tequila, garlic, and smoky chipotle pepper and then skewered on spears of sugar cane. For a heartier dish, try the casserole of slow-steamed lamb with *guajillo* adobo and pinto beans. For dessert, the chocolate tamale is a brownie-dough delight, redolent with bittersweet chocolate flavor. Before you opt for a margarita or one of the 60 sipping tequilas, consider a refreshing Michelada (your choice of beer with lime juice in a chile- and-salt-dusted glass) or a bittersweet Adobopolitan (tequila, Cointreau, and hibiscus tea).

1610 N. Wells St. © **312/266-7999.** Reservations recommended. Main courses $12–$18. AE, DC, MC, V. Mon–Thurs 5:30–10pm; Fri 5:30–11pm; Sat 12–2:30pm and 5:30–11:30pm; Sun 12–9:30pm. Bus: No. 22, 36, or 156.

Bistrot Margot ★★ *Finds* FRENCH/BISTRO   Bistrot Margot is not only one of the best restaurants in Old Town—it's also one of the better French bistros in town. It can get very busy and loud, and the tables are quite close together, but, for many, that only adds to its charm. This is true bistro dining—very casual and never stuffy. Starters include out-of-this-world mussels in white wine with fresh herbs, escargot in garlic butter, country-style paté, and crab cake in mustard sauce. Don't skip the salad course, either (in warm weather go for the light, refreshing Belgian endive with spicy walnuts, blue cheese, and apples). Specials are usually a best bet for the main course. But the usual suspects (roasted chicken with garlic, lemon, herbs, and pommes frites; rack of lamb with Dijon mustard and garlic bread crumbs; and a terrific steak frites) are proof that, when done right, it's hard to beat classic French cuisine. On warm summer nights, the restaurant sets about half a dozen tables on the sidewalk, which, on this colorful stretch of Wells Street, makes for a truly memorable meal.

1437 N. Wells St. © **312/587-3660.** Reservations recommended. Main courses $13–$20. AE, DC, MC, V. Sun–Mon 5–9pm; Tues–Thurs 5–10pm; Fri–Sat 5–11pm. Subway/El: Red Line to Clark/Division or Brown Line to Sedgwick.

Café Ba-Ba-Reeba! ★ SPANISH/TAPAS   One of the city's first tapas restaurants, Café Ba-Ba-Reeba! is still going strong, thanks to its location on bustling Halsted Street, near the Armitage Avenue shopping strip. The clientele tends to be young and comes to the restaurant in groups, so be prepared: Loud conversations and tipsy toasts over pitchers of sangria may surround you.

Café Ba-Ba-Reeba! isn't breaking any new ground with its menu, but tapas lovers will see plenty of favorites, including *patatas con alioli* (garlic potato salad), *gambas a la plancha* (shrimp with lemon and garlic), and *queso de cabra al horno* (baked goat cheese with tomato sauce). The chicken and chorizo-sausage brochettes, served with a garlic-cumin mayonnaise, are one of the house specialties. There's also a good selection of paellas, as well as some full-size entrees for those who don't want to go the tapas route. The vibrantly decorated cafe makes an excellent, efficient choice for pre- or posttheater dining if you're headed to Steppenwolf Theatre, a few blocks south, for a play.

2024 N. Halsted St. (at Armitage Ave.). © **773/935-5000.** Limited number of reservations accepted. Tapas $3.25–$7.95; main courses $11–$16. AE, DC, DISC, MC, V. Sun–Thurs noon–10pm; Fri–Sat noon–midnight. Subway/El: Red or Brown line to Fullerton, or Brown Line to Armitage.

Don Juan on Halsted ★★ MEXICAN   Chef Patrick Concannon has the right culinary pedigree—he's done time at Charlie Trotter's and other top

Chicago restaurants—but this time he's drawing on his family ties: The original Don Juan was opened by his mother in the suburb of Edison Park almost 20 years ago. This inviting space has pale yellow and orange walls and terra-cotta floor tiles. The outdoor courtyard fills up early in nice weather.

The menu mixes traditional Mexican flavors with unexpected ingredients. There's a new take on buffalo wings: chicken wings dipped in chipotle pepper sauce and covered with sesame seeds, served with bleu cheese sauce. The tuna tartare—now a staple of many high-end restaurants—is served here with tortilla chips, avocado, jicama, and mango sauce. Entrees include lamb shank, duck confit, and garlic-roasted chicken breast.

In a nod to late-night diners, the menu includes a taqueria section open after the regular kitchen is closed. Eight new takes on the taco (all under $4) include barbecued veal, shrimp and bacon, grilled lamb, and vegetarian.

1729 N. Halsted St. (between North Ave. and Willow St.). © 312/981-4000. Reservations accepted. Main courses $12–$20. AE, DC, DISC, MC, V. Mon–Thurs 5pm–midnight; Fri–Sat 5pm–1am; Sun 5–10pm. Subway/El: Red Line to North/Clybourn.

Escargot ★★ *Finds* CONTEMPORARY FRENCH   A reflection of changing economic times, this restaurant was transformed last year from the upscale Aubriot into the more affordable Escargot. Chef Eric Aubriot has simplified his presentations and ingredients so that no entree costs more than $20—and so far the change has been a hit with locals, from older couples to families with children. The cheery dining room—with translucent green chairs and glass panels painted with brightly colored sunflowers—is particularly welcoming. Appetizers are mostly familiar French favorites (foie gras, salads, and—of course—escargot). Entrees blend unexpected ingredients without ever veering too far from the familiar. Recent choices included sautéed skate wing with a lobster vegetable ragout; artichoke-and-ricotta crepes with tomato marmalade and olive tapenade; and risotto with carrot juice, herbs, and tarragon sauce. An upstairs lounge, **Eau,** is aimed at a younger set, with tapas-sized nibbles and sleek contemporary decor.

1962 N. Halsted St. © 773/281-4211. Main courses $16–$19. AE, DC, DISC, MC, V. Tues–Thurs 5:30–10pm; Fri–Sat 5:30–10:30pm; Sun 5:30–9:30pm. Subway/El: Brown Line to Armitage. Bus: No. 8.

INEXPENSIVE

Goose Island Brewing Company AMERICAN PUB   Some of the best beer in Chicago is manufactured at this comfy, award-winning microbrewery in the Clybourn corridor (an impressive cast of professional beer critics agrees). In the course of a year, Goose Island brewmeister Greg Hall (whose dad, John, is the pub/brewery's owner) produces about 100 varieties of lagers, ales, stouts, pilsners, and porters that change with the seasons. Normally a pint costs $4 (ale of the day, $3), but a 6-ounce sampler glass is only $1, making a tasting session a fun evening's entertainment. For a behind-the-scenes look, you can tour the brewing facility every Sunday at 3pm ($3, which includes tastings afterward).

For many years, the food here didn't live up to the beer. But fans of the foamy are now dining at the Goose with almost the same gusto they devote to their guzzling. Cut-above bar food includes burgers (including a killer, dragon-breath-inducing Stilton burger with roasted garlic), sandwiches (pulled pork, catfish po' boy, chicken Caesar), and some serious salads. Goose Island is also known for its addictive homemade potato chips, fresh-brewed root beer, and orange cream soda. The zero-attitude, come-as-you-are ambience is very refreshing for a lazy afternoon pit stop or a casual lunch or dinner. A second location at 3535 N. Clark St. in Wrigleyville (© 773/832-9040) has an enclosed beer garden.

1800 N. Clybourn Ave. (at Sheffield Ave.). © 312/915-0071. www.gooseisland.com. Reservations recommended on weekends. Sandwiches $7.50–$9.95; main courses $11–$17. AE, DC, DISC, MC, V. Mon–Fri 11:30am–1am; Sat 11am–2am; Sun 11am–midnight; main dining room closes at 10pm daily. Subway/El: Red Line to North/Clybourn.

La Creperie ★★ *Finds* FRENCH   Germain and Sara Roignant have run this intimate gem of a cafe since 1972, never straying from the reasonably priced crepes that draw repeat customers aplenty. The decor is heavy on '70s-era brown, but if you find the main dining room too dark, head to the back patio (enclosed in colder months), which sparkles with strings of white lights. Onion soup, paté, and escargots are all good starters, but the highlights here are the whole-wheat crepes—each prepared on a special grill that Germain imported from his native Brittany. Single-choice fillings include cheese, tomato, egg, or ham; tasty duets feature chicken and mushroom or broccoli and cheese. Beef bourguignon, coq au vin, or curried chicken are the more adventurous crepe combinations. Non-crepe offerings are few: orange roughy and steak frites. Don't leave without at least sharing one of the dessert crepes, which tuck anything from apples to ice cream within their warm folds. The restaurant officially discontinued its three-course prix-fixe meal a few years ago, but they still offer it to in-the-know customers, so ask about it if you plan on going whole-hog.

2845 N. Clark St. (½ block north of Diversey Pkwy.). © 773/528-9050. Reservations accepted. Main courses $5.50–$15. AE, DC, DISC, MC, V. Tues–Fri 11:30am–3:30pm and 5–11pm; Sat 11am–11pm; Sun 11am–9:30pm. Subway/El: Brown Line to Diversey.

Potbelly Sandwich Works *Value* SANDWICHES   It doesn't seem to matter what time I stop by Potbelly; there's invariably a line of hungry 20- and 30-somethings waiting to get their sandwich fix. Yes, there's a potbelly stove inside, as well as a player piano and other Old West saloon–type memorabilia, but go here for the mouthwatering made-to-order namesake comestibles (that's all they serve). Prepared on homemade sub rolls stuffed with your choice of turkey, Italian meats, veggies, pizza ingredients, and more, and layered with lettuce, tomato, onion, pickles, and Italian seasonings, they're warmed in a countertop toaster oven. Even with all the fixin's, each is under $5 (unlike the massive subs found at many other spots, Potbelly's are the more the size of normal sandwiches). Tempting milkshakes keep the blender mighty busy. And the good news about those lines: The behind-the-counter staff are experts at keeping things moving, so you never end up waiting too long. Potbelly has other locations at 190 N. State St. (© 312/683-1234) and in The Shops at North Bridge, 520 N. Michigan Ave. (© 312/527-5550), which are convenient to the Loop and Mag Mile.

2264 N. Lincoln Ave. (between Belden Ave. and Webster St.). © 773/528-1405. Reservations not accepted. Main courses $3.50–$5.50. Cash only. Subway/El: Brown Line to Fullerton.

RoseAngelis ★★ *Value* NORTHERN ITALIAN   What is it about RoseAngelis that keeps me coming back, when there's not exactly a shortage of Italian restaurants in this city? The secret is simple: This is neighborhood dining at its best, a place with reliably good food and very reasonable prices. Tucked in a residential side street in Lincoln Park, the restaurant fills the ground floor of a former private home, with a charming series of cozy rooms and a garden patio. The menu emphasizes pasta (my favorites are the rich lasagna and the ravioli al Luigi, filled with ricotta and served with a sun-dried-tomato cream sauce). The garlicky chicken Vesuvio is excellent, but it's not offered on Friday and Saturday nights because of preparation time. While RoseAngelis is not a vegetarian restaurant

Finds   **Taste of Thai**

Thai restaurants are to Chicago what Chinese restaurants are to many other American cities: ubiquitous, affordable, and perfect for a quick meal that offers a taste of the exotic. If you've never tried Thai, Chicago is a great place to start. Good introductory dishes are pad thai noodles topped with minced peanuts, or the coconut-based mild yellow curry.

Arun's (p. 153) and **Erawan** (p. 132) are the city's reigning gourmet interpreters of Thai cuisine, but many other low-key places are scattered throughout the residential neighborhoods. Most entrees at these spots don't go much beyond $10. A staple of the River North dining scene (and the 1st place I ever tried Thai food) is the bright and airy **Star of Siam**, 11 E. Illinois St., at North State Street (© **312/670-0100**). **Amarit**, a few blocks off the Magnificent Mile at 1 E. Delaware Place, at State Street (© **312/649-0500**), consistently delivers top-quality noodles, curries, and Thai iced tea, even if the decor runs toward the shabby. **Thai Classic**, 3332 N. Clark St. at Roscoe Street (© **773/404-2000**), conveniently located between the busy Belmont/Clark intersection and Wrigley Field, offers an excellent all-you-can-eat buffet on weekends, if you want to try a taste of everything. If you're wandering the Lakeview neighborhood, a good stop is the **Bamee Noodle Shop**, 3120 N. Broadway at Wellington Street (© **773/281-2641**), which offers a good selection of "Noodles on Plates" and "Noodles on Bowls," as well as a number of soups and fried-rice combinations.

per se, there's no red meat on the menu, and many of the pastas are served with vegetables rather than meat. Finish up with the deliciously decadent bread pudding with warm caramel sauce, one of my favorite desserts in the city (and big enough to share). I suggest stopping by on a weeknight because you'll be fighting lots of locals on weekend nights (when you'll wait 2 hr. for a table).

1314 W. Wrightwood Ave. (at Lakewood Ave.). © **773/296-0081**. Reservations accepted for parties of 8 or more. Main courses $9.95–$15. DISC, MC, V. Tues–Thurs 5–10pm; Fri–Sat 5–11pm; Sun 4:30–9pm. Subway/El: Red Line to Fullerton.

Sai Café ⭐ SUSHI/JAPANESE   Chicago has had an infusion of high-style sushi bars in recent years, but the low-key Sai Café continues to be a popular place for Lincoln Park residents more interested in food than funky decor. This is truly a neighborhood restaurant, just off the chic Armitage Avenue shopping corridor (star chef Charlie Trotter is a regular here, which is certainly a good sign). A la carte selections come by the piece or maki-mono style, which pairs anything from tuna and avocado to flying-fish eggs and scallions, and then wraps it all up in rice and a thin sheet of dried seaweed. Combo plates feature different meat, fish, and vegetables that can be dressed in tempura or teriyaki, or served sashimi style. Sai Café also offers a large selection of noodle and rice dishes.

2010 N. Sheffield Ave. (at Armitage Ave.). © **773/472-8080**. Main courses $16–$24 (a la carte sushi $3.75–$6.95 per piece). AE, DC, MC, V. Mon–Thurs 4:30–11pm; Fri–Sat 4:30pm–midnight; Sun 3:30–10pm. Subway: Brown Line to Armitage.

Twin Anchors ⭐ BARBECUE   A landmark in Old Town since the end of Prohibition, Twin Anchors manages to maintain the flavor of old Chicago. It's a friendly, family-owned pub with Frank Sinatra on the jukebox and on the walls (he apparently hung out here on swings through town in the 1960s). It's a totally unpretentious place with a long mahogany bar up front and a modest dining room in back with red Formica-topped tables crowded close. Of course, you don't need anything fancy when the ribs—the fall-off-the-bone variety—come this good. Even nonmeat eaters may be swayed if they allow themselves one bite of the enormous slabs of tender baby back pork ribs. (Go for the zesty sauce.) All of this means that you should prepare for a long wait on weekends. Ribs and other entrees come with coleslaw and dark rye bread, plus your choice of baked potato, tasty fries, and the even-better crisp onion rings. For dessert, there's a daily cheesecake selection.

1655 N. Sedgwick St. (1 block north of North Ave.). ☎ **312/266-1616.** Reservations no accepted. Main courses $9.95–$20; sandwiches $3.50–$7.50. AE, DC, DISC, MC, V. Mon–Thurs 5–11:30pm; Fri 5pm–12:30am; Sat noon–12:30am; Sun noon–10:30pm. Subway/El: Brown Line to Sedgwick.

7 Wrigleyville & the North Side

The area surrounding Wrigley Field has a long history as a working-class neighborhood. But Wrigleyville quickly gentrified as developers built new town houses and apartments. And with that affluence has come several popular restaurants spanning a range of culinary offerings and prices.

VERY EXPENSIVE

Arun's ⭐⭐⭐ THAI   It has been called the best Thai restaurant in the city—possibly the country. Here, chef/owner Arun Sampanthavivat prepares a refined version of traditional Thai cuisine, authentic and flavorful but not palate-scorching. The only downside is its out-of-the-way location—you can get here by public transportation, but I recommend a taxi at night when the bus schedules are less reliable.

The 12-course chef's menu is your only option here, and different tables receive different dishes on a given night. This sequential banquet begins with degustation-style appetizers, followed by four family-style entrees and two desserts. You might see courses of various delicate dumplings accented with edible, carved dough flowers; an alchemist's Thai salad of bitter greens and peanuts with green papaya, tomatoes, chiles, and sticky rice; and a medley of clever curries, including a surprisingly delightful sea bass and cabbage sour curry. When classic dishes appear, such as pad thai, they're always above the norm. Hope your dessert selections include the sticky rice with papaya (don't tell them if you're celebrating an occasion or they may serve you chocolate cake). The menu is paired with an award-winning wine list, and the restaurant provides a smoke-free environment.

4156 N. Kedzie Ave. (at Irving Park Rd.). ☎ **773/539-1909.** Reservations required with credit card. 12-course chef's menu $85. AE, DC, DISC, MC, V. Sun and Tues–Thurs 5–9pm; Fri–Sat 5–10pm. Subway/El and bus: Blue Line to Irving Park, and then transfer to eastbound no. 80 bus; or Brown Line to Irving Park, and then transfer to westbound no. 80 bus.

EXPENSIVE

Yoshi's Café NOUVELLE/FRENCH/BISTRO   Yoshi Katsumura has been a familiar name on the Chicago restaurant scene thanks to the intimate, refined restaurant he operated for years. But when he found the demand for special-occasion dining falling off, Yoshi shifted gears and reinvented his restaurant as a casual bistro. The result has proven a hit with the neighborhood; in fact, weekends can be chaotic. The new Yoshi's is comfortable and casual (even if the pastel decor does kind of remind some of a hotel coffee shop), with an intriguing menu that reflects both Yoshi's native Japan and his French training. Spring rolls come filled with chicken, mushrooms, and goat cheese, while a leek-and-brie tart is livened up with shiitake mushrooms. Vegetable and shrimp tempura show up on the entree list side by side with steak frites au poivre and Dover sole meunière. There are always a number of vegetarian options, ranging from pasta to grilled tofu with brie and basil topped with sweet sesame paste and miso sauce.

3257 N. Halsted St. (at Aldine St.). ℂ 773/248-6160. Reservations recommended. Main courses $13–$27. AE, DC, MC, V. Tues–Thurs 5–10:30pm; Fri–Sat 5–11pm; Sun 11am–2:30pm and 5–9:30pm. Subway/El: Red Line to Belmont.

MODERATE

Mia Francesca ITALIAN   It has been open since 1992, but Mia Francesca remains one of the hardest tables to get in Chicago. Unless you plan on arriving as the doors open, be prepared to wait. By 7pm, that wait often exceeds an hour and can drag on to 3 hours as the night wears on (the locals have an advantage: They put their names in and then go back to their apartments and have the hostess call when their table is ready). The addition of a second-floor dining room has eased things a bit, but "Mia" remains an exceedingly fashionable place. They come for the scene, but it's the food—unpretentious but never dull—that keeps locals coming back. Tables are packed close together, so you can't help eavesdropping on your neighbors—and checking out their food. The menu changes weekly, but you can count on thin-crust individual pizzas, excellent pastas and chicken, veal, and fish dishes nightly.

For a less frenzied atmosphere with mostly the same menu, try the other locations—**Francesca's on Taylor,** 1400 W. Taylor St. in Little Italy (ℂ 312/829-2828), and **Francesca's Bryn Mawr,** 1039 W. Bryn Mawr Ave. just north of Wrigleyville (ℂ 773/506-9261)—which both accept reservations.

3311 N. Clark St. (1½ blocks north of Belmont Ave.). ℂ 773/281-3310. www.miafrancesca.com. Reservations not accepted. Main courses $9.95–$23. AE, MC, V. Sun–Thurs 5–10:30pm; Fri–Sat 5–11pm. Subway/El: Red Line to Belmont.

INEXPENSIVE

Ann Sather ★★ SWEDISH/AMERICAN/BREAKFAST   A sign hanging by Ann Sather's door bears the following inscription: "Once one of many neighborhood Swedish restaurants, Ann Sather's is the only one that remains." It's a real Chicago institution, where you can enjoy Swedish meatballs with buttered noodles and brown gravy, or the Swedish sampler of duck breast with lingonberry glaze, meatball, potato-sausage dumpling, sauerkraut, and brown beans. All meals are full dinners, including appetizer, main course, vegetable, potato, and dessert. Sticky cinnamon rolls are a highlight of Sather's popular (and very affordable) weekend brunch menu (it can get frenzied, but you'll be fine if you get here before 11am). The people-watching is priceless here: a cross section of gay and straight, young and old, from club kids to elderly couples.

There are several other branches that serve only breakfast and lunch: a restaurant in Andersonville, at 5207 N. Clark St. (ℂ 773/271-6677), and smaller cafes in Lakeview, at 3411 N. Broadway (ℂ 773/305-0024) and 3416 N. Southport Ave. (ℂ 773/404-4475).

929 W. Belmont Ave. (between Clark St. and Sheffield Ave.). ℂ 773/348-2378. Reservations accepted for parties of 6 or more. Main courses $7–$12. AE, DC, MC, V. Sun–Thurs 7am–10pm; Fri–Sat 7am–11pm. Free parking with validation. Subway/El: Red Line to Belmont.

Hi Ricky Asia Noodle Shop & Satay Bar ★ *Value* ASIAN/THAI   Hi Ricky offers a continent-hopping menu of dishes from Thailand, Japan, Indonesia, China, and Vietnam in a hip setting. The dishes feature fresh ingredients, generous portions, and reasonable prices. This big, airy restaurant, installed in a former auto shop, has an industrial look with down-turned woks inventively employed as light fixtures along the open grill. Given the restaurant's name, you'll want to begin with an order or two of satay: You've got seven to choose from, or you can go for a sampler and try all of them (chicken, lamb, shrimp, tofu, and more). Main courses include spicy drunken noodles (broad noodles stir-fried with basil, greens, tomato, sprouts, and hot pepper—and a choice of tofu or a variety of meats) and the Malaysian Hokkien noodles (spicy curry fried egg and rice noodles with a choice of meats). There's also a full bar, specializing in tropical-inspired cocktails. Other locations are in Wicker Park at 1852 North Ave. (𝒞 **312/276-8300**), and near downtown at 941 W. Randolph St. (𝒞 **312/491-9100**).

3730 N. Southport Ave. (between Irving Park Rd. and Addison St.). 𝒞 **773/388-0000**. Reservations not accepted. Main courses $6.95–$11. AE, DISC, MC, V. Mon–Thurs 11:30am–10pm; Fri 11:30am–11pm; Sat noon–11pm; Sun noon–10pm. Subway/El: Brown Line to Southport.

Penny's Noodle Shop ★ *Value* ASIAN/THAI   Predating many of Chicago's pan-Asian noodle shops, Penny's has kept its loyal following even as others have joined the fray. Penny Chiamopoulous, a Thai native, has assembled a concise menu of delectable dishes, all of them fresh and made to order—and all at prices that will make you do a double-take. The two dining rooms are clean and spare; single diners can usually find a seat along the bar that wraps around the grill. The Thai spring roll, filled with seasoned tofu, cucumber, bean sprouts, and strips of cooked egg, makes a refreshing starter. Of course, noodles unite everything on the menu, so your main decision is choosing among the options (crispy wide rice, rice vermicelli, Japanese udon, and so on) served in a soup or spread out on a plate. There are several barbecued pork and beef entrees, and plenty of options for vegetarians.

The original Penny's, tucked under the El tracks at 3400 N. Sheffield Ave. near Wrigley Field (𝒞 **773/281-8222**), is small and often has long waits; you stand a better chance of scoring a table at the Diversey Avenue location or the one in Wicker Park, at 1542 N. Damen Ave. (𝒞 **773/394-0100**). All locations are BYOB.

950 W. Diversey Ave. (at Sheffield St.). 𝒞 **773/281-8448**. Reservations not accepted. Main courses $4.50–$7.95. MC, V. Sun and Tues–Thurs 11am–10pm; Fri–Sat 11am–10:30pm. Subway/El: Brown Line to Diversey.

8 Wicker Park/Bucktown

The booming Wicker Park/Bucktown area followed closely in the race to gentrification on the heels of Lincoln Park and Wrigleyville. First came the artists and musicians who were then followed by armies of yuppies and young families—all attracted by cheap rents and real estate. The result is a now-established happening scene, which includes some of the city's hippest restaurants and clubs. Get yourself to the nexus of activity at the intersection of North, Damen, and Milwaukee avenues, and you won't have to walk more than a couple of blocks in any direction to find a hot spot. Cab fares from downtown are reasonable, or you can take the El's Blue Line to Damen.

EXPENSIVE

Cafe Absinthe ★★ ECLECTIC   For most Chicagoans, alleys function as a place to store garbage until the sanitation crews come along, keeping the sidewalks clear. Cafe Absinthe uses its alley as the restaurant entrance. Looks can be deceiving because Absinthe is no dive. On the contrary, it has become one of Chicago's hippest eateries, both because its out-of-the-way location attracts trendy types and because of the moody atmosphere. The darkly lit interior sets a subdued tone, with jazz playing in the background and model-types sipping Cosmopolitans at the bar. The menu changes daily; on a typical evening, Absinthe will offer such appetizers as grilled ostrich filet with confit onion, fresh figs, and mandarin oranges, or brie cooked *en croute* with hazelnuts, blackberry preserves, and spiced strawberries. Main courses include wasabi-seared tuna with oriental vegetable roll and Pernod-glazed rack of lamb with fluffy macadamia nut couscous. The dessert menu is every bit as tempting, from the selection of flavored crème brûlées to the chocolate-and-hazelnut mousse served in a martini glass.

1954 W. North Ave. (at Damen and Milwaukee aves.). ℂ 773/278-4488. Reservations recommended. Main courses $17–$27. AE, DC, DISC, MC, V. Mon–Thurs 5:30–10pm; Fri–Sat 5:30–11pm; Sun 5:30–9pm. Subway/El: Blue Line to Damen.

Mas ★★ LATIN AMERICAN   Urban, cozy, and dark, "nuevo Latino" Mas is almost always packed with faithful regulars who come for the Latin cocktails and modern takes on traditional Central and South American cuisine. The "primero" list includes spicy lime-marinated tuna tacos with papaya, rosemary, and Dijon salsa; and a succulent ceviche of the day (such as yellowtail snapper with smoked poblano chile or blue marlin with rum and vanilla). Entrees worth the wait include chile-cured pork tenderloin over smoky white beans; the achiote-roasted mako shark with crawfish-lentil salsa and avocado salad; and traditional Brazilian *xinzim* (shrimp and chicken stew with coconut broth and black beans). Out-of-the-ordinary desserts include lightly fried pound cake with fresh plum compote, roasted hazelnuts, and caramel-praline ice cream. At the bar, try a Brazilian *caipirinha* (made with sugar, lime, and *cachaça*, a brandy made from sugar cane), a guava *batida* (an alcoholic version of a fruit smoothie), or a Peruvian Pisco sour. The margaritas are also very good. The wine list emphasizes selections from Spain, Argentina, and Chile. They also serve a refreshingly different brunch.

With long waits on weekends (there are no reservations) and plenty of loud conversation, Mas may not be to everyone's taste. They do offer the same menu at its second location, **Otro Mas**, at 3651 N. Southport Ave., ℂ **773/348-3200.**

1670 W. Division St. ℂ 773/276-8700. www.masrestaurant.com. Reservations not accepted. Main courses $17–$27. AE, DC, MC, V. Mon–Thurs 5:30–10:30pm; Fri–Sat 5:30–11:30pm; Sun 11am–2pm and 5:30–10pm. Subway/El: Blue Line to Damen.

Meritage Café and Wine Bar ★★ CONTEMPORARY AMERICAN   Meritage opened a few years back with an emphasis on Pacific Northwest cuisine; with a change in chefs, the menu selections have become more broad. Nonetheless, the lovely decor remains the draw for me. The front room, with tables opposite a long wood bar, has the feel of a hip wine bar. But the place to sit is the romantic patio, lit by overhead lights; the entire space is covered and heated in winter, so you don't have to wait for good weather to enjoy the atmosphere.

DINING ◆
Bongo Room **25**
Café Absinthe **16**
Club Lucky **12**
Jane's **7**
Le Bouchon **3**
Mas **28**
Meritage Café &
  Wine Bar **2**
Mirai Sushi **26**
MOD **20**

Northside Café **13**
Piece **17**
Silver Cloud **11**
Soju **18**
Soul Kitchen **21**
Spring **19**
NIGHTLIFE ●
Big Wig **29**
The Borderline **6**
The Bucktown Pub **9**
Danny's Tavern **4**

Davenport's Piano Bar
  & Cabaret **24**
Double Door **23**
Get Me High Lounge **10**
Leopard Lounge **8**
The Map Room **1**
Marie's Riptide Lounge **5**
The Note **14**
Phyllis' Musical Inn **27**
Red Dog **15**
Sinibar **22**

The menu offers a fair variety of seafood (ahi tuna, crab, scallops) and wild game shows up both in entrees and appetizers (the grilled ostrich with bacon, Brussels sprouts, and brie is a good off-the-beaten-path choice). Many entrees put a modern twist on the meat-starch-vegetable formula: roast duck breast is served with mashed potatoes and green beans, topped with a kumquat-cherry reduction. An apple caramel Dutch pancake and chocolate mousse cake are among the comfort-food desserts. Don't forget to try a glass of the restaurant's namesake wine; the servers can also point the way to the best food-wine pairings.

2118 N. Damen Ave. ⓒ 773/235-6434. www.meritagecafe.com. Reservations recommended. Main courses $16–$28. AE, DC, MC, V. Mon–Thurs 5:30–10pm; Fri–Sat 5:30–11pm; Sun 5–9pm. Subway/El: Blue Line to Damen.

Mirai Sushi ★★ SUSHI/JAPANESE For now, Miae Lim's stylish Mirai (translation: "the future") surfs atop the crest of Chicago's sushi tsunami. Blending a serious devotion to sushi and sake with a decidedly youthful, funky-chic ambience, Mirai is one hot destination for cold raw fish (it serves other Japanese fare as well). The futuristic second-floor sake lounge is the hippest place in town to slurp down sushi, chilled sakes, and "red ones," the house cocktail of vodka with passion fruit, lime, and cranberry juices. The bright, smoke-free main-floor dining room offers a comparatively traditional environment.

Fish is flown in daily for the sushi bar, where several chefs are hard at work master-crafting a lovely list of offerings—from the beginner sushi standards such as California roll and *ebi* (boiled shrimp) to escalating classifications of tuna, three additional shrimp varieties, five types of salmon, a half-dozen varieties of fresh oysters, and a tantalizing list of four caviars (in addition to the four roes offered). The informative sake menu of about a dozen selections opens up a new world to diners accustomed to the generic carafe of heated sake.

2020 W. Division St. ⓒ 773/862-8500. Reservations recommended. Main courses $13–$21. AE, DC, DISC, MC, V. Sun–Wed 5–10pm; Thurs–Sat 5–11pm. Upstairs lounge open until 2am. Subway/El: Blue Line to Division.

MOD ★★★ CONTEMPORARY AMERICAN A 21st-century American restaurant unlike any other in Chicago, MOD's main draw is its postindustrial, MTV-style decor: circular recycled foam banquettes covered in clear vinyl, egg-shaped chairs, inflatable lamps, and a floor made from recycled tires. See it to believe it. The "modern American" menu, which offers some globally influenced selections, is a little more down-to-earth, with an emphasis on organic ingredients. First courses include a "ham and eggs" dish (Parma prosciutto, poached swan creek egg, ciabatta crostini, and ravida estate oil), and hand-chopped spicy tuna on ice with crispy lentil pappadams. The salads are equally intriguing: arugula with Mission figs, toasted hazelnuts and sheep's-milk cheese, for instance. Entrees include a crispy duck confit with grilled nectarines and a rosemary broth, and clams with grilled fennel sausage, roasted tomato, little ear pasta, and olive oil. The mascarpone "mac and cheese" is a signature side dish. Desserts include a toasted hazelnut napoleon with vanilla bean–scented raspberries and Frangelico mousse. Call far in advance for a table. And dress to impress.

1520 N. Damen Ave. (1 block south of North Ave.). ⓒ 773/252-1500. Reservations recommended. Main courses $16–$27. AE, DC, DISC, MC, V. Sun–Mon 5–10pm; Tues–Thurs 5–11pm; Fri–Sat 5pm–midnight; lounge and bar menu available until midnight Tues–Thurs and until 1am Fri–Sat. Subway/El: Blue Line to Damen.

Soul Kitchen ☆ CAJUN/CARIBBEAN/LATIN AMERICAN/SOUTHERN
Situated at the center of the Bucktown/Wicker Park scene, colorful Soul Kitchen
epitomizes the hip artsiness of the neighborhood. Specializing in the cuisine of
the American South with Caribbean, Latin American, and Creole influences,
the concept here is as funky and diverse as the crowd.

Soul Kitchen boasts of its "loud food, spicy music." The 1960s and 1970s
soul and funk tunes spun here might be a bit much for some diners, but they
add to the lively ambience. Starters include stuffed shrimp with corn-bread
dressing and rémoulade sauce, and wilted spinach salad with crispy crawfish,
mushrooms, and warm andouille dressing. Entrees range from braised lamb
shanks with ancho chile–honey glaze, cumin-roasted carrots, and crispy polenta,
to jerk chicken with black beans, sweet potatoes, plantains, and coconut milk.
For a sweet touch of Nawlins, finish with chocolate chess pie with bourbon ice
cream and pecan praline. This is my pick for funkiest brunch in town: The
lemon-bread French toast with oranges, bananas, raspberries, blueberries, and
Bavarian cream tops the hit parade. Expect to wait for a table, perhaps with a
playful house cocktail at the long, undulating bar.

1576 N. Milwaukee Ave. (at Damen and North aves.). ✆ 773/342-9742. Reservations not accepted. Main
courses $15–$24. AE, MC, V. Sun–Thurs 5–10:30pm; Fri–Sat 5–11:30pm; Sun brunch 10am–2pm. Subway/El:
Blue Line to Damen.

Spring ☆☆☆ CONTEMPORARY AMERICAN   This former Russian bath-
house has been transformed into an oasis of Zen calm and soothing, neutral colors. Chef Shawn McClain is Chicago's newest culinary celebrity, and his
restaurant has been attracting national attention since it opened in 2001. Spring
is not a scene; diners step down into a dining room hidden from the street, sink
into the banquettes that zigzag across the center of the room, and concentrate
on the food. Unlike other chefs who feel pressured to keep outdoing themselves,
McClain sticks to a focused menu, with a heavy emphasis on seafood and pan-
Asian preparations. Appetizers include an aromatic lemon grass–red curry broth
with rice noodles, and sea scallop–and-potato ravioli with sautéed mushrooms
and truffle essence. Most of the entrees are seafood-based: New Zealand snapper with lemon couscous and fennel salad, or the braised baby monkfish and
escargots with roasted eggplant in smoked tomato bouillon, for example.
Among the nonfish options, beef short-rib pot stickers spiced up with Korean
seasonings stand out. Desserts also go the Asian route, focusing on seasonal
fruits, although the coconut mochi brûlée with warm pineapple puts a whole
new twist on rice pudding.

2039 W. North Ave. (at Milwaukee Ave.). ✆ 773/395-7100. Reservations recommended. Main courses
$16–$25. AE, DC, DISC, MC, V. Tues–Thurs 5:30–10pm; Fri–Sat 5:30–11pm; Sun 5:30–9pm. Subway: Blue Line
to Damen.

MODERATE

Club Lucky ☆ _Value_ TRADITIONAL ITALIAN   Club Lucky seems to have
been carved from a local 1950s-era corner tavern with a catering business in the
back room. In fact, the place was designed to look like that, with plenty of Naugahyde banquettes, a Formica-topped bar and tables, and Captain Video ceiling
fixtures. The scene here is youngish and fairly dressy; expect to wait for a seat
(but that just gives you time to order one of the signature martinis).

You might or might not take to the scene, but the food does not disappoint.
Prices overall are moderate, especially considering the generous family-style
portions. The large calamari appetizer—"for two," the menu says—will almost

certainly keep you in leftover land for a day or two. The menu offers real Italian home-style cooking, such as *pasta e fagioli* (thick macaroni-and-bean soup—really a kind of stew). Or, try the rigatoni with veal meatballs, served with steamed escarole and melted slabs of mozzarella, or the spicy grilled boneless pork chops served with peppers and roasted potatoes. The lunch menu includes about a dozen Italian sandwiches, such as scrambled eggs and pesto, meatball, and Italian sausage.

1824 W. Wabansia Ave. (1 block north of North Ave., between Damen and Ashland aves.). ℭ 773/227-2300. www.club-lucky.com. Reservations accepted for parties of 6 or more. Sandwiches $6.96–$8.95; main courses $8.95–$18. AE, DC, DISC, MC, V. Mon–Thurs 11:30am–11pm; Fri 11:30am–midnight; Sat 5pm–midnight; Sun 2–10pm; cocktail lounge open later. Subway/El: Blue Line to Damen.

Jane's ★ *Finds* ECLECTIC   Jane's has long been ignored by snobbish dining critics, which is all the more reason to love this inconspicuous charmer. This does not, however, mean that snagging a table at Jane's is an easy feat. On the contrary, this is a hugely popular destination among Wicker Park/Bucktown habitués, who'd prefer to keep it a secret. (Wait for your table at the Bucktown Pub or the Leopard Lounge, two of Bucktown's friendliest bars, which are across the street and next door, respectively.)

More than anything else, it may be the cozy ambience that attracts diners. Jane's is ensconced in an old house that has been gutted and rehabbed to create an open, two-story space with just 16 tables. (In summer, seven more are set up on an outside patio.) The menu offers piquant, upscale comfort food prepared simply and with loving care. The salads are standouts. Try the mesclun greens with pear, blue cheese, pecans, and balsamic vinaigrette. Tasty entrees include seared sea bass with mashed potatoes, arugula, caramelized pearl onions, and mushroom coulis; and an excellent garden burger with wild mushrooms and Monterey Jack cheese, served with mashed potatoes.

1655 W. Cortland St. (1 block west of Ashland Ave.). ℭ 773/862-5263. Reservations recommended but on a limited basis. Main courses $9–$22. MC, V. Mon–Thurs 5–10pm; Fri 5–11pm; Sat 11am–11pm; Sun 11am–10pm. Subway/El: Blue Line to Damen (walk 3 blocks north on Damen Ave., 4 blocks east on Cortland St.).

Le Bouchon ★★ *Finds* FRENCH/BISTRO   Opened in 1994, Jean-Claude Poilevey's trend-setting Le Bouchon was a well-received precursor of the bistro boom. This tiny storefront restaurant quickly caught on for the intimate yet boisterous atmosphere and authentic bistro fare at reasonable prices.

Whatever the season, the food here is fairly heavy, although specials are lighter in warmer months. Poilevey could pack this place every night just with regulars addicted to the house specialty of roast duck for two bathed in Grand Marnier–orange marmalade sauce. The fare covers bistro basics, with starters including steamed mussels in white wine and herbs, country paté, onion tart, codfish *brandade* (a pounded mixture of cod, olive oil, garlic, milk, and cream), and *salade Lyonnaise* (greens with bacon lardons, croutons, and poached egg). The authenticity continues in the entree department, with steak frites, sautéed rabbit in white wine, veal kidneys in mustard sauce, and garlicky frog legs on the bill of fare. The sounds of prominent music and voices from closely packed tables create an atmosphere that some perceive as cozy and romantic, and others as claustrophobic and noisy. There's a small bar where you can wait—something you can expect even if you have a reservation.

1958 N. Damen Ave. (at Armitage Ave.). ℭ 773/862-6600. www.lebouchonofchicago.com. Reservations recommended. Main courses $13–$15. AE, DC, DISC, MC, V. Mon–Thurs 5:30–11pm; Fri–Sat 5pm–midnight. Subway/El and bus: Blue Line to Damen and transfer to bus no. 50.

Soju KOREAN   Funky-chic Soju is a welcome destination for accessible Korean food, which isn't easy to find in Chicago outside of certain Korean neighborhoods on the north side of the city. The menu is slightly Americanized with a few Sushi 101 items, and the traditional barbecued beef and pork aren't served with lettuce wrappers, but otherwise Soju delivers tasty Korean fare in a casual, urban setting a step above neighborhood ethnic dining (priced accordingly).

Soju's menu is broken down into American-style courses. The kimchi-rice flour pancakes have a creamy, doughy texture spiked with the crunch of fermented vegetables and served with a soy-and-sesame dipping sauce. The pumpkin soup is an oddity, but the brothy *suun-dubu* (spicy soft tofu casserole) is an earthy delight, contrasting the crunch of cabbage with the softness of tofu, and finishing with a hint of fire. The signature house chicken entree is sauced with *soju* (a vodkalike Korean liquor). The classic *bibimbop* (mixture of rice and vegetables) can be ordered with beef, chicken, or tofu. The latter is a good vegetarian option, as is "Boys' noodles," a tasty texture and flavor medley that tosses cold rice noodles with shredded cabbage, scallions, and spicy bean sauce.

1745 W. North Ave. (?) **773/782-9000.** www.sojuchicago.com. Reservations for large parties only. Main courses $11–$15. AE, DC, MC, V. Mon–Thurs 6–10pm; Fri–Sat 6–11pm. Subway/El: Blue Line to Damen.

INEXPENSIVE

Northside Café AMERICAN/BURGERS   Among the best cheap eats in the city, Northside cooks up great burgers, sandwiches, and salads, all for less than $10. This is strictly neighborhood dining, without attitude and little in the way of decor; the back dining room looks like a rec room circa 1973, complete with a fireplace, pinball machines, and a pool table. In nice weather, Northside opens up its large front patio for dining, and a skylit cover keeps it in use during the winter. You're always sure to find entertaining people-watching, as Northside attracts all sorts. During the week, it's more of a neighborhood hangout, while on weekends, a touristy crowd from Lincoln Park and the suburbs piles in. A limited late-night menu is available from 10pm to 1am.

1635 N. Damen Ave. (at North and Milwaukee aves.). (?) **773/384-3555.** Reservations not accepted. Menu items $5.95–$11. AE, DC, DISC, MC, V. Sun–Fri 11:30am–2am; Sat 11am–3am. Subway/El: Blue Line to Damen.

Piece ⭐ *Kids* AMERICAN/PIZZA   Ever since its debut a year ago, Piece has been convincing deep-dish-loving Chicagoans that thin-crust pizza deserves respect. A casual, welcoming hangout, Piece makes a great family lunch stop during the day; at night, it becomes a convivial scene full of young singles sipping one of the restaurant's seasonal microbrew beers. The large, airy dining room—a former garage that's been outfitted with dark wood tables and ceiling beams—is flooded with light from the expansive skylights overhead; even when it's crowded (as it gets on weekend evenings), the soaring space above keeps the place from feeling claustrophobic.

Piece offers a selection of salads and sandwiches on satisfyingly crusty bread, but pizza in the style of New Haven, Connecticut (hometown of one of the owners), is the house specialty. You pick from three styles: plain (tomato sauce, Parmesan cheese, and garlic), red (tomato sauce and mozzarella), or white (olive oil, garlic, and mozzarella), then add on your favorite toppings. Sausage and/or spinach work well with the plain or red, but the adventurous shouldn't miss the house specialty: clam and bacon on white pizza.

1927 W. North Ave. (at Milwaukee Ave.). ℂ **773/772-4422**. Reservations not accepted. Main courses $6.95–$15. AE, DISC, MC, V. Mon–Thurs 11:30am–11pm; Fri–Sat 11:30am–12:30am; Sun 11am–11pm. Subway: Blue Line to Damen.

Silver Cloud ★★ AMERICAN   The motto of this casual cafe is "Food like Mom would make if she was gettin' paid." Silver Cloud is comfort food central, with a laid-back pub-meets-diner decor and suitably attitude-free clientele. If intimate conversation is your priority, try to snag one of the roomy red leather booths. While the food isn't extraordinary, the restaurant does deliver consistently reliable home-style favorites: chicken potpie, grilled-cheese sandwiches, pot roast, even sloppy joes with a side of tater tots; retro desserts include Frito pie and s'mores. While Silver Cloud attracts a mix of families, couples, and groups of friends during the day and early evening hours, it becomes more of a cocktail lounge at night—serving up specialty martinis and allowing smoking after 10pm. A warning for those with sensitive ears: The jukebox volume gets turned up at night, too. The Sunday brunch is especially popular; the "Hangover" specials attract a fair amount of hip young things recovering from nightly adventures.

1700 N. Damen Ave. (at Wabansia St.). ℂ **773/489-6212**. Reservations accepted. Main courses $6.50–$10 lunch, $8–$12 dinner. AE, DC, MC, V. Mon–Thurs 11:30am–12am; Fri 10am–2am; Sat 10am–3am; Sun 10am–midnight. Subway: Blue Line to Damen.

Exploring Chicago

Chicago may still be stereotyped as the home of sausage-loving, overweight guys who babble on endlessly about "da Bears" or "da Cubs," but in reality the city offers some of the most sophisticated cultural and entertainment options in the country. You'll have trouble fitting in all of Chicago's museums, which offer everything from action (the virtual-reality visit to the Milky Way galaxy at the Adler Planetarium) to quiet contemplation (the Impressionist masterpieces at the Art Institute of Chicago). Gape at Sue, the biggest T-rex fossil ever discovered, at the Field Museum of Natural History, or be entranced by the colorful world of the Butterfly Haven at the Peggy Notebaert Nature Museum. Stroll through picture-postcard Lincoln Park Zoo on the Near North Side, and then enjoy the view from the top of the Ferris wheel on historic Navy Pier.

Best of all for visitors, the majority of the places you'll want to visit are in or near downtown, making it easy to plan your day and get from place to place. And because this is a town with a thriving tourist economy, you'll have plenty of visitor-friendly options: walking tours of famous architecture; boat cruises on Lake Michigan; even bus tours of notorious gangster sites. If you're lucky enough to visit when the weather's nice, you can join the locals at our parks and the beaches along Lake Michigan.

Extensive public transportation makes it simple to reach almost every tourist destination, but some of your best memories of Chicago may come from simply strolling the sidewalks. Chicago's neighborhoods each have their own distinct style and look, and you'll have a more memorable experience if you don't limit yourself solely to the prime tourist spots. And if you *really* want to talk about da Bears or da Cubs, chances are you'll find someone more than happy to join in.

SUGGESTED ITINERARIES
If You Have 1 Day

If you have only a day in Chicago, sample some of the city's most distinctive areas. Assuming that you'll be visiting during nice weather, start the day in **the Loop,** either on a self-guided tour or one organized by the **Chicago Architecture Foundation** (the early-skyscraper tour is a good primer). Thanks to the Great Fire of 1871 and the determination to rebuild, Chicago has been a world leader in architecture for more than a century. If you're a shopper, spend the afternoon scoping out **Michigan Avenue** or strolling among the boutiques on **Armitage Avenue.** Or, if you're here in the summer, take the El uptown (along with a whole lot of business types taking a "long lunch") and spend the afternoon watching a Cubs game at historic **Wrigley Field.** If the weather's lousy, head indoors to one of the city's great museums, such as the **Art Institute,** the **Field Museum of Natural History,** the **Shedd**

Aquarium, or the **Adler Planetarium.** To top off the day, catch a play at one of the city's top theaters: **Goodman, Chicago Shakespeare,** or **Steppenwolf.**

If You Have 2 Days

Spend the first day in the downtown area. Walk around **the Loop** (as mentioned above) to see the buildings and the city's extensive sculpture collection. If it's a Saturday, get free tickets at the Chicago Cultural Center for the **Loop Tour Train,** which offers a guided overview of the city from the century-old elevated train (on any other day of the week, you can hop the El yourself for the same views, without the commentary). Next, visit one or two of the city's premier museums. Finish off the day with a shopping trip up the **Magnificent Mile** (and maybe a trip to the top of the **Hancock Building**) or a gallery-hopping expedition in **River North.** Both areas have plenty of excellent restaurants for dinner. If you've still got the energy, take an evening stroll along **Navy Pier** and a spin on the Ferris wheel. Then pick a boat along the dock for a nighttime cruise and view the shimmering skyline from the lake.

On the second day, head for a neighborhood on the **North Side,** such as the Gold Coast, Lincoln Park, or Wicker Park, and explore. In the afternoon, you won't be far from **Wrigley Field,** where you can see the Cubs play. In the evening, dine at one of the many ethnic restaurants along Clark Street or Southport Avenue. Spend the rest of the evening at one of the big-name theaters or perhaps at a more offbeat show in the Wrigleyville area.

If You Have 3 Days

Begin the third day with a trip to **Hyde Park,** where you can see the University of Chicago and Frank Lloyd Wright's Robie House, among other sights. Then spend a few hours at the fascinating **Museum of Science and Industry.** If you have time left, you could head back north and visit another museum. One worthy candidate is the **Mexican Fine Arts Center Museum** in Pilsen, a vibrant Hispanic community south of the Loop that has wonderful outdoor murals and some charming bakeries along 18th Street. If it's a nice day, however, walk up North Michigan Avenue or cross over to **Oak Street Beach** for a stroll (or roll, with a rented bike or blades) along the lake up to Fullerton Avenue, where you can wander around the zoo and the conservatory, or the **Peggy Notebaert Nature Museum.** If you have an extra couple of hours of daylight, jump in a cab and head for nearby **Armitage Avenue,** lined with some of Chicago's most unique boutiques and retail shops. Choose one of the neighborhood's many good restaurants for dinner and then one of its **jazz or blues clubs** for a finale.

1 In & Around the Loop: The Art Institute, the Sears Tower & Grant Park

The heart of the Loop is Chicago's business center, where you'll find such finance fascinations as the Chicago Board of Trade, the world's largest commodities, futures, and options exchange, and some of the city's most famous early skyscrapers (not to mention the Sears Tower). If you're looking to soak in a real big-city experience, wander the area on a bustling weekday (just make sure you don't get knocked down by a commuter rushing to catch the train). The Loop is also home to one of the city's top museums, the Art Institute of Chicago, as well as a number of cultural institutions: Symphony Center (home of the world-class Chicago Symphony Orchestra), the Auditorium Theatre, the Civic Opera House, the Goodman Theatre, and two fabulously restored historic theaters along Randolph Street. On the eastern edge of the Loop in Grant Park, three popular museums are conveniently located within a quick stroll of each other on a landscaped Museum Campus. Busy Lake Shore Drive, which brings cars zipping past the Museum Campus, was actually rerouted a few years ago to make the area easier to navigate for pedestrians (talk about a visitor-friendly city!)

THE TOP ATTRACTIONS IN THE LOOP

Art Institute of Chicago ★★★ *Kids* You can't (and shouldn't) miss the Art Institute: The signature pair of bronze lions that flank the museum's main entrance are perfect rendezvous points, and there is always a throng of people sitting on the steps on nice days. Finding the museum is easy—it's deciding what to see that is hard. Choose a medium and a century and the Art Institute has the works in its collection to captivate you: Japanese *ukiyo-e* prints, ancient Egyptian bronzes and Greek vases, 19th-century British photography, masterpieces by most of the greatest names in 20th-century sculpture, or modern American textiles. For a good general overview of the museum's collection, take the free "Highlights of the Art Institute" tour, offered at 2pm on Saturdays, Sundays, and Tuesdays.

If you've got limited time, you'll want to head straight to the museum's renowned collection of **Impressionist art** ★★★ (including one of the world's largest collections of Monet paintings); this is one of the most popular areas of the museum, so arriving early pays off. Among the treasures, you'll find Seurat's pointillist masterpiece *Sunday Afternoon on the Island of La Grande Jatte*. Your second must-see areas are the galleries of **European and American contemporary art** ★★, ranging from paintings, sculptures, and mixed-media works from Pablo Picasso, Henri Matisse, and Salvador Dalí through Willem de Kooning, Jackson Pollock, and Andy Warhol. Visitors are sometimes surprised when they discover many of the icons that hang here. (Grant Wood's *American Gothic* and Edward Hopper's *Nighthawks* are two that bring double takes from many visitors.)

Other recommended exhibits are the collection of delicate mid-19th-century **glass paperweights** in the museum's famous Arthur Rubloff collection and the great hall of **European arms and armor** ★ dating from the 15th to 19th centuries. Composed of more than 1,500 objects, including armor, horse equipment, swords and daggers, polearms, and maces, the collection is one of the most important assemblages of its kind in the country. (If you do head down here, don't miss Marc Chagall's stunning stained-glass windows at the end of the gallery.)

The Art Institute goes the extra mile to entertain kids. The **Kraft Education Center** on the lower level features interactive exhibits for children and has a list of "gallery games" to make visiting the museum more fun. When I was a kid, I was entranced by the **Thorne Miniature Rooms** ★, filled with tiny reproductions of furnished interiors from European and American history (heaven for a dollhouse fanatic).

The museum also has a cafeteria and an elegant full-service restaurant, a picturesque courtyard cafe (open June–Sept), and a large shop. There is a busy schedule of lectures, films, and other special presentations, as well as guided tours, to enhance your viewing of the art. The museum also has a research library. Allow 3 hours.

Central Chicago Attractions

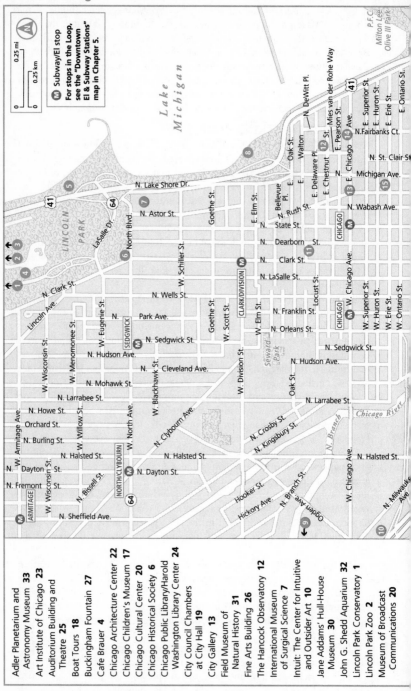

Adler Planetarium and Astronomy Museum **33**
Art Institute of Chicago **23**
Auditorium Building and Theatre **25**
Boat Tours **18**
Buckingham Fountain **27**
Cafe Brauer **4**
Chicago Architecture Center **22**
Chicago Children's Museum **17**
Chicago Cultural Center **20**
Chicago Historical Society **6**
Chicago Public Library/Harold Washington Library Center **24**
City Council Chambers at City Hall **19**
City Gallery **13**
Field Museum of Natural History **31**
Fine Arts Building **26**
The Hancock Observatory **12**
International Museum of Surgical Science **7**
Intuit: The Center for Intuitive and Outsider Art **10**
Jane Addams' Hull-House Museum **30**
John G. Shedd Aquarium **32**
Lincoln Park Conservatory **1**
Lincoln Park Zoo **2**
Museum of Broadcast Communications **20**

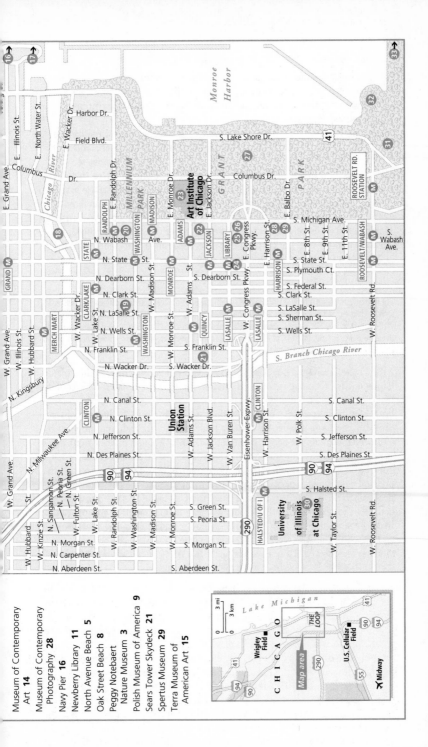

Museum of Contemporary Art **14**
Museum of Contemporary Photography **28**
Navy Pier **16**
Newberry Library **11**
North Avenue Beach **5**
Oak Street Beach **8**
Peggy Notebaert Nature Museum **3**
Polish Museum of America **9**
Sears Tower Skydeck **21**
Spertus Museum **29**
Terra Museum of American Art **15**

Tips **Insider Tips for Touring the Art Institute**

If you want to enjoy your favorite masterpieces in something resembling peace and quiet, put some thought into the timing of your visit to the Art Institute, a museum so popular that it draws as much traffic as our jammed expressways.

Some tips for avoiding the rush hour: Many people don't realize the museum is open on Mondays; so keep this secret to yourself, and visit when the galleries are relatively subdued. Wednesdays are a close second. Tuesdays tend to draw the masses because the Art Institute is free that day and open late (until 8pm). Try to arrive when the doors open in the morning or else during the lunchtime lull. Another tip: If the Michigan Avenue entrance is crowded, head around to the entrance on the Columbus Drive side, which is usually less congested and is more convenient to the Grant Park underground parking garage. There's a small gift shop near the Columbus Drive entrance, too, if the main shop is too bustling.

---

111 S. Michigan Ave. (at Adams St.). © 312/443-3600. www.artic.edu. Suggested admission $10 adults; $6 seniors, children, and students with ID. Additional cost for special exhibitions. Free admission Tues. Mon, Wed–Fri, and holidays 10:30am–4:30pm; Tues 10:30am–8pm; Sat–Sun 10am–5pm. Closed Thanksgiving and Dec 25. Bus: No. 3, 4, 60, 145, 147, or 151. Subway/El: Green, Brown, Purple, or Orange line to Adams, or Red Line to Monroe/State or Jackson/State.

City Council Chambers at City Hall The public meetings of the volatile Chicago City Council make great theater for political junkies. The council meets in a massive building that takes up an entire city block, encompassing both City Hall and the County Building. (You can't miss it: Its columns are probably the most massive of any city building—75 ft. high and crowned by Corinthian capitals the height of an entire floor.) Although politics aren't quite as colorful under Mayor Richard M. Daley as they were under his dad, when a hot-button issue is being debated, factions can still get down and dirty, and the political posturing of the 50 aldermen (the name given to the city council members) can make for the best kind of theatrics. Call ahead to find out when the council is in session. City Hall tours also can be arranged for groups; call to make a reservation (© **312/744-9617**). Allow 1 hour.

Washington, LaSalle, Randolph, and Clark sts. © 312/744-6800. www.ci.chi.il.us/CityCouncil. Free admission. Open when City Council is in session. Bus: No. 20, 56, 131, 156, or 157. Subway/El: Brown, Green, Orange, or Purple line to Clark, or Red or Blue line to Washington.

Sears Tower Skydeck *Overrated* First Sears sold the building and moved to cheaper suburban offices in 1992. Then the skyscraper got an ego blow when the Petronas Towers in Kuala Lumpur, Malaysia, went up and laid claim to the title of world's tallest buildings. (The Sears Tower has since put up a 22-ft. antenna in an attempt to win back the title.) Tallest-building posturing aside, this is still a great place to orient yourself to the city, but I wouldn't put it on the top of must-see sights for anyone with limited time (and limited patience for crowds).

The view from the 103rd-floor Skydeck is everything you'd expect it to be—once you get there. Unfortunately, you're often stuck in a very long, very noisy line, so by the time you make it to the top, your patience could be as thin as the atmosphere up there. (Come in the late afternoon to avoid most of the crowds.) On a clear day, visibility extends up to 50 miles, and you can catch glimpses of four surrounding states. Despite the fact that it's called a "skydeck," you can't actually walk outside. Recent upgrades include multimedia exhibits on Chicago history and *Knee High Chicago,* an exhibit for kids. The 70-second high-speed elevator trip will feel like a thrill ride for some, but it's a nightmare for anyone with even mild claustrophobia. Allow 1 to 2 hours, depending on the length of the line.

233 S. Wacker Dr. (enter on Jackson Blvd.). © 312/875-9696. www.sears-tower.com. Admission $9.50 adults, $7.75 seniors, $6.75 children 3–12, free for children under 3 and military with active-duty ID. May–Sept daily 10am–10pm; Oct–April daily 10am–8pm. Bus: No. 1, 7, 126, 146, 151, or 156. Subway/El: Brown, Purple, or Orange line to Quincy, or Red or Blue line to Jackson; then walk a few blocks west.

THE LOOP SCULPTURE TOUR

Downtown Chicago is a veritable "museum without walls." Examples of public art—in the form of traditional monuments, murals, and monumental contemporary sculpture—are located widely throughout the city, but their concentration within the Loop and nearby Grant Park is worth noting. The best known of these works are by 20th-century artists, including Picasso, Chagall, Miró, Calder, Moore, and Oldenburg.

With the help of a very comprehensive booklet, *Loop Sculpture Guide* ($3.95 at the gift shop in the Chicago Cultural Center, 78 E. Washington St.), you can steer yourself through Grant Park and much of the Loop to view some 100 examples of Chicago's monumental public art. It provides locations and descriptions of 37 major works, including photographs, plus about 60 other nearby sites.

You also can conduct a self-guided tour of the city's public sculpture by following our "Loop Sculpture Tour" map (p. 171).

The single-most-famous sculpture is **Pablo Picasso's** *Untitled,* located in Daley Plaza and constructed out of Cor-Ten steel, the same gracefully rusting material used on the exterior of the Daley Center behind it. Viewed from various perspectives, its enigmatic shape alternately suggests that of a woman, bird, or dog. Perhaps because it was the button-down Loop's first monumental modern sculpture, its installation in 1967 was met with hoots and heckles, but today "The Picasso" enjoys semiofficial status as the logo of modern Chicago. It is by far the city's most popular photo opportunity among visiting tourists. At noon on weekdays during warm-weather months, you'll likely find a dance troupe, musical group, or visual-arts exhibition there as part of the city's long-running "Under the Picasso" multicultural program. Call © **312/346-3278** for event information.

GRANT PARK

Thanks to architect Daniel Burnham and his coterie of visionary civic planners—who drafted the revolutionary 1909 Plan of Chicago—the city boasts a

Oprah in Person

Oprah Winfrey tapes her phenomenally successful talk show at Harpo Studios, 1058 W. Washington Blvd., just west of the Loop. If you'd like to be in her studio audience, you'll have to plan ahead: Reservations are taken by phone only (© **312/591-9222**), at least one month in advance.

wide-open lakefront park system unrivaled by most major metropolises. Modeled after the gardens at Versailles, Grant Park is Chicago's front yard, composed of giant lawns segmented by *allées* of trees, plantings, and paths, and pieced together by major roadways and a network of railroad tracks. Covering the greens are a variety of public recreational and cultural facilities (although these are few in number and nicely spread out, a legacy of mail-order magnate Aaron Montgomery Ward's *fin de siècle* campaign to limit municipal buildings in the park). Incredibly, the entire expanse was created from sandbars, landfill, and Chicago Fire debris; the original shoreline extended all the way to Michigan Avenue.

The immense **Buckingham Fountain,** accessible along Congress Parkway, is the baroque centerpiece of the park, composed of pink Georgia marble and patterned after—but twice the size of—the Latona Fountain at Versailles, with adjoining esplanades beautified by rose gardens in season. From April through October, the fountain spurts columns of water up to 150 feet in the air every hour on the hour; beginning at 4pm, a whirl of colored lights and dramatic music amps up the drama (the fountain shuts down at 11pm). Concession areas and bathrooms are available on the plaza.

The northwest corner of Grant Park (bordered by Michigan Ave. and Randolph St.) is the site of **Millennium Park,** one of the city's grandest recent public-works projects. Who cares that the park cost hundreds of millions more than it was supposed to, or the fact that it's finally opening a whole four years after the actual millennium? It's a winning combination of beautiful landscaping, elegant architecture (the classically inspired Peristyle), and public entertainment spaces (an ice rink, the music and dance theater). The park's centerpiece is the dramatic, Frank Gehry–designed **Music Pavilion,** featuring massive curved ribbons of steel. The Grant Park Symphony Orchestra and Chorus stages a popular series of free outdoor classical music concerts here most Wednesday through Sunday evenings in the summer. For a schedule of concert times and dates, contact the **Grant Park Music Festival** (© 312/742-7638).

Through the summer, Grant Park is taken over by a variety of music and food festivals. Annual events that draw big crowds include a blues music festival (in June) and a jazz festival (Labor Day). The **Taste of Chicago** (© 312/744-3315), purportedly the largest food festival in the world (the city estimates its annual attendance at around 3½ million), takes place every summer for 10 days around the July 4th holiday. Local restaurants serve up more ribs, pizza, hot dogs, and beer than you'd ever want to see, let alone eat. (See chapter 3 for a comprehensive listing of summer events in Grant Park.)

Scattered about the park are a number of sculptures and monuments, including the heroic sculptures of two Native Americans on horseback entitled *The Bowman and The Spearman* (at Congress Pkwy. and Michigan Ave.), which has become the park's trademark since it was installed in 1928, as well as likenesses of Copernicus, Columbus, and Lincoln, the latter by the great American sculptor Augustus Saint-Gaudens, located on Congress Parkway between Michigan Avenue and Columbus Drive. On the western edge of the park, at Adams Street, is the **Art Institute** (see above), and at the southern tip in the newly redesigned Museum Campus are the Field Museum of Natural History, the Adler Planetarium, and the Shedd Aquarium (see below for all three).

To get to Grant Park, take bus no. 3, 4, 6, 60, 146, or 151. If you want to take the subway or the El, get off at any stop in the Loop along State or Wabash, and walk east.

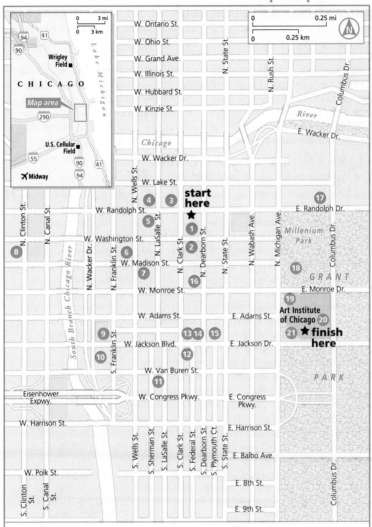

1 *Untitled ("The Picasso")*, Pablo Picasso (1967)

2 *Chicago*, Joan Miro (1981)

3 *Monument with Standing Beast*, Jean Dubuffet (1984)

4 *Freeform*, Richard Hunt (1993)

5 *Flight of Daedalus and Icarus*, 120 N. LaSalle St., Roger Brown (1990)

6 *Dawn Shadows*, Louise Nevelson (1983)

7 *Loomings and Knights and Squires*, Frank Stella

8 *Batcolumn*, Claes Oldenburg (1977)

9 *The Universe*, Alexander Calder (1974)

10 *Gem of the Lakes*, Raymond Kaskey (1990)

11 *San Marco II*, Ludovico de Luigi (1986)

12 *The Town-Ho's Story*, Frank Stella (1993)

13 *Ruins III*, Nita K. Sutherland (1978)

14 *Flamingo*, Alexander Calder (1974)

15 *Lines in Four Directions*, Sol Lewitt (1985)

16 *The Four Seasons*, Marc Chagall (1974)

17 *Untitled Sounding Sculpture*, Harry Bertoia (1975)

18 *Alexander Hamilton*, Bela Lyon Pratt (1918)

19 *Large Interior Form*, Henry Moore (1983)

20 *Celebration of the 200th Anniversary of the Founding of the Republic*, Isamu Noguchi (1976)

21 *The Fountain of the Great Lakes*, Lorado Taft (1913)

MORE ATTRACTIONS IN THE LOOP

Fashion and glamour might have moved north to the Magnificent Mile, but Chicago's grandest stretch of boulevard is still Michigan Avenue, south of the river. From a little north of the Michigan Avenue bridge all the way down to the Field Museum, South Michigan Avenue runs parallel to Grant Park on one side and the Loop on the other. A stroll along this boulevard in any season offers both visual and cultural treats. Particularly impressive is the great wall of buildings from Randolph Street south to Congress Parkway (beginning with the Chicago Cultural Center and terminating at the Auditorium Building) that architecture buffs refer to as the "Michigan Avenue Cliff."

ALONG SOUTH MICHIGAN AVENUE

The following attractions are listed from north to south.

Chicago Cultural Center ★ *Finds*   Built in 1897 as the city's public library, and transformed into a showplace for visual and performing arts in 1991, the Chicago Cultural Center is an overlooked civic treasure. Its basic beaux arts exterior conceals a sumptuous interior of rare marble, fine hardwood, stained glass, polished brass, and mosaics of Favrile glass, colored stone, and mother-of-pearl inlaid in white marble. The crowning centerpiece is Preston Bradley Hall's majestic Tiffany dome, said to be the largest of its kind in the world.

The building also houses one of the Chicago Office of Tourism's visitor centers, which makes it an ideal place to kick-start your visit. If you stop in to pick up tourist information and take a quick look around, your visit won't take longer than half an hour. But the Cultural Center also hosts an array of art exhibitions, concerts, films, lectures, and other special events (many free), which might convince you to extend your time here. A long-standing tradition is the 12:15pm Dame Myra Hess Memorial classical concert every Wednesday in the Preston Bradley Hall. Other ongoing programs include a monthly cultural festival—which highlights a different city or country over a weekend with art, theater, and film.

Guided architectural tours of the Cultural Center are offered Wednesday, Friday, and Saturday at 1:15pm. For information, call ✆ **312/744-8032.**
Allow a half-hour.

78 E. Washington St. ✆ **312/744-6630,** or 312/FINE-ART for weekly events. Fax 312/744-2089. www.ci.chi. il.us/tour/culturalcenter. Free admission. Mon–Wed 10am–7pm; Thurs 10am–9pm; Fri 10am–6pm; Sat 10am–5pm; Sun 11am–5pm. Closed holidays. Bus: No. 3, 4, 20, 56, 60, 127, 131, 145, 146, 147, 151, or 157. Subway/El: Brown, Green, Orange, or Purple line to Randolph, or Red Line to Washington/State.

Chicago Architecture Center   Chicago's architecture is one of the city's main claims to fame, and a quick swing through this center will help you understand why. Run by the well-regarded Chicago Architecture Foundation, it's conveniently located across the street from the Art Institute. Still trying to figure out the difference between Prairie School and postmodern? Stop in here for a quick lesson. Exhibits include a scale model of downtown Chicago, profiles of the

---

Moments Photo Op

For a great photo op, walk on Randolph Street toward the lake in the morning. That's when the sun, rising in the east over the lake, hits the cliff of buildings along South Michigan Avenue—giving you the perfect backdrop for an only-in-Chicago picture.

South Michigan Avenue & Grant Park Attractions

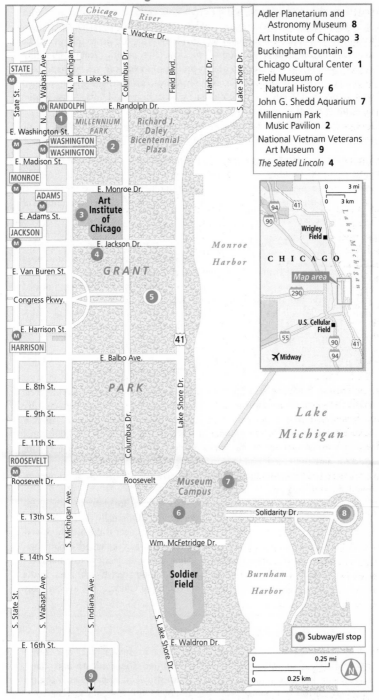

Adler Planetarium and Astronomy Museum **8**
Art Institute of Chicago **3**
Buckingham Fountain **5**
Chicago Cultural Center **1**
Field Museum of Natural History **6**
John G. Shedd Aquarium **7**
Millennium Park Music Pavilion **2**
National Vietnam Veterans Art Museum **9**
The Seated Lincoln **4**

Chicago River
E. Wacker Dr.
STATE
Chicago River
E. Lake St.
RANDOLPH
E. Randolph Dr.
State St.
Wabash Ave.
N. Michigan Ave.
N.
Columbus Dr.
Field Blvd.
Harbor Dr.
S. Lake Shore Dr.
E. Washington St.
MILLENNIUM PARK
Richard J. Daley Bicentennial Plaza
WASHINGTON
WASHINGTON
E. Madison St.
MONROE
ADAMS
E. Adams St.
E. Monroe Dr.
Art Institute of Chicago
JACKSON
E. Jackson Dr.
GRANT
Monroe Harbor
E. Van Buren St.
Congress Pkwy.
E. Harrison St.
HARRISON
41
E. Balbo Ave.
PARK
Lake Shore Dr.
E. 8th St.
E. 9th St.
Columbus Dr.
E. 11th St.
Lake Michigan
ROOSEVELT
Roosevelt Dr.
Roosevelt
Museum Campus
S. Michigan Ave.
E. 13th St.
Solidarity Dr.
E. 14th St.
Wm. McFetridge Dr.
S. State St.
S. Wabash Ave.
S. Indiana Ave.
Soldier Field
Burnham Harbor
S. Lake Shore Dr.
E. 16th St.
E. Waldron Dr.
M Subway/El stop

0   3 mi
0   3 km
94
41
90
Wrigley Field
Lake Michigan
CHICAGO
Map area
290
U.S. Cellular Field
55
90
41
Midway
94

0   0.25 mi
0   0.25 km
N

people and buildings that shaped the city's look, and a searchable database with pictures and information on many of Chicago's best-known skyscrapers. "Architecture ambassadors" are on hand to provide information on tours run by the foundation (see "Sightseeing Tours," p. 209). Two galleries feature changing exhibits about ongoing Chicago design projects—so you can see firsthand how local architecture continues to evolve. There's also an excellent gift shop filled with architecture-focused books, decorative accessories, and gifts. Allow a half-hour, more if you want to browse in the store.

224 S. Michigan Ave. ⓒ 312/922-3432. www.architecture.org. Free admission. Daily 9:30am–5pm. Bus: No. 3, 4, 60, 145, 147, or 151. Subway/El: Brown, Green, Purple, or Orange line to Adams, or Red Line to Jackson.

Fine Arts Building A worthwhile brief stop for architecture and history buffs, this 1885 building was originally a showroom for Studebaker carriages. In 1917, it was converted into an arts center with offices, shops, two theaters, and studios for musicians, artists, and writers. Its upper stories sheltered a number of well-known publications *(The Saturday Evening Post, Dial)* and provided offices for such luminaries as Frank Lloyd Wright, sculptor Lorado Taft, and L. Frank Baum, author of *The Wonderful Wizard of Oz.* Harriet Monroe published her magazine, *Poetry,* here and first introduced American readers to Carl Sandburg, T. S. Eliot, and Ezra Pound. Before the literary lions prowled its halls, the building also served for a short time as a rallying base for suffragettes. Located throughout the building are a number of interesting studios and musical instrument shops. Take at least a quick walk through the marble-and-wood lobby, then take the vintage elevator to the top floor to see the spectacular murals. Allow a half-hour.

410 S. Michigan Ave. ⓒ 312/427-7602. Free admission. Daily 7am–10pm. Bus: No. 3, 4, 60, 145, 147, or 151. Subway/El: Brown, Green, Purple, or Orange line to Adams, or Red Line to Jackson.

Auditorium Building and Theatre ★★ A truly grand theater with historic landmark status, the Auditorium is worth a visit to experience late-19th-century Chicago opulence. Designed and built in 1889 by Louis Sullivan and Dankmar Adler, the Auditorium was a wonder of the world: the heaviest (110,000 tons) and most massive modern edifice on earth, the most fireproof building ever constructed, and the tallest building in Chicago. It was also the first large-scale building to be electrically lighted, and its theater was the first in the country to install air-conditioning.

The 4,000-seat theater, which today is the scene for Broadway touring musicals, is a marvel of visionary design and engineering. Originally the home of the Chicago Opera Company, Sullivan and Adler's masterpiece is defined by powerful arches lit by thousands of bulbs and features Sullivan's trademark ornamentation—in this case, elaborate golden stenciling and gold plaster medallions. It's equally renowned for otherworldly acoustics and unobstructed sight lines. In the days when the Auditorium was the leading theater of Chicago, the hydraulically

---

(Fun Fact Did You Know?

The two bronze sculptures of Indian warriors on horseback that flank Congress Parkway at Michigan Avenue were titled *The Bowman and The Spearman* by Yugoslavian sculptor Ivan Mestrovic. It appears as if their bow and arrow and spear have been removed, but the omission is actually intentional: Mestrovic aimed to make an antiwar statement.

Value **Museum Free Days**

Plan your time in Chicago carefully and you can save yourself admission fees to some of the city's major museums. However, keep in mind that you will still have to pay for special exhibitions and films on free days.

Monday: Adler Planetarium (Sept–Feb only), Field Museum of Natural History (Sept–Feb only), Museum of Science and Industry (Sept–Feb only), Shedd Aquarium (Sept–Feb, Oceanarium admission extra)

Tuesday: Adler Planetarium (Sept–Feb only), Art Institute of Chicago, Field Museum of Natural History (Sept–Feb only), International Museum of Surgical Science, Museum of Contemporary Art, Museum of Science and Industry (Sept–Feb only), Terra Museum of American Art, Shedd Aquarium (Sept–Feb, Oceanarium admission extra)

Thursday: DuSable Museum of African-American History, Chicago Children's Museum (5–8pm only), Terra Museum of American Art

Friday: Spertus Museum

Always Free: Chicago Cultural Center, Garfield Park Conservatory, David and Alfred Smart Museum of Art, Jane Addams Hull-House Museum, Lincoln Park Conservatory, Lincoln Park Zoo, Martin D'Arcy Gallery of Art, Mexican Fine Arts Center Museum, Museum of Contemporary Photography, Newberry Library

operated stage could be lowered from view, creating a ballroom capable of accommodating 8,000 guests.

Owned since 1946 by Roosevelt University, the Auditorium has had a roller-coaster history. Originally the site of a 400-room luxury hotel and commercial office space, it fell on hard times during the Depression and closed in 1941. During World War II, the building sheltered GIs, and its theater stage was turned into a bowling alley. The theater reopened in 1967 following a $3 million renovation made possible through the fundraising efforts of the nonprofit Auditorium Theatre Council. Remnants of the building's halcyon days remain. Don't miss the lobby fronting Michigan Avenue, with its faux ornamental marble columns, molded ceilings, mosaic floors, and Mexican onyx walls. Another inside tip: Take the elevator to the school's 10th-floor library reading room and have a look at what was once the city's first top-floor dining room. Its palatial, barrel-vaulted ceiling, and marvelous views of Grant Park and the lake will make you want to brush up on your Dewey Decimal System.

The best way to see everything is to take a 1-hour guided tour, offered on Mondays between 10am and 4pm (call ✆ **312/431-2354** to make reservations). Tours cost $6 for adults, $3 for seniors and students.

Allow a half-hour, one hour if you take the guided tour.

50 E. Congress Pkwy. ✆ **312/922-2110.** www.auditoriumtheatre.org. For ticket reservations or box-office information, call Ticketmaster at ✆ 312/902-1500. Bus: No. 145, 147, or 151. Subway/El: Brown, Green, Orange, or Purple line to Library/Van Buren, or Red Line to Jackson.

Museum of Contemporary Photography   Ensconced in a ground-floor space at Columbia College—a progressive arts- and media-oriented institution that boasts the country's largest undergraduate film department and a highly respected photojournalism-slanted photography department—the Museum of Contemporary Photography is the only museum in the Midwest of its ilk. As the name indicates, it exhibits, collects, and promotes modern photography, with a special focus on American works from 1959 to present. Rotating exhibitions showcase images by both nationally recognized and "undiscovered" regional artists. Related lectures and special programs are scheduled during the year. Allow 1 hour.

600 S. Michigan Ave. (€) **312/344-7104.** www.mocp.org. Free admission. Mon–Wed and Fri 10am–5pm; Thurs 10am–8pm; Sat noon–5pm. Bus: No. 6, 146, or 151. Subway/El: Red Line to Harrison.

Spertus Museum   The Spertus Museum, an extension of the Spertus Institute of Jewish Studies, showcases intricately crafted and historic Jewish ceremonial objects, textiles, coins, paintings, and sculpture, tracing 5,000 years of Jewish heritage. Though small in scale, the Zell Holocaust Memorial exhibit is particularly moving, featuring a video montage of Holocaust victims with a Chicago connection and a display of related artifacts and documents. The Artifact Center is a great spot for kids; it's a re-creation of a Middle Eastern archaeological dig, where children can search for buried treasures (reserved for school groups in the mornings, it's open to the public in the afternoon). The institute's Asher Library boasts one of the largest collections of Jewish books, periodicals, videos, and music in the country. The Bariff Shop for Judaica carries a large selection of art, books, music, videos, and contemporary and traditional Jewish ceremonial gifts. Allow 1 hour.

618 S. Michigan Ave. (€) **312/322-1747.** www.spertus.edu. Admission $5 adults; $3 seniors, students, and children; $10 maximum family rate. Free admission Fri. Sun–Wed 10am–5pm; Thurs 10am–7pm; Fri 10am–3pm. Bus: No. 3, 4, 6, 145, 147, or 151. Subway/El: Red Line to Harrison, or Brown, Purple, Orange, or Green line to Adams. Validated parking in nearby lots.

ELSEWHERE IN THE LOOP

Chicago Public Library/Harold Washington Library Center   A massive, hulking building that looks like an Italian Renaissance fortress, the main public library for the city of Chicago is the largest public library in the world. Named for the city's first and only African-American mayor, who died of a heart attack in 1987 at the beginning of his second term in office, the building fills an entire city block at State Street and Congress Parkway. The interior design has been criticized for being somewhat cold (you have to go up a few floors before you even see any books), but the stunning 52-foot glass-domed winter garden on the top floor is worth a visit. On the second floor is another treasure: the vast Thomas Hughes Children's Library, which makes an excellent resting spot for families with young children. The library offers an interesting array of events and art exhibitions worth checking out. A 385-seat auditorium is the setting for a unique mix of dance and music performances, author talks, and children's programs. Allow a half-hour.

400 S. State St. (€) **312/747-4300.** www.chipublib.org. Free admission. Mon–Thurs 9am–7pm; Fri–Sat 9am–5pm; Sun 1–5pm. Closed holidays. Bus: No. 2, 6, 11, 29, 36, 62, 145, 146, 147, or 151. Subway/El: Red Line to Jackson/State, or Brown Line to Van Buren/Library.

2 The Earth, the Sky & the Sea: The Big Three in the Grant Park Museum Campus

With terraced gardens and broad walkways, the Museum Campus at the southern end of Grant Park makes it easy for pedestrians to visit three of the city's most beloved institutions: our natural history museum, aquarium, and planetarium.

Value Museums for Less

If you're planning on visiting lots of Chicago museums, you should invest in a CityPass, a prepaid ticket that gets you into the biggest attractions (The Art Institute, Field Museum of Natural History, Shedd Aquarium, Adler Planetarium, Museum of Science and Industry, and Hancock Observatory). The cost at press time was $49 for adults and $38 for children, which is about 50% cheaper than paying all the museums' individual admission fees. You can buy a CityPass at any of the museums listed above, or purchase one online before you get to town (www.citypass.net). Also, see the "Museum Free Days" box, above, for schedules of when some of these museums are free.

The campus is about a 15- to 20-minute walk from the Loop, and is easily reached by bus or subway (a trolley runs from the Roosevelt Rd. El stop). To get to the Museum Campus from the Loop, head east across Grant Park on East Balbo Drive from South Michigan Avenue, and then trek south along the lakeshore path to the museums. Or, you can make your approach on the path that begins at 11th Street from South Michigan Avenue. Follow 11th to the walkway that spans the Metra tracks. Cross Columbus Drive and then pick up the path that will take you under Lake Shore Drive and into the Museum Campus. The CTA no. 146 bus will take you from downtown to all three of these attractions. Call ℂ **836-7000** (from any city or suburban area code) for the stop locations and schedule.

Adler Planetarium and Astronomy Museum ★★   The building is historic, but some of the attractions here will captivate the most jaded video-game addict. The zodiacal 12-sided structure sits on a promontory at the end of ornamental Solidarity Drive, just up the road from the aquarium. The first planetarium in the Western Hemisphere, it was founded by Sears, Roebuck and Co. executive Max Adler, who imported a Zeiss projector from Germany in 1930.

The good news for present-day visitors is that the planetarium has been updated since then. A $40 million expansion and renovation, completed in 1999, added the 60,000-square-foot Sky Pavilion, which should be your first stop. The don't miss experience is the **StarRider Theater** ★★, which takes you on an interactive virtual-reality trip through the Milky Way and into deep space, featuring a computer-generated 3D-graphics projection system and controls in the armrest of each person's seat. Six high-resolution video projectors form a seamless image on the domed ceiling—you'll feel like you're literally floating in space. If you're looking for more entertainment, the **Sky Theater** shows movies with an astronomical bent (*Skywatchers of Africa* looks at the way different African cultures have interpreted the sky, and *Images of the Infinite* highlights discoveries from the Hubble Telescope). The planetarium's exhibit galleries feature a variety of displays and interactive activities designed to foster understanding of our solar system and more. The best current exhibit is ***Bringing the Heavens to Earth*** ★, which traces the ways different cultures have tried to make sense of astronomical phenomena. The planetarium's signature exhibit, ***From the Night Sky to the Big Bang***, traces changing views of the cosmos over 1,000 years and features artifacts from the planetarium's extensive collection of historical astronomical instruments (all of which can get a bit boring for kids unless they're real astronomy nuts).

The museum's cafe provides views of the lakefront and skyline. On the first Friday evening of the month, visitors can view dramatic close-ups of the moon, the planets, and distant galaxies through a closed-circuit monitor connected to the planetarium's Doane Observatory telescope.

Allow 2 hours, more if you want to see more than one show.

1300 S. Lake Shore Dr. (€) **312/922-STAR**. Fax 312/922-2257. www.adlerplanetarium.org. Admission (including 1 show) $13 adults, $12 seniors, $11 children 4–17, free for children under 4. Free admission Mon and Tues Sept–Feb only. Mon–Fri 9:30am–4:30pm, Sat–Sun 9am–4:30pm; from June 1–Sept 1 Sat–Wed until 6pm and Thurs–Fri until 9pm; 1st Fri of every month until 10 pm. StarRider Theater and Sky Shows at numerous times throughout the day; call (€) 312/922-STAR for current times. Bus: No. 12, 127, or 146.

Field Museum of Natural History ★★★ *Kids*   Is it any wonder that Steven Spielberg thought the Field Museum of Natural History suitable home turf for the intrepid archaeologist and adventurer hero of his *Indiana Jones* movies? Spread over the museum's 9 acres of floor space are scores of permanent and temporary exhibitions—some interactive, but most requiring the old-fashioned skills of observation and imagination. But navigating all the disparate exhibits can be daunting.

You'll start out in the grand Stanley Field Hall, which you enter from either the north or south end. Standing proudly at the north side is the largest, most complete *Tyrannosaurus rex* fossil ever unearthed. Named **Sue** ★★★ for the paleontologist who found the dinosaur in 1990 in South Dakota, the specimen was acquired by the museum for a cool $8.4 million following a high-stakes bidding war. The real skull is so heavy that a lighter copy had to be mounted on the skeleton; the actual one is displayed nearby.

Families should head downstairs for two of the most popular kid-friendly exhibits. The pieces on display in ***Inside Ancient Egypt*** ★★ were brought to the museum in the early 1900s, after researchers in Saqqara, Egypt, excavated two of the original chambers from the tomb of Unis-ankh, son of the Fifth Dynasty ruler Pharaoh Unis. This *mastaba* (tomb) of Unis-ankh now forms the core of a spellbinding exhibit that realistically depicts scenes from Egyptian funeral, religious, and other social practices. Visitors can explore aspects of the day-to-day world of ancient Egypt, viewing 23 actual mummies and realistic burial scenes, a living marsh environment and canal works, the ancient royal barge, a religious shrine, and a reproduction of a typical marketplace of the period. Many of the exhibits allow hands-on interaction, and there are special activities for kids, such as making parchment from living papyrus plants.

Next to the Egypt exhibit, you'll find ***Underground Adventure*** ★★, a "total immersion environment" populated by giant robotic earwigs, centipedes, wolf spiders, and other subterranean critters. The Disneyesque exhibit is a big hit with kids, but—annoyingly—requires an extra admission charge ($5 on top of regular admission for adults, $2 for kids).

You might be tempted to skip the "peoples of the world" exhibits, but, trust me—some are not only mind-opening, but they're also great fun. ***Traveling the Pacific*** ★ is hidden up on the second floor, but it's definitely worth a stop. Hundreds of artifacts from the museum's oceanic collection re-create scenes of island life in the South Pacific (there's even a full-scale model of a Maori meeting house). ***Africa*** ★, an assemblage of African artifacts and provocative, interactive multimedia presentations, takes viewers to Senegal, to a Cameroon palace, to the savanna and its wildlife, and on a "virtual" journey aboard a slave ship to the Americas. Native Chicagoans will quickly name two more signature highlights: the taxidermies of ***Bushman*** (a legendary lowland gorilla who made international headlines while at the city's Lincoln Park Zoo) and the *Man-Eating Lions of Tsavo* (the pair of male lions who munched nearly 140 British railway workers constructing a bridge in East Africa in 1898; their story is featured in the film *The Ghost and the Darkness*).

The museum hosts special traveling exhibits (recent blockbusters included shows on Cleopatra and the jewels of Russia), as well as numerous lectures, book signings, multiethnic musical and dance performances, storytelling events, and family activity days throughout the year. The Corner Bakery cafe, located just off the main hall, is a cut above the usual museum victuals (to avoid the lunchtime lines, pick up one of the premade salads or sandwiches and head for the cash register). Families also flock to the McDonald's on the lower level. Allow 3 hours.

Roosevelt Rd. and Lake Shore Dr. ℂ **312/922-9410** or 312/341-9299 TDD (for hearing-impaired callers). www.fmnh.org. Admission $10 adults; $7 seniors, children 3–11, and students with ID; free for teachers, armed-forces personnel in uniform, and children 2 and under. Free admission mid-Sept–Feb. Daily 9am–5pm. Open Thurs to 8pm June 17–Aug 26. Closed Dec 25 and Jan 1. Bus: No. 6, 10, 12, 130, or 146.

John G. Shedd Aquarium ★★★   The Shedd is a city treasure and well deserving of its title as world's largest indoor aquarium. A mix of standard aquarium tanks and elaborate new habitats, this marble octagon building is filled with thousands of denizens of river, lake, and sea. The only problem with the Shedd is its steep admission price. You can keep your costs down by buying the "Aquarium Only" admission, but then you'll be missing some of the most stunning exhibits.

The first thing you'll see as you enter is the **Caribbean Coral Reef** ★. This 90,000-gallon circular tank occupies the beaux arts–style central rotunda, entertaining spectators who press up against the glass to ogle divers feeding nurse sharks, barracudas, stingrays, and a hawksbill sea turtle. New technology includes an enhanced sound system and a roving camera connected to video monitors mounted on the tank's periphery, which gives visitors close-ups of the animals inside. It's worth sticking around to catch one of the daily feedings, when a diver swims around the tank and (thanks to a microphone) talks about the species inside and their eating habits.

The exhibits surrounding the Caribbean coral reef re-create different marine habitats around the world. The best is *Amazon Rising: Seasons of the River* ★, a recreation of the Amazon basin that showcases far more than fish (although you'll get to see some sharp-toothed piranhas as well).

You'll pay extra to see the other Shedd highlights, but they're quite impressive, so I'd suggest shelling out for at least one. The *Oceanarium* ★★★, with a wall of windows revealing the lake outside, re-creates a Pacific Northwest coastal environment and creates a stunning optical illusion of one uninterrupted

---

Tips **Walker's Warning**

While Chicago is a great city to explore on foot, Lake Shore Drive is no place for pedestrians. People have been seriously injured and even killed attempting to dodge the traffic on this busy road. Near Grant Park, cross only in crosswalks at Jackson Boulevard or Randolph, East Monroe, or East Balbo drives, or by using the underpass on the Museum Campus. North of the river, utilize underpasses or bridges at East Ohio Street, Chicago Avenue, Oak Street, and North Avenue.

The Pride of Prairie Avenue

Prairie Avenue, south of the Loop, was the city's first "Gold Coast," and its most famous address is **Glessner House,** a must-see for anyone interested in architectural history. The only surviving Chicago building designed by Boston architect Henry Hobson Richardson, it represented a dramatic shift from traditional Victorian architecture when it was built in 1886 (and inspired a young Frank Lloyd Wright).

The imposing granite exterior gives the home a forbidding air (railway magnate George Pullman, who lived nearby, complained, "I do not know what I have ever done to have that thing staring me in the face every time I go out my door."). But step inside, and the home turns out to be a welcoming, cozy retreat, filled with Arts and Crafts furnishings. For an illustration of the Glessner House exterior, see "Richardsonian Romanesque (1870–1900)," on p. 14.

Visits to Glessner House are by guided tour only. Tours are given Wednesday through Sunday at 1, 2, and 3pm year-round (except major holidays). Tours are first-come, first-served, with no advance reservations except for groups of 10 or more. 1800 S. Prairie Ave. ✆ **312/326-1480.** www.glessnerhouse.org. $7 adults, $6 students and seniors, $4 children 5 to 12. Bus: No. 1, 3, or 4 from Michigan Avenue at Jackson Boulevard (get off at 18th St.).

expanse of sea. On a fixed performance schedule in a large pool flanked by an amphitheater, a crew of friendly trainers puts dolphins through their paces of leaping dives, breaches, and tail walking. Check out the Oceanarium schedule as soon as you get to the Shedd; seating space fills up quick for the shows, so you'll want to get there early. If you're visiting during a summer weekend, you may also want to buy your Oceanarium ticket in advance to made sure you can catch a show that day. The newest signature exhibit is *Wild Reef—Sharks at Shedd* 👍👍, a series of 26 interconnected habitats that house a Philippine coral reef patrolled by sharks and other predators. The floor-to-ceiling windows bring those toothy swimmers up close and personal (they even swim over your head at certain spots).

If you want a quality sit-down meal in a restaurant with a spectacular view of Lake Michigan, check out Soundings, right there inside the aquarium.

Allow 2 to 3 hours.

1200 S. Lake Shore Dr. ✆ **312/939-2438.** www.sheddaquarium.org. All-Access Pass (to all exhibits) $21 adults, $15 seniors and children 3–11; admission to aquarium and either *Oceanarium* or *Wild Reef,* $17 adults, $13 seniors and children 3–11; aquarium only $8 adults, $6 children and seniors. Free admission to aquarium Mon and Tues Oct–Feb. Summer Fri–Wed 9am–6pm, Thurs 9am–10pm; fall–spring Mon–Fri 9am–5pm, Sat–Sun 9am–6pm. Bus: No. 6, 10, 12, 130, or 146.

3 North of the Loop: The Magnificent Mile & Beyond

North of the Chicago River are a number of attractions you should not overlook, including several museums and buildings, the city's greatest park, a zoo, and one of the world's most impressive research libraries. Most of these sites are either on the Magnificent Mile (North Michigan Ave.) and its surrounding blocks or not too far from there, on the Near North Side.

The Hancock Observatory ★★   While not as famous as the Sears Tower, for many locals the Hancock remains the archetypal Chicago skyscraper, with its bold, tapered shape and exterior steel cross-bracing design. The Hancock Observatory delivers an excellent panorama of the city and an intimate view over nearby Lake Michigan and the various shoreline residential areas. The view from the top of Chicago's third-tallest building is enough to satisfy, but some high-tech additions to the experience include "talking telescopes" with sound effects and narration in four languages, history walls illustrating the growth of the city, and the Skywalk open-air viewing deck—a "screened porch" that allows visitors to feel the rush of the wind at 1,000 feet. On a clear day you can see portions of the three states surrounding this corner of Illinois (Michigan, Indiana, and Wisconsin), for a radius of 40 to 50 miles. The view up the North Side is particularly dramatic, stretching from the nearby Oak Street and North Avenue beaches, along the green strip of Lincoln Park, to the line of high-rises you can trace up the shoreline until they suddenly halt just below the boundary of the northern suburbs. A high-speed elevator carries passengers to the observatory in 40 seconds, and the entrance and observatory are accessible for people with disabilities. Allow 1 hour.

"Big John," as it's referred to by some locals, also has a sleek restaurant, the Signature Room at the 95th, with an adjoining lounge. For about the same cost as the observatory, you can take in the views from the latter with a libation in hand.

94th floor of the John Hancock Center, 875 N. Michigan Ave. (enter on Delaware St.). © **888/875-VIEW** or 312/751-3681. Fax 312/751-3675. www.hancock-observatory.com. Admission $9.75 adults, $7.75 seniors, $6 children 5–12, free for children under 4 and military personnel in uniform or with active-duty cards. Daily 9am–11pm. Bus: No. 125, 145, 146, 147, or 151. Subway/El: Red Line to Chicago/State.

Museum of Contemporary Art ★★   The MCA claims to be the largest contemporary art museum in the country, emphasizing experimentation in a variety of media—painting, sculpture, photography, video and film, dance, music, and performance. But much of the space seems to be taken up with theaters and hallways; seeing the actual art won't take you long. Sitting on a front-row piece of property between the lake and the historic Water Tower, the gloomy, imposing building (designed by Berlin's Josef Paul Kleihues) looks like something out of Communist Russia, but the interior spaces are more vibrant, with a sun-drenched two-story central corridor, elliptical staircases, and three floors of exhibition space. The MCA has tried to raise its national profile to the level of New York's Museum of Modern Art by hosting major touring retrospectives of working artists such as Cindy Sherman and Chuck Close.

You can see the MCA's highlights in about an hour, although art lovers will want more time to wander (especially if a high-profile exhibit is in town). Your first stop should be the handsome barrel-vaulted galleries on the top floor, dedicated to pieces from the permanent collection. For visitors who'd like a little

---

Moments **Summer Solstice**

If you're here in mid-June, don't miss the **Museum of Contemporary Art's** annual **Summer Solstice** celebration (© **312/280-2660**), a 24-hour festival of contemporary art and music. During the daylight hours, there are plenty of hands-on activities for kids; after dark, the museum turns into an avant-garde nightclub. After a night of nonstop performances, soak in the sunrise over the lake before crashing back at your hotel.

> **Fun Fact** Rock Around the World
>
> The impressive, gothic **Tribune Tower,** just north of the Chicago River on
> the east side of Michigan Avenue, is home to one of the country's media
> giants and the *Chicago Tribune* newspaper. But it's also notable for an
> array of architectural fragments jutting out from the exterior. The collec-
> tion was started shortly after the building's completion in 1925 by the
> newspaper's notoriously despotic publisher, Robert R. McCormick, who
> gathered them during his world travels. *Tribune* correspondents then
> began supplying building fragments that they acquired on assignment.
> Each one now bears the name of the structure and country whence it
> came. There are 138 pieces in all, including chunks and shards from the
> Great Wall of China, the Taj Mahal, the White House, the Arc de Triom-
> phe, the Berlin Wall, the Roman Colosseum, London's Houses of Parlia-
> ment, the Great Pyramid of Cheops in Giza, Egypt, and the original tomb
> of Abraham Lincoln in Springfield, IL.

guidance for making sense of the rather challenging works found here, there is
an audio tour for rent as well as a free tour (1 and 6pm Tues; 1pm Wed–Fri;
11am, noon, 1, and 2pm Sat–Sun). In addition to a range of special activities
and educational programming, including films, performances, and a lecture
series in a 300-seat theater, the museum features Puck's at the MCA, a cafe operated by Wolfgang Puck of Spago restaurant fame, with seating that overlooks a
1-acre terraced sculpture garden. There's also a store, Culturecounter, with one-
of-a-kind gift items, that's worth a stop even if you don't make it into the
museum. The museum's First Fridays program, featuring after-hours performances, live music, and food and drink, takes place the first Friday of every
month. Allow 1 to 2 hours.

220 E. Chicago Ave. (1 block east of Michigan Ave.). © 312/280-2660. Fax 312/397-4095. www.mca
chicago.org. Admission $10 adults, $6 seniors and students with ID, free for children under 12. Free admission on Tues. Tues 10am–8pm; Wed–Sun 10am–5pm. Bus: No. 3, 10, 11, 66, 125, 145, 146, or 151. Subway/El:
Red Line to Chicago/State.

Navy Pier ★ *Kids* Built during World War I, this 3,000-foot-long pier was
used by the Navy during World War II as a training center for pilots. But any
military aura is long gone, now that the place has been transformed into a
bustling tourist mecca. A combination of carnival, food court, and boat dock,
the pier makes a fun place to stroll (if you don't mind crowds), but you'll have
to walk all the way to the end to get the best views back to the city.

Midway down the pier are the Crystal Gardens, with 70 full-size palm trees,
dancing fountains, and other flora in a glass-enclosed atrium; a white-canopied
open-air Skyline Stage that hosts concerts, dance performances, and film screenings; a carousel; and a 15-story Ferris wheel that's a replica of the original that
debuted at Chicago's 1893 World's Fair. The 50 acres of pier and lakefront property also are home to the **Chicago Children's Museum** (p. 208), a **3D IMAX
theater** (© 312/595-5629), a small ice-skating rink, and the **Chicago Shakespeare Theatre** (p. 254). The shops tend to be bland and touristy (except for
independently owned Barbara's Bookstore [p. 236]). Dining options include a
food court, an outpost of Lincoln Park's popular Charlie's Ale House, and the
white-tablecloth seafood restaurant Riva. You also find a beer garden with live

music; Joe's Be-Bop Cafe & Jazz Emporium (run by Joe and Wayne Segal of Jazz Showcase fame); a Southern-style barbecue restaurant with live music nightly; and Bubba Gump Shrimp Co. & Market, a casual family seafood joint. Summer is one long party at the pier, with fireworks on Wednesday and Saturday evenings.

The **Smith Museum of Stained Glass Windows** may sound rather dull, but decorative art aficionados shouldn't miss this remarkable installation of more than 150 stained-glass windows set in illuminated display cases. Occupying an 800-foot-long expanse on the ground floor of Navy Pier, the free museum features works by Frank Lloyd Wright, Louis Sullivan, John LaFarge, and Louis Comfort Tiffany.

Navy Pier hosts a variety of conventions and trade shows, including an international art exposition in May, pro-tennis exhibitions, and a flower and garden show. There's something for everyone, but the commercialism of the place might be too much for some people. If that's the case for you, take the half-mile stroll to the end of the pier, east of the ballroom, where you can find a little respite and enjoy the wind, the waves, and the city view, which is the real delight of a place like this. Or unwind in **Olive Park,** a small sylvan haven with a sliver of beach that lies just to the north of Navy Pier.

You'll find, moored along the south dock, more than half a dozen different sailing vessels, including a couple of dinner cruise ships, the pristine white-masted tall ship *Windy,* and the 70-foot speedboats *Seadog I, II,* and *III.* In the summer months, water taxis speed between Navy Pier and other Chicago sights. For more specifics on sightseeing and dinner cruises, see "Lake & River Cruises" on p. 210. Allow 1 hour.

600 E. Grand Ave. (at Lake Michigan). ✆ **800/595-PIER** (outside 312 area code), or 312/595-PIER. www.navypier.com. Free admission. Summer Sun–Thurs 10am–10pm, Fri–Sat 10am–midnight; fall–spring Mon–Sat 10am–10pm, Sun 10am–7pm. Bus: No. 29, 56, 65, 66, 120, or 121. Parking: Rates start at $9.50 for the 1st hr. and go up to $17.50 for up to 8 hr. However, the lots fill quickly. Valet parking is $7 with a restaurant validation. There are also surface lots west of the pier, and free trolley buses make stops on Grand Ave. and Illinois St. from State St. Subway/El: Red Line to Grand/State; transfer to city bus or board a free pier trolley bus.

Newberry Library   The Newberry Library is a bibliophile's dream. Established in 1887 at the bequest of the Chicago merchant and financier Walter Loomis Newberry, the noncirculating research library today contains many rare books and manuscripts (such as Shakespeare's 1st folio and Jefferson's copy of *The Federalist Papers*), housed in a comely five-story granite building. The library is also a major destination for genealogists digging at their roots, with holdings that are open free to the public (over the age of 16 with a photo ID). The collections include more than 1.5 million volumes and 75,000 maps, many of which are displayed during an ongoing series of public exhibitions. For an overview, take a free 1-hour tour Thursday at 3pm or Saturday at 10:30am. The Newberry also sponsors a series of concerts (including those by its resident early music ensemble, the Newberry Consort), lectures, and children's story hours throughout the year, and operates a fine bookstore. One popular annual event is the Bughouse Square debates. Held across the street in Washington Square Park, the debates re-create the fiery soapbox orations of the left-wing agitators in the 1930s and 1940s. Chicago's favorite son Studs Terkel, the Pulitzer Prize–winning oral historian, often emcees the hullabaloo. Allow a half-hour.

60 W. Walton St. (at Dearborn Pkwy.). ✆ **312/943-9090** or 312/255-3700 for programs. www.newberry.org. Reading room Tues–Thurs 10am–6pm; Fri–Sat 9am–5pm. Bus: No. 22, 36, 125, 145, 146, 147, or 151. Subway/El: Red Line to Chicago/State. Validated parking available at Clark and Chestnut sts.

Terra Museum of American Art ✦ *Finds*   Sandwiched between high-rises on
North Michigan Avenue, in the heart of the city's most prestigious retail district,
the Terra's narrow rectangular building is passed without so much as a glance by
droves of shoppers making a beeline for Crate & Barrel or Water Tower Place.
But this unique art repository is well worth a visit.

The core of the Terra's holdings was originally the private collection of Daniel
Terra, a wealthy industrialist and rainmaker for Ronald Reagan who founded his
eponymous museum in north-suburban Evanston in 1980. Moved to the present location in 1987, its excellent collection has grown to include some 700
pieces of American art from the late 18th century to the present. (Another 200
works reside at the Terra's sister museum, Musée d'Art Américain, in Giverny,
France.) Many of the paintings and prints, and a limited number of sculptures,
on display are by American artists whose names will assuredly draw a blank—
but that's part of the Terra's appeal. The other part is coming across works by
household names such as Mary Cassatt, Winslow Homer, Andrew Wyeth, John
Singer Sargent, James McNeill Whistler, and Edward Hopper. The museum is
particularly known for its outstanding American Impressionism collection. And,
from time to time, the Terra can bowl you over with a truly stellar traveling
exhibition, so it's worth checking out the museum's website before you come to
town. Allow 1 hour.

664 N. Michigan Ave. (near Erie St.). ✆ 312/664-3939. Fax 312/664-2052. www.terramuseum.org. Admission $5 adults; $3.50 seniors, students, educators; free for children under 12 and veterans with valid ID. Free
admission on Tues, Thurs, and 1st Sun of each month. Tues 10am–8pm; Wed–Sat 10am–6pm; Sun noon–5pm.
Bus: No. 3, 11, 125, 145, 146, 147, or 151. Subway/El: Red Line to Grand/State or Chicago/State.

4 Lincoln Park Attractions

Lincoln Park is the city's largest park, and certainly one of the longest. Straight
and narrow, Lincoln Park begins at North Avenue and follows the shoreline of
Lake Michigan northward for several miles. Within its elongated 1,200 acres are
a world-class zoo, a half-dozen bathing beaches, a botanical conservatory, two
excellent museums, a golf course, and the usual meadows, formal gardens, sporting fields, and tennis courts typical of urban parks. To get to the park, take bus
no. 22, 145, 146, 147, 151, or 156.

The **statue of the standing Abraham Lincoln** (just north of the North Ave.
and State St. intersection) in the park that bears his name is one of two in
Chicago by Augustus Saint-Gaudens (the seated Lincoln is in Grant Park).
Saint-Gaudens also did the Bates Fountain near the conservatory.

Cafe Brauer   This landmark 1900 building, a fine example of Chicago's
Prairie School of architecture, is not technically open to the public, except for a
cafe and ice-cream parlor on the ground floor. But the Great Hall on the second
floor, flanked by two curving loggias, is one of the city's most popular wedding
reception spots, so if you stop by on a weekend, chances are you can sneak a
peek while the caterers are setting up. Even if you don't make it inside, Cafe
Brauer makes a nice stopping-off point during a walk around the park. Sit and
sip a coffee, or rent a paddleboat at the edge of the lovely South Pond ($10 per
half-hr.). Best of all, though, is the picture-postcard view from the adjacent
bridge spanning the pond of the John Hancock Center and neighboring skyscrapers beyond Lincoln Park's treetops. Allow a quarter-hour, longer for a paddleboat ride.

2021 Stockton Dr. ✆ 312/742-2400. Daily 10am–5pm. Bus: No. 151 or 156.

Chicago Historical Society ✿   At the southwestern tip of Lincoln Park stands one of Chicago's oldest cultural institutions (founded in 1856), but one that has successfully brought its exhibits into the 21st century. Inside the Historical Society's lovely redbrick and glass-walled building, you'll find well-designed displays of significant objects, artifacts, and artwork—but the overall effect is instructive rather than interactive (this isn't the place to bring young children).

Casual visitors can get a good overview of the highlights in about an hour; history buffs will need more time. The must-see permanent exhibit is *A House Divided: America in the Age of Lincoln* ✿✿, which explores the institution of slavery in America and the devastation of the Civil War (items on display include the bed that Lincoln died in and an original copy of the 13th amendment abolishing slavery, signed by Honest Abe himself). Another highlight is the CHS's **costume collection** ✿, which includes clothing worn by George Washington, John Adams, and, of more current vintage, one of Michael Jordan's uniforms, along with numerous gowns by contemporary fashion designers (pieces from the collection are displayed on a rotating basis). Other worthy stops are the Charles F. Murphy **architectural study center,** featuring one of the nation's largest collections of architectural working drawings; the decorative and industrial-arts collection, including stained-glass designs by Frank Lloyd Wright and Louis Sullivan; and *We the People,* a permanent exhibit that explores how "ordinary people" founded the United States. (After your visit, head a few blocks away to North Ave. Beach, the best beach in the city, and or wander the neighboring residential streets of the exclusive Gold Coast.)

The Historical Society also sponsors lectures, symposia, and seminars; film screenings; family programs; historical reenactments and performances by local theater companies; and music concerts on the beautiful plaza overlooking Lincoln Park. On the ground floor of the museum, past the gift shop, is Big Shoulders Cafe, entered through a flora- and fauna-decorated terra-cotta arch removed from the old Stockyard Bank and reassembled here. The museum's website is worth checking out before your visit, especially the impressive online "exhibit" on the Great Chicago Fire. Allow 1 to 2 hours.

1601 N. Clark St. (at North Ave.). ✆ **312/642-4600.** www.chicagohistory.org. Admission $5 adults, $3 seniors and students, $1 children 6–12, free for children under 6. Free admission on Mon. Mon–Sat 9:30am–4:30pm; Sun 12–5pm. Research center Tues–Sat 10am–4:30pm. Bus: No. 11, 22, 36, 72, 151, or 156.

The Elks Veterans Memorial   Combine your trip to the Lincoln Park Zoo or Nature Museum with a friendly 30-minute tour of the Elks Memorial, an architectural gem just a short walk up Cannon Drive. As you step through the ornate 1,000-pound bronze doors, you'll be asked to sign the guest register. A quick peek at its pages reveals that, by far, the majority of your fellow visitors are out-of-state Elks.

First you'll be shown the rotunda, with its marble floors and columns fashioned from 26 kinds of marble from six countries. The 12 allegorical murals above your head are by American artist Eugene Savage. The 100-foot-high domed ceiling and the four statues, *Charity, Justice, Brotherly Love,* and *Fidelity,* by American sculptor James Earle Fraser, are adorned liberally with 24-carat gold leaf. As you move into the adjoining Grand Reception Room, check out the three panels in the entryway by Edwin Blashfield. The Reception Room itself is an opulent chamber softly illuminated by colored-glass overlay windows. Bold, imaginative murals by Savage cover the walls and ceilings. If this grandeur has piqued your interest in the doings of the Benevolent and Protective Order of Elks, proceed downstairs to the archives, where you'll find historical photographs, displays of pin-back buttons, and medals from the past hundred years or so. Especially charming is a series of miniature replicas of Elks Tournament of Roses Parade floats. Allow a half-hour.

2750 N. Lakeview Ave. (at Diversey Pkwy.). (✆) **773/755-4700.** Free admission. Open year-round Mon–Fri 9am–5pm; Apr 15–Nov 15 Sat–Sun 10am–5pm. Bus: No. 76, 151, 152, or 156.

Lincoln Park Conservatory ⭐ Just beyond the zoo's northeast border is a lovely botanical garden housed in a soaring glass-domed structure. Inside are four great halls filled with thousands of plants. If you're visiting Chicago in the wintertime, I can't think of a better prescription for mood elevation than the conservatory's lush haven of greenery. The Palm House features giant palms and rubber trees (including a 50-ft. fiddle leaf rubber tree dating from 1891), the Fernery nurtures plants that grow close to the forest floor, and the Tropical House is a shiny symphony of flowering trees, vines, and bamboo. The fourth environment is the Show House, where seasonal flower shows are held.

Even better than the plants inside, however, might be what lies outside the front doors. The expansive lawn with its French garden and lovely fountain on the conservatory's south side is one of the best places in town for an informal picnic (especially nice if you're visiting the zoo and want to avoid the congestion at its food concession venues).

The Lincoln Park Conservatory has a sister facility on the city's West Side, in Garfield Park, that is much more remarkable. In fact, the 2-acre **Garfield Park Conservatory,** 300 N. Central Park Ave. ((✆) **312/746-5100**), designed by the great landscape architect Jens Jensen in 1907, is one of the largest gardens under glass in the world. It's open 365 days a year from 9am to 5pm. Unfortunately, a rather blighted neighborhood with a high crime rate surrounds the conservatory. If you want to see it, I advise driving there and forgoing public transportation.

Allow a half-hour for the Lincoln Park Conservatory.

Fullerton Ave. (at Stockton Dr.). (✆) 312/742-7736. Free admission. Daily 9am–5pm. Bus: No. 73, 151, or 156.

Lincoln Park Zoo ⭐⭐⭐ *Value* This is one of Chicago's don't-miss attractions (especially if the weather is decent), and because it's free, it's worth at least a quick stop during a stroll through Lincoln Park. But you'll probably want to wander for a while. The term "zoological gardens" truly fits here: Landmark Georgian Revival brick buildings and modern structures sit among gently rolling pathways, verdant lawns, and a kaleidoscopic profusion of flower gardens. A complete tour of the various habitats takes all of 2 or 3 hours—a convenience factor even more enticing when you consider that the nation's oldest zoo (it was founded in 1868) stays open 365 days a year and is one of the last free zoos in the country. The late Marlon Perkins, legendary host of the *Mutual of Omaha's Wild Kingdom* TV series, got his start here as the zoo's director, and filmed a pioneering TV show called *Zoo Parade* (*Wild Kingdom*'s predecessor) in the basement of the old Reptile House.

The zoo has taken on an ambitious modernization campaign, which is good news for animal lovers. While many zoo residents used to wander listlessly in stark concrete pens, exhibits have been renovated and expanded to reflect natural habitats. For years, the zoo's star attraction has been the **Great Ape House** ⭐⭐⭐, which will reopen in the summer of 2004 after a complete renovation. Lincoln Park Zoo has had remarkable success breeding gorillas and chimpanzees, and watching these ape families interact can be mesmerizing (and touching). The new **Regenstein African Journey** ★★ is home to elephants, giraffes, rhinos, and other large mammals; large glass-enclosed tanks allow visitors to go face-to-face with swimming pygmy hippos and (not for the faint of heart) a rocky ledge filled with Madagascar hissing cockroaches.

The **Small Mammal–Reptile House** is a state-of-the-art facility, housing 200 species and featuring a glass-enclosed walk-through ecosystem simulating river, savanna, and forest habitats. The popular **Sea Lion Pool,** situated in the center of the zoo and home to harbor seals, gray seals, and California sea lions, features an underwater viewing area spanning 70 feet and an updated amphitheater. If you're here for a while and need nourishment, the Park Place Café is a food court located in a historic building that originally was Chicago's first aquarium. The Mahon Theobold Pavilion features a sprawling indoor gift shop and a unique rooftop eatery called Big Cats Café that opens at 8am (1 hr. before the exhibits do) and serves fresh-baked muffins and scones, focaccia sandwiches, salads, and flatbreads.

Allow 2 to 3 hours. For the adjoining children's zoo, see "Kid Stuff," on p. 208.

2200 N. Cannon Dr. (at Fullerton Pkwy.). © **312/742-2000.** www.lpzoo.com. Free admission. Year-round Mon–Fri 10am–5pm, grounds open at 9am; fall–spring Sat–Sun 10am–6:30pm. Bus: No. 151 or 156. Free trolley service from area CTA stations and parking garages on Sat–Sun and holidays 11am–7pm.

Peggy Notebaert Nature Museum ★ *Kids*   Built into the rise of an ancient sand dune—once the shoreline of Lake Michigan—Chicago's newest museum bills itself as "an environmental museum for the 21st century." Throughout, the focus is on interactivity, making this a good stop for active kids.

Shaded by huge cottonwoods and maples, the sand-colored exterior with its horizontal lines composed of interlocking trapezoids itself resembles a sand dune. Rooftop-level walkways give strollers a view of birds and other urban wildlife below. Paths wind through gardens planted with native Midwestern wildflowers and grasses, and trace the shore of the newly restored North Pond.

Inside, large windows create a dialogue between the outdoor environment and the indoor exhibits designed to illuminate it. Don't miss the **Butterfly Haven** ★★, a greenhouse habitat where about 25 Midwestern species of butterflies and moths carry on their complex life cycles (wander through as a riot of color flutters all around you). Another top exhibit is **City Science** ★, a 3,000-square-foot, two-story "house" with functional rooms where visitors can view the pipes and ducts that connect our homes with power sources miles away. **Water Lab** is a model river system demonstrating the uses and abuses that a waterway undergoes as it meanders from rural to urban environments. It's probably safe to say that the **Children's Gallery** is the only place in town where kids

---

⌒*Moments* **A Great View**

After a visit to the Lincoln Park Zoo or the Peggy Notebaert Nature Museum, take a quick stroll on Fullerton Avenue to the bridge that runs over the lagoon (just before you get to Lake Shore Dr.). Standing on the south side of Fullerton Avenue, you'll have a great view of the Chicago skyline and Lincoln Park—an excellent backdrop for family souvenir photos. This path can get very crowded on summer weekends, so I suggest trying this photo op during the week.

can clamber in and out of a model ground-squirrel town or explore a beaver lodge from the inside.

The sunny Butterfly Cafe offers fresh, healthy meals cafeteria-style. In summer, get there early to enjoy coffee and a muffin—and the lovely surroundings—with joggers and other locals.

Allow 1 hour.

Fullerton Ave. and Cannon Dr. © 773/871-2668. www.chias.org. Admission $7 adults, $5 seniors and students, $4 children ages 3–12, free for children under 3. Mon–Fri 9am–4:30pm; Sat–Sun 10am–5pm. Closed Thanksgiving, Dec 25, and Jan 1. Bus: No. 151 or 156.

5 Exploring Hyde Park: The Museum of Science and Industry & More

Birthplace of atomic fission, home to the University of Chicago, and site of the popular Museum of Science and Industry, Hyde Park is worth a trip south of the Loop. You should allow at least half a day to explore the campus and neighborhood, one of Chicago's most successfully integrated; set aside a full day if you want to explore museums as well.

SOME HYDE PARK HISTORY   When Hyde Park was settled in 1850, it became Chicago's first suburb. A hundred years later, in the 1950s, Hyde Park added another first to its impressive resume, one that the current neighborhood is not particularly proud of: an urban-renewal plan. At the time, a certain amount of old commercial and housing stock was demolished rather than rehabilitated— just those kinds of buildings that would be much prized today—and was replaced by projects and small shopping malls that actually make some corners of Hyde Park look more suburban, in the modern sense, than they really are.

What Hyde Park does have to be proud of is that, in racially balkanized Chicago, this neighborhood has found an alternative vision. As Southern blacks began to migrate to Chicago's South Side during World War I, many whites fled. But most whites here, especially those who wanted to stay near the university, chose integration as the only realistic strategy to preserve their neighborhood. The 2000 census proved that integration still works; about 40% of the residents are white and 37% are black; there is also a significant Asian population. Hyde Park is decidedly middle-class, with pockets of true affluence in Kenwood that reflect the days when the well-to-do moved here in the beginning of the 20th century to escape the decline of Prairie Avenue. Among Hyde Park–Kenwood's well-known black residents in recent years were the late Elijah Muhammad, Muhammad Ali, and, currently, Louis Farrakhan, along with numerous other Nation of Islam families who continue to worship in a mosque, formerly a Greek Orthodox cathedral, that is one of the neighborhood's architectural landmarks. The late Mayor Harold Washington also lived here. Surrounding this unusual enclave, however, are many marginal blocks where poverty and slum housing abound. For all its nobility, Hyde Park's achievement in integration merely emphasizes that even more unwieldy than racial differences are socioeconomic ones.

Through its fight for self-preservation, Hyde Park has gained a reputation as an activist community. A certain vitality springs from acts of coping with the world as you find it, and it is this element that distinguishes Hyde Park from other middle-class neighborhoods in Chicago. Hyde Park is, in a word, cosmopolitan.

The University of Chicago is widely hailed as one of the more intellectually exciting institutions of higher learning in the country and has been home to

Hyde Park Attractions

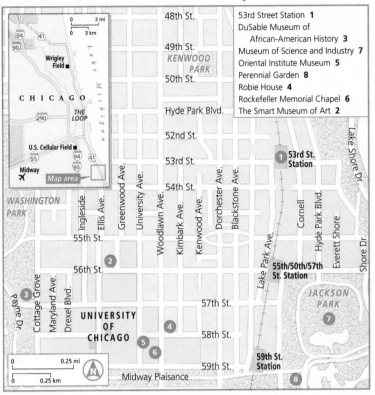

some 73 Nobel laureates. The year the university opened its doors, 1892, was a big one for Hyde Park, but 1893 was even bigger. In that year, Chicago, chosen over other cities in a competitive international field, hosted the World's Columbian Exposition, commemorating the 400th anniversary of Columbus's arrival in America.

To create a fairground, the landscape architect Frederick Law Olmsted was enlisted to fill in the marshlands along Hyde Park's lakefront and link what was to become Jackson Park to existing Washington Park on the neighborhood's western boundary with a narrow concourse called the Midway Plaisance. On the resulting 650 acres—at a cost of $30 million—12 exhibit palaces, 57 buildings devoted to U.S. states and foreign governments, and dozens of smaller structures were constructed under the supervision of architect Daniel Burnham. Most of the buildings followed Burnham's preference for the Classical Revival style and exterior surfaces finished in white stucco. With the innovation of outdoor electric lighting, the sparkling result was the "White City," which attracted 27 million visitors in a single season, running from May 1 to October 31, 1893. The exposition sponsors, in that brief time, had remarkably recovered their investment, but within a few short years of its closing, most of the fair's buildings were destroyed by vandalism and fire. Only the Palace of Fine Arts, occupying the eastern tip of the midway, survives to this day, and it now houses the Museum of Science and Industry.

Did You Know?

The world's first Ferris Wheel was built on Hyde Park's Midway during the World's Columbian Exposition in 1893. It was eventually dynamited and sold for scrap metal.

GETTING THERE   From the Loop, the ride to Hyde Park on the **no. 6 Jeffrey Express bus** takes about 30 minutes. The bus originates on Wacker Drive, travels south along State Street, and ultimately follows Lake Shore Drive to Hyde Park. The bus runs from early morning to late evening 7 days a week, with departures about every 5 minutes on weekdays and every 10 minutes on weekends and holidays. The southbound express bus adds a surcharge of 25¢ to the normal fare of $1.50 (there's no surcharge if you use a CTA transit card). The **no. 1 local bus** originates at Union Station on Jackson Boulevard and Canal Street and takes about an hour.

For a faster trip, take the **Metra Electric train** on the South Chicago line, which goes from downtown to Hyde Park in about 15 minutes. Trains run every hour (more frequently during rush hr.) Monday through Saturday from 5:15am to 12:50am, and every 30 to 90 minutes on Sunday and holidays from 5am to 12:55am. Downtown stations are at Randolph Street and Michigan Avenue, Van Buren Street and Michigan Avenue, and Roosevelt Road and Michigan Avenue (near the Museum Campus in Grant Park). Printed schedules are available at the stations. The fare is approximately $2 each way.

For CTA bus and Metra train information, call ✆ **836-7000** (from any city or suburban area code).

For taxis, dial ✆ **312/TAXI-CAB** (✆ 312/829-4222) for **Yellow Cab** or ✆ **312/CHECKER** (✆ 312/243-2537) for **Checker.** The one-way fare from downtown is around $15.

A SUGGESTED ITINERARY   A long 1-day itinerary for Hyde Park should include the following: a walk through the U of C campus (including a stroll along the Midway Plaisance); a visit to the Museum of Science and Industry (for families), Frank Lloyd Wright's Robie House, or one of the other local museums; and lunch or dinner in the neighborhood's commercial center.

THE TOP ATTRACTIONS

DuSable Museum of African-American History   The DuSable Museum is a repository of the history, art, and artifacts pertaining to the African-American experience and culture. Named for Chicago's first permanent settler, Jean Baptiste Point du Sable, a French-Canadian of Haitian descent, it is admirable not so much for its collections and exhibits as for the inspiring story behind its existence. Founded in 1961 with a $10 charter and minimal capital, the museum began in the home of Dr. Margaret Burroughs, an art teacher at the city's Du Sable High School. In 1973, as a result of a community-based campaign, the museum took up residence in its present building (a former parks administration facility and police lockup) on the eastern edge of Washington Park. With no major endowment to speak of, the DuSable Museum has managed to accumulate a respectable collection of more than 13,000 artifacts, books, photographs, art objects, and memorabilia. Its collection of paintings, drawings, and sculpture by African-American and African artists is excellent.

In 1993, the DuSable Museum added a 25,000-square-foot wing named in honor of the city's first and only African-American mayor, Harold Washington. The permanent exhibit on Washington contains memorabilia and personal effects, and surveys important episodes in his political career. More recent is a permanent exhibit called *Blacks in Aviation,* which celebrates the achievements of the legendary Tuskegee Airmen and features such items as the flight jacket of Major Robert H. Lawrence, the nation's first African-American astronaut.

The museum also has a gift shop, a research library, and an extensive program of community-related events, such as a jazz and blues music series, poetry readings, film screenings, and other cultural events, all of which are presented in a 466-seat auditorium. Allow 1 to 2 hours.

740 E. 56th Place. (℃) 773/947-0600. www.dusablemuseum.org. Admission $3 adults, $2 students and seniors, $1 children 6–12, free for children under 6. Free admission Sun. Mon–Fri 10am–5pm; Sat–Sun noon–5pm. Closed Thanksgiving, Dec 25, and Jan 1. Bus: No. 3, 4, or 55. Subway/El: Red Line to 55th or 63rd in Washington Park.

The Museum of Science and Industry ★★★ *Kids*   Even if you don't plan on spending the day in Hyde Park, you'll pass through the neighborhood on your way to one of Chicago's most popular tourist attractions. The massive Museum of Science and Industry is the granddaddy of interactive museums, with some 2,000 exhibits. You should plan on spending at least a couple of hours here, and a comprehensive visit can take all day, especially if you catch an Omnimax movie while you're here. Although it's quite a distance from the rest of Chicago's tourist attractions, it's easy enough to get here without a car; your best options are the no. 6 Jeffrey Express bus or the Metra Electric train from downtown (the no. 10 bus runs from downtown to the museum's front entrance during the summer).

While the museum is constantly adding new exhibits to cover the latest scientific breakthroughs, you shouldn't miss certain tried-and-true exhibits that have been here for years and epitomize the museum for Chicagoans. The **U-505** ★★★, a German submarine that was captured in 1944 and brought to the museum 10 years later, brings home the claustrophobic reality of underwater naval life. The full-scale **Coal Mine** ★★, which dates back to 1934, now

---

Tips   Hyde Park Bites

When you're ready to take a break, Hyde Park has an eclectic selection of restaurants to choose from. As in any university town, you'll find plenty of affordable, student-friendly hangouts. The most famous University of Chicago gathering spot is **Jimmy's Woodlawn Tap** (p. 284), 1172 E. 55th St. (℃ 773/ 643-5516). This 50-year-old bar and grill doesn't offer much in the way of atmosphere (and be prepared for cigarette smoke), but the hamburgers and sandwiches are cheap, and the person sitting next you might just be a Nobel Prize-winning professor. Another casual spot near campus is **Medici,** 1327 E. 57th St. (℃ 773/667-7394), where a few generations' worth of students have carved their names into the tables while chowing down on pizza, the house specialty. **Calypso Café,** 5211 S. Harper St., near the Metra train tracks (℃ 773/955-0229), serves up conch chowder, jerk chicken, and other Caribbean favorites in a bright, funky setting. A few blocks south, you'll find **La Petite Folie,** 1504 E. 55th St. (℃ 773/493-1394), a French bistro that offers refined escape from student life.

incorporates modern mining techniques into the exhibit—but the best part is the simulated trip down into a dark, mysterious mine. Get to these exhibits quickly after the museum opens because they attract amusement-park-length lines during the day.

Kids who love planes, trains, and automobiles shouldn't miss *All Aboard the Silver Streak,* a refurbished Burlington Pioneer Zephyr train with on-board interactive exhibits; the massive model train exhibit that makes up *The Great Train Story;* or *Take Flight,* an aviation exhibit featuring a full-size 727 airplane that revs up its engines and replays the voice recordings from a San Francisco–Chicago flight periodically throughout the day. Computer addicts should be entranced by **Networld,** which offers a flashy immersion into the Internet (with plenty of interactive screens). More low-tech—but fascinating—is the giant walk-through **model of the human heart** ⌀. Well-designed educational exhibits include *AIDS: The War Within* (which was the 1st permanent museum exhibit on the immune system and HIV) and *Reusable City,* which teaches children ecological tips with implements that they might find in their own backyard. Older children with a creative streak will enjoy *Enterprise,* which lets visitors take on the role of CEO for a day as they immerse themselves in the goings-on of a virtual company.

And, not to be sexist, but girls (myself included) love **Colleen Moore's Fairy Castle** ⌀, a lavishly decorated miniature palace filled with priceless treasures (yes, those are real diamonds and pearls in the chandeliers). The castle is hidden away on the lower level. Also tucked away in an inconspicuous spot—along the Blue stairwell between the Main Floor and the Balcony—are the *Human Body Slices,* actual slivers of human cadavers that are guaranteed to impress teenagers in search of something truly gross.

A major newer addition to the museum is the **Henry Crown Space Center** ⌀⌀, where the story of space exploration is documented in copious detail, highlighted by a simulated space-shuttle experience through sight and sound at the center's five-story Omnimax Theater. The theater offers double features on the weekends; call for show times.

When you've worked up an appetite, you can visit one of the museum's five restaurants, including a Pizza Hut and an ice-cream parlor, and there are also two gift shops. Allow 3 hours.

57th St. and Lake Shore Dr. ⌀ **800/468-6674** outside the Chicago area, 773/684-1414, or TTY 773/684-3323. www.msichicago.org. Admission to museum only, $9 adults, $7.50 seniors, $5 children 3–11, free for children under 3. Free admission Mon and Tues Sept 15–Nov 25 and Jan–Feb. Combination museum and Omnimax Theater $15 adults, $12.50 seniors, $10 children 3–11, free for children under 3 on an adult's lap. Omnimax Theater only, evening shows $10 adults, $8 seniors, $6 children, free for children under 3 on an adult's lap. Mon–Sat 9:30am–4pm, Sun 11am–4pm. Closed Christmas. Bus: No. 6, 10, 55, 151, or 156.

Oriental Institute Museum ⌀⌀ *Finds*   Near the midpoint of the campus, a few blocks from Rockefeller Memorial Chapel, is the Oriental Institute, housing one of the world's major collections of Near Eastern art. This is no dry, dusty academic retreat, thanks to a major renovation and expansion that has enhanced all the exhibits and brought the galleries into the 21st century.

Your first stop should be the **Egyptian Gallery** ⌀⌀, which showcases the finest objects among the 35,000 artifacts from the Nile Valley held by the museum. At the center stands a monumental 17-foot solid-quartzite statue of King Tutankhamen, the boy king who ruled Egypt from about 1335 to 1324 B.C. The largest Egyptian sculpture in the Western Hemisphere (tipping the scales at 6 tons), Oriental Institute excavated it in 1930. The surrounding exhibits, which document the life and beliefs of Egyptians from 5000 B.C. to the 8th century A.D., have a wonderfully accessible approach that emphasizes themes, not chronology. Among them are: mummification (there are 14 mummies on display—five people and nine animals, including hawks, an ibis, a shrew, and a baby crocodile), kingship, society, and writing (including a deed for the sale of a house, a copy of the *Book of the Dead,* and a schoolboy's homework).

The Oriental Institute also houses the nation's premier archaeological collection of artifacts from civilizations that once flourished in what is now Iran on display in the **Persian Gallery** 🔎. The gallery displays approximately 1,000 objects dating from the Archaic Susiana Period (ca. 6800 B.C.) to the Islamic Period (ca. A.D. 1000). Other galleries are filled with artifacts from Sumer, ancient Palestine, Israel, Anatolia, Nubia, and Mesopotamia (including a re-creation of a royal courtyard of Assyrian King Sargon II).

The excellent gift shop, called the Suq, stocks many one-of-a-kind items, including reproductions of pieces in the museum's collection. Allow 2 hours.

1155 E. 58th St. (at University Ave.). Ⓒ 773/702-9514. www.oi.uchicago.edu. Free admission; suggested donation $5 adults, $2 children. Tues and Thurs–Sat 10am–4pm; Wed 10am–8:30pm; Sun noon–4pm. Bus: No. 6.

Robie House ⭐⭐   One of Frank Lloyd Wright's finest works, the Robie House is considered among the masterpieces of 20th-century American architecture. The open layout, linear geometry of form, and craftsmanship are typical of Wright's Prairie School design. Completed in 1909 for inventor Frederick Robie, a bicycle and motorcycle manufacturer, the home is also notable for its exquisite leaded- and stained-glass doors and windows. It's also among the last of his Prairie School–style homes: During its construction, Wright abandoned both his family and his Oak Park practice to follow other pursuits, most prominently the realization of his Taliesin home and studio in Spring Green, Wisconsin. Docents from Oak Park's Frank Lloyd Wright Home and Studio Foundation lead tours here, even though the house is undergoing a massive, 10-year restoration (the house will be open throughout the process, but your photos may include plenty of scaffolding). A Wright specialty bookshop is located in the building's former three-car garage—which was highly unusual for the time in which it was built. Allow 2 hours.

5757 S. Woodlawn Ave. (at 58th St.). Ⓒ 773/834-1847. Admission $9 adults, $7 seniors and children 7–18. Mon–Fri tours at 11am, 1pm, and 3pm; Sat–Sun every half-hr. 11am–3:30pm. Bookshop open daily 10am–5pm. Bus: No. 6.

Rockefeller Memorial Chapel   The Rockefeller Memorial Chapel is just across from Robie House. Did someone say chapel? This is false modesty, even for a Rockefeller. When the university first opened its doors, the students sang the following ditty:

> *John D. Rockefeller, wonderful man is he*
> *Gives all his spare change to the U of C.*

John D. was a generous patron, indeed. He founded the university (in cooperation with the American Baptist Society), built the magnificent mini-cathedral that now bears his name, and shelled out an additional $35 million in donations to the institution over the course of his lifetime. Designed by Bertram Goodhue, an architect known for his ecclesiastical buildings—including Cadet Chapel at West Point and New York City's St. Thomas Church—the Memorial Chapel was dedicated in 1928.

Finds **More Frank Lloyd Wright Homes**

In addition to Robie House, several of Wright's earlier works, still privately owned, dot the streets of Hyde Park, such as the **Heller House,** 5132 S. Woodlawn Ave. (1897); the **Blossom House,** 1332 E. 49th St. (1882); and the **McArthur House,** 4852 S. Kenwood Ave. (1892). *Note:* The above-named houses are not open to the public, so they should only be admired from the outside.

In keeping with the rest of the campus, which is patterned after Oxford, it is reminiscent of English Gothic structures but was built from limestone and with modern construction techniques. Its most outstanding features are the circular stained-glass window high above the main altar (the windows, in general, are among the largest of any church or cathedral anywhere) and the world's second-largest carillon, which was donated by John D. Rockefeller Jr. in 1932 in memory of his mother, Laura. The chapel's organ is nearly as impressive, with four manuals, 126 stops, and more than 10,000 pipes.

Choir concerts, carillon performances, and other musical programs are presented throughout the year, usually for a small donation. The building is open to the public; in-depth tours can be arranged through the university's Office of Special Events at (🕻 773/702-9636. Tours of the carillon are done during the academic year; call the office to find out times. Allow a half-hour.

5850 S. Woodlawn Ave. (🕻 773/702-2100. http://rockefeller.uchicago.edu. Free admission. Daily 8am–4pm (except during religious services). Bus: No. 6.

The Smart Museum of Art 🟊   The University of Chicago's fine arts museum looks rather modest, but it packs a lot of talent into a compact space. Its permanent collection of more than 7,000 paintings and sculptures spans Western and Eastern civilizations and ranges from classical antiquity to the present day. Bona fide treasures include ancient Greek vases, Chinese bronzes, and Old Master paintings; Frank Lloyd Wright furniture; Tiffany glass; sculptures by Degas, Matisse, and Rodin; and 20th-century paintings and sculptures by Mark Rothko, Arthur Dove, Mexican muralist Diego Rivera, Henry Moore, and Chicago sculptor Richard Hunt. Built in 1974, the contemporary building doesn't really fit in with the Gothic style of other campus buildings, but its sculpture garden and outdoor seating area make a nice place for quiet contemplation. The museum also has a gift shop and cafe. Allow 1 hour.

5550 S. Greenwood Ave. (at E. 55th St.). (🕻 773/702-0200. http://smartmuseum.uchicago.edu. Free admission; donations welcome. Tues–Wed and Fri 10am–4pm; Thurs 10am–8pm; Sat–Sun 11am–5pm. Closed holidays. Bus: No. 6.

EXPLORING THE UNIVERSITY OF CHICAGO

Walking around the Gothic spires of the University of Chicago campus is bound to conjure up images of the cloistered academic life. Allow at least an hour to stroll through the grassy quads and dramatic stone buildings (if the weather's nice, do as the students do and vegetate for a while on the grass). If you're visiting on a weekday, your first stop should be the university's **Visitors Information Desk** (🕻 773/702-9739), located on the first floor of Ida Noyes Hall, 1212 E. 59th St., where you can pick up campus maps and get information on university events. The center is open Monday through Friday from 10am to

7pm. The university also offers free architecture tours on Saturdays (paid tours can be arranged for other days); call the **Office of Special Events** (© **773/702-9636**). If you stop by on a weekend when the Visitors Information Desk is closed, you can get the scoop on campus events at the **Reynolds Clubhouse** student center (© **773/702-8787**).

Start your tour of the campus at the **Henry Moore statue,** *Nuclear Energy,* on South Ellis Avenue between 56th and 57th streets. It's next to the Regenstein Library, which marks the site of the old Stagg Field, where, on December 2, 1942, the world's first sustained nuclear reaction was achieved in a basement laboratory below the field. Then turn left at 57th Street until you reach the grand stone Hull Gate; walk straight to reach the main quad, or turn left through the column-lined arcade to reach **Hutchinson Court** (designed by John Olmsted, son of revered landscape designer Frederick Law Olmsted). The Reynolds Clubhouse, the university's main student center, is located here; you can take a break at the C-Shop cafe or settle down at a table at Hutchinson Commons, a dining room/hangout spot right next to the cafe which will bring to mind the grand dining halls of Oxford or Cambridge.

Other worthy spots on campus include the charming, intimate **Bond Chapel,** located behind Swift Hall on the main quad, and the blocks-long **Midway Plaisance,** a wide stretch of green that was the site of carnival sideshow attractions during the World's Columbian Exposition in 1893 (the term "midway" has been used ever since to refer to carnivals in general).

The **Seminary Co-op Bookstore,** 5757 S. University Ave. (© **773/752-4381;** www.semcoop.com), is a treasure trove of academic and scholarly books. Its selection of more than 100,000 titles has won it an international reputation as "the best bookstore west of Blackwell's in Oxford." It's open Monday through Friday from 8:30am to 9pm, Saturday from 10am to 6pm, and Sunday from noon to 6pm.

ENJOYING THE OUTDOORS IN HYDE PARK

Hyde Park is not only a haven for book lovers and culture aficionados—the community also has its open-air attractions. A number of worthy outdoor environments are located near Lake Michigan, including **Lake Shore Drive** itself, where many stately apartment houses follow the contour of the shoreline. A very suitable locale for a quiet stroll during the day is **Promontory Point,** at 55th Street and Lake Michigan, a bulb of land that juts into the lake and offers a good view of Chicago to the north and the seasonally active 57th Street beach to the south.

Farther south, just below the Museum of Science and Industry, is **Wooded Island** in Jackson Park, the site of the Japanese Pavilion during the Columbian Exposition and today a lovely garden of meandering paths. The **Perennial Garden** in Jackson Park is at 59th Street and Stony Island Avenue, where more than 180 varieties of flowering plants display a palette of colors that changes with the seasons.

6 More Museums

Chicago has a slew of smaller museums devoted to all manner of subjects. Many of their collections preserve the stories and heritage of a particular immigrant group that has become inseparable from the history of the city as a whole.

City Gallery 🔍   Along with the pumping station across the street, the Chicago Water Tower is one of only a handful of buildings to survive the Great Chicago Fire of 1871. It has long been a revered symbol of the city's resilience and fortitude, although today—more than 130 years after it first rose to a once-mighty height of 154 feet—the Water Tower is dwarfed by the high-rise shopping centers and hotels of North Michigan Avenue. The Gothic-style limestone building now has been reinvented as an art gallery. The spiffed-up interior is intimate and sunny, and it's a refreshing pit stop of culture on your way to the Water Tower shopping center or pumping-station tourist information center across the street. Exhibits have included works by Chicago-based photographer Victor Skrebneski. Allow a half-hour.

806 N. Michigan Ave. (between Chicago Ave. and Pearson St.). © **312/742-0808**. Free admission. Mon–Sat 10am–6:30pm; Sun 10am–5pm. Bus: No. 3, 11, 145, 146, 147, or 151.

Historic Pullman ★★   Railway magnate George Pullman may have been a fabulously wealthy industrialist, but he fancied himself more enlightened than his 19th-century peers. So when it came time to build a new headquarters for his Pullman Palace Car Company, he dreamed of something far more than the standard factory surrounded by tenements. Instead, he built a model community for his workers, a place where they could live in houses with indoor plumbing and abundant natural light—amenities almost unheard of for industrial workers in the 1880s. Pullman didn't do all this solely from the goodness of his heart; he hoped that the town named after him would attract the most skilled workers (who would be so happy that they wouldn't go on strike). As one of the first "factory towns," Pullman caused an international sensation and was seen as a model for other companies to follow. The happy workers that Pullman envisioned, however, did go on strike in 1894, frustrated by the company's control of every aspect of their lives.

Today, the Pullman district makes a fascinating stop for anyone with a historical or architectural bent. While many of the homes are private residences, a number of public buildings still stand (including the lavish Hotel Florence, the imposing Clock Tower, and the two-story colonnaded Market Hall). Although a fire damaged some buildings in the late 1990s, Pullman has thankfully been recognized as a unique historic site, and much-needed repairs are being finished up. You can walk through on your own during opening hours (stop by the Visitor Center for a map), or take a guided a tour at 12:30 or 1:30pm on the first Sunday of the month from May through October ($4 adults, $3.50 seniors).

11141 S. Cottage Grove Ave. © **773/785-8901**. www.pullmanil.org. Mon–Fri 12–2pm; Sat 11am–2pm; Sunday 12–3pm. Train: Metra Electric line to Pullman (111th St.), turn right on Cottage Grove Ave. and walk 1 block to the Visitor Center.

International Museum of Surgical Science ★ *Finds*   After you've done the Field Museum and the Art Institute, it might be time for something a little more offbeat. This unintentionally macabre shrine to medicine is my pick for the weirdest tourist attraction in town. Not for the faint of stomach, it is run by the International College of Surgeons and is housed in a historic 1917 Gold Coast mansion designed by the noted architect Howard Van Doren Shaw, who modeled it after Le Petit Trianon at Versailles. Displayed throughout its four floors are surgical instruments, paintings, and sculptures depicting the history of surgery and healing practices in Eastern and Western civilizations. The exhibits are old-fashioned (no interactive computer displays here!), but that's part of the museum's odd appeal.

You'll look at your doctor in a whole new way after viewing the trepanned skulls excavated from an ancient tomb in Peru. The accompanying tools were used to bore holes in patients' skulls, a horrific practice thought to release the evil spirits causing their illness (some skulls show signs of new bone growth, meaning that some lucky headache-sufferers actually survived this low-tech surgery). There are also battlefield amputation kits, a working iron-lung machine in the polio exhibit, and oddities such as a stethoscope designed to be transported inside a top hat. Other attractions include an apothecary shop and dentist's office (ca. 1900), re-created in a historic street exhibit, and the hyperbolically titled "Hall of Immortals," a sculpture gallery depicting 12 historic figures in medicine, from Hippocrates to Madame Curie.

1524 N. Lake Shore Dr. (between Burton Place and North Ave.). (ℂ) **312/642-6502**. www.imss.org. Admission $6 adults, $3 seniors and students. Free admission Tues. Tues–Sat 10am–4pm. Bus: No. 151.

Intuit: The Center for Intuitive and Outsider Art   Chicago is home to an active community of collectors of so-called "outsider art," a term attached to a group of unknown, unconventional artists who do their own artwork without any formal training or connection to the mainstream art world. Often called folk or self-taught artists, their work is highly personal and idiosyncratic, and they work in a range of media, from bottle caps to immense canvases. Intuit was founded in 1991 to bring attention to these artists through exhibitions and educational lectures. Housed in the warehouse district northwest of the Loop, with two galleries and a performance area, Intuit is slowly gaining a higher profile on the city's art scene. The museum offers a regular lecture series, and if you time your visit right, you might be here for one of the center's tours of a private local art collection. Guided tours of the museum are available at 1pm on the first Saturday of every month. Allow 1 hour.

756 N. Milwaukee Ave. (at Chicago and Ogden aves.). (ℂ) **312/243-9088**. http://outsider.art.org. Free admission. Wed–Sat noon–5pm. Bus: No. 56 or 66. Subway/El: Blue Line to Chicago.

Jane Addams Hull-House Museum   Three years after the Haymarket Riot, a young woman named Jane Addams bought an old mansion on Halsted Street that had been built in 1856 as a "country home" but was now surrounded by the shanties of the immigrant poor. Here, Addams and her co-worker, Ellen Gates Starr, launched the American settlement-house movement with the establishment of Hull House, an institution that endured on this site in Chicago until 1963. (It continues today as a decentralized social-service agency known as Hull House Association.) In that year, all but two of the settlement's 13 buildings, along with the entire residential neighborhood in its immediate vicinity, were demolished to make room for the new University of Illinois at Chicago campus, which now owns the museum buildings. Of the original settlement, what remain today are the Hull-House Museum, the mansion itself, and the residents' dining hall, snuggled among the ultramodern, poured-concrete buildings of the university campus. Inside are the original furnishings, Jane Addams's office, and numerous settlement maps and photographs. Rotating exhibits re-create the history of the settlement and the work of its residents, showing how Addams was able to help transform the dismal streets around her into stable inner-city environments worth fighting over. Allow a half-hour.

University of Illinois at Chicago, 800 S. Halsted St. (at Polk St.). (ℂ) **312/413-5353**. www.uic.edu/jaddams/ hull/hull_house. Free admission. Tues–Fri 10am–4pm; Sun noon–5pm. Bus: No. 8. Subway/El: Blue Line to Halsted/University of Illinois.

Mexican Fine Arts Center Museum ⭐ *Kids*   Chicago's vibrant Pilsen neighborhood, just southwest of the Loop, is home to one of the nation's largest Mexican-American communities. Ethnic pride emanates from every doorstep, taqueria, and bakery, and the multitude of colorful murals splashed across build-ing exteriors and alleyways. But this building, the largest Latino cultural insti-tution in the country, may be the neighborhood's most prized possession. That's quite an accomplishment, given that the Mexican Fine Arts Center Museum was founded in 1987 by a passel of public schoolteachers who pooled $900 to get it started.

This is truly a living museum. There are wonderful exhibits to be sure, show-casing Mexican and Mexican-American visual and performing artists, and often drawing on the museum's permanent collection of more than 2,400 works. But it's the visiting artists, festival programming, and community participation that make the museum really shine. Its Day of the Dead celebration, which runs for about 8 weeks beginning in September, is one of the most ambitious in the coun-try. The Del Corazon Mexican Performing Arts Festival, held in the spring, fea-tures programs by local and international artists here and around town. And the Sor Juana Festival, presented in the fall, honors Mexican writer and pioneering feminist Sor Juana Ines de la Cruz with photography and painting exhibits, music and theater performances, and poetry readings by Latino women.

The museum is very family oriented, offering a deluge of educational work-shops for kids and parents. It also has a splendid gift shop, and it stages a holi-day market, featuring items from Mexico, on the first weekend in December. Allow 1 hour.

1852 W. 19th St. (a few blocks west of Ashland Ave.). ℂ **312/738-1503.** www.mfacmchicago.org. Free admission. Tues–Sun 10am–5pm. Bus: No. 9. Subway/El: Blue Line to 18th St.

National Vietnam Veterans Art Museum ★★ *(Finds)* This museum houses one of the most stirring art collections anywhere—and the only one of its kind in the world—telling the story of the men who fought in Vietnam. Since the war, many of the veterans made art as personal therapy, never expecting to show it to anyone, but in 1981, a small group of them began showing their works together in Chicago and in touring exhibitions. The collection has grown to more than 700 paintings, drawings, photographs, and sculptures from all over the country and other countries, including Vietnam. Titles such as *We Regret to Inform You, Blood Spots on a Rice Paddy,* and *The Wound* should give you an idea of the power of the images in this unique legacy to the war. Housed in a former warehouse in the Prairie Avenue district south of the Loop, the museum is mod-ern and well organized. An installation suspended from the ceiling, ***Above & Beyond*** ✵, comprises more than 58,000 dog tags with the names of the men and women who died in the war—the emotional effect is similar to that of the Wall in Washington, D.C. The complex also houses a small theater, a cafe open for breakfast and lunch, a gift shop, and an outdoor plaza with a flagpole that has deliberately been left leaning because that's how veterans saw them in com-bat. Allow 1 hour.

1801 S. Indiana Ave. (at 18th St.). ℂ **312/326-0270.** www.nvvam.org. Admission $5 adults, $4 seniors and students with ID. Tues–Fri 11am–6pm; Sat 10am–5pm; Sun noon–5pm. Closed major holidays. Bus: No. 3 or 4.

Polish Museum of America One million people of Polish ancestry live in Chicago, giving the city the largest Polish population outside of Warsaw. So it's no surprise that Chicago is the site of the Polish Museum of America, located in the neighborhood where many of the first immigrants settled. The museum has one of the most important collections of Polish art and historical materials out-side Poland (it is also the largest museum in the United States devoted exclu-sively to an ethnic group). The museum's programs include rotating exhibitions, films, lectures, and concerts, and a new permanent exhibit about Pope John Paul II. There is also a library with a large Polish-language collection, and archives where visitors can research genealogical history (call in advance if you want to look through those records). Allow a half-hour.

984 N. Milwaukee Ave. (at Augusta Blvd.). © 773/384-3352. http://pma.prcua.org. Suggested donation $3 adults, $2 students, $1 children. Fri–Wed 11am–4pm. Subway/El: Blue Line to Division.

7 Exploring the 'Burbs

Like any good American metropolis, Chicago is surrounded by an ever-expanding ring of suburbs. While many of those towns are cookie-cutter communities filled with subdivisions and strip malls, other surrounding towns trace their origins as far back as Chicago does, and some of these places have managed to retain their original character. If you're in town for a while, or if you're staying with friends and relatives in the suburbs, it's worth venturing beyond the city limits to check out some of the sights in the surrounding areas. For a map of the greater Chicagoland area, see p. 63.

OAK PARK

Architecture and literary buffs alike make pilgrimages to Oak Park, a near suburb on the western border of the city that is easily accessible by car or train. The reason fans of both disciplines flock to this same small town is that Ernest Hemingway was born and grew up here and Frank Lloyd Wright spent a great deal of his career designing the homes that line the well-maintained streets.

GETTING THERE

BY CAR   Oak Park is 10 miles due west of downtown Chicago. By car, take the Eisenhower Expressway west (I-290) to Harlem Avenue (Ill. 43) and exit north. Continue on Harlem north to Lake Street. Take a right on Lake Street and continue to Forest Avenue. Turn left here, and immediately on your right you'll see the **Oak Park Visitor Center** (see below).

BY PUBLIC TRANSPORTATION   Take the Green Line west to the Harlem stop, roughly a 25-minute ride from downtown. Exit the station onto Harlem Avenue, and proceed north to Lake Street. Take a right on Lake Street to Forest Avenue, and then turn left to the **Oak Park Visitor Center** (see below).

BY TOUR   The **Chicago Architecture Foundation** runs guided tours from downtown Chicago to Oak Park on a regular basis. For details, see "Architecture Tours" later in this chapter.

VISITOR INFORMATION

The **Oak Park Visitor Center,** 158 Forest Ave. (© **708/848-1500**), is open daily from 10am to 5pm April through October, and from 10am to 4pm November through March. Stop here for orientation, maps, and guidebooks. There's a city-operated parking lot next door. From the center, the heart of the historic district and the Frank Lloyd Wright Home and Studio is only a few blocks away.

SITES

Frank Lloyd Wright Home and Studio ★★★   For the first 20 years of Wright's career, this remarkable complex served first and foremost as the sanctuary from which Wright was to design and execute more than 130 of an extraordinary output of 430 completed buildings. The home began as a simple shingled cottage that Wright built for his bride in 1889 at the age of 22, but it became a work in progress, as Wright remodeled it constantly until 1911 (he left

The (Frank Lloyd) Wright Stuff

Oak Park has the highest concentration of houses or buildings any-where designed and built by Frank Lloyd Wright, probably the most influential American architect. People come here to marvel at the work of a man who saw his life as a twofold mission: to wage a single-handed battle against the ornamental excesses of architecture, Victo-rian in particular, and to create in its place a new form that would be at the same time functional, appropriate to its natural setting, and stimulating to the imagination.

Not everyone who comes to Oak Park shares Wright's architectural philosophy. But scholars and enthusiasts admire Wright for being con-sistently true to his own vision, out of which emerged a unique and genuinely American architectural statement. The reason for Wright's success could stem from the fact that he himself was a living exemplar of a quintessential American type. In a deep sense, he embodied the ideal of the self-made and self-sufficient individual who had survived, even thrived, in the frontier society—qualities that he expressed in his almost-puritanical insistence that each spatial or structural form in his buildings serve some useful purpose. But he was also an aesthete in Emersonian fashion, deriving his idea of beauty from natural environ-ments, where apparent simplicity often belies a subtle complexity.

The three principal ingredients of a tour of Wright-designed struc-tures in Oak Park are the **Frank Lloyd Wright Home and Studio Tour, the Unity Temple Tour,** and a **walking tour**—guided or self-guided—to view the exteriors of homes throughout the neighborhood that were built by the architect. Oak Park has, in all, 25 homes and buildings by Wright, constructed between the years 1892 and 1913, which consti-tute the core output of his Prairie School period.

there in 1909). During this highly fertile period, the house was Wright's show-case and laboratory, but it also embraces many idiosyncratic features molded to his own needs rather than those of a client. With many add-ons—including a barrel-vaulted children's playroom and a studio with an octagonal balcony sus-pended by chains—the place has a certain whimsy that others might have found less livable. This, however, was not an architect's masterpiece, but the master's home, and every room in it can be savored for the view it reflects of the work-ings of a remarkable mind. The Home and Studio Foundation has restored the residence and studio to its 1909 vintage. Allow 2 hours.

951 Chicago Ave. ℂ **708/848-1976.** www.wrightplus.org. Admission $9 adults, $7 seniors and children 7–18, free for children under 7. Combined admission for Home and Studio tour and guided or self-guided his-toric district tour (see below) $15 adults, $11 seniors and children 7–18. Admission to home and studio is by guided tour only; tours depart from the Ginkgo Tree Bookshop Mon–Fri 11am, 1pm, and 3pm; Sat–Sun every 20 min. 11am–3:30pm. Facilities for people with disabilities are limited; please call in advance.

HISTORIC DISTRICT WALKING TOURS
An extensive tour of the neighborhood surrounding the Frank Lloyd Wright Home and Studio leaves from the **Ginkgo Tree Bookshop,** 951 Chicago Ave., on weekends from 10:30am to 4pm (tour times are somewhat more limited

Oak Park Attractions

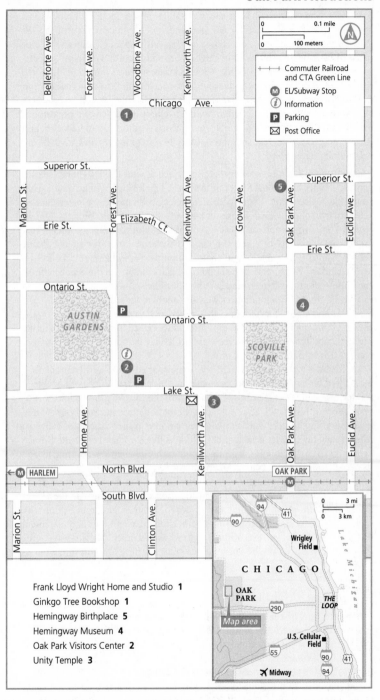

Frank Lloyd Wright Home and Studio **1**
Ginkgo Tree Bookshop **1**
Hemingway Birthplace **5**
Hemingway Museum **4**
Oak Park Visitors Center **2**
Unity Temple **3**

Nov–Feb). The tour lasts 1 hour and costs $9 for adults and $7 for seniors and children 7 to 18, and is free for children under 7. If you can't make it to Oak Park on the weekend, you can follow a self-guided map and audiocassette tour of the historic district (recorded in English, French, Spanish, German, Japanese, and Italian). Available at the Ginkgo Tree Bookshop from 10am to 3:30pm, the self-guided tour costs $9 for adults and $7 for seniors and children. In addition to Wright's work, you will see that of several of his disciples, as well as some very charming examples of the Victorian styling that he so disdained. A more detailed map selling for $3 at the bookshop, "Architectural Guide Map of Oak Park and River Forest," includes text and photos of all 80 sites of interest in Oak Park and neighboring River Forest.

Unity Temple ⭐   After fire destroyed its church around 1900, a Unitarian/Universalist congregation asked one of its members, Frank Lloyd Wright, to design an affordable replacement. Using poured concrete with metal reinforcements—a necessity, owing to the small budget of $40,000 allocated for the project—Wright created a building that on the outside seems as forbidding as a mausoleum but that inside contains in its detailing the entire architectural alphabet of the Prairie School that has since made Wright's name immortal. Following the example of H. H. Richardson, Wright placed the building's main entrance on the side, behind an enclosure—a feature often employed in his houses as well—to create a sense of privacy and intimacy. Front entrances were too anonymous for these two architects. Wright complained, furthermore, that other architectural conventions of the church idiom, such as the nave in the Gothic-style cathedral across from the future site of Unity Temple, were overpowering. Of that particular church, he commented that he didn't feel a part of it.

Yet his own vision in this regard was somewhat confused and contradictory. He wanted Unity Temple to be "democratic." But perhaps Wright was unable to subdue his own personal hubris and hauteur in the creative process, for the ultimate effect of his chapel, and much of the building's interior, is very grand and imperial. Unity Temple is no simple meetinghouse in the tradition of Calvinist iconoclasm. Instead, its principal chapel looks like the chamber of the Roman Senate. Even so, the interior, with its unpredictable geometric arrangements and its decor reminiscent of Native American art, is no less beautiful.

Wright used color sparingly within Unity Temple, but the pale, natural effects that he achieved are owed in part to his decision to add pigment to the plaster rather than use paint. Wright's use of wood for trim and other decorative touches is still exciting to behold; his sensitivity to grain and tone and placement was akin to that of an exceptionally gifted woodworker. Wright was a true hands-on, can-do person; he knew the materials he chose to use as intimately as

---

⸨ *Tips* **The Wright Plus Tour**

Die-hard fans of the architect will want to plan to be in town the third Saturday in May for the annual Wright Plus Tour, during which the public can tour several Frank Lloyd Wright–designed homes and several other notable Oak Park buildings, in both the Prairie School and the Victorian styles, in addition to Wright's home and studio and the Unity Temple. The tour includes 10 buildings in all. Tickets go on sale March 1 and can sell out within 6 weeks. Call ✆ **708/848-1976** (Frank Lloyd Wright Home and Studio) for details and ticket information.

the artisans who carried out his plans. And his stunning, almost-minimalist use of form is what still sets him apart as a relevant and brilliant artist. Other details to which the docent guide will call your attention, as you complete a circuit of the temple, are the great fireplace, the pulpit, the skylights, and the clerestory (gallery) windows. Suffice it to say, Unity Temple—only one of Wright's masterpieces—is counted among the 10 greatest American architectural achievements. Allow a half-hour.

875 Lake St. (C) 708/383-8873. http://unitytemple.org. Self-guided tours $6 adults; $3 seniors, children, and students with ID. 45-min. guided tours Sat–Sun on the hr. 1–3pm at no extra charge. Mon–Fri 10:30am–4:30 pm; Sat–Sun 1–4pm. Church events can alter the schedule; call in advance.

ON THE TRAIL OF HEMINGWAY

Frank Lloyd Wright might be Oak Park's favorite son, but the town's most famous native son is Ernest Hemingway. Maybe because Hemingway left when he had the chance and didn't write much about the town of his boyhood, Oak Park only recently has begun to rally around the memory of the Nobel and Pulitzer Prize–winning writer with the opening of a **Hemingway Museum,** 200 N. Oak Park Ave. ((C) **708/848-2222**). A portion of the ground floor of this former church, now the Oak Park Arts Center, is given over to a small but interesting display of Hemingway memorabilia. A 6-minute video sheds considerable light on Hemingway's time in Oak Park, where he spent the first 18 years of his life, and is particularly good on his high school experiences. The museum is open Sunday through Friday from 1 to 5pm, and Saturday from 10am to 5pm.

To see where Hemingway was born, on July 21, 1899, continue up the block to 339 N. Oak Park Ave., the home of his maternal grandparents. A local foundation recently purchased the home to serve as a museum and restored it to reflect its appearance during Hemingway's boyhood in time for the centenary of his birth in 1999. Hemingway's actual boyhood home, still privately owned, is located several blocks from here, not far from the Wright Home and Studio, at 600 N. Kenilworth Ave. The hours at the Hemingway Birthplace museum are the same as the Hemingway Museum above; an admission price of $7 for adults and $5 for seniors and children (free for children under 5) covers both museums.

THE NORTH SHORE

Between Chicago and the state border of Wisconsin to the north is one of the nation's most affluent residential areas, a swath of suburbia known as the North Shore. Although towns farther to the west like to co-opt the name for its prestige value, the North Shore proper extends from Evanston, Chicago's nearest neighbor to the north, along the lakefront to tony Lake Forest, originally built as a resort for Chicago's aristocracy. Dotted with idyllic, picture-perfect towns such as Kenilworth, Glencoe, and Winnetka, this area has long attracted filmmakers such as Robert Redford, who filmed *Ordinary People* in Lake Forest, and the North Shore's own John Hughes, who has shot virtually every one of his popular coming-of-age comedies (*Sixteen Candles, Ferris Bueller's Day Off, Home Alone,* and so on) here.

Although a Metra train line extends all the way to Lake Forest and neighboring Lake Bluff, I highly recommend that you rent a car and drive northward along **Sheridan Road,** which wends its leisurely way through many of these communities, past palatial homes and mansions designed in a startling array of architectural styles. Next to Lake Shore Drive in Chicago, there is no more impressive stretch of roadway in the entire metropolitan area.

EXPLORING EVANSTON

Despite being a place much frequented by Chicagoans, Evanston, the city's oldest suburb, retains an identity all its own. A unique hybrid of sensibilities, it manages to combine the tranquility of suburban life with a highly cultured, urban charm. It's great fun to just wander amid the hip shops and cafes located in its downtown area or along funky Dempster Street at its southern end. **Northwestern University** (© 847/491-3741; www.northwestern.edu) makes its home here on a beautiful lakefront campus, and many of its buildings—such as Alice Millar Chapel, with its sublime stained-glass facade, and the Mary and Leigh Block Gallery, a fine arts haven that offers a top-notch collection and always-intriguing temporary exhibitions—are well worth several hours of exploration in their own right.

Evanston was also the home of Frances Willard, founder of the Women's Christian Temperance Union. **Willard House,** 1730 Chicago Ave. (© 847/ 328-7500), is open to visitors on the first Sunday of every month ($5). Nine of the 17 rooms in this old Victorian "Rest Cottage" (as Willard called it) have been converted into a museum of period furnishings and temperance memorabilia. Among her personal effects is the bicycle that she affectionately called "Gladys" and learned to ride late in life, in the process spurring women across the country to do the same. The headquarters of the WCTU is still located on the site.

Another interesting house museum is the former **mansion of Charles Gates Dawes,** a wealthy financier who served as vice president under Calvin Coolidge and won the Nobel Peace Prize in 1925 for his smooth handling of German reparations on behalf of the League of Nations following World War I. It now houses the **Evanston Historical Society,** 225 Greenwood St. (© 847/475-3410), which provides tours of this restored century-old landmark Thursday through Sunday from 1pm to 5pm ($5).

Neither cultural nor recreational facilities are lacking in Evanston. The unusual and informative **Mitchell Museum of the American Indian** is located in a large gallery at 2600 Central Park Ave. (© 847/475-1030), with a collection ranging from stoneware tools and weapons to the work of contemporary Native American artists. The museum is open Tuesday through Saturday from 10am to 5pm, and Sunday from 12 to 4pm. It's closed on holidays and during the last two weeks of August. Admission is $5 for adults, $2.50 for seniors and children. Call in advance to arrange a volunteer-led tour.

For a bit of serenity, head to **Grosse Point Lighthouse and Maritime Museum,** 2601 Sheridan Rd. (© 847/328-6961), a historic lighthouse built in 1873, when Lake Michigan still teemed with cargo-laden ships. Tours of the lighthouse, situated in a nature center, take place on weekends from June to September.

OTHER AREA ATTRACTIONS

Baha'i House of Worship   Up the road from Evanston in Wilmette is the most visited of all the sights in the northern suburbs, the Baha'i House of Worship, an ethereal edifice that seems not of this earth. The gleaming white stone temple, designed by the French Canadian Louis Bourgeois and completed in 1953, is essentially a soaring nine-sided 135-foot dome, draped in a delicate lacelike facade, that strongly reveals the Eastern influence of the Baha'i faith's native Iran. Surrounded by formal gardens, it is one of seven Baha'i temples in the world, and the only one in the Western Hemisphere. The dome's latticework

> **Moments   A Suburban Respite**
>
> If you've made it up to the Baha'i Temple, take a stroll across Sheridan Road to **Gilson Park** for a taste of north suburban life. Check out the sailors prepping their boats for a day cruise, families picnicking and playing Frisbee, and kids frolicking on the sandy beach. Access to the beach is restricted in the summer, but in the fall and spring you're welcome to wander (just don't expect to take a dip in the frigid water).

is even more beautiful as you gaze upward from the floor of the sanctuary, which, during the day, is flooded with light. Temple members offer informal tours of the building and exhibits to anyone who inquires. Allow a half-hour.

100 Linden Ave. (at Sheridan Rd.), Wilmette. © **847/853-2300.** www.us.bahai.org/how. Free admission. Visitor center daily May–Sept 10am–10pm; Oct–Apr 10am–5pm. Devotional services are held Mon–Sat at 12:15pm and Sun at 1:15pm (with choral accompaniment). To get there from Chicago, take the Red Line of the El north to Howard St. Change trains for the Evanston train and go to the end of the line, Linden Ave. (Or take the Purple/Evanston Express and stay on the same train all the way.) Turn right on Linden and walk 2 blocks east. If you're driving, take the Outer Dr. (Lake Shore Dr.) north, which feeds into Sheridan Rd.

Chicago Botanic Garden ★★ *Value*   Despite its name, the world-class Chicago Botanic Garden is located 25 miles north of the city in the suburb of Glencoe. Owned by the Forest Preserve District of Cook County and managed by the 110-year-old Chicago Horticultural Society, this 385-acre living preserve includes eight large lagoons and a variety of distinct botanical environments—from the Illinois prairie to an English walled garden to a three-island Japanese garden. Also on the grounds are a large fruit and vegetable garden, an "enabling garden" (which shows how gardening can be adapted for people with disabilities), and a 100-acre old-growth oak woodland. If you're here in the summer, don't miss the extensive rose gardens (just follow the bridal parties who flock here to get their pictures taken). The Botanic Garden also has an exhibit hall, an auditorium, a museum, a library, education greenhouses, an outdoor pavilion, a carillon, a cafe, a designated bike path, and a garden shop. Carillon concerts take place at 7pm Monday evenings from late June through August, with a preliminary hour-long tour.

Every summer, the Botanic Garden stages a special outdoor exhibition (one year giant animal-shaped topiaries were placed in unexpected locations throughout the grounds; another year, model railroads wound through miniature versions of American national parks). Check the website or call for event schedules. Allow 3 hours.

1000 Lake-Cook Rd. (just east of Edens Expressway/I-94), Glencoe. © **847/835-5440.** www.chicago-botanic.org. Free admission. Daily (except Christmas) 8am–sunset. Tram tours offered Apr–Oct. From Chicago, take Sheridan Rd. north along Lake Michigan or the Edens Expwy. (I-94) to Lake-Cook Rd. Parking $8.75 daily.

Ravinia Festival ★★ *Finds*   Want to know where the natives get away from it all? Come summertime, you'll find us chilling on the lawn at Ravinia, the summer home of the highly regarded Chicago Symphony Orchestra in suburban Highland Park. The season runs from mid-June to Labor Day and includes far more than classical concerts: You can also catch pop acts, dance performances, operatic arias, and blues concerts. Tickets are sold to both the covered pavilion, where you get a reserved seat and a view of the stage, and the lawn, which is the real joy of Ravinia: sitting under the stars and a canopy of leafy branches while listening to music and indulging in an elaborate picnic (it's a local tradition to try to outdo everyone else by bringing candelabras and fine china). I've been here for everything from Beethoven symphonies to folky singer-songwriters, and the setting has been magical every time. The lawn to the left of the stage is a popular place for families to spread out, but I'm partial to the tree-filled area on the right (the lights projected into the branches create a dramatic effect after the sun sets).

Don't let the distance from downtown discourage you from visiting, because Ravinia is served by an extremely convenient public-transportation system. Any evening a concert is scheduled, a special Ravinia Metra commuter train leaves at 5:50pm from the North Western train station at Madison and Canal streets (just west of the Loop). The train stops directly at the festival at 6:30pm, plenty of time to enjoy a picnic before an 8 o'clock showtime. After the concert, trains wait right outside the gates to take commuters back to the city. The round-trip train fare is $5, a real bargain considering that traffic around the park can be brutal.

Dining options available at the park range from the fine-dining restaurant **Mirabelle** (© 847/432-7550 for reservations) to prepacked picnic spreads from the **Gatehouse,** featuring gourmet items to go. For $10, you can rent a pair of lawn chairs and a table from booths set up near the park entrance. In case you're wondering about the weather conditions at concert time, dial Ravinia's Weather Line (© **847/433-5010**).

Green Bay and Lake-Cook roads, Highland Park. © **847/266-5100** or 312/RAVINIA. www.ravinia.org. Tickets: Pavilion $15–$50; lawn $10. Most concerts are held in the evening.

THE NORTH & NORTHWEST SUBURBS

Of course, the North Shore is only one slice of life north of Chicago. To its west lies a sprawling thicket of old and new suburbs, from the bucolic environs of equestrian-minded **Barrington** and its ring of smaller satellite communities in the far northwest, to near-northwest shopping mecca **Schaumburg,** home to the gigantic Woodfield Mall.

A more pastoral option for visitors with spare time on their hands might be a day trip to the **historic village of Long Grove,** about 30 miles northwest of Chicago. Settled in the 1840s by German immigrants and pioneers traveling west from New England, Long Grove has assiduously preserved its old-fashioned character. Set amid 500 acres of oak- and hickory-tree groves, the village maintains nearly 100 specialty stores, galleries, and restaurants, many of which are housed in former smithies, wheelwright barns, and century-old residences. (Don't skip the Long Grove Confectionery Company, something of a local institution.) Thanks to a recent ordinance, all new buildings constructed in the shopping district must conform to the architecture of the early 1900s. The village hosts several cultural and entertainment events, festivals, and art fairs throughout the year. The biggest and best is the annual Strawberry Festival, held during the last weekend in June. Call the village's information center (© **847/ 634-0888**) for updates on coming events. To get there from the Chicago Loop, take the I-94 tollway north until it separates at I-90, another tollway that travels in a northwest direction. Follow I-90 until you reach Route 53, and drive north on 53 until it dead-ends at Lake-Cook Road. Take the west exit off 53 and follow Lake-Cook Road to Hicks Road. Turn right on Hicks Road and then left on Old McHenry Road, which will take you right into the center of town.

Arlington International Racecourse   With its gleaming-white, palatial, six-story grandstand and lush gardens, this racecourse is one of the most beautiful showcases for thoroughbred horse racing in the world. It has a storied history stretching back to 1927, and its track has been graced by such equine stars as Citation, Secretariat, and Cigar. The track's annual Arlington Million (the sport's 1st million-dollar race) has attracted the top jockeys, trainers, and horses in past years and recently became part of the new World Series Racing Championship, which includes the Breeders Cup races. Arlington's race days are thrilling to behold, with all of racing's time-honored pageantry on display—from the bugler in traditional dress to the parade of jockeys.

Arlington likes to say that it caters to families, and it must be said that the ambience here is more Disney than den of iniquity.

2200 W. Euclid Ave., Arlington Heights. ℂ 847/255-4300. www.arlingtonpark.com. Gates open at 11am Wed–Sun. Season runs May–Sept. Admission $5 adults, $3–$6 for reserved seating. Take the Kennedy (I-94) Expressway to the I-90 tollway and exit north on Rte. 53. Follow 53 north until you reach the Euclid exit. Or, take the Metra train line to its Arlington Heights stop, which is within walking distance of the racecourse. Free parking.

THE WESTERN SUBURBS

So many corporations have taken to locating their offices beyond the city limits that today more people work in the suburbs than commute into Chicago. Much of the suburban sprawl in counties such as DuPage and Kane consists of seas of aluminum-sided houses that seem to sprout from cornfields overnight. But there are also some lovely older towns, such as upscale **Hinsdale** and, much farther west, the quaint tandem of **St. Charles** and **Geneva,** which lie across the Fox River from each other. Perhaps there is no more fitting symbol of this booming area than the city of **Naperville.** A historic, formerly rural community with a Main Street U.S.A. downtown district worthy of Norman Rockwell, Naperville has exploded from a population of about 30,000 residents in the early 1970s to approximately 130,000 today—which makes it the third-largest municipality in the state. Naperville maintains a collection of 19th-century buildings in an outdoor setting known as Naper Settlement, and its river walk is the envy of neighboring village councils. But much of its yesteryear charm seems to be disappearing bit by bit as new subdivisions and strip malls ooze forth across the prairie.

Brookfield Zoo ★★ *Kids*   Brookfield is the Chicago area's largest zoo. In contrast to the rather efficient Lincoln Park Zoo, Brookfield is spacious, spreading out over 216 acres with 2,700 animal residents—camels, dolphins, giraffes, baboons, wolves, tigers, green sea turtles, Siberian tigers, snow leopards, and more—living in naturalistic environments that put them side by side with other inhabitants of their regions. These creative indoor and outdoor settings—filled with activities to keep kids interested—are what set Brookfield apart. One of the newest exhibits, *The Living Coast* ★★, explores the western coast of Chile and Peru and includes everything from a tank of plate-size moon jellies to a rocky shore where Humboldt penguins swim and nest as Inca terns and gray gulls fly freely overhead. Other impressive exhibits include *The Swamp* ★, which re-creates the bioregions of a southern cypress swamp and an Illinois river scene and discusses what people can do to protect wetlands, and *Habitat Africa!* ★, a multiple ecosystem exhibit-in-progress that eventually will encompass 30 acres—about the size of the entire Lincoln Park Zoo. The thrills here aren't always high concept: Some of my favorite exhibits are the *Australia House,* where fruit bats flit around your head, and *Tropic World,* where you wander at tree-top level with monkeys. The dolphins at the *Seven Seas Panorama* ★★ put on an amazing show that has been a Brookfield Zoo fixture for years. If you go on a weekend, buy tickets to the dolphin show at least a couple of hours before the one you plan to attend because they tend to sell out quickly.

The new **Hamill Family Play Zoo** is a wonderful stop for kids, a place where they not only get to pet animals, but also can build habitats, learn how to plant a garden, and even play animal dress-up. The only catch: You will have to pay a separate admission fee ($3 adults, $2 children). Allow 3 hours.

First Ave. and 31st St., Brookfield. © **708/485-0263.** www.brookfieldzoo.org. Regular admission $8 adults, $4 seniors and children 3–11. Parking $8. Free admission Tues and Thurs Oct–Mar. Summer daily 9:30am–6pm; fall–spring daily 10am–5pm. Take the Stevenson (I-55) and Eisenhower (I-290) expressways 14 miles west of the Loop. Bus: No. 304 or 311.

8 Kid Stuff

Chicago has plenty of places to take the kids—places, in fact, that make every effort to turn a bored child into a stimulated one. All of the city's museums are leaders in the "please touch me" school of interactive exhibitions, with buttons and lights and levers and sounds and bright colors, and activities for kids at special exhibitions.

Chicago Children's Museum ★★ Since the Chicago Children's Museum moved to Navy Pier in 1996, it has become one of the most popular cultural attractions in the city. The museum has areas especially for preschoolers as well as for children up to age 10, and several permanent exhibits allow kids a maximum of hands-on fun. *Dinosaur Expedition* re-creates an expedition to the Sahara, allowing kids to experience camp life, conduct scientific research, and dig for the bones of Suchomimus, a Saharan dinosaur discovered by Chicago paleontologist Paul Sereno (a full-scale model stands nearby). *Face to Face: Dealing with Prejudice and Discrimination* is a multimedia display that helps kids identify prejudice and find ways to deal with it. There's also a **three-level schooner** that children can board for a little climbing, from the crow's nest to the gangplank; *PlayMaze,* a toddler-scale cityscape with everything from a gas station to a city bus that children under 5 can touch and explore; and an **arts-and-crafts area** where visitors can create original artwork to take home. Allow 2 to 3 hours.

Navy Pier, 700 E. Grand Ave. © **312/527-1000.** www.chichildrensmuseum.org. Admission $7 adults and children, $6 seniors. Free admission Thurs 5–8pm. Tues–Wed and Fri–Sun 10am–5pm; Thurs 10am–8pm. Bus: No. 29, 56, 65, or 66. Subway/El: Red Line to Grand/State; transfer to city bus or Navy Pier's free trolley bus.

Lincoln Park Pritzker Children's Zoo & Farm-in-the-Zoo ★ *Value* After hours of looking at animals from afar in the rest of the Lincoln Park Zoo, kids can come here for some hands-on experience. Children are encouraged to come touch a variety of small animals—hedgehogs, iguanas, rabbits—under the supervision of zookeepers. There's also a very popular glass-walled animal nursery, where zoo docents and keepers care for the babies of more exotic species—often, this means gorillas and chimpanzees—who are ill, born weak, or rejected by their mothers. The Conservation Station has interactive exhibits and workshop activities focusing on wildlife and environmental preservation. The adjacent outdoor portion of the Children's Zoo has owls, otters, and other small critters in winding habitats sculpted from concrete.

The newly renovated Farm-in-the-Zoo is a working reproduction of a Midwestern farm, complete with a white-picket-fenced barnyard, chicken coops, and demonstrations of butter churning and weaving. Of course, you'll also spot plenty of livestock, including cows, sheep, and pigs. Inside the Main Barn (filled with interactive exhibits), the main attraction is the huge John Deere tractor that kids can climb up into and pretend to drive. (Can you say photo opportunity?) Allow 1 hour.

2200 N. Cannon Dr. © 312/742-2000. Free admission. Daily 9am–5pm. Bus: No. 151 or 156.

Six Flags Great America ✫ One of the Midwest's biggest theme/amusement parks, Six Flags is located midway between Chicago and Milwaukee on I-94 in Gurnee, Illinois. The park has more than 100 rides and attractions and is a favorite of roller-coaster devotees. There are a whopping 10 of them here, including the nausea-inducing Déjà Vu, where riders fly forwards and backwards over a twisting, looping inverted steel track, and Superman, where you speed along hanging headfirst (with your legs dangling). Other don't-miss rides for the strong of stomach include the Iron Wolf, where you do corkscrew turns and 360-degree loops while standing up, and the American Eagle, a classic wooden coaster. Because this is a place that caters to families, you'll also find plenty to appeal to smaller visitors. The Looney Tunes National Park is full of kiddie rides with a cartoon theme; other worthwhile stops include the double-decker carousel and bumper cars. Six Flags also has live shows, IMAX movies, and restaurants. If you take the trouble to get out here, allow a full day.

I-94 at Rte. 132 East., Gurnee. © 847/249-4636. www.sixflags.com. Admission (including unlimited rides, shows, and attractions) $40 adults, $30 seniors and children under 54" tall, free for children 3 and under. Open seasonally, May 10am–7pm; June–Aug 10am–9pm; Sept–Oct 10am–7pm, daily. Parking $10. Take I-94 or I-294 West to Rte. 132 (Grand Ave.). Approximate driving time from Chicago city limits is 45 min.

9 Sightseeing Tours

If you're in town for a limited amount of time, an organized tour may be the best way to get a quick overview of the city's highlights. Some tours—such as the boat cruises on Lake Michigan and the Chicago River—can give you a whole new perspective on the city's landscape. Because Chicago caters to sophisticated travelers from all over the world, many tours go beyond simple sightseeing to explore important historical and architectural landmarks in depth. These specialized tours can help you appreciate buildings or neighborhoods that you might have passed by otherwise without a second glance.

CARRIAGE RIDES

Noble Horse (© 312/266-7878) maintains the largest fleet of antique horse carriages, stationed around the old Water Tower Square at the northwest corner of Chicago and Michigan avenues. Each of the drivers, outfitted in black tie and top hat, has his or her own variation on the basic Magnificent Mile itinerary (you can also do tours of the lakefront, river, Lincoln Park, and Buckingham Fountain). The charge is $30 for each half-hour for up to four people. The coaches run year-round, with convertible coaches in the warm months and enclosed carriages furnished with wool blankets on bone-chilling nights. There are several other carriage operators, all of whom pick up riders in the vicinity.

ORIENTATION TOURS

Chicago Trolley Company Chicago Trolley Company offers guided tours on a fleet of rubber-wheeled "San Francisco–style" trolleys that stop at a number of popular spots around the city, including Navy Pier, the Grant Park museums, the Museum of Science and Industry, Lincoln Park Zoo, and the cluster of theme restaurants in River North (Hard Rock Cafe, Planet Hollywood, and so on). You can stay on for the full 1½-hour ride or get on and off at each stop. The same

---

(*Tips* **Ticket to Ride**

One of the most distinctive ways to tour the city is by hopping aboard one of our iconic El trains. Although you can ride anytime yourself for $1.50, a guided train tour will give you new insights on the buildings outside the windows. The city's **Office of Tourism** runs a 40-minute train tour of the Loop on Saturdays at 11:35, 12:15, 12:55, and 1:35 from May through September; tickets are free, but must be picked up on the day of the tour at the Chicago Cultural Center, 77 E. Randolph St., a block east of the Randolph and Wabash station where the tour starts (© **312/744-2400**).

---

company also operates the **Chicago Double Decker Company,** which has a fleet of London-style, red, two-story buses. The buses follow the same route as the trolleys; if you buy an all-day pass, you can hop from bus to trolley at any point.

© **773/648-5000.** www.chicagotrolley.com. All-day hop-on, hop-off pass $20 adults, $17 seniors, $10 children 3–11. Family package (2 adults, 2 children) $54. Daily 9am–5pm year-round (in the winter the vehicles are enclosed and heated).

Gray Line   Part of a company that offers bus tours worldwide, Gray Line Chicago offers professional tours in well-appointed buses. A basic guided tour of the city takes 1½ hours; more extensive trips run 4 to 5 hours and include lunch. Some tours also include a cruise on Lake Michigan or a visit to the Sears Tower Skydeck. Gray Line also operates a trolley that runs through downtown Wednesday through Sunday; an all-day pass costs $20 for adults and $10 for children.

27 E. Monroe St., Suite 515. © **800/621-4153** or 312/251-3107. www.grayline.com. Tours cost $16–$45.

LAKE & RIVER CRUISES

Getting out on the lake is a great way to take in Chicago's incredible skyline from a whole new vantage point. Don't forget that you're always going to be at the mercy of the weather if you book in advance: I've taken sightseeing cruises in the rain (most boats have plenty of covered areas for just this reason), and twice I've gone to parties on expensive dinner cruise boats that never left the dock because the lake was too choppy. But when the weather cooperates, the sight of sunlight or moonlight sparkling off the city's skyscrapers never fails to thrill.

Chicago from the Lake   This company runs two different cruises: a 90-minute tour of architecture along the Chicago River, and historical cruises that travel on the lake and river to explore the development of the city. Complimentary coffee (Starbucks, no less), lemonade, cookies, and muffins are served. For tickets, call or stop by the company's ticket office, located on the lower level on the east end of River East Plaza. Advance reservations are recommended.

Departing from Ogden Slip adjacent to River East Plaza (formerly North Pier) at the end of E. Illinois St. © **312/527-1977.** www.chicagoline.com. Tickets $25 adults, $22 seniors, $14 children 7–18, free for children under 7. Daily May–Oct.

Mystic Blue Cruises   A more casual alternative to fancy dinner cruises, this is promoted as more of a "fun" ship (that means DJs at night, although you'll have to put up with some kind of "live entertainment" no matter when you sail). Daily lunch and dinner excursions are available, as well as midnight weekend voyages. The same company offers more formal (and expensive) cruises aboard the **Odyssey,** and motorboat rides on the 70-passenger **Seadog,** if you really want to feel the water in your face.

Departing from Navy Pier. ℭ 877/299-7783. www.mysticbluecruises.com. Lunch cruises $28–$31, dinner $55–$60, midday cruise $22, moonlight cruise $28. Cruises run year-round.

Shoreline Sightseeing   Shoreline schedules 30-minute lake cruises every half-hour from its three dock locations: the Shedd Aquarium, Navy Pier, and Buckingham Fountain in Grant Park. Shoreline has also gotten in on the popularity of architecture tours by offering its own version, narrated by an architectural guide (with higher prices than their regular tours). A water taxi also runs every half-hour from Navy Pier to both the Sears Tower and the Shedd Aquarium. One-way tickets for the water taxi are $6 for adults, $5 for seniors, and $3 for children under 12; all-day passes cost $12 for adults and $6 for children.

Departing from Navy Pier, Shedd Aquarium, and Buckingham Fountain in Grant Park. ℭ 312/222-9328. www.shorelinesightseeing.com. Tickets $10 adults, $9 seniors, $5 children under 12; architectural tours $18–20 adults, $17 seniors, $7–$8 children under 12. Daily May 1–Sept 30.

The Spirit of Chicago   This luxury yacht offers a variety of wining-and-dining harbor cruises, from a lunch buffet to the "Moonlight Dance Party." This can be a fairly pricey night out if you go for the whole dinner package; the late-night moonlight cruises are a more affordable option for insomniacs.

Departing from Navy Pier. ℭ 312/836-7899. www.spiritcruises.com. Lunch cruises $35–45, dinner (seated) $70–$100, sunset and midnight cruises $32. Ask about children's rates. Daily year-round.

Wendella Sightseeing Boats   Wendella is the granddaddy of all sightseeing operators in Chicago. Started in 1935, it's run by the original owner's son, Bob Borgstrom, whose own two sons serve as captains. You won't find a more authoritative source on the Chicago River than Borgstrom.

Wendella operates a 1-hour tour along the Chicago River, and a 1½-tour along the river and out onto Lake Michigan. (One of the most dramatic events during the boat tours is passing through the locks that separate the river from the lake.) Boats run from late April to early October. The 2-hour sunset tour runs Memorial Day to Labor Day starting at 7:45pm. Scheduling for cruises depends on the season and the weather, but cruises usually leave every hour during the summer.

Departing from Michigan Ave. and Wacker Dr. (on the north side of the river at the Wrigley Building). ℭ 312/337-1446. www.wendellaboats.com. Tickets $16 adults, $14 seniors, $8 children under 12. Daily Apr–Oct.

Windy   One of the more breathtaking scenes on the lake is watching this tall ship approach the docks at Navy Pier. The 148-foot-long, four-masted schooner (and its new sister ship, the *Windy II*) sets sail for 90-minute cruises two to five times a day, both day and evening. Of course, the boats are at the whims of the wind, so every cruise charts a different course. Passengers are welcome to help raise and trim the sails and occasionally take turns at the ship's helm (with the captain standing close by). The boats are not accessible for people with disabilities.

Departing from Navy Pier. ℭ 312/595-5555. Tickets $25 adults, $15 seniors and children under 12. Tickets go on sale 1 hr. before the 1st sail of the day at the boat's ticket office, on the dock at Navy Pier. Reservations (except for groups) are not accepted. Call for sailing times.

SPECIAL-INTEREST TOURS
ARCHITECTURE TOURS

Chicago is the first city of architecture, and the **Chicago Architecture Foundation (CAF),** 224 S. Michigan Ave. (ℭ **312/922-3432,** or 312/922-TOUR for recorded information; www.architecture.org), offers first-rate guided programs, led by nearly 400 trained and enthusiastic docents. The foundation offers walking, bike, boat, and bus tours to more than 60 architectural sites and environments in and around Chicago. The foundation also has another tour center in the John Hancock Center, 875 N. Michigan Ave. Below is a sampling of their offerings.

BY BOAT   Perhaps the CAF's most popular tour is its 1½-hour **Architecture River Cruise,** which glides along both the north and the south branches of the Chicago River. Although you can see the same 50 or so buildings that the cruise covers on your own by foot, traveling by water lets you enjoy the buildings from a unique perspective. The excellent docents also provide interesting historical details, as well as some fun facts (David Letterman once called the busts of the nation's retailing legends that face the Merchandise Mart the "Pez Hall of Fame"). The cruise points out both landmark buildings, such as the Gothic 1925 Tribune Tower, and contemporary ones, including the late-1980s NBC Tower, constructed in wedding-cake style in homage to the city's old zoning codes mandating that sunlight reach down to the street.

The docents generally do a good job of making the cruise enjoyable for visitors with all levels of architectural knowledge. In addition to pointing out famous buildings—Marina City, the Civic Opera House, the Sears Tower, to name a few—they approach the sites thematically, explaining, for example, how Chicagoans' use of and attitudes toward the river have changed over time.

Tickets are $23 per person weekdays, $25 on weekends and holidays, and are scheduled hourly every day May through October from 11am to 3pm. The trips are extremely popular, so purchase tickets in advance through **Ticketmaster** (✆ **312/902-1500;** www.ticketmaster.com/Illinois), or avoid the service charge and buy your tickets at one of the foundation's tour centers, 224 S. Michigan Ave. or the John Hancock Center, or from the boat launch on the southeast corner of Michigan Avenue and Wacker Drive.

BY BUS   Reservations are required for all bus tours, although walk-ins are welcome if there's space.

Highlights by Bus is a 3½-hour tour offered Saturdays at 9:30am that covers the Loop, Hyde Park, and the Gold Coast, plus several other historic districts. The tour includes a visit to the interior of Frank Lloyd Wright's Robie House. Tickets are $30 per person; tours depart from the Chicago Architecture Center at 224 S. Michigan Ave. To keep up with popular demand, the foundation adds Sunday morning tours periodically throughout the year.

A 4-hour bus tour of Frank Lloyd Wright sights in **Oak Park** is offered once a month on Saturday from May to October ($30). The tour includes walks through three neighborhoods and commentary on more than 25 houses—but does not take visitors inside Wright's home and studio. A separate 4-hour bus tour takes Wright fans inside the master's home and Oak Park's Unity Temple ($40). Both tours leave from the Chicago Architecture Center.

The foundation also offers special theme bus tours periodically throughout the year (recent subjects included Chicago movie palaces and historic churches).

ON FOOT   If you prefer exploring on your own two feet, the CAF offers a variety of guided walking tours. For first-time visitors, I highly recommend two tours that give an excellent introduction to the dramatic architecture of the Loop: **Historic Skyscrapers,** which covers buildings built between 1880 and 1940, including the Rookery and the Chicago Board of Trade, and **Modern Skyscrapers,** which includes modern masterpieces by Mies van der Rohe and

> **Finds** **The Wright Stuff in the Gold Coast**
>
> Architecture junkies may also want to visit the **Charnley-Persky House** (© **312/915-0105** or 312/573-1365), designed by Frank Lloyd Wright and Louis Sullivan in 1891. The house is located in the Gold Coast at 1365 N. Astor St. and makes a nice highlight during an informal walking tour of the area. One-hour tours are offered on Wednesdays at noon (free) and Saturdays April through November at 10am and 1pm ($5); no reservations are accepted.

postmodern works by contemporary architects. The 2-hour tours cost $12 each ($20 for both) for adults and $9 each ($15 for both) for seniors and students. The tours are offered daily and depart from the Chicago Architecture Center at 224 S. Michigan Ave. Call © **312/922-TOUR** for exact tour times.

The CAF also offers more than 50 **neighborhood tours,** visiting the Gold Coast, River North, Grant Park, Old Town, the Jackson Boulevard Historic District, and even the Lincoln Park Zoo. Most cost $5 to $10 and last a couple of hours. Call © **312/922-TOUR** for details.

The **Chicago Historical Society** offers walking tours every summer of the neighborhoods surrounding the museum: the **Gold Coast, Old Town,** and **Lincoln Park.** Led by CHS docents, they average about four per month June through August. Day and evening tours are available, and a few specialty walking tours usually are offered as well. Tours are $10 per tour or $25 for a combination of any three tours. Registration is recommended but not required. Tours depart from the CHS museum at Clark Street and North Avenue, and light refreshments are served immediately afterward. Call © **312/642-4600** for updates.

The museum also offers three or four daylong bus tours, called **"Exploring Chicago,"** from May to July that cover unique themes or aspects of the metropolitan area's history. Led by historians and scholars, they take place in the city and surrounding areas. Tours are different every year, so call the Historical Society (© **312/642-4600**) for updates (the tours usually are tied in to exhibits at the museum). Prices vary but are usually about $60 per person. Tours depart from the Historical Society's museum at Clark Street and North Avenue, and include lunch and light refreshments.

CEMETERY TOURS

Don't be scared away by the creepy connotations. Some of Chicago's cemeteries are as pretty as parks, and they offer a variety of intriguing monuments that are a virtual road into the city's history. There's also something undeniably peaceful about strolling these places, which offer an escape from the nonstop bustle of downtown.

One of the best area cemeteries is **Graceland,** stretching along Clark Street in the Swedish neighborhood of Andersonville, where you can view the tombs and monuments of many Chicago notables. When Graceland was laid out in 1860, public parks as such did not exist. The elaborate burial grounds that were constructed in many large American cities around this same time had the dual purpose of relieving the congestion of the municipal cemeteries closer to town and providing pastoral recreational settings for the Sunday outings of the living. Indeed, cemeteries like Graceland were the precursors of such great municipal green spaces as Lincoln Park. Much of Lincoln Park, in fact, had been a public cemetery since Chicago's earliest times. (Many who once rested there were rein-terred in Graceland when the plans for building Lincoln Park went forward.)

The Chicago Architecture Foundation (𝄐 **312/922-TOUR**) offers walking tours of Graceland on selected Sundays during August, September, and Octo-ber. The tour costs $10 per person and lasts about 2 hours. Among the points of interest in these 121 beautifully landscaped acres are the Ryerson and Getty tombs, famous architectural monuments designed by Louis Sullivan. Sullivan himself rests here in the company of several of his most distinguished colleagues: Daniel Burnham, Ludwig Mies van der Rohe, and Howard Van Doren Shaw. Some of Chicago's giants of industry and commerce are also buried at Grace-land, including Potter Palmer, Marshall Field, and George Pullman. The Chicago Architecture Foundation offers tours of some other cemeteries, as well, including Rosehill Cemetery, suburban Lake Forest Cemetery, and Oak Woods Cemetery, the final resting place for many of Chicago's most famous African-American figures, including Jesse Owens, Ida B. Wells, and the late Mayor Harold Washington.

GANGSTER TOURS

Untouchable Tours, or so-called "Gangster Tours," 10924 S. Prospect Ave., Chicago, IL 60643 (𝄐 **773/881-1195;** www.gangstertour.com), is the only bus tour that takes you to all of the city's old hoodlum hangouts from the Prohibi-tion era. The focus is definitely more on entertainment (the guides appear in costume and role-play their way through the tour) than a seriously historic take on the era, but the bus trip gives you a pretty thorough overview of the city, in addition to the gangster hot spots. You'll see O'Bannion's flower shop, the site of the St. Valentine's Day massacre, plus much more. The cost is $24 for adults, $18 for children. Tours, which depart from the **Rock 'n' Roll McDonald's** at Clark and Ohio streets (the east side of the restaurant), run Monday through Wednesday at 10am; Thursday at 10am and 1pm; Friday at 10am, 1pm, and 7:30pm; Saturday at 10am, 1pm, and 5pm; and Sunday at 10am and 1pm.

GHOST TOURS

Another offbeat way to experience the real "spirit" of Chicago is to take a nar-rated **supernatural bus tour** of cemeteries, murder sites, Indian burial grounds, haunted pubs, and other spooky places. Richard Crowe, who bills himself as a "professional ghost hunter," spins out ghost stories, legends, and lore on the 4-hour trip, held both day and night (afraid of the dark?). Tickets are $35 per person, and the tour begins at **Goose Island Restaurant,** 1800 N. Clybourn Ave. (a short walk from the North/Clybourn El station on the Red Line). Two-hour **supernatural boat excursions** are available for $24 per person in July and August through Labor Day weekend, and board at 10:30pm from the Mercury boat dock at Michigan Avenue and Wacker Drive. Reservations are required for each tour; call 𝄐 **708/499-0300** or visit www.ghosttours.com. As you can imag-ine, Crowe's tours get especially popular around Halloween, so you'll definitely want to reserve well ahead of time.

NEIGHBORHOOD TOURS

It's a bit of a cliché to say that Chicago is a city of neighborhoods, but if you want to see what really makes Chicago special, that's where you have to go. And if you're a bit intimidated by public transportation and getting around a less tourist-friendly area of the city, an escorted tour is the perfect way to see places you'd otherwise miss. Sponsored by the city's Department of Cultural Affairs,

Chicago Neighborhood Tours (© 312/742-1190; www.chgocitytours.com) are 4- to 5-hour, narrated bus excursions to about a dozen diverse communities throughout the city. Embarking from the Chicago Cultural Center, 77 E. Randolph St., every Saturday (not on major holidays—call first; and not during Jan, generally), the tours visit different neighborhoods, from Chinatown and historic Bronzeville on the South Side to the ethnic enclaves of Devon Avenue and Uptown on the North Side. Neighborhood representatives serve as guides and greeters along the way as tour participants visit area landmarks, murals, museums, and shopping districts. Tickets (including a light snack) are $25 for adults and $20 for seniors, students, and children 8 to 18. Several specialty tours are also offered on a regular basis, including Gay and Lesbian History; Great Chicago Fire; Roots of Blues, Gospel, & Jazz; Threads of Ireland; Jewish Legacy; and an Ethnic Cemetery tour. These tours, which generally run about 4 to 6 hours and include lunch, are more expensive ($50 adults, $45 seniors and children).

Groups can arrange tours of Chicago's **"Black Metropolis,"** the name given to a South Side area of Bronzeville where African Americans created a flourishing business and artistic community after World War II. Contact **Tour Black Chicago** (© 312/332-2323; www.tourblackchicago.com) for more information.

10 Staying Active

Perhaps because Chicago's winters can be so brutal, Chicagoans take their summers very seriously. In the warmer months, with the wide blue lake and the ample green parks, it's easy to think that the city is one big grown-up playground. Whether your fancy is watersports or land-based ones, you'll probably be able to find it here. The park district can be reached at © 312/742-PLAY; for questions about the 29 miles of beaches and parks along Lake Michigan, call the park district's lakefront region office at © 312/747-2474.

Another handy resource is *Windy City Sports* (© 312/421-1551; www. windycitysportsmag.com), a free monthly publication that you'll find at many retail shops, grocery stores, and bars and cafes.

BEACHES

Public beaches line Lake Michigan all the way up north into the suburbs and Wisconsin, and southeast through Indiana and into Michigan. The most well known is **Oak Street Beach,** the location of which at the northern tip of the Magnificent Mile creates some interesting sights as sun worshippers sporting swimsuits and carting coolers make their way down Michigan Avenue. The most popular is **North Avenue Beach,** about 6 blocks farther north, which has developed into a volleyball hot spot and recently rebuilt its landmark steamship-shaped beach house and added a Venice Beach–style outdoor gym; this is where the Lincoln Park singles come to play, check each other out, and fly by on bikes and in-line skates. **Hollywood-Ardmore Beach** (officially Kathy Osterman Beach), at the northern end of Lake Shore Drive, is a lovely crescent that's less congested and has steadily become more popular with gays who've moved up the lakefront from the Belmont Rocks, a longtime hangout. For more seclusion, try **Ohio Street Beach,** an intimate sliver of sand in tiny Olive Park, just north of Navy Pier, which, incredibly enough, remains largely ignored despite its central location. If you have a car, head up to **Montrose Beach,** a beautiful unsung treasure about midway between North Avenue Beach and Hollywood-Ardmore Beach (with plenty of free parking). Long popular with the city's Hispanic community, it has an expanse of beach mostly uninterrupted by piers or jetties, and a huge adjacent park with soccer fields and one big hill great for kite fly-ing—even a small bait shop where anglers can go before heading for a nearby long pier designated for fishing.

If you've brought the pooch along, you might want to take him for a dip at the **doggie beach** south of Addison Street, at about Hawthorne and Lake Shore Drive—although this minute spot aggravates some dog owners because it's situ-ated in a harbor where the water is somewhat fouled by gas and oil from nearby boats. *A tip:* Try the south end of North Avenue Beach in early morning, before it opens to the public for the day. (Also consider that, in off-season, all beaches are fair game for dogs. The police won't hassle you, I promise.)

Beaches are officially open with a full retinue of lifeguards on duty beginning about June 20, though swimmers can wade into the chilly water Memorial Day to Labor Day. Only the bravest souls venture into the water before July, when the temperature creeps up enough to make swimming an attractive proposition. Please take note that the entire lakefront is not beach, and don't go doing any-thing stupid such as diving off the rocks.

BIKING

Biking is a great way to see the city, particularly along the lakefront bike path that extends for more than 18 miles. The stretch between Navy Pier and North Avenue Beach gets extremely crowded in the summer (you're jostling for space with in-line skaters, joggers, and dawdling pedestrians). If you're looking to pick up some speed, I recommend biking south—once you're past the Museum Campus, the trail is relatively wide open, and you can zip all the way to Hyde Park. If you want a more leisurely tour with good people-watching potential, head north (through the crowds) and be patient—once you pass Belmont Har-bor, the traffic lets up somewhat. Ride all the way to Hollywood Beach (where the lakefront trail ends) for a good, but not exhausting, workout.

To rent bikes, try **Bike & Roll,** which has locations at Navy Pier (© 312/ 595-9600) and North Avenue Beach (© 773/327-2706). Open from 8am to 10pm May through October (weather permitting), Bike & Roll stocks moun-tain and touring bikes, kids' bikes, strollers, and—most fun of all—quadcycles, which are four-wheeled contraptions equipped with a steering wheel and canopy that can accommodate four or five people. Rates for bikes are $9.75 an hour, $34 a day, with helmets, pads, and locks included. Quadcycles rent for $20 per hour. Both locations offer free lakefront bike tours daily; tours start at 1:30pm and run about 2½ hours. There's a 15-person maximum per tour (and they usu-ally fill up), so call in advance to make a reservation.

Both the park district (© 312/742-PLAY) and the **Chicagoland Bicycle Fed-eration** (© 312/42-PEDAL; www.chibikefed.org) offer free maps that detail popular biking routes. The latter, which is the preeminent organization for cyclists in Chicago, also sells a much larger, more extensive map for $6.95 that shows routes within a seven-county area. They sponsor a number of bike rides throughout the year, including the highly enjoyable **Boulevard Lakefront Tour,** held in late June, which follows the historic circle of boulevards that had their genesis in the Chicago Plan of 1909. It starts in Hyde Park at the University of Chicago campus.

A word of caution: Never head anywhere on the city's streets without first strapping on a helmet. Chicago Mayor Richard M. Daley is an avid cyclist him-self and has tirelessly promoted the addition of designated bike lanes along many main thoroughfares. But, that said, most cabbies and drivers tend to ignore them. Bike with extreme caution on city streets (you can get a ticket for biking on the sidewalk) and stick to the lakefront path if you're not an expert rider. Locking your bike anywhere you go is a no-brainer.

ICE SKATING

The city's premier skating destination is the **McCormick-Tribune Ice Rink** at Millennium Park, 55 N. Michigan Ave. (© **312/742-5222**). The location is unbeatable; you're skating in the shadows of grand skyscrapers and within view of the lake. The rink is open daily from 9am to 9pm November through March. Admission is free, and skate rentals are $5.

The park district runs dozens of other skating surfaces throughout the city, both along the lakefront and in neighborhood parks. Call © **312/742-PLAY** for locations. There's also a relatively small rink at **Navy Pier,** 600 E. Grand Ave. (© **312/595-PIER**).

IN-LINE SKATING

The wheeled ones have been taking over Chicago's sidewalks, streets, and bike paths since the early 1990s. Numerous rental places have popped up, and several sporting-goods shops that sell in-line skates also rent them. The rentals generally include helmets and pads. **Bike & Roll,** with locations at Navy Pier (© **312/595-9600**) and North Avenue Beach (© **773/327-2706**), charges $9.75 an hour or $34 a day (you can have the skates 8am–10pm). A second spot is **Londo Mondo,** 1100 N. Dearborn St. (© **312/751-2794**), on the Gold Coast, renting blades for $7 an hour or $20 a day.

The best route to skate is the lakefront trail that leads from Lincoln Park down to Oak Street Beach. Beware, though, that those same miles of trail are claimed by avid cyclists—I've seen plenty of collisions between 'bladers and bikers. Approach Chicago lakefront traffic as carefully as you would a major expressway.

SAILING

It seems a shame just to sit on the beach and watch all those beautiful sailboats gliding across the lake. Go on, get out there. The **Chicago Sailing Club,** in Belmont Harbor (© **773/871-7245,** www.chicagosailingclub.com), rents J-22 and J-30 boats from 9am to sunset, weather permitting, May through October. A J-22 holds four or five adults. Rates for a J-22 range from $35 to $55 an hour ($10 extra for a skipper). A J-30 accommodates up to 10 people and can sail at night. Rates are $70 to $90 per hour, plus $20 per hour for a skipper. If you want to take the boat out without a skipper, you need to demonstrate your skills first (for an additional $10 checkout fee). Reservations are recommended. Charters are also available.

SWIMMING

The Chicago Park District maintains about 30 indoor pools for lap swimming and general splashing around, but none are particularly convenient to downtown. The lakefront is open for swimming until 9:30pm Memorial Day to Labor Day in areas watched over by lifeguards (no swimming off the rocks, please). But be forewarned: The water is usually freezing. A good place for lake swimming is the water along the wall beginning at Ohio Street Beach, located slightly northwest of Navy Pier. The Chicago Triathlon Club marks a course here each summer with a buoy at both the ¼- and ½-mile distance. This popular swimming route follows the shoreline in a straight line. The water is fairly shallow. For more information, call the park district's beach and pool office (© **312/742-PLAY**).

11 In the Grandstand: Watching Chicago's Athletic Events

Alas, Chicago's professional sports glory has faded since the days when Michael Jordan was the most recognized athlete in the world. Now most of our teams rarely rise above mediocre, despite a few high points—such as Sammy Sosa making home-run history for the Cubs. But Chicago fans are nothing if not loyal, and, for that reason, attending a home game in any sport is an uplifting experience. And look on the bright side: Now that our teams aren't doing so well, it's a lot easier to get tickets to games.

BASEBALL

Baseball is imprinted in the national consciousness as part of Chicago, not because of victorious dynasties, but rather because of the opposite—the Black Sox scandal of 1919 and the perennially losing Cubs.

Let's start with the **Chicago Cubs.** The Cubbies haven't made a World Series appearance since 1945 and haven't been World Champs since 1908, but when the team plays in so perfect a place as Wrigley Field, with its ivy-covered outfield walls, its hand-operated scoreboard, its view of the shimmering lake from the upper deck, and its "W" or "L" flag announcing the outcome of the game to the unfortunates who couldn't attend, how could anyone stay away? After all the strikes and temper tantrums and other nonsense, Wrigley has managed to hold on to something like purity. Yes, *Chicago Tribune*–owned Wrigley finally installed lights a decade ago, but by agreement with the residential neighborhood it occupies, the Cubs still play most games in the daylight, as they should. Because Wrigley is small, just about every seat is decent.

No matter how the Cubs are doing, tickets ($12–$36) go fast; most weekend and night games are sold out by Memorial Day. Your best bet is to hit a weekday game, or try your luck buying a ticket on game day outside the park (you'll often find some season-ticket holders looking to unload a few seats).

Wrigley Field, 1060 W. Addison St. (© **773/404-CUBS;** www.cubs.mlb.com), is easy to reach. Take the Red Line to the Addison stop, and you're there. You could also take the no. 22 bus, which runs up Clark Street. To order tickets in person, stop by the ticket windows at Wrigley Field, Monday through Friday from 9am to 6pm, Saturday from 9am to 4pm, and on game days. Call © **800/THE-CUBS** for tickets through **Ticketmaster,** and you can also order online through the Cubs website. About a dozen tours of the ballpark are led each season; tickets are $15 and are sold through the Wrigley Field ticket office or Ticketmaster.

Alas, the **Chicago White Sox** can't count on the same kind of loyalty as the Cubs. Longtime fans rue the day owner Jerry Reinsdorf (who is also majority owner of the Bulls) replaced the admittedly dilapidated Comisky Park with a concrete behemoth that lacks the yesteryear charm of its predecessor (it's now known as **U.S. Cellular Field**). That said, sightlines at the new stadium are spectacular from every seat (if you avoid the vertigo-inducing upper-deck seats), and every conceivable amenity—from above-average ballpark food concessions to shops to plentiful restrooms—has been provided for your ease and enjoyment. The endearing quality about the White Sox is their blue-collar, working-class aura with which so many Cubs-loathing South Siders identify. Games are rarely sellouts—a residual effect, presumably, of Reinsdorf's sterile stadium and the blighted neighborhood that surrounds it. All of this makes it a bargain deal for bona fide baseball fans. Tickets cost $12 to $26 and are half-price on Mondays (kids get in for $1 on certain Sun games).

U.S. Cellular Field is at 333 W. 35th St. (© **312/674-1000;** www.whitesox. mlb.com), in the South Side neighborhood of Bridgeport. To get Sox tickets, call **Ticketmaster** at © **866/SOX-GAME** or visit the ticket office, open Monday through Friday from 10am to 6pm, Saturday and Sunday from 10am to 4pm, except on game days, when it opens at 9am. To get to the ballpark by subway/El, take the Red Line to Sox/35th Street.

BASKETBALL

Do not mention the name Jerry Reinsdorf or Jerry Krause to a Chicago sports fan unless you want to be pummeled like a speed bag. The owner and general manager, respectively, of the **Chicago Bulls** were—fairly or not—castigated by the public and local press after dismantling the world-famous six-time NBA championship Chicago Bulls following the 1998 season. We had grown to take for granted the frenzied celebrations in the street that inevitably occurred each June in the wake of the latest championship crown. It was a wonderful boost for a perennially pessimistic sports-loving metropolis, and a rare, indelible moment when the city's white and black populations seemed to embrace in simple camaraderie and festivity.

So you can imagine what a jolt it has been to hear about the Bulls losing 5, 10, or 15 games in a row, year after year. The **United Center,** 1901 W. Madison St. (© **312/455-4500;** www.chicagosports.com), where the Bulls play, feels like an airplane hangar–size funeral parlor these days. For the time being, tickets, once impossible to come by, are worth about as much as the paper they're printed on. So grab yourself a courtside seat—there are plenty to go around.

The **DePaul Blue Demons,** the local college team and an NCAA tournament selection last season, are a far better bet for a good game. They play mostly at the **Allstate Arena,** 6920 N. Mannheim Rd., Rosemont (© **773/325-7526**), although some of their games are at the United Center.

FOOTBALL

The **Chicago Bears** play at a newly renovated **Soldier Field,** Lake Shore Drive and 16th Street (© **847/615-2327;** www.chicagobears.com). Although the project was controversial (raising the usual uproar about tax dollars being used to fund a privately owned sports team), the original stadium, built to commemorate the soldiers of World War I, was undeniably shabby and low on amenities. The stadium's most distinctive feature—its classically-inspired colonnade—was retained, but a giant addition that looks somewhat like a spaceship was crammed awkwardly on top. Architecturally, it's a disaster. But from a comfort perspective, the place is much improved—although that doesn't impress long-time fans that prided themselves on surviving blistering cold game days and horrifying bathrooms.

Bears fans still reminisce about the 1985 Mike Ditka–led team's NFL championship like it happened yesterday. But the current Bears are no longer the notorious "Monsters of the Midway" who battered opponents into submission under the aegis of NFL founding father and legendary coach George "Papa Bear" Halas. Nor are they the gridiron warriors immortalized by hard-hitting linebacker Dick Butkus, or the fun-loving "Shufflin' Crew" led by Hall of Fame running back Walter Payton, the league's all-time rushing leader. But there is still something quintessentially Chicago about grilling up ribs and brats in the parking lot before the Bears go to battle against our arch enemy, the Green Bay Packers. Just make sure you dump a pint of peppermint schnapps in that thermos of hot chocolate before you experience "Bear Weather" for the first time.

The **Northwestern Wildcats** play Big Ten college ball at **Ryan Field,** 1501 Central St., in nearby Evanston (© **847/491-CATS**).

HOCKEY

The **Chicago Blackhawks** have a devoted, impassioned following of fans that work themselves into a frenzy with the first note of the "Star Spangled Banner." But don't expect any heroics on ice along the lines of past Hawks legends such as Bobby Hull and Tony Esposito. Any player that turns into a star and, hence, earns the right to restructure his contract for a higher salary is immediately traded by penny-pinching owner Bill Wirtz—derided by fans and local sportswriters as "Dollar Bill." The Blackhawks play at the **United Center,** 1901 W. Madison St. (© **312/455-4500;** www.chicagoblackhawks.com).

For a more affordable and family-friendly experience, catch the semipro **Chicago Wolves** at Allstate Arena (© **847/724-GOAL,** www.chicagowolves. com). The team has been consistently excellent over the past few years, and the games are geared toward all ages, with fireworks before the show and plenty of on- and off-ice entertainment.

HORSE RACING

Thoroughbred racing happens at **Arlington International Racecourse** (p. 206), 2200 W. Euclid Ave., in Arlington Heights (© **847/255-4300;** www.arlington park.com), and **Hawthorne Race Track,** 3501 S. Laramie Ave., in Stickney (© **708/780-3700**).

SOCCER

Chicago's major-league soccer team, the **Chicago Fire,** plays at Soldier Field from late May through October (© **888/MLS-FIRE;** www.chicago-fire.com). Games have a family feel, with plenty of activities for kids and affordable ticket prices ($15–$30).

9

Shopping

The art of merchandising has a rich history in Chicago. The original Marshall Field operated his namesake department store under the motto "Give the lady what she wants," pioneering many customer-service policies that are now standard (such as hassle-free returns). Catalogs from Chicago-based Sears and Montgomery Ward made clothes, books, and housewares accessible to even the most remote frontier towns. East to west, or back the other way, just about everything passed through Chicago.

Today, Montgomery Ward is no more, but Sears recently opened a new flagship store in the heart of the Loop, signaling the continued vitality of downtown Chicago as a shopping destination. From the fine furniture showrooms at the imposing Merchandise Mart to the "who's who" of designer boutiques lining Oak Street and Michigan Avenue, the quality of stores is top-notch. Because so many of the best are concentrated in one easy-to-walk area, the convenience is unmatched.

This chapter concentrates on the Magnificent Mile, State Street, and several trendy neighborhoods, where you'll find one-of-a-kind shops and boutiques that make shopping such an adventure.

SHOPPING HOURS As a general rule, store hours are 10am to 6 or 7pm Monday through Saturday, and noon to 6pm Sunday. Neighborhood stores tend to keep later hours, as do some of the stores along Michigan Avenue, which cater to after-work shoppers as well as tourists. Almost all stores have extended hours during the holiday season. Nearly all the stores in the Loop are open for daytime shopping only, generally from 9 or 10am to no later than 6pm Monday through Saturday. (The few remaining big downtown department stores have some selected evening hours.) Many Loop stores not on State Street are closed Saturday; on Sunday, the Loop—except for a few restaurants, theaters, and cultural attractions—is shut down pretty tight.

SALES TAX You might do a double take after checking the total on your purchase: At 8.75%, the state and local sales tax on nonfood items is one of the steepest in the country.

1 Shopping the Magnificent Mile

The nickname "Magnificent Mile"—hyperbole to some, an understatement to others—refers to the roughly mile-long stretch of North Michigan Avenue between Oak Street and the Chicago River.

The density of the area's first-rate shopping is, quite simply, unmatched anywhere. Even jaded shoppers from other worldly capitals are delighted at the ease and convenience of the stores concentrated here. Taking into account that tony Oak Street (see below) is just around a corner, the overall area is a little like New York's Fifth Avenue and Beverly Hills's Rodeo Drive rolled into one. Whether your passion is Bulgari jewelry, Prada bags, or Salvatore Ferragamo footwear, you'll find it on this stretch of concrete. And don't think you're seeing everything by walking down the street; Michigan Avenue is home to several indoor, high-rise malls, where plenty more boutiques and restaurants are tucked away. Window-shoppers and people-watchers will find plenty to amuse themselves because this is the city's liveliest corridor: The sidewalks are packed in the summer and on weekends with hordes of shoppers strolling up and down the avenue and pausing to enjoy the many street performers who enliven this strip.

For the ultimate Mag Mile shopping adventure, start at one end of North Michigan Avenue and try to work your way to the other. In this section are listed some of the best-known shops on the avenue and on nearby side streets.

A NORTH MICHIGAN AVENUE SHOPPER'S STROLL

This shopper's stroll begins at Oak Street at the northern end of the avenue and heads south toward the river. It just hits the highlights; you're sure to find much more to tickle your fancy and tempt your wallet as you meander from designer landmarks to well-known chain stores. North Michigan Avenue's four vertical malls—each a major shopping destination in its own right—are discussed below under "The Magnificent Malls."

The parade of designer names begins at the intersection of Michigan Avenue and Oak Street, including a couple housed in The Drake hotel, such as the legendary Danish silversmith **Georg Jensen,** 959 N. Michigan Ave. (© **312/642-9160**), known for outstanding craftsmanship in sterling silver and gold, including earrings, brooches, watches, tie clips, and flatware; and **Chanel,** 935 N. Michigan Ave. (© **312/787-5500**).

The newest luxury emporium in town is the spacious **Louis Vuitton** store at 919 N. Michigan Ave. (© **312/944-2010**), where you'll find trendy handbags and the company's distinctive brown-and-gold luggage. A few doors down is famed Italian jeweler **Bulgari,** 909 N. Michigan Ave. (© **312/255-1313**), which sells timepieces, necklaces, bracelets, rings, and silver gift items. Just across the street is **900 North Michigan,** commonly referred to as the Bloomingdale's building (see "The Magnificent Malls," below).

Just south of the Hancock Center and across the street is **Plaza Escada,** 840 N. Michigan Ave. (© **312/915-0500**), an elegant building between Chestnut and Pearson streets that houses the country's most comprehensive collection of apparel and accessories from German design house Escada (this is where you'll see the local society ladies shopping for their charity-ball gowns).

Giorgio Armani's sleek boutique, at 800 N. Michigan Ave. in the Park Hyatt Hotel (© **312/751-2244**), faces the park that overlooks the historic Water Tower. Just around the corner, also at 800 N. Michigan Ave. but with an entrance on Chicago Avenue, is the first American store from Canadian knitwear manufacturer **Marlowe** (© **312/988-9398**). Don't come here looking for a simple pullover; the shop looks like a modern art gallery, with prices that are closer to Armani than Banana Republic. Across the street, a few doors west of Michigan Avenue, is one of Chicago's hottest family destinations: **American Girl Place,** at 111 E. Chicago Ave. (© **877/AG-PLACE**). The three-story doll emporium attracts hordes of young girls (and parents) hooked on the popular mail-order company's line of historic character dolls. A stage show brings stories from the American Girl books to life, and the store's cafe is a nice spot for a special mother-daughter lunch or afternoon tea.

Magnificent Mile Shopping

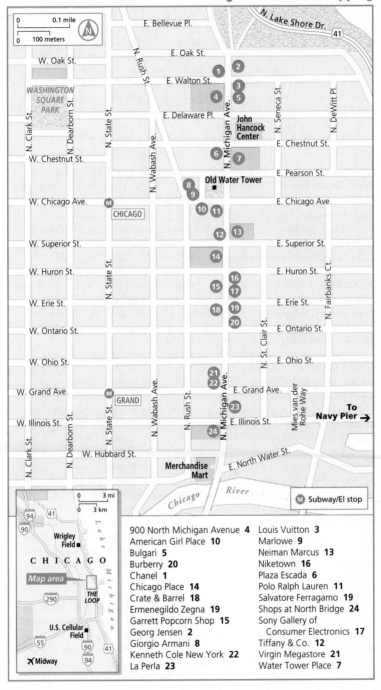

900 North Michigan Avenue **4**
American Girl Place **10**
Bulgari **5**
Burberry **20**
Chanel **1**
Chicago Place **14**
Crate & Barrel **18**
Ermenegildo Zegna **19**
Garrett Popcorn Shop **15**
Georg Jensen **2**
Giorgio Armani **8**
Kenneth Cole New York **22**
La Perla **23**

Louis Vuitton **3**
Marlowe **9**
Neiman Marcus **13**
Niketown **16**
Plaza Escada **6**
Polo Ralph Lauren **11**
Salvatore Ferragamo **19**
Shops at North Bridge **24**
Sony Gallery of
    Consumer Electronics **17**
Tiffany & Co. **12**
Virgin Megastore **21**
Water Tower Place **7**

(Moments   Resting at Crate & Barrel

Need a quick break during your shopping spree? The overstuffed couches on the third and fourth floors of Crate & Barrel practically beg to be tested out—and there are always as least a few weary shoppers slumped against the piles of pillows. Go ahead and rest awhile; the store's staff won't bug you. Make sure you stop by the terrace on the fourth floor for a bird's-eye view of bustling Michigan Avenue and enjoy a moment of contemplation before rejoining the hordes below.

The next block of Michigan Avenue has a New York vibe, thanks to the world's largest **Polo Ralph Lauren** (© 312/280-1655), a four-floor, wood-paneled mini-mansion, and **Tiffany & Co.** (© 312/944-7500), with its signature clock, jewels, and tabletop accessories (if you want to get your hands on one of the distinctive robin's-egg blue shopping bags without spending a fortune, the $50 sterling-silver key chains are the least expensive items in the store).

A few doors south are **Neiman Marcus,** 737 N. Michigan Ave. (© 312/642-5900), and, at 669 N. Michigan Ave. (© 312/642-6363), the hugely popular **Niketown,** a multilevel complex that helped pioneer the concept of retail as entertainment. A little farther south is a haven for reluctant male shoppers: the **Sony Gallery of Consumer Electronics,** 663 N. Michigan Ave. (© 312/943-3334), where the latest high-tech gadgets are displayed in a museumlike setting (head up to the 2nd floor to try out the newest PlayStation games).

Across the street, you'll probably see a line of people trailing out from the **Garrett Popcorn Shop,** 670 N. Michigan Ave. (© 312/944-2630), a 50-year-old landmark. Join the locals in line and pick up some caramel corn for a quick sugar rush.

At the intersection of Michigan Avenue and Erie Street is the appropriately barrel-shaped **Crate & Barrel,** 646 N. Michigan Ave. (© 312/787-5900). Crate & Barrel was started in Chicago, so this is the company's flagship location. Countless varieties of glassware, dishes, cookware, and kitchen gadgets for everyday use line the shelves. The top two floors are devoted to furniture.

Sharing the same address, at 645 N. Michigan Ave., are two big names in Italian fashion: shoemaker **Salvatore Ferragamo** (© 312/397-0464), which also sells men's and women's clothing; and **Ermenegildo Zegna** (© 312/587-9660), designer of finely tailored menswear. Continuing south, you'll find **Burberry,** 633 N. Michigan Ave. (© 312/787-2500), where the classic beige plaid has moved beyond trench coats to show up on chic purses, shoes, and bathing suits (if you're looking for luxury souvenirs, check out the collection of baby clothes and dog accessories).

Two shops are pulling younger, hipper shoppers into the renovated ground-floor retail wing of the Chicago Marriott: the **Virgin Megastore** (© 312/645-9300), which, true to its name, has stockpiled a megacollection of CDs, videos, DVDs, books, and interactive games; and **Kenneth Cole New York** (© 312/644-1163), offering a line of contemporary shoes for women and men, along with men's sportswear and suits. Across the street, at 535 N. Michigan Ave., is **La Perla** (© 312/494-0400), home of very trendy and very expensive Italian lingerie.

THE MAGNIFICENT MALLS

WATER TOWER PLACE   Chicago's first—and still busiest—vertical mall is Water Tower Place, a block-size, marble-sheathed building at 835 N. Michigan Ave. (© 312/440-3165), between East Pearson and East Chestnut streets. The mall's seven floors contain about 100 stores that reportedly account for roughly half of all the retail trade transacted along the Magnificent Mile. The mall also houses a dozen different cafes and restaurants.

Water Tower was the first big indoor mall to open downtown (in 1975), and 20 years ago its glass elevators and shiny gold trim gave the place a glamorous air. These days, after some recent renovations, the spiffed-up mall remains popular, but doesn't have much to distinguish it from any other upscale shopping center. Water Tower is a magnet for suburban teenagers (just like your mall back home!), and can get quite crowded during prime summer tourist season. Most of its stores are part of national chains (Gap, Victoria's Secret, etc.). But there are a few shops that make it worth a stop, including hip young designs from the British store **French Connection** (5th floor; © 312/932-9460) and wearable women's clothing at **Eileen Fisher** (2nd floor; © 312/943-9190). The department stores anchoring the mall are the Mag Mile outpost of the Loop's famed **Marshall Field's** (floors one to eight; © 312/335-7700) and a **Lord & Taylor** (floors one to seven; © 312/787-7400). One of Water Tower's best features is the funky food court **foodlife** (see listing, p. 130).

900 NORTH MICHIGAN   The most upscale of the Magnificent Mile's three vertical malls, 900 North Michigan (often called the Bloomingdale's building, for its most prominent tenant) avoids the tumult of Water Tower Place by appealing to a more well-heeled shopper. In addition to about 70 stores are a few good restaurants and a nice movie multiplex on the lower level. For mall information, call © 312/915-3916.

The Chicago outpost of **Gucci** (ground floor; © 312/664-5504) has the same hip attitude as the label's sexy clothing and much-in-demand purses. Also on the ground floor is **MaxMara** (© 312/475-9500), the Italian women's fashion house known for elegantly constructed coats and separates (some of which will cost you about as much as a flight to Italy). Other goodies worth checking out include funky European footwear at **Charles David** (2nd floor; © 312/944-9013), amazingly intricate French glassware at **Lalique** (ground floor; © 312/867-1787), silver and crystal splurge items at **Christofle** (ground floor; © 312/664-9700), and lovely hats made by a local designer at **Linda Campisano Millinery** (6th floor; © 312/337-1004).

Tips   Lunch on the Mag Mile

When I worked just off Michigan Avenue, my favorite spot for lunch was the Food Court on the eighth floor of Chicago Place. A bright, airy space with a fountain and palm trees, it's my pick for the best cheap eats in the area. You'll find the usual mall favorites **(Subway, Taco Bell, Wendy's)**, but healthier dishes are available at **Pattie's Quick and Lite** (salads, wraps, pasta) and **Pita Pavilion** (Mediterranean). My true downfall, though, were always the crispy french fries at the **Great Steak and Potato Company.** Grab one of the tables behind Pita Pavilion for a great Michigan Avenue view.

CHICAGO PLACE   Chicago Place, 700 N. Michigan Ave. (✆ **312/266-7710**), has been looking for an identity ever since opening in 1991. Although it is home to **Saks Fifth Avenue** (✆ **312/944-6500**), the rest of the stores are not as upscale; they include a three-floor **Ann Taylor** (1st, mezzanine, and 2nd floors; ✆ **312/335-0117**) and the companion furniture stores **Retrospect** (5th floor; ✆ **312/440-1270**), for traditional home furnishings, and **Room and Board** (6th and 7th floors; ✆ **312/266-0656**), for contemporary styles. The mall has also attracted a good selection of import stores, the best of which are **Joy of Ireland,** where you can also stop for a spot of tea in the afternoon (✆ **312/664-7290**), **Design Toscano** (✆ **312/587-1199**), and **Russian Creations** (✆ **312/573-0792**).

THE SHOPS AT NORTH BRIDGE   The newest addition to the Mag Mile shopping scene is this mall at 520 N. Michigan Ave. The anchor of the development is a four-story **Nordstrom** (✆ **312/464-1515**). The mall includes the first Chicago locations for **A/X Armani Exchange** (✆ **312/467-5702**), Giorgio Armani's younger and more affordable line, and **Tommy Bahama** (✆ **312/644-8388**), which sells upscale tropical gear (plenty of Hawaiian-style prints and bright colors). Moms and their kids can get decked out in fun, colorful outfits at **Oilily** (✆ **312/822-9616**). The third floor is devoted to children's shops, the best of which is **The Lego Store** (✆ **312/494-0760**)—look for the replicas of Chicago landmarks built out of those distinctive colored-plastic blocks. Future Easy Riders can get decked out in minisized motorcycle gear at the **Harley-Davidson** children's store (✆ **312/755-9520**).

CHIC SHOPPING ON NEARBY OAK STREET

Oak Street has long been a symbol of exclusive designer-label shopping; if a store has an Oak Street address, you can count on its being expensive. This posh, 1-block stretch of exclusive shops is located at the northern tip of the Magnificent Mile, where Michigan Avenue ends and Lake Shore Drive begins. While some big-name boutiques (such as Giorgio Armani) have left Oak Street for higher-traffic locations on Michigan Avenue, this stretch of converted town houses is still well worth a stroll—for people-watching, if nothing else (this is Main St. for Chicago socialites). Most of Oak Street is closed on Sunday, except during the holiday season.

Without a doubt, the top independent designer shop in Chicago is **Ultimo,** 114 E. Oak St. (✆ **312/787-1171**), which carries both men's and women's clothing and accessories. Although the store has had its ups and downs recently (ever since the founder and longtime owner sold it), this is still the place to find hot, up-and-coming designers before they show up in department stores. Ultimo's distinctive lush, red interior also is a welcome change from the minimalist design of so many other designer boutiques.

Oak Street is home to several fancy footwear moguls: Italian shoemaker **Tod's,** 121 E. Oak St. (✆ **312/943-0070**); **Donald J Pliner,** 106 E. Oak St. (✆ **312/202-9600**), whose eponymous founder got his start in Chicago; and elegant French designs from **Robert Clergerie,** 56 E. Oak St. (✆ **312/867-8720**), displayed in a sleek, modern setting. Shoes, stationery—and most importantly, handbags—are available at **kate spade,** 101 E. Oak St. (✆ **312/654-8853**), along with the Jack Spade line of men's accessories. The priciest accessories on this very pricey block are probably to be found at French luxury house **Hermès of Paris,** 110 E. Oak St. (✆ **312/787-8175**).

Finds An Oak Street Bargain

Oak Street is not the place to come shopping for bargains—with one exception: **Bravco,** 43 E. Oak St. (© 312/943-4305), a crowded, narrow drugstore that seems out of place among the hip boutiques, is the favorite spot of Chicago hairstylists and makeup artists. You'll find an excellent selection of professional hair and beauty products (including Aveda, Sebastian, and Bumble and Bumble) here for much less than they cost at salons. Even if you haven't heard of some of the brands, trust us—if Bravco carries them, they're hot.

Thread-count fanatics swear by the sheets from **Pratesi,** 67 E. Oak St. (© **312/943-8422**), and **Frette,** 41 E. Oak St. (© **312/649-3744**), both of which supply linens to the top hotels in Europe (and where sheet sets cost more than what some people pay in rent). Other shops include **Loro Piana,** 45 E. Oak St. (© **312/664-6644**), for Italian cashmere and wool clothing, and **Marina Rinaldi,** 113 E. Oak St. (© **312/867-8700**), a division of Italian clothing company MaxMara that specializes in women's clothing sizes 12 and above (making this a welcome respite from the fashion-model-size clothes at surrounding boutiques). **Dunhill,** 55 E. Oak St. (© **312-467-4455**), sells upscale British menswear; there's even an old-style barbershop inside.

Anchoring the western end of the block are two haute heavyweights: **Barneys New York,** 25 E. Oak St. (© **312/587-1700**), for chic clothing, stellar shoe selection, and always-interesting home accessories (prepare for attitude from the sales staff if you're not dressed to impress); and stratospherically hip Italian designer **Prada,** 30 E. Oak St. (© **312/951-1113**), which offers three floors of sleek, postmodern fashions for men and women, and plenty of the designer's signature handbags.

2 More Shopping Neighborhoods

STATE STREET & THE LOOP

This was Chicago's first great shopping district—by World War I, seven of the largest and most lavish department stores in the world were competing for shoppers' loyalties along a half-mile stretch between Randolph Street and Congress Parkway. The area has now been eclipsed by Michigan Avenue, and State Street now is lined with discount stores and fast-food outlets. But it's still worth visiting because of the two grand old department stores that remain: **Marshall Field & Co.,** 111 N. State St., at Randolph Street (© **312/781-1000**); and **Carson Pirie Scott & Co.,** a few blocks south, at 1 S. State St., at the corner of Madison Street (© **312/641-7000**). Both buildings are city landmarks and attractions in themselves. Architecturally speaking, the Louis Sullivan–designed Carson's is the more celebrated of the two; however, Field's State Street store remains one of the world's largest, occupying an entire city block and featuring the largest Tiffany glass mosaic dome in the United States. If you're in Chicago between Thanksgiving and New Year's, a visit to Marshall Field's to see the holiday windows and to have lunch under the Great Tree in the Walnut Room is in keeping with local tradition.

Although State Street has not recaptured the glamour of decades past, it manages to draw crowds of loyal customers from the Loop's office towers and

> **Tips   Point Zero**
>
> If the quick change from north to south in the Loop confuses you, keep in mind that in Chicago, point zero for the purpose of address numbering is the intersection of State and Madison streets.

Chicagoans turned off by Michigan Avenue's snob factor. There's no better example of the street's revival than the 2001 opening of a new **Sears** store (© **312/373-6000**) at the corner of State and Madison streets and a large **Old Navy** store at Washington and State streets (© **312/551-0522**).

RIVER NORTH

Along with becoming Chicago's primary art-gallery district, River North—the area west of the Magnificent Mile and north of the Chicago River—has attracted many interesting home-design shops, concentrated on Wells Street from Kinzie Street to Chicago Avenue. The neighborhood even has a mall of its own—**The Shops at the Mart** (© **312/527-7990**)—in the Merchandise Mart, at Wells and Kinzie streets, with a standard collection of chain stores.

The rest of the **Merchandise Mart,** the world's largest commercial building, houses mostly interior design showrooms—which are open only to professional designers. The massive complex was built in 1930 by Marshall Field & Company, and bought in 1945 by Joseph P. Kennedy (JFK's dad); the Kennedy family ran the Mart until the late 1990s. The only way for visitors to get a sense of the whole massive complex is to take a public tour, usually offered Fridays at 1pm ($10 adults; © **312/527-7762**).

Not all of the furniture trade in Chicago is confined to the Merchandise Mart. In River North, you'll find **Manifesto,** 755 N. Wells St., at Chicago Avenue (© **312/664-0733**), offering custom-designed furniture, as well as imports from Italy and Austria, and **Mig & Tig,** 549 N. Wells St., at Ohio Street (© **312/644-8277**), a charming furniture and decorative-accessories shop. **Sawbridge Studios,** 153 W. Ohio St. (© **312/828-0055**), between LaSalle and Wells streets, purveys exquisite handcrafted furniture, accessories, and gift items from artisans across America in a handsome, lofted, gallery-type space with exposed brick walls. **Michael FitzSimmons Decorative Arts,** 311 W. Superior St. (© **312/787-0496**), is one of the top dealers anywhere for furniture and furnishings dating to the Arts and Crafts period.

Creative types will find their imaginations running wild with homemade projects at the three-level **Paper Source,** 232 W. Chicago Ave., at Franklin Street (© **312/337-0798**). Artists, designers, and other paper fetishists can choose among reams of exotic and unusual paper, as well as journals, gift items, handmade wedding albums, and a roomful of fun rubber stamps.

ART GALLERY HOPPING

Since the 1960s, when the Chicago Imagists (painters Ed Paschke, Jim Nutt, and Roger Brown among them) attracted international attention with their shows at the Hyde Park Art Center, the city has been a fertile breeding ground for emerging artists and innovative art dealers. The primary gallery district today is concentrated in the River North neighborhood, where century-old, redbrick warehouse buildings have been converted into lofty exhibition spaces. More recently, a new generation of gallery owners has set up shop in the rapidly gentrifying West Loop neighborhood, where you'll tend to find more cutting-edge work. The River North gallery district is an easy walk from many hotels; the West Loop may seem a little farther afield, but it's only a short cab ride from downtown (you can also take the bus, but I'd recommend a taxi at night).

The River North gallery season officially gets underway on the first Friday after Labor Day in September. Besides fall, another great time to visit the district is from mid-July to early September, when the Chicago Art Dealers Association presents the Absolut Vodka–sponsored **Absolut Visions,** an annual lineup of programs tailored to the public. Early September also offers the annual **Around the Coyote** festival in Wicker Park/Bucktown (call ℂ **773/342-6777** for information), when scores of artists open their studios to the public.

The *Chicago Reader,* a free weekly newspaper available at many stores, taverns, and cafes on the North Side, publishes a very comprehensive listing of current gallery exhibitions, as does the *Chicago Gallery News,* a quarterly published by the Chicago Art Dealers Association (ℂ **312/649-0065**) that is available free at the city's three visitor information centers.

Below is a sampling of recommended galleries around the city.

Alan Koppel Gallery   Open since 1995, this expansive galley showcases modern and contemporary works of art, as well as French and Italian furniture from the '20s through the '50s (in a separate area). Koppel also specializes in 20th-century photography, so if you're hankering for something by Diane Arbus, Man Ray, or Walker Evans, this is the place to look. 210 W. Chicago Ave. ℂ **312/640-0730**. Subway/El: Brown or Red line to Chicago.

Aldo Castillo Gallery   Aldo Castillo left his native Nicaragua in 1976, shortly after the Sandinistas began their revolution against the Somoza regime. He arrived in Chicago in 1985 and, 8 years later, appalled at the lack of attention given to Latin American art, opened his eponymous gallery in Lakeview, moving to his present River North location in 1993. Castillo continues to promote a range of work by emerging artists and established masters from Latin America, Spain, and Portugal. 233 W. Huron St. ℂ **312/337-2536**. Subway/El: Brown or Red line to Chicago.

Ann Nathan Gallery   Ann Nathan, who started out as a collector, shows exciting (and sometimes outrageous) pieces in clay, wood, and metal—along with paintings, photographs, and "functional art" (pieces that blur the line between furniture and sculpture). Nathan's space in the center of the River

---

⌐ Fun Fact Jewelers' Row

It's not quite as impressive as the Big Apple's diamond district, but Chicago's own "Jewelers' Row" is certainly worth a detour for rock hunters. Half a dozen high-rises along the Wabash Avenue El tracks in the heart of the Loop service the wholesale trade, but the one at 5 S. Wabash Ave. opens its doors to customers off the street. There's a mall-like retail space on the ground floor, crammed with tiny booths manned by smooth-talking reps hawking their wares, and you can grab a map here for a self-guided tour of the rest of the building's tenants. It's quite an experience because many are closet-size cubbyholes with hunched-over geezers who look as if they've been eyeballing solitaire and marquise cuts since the Roosevelt administration—Teddy, that is.

North district is one of the most beautiful in the city. 218 W. Superior St. ☎ 312/664-6622. Subway/El: Brown or Red line to Chicago.

Carl Hammer Gallery   A former schoolteacher and one of the most venerated dealers in Chicago, Carl Hammer touts his wares as "contemporary art and selected historical masterworks by American and European self-taught artists"—but it's the "self-taught" part that warrants emphasis. Hammer helped pioneer the field known as "outsider art," which has since become a white-hot commodity in the international art world. 740 N. Wells St. ☎ 312/266-8512. Subway/El: Brown or Red line to Chicago.

Donald Young Gallery   Internationally renowned on the contemporary art scene since the late 1970s, when he teamed with ex-partner and ex-wife Rhona Hoffman (listed below), Young returned to Chicago to much applause in 1999 after an 8-year residency in Seattle. His very dramatic West Loop gallery is a haven for critically important artists working in video, sculpture, photography, painting, and installation, including Anne Chu, Gary Hill, Martin Puryear, Bruce Nauman, Cristina Iglesias, Robert Mangold, and Charles Ray. 933 W. Washington St. ☎ 312/455-0100. Bus: No. 20 (Madison).

Vedanta Gallery   Owner Kavi Gupta (a former investment banker) is widely credited with kicking off the West Loop art scene when he developed this property as a home for new galleries. Vedanta specializes in contemporary art by national and international emerging artists, so you never quite know what you're going to see here. Also worth checking out in the same building are **Thomas McCormick Gallery** (☎ 312/226-6800) and **Kraft/Lieberman Gallery** (☎ 312/948-0555). 835 W. Washington St. ☎ 312/432-0708. Bus: No. 20 (Madison).

G.R. N'Namdi Gallery   George N'Namdi founded his gallery, which specializes in African-American artists, 2 decades ago in the Detroit area. His son Jumaane operates this second location. Artists they've helped bring to the attention of museums and art collectors include James Vanderzee, Al Loving, Edward Clark, Robert Colescott, and local photographer Rashid Johnson. 110 N. Peoria St. ☎ 312/563-9240. Bus: No. 20 (Madison).

Marx-Saunders Gallery   Chicago is home to a trio of world-class galleries dealing in contemporary glass-art sculpture. Fortunately for glass-art lovers, they're within footsteps of each other along Superior Street in River North: **Habatat Galleries Chicago,** 222 W. Superior St. (☎ 312/440-0288); **Portia Gallery,** 207 W. Superior St. (☎ 312/932-9500); and Marx-Saunders Gallery. The last houses the city's largest showcase of glass art and features world-famous artists past and present (William Morris, Mark Fowler, Therman Statom, and Hiroshi Yamano), as well as newcomers. 230 W. Superior St. ☎ 312/573-1400. Subway/El: Brown or Red line to Chicago.

Maya Polsky Gallery   Gallery owner Maya Polsky deals in international contemporary art, and also represents some leading local artists—including Chicago's most famous living artist, Ed Paschke. But she's best known for the contemporary and postrevolutionary art of Russia, including the work of such masters as Natalya Nesterova and Sergei Sherstiuk. 215 W. Superior St. ☎ 312/440-0055. Subway/El: Brown or Red line to Chicago.

Rhona Hoffman Gallery   Like her former partner and spouse, Donald Young, the New York–born Hoffman maintains a high profile on the international contemporary art scene. She launched her gallery in 1983 and, from the start, sought national and international artists, typically young and cutting-edge artists who weren't represented elsewhere in Chicago. Today she is the purveyor of such blue-chip players as Cindy Sherman, Sol LeWitt, and Jenny Holzer; she has also added young up-and-comers such as Dawoud Bey. 118 N. Peoria St. ℂ 312/455-1990. Bus: No. 20 (Madison).

Richard Gray Gallery   Richard Gray is the dean of art dealers in Chicago. He founded his gallery in 1963, has been president of the Art Dealers Association of America and chairman of the board at the University of Chicago's Smart Museum of Art, and operates a second gallery in New York. Specializing in paintings, sculpture, and drawings by leading artists from the major movements in 20th-century American and European art, Gray and his son, Paul, who now runs the Chicago gallery, have shown the work of such luminaries as Pablo Picasso, Jean Dubuffet, Willem de Kooning, Alexander Calder, Claes Oldenberg, Joan Miró, and Henri Matisse. John Hancock Center, 875 N. Michigan Ave., Suite 2503. ℂ 312/642-8877. Subway/El: Red Line to Chicago.

Wood Street Gallery & Sculpture Garden   The most appealing and enduring gallery in Wicker Park is undoubtedly Wood Street, a lovely, expansive second-floor space dealing in contemporary sculpture, figurative and narrative paintings, and manipulated photography (there's also a sculpture garden next to the building). Owner Mary O'Shaughnessy makes a point of emphasizing local and national emerging and midcareer artists. 1239 N. Wood St. (just north of Division St.). ℂ 773/227-3306. Subway/El: Blue Line to Division.

Zolla/Lieberman Gallery   Bob Zolla and Roberta Lieberman kicked off the River North revival when they opened their gallery here in 1976. Today, Zolla/ Lieberman represents a wide range of artists—including sculptor Deborah Butterfield, installation artist Vernon Fisher, and painter Terence LaNoue—and this gallery is generally considered the *grande dame* of the area. 325 W. Huron St. (at Orleans St.). ℂ 312/944-1990. Subway/El: Brown Line to Chicago.

LINCOLN PARK

The North Side neighborhood of Lincoln Park has a variety of unique specialty shops that make it easy to browse through this leafy, picturesque community. While many of the shops on Michigan Avenue are branches of national chains and offer few surprises, the shops and boutiques in Lincoln Park tend to be locally owned and offer unique and interesting wares. Shops are located on the primary commercial arteries running through the area, including Armitage Avenue, Webster Avenue, Halsted Street, Clark Street, and Lincoln Avenue.

ARMITAGE AVENUE   Armitage Avenue has emerged as a shopping destination in its own right, thanks to an influx of wealthy young professionals who have settled into historic town homes on the neighboring tree-lined streets. The shops and boutiques here—which sell everything from artisan-made apparel to offbeat gifts—are geared toward a sophisticated, well-heeled shopper, and make for great browsing. As you stroll the area, you will feel part of a community, with neighbors greeting each other and catching up on the street corners. Most of the shops are concentrated between Halsted Street and Clybourn Avenue.

Here you'll find **Urban Gardener,** 1006 W. Armitage Ave. (ℂ 773/477-2070), a two-story garden shop in an old Victorian row house with lovely displays of gardening books and tools, topiaries, garden furniture, and other gifts; **Lori's Designer Shoes,** 824 W. Armitage Ave. (ℂ 773/281-5655), for a great selection of shoes at great prices (p. ###); and the jaw-droppingly beautiful **Tabula Tua,** 1015 W. Armitage Ave. (ℂ 773/525-3500), with everything you need to set the perfect table.

Finds **Pamper Yourself**

When all that Armitage Avenue shopping gets just *too* exhausting, take a break at one of the beauty stores concentrated within a few blocks of each other on Halsted Street. **Endo-Exo Apothecary,** 2034 N. Halsted St. (© 773/525-0500), lined with vintage wood cabinets, is a peaceful retreat that stocks a number of specialty skin-care and make-up lines; they'll even give you a complimentary makeover. The mood is more flashy and hip at **Fresh,** 2040 N. Halsted St. (© 773/404-9776), where the sleek shelves are filled with skin treatments, at-home spa supplies, and their own line of cosmetics; test out some of the aromatic products and you'll feel instantly rejuvenated. Now that you're freshened up and made over . . . it's time to get back to shopping!

A number of clothing and accessories stores cater to the hip young women who live in the area. **Celeste Turner,** 859 W. Armitage Ave. (© 773/549-3390), offers sophisticated suits, dresses, and eveningwear from up-and-coming designers. **Art Effect,** 934 W. Armitage Ave. (© 773/929-3600), which bills itself as a "modern-day general store," stocks everything from cute blouses and creative jewelry to handmade picture frames, which makes for fun browsing. Bargain hunters shouldn't miss **Fox's,** 2150 N. Halsted St. (© 773/281-0700), a perennially crowded shop that offers designer clothing at a steep discount. The downside: Most clothing labels are cut out, so you might not know exactly which A-list name you're buying. But Chicago fashion insiders flock here; as I heard one woman say recently as she shopped at Fox's: "Too often, I stock up at Sak's, then find the same thing here for less." Another great stop for designer clothes at real-people prices is the consignment shop **McShane's Exchange,** 815 W. Armitage Ave. (© 773/525-0282, see listing on p. 245). And don't miss the boutique of local-gal-made-good **Cynthia Rowley,** 808 W. Armitage Ave. (© 773/528-6160).

LAKEVIEW

Shoppers will find elements of both prosperous Lincoln Park and alternative-ish Wicker Park when they're wandering along Lakeview's principal avenues.

BELMONT AVENUE & CLARK STREET   Radiating from the intersection of Belmont Avenue and Clark Street is a string of shops catering to rebellious kids on tour from their homes in the 'burbs (the Dunkin' Donuts on the corner is often referred to as "Punkin' Donuts" in their honor).

One constant in the ever-changing youth culture has been the **Alley,** 858 W. Belmont Ave., at Clark Street (© 773/525-3180), an "alternative shopping complex" selling everything from plaster gargoyles to racks of leather jackets. It has separate shops specializing in condoms, cigars, and bondage wear.

All the latest men's (and some women's) fashion styles—from names such as Fresh Jive, Fuct, and Diesel—can be found under the same roof at the multiroom building housing the **Aero** and **Untitled** shops, 2707 N. Clark St. (© 773/404-9225). Whether you're into tight, fitted fashion or the layered, droopy-pants look, it's here. **Tragically Hip,** a storefront women's boutique at 931 W. Belmont Ave. (© 773/549-1500), next to the Belmont El train stop, has outlasted many other similar purveyors of cutting-edge women's apparel.

Or, you can get plugged into what the kids are reading at **Chicago Comics,** 3244 N. Clark St. (© 773/528-1983), the industry's 1998 pick for best comics shop in the country. Besides the usual superhero titles, you'll find lots of European and Japanese comics, along with underground books and 'zines.

SOUTHPORT AVENUE   Another strip worth a stroll is the gentrified retail row along Southport Avenue, a few blocks west of Wrigley Field. With the Music Box Theater at 3733 N. Southport Ave., north of Addison Street, as its anchor, the area has an interesting mix of quirky and artsy merchants and restaurateurs. **P.O.S.H.,** 3729 N. Southport Ave., between Waveland Avenue and Grace Street (© 773/529-7674), offers never-used vintage silver and commercial-grade china from European and American hotels and restaurants that make for fun, quirky tableware. A new boutique catering to hip young women with plenty of disposable income is **Krista K,** 3458 N. Southport Ave. (© 773/248-1967), which stocks hot newer designers that aren't widely available in Chicago.

WICKER PARK/BUCKTOWN
Note: For a map of this area, see p. 157.

The go-go gentrification of the Wicker Park/Bucktown area has been followed by not only a rash of restaurants and bars, but also retailers with an artsy bent that reflect the neighborhood's bohemian spirit. Mixed in with old neighborhood businesses, such as discount furniture stores and religious icon purveyors, is a proliferation of antique-furniture shops, too-cool-for-school clothing boutiques (see the box "Chic Boutiques," below), and eclectic galleries and gift emporiums.

The friendly modern-day Marco Polos at **Pagoda Red,** 1714 N. Damen Ave., second floor (© 773/235-1188), have imported beautiful (and expensive) antique furniture and art objects, including Chinese concubine beds, painted Tibetan cabinets, Burmese rolling water vessels, cast-iron lotus bowls, bronze Buddhas, and Chinese inspiration stones. The three women who opened the upscale bazaar **Embelezar** a few years ago at 1639 N. Damen Ave. (© 773/645-9705) purvey exotic merchandise from around the world, both old and new, including the famous Fortuny silk lamps—hand-painted in Venice at the only studio allowed to reproduce the original Fortuny designs. You'll find a well-edited selection of home accessories and jewelry at **Lille,** 1923 W. North Ave. (© 773/342-0563). The airy, white space looks like an art gallery, with pieces from internationally known designers (Lulu de Kwiatkowski handbags, Christian Tortu vases) alongside plenty of quirky objects.

Hip young dudes will find everything for the well-dressed 21st-century man at **Apartment Number 9,** 1804 N. Damen Ave. (© 773/395-2999), a shop that specializes in trendy—but not outrageous—modern menswear. And really

---

Moments   **Taking a Break in Wicker Park**

When you're ready to rest your weary self, settle down at a local coffeehouse and soak in Wicker Park's artsy vibe. **Earwax Café,** 1564 N. Milwaukee Ave. (© 773/772-4019), attracts the jaded and pierced set with a no-frills, slightly gritty atmosphere. **Filter,** across the street at 1585 N. Milwaukee Ave. (© 773/227-4850), is a little more welcoming; comfy couches fill the main dining room, which features paintings by local artists. Both cafes are near the bustling intersection of North, Milwaukee, and Damen avenues—the heart of Wicker Park—and draw a steady stream of locals. It's here you'll realize that Wicker Park is really just a small town—with cooler hair and funkier shoes.

Chic Boutiques

In the not-so-distant past, local fashion addicts fled to the coasts to shop for cutting-edge designer duds. Those days are over. Chicago has come into its own fashion-wise as a new generation of boutiques has sprung up, offering a fresh array of unique accouterments. These are some of the best.

The cozy, minimalist **Chasalla** boutique, 70 E. Oak St. (© **312/640-1940**), specializes in clothing from designers' younger, slightly more-affordable labels, including Versace's Versus, D&G, Hugo Red Label, Cinque, and GFF Gianfranco Ferre.

Just around the corner from chic Oak Street is the newest fashionista haven, **Ikram,** 873 Rush St. (© **312/587-1000**). Run by Ikram Goldman, a former saleswoman at well-known women's clothing store Ultimo, the shop stocks all the big names, from Valentino to Yves St. Laurent—and whatever else *Vogue* has declared "hot" for the season. But tucked among the high-priced pieces are jewelry, stationery, and decorative accessories that give the place a personal touch.

Clever Alice, 2248 N. Clark St. (© **773/665-0555**), used to be Lincoln Park's best-kept secret, when it was tucked away on the lower level of a town house. Now that the store has moved upstairs, with a bright, airy interior and large display windows, it's attracting more attention. Loyal fans love the body-conscious, European-inspired clothing and fun accessories.

With white-hot designers including Tocca, Plein Sud, St. Vincent, and Barbara Bui Initials filling the racks, it's no wonder that business is booming at **Jolie Joli,** 2131 N. Southport Ave. (© **773/327-4917**). Located in an uninteresting stretch near the Clybourn Corridor but well worth seeking out, the boutique offers killer men's and women's wear by NY Industrie, playful frocks by Shoshanna, and racks of other garb by hard-to-find labels.

Wicker Park's **p45,** 1643 N. Damen Ave. (© **773/862-4523**), is a gold mine of urbane and cutting-edge fashion for men and women. Word about the store's unique mix of hip national labels (Michelle Mason,

hip dudes should stop by **Quimby's,** 1854 W. North Ave. (© **773/342-0910**), the source for every kind of obscure, alternative, and possibly offensive comic, magazine, and self-published 'zine.

3 Shopping A to Z

Chicago has shops selling just about anything you could want or need, be it functional or ornamental, whimsical or exotic. Although the following list only scratches the surface, it will give you an idea of the range of merchandise available. You'll find more shops in many of these categories, such as apparel and gifts, covered in the earlier sections of this chapter.

ANTIQUES

The greatest concentration of antiques businesses, from packed-to-the-rafters malls to idiosyncratic individual shops, can be found on Belmont Avenue west

Rebecca Danenberg, Colovos, Catherine, and M Collection) and local designers (Amy Zoller, Urban Armor by Sandy Neal, and Regan Wood) has spread far and wide since the boutique's 1997 opening. Innovative fashions from emerging young designers are draped all over this slick lofted space.

Browsing **Robin Richman,** 2108 N. Damen Ave. (© 773/278-6150), feels more like poking around a big, antiques-filled closet than shopping for threads in Bucktown. The walls of this tiny storefront are adorned with balls of string, vintage diaries, and artful handmade wire hangers. While Richman carries a small assortment of men's and women's separates (mostly loose, unstructured pieces), the big draw here is her exquisite sweaters.

Very few retail outlets can successfully mix the haute designs of a British-style queen like Vivienne Westwood with quirky skater T's and street-savvy cargo pants, but Nigeria native Obi Nwazota has done just that at his spare Wicker Park boutique, **Softcore,** 1420 N. Milwaukee Ave. (© 773/276-7616). The 31-year-old architect and designer's sense of style is urban, nonconformist, and no-holds-barred.

Kim Hiley, the owner of **Tribeca,** 2480½ N. Lincoln Ave. (© 773/528-5958), describes her style as "the kind of clothes you might wear on a date." While she doesn't eschew the essential blacks and grays, her racks are lined with pastels, oranges, teals, and flowery, exotic patterns. The store is bright, cutesy, and essentially feminine, catering more to the style sensibilities of corporate Lincoln Park 20-somethings than hipster Wicker Park club hoppers. Hiley recently opened a second location at 1013 W. Armitage Ave. (© 773/296-2997).

Lincoln Park 20- and 30-somethings flock to **Shopgirl,** 1206 W. Webster Ave. (© 773/935-SHOP) to pick up the latest looks from trendy lines such as Trina Turk and Theory. It's a girly gathering place (pink walls, glittery chandeliers) with three-digit price tags, but it still has the feel of a neighborhood hangout, thanks to the friendly staff.

of Southport Avenue, or stretching north and south of Belmont Avenue along intersecting Lincoln Avenue. Here are a few others.

Architectural Artifacts, Inc. *(Finds* Chicago has a handful of salvage specialists that cater to the design trades and retail customers seeking an unusual architectural piece for their homes. This one is the best and well worth seeking out at its location next to the Metra train line in the far-northwest corner of the city's Lakeview neighborhood. Its brightly lit, well-organized, cavernous showroom features everything from original mantels, garden ornaments, and vintage bathroom hardware to American and French Art Deco lighting fixtures. Shoppers may also come across portions of historically significant buildings. 4325 N. Ravenswood Ave. (east of Damen Ave. and south of Montrose Ave.). © 773/348-0622. Subway/El: Brown Line to Irving Park.

Broadway Antique Market Want to shop vintage like a pro? Visiting Hollywood prop stylists and local interior designers flock here to find 20th-century antiques in near-perfect condition. In this two-level, 20,000-square-foot vintage megamart, you'll spot both pricey pieces (for example, an Arne Jacobsen egg chair) and affordable collectibles for less than $100 (Roseville pottery, Art Deco barware, Peter Max scarves). 6130 N. Broadway (½ mile north of Hollywood Ave. and Lake Shore Dr.). © 773/743-5444. Subway/El: Red Line to Granville.

Jay Robert's Antique Warehouse This mammoth space boasts 60,000 square feet of fine furniture, as well as fireplaces, stained glass, and an impressive selection of antique clocks. 149 W. Kinzie St. (at LaSalle St.). © 312/222-0167. Subway/El: Brown Line to Merchandise Mart.

Modern Times A few antiques shops have opened to furnish the wave of lofts that has washed over trendy Wicker Park. This one specializes in the major designers of home furnishings from the 1930s to the 1960s, plus lighting fixtures of all types and some jewelry. 1538 N. Milwaukee Ave. (between Division St. and North Ave.). © 773/772-8871. Subway/El: Blue Line to Damen.

Salvage One Everything and the kitchen sink are for sale at this sprawling source for the home handyperson: doors, mantels, tubs, stained glass, and light fixtures. 1840 W. Hubbard St. (at Damen Ave.). © 312/733-0098. Bus: No. 65 (Grand Ave.).

BOOKS

Abraham Lincoln Book Shop This bookstore is truly the land of Lincoln, with one of the country's most outstanding collections of Lincolniana, from rare and antique books about the 16th president to collectible signatures, letters, and other documents illuminating the lives of other U.S. presidents and historical figures. The shop carries new historical and academic works, too. 357 W. Chicago Ave. (between Orleans and Sedgwick sts.). © 312/944-3085. Subway/El: Brown Line to Chicago.

Afrocentric Bookstore Located in the Chicago Music Mart, this bookstore houses more than 10,000 titles on African and African-American life, as well as magazines, greeting cards, and other gift items. The store also hosts author visits. 333 S. State St. (at Jackson Blvd.). © 312/939-1956. Subway/El: Red Line to Jackson.

Barbara's Bookstore This haven for small, independent press titles also has extensive selections of everything current. In addition, it has a well-stocked children's section, with sitting areas for the tots to peruse the books. If you enjoy author readings, call the store to see if your visit coincides with that of one of your favorite writers. Two other branches are a small tourist-targeted shop at Navy Pier, 700 E. Grand Ave. (© 312/222-0890), and a shop in Oak Park at 1100 Lake St. (© 708/848-9140). 1350 N. Wells St. (between Division St. and North Ave.). © 312/642-5044. Subway/El: Brown Line to Sedgwick.

Barnes & Noble Barnes & Noble opened its first downtown store in the heart of the Gold Coast a few years ago. The two-level store comes complete with a cafe, in case you get the munchies while perusing the miles of books. The store also hosts readings, book groups, and other special events. There's another store in Lincoln Park, at 659 W. Diversey Ave., 1 block west of Clark Street (© 773/871-9004), and one at 1441 W. Webster Ave., at Clybourn Avenue (© 773/871-3610). 1130 N. State St. (at Elm St.). © 312/280-8155. Subway/El: Red Line to Clark/Division.

Borders You couldn't ask for a better location, right across from Water Tower Place. This place is like a minidepartment store, with books, magazines, CDs, and computer software spread over four floors, and a cafe with a view overlooking the Mag Mile. You'll also find author readings, book signings, and other special events. There's also a new Borders in the Loop at 150 N. State St., at Randolph Street (📞 **312/606-0750**), and one in Lincoln Park at 2817 N. Clark St., at Diversey Avenue (📞 **773/935-3909**). 830 N. Michigan Ave. (at Pearson St.). 📞 **312/573-0564**. Subway/El: Red Line to Chicago.

Children in Paradise Bookstore *Kids*   This is Chicago's largest children's bookstore, with storytelling hours Tuesday and Wednesday and special events on Saturday. 909 N. Rush St. (between Delaware Place and Walton St.). 📞 **312/951-5437**. Subway/El: Red Line to Chicago.

Powell's Bookstore   Used books, especially from scholarly and small Chicago presses, dog-eared paperbacks, and hardcover classics fill the shelves. There are also outlets in Lakeview at 2850 N. Lincoln Ave. (📞 **773/248-1444**), and Hyde Park at 1501 E. 57th St. (📞 **773/955-7780**). 828 S. Wabash Ave. (between 8th and 9th sts.). 📞 **312/341-0748**. Subway/El: Red Line to Harrison.

Prairie Avenue Bookshop   This South Loop store does Chicago's architectural tradition proud with the city's finest stock of architecture, design, and technical books. 418 S. Wabash Ave. (between Congress Pkwy. and Van Buren St.). 📞 **312/922-8311**. Subway/El: Red Line to Jackson.

Seminary Co-op Bookstore   A classic campus bookstore located near the University of Chicago, this shop has extensive philosophy and theology sections and is one of the premier academic bookstores in the country. 5757 S. University Ave. (between 57th and 58th sts.). 📞 **773/752-4381**. Bus: No. 69 (Jeffrey Express).

Unabridged Books   This quintessential neighborhood bookseller in the area known as Boys Town has strong sections in gay and lesbian literature, travel, film, and sci-fi. Yellow tags hanging from the shelves penned with smartly written reviews indicate staff favorites. The shop hosts frequent author readings and a gay men's book club. 3251 N. Broadway (between Belmont Ave. and Addison St.). 📞 **773/883-9119**. Subway/El: Red Line to Addison.

Women & Children First *Kids*   This feminist and children's bookstore holds the best selection in the city of titles for, by, and about women. Co-owner Linda Bubon holds a children's storybook hour every Wednesday at 10:30am; several book groups meet regularly as well, including one for mothers and daughters. The store also hosts frequent readings by the likes of Gloria Steinem, Amy Tan, and Alice Walker. 5233 N. Clark St. (between Foster and Bryn Mawr aves.). 📞 **773/769-9299**. wcfbooks@aol.com. Subway/El: Red Line to Berwyn.

CANDY, CHOCOLATES & PASTRIES

Bittersweet   Run by Judy Contino, one of the city's top pastry chefs and bakers of all things sweet, this Lakeview cafe and shop is sought out by brides-to-be and trained palates who have a yen for gourmet cakes, cookies, tarts, and ladyfingers. The rich chocolate mousse cake, a specialty of the house, is out of this world. 1114 W. Belmont Ave. 📞 **773/929-1100**. Subway/El: Red Line to Belmont.

Ghirardelli Chocolate Shop & Soda Fountain   This Midwest outpost of the famed San Francisco chocolatier, just a half block off the Mag Mile, gets swamped in the summer, but they've got their soda fountain assembly line down to a science. Besides the incredible hot-fudge sundaes, there's a veritable mudslide of chocolate bars, hot-cocoa drink mixes, and chocolate-covered espresso beans to tempt your sweet tooth. 830 N. Michigan Ave. 📞 **312/337-9330**. Subway/El: Red Line to Chicago.

Margie's Candies *Value*   This family-run candy and ice-cream shop hasn't changed much since it opened in 1921. It still offers some of the city's finest handmade fudge, whether it comes in a box or melted over a banana split served in a clamshell dish. The store is known for its turtles—chocolate-covered pecan and caramel clusters—and may be the only place in the city still selling rock candy on wooden sticks. 1960 N. Western Ave. (just north of Armitage Ave.). *C* 773/384-1035. Subway/El: Blue Line to Western.

Sweet Thang   If you're bopping around Wicker Park, don't miss Bernard Runo's Euro-style cafe for a tasty treat. Runo, a classically trained pastry chef who has worked in the kitchens of the city's best hotels and learned his trade in France, imports most of the ingredients for his croissants, cookies, tarts, and other pastries from across the pond. The cafe has a *laissez-faire* atmosphere, with red distressed walls covered with abstract art and Parisian-style tables and chairs that are set outside in warm weather. 1921 W. North Ave. *C* 773/772-4166. Subway/El: Blue Line to Damen.

Vosges Haut-Chocolat *Finds*   Chocolatier Katrina Markoff studied at Le Cordon Bleu in Paris and honed her skills throughout Europe and Asia. Her exotic gourmet truffles—with fabulous names such as absinthe, mint julep, wink of the rabbit, woolloomooloo, and ambrosia—are made from premium Belgian chocolate and infused with rare spices, seasonings, and flowers from around the world. The store—which looks more like a modern art gallery than a chocolatier—includes a gourmet hot chocolate bar, where you're welcome to sit and sip. 520 N. Michigan Ave. (in The Shops at North Bridge). *C* 312/644-9450. Subway/El: Red Line to Grand.

COLLECTIBLES

F.A.M.E   Movie buffs will have a field day browsing through the thousands of posters, film stills, and lobby cards at this Wicker Park shop. The name refers to the store's specialty areas (Film, Art, Music, and "Etc."), but it's the movie posters that take up most of the space—you could spend hours flipping through them all. Rare originals come with three-digit price tags, but there are also plenty of affordable reprints of current hits and campy little-known gems from the '50s and '60s. 1941 W. North Ave. (at Milwaukee Ave.). *C* 773/384-4708. Subway/El: Blue Line to Damen.

Quake Collectibles   Off the beaten tourist path in the rapidly gentrifying Lincoln Square area, this temple to all things kitschy includes an impressive vintage lunch-box collection and ample stacks of old fan magazines, à la *Teen Beat* with Shaun Cassidy tossing his feathered tresses while he does the "Do Run Run" in a bubble-gum pop-glamour spread. 4628 N. Lincoln Ave. (north of Wilson Ave.). *C* 773/878-4288. Subway/El: Blue Line to Western.

Uncle Fun *Finds*   Whenever I'm looking for a quirky Christmas stocking-stuffer or the perfect gag gift, I know Uncle Fun will come through for me (my sister is still raving about the Scooby Doo socks I bought for her a few years ago). Bins and cubbyholes are stuffed full of the standard joke toys (rubber-chicken key chains and chattering wind-up teeth), but you'll also find every conceivable modern pop-culture artifact, from Jackson Five buttons to demon-on-wheels *Speed Racer*'s Mach-Five model car. 1338 W. Belmont Ave. (near Southport Ave.). *C* 773/477-8223. Subway/El: Red or Brown line to Belmont.

DEPARTMENT STORES

Bloomingdale's   The first Midwestern branch of the famed New York department store, Bloomingdale's is on par in terms of size and selection with

Marshall Field's Water Tower store. Among its special sections is the one for its souveniresque Bloomingdale's logo merchandise. 900 N. Michigan Ave. (at Walton St.). © 312/440-4460. Subway/El: Red Line to Chicago.

Carson Pirie Scott & Co.   Carson's still appeals primarily to working- and middle-class shoppers. But this venerable Chicago institution that was almost wiped out by the Chicago Fire has made a recent bid to capture the corporate trade, adding a number of more upscale apparel lines, plus a trendy housewares department, to appeal to the moneyed crowd that works in the Loop. 1 S. State St. (at Madison St.). © 312/641-7000. Subway/El: Red Line to Monroe.

Lord & Taylor   Lord & Taylor, one of two large department stores in Water Tower Place (see Marshall Field's, below), carries about what you'd expect: women's, men's, and children's clothing; cosmetics; and accessories. The formerly crowded first floor has gotten an upscale makeover, although the offerings remain fairly affordable. The store's star department is definitely shoes, for its good selection and sales. Water Tower Place, 835 N. Michigan Ave. © 312/787-7400. Subway/El: Red Line to Chicago.

Marshall Field's   Although it's now owned by Minneapolis-based Target Corporation, Chicagoans still consider Marshall Field's their "hometown" department store. The flagship store, which covers an entire block on State Street, is second in size only to Macy's in New York City. Within this overwhelming space, shoppers will find areas unusual for today's homogeneous department stores, such as the Victorian antique-jewelry department and a gallery of antique-furniture reproductions. Store craftspeople are still on hand to fix antique clocks, repair jewelry, and restore old paintings. A basement marketplace offers gourmet goodies, including a bakery and upscale cafeteria.

The breadth is what makes this store impressive; shoppers can find a rainbow of shirts for under $20, a floor or so away from the 28 Shop, the Field's homage to designer fashion. For a sophisticated take on the latest trends at a more affordable price, look for clothes from Field's own label, 111 State. The recently expanded shoe department is huge, with everything from killer high heels (at killer prices) to slippers and casual sandals.

The Water Tower store—the mall's primary anchor—is a scaled-down but respectable version of the State Street store. Its eight floors are actually much more manageable than the enormous flagship, and its merchandise selection is still vast (although this branch tends to focus on the more expensive brands). 111 N. State St. (at Randolph St.). © 312/781-1000. Subway/El: Red Line to Washington. Water Tower Place, 835 N. Michigan Ave. (at Pearson St.). © 312/335-7700. Subway/El: Red Line to Chicago.

Neiman Marcus   Yes, you'll pay top dollar for designer names here—the store does, after all, need to live up to its Needless Mark-up moniker—but Neiman's has a broader price range than many of its critics care to admit. It also has some mighty good sales. The four-story store, a beautiful environment in its own right, sells cosmetics, shoes, furs, fine and fashion jewelry, and men's and children's wear. On the top floor is a fun gourmet food department, as well as a pretty home-accessories area. Neiman's has two restaurants: one relaxed, the other a little more formal. 737 N. Michigan Ave. (between Superior St. and Chicago Ave.). © 312/642-5900. Subway/El: Red Line to Chicago.

Nordstrom   The newest arrival on the Chicago department store scene, Nordstrom has upped the stakes with its spacious, airy design and trendy touches (wheatgrass growing by the escalators, funky music playing on the stereo system). The company's famed shoe department is large but not overwhelming;

more impressive is the cosmetics department, where you'll find a wide array of smaller labels and an "open sell" environment (meaning you're encouraged to try on makeup without a salesperson hovering over you). In keeping with the store's famed focus on service, a concierge can check your coat, call a cab, or make restaurant reservations. The Shops at North Bridge, 55 E. Grand Ave. (at Rush St.). © 312/464-1515. Subway/El: Red Line to Grand.

Saks Fifth Avenue   Saks Fifth Avenue might be best known for its designer collections—Valentino, Chloe, and Giorgio Armani, to name a few—but the store also does a swell job of buying more casual and less expensive merchandise. Check out, for example, Saks's own Real Clothes or The Works women's lines. Plus, the store has very good large-size and petite women's apparel departments. A men's department recently opened in a separate building across Michigan Avenue. Don't forget to visit the cosmetics department, where Saks is known, in particular, for its fragrance selection. Chicago Place, 700 N. Michigan Ave. (at Superior St.). © 312/944-6500. Subway/El: Red Line to Chicago.

MAPS & TRAVEL GEAR
Rand McNally Map and Travel Store   Map lovers will be satiated. The store also stocks, among its 10,000-item inventory, travel guides, videotapes, globes, and travel supplies and gift items from around the world. 444 N. Michigan Ave. (at Illinois St.). © 312/321-1751. Subway/El: Red Line to Grand.

The Savvy Traveller   Smart travelers buy their Frommer's guidebooks here. This Loop specialty store carries just about everything a traveler might need, from maps to rain gear to games that keep the kids occupied on long car trips. 310 S. Michigan Ave. (between Van Buren St. and Jackson Blvd.). © 312/913-9800. Subway/El: Red Line to Jackson.

MUSIC
Beat Parlor   If the idea of hanging out where the local DJs do appeals to you, then Beat Parlor is your place. In the city where house music was born, Howard Bailey's Bucktown shop sells lots of it, plus plenty of hip-hop and local DJs' mix tapes, on CD and vinyl. The store's two turntables are always in use by cutters checking out new merchandise. 1653 N. Damen Ave. © 773/395-CUTS. Subway/El: Blue Line to Damen.

Clubhouse   Alyse Matlak opened Clubhouse next door to Chicago's premier rock venue, Metro, in 1993—but back then it sold only pop-culture merchandise such as T-shirts and patches. Matlak still carries that stuff, but the store has since added an inventory of ska and punk records, CDs, and tapes. Almost the entire selection is new music, much of it of the underground variety. 3728 N. Clark St. © 773/549-2325. Subway/El: Red Line to Addison.

Dusty Groove America   In 1996, using a rickety old PC, Rick Wojcik and John Schauer founded an online record store at www.dustygroove.com. Since then, the operation has expanded in both cyberspace and the real world. Dusty Groove covers a lot of ground, selling soul, funk, jazz, Brazilian, lounge, Latin, and hip-hop music on new and used vinyl and all new CDs. For the most part, all selections are either rare or imported, or both. 1120 N. Ashland Ave. ((© 773/342-5800. Subway/El: Blue Line to Division.

Jazz Record Mart   This is possibly the best jazz record store in the country. The first of four rooms houses the "Killer Rack," a display of albums that the store's owners consider essential to any jazz collection. Besides jazz, there are bins filled with blues, Latin, and "New Music"; the albums in the record rooms are filed alphabetically and by category (vocals, big band, and so on), and there are a couple of turntables to help you spend wisely. Jazz Record Mart also features a stage, with seating for 50, where local and national artists coming through town entertain with in-store performances. 444 N. Wabash Ave. (at Grand Ave.). (Ⓒ 312/222-1467. Subway/El: Red Line to Grand.

New Sound Gospel   Chicago is the birthplace of gospel music, but when Lee Johnson opened New Sound Gospel 20 years ago, few people were selling it. That has all changed, thanks to the recent resurgence in gospel led by Kirk Franklin, whose platinum albums have crossed over into mainstream success. All the major labels now have gospel music divisions, and the rising tide has helped store owners like Johnson, who has since opened a second location at 10723 S. Halsted St. (Ⓒ 773/785-8001). Both brim with records, CDs, and tapes, from gospel's greatest legend, Mahalia Jackson, to groups with names such as Gospel Gangstaz. 5958 W. Lake St. (Ⓒ 773/261-1115. Subway/El: Green Line to Austin.

Reckless Records   The best all-round local record store for music that the cool kids listen to, Reckless Records wins Brownie points for its friendly and helpful staff. You'll find new and used CDs and albums in a variety of genres (psychedelic and progressive rock, punk, soul, and jazz) here, along with 'zines and a small collection of DVDs. There's also a location in Wicker Park, at 1532 N. Milwaukee Ave. ((Ⓒ 773/235-3727). 3157 N. Broadway (at Belmont Ave.). (Ⓒ 773/404-5080. Subway/El: Red or Brown Line to Belmont.

PAPER & STATIONERY

All She Wrote   One of the many owner-operated specialty shops along Armitage Avenue, All She Wrote stocks a fun mix of cards and notepaper, all with a lighthearted, whimsical feel. 825 W. Armitage Ave. (1 block west of Halsted St.). (Ⓒ 773/529-0100. Subway/El: Red Line to North/Clybourn.

Fly Paper *Finds*   Located on a busy stretch of Southport in the Wrigleyville neighborhood, Fly Paper has one of the most offbeat and artsy selections of greeting cards in the city, as well as other novelty and gift items. **Paper Boy,** a 10-minute walk away at 1351 W. Belmont Ave. ((Ⓒ 773/388-8811), is under the same ownership and features a similarly eclectic collection. 3402 N. Southport Ave. (between Belmont Ave. and Addison St.). (Ⓒ 773/296-4359. Subway/El: Brown Line to Southport.

The Heartworks   This Old Town shop is another good source for cards, paper goods, journals, photo albums, and impulse gift items. 1704 N. Wells St. (between North and Lincoln aves.). (Ⓒ 312/943-1972. Subway/El: Brown Line to Sedgwick.

Paper Source   The acknowledged leader of stationery stores in Chicago, Paper Source is now expanding throughout the country (with locations from Boston to Beverly Hills). The store's claim to fame is its collection of handmade paper in a stunning variety of colors and textures. You'll also find one-of-a-kind greeting cards and a large collection of rubber stamps for personalizing your own paper at home. The River North shop is the store's headquarters, but there's also a location in the trendy Armitage shopping district, at 919 W. Armitage Ave. ((Ⓒ 773/525-7300). 232 W. Chicago Ave. (at Franklin St.). (Ⓒ 312/337-0798. Subway/El: Red or Brown Line to Chicago.

The Watermark   Chicago socialites come here to order their engraved invitations, but this stationery store also carries an intriguing selection of handmade greeting cards for all occasions. 109 E. Oak St. (1 block from Michigan Ave.). (Ⓒ 312/337-5353. Subway/El: Red Line to Clark/Division.

SALONS & SPAS

Charles Ifergan   One of Chicago's top hair salons, Charles Ifergan caters to the ladies-who-lunch, and his rates, which vary according to the seniority of the stylist, are relatively high. If you're a little daring, you can get a cut for the price of the tip. On Tuesday and Wednesday evenings, junior stylists do their thing gratis—under the watchful eye of Monsieur Ifergan (call ✆ **312/640-7444** between 10am and 4pm to make an appointment for that night). 106 E. Oak St. (between Michigan Ave. and Rush St.). ✆ **312/642-4484.** Subway/El: Red Line to Chicago.

Kiva   Named for the round ceremonial space used by Native Americans for quietness, cleansing, and relaxation of the spirit, Kiva is the city's reigning "super spa." The two-floor, 6,000-square-foot space offers spa, salon, nutrition, and apothecary services, and a nutritional juice and snack bar in a setting that evokes its namesake inspiration. The round first-floor salon is equipped with a massive granite circular counter surrounded by hair-care, facial, and aromatherapy products, and body massage oils. Water Tower Place, 196 E. Pearson St. ✆ **312/840-8120.** Subway/El: Red Line to Chicago.

Ren   This Lincoln Park massage haven, handsomely designed in an organic, Zen-like style complete with ambient mood music, offers a range of massage therapies, from the ever-popular Swedish massage to an advanced muscle-therapy version that uses deep-tissue massage to remove muscular discomfort and pain. Finish any session with a private "rain shower" to extend your state of blissful relaxation. 2204 N. Clark St. ✆ **773/525-1515.** Bus: No. 22 (Clark St.) or 36 (Broadway).

Salon Buzz   This hip coiffure parlor, operated by wizardly stylist Andreas Zafiriadis (who has wielded his scissors in Paris, Greece, New York, and California), is the hair salon of the moment, especially for young women in less-than-conservative creative professions. 1 E. Delaware Place (at State St.). ✆ **312/943-5454.** Subway/El: Red Line to Chicago.

Studio 110   Another hip salon catering to the city's bright young things, Studio 110 adds a dash of humor the hairstyling business (witness the shiny disco balls overhead). Yes, you'll see plenty of glamorous gals here, but the staff is friendly and attitude-free. The salon also offers facials, manicures, and pedicures. 110 E. Delaware Place. ✆ **312/337-6411.** Subway/El: Red Line to Chicago.

Tiffani Kim Institute   Occupying a modern three-story building in the heart of River North's art-gallery district, the Tiffani Kim Institute has to be seen to be believed. This sanctuary for women provides salon, spa, wellness, and cosmetic surgery treatments—not to mention a fashion and bridal boutique. Treatments include such faves as a detox seaweed body wrap, Asian ear candling, acupuncture and Chinese herbal medicine, and the "Serenity Stone Massage," a Tiffani Kim specialty in which smooth massage stones are warmed in a thermal unit to 135°F (57°C) and then used as tools in a Swedish-style massage. 310 W. Superior St. ✆ **312/943-8777.** Subway/El: Red or Brown line to Chicago.

Truefitt & Hill *Finds*   Women have their pick of hair and beauty salons, but men don't often come across a place like Truefitt & Hill, the local outpost of a British barbershop listed in the *Guinness Book of World Records* as the oldest barbershop in the world. You'll pay a steep price for a haircut here ($40 and up), but the old-world atmosphere is dead-on, from the bow-tied barbers to the antique chairs. Services include lather shaves, manicures, massages, and shoe shines. Up front, the apothecary sells imported English shaving implements and toiletries. 900 N. Michigan Ave., 6th floor. ✆ **312/337-2525.** Subway/El: Red Line to Chicago.

Urban Oasis *Finds*   After a long day of sightseeing, try a soothing massage in a subdued, Zen-like atmosphere. The ritual begins with a steam or rain shower in a private changing room, followed by the spa treatment you elect—various forms of massage (including a couples' massage, in which you learn to do it yourself), an aromatherapy wrap, or an exfoliating treatment. Fruit, juices, or herbal teas are offered on completion. 12 W. Maple St., 3rd floor (between Dearborn and State sts.). ℂ 312/587-3500. Subway/El: Red Line to Clark/Division.

SHOES

Alternatives   Yes, you'll see plenty of black shoes here. But this locally owned shoe-store chain offers far more than Doc Marten wannabe designs; you'll find cutting-edge styles for men and women that are more affordable than you'd find in the designer boutiques. In addition to the tourist-friendly location off the Magnificent Mile, there's also a shop at 1969 N. Halsted St. (ℂ 312/943-1591), near the Armitage Avenue shopping district. 942 Rush St. (at Delaware St.). ℂ 312/266-1545. Subway/El: Red Line to Chicago.

Avventura   Michael Jordan and Sammy Sosa are fans of this upscale men's-only footwear boutique, but you don't have to have huge feet to find a perfect fit here. With prices starting at about $175, Avventura offers boots, loafers, slip-ons, sandals, and two-tone spectators in every material imaginable, from leather and crocodile to lizard and stingray. Water Tower Place, 835 N. Michigan Ave. ℂ 312/337-3700. Subway/El: Red Line to Chicago.

Donald J Pliner   Light and airy, with Tibetan rugs, giant mirrors, and a polished hardwood floor, hometown retail hero Donald Pliner's Oak Street boutique evokes a contemporary art gallery. In fact, he peppers the place with his signature wooden pig figurines. But Pliner's shoe selection goes above and beyond whimsical. Cowboy boots, in basic black and outrageously funky colors, fly off the shelves. He also offers mules—in leopard and cow prints, no less—as well as many styles in colored furs. 106 E. Oak St. ℂ 312/202-9600. Subway/El: Red Line to Chicago.

G'Bani   On the corner of Oak and State, this funky, European-style boutique caters to men and women unfulfilled by designs made for the masses. The owner, a former fashion buyer for several high-style stores abroad, sells upscale clothing and shoes (priced $120–$900) often skewed toward fit fashionistas in their 20s through their 40s. 949 N. State St. ℂ 312/440-1718. Subway/El: Red Line to Chicago.

Lori's Designer Shoes *Value*   Lori's looks like a local version of Payless Shoes, with shoeboxes stacked on the floor and women surrounded by piles of heels and boots that they try on and trade in search of the perfect fit. But the designer names on most of those shoes prove that this is a step above your typical discount store. (I have friends from New York who make pilgrimages to Lori's whenever they're in town on business—no matter how short their trip is.) A mecca for shoe-obsessed fashion slaves, Lori's stocks all the latest styles, at prices that average 10% to 30% below department-store rates. 824 W. Armitage Ave. (between Sheffield Ave. and Halsted St.). ℂ 773/281-5655. Subway/El: Brown Line to Armitage.

Stuart Weitzman   Strappy high-heeled sandals from this shoe seller to the stars make regular appearances on the red carpet at the Academy Awards and other A-list celebrity events. Go to Stuart Weitzman for shoes that make a dramatic impression—on your feet and on your wallet. You'll find lots of special-occasion heels here, as well as some lovely knee-high boots. 900 N. Michigan Ave. ℂ 312/943-5760. Subway/El: Red Line to Chicago.

Tod's Opened in late 1999, the Chicago outpost of princely Italian footwear fave, Tod's has already emerged as a stronghold on fashion-forward Oak Street. Characterized by detailed workmanship and top-quality material, the Tod's lines include their popular calfskin moccasin driving shoe, high-heeled sandals, balle-rina-style shoes, and mules in various colors. (And that's to say nothing of their trademark fab handbags.) 121 E. Oak St. ✆ 312/943-0070. Subway/El: Red Line to Chicago.

SPORTING GOODS

Active Endeavors This store is a good source for camping gear, running shoes, and everyday sporty apparel. 935 W. Armitage Ave. (between Sheffield Ave. and Halsted St.). ✆ 773/281-8100. Subway/El: Brown Line to Armitage.

Niketown *Overrated* When Niketown opened almost 10 years ago, it was truly something new: a store that felt more like a funky sports museum than a place hawking running shoes. In the days when Michael Jordan was the city's reigning deity, Niketown was the place to bask in his glory. These days, Niketown is no longer unique to Chicago (it's sprung up in cities from Atlanta to Honolulu), and the store's celebration of athletes can't cover up the fact that the ultimate goal is to sell expensive shoes. But the crowds keep streaming in—and snatching up products pitched by Niketown's new patron saint, Tiger Woods. 669 N. Michigan Ave. ✆ 312/642-6363. Subway/El: Red Line to Grand.

Sportmart The largest sporting-goods store in the city, the flagship store of this chain offers seven floors of merchandise, from running apparel to camping gear. Sports fans will be in heaven in the first- and fifth-floor team merchandise departments, where Cubs, Bulls, and Sox jerseys abound. Cement handprints of local sports celebs dot the outside of the building; step inside to check out the prints from Michael Jordan and White Sox slugger Frank Thomas. 620 N. LaSalle St. (at Ontario St.). ✆ 312/337-6151. Subway/El: Red Line to Grand.

Vertel's Here's a store that takes running seriously. Shoe shoppers are advised to bring their old shoes and invest at least half an hour while the salespeople help fit you for a new pair, including letting you do a lap on the sidewalk out front. The store also stocks running apparel and accessories, as well as swimwear. 2001 N. Clybourn Ave. (between North and Fullerton aves.). ✆ 773/248-7400. Subway/El: Brown Line to Armitage.

TOYS

Fantasy Headquarters *Finds* Not exactly a toy store, this sprawling costume shop that covers an entire city block is nonetheless devoted to make-believe and is just as fun. The store stocks more than a million items, including 800 styles of masks (priced $1–$200) and all the accessories and makeup needed to complete any costume. There's also a full-service wig salon. 4065 N. Milwaukee Ave. (west of Cicero Ave.). ✆ 773/777-0222. Subway/El: Blue Line to Irving Park.

Saturday's Child You'll know from the vintage decor (wood floors, a pressed-tin ceiling) that this is no cookie-cutter modern shop. Instead, this is a place that values classic designs over the latest electronic gadgets. The clever toys range from rubber snakes and frogs to sidewalk chalk and kids' large-face wristwatches. 2146 N. Halsted St. (south of Webster Ave.). ✆ 773/525-8697. Subway/El: Brown Line to Armitage.

Toyscape The proprietors bar the door to Barbie at this cluttered Lakeview toyshop. Their tastes run to good old-fashioned wooden toys, musical instruments, and puppets, most of which don't require batteries. 2911 N. Broadway (between Diversey Pkwy. and Belmont Ave.). ✆ 773/665-7400. Subway/El: Brown Line to Diversey.

VINTAGE FASHION/RESALE SHOPS

Beatnix   This solid vintage store, good for day-to-day and dress-up items, also vends a huge selection of old tuxes. Both men's and women's apparel is available. 3400 N. Halsted St. (at Roscoe St.). ☎ 773/281-6933. Subway/El: Red Line to Addison.

The Daisy Shop   A significant step up from your standard vintage store, The Daisy Shop specializes only in couture fashions. These designer duds come from the closets of the city's most stylish socialites and carry appropriately hefty price tags. Even so, paying hundreds of dollars for a pristine Chanel suit or Louis Vuitton bag can still be considered a bargain, and well-dressed women from throughout the world stop by here in search of the perfect one-of-a-kind item. 67 E. Oak St. (between Michigan Ave. and Rush St.). ☎ 312/943-8880. Subway/El: Brown Line to Sedgwick.

Flashy Trash *(Finds*   One of the best vintage stores anywhere, Flashy Trash mixes used and new clothing, from Todd Oldham jeans to used tuxes to dress-up accessories such as feather boas, wigs, and jewelry. Naturally, Halloween is a busy time here, but the salesclerks are always in one costume or another. 3524 N. Halsted St. (between Belmont Ave. and Addison St.). ☎ 773/327-6900. Subway/El: Red Line to Addison.

Hollywood Mirror   You'll find two floors of fun, recycled stuff, including lots of blue jeans on the first floor and 1950s furniture and lamps in the basement. Sure, some of the '70s disco suits will appeal only to ironic club kids, but the selection of clothes is so large that a patient search through the racks is usually rewarded with a great wool jacket or classic pinstriped blouse. Don't miss the huge collection of so-out-they're-in-again bowling shirts (many are monogrammed, so you might find one that literally has your name on it). 812 W. Belmont Ave. (at Clark St.). ☎ 773/404-4510. Subway/El: Red Line to Belmont.

McShane's Exchange *(Finds*   This consignment shop has a selection that's a few steps above the standard thrift store, and for designer bargains it can't be beat. The store expands back through a series of cramped rooms (you'll miss the best stuff if you don't wander beyond the front room), with clothes organized by color, making it easy to scope out the perfect black dress. The longer a piece stays in stock, the lower the price drops—and I've done plenty of double-takes at the price tags here: Calvin Klein coats, Prada sweaters, and Armani jackets all going for well under $100. If that's not tempting enough, you'll also find barely used shoes and purses. McShane's also has another location at 1141 W. Webster St. (☎ 773/525-0211), with a similar selection. 815 W. Armitage Ave. (at Halsted St.). ☎ 773/525-0282. Subway/El: Brown Line to Armitage.

Ragstock *(Value*   Located above Hollywood Mirror, this branch of the Minneapolis-based thrift-store chain has everything for the slacker on the go—at decent prices. You'll find new stuff mixed in too. 812 W. Belmont Ave., enter in the alley (at Clark St.). ☎ 773/868-9263. Subway/El: Red Line to Belmont.

Una Mae's Freak Boutique   Go for the name, stay for the gear. Here's a Wicker Park down-and-funky blast from the past. 1422 N. Milwaukee Ave. (2 blocks south of North Ave.). ☎ 773/276-7002. Subway/El: Blue Line to Damen.

Wisteria   This is a very fun and lovely store (great hats and handbags) in the thick of the trendy North Southport Avenue corridor, right next door to the marvelous old Music Box Theatre revival cinema house. 3715 N. Southport Ave. ☎ 773/880 5868. Subway/El: Brown Line to Southport.

WINE & LIQUOR

Binny's Beverage Depot *Value*   This River North purveyor of fermented libations is housed in a delightfully no-frills warehouse space, and it offers an enormous selection of wine, beer, and spirits—often at discounted prices. Binny's has a second, smaller location at 3000 N. Clark St. (✆ **773/935-9400**). 213 W. Grand Ave. ✆ **312/332-0012**. Subway/El: Red Line to Grand.

House of Glunz *Finds*   Not only is this Chicago's oldest wine shop, but it's also the oldest in the Midwest, with an inventory of 1,500 wines dating back to 1811. The shop periodically cracks open a few of its vintage wines for special wine-tasting events, but not all the selections here are rare or expensive. There's a stock of modern wines from California and Europe, and the knowledgeable owners are able to steer you to the right bottle to fit your budget. 1206 N. Wells St. ✆ **312/642-3000**. Subway/El: Brown Line to Sedgwick.

Sam's Wines & Spirits   Believe it or not, this football-field-size warehouse store evolved from a modest packaged-goods store. Today the family-owned operation is the best-stocked wine and spirits merchant in the city and offers pleasant, friendly service. It also features a superb cheese selection in the on-site Epicurean shop. 1720 N. Marcey St. (near Sheffield and Clybourn aves.). ✆ **800/777-9137** or 312/664-4394. www.samswine.com. Subway/El: Red Line to North/Clybourn.

10

Chicago After Dark

Chicago's bustling energy isn't confined to daylight hours. The city offers something for everyone—from discriminating culture vultures to hardcore club-hoppers. But nightlife here has a distinctly low-key, Midwestern flavor. The Chicago Symphony Orchestra and the Lyric Opera of Chicago are world-class performing arts institutions, but their audiences aren't snobby and newcomers are welcome. Chicago's thriving theater scene was built by performers who valued gritty realism and a communal work ethic; from the big-league Steppenwolf and Goodman theaters down to the scrappy storefront companies that keep springing up throughout town, that down-to-earth energy is still very much a part of theater here. Chicago also has a thriving music scene, with clubs devoted to everything from jazz and blues to alternative rock, reggae, and Latin beats. Music and nightclub haunts are scattered throughout the city, but many are concentrated in River West, Lincoln Park, Lakeview, and Wicker Park.

While the city has its share of see-and-be-seen spots, Chicagoans in general are not obsessed with getting into the latest hot club. We'd much rather hang out with our buddies at a neighborhood bar. To join us, you only have to pick a residential area and wander. You don't have to go far to find a tavern filled with locals and maybe a pool table or a dartboard or two.

For up-to-date entertainment listings, check the local newspapers and magazines, particularly the "Friday" and "Weekend Plus" sections of the two dailies, the *Chicago Tribune* and the *Chicago Sun-Times;* the *Chicago Reader* or *New City,* two free weekly tabloids with extensive listings; and the monthly *Chicago* magazine. The *Tribune's* entertainment-oriented website, **www.metromix.com**; the *Reader's* website, **www.chireader.com**; and the local Citysearch website, **www.chicago.citysearch.com**, are also excellent sources of information, with lots of opinionated reviews. The "Entertainment and Night Life" section of Out Chicago's website, **www.outchicago.org**, provides a directory of links to bars, clubs, and performing-arts venues that welcome gay and lesbian visitors.

Note: For a map of nightlife in the Wicker Park and Bucktown areas, please see the map "Dining & Nightlife in Wicker Park/Bucktown" on p. 157. A map of after dark establishments in the Lincoln Park and Wrigleyville neighborhoods is in this chapter on p. 264.

1 The Performing Arts

Chicago is a regular stop on the big-name entertainment circuit, whether it's the national tour of Broadway shows such as *Rent* and *Cabaret* or pop music acts such as U2 or the Dave Matthews Band (both of whom sell out multiple nights at stadiums when they come to town). High-profile shows such as Disney's *Aida* and Mel Brooks's stage version of *The Producers* had their first runs here before moving on to New York. Thanks to extensive renovation efforts, performers now have some impressive venues where they can strut their stuff. The **Auditorium Theatre,** at 50 E. Congress Pkwy., between Michigan and Wabash avenues (✆ 312/922-2110; www.auditoriumtheatre.org) is my pick for the most beautiful theater in Chicago—and it's a certified national landmark, too. Built in 1889 by Louis Sullivan and Dankmar Adler, this grand hall hosts mostly musicals and dance performances. Even if you don't catch a show here, stop by for a tour (for more details, see p. 174).

The city's other great historic theaters are concentrated in the North Loop. The **Ford Center for the Performing Arts/Oriental Theater,** at 24 W. Randolph St. (✆ 312/782-2004), and the **Cadillac Palace Theater,** at 151 W. Randolph St. (✆ 312/384-1510), book major touring shows and are well worth a visit for arts buffs. The Oriental's fantastical Asian look includes elaborate carvings almost everywhere you look; dragons, elephants, and griffins peer down at the audience from the gilded ceiling. The Palace features a profusion of Italian marble surfaces and columns, gold-leaf accents à la Versailles, huge decorative mirrors, and crystal chandeliers.

The **Shubert Theatre,** 22 W. Monroe St. (✆ 312/977-1700) was built in 1906 as a home for vaudeville; today it books mostly big-name musicals and sometimes comedy performers. The **Chicago Theatre,** 175 N. State St., at Lake Street (✆ 312/443-1130), is a 1920s music palace reborn as an all-purpose entertainment venue, hosting everything from pop acts and magicians to stand-up comedy. **Arie Crown Theater,** in the McCormick Place convention center at 23rd Street and Lake Shore Drive (✆ 312/791-6190), books musicals and pop acts; a renovation has improved what were terrible acoustics (Elton John once interrupted a performance to complain about the sound), but this is still a massive, somewhat impersonal hall. Since all these theaters are quite large, be aware that the cheaper seats will be in nosebleed territory.

Symphony Center, 220 S. Michigan Ave., between Adams Street and Jackson Boulevard (✆ 312/294-3000), is the building that encompasses Orchestra Hall, home of the Chicago Symphony Orchestra. Expanded and renovated a few years back, the building now includes a six-story skylit arcade, recital spaces, and the fine-dining restaurant Rhapsody (p. 115). While the CSO is the main attraction, the Symphony Center hosts a series of piano recitals, classical and chamber music concerts, a family matinee series, and the occasional jazz or pop artist.

Chicago has a few other major venues for traveling shows, but they are not as convenient for visitors. The **Rosemont Theatre,** 5400 River Rd. in Rosemont, near O'Hare Airport (✆ 847/671-5100), is a top suburban stop for musicals and concerts. The **North Shore Center for the Performing Arts in Skokie,**

Tips **Finding a Better Seat**

Most of Chicago's grand old theaters have balconies that go way, way up toward the ceiling—and if you're stuck in the cheap seats, you'll be straining to see what's happening on stage. While theaters are very strict about checking tickets when you arrive, the ushers relax during intermission. So scope out empty seats during the first act, and then move down to better (and much pricier) spots for the rest of the show (I've had great success with this tactic at the Auditorium Theatre, which is so huge that it rarely sells out).

9501 Skokie Blvd. in the northern suburb of Skokie (© **847/673-6300**), is home to the well-respected Northlight Theater, the Skokie Valley Symphony Orchestra, and a series of touring acts, including comics, dance troupes, and children's programs.

CLASSICAL MUSIC

For current listings of classical music concerts and opera, call the **Chicago Dance and Music Alliance** (© **312/987-1123**).

Chicago Symphony Orchestra ★★   The Chicago Symphony Orchestra (CSO) is being led into its second century by music director Daniel Barenboim, and it remains among the best in the world—a legacy of the late maestro Sir Georg Solti, who captured a record-breaking 31 Grammy awards for his CSO recordings and showcased the orchestra at other major musical capitals during frequent international tours. Barenboim has proven a worthy successor to the baton, a talented conductor and pianist prodigy whom the CSO recruited from the Orchestre de Paris after Solti's death in 1997. Staking out his own legacy in the renovated and expanded Symphony Center complex (see the description of this complex above), he has steadily introduced more modern works by 20th-century composers into the orchestra's repertoire. But you will certainly not be disappointed by the CSO's treatment of crowd-pleasing Beethoven or Brahms.

Classical is far from the only kind of music on tap here, however. The "Symphony Center Presents" series has included some of the top jazz, world beat, Latin, and cabaret artists in the world in recent years.

Although in high demand, good seats for all concerts often become available on concert days. Call Symphony Center or stop by the box office to check availability.

Summertime visitors have an opportunity to hear a CSO performance at the delightful **Ravinia Festival** ★★ (© **847/266-5100**) in suburban Highland Park, led by music director Christoph Eschenbach. (For more information, see p. 205.)

The **Civic Orchestra of Chicago,** the training orchestra of the Chicago Symphony since 1919, is also highly regarded and presents free programs at Orchestra Hall. The **Chicago Symphony Chorus** also performs there. Orchestra Hall, in Symphony Center, 220 S. Michigan Ave. © 312/294-3000. www.cso.org. Tickets $10–$90; box seats $165. Subway/El: Red Line to Jackson.

Grant Park Symphony and Chorus (Value)   A great Chicago event from late June through August is the series of free outdoor classical music concerts given by this summer orchestra, as well as a number of visiting artists, performing in Grant Park just a block from Lake Michigan. This year marks the symphony's first at the Frank Gehry–designed Millennium Park Music Pavilion (opening only 4 years behind schedule!). Featuring Gehry's signature sinuous lines, the pavilion is surrounded by dramatic ribbons of curved steel. The Grant Park Symphony will not only look better than ever, it should sound great, too—thanks to a state-of-the-art sound system. Concerts are held Wednesday through Sunday, with most performances beginning at 7:30 p.m. Seats (about 4,000 of them) are reserved for subscribers, but unclaimed places are offered to the public 15 minutes before the concert starts. But there's plenty of lawn seating; bring a blanket and enjoy a picnic dinner. Millennium Park Music Pavilion, at the corner of Michigan Ave. and Randolph St. © 312/742-4763. www.grantparkmusicfestival.com. Subway/El: Red Line to Washington/State or Brown, Orange, or Green line to Randolph//Wabash.

ADDITIONAL OFFERINGS

The **Apollo Chorus of Chicago** (✆ 312/427-5620; www.apollochorus.org) is best known for its annual holiday-season performance of Handel's *Messiah* at Orchestra Hall. Founded in 1872, 1 year after the Great Chicago Fire, the oldest all-volunteer civic chorus in the country began life as an all-male chorus but now is composed of men and women. They stage concerts throughout the year at various venues.

Bella Voce (✆ 312/461-0723; www.bellavoce.org) is an a cappella choir that re-creates ("imitates" doesn't do justice to the performers' amazing skills) the musical style of 16th-century English religious singers. Their repertoire used to be mainly liturgical, but it has grown to include an eclectic array of works, from Eastern European and Chinese folk songs to 20th-century ecclesiastical pieces. Performances take place mostly in churches across the Chicago area from October to May.

The **Chicago Chamber Musicians** (✆ 312/225-5226; www.chicagochambermusic.org), a 14-member ensemble drawn from performers from the CSO and Northwestern and DePaul universities, presents chamber music concerts at various locales around the city. While the season runs October through May, you can always find the CCM performing free noontime concerts on the first Monday of the month (except Sept and Mar) at the Chicago Cultural Center. The **Chicago String Quartet,** in residence at DePaul, is also affiliated with the group.

The **Chicago Sinfonietta** (✆ 312/236-3681; www.chicagosinfonietta.org), with its racially diverse 45-member orchestra and a wide-ranging repertoire, seeks to broaden the audience for classical music. In the past, the group has followed a Beethoven piano concerto with a piece featuring a steel drum. Playing about 15 times a year at Orchestra Hall and other venues throughout the city, the orchestra often takes a multimedia approach to its multicultural mission, accompanying its performances with art slides from the Art Institute and the Mexican Fine Arts Center Museum.

Music of the Baroque (✆ 312/551-1414; www.baroque.org), a small orchestra and chorus that pulls members from both the CSO and the Lyric Opera orchestra and that features professional singers from across the country, performs the music of the 16th, 17th, and 18th centuries, appropriately in Gothic church settings in Chicago neighborhoods. The group has made several recordings and has introduced works by Mozart and Monteverdi to Chicago audiences.

A critically acclaimed chamber music ensemble, the Grammy-nominated **Vermeer Quartet** actually makes its home at Northern Illinois University in De Kalb, about 60 miles west of Chicago. But it's considered the city's top string quartet by many because of its long-running connection with **Performing Arts Chicago** (✆ 773/722-5463), a nonprofit group that stages theater and concert events (many by international avant-garde troupes) throughout the year. Its repertoire ranges from works by Mozart to Haydn to modern composers. Call for details on upcoming concerts.

OPERA

Chicago Opera Theater The "other" opera company in town, Chicago Opera Theater, doesn't get all the big names, but it does make opera accessible to a wider audience with an emphasis on American composers and performers who sing in English. It also helps that tickets are less expensive and more plentiful than

---

Tips **A Do-It-Yourself *Messiah***

Fancy yourself an ecclesiastical crooner? Should you be in town over the holidays, don't skip the LaSalle Talman **Do-It-Yourself *Messiah*,** an extraordinarily popular and rousing rendition of the Handel classic. Now staged at the opulent Civic Opera House (although, for years, Orchestra Hall provided the setting), the program enlists audience members as part of a 3,500-voice chorus, which is accompanied by a volunteer orchestra and four professional soloists. The roof-raising aural power that fills the theater guarantees goose bumps. This is a hot, hot, hot ticket, so call early for reservations at ⓒ **773/776-4300** (www.lasallebank.com/messiah).

---

those to the Lyric Opera. The company performs three operas a year (Apr, June, and Oct), which usually run the gamut from classical tragedies by Handel to 20th-century satirical works. No matter what the bill, the talent and production values are top-notch (a recent production of two 20th-century Czech operas featured English text by playwright Tony Kushner and sets by illustrator Maurice Sendak). Chicago Opera Theater also runs a family opera program. Athenaeum Theatre, 2936 N. Southport Ave. (at Lincoln Ave.). ⓒ **312/704-8414.** www.ChicagoOperaTheater.org. Tickets $35–$75 adults, children half price. Subway/El: Brown Line to Wellington.

Lyric Opera of Chicago ✮✮   One of the top American opera companies, the Lyric attracts the very best singers in the world for its lavish productions. The Lyric's talented musicians and performers satisfy the opera snobs, while newcomers are often swept away by all the grand opera dramatics (English supertitles make it easy to follow the action). Opening night in September remains the quasi-official kickoff of the Chicago social season, but don't be scared off by the snooty factor; audiences here are relatively casual (to the dismay of all those opera snobs). The company has a strong commitment to new American works (the Lyric's production of *A View from the Bridge*, based on the Arthur Miller play, was picked up by the Metropolitan Opera for its 2002–03 season).

The Lyric Opera performs in the handsome 3,563-seat Art Deco Civic Opera House, the second-largest opera house in the country, built in 1929. If you're sitting in one of the upper balconies, you'll definitely want to bring binoculars (if you're nice, the regulars sitting nearby may lend you theirs). There's only one problem with catching a show at the Lyric: the season, which runs through early March, sells out way in advance. Single tickets are sometimes available a few months in advance. Your other option is to call the day of a performance, when you can sometimes buy tickets that subscribers have turned in because they won't be using them.

If you're in town in February or March, you can check out the theater by taking a tour (tours are only offered during those months; call ⓒ **312/827-5685**). The opera has an adjunct, the Lyric Opera Center for American Artists, which in spring and summer gives performances in smaller venues around town. Civic Opera House, at Madison St. and Wacker Dr. ⓒ **312/332-2244.** Fax 312/332-8120. www.lyricopera.org. Tickets $26–$125. Subway/El: Brown Line to Washington.

DANCE

Chicago's dance scene is lively, but unfortunately it doesn't attract the same crowds as our theaters or music performances. So although some of our resident dance troupes have international reputations, they spend much of their time touring to support themselves. Although visiting companies such as the American Ballet Theatre and the Dance Theater of Harlem stop in Chicago for limited engagements, dance performances in Chicago tend to occur in spurts throughout the year. Depending on the timing of your visit, you may have a choice of dance performances—or there may be none at all.

Many local dance troupes also face the challenge of finding places to perform; until recently, the city had no major dance venue. That situation will finally be resolved thanks to Millennium Park—the high-profile cultural and recreational center in Grant Park—which features a state-of-the-art 1,500-seat music and dance theater. If all goes as planned, many of the troupes listed here will be performing at the theater this year. For complete information on local dance performances, call the Chicago Dance and Music Alliance information line at ℂ 312/987-1123. Another phenomenon that has enlivened the local scene is the scintillating **Chicago Human Rhythm Project** (ℂ 773/296-1108). An annual tap-dance festival and nonprofit foundation created in 1990, it brings together tap and percussive dancers from all over the world for a series of workshops and outreach programs in July and August at locations throughout the city and suburbs. The Athenaeum Theatre, 2936 N. Southport Ave. (at Lincoln Ave.), hosts the annual **Dance Chicago,** a highly engaging month-long festival showcasing the talents of up-and-coming contemporary dance companies and choreographers. It usually takes place in October or November. Call the theater at ℂ 773/935-6860 for information.

Ballet Chicago Under artistic director Daniel Duell, a former New York City Ballet dancer, the group is notable for its specialty, the ballets of Balanchine. The ballet performs one full-length story ballet a year, usually in April or May. 218 S. Wabash Ave. For administrative purposes only (not the address where they perform). ℂ 312/251-8838. www.balletchicago.org. Tickets $10–$25.

The Dance Center–Columbia College Chicago *(Finds)* Columbia College, a liberal-arts institution specializing in the arts and media, has been growing by leaps and bounds in recent years. Its Dance Center—the hub of Chicago's modern dance milieu—features an intimate "black box" 275-seat performance space with stadium seating and marvelous sight lines. The center hosts at least a dozen performances a year by both international and national touring groups and homegrown choreographers. 1306 S. Michigan Ave. ℂ 312/344-8300. www.dancecenter. org. Tickets $20. Bus: No. 151. Subway/El: Red Line to Roosevelt.

Hubbard Street Dance Chicago If you're going to see just one dance performance while you're in town, make it Hubbard Street. Chicago's best-known dance troupe mixes jazz, modern, ballet, and theater dance into an exhilarating experience. Sometimes whimsical, sometimes romantic, the crowd-pleasing 22-member ensemble incorporates a range of dance traditions, from Kevin O'Day to Twyla Tharp, who has choreographed pieces exclusively for Hubbard Street. Although the troupe spends most of the year touring, it has regular 2- to 3-week Chicago engagements in the fall and spring. In the summer, the dancers often perform at Ravinia Festival, the Chicago Symphony Orchestra's lovely outdoor pavilion in north-suburban Highland Park (p. 205). Offices at 1147 W. Jackson Blvd. ℂ 312/850-9744. www.hubbardstreetdance.com. Tickets $25–$70.

Joffrey Ballet of Chicago While this major classical company concentrates on touring, the Joffrey schedules about 6 weeks of performances a year in its hometown. Led by co-founder and artistic director Gerald Arpino, the company is committed to the classic works of the 20th century. Its repertoire extends from the ballets of Arpino, Robert Joffrey, Balanchine, and Jerome Robbins to the cutting-edge works of Alonzo King and Chicago choreographer Randy Duncan. The Joffrey continues to draw crowds to its popular rock ballet, *Billboards,* which is set to the music of Prince, and continues to tour internationally. The company is usually in town in the spring (March or April), October, and December, when it stages a popular rendition of the holiday favorite *The Nutcracker.* Offices at 70 E. Lake St. ℂ 312/739-0120. www.joffreyballet.org. Tickets $30–$75.

Muntu Dance Theatre of Chicago   The tribal costumes, drumming, and energetic moves of this widely touring group, which focuses on both traditional and contemporary African and African-American dance, are always a hit with audiences. The company performs in town several times a year in a variety of venues. Offices at 6800 S. Wentworth Ave. ℂ 773/602-1135. www.muntu.com. Tickets $10–$20.

River North Dance Company   Chicago can be a brutal testing ground for start-up dance companies, who have to struggle to find performance space and grab publicity. But the odds didn't buckle the well-oiled knees of the River North Dance Company. This talented jazz dance ensemble performs programs of short, Broadway-style numbers by established and emerging choreographers. You never know where they'll pop up next, though, so call for information on upcoming shows. Offices at 1016 N. Dearborn St. ℂ 312/944-2888. www.rivernorthchicago.com. Tickets $20–$35.

THEATER

Ever since the Steppenwolf Theatre Company burst onto the national radar in the 1970s and early 1980s with gritty, in-your-face productions of Sam Shepard's *True West* and Lanford Wilson's *Balm in Gilead,* Chicago has been known as a theater town. As Broadway produced a steady stream of bloated, big-budget musicals with plenty of special effects but little soul, Chicago theater troupes gained respect for their risk-taking and no-holds-barred emotional style. Some of Broadway's most acclaimed dramas in recent years (Goodman Theatre's revival of *Death of a Salesman* and Steppenwolf's *The Grapes of Wrath,* to name just two) have been hatched on Chicago stages. Steppenwolf and Goodman have led the way in forging Chicago's reputation as a regional theater powerhouse, but a host of other performers are creating their own special styles. With more than 200 theaters, Chicago might have dozens of productions playing on any given weekend—and seeing a show here is on my must-do list for all visitors.

Two of the biggest stars of the local theater scene entered the 21st century in new, custom-built homes downtown. The **Goodman Theatre,** hidden from view behind the Art Institute of Chicago for years, moved to a new theater complex on Dearborn Street, just north of Randolph Street, in the fall of 2000. A bit farther to the east, the marvelous **Chicago Shakespeare Theatre** company performs in a welcoming space on Navy Pier that the Bard himself would recognize—its design is based on the theater where his plays were originally performed. It's not just highbrow stuff that's flourishing downtown; the **Noble Fool Theater** offers an eclectic selection of comedy and cabaret entertainment in its new home at Randolph and State streets, in a building recently renovated by the School of the Art Institute of Chicago.

The listings below represent only a fraction of the city's theater offerings. For a complete listing of current productions playing on a given evening, check the comprehensive listings in the two free weeklies, the *Reader* (which reviews just about every show in town) and *New City,* or the Friday sections of the two dailies. The **League of Chicago Theatres'** website (www.chicagoplays.org) also lists all theater productions playing in the area.

GETTING TICKETS

To order tickets for many plays and events, call **Ticketmaster Arts Line** (✆ **312/ 902-1500**), a centralized phone-reservation system that allows you to charge full-price tickets (with an additional service charge) for productions at more than 50 Chicago theaters. Individual box offices will also take credit-card orders by phone, and many of the smaller theaters will reserve seats for you with a simple request under your name left on their answering machines. For hard-to-get tickets, try the **Ticket Exchange** (✆ **800/666-0779** outside Chicago, or 312/ 902-1888).

HALF-PRICE TICKETS   For half-price tickets on the day of the show (on Fri. you can also purchase tickets for weekend performances), drop by one of the **Hot Tix** ticket centers (✆ **312/977-1755**), located in the Loop at 78 W. Randolph St. (just east of Clark St.); at the Water Works Visitor Center, 163 E. Pearson St.; in Lincoln Park at Tower Records, 2301 N. Clark St.; and in several suburban locations. Hot Tix also offers advance-purchase tickets at full price. Tickets are not sold over the phone. The Hot Tix website (www.hottix.org) lists what's on sale for that day beginning at 10am.

In addition, a few theaters offer last-minute discounts on their leftover seats. Steppenwolf Theatre Company often has half-price tickets on the day of a performance; call or stop by the box office 1 hour before showtime. The "Tix at Six" program at the Goodman Theatre offers half-price, day-of-show tickets; many of them are excellent seats that have been returned by subscribers. Tickets go on sale at the box office at 6pm for evening performances, noon for matinees.

DOWNTOWN THEATERS

Chicago Shakespeare Theatre on Navy Pier   This group's relatively new home is a visually stunning, state-of-the-art jewel. The centerpiece of the glass-box complex, which rises seven stories, is a 525-seat courtyard-style theater patterned loosely after the Swan Theater in Stratford-upon-Avon. The complex also houses a 180-seat studio theater, an English-style pub, and lobbies with commanding views of Lake Michigan and the Chicago skyline. But what keeps subscribers coming back is the talented company of actors, including some of the finest Shakespeare performers in the country.

The main theater presents three plays a year—almost always by the Bard—with founder and artistic director Barbara Gaines usually directing one of the shows. Chicago Shakespeare also hosts special short-run performances, such as a recent production of *Hamlet* by acclaimed British director Peter Brook and a lecture by British actor Derek Jacobi. We Shakespeare Theatre subscribers are a very loyal lot, so snagging tickets can be a challenge; reserve well in advance, if possible. If you have a choice of seats, avoid the upper balcony—the tall chairs are fairly uncomfortable and you have to lean way over the railing to see all the action on stage—definitely not recommended for anyone with a fear of heights. 800 E. Grand Ave. ✆ 312/595-5600. www.chicagoshakes.com. Tickets $48–$58. Subway/El: Red Line to Grand, then bus no. 29 to Navy Pier. Guaranteed parking in attached garage at 40% discount.

Goodman Theatre ✭   The Goodman is the dean of legitimate theaters in Chicago. Under artistic director Robert Falls, the Goodman produces both original productions—such as Horton Foote's *The Young Man from Atlanta* before it went directly to Broadway—and familiar standards, including everything from

Shakespeare to musicals. Its acclaimed revival of Arthur Miller's *Death of a Salesman,* starring Brian Dennehy, not only made it to the Broadway stage in 1999, but won four Tonys—more than any other production. The theater has nurtured the talents of solo artists Spalding Gray and John Leguizamo, and hosted such acclaimed actors as Denzel Washington, William Hurt, Sigourney Weaver, Chita Rivera, and Rip Torn. Productions at the Goodman are always solid; you may not see anything revolutionary, but you'll get some of the best actors in the city and top-notch production values.

In 2000, the Goodman moved into a new, custom-designed home in the North Loop (you'll see the side of the building glowing with different colors in the evenings). The new mixed-use complex is a total-gut rehab of the historic Harris and Selwyn theaters, a pair of former rococo movie houses. But none of the historic bric-a-brac has been retained; the new building has a very modern, minimalist feel. The centerpiece—the 830-seat Albert Ivar Goodman Theatre—is a brand-new limestone-and-glass structure. Connected to the main theater is another addition, a cylindrical, glass-walled building housing retail operations, the 400-seat Owen Theatre, and restaurant Petterino's (p. 115).

One tradition that made the move to the Goodman's new home is the production of *A Christmas Carol,* a perennial holiday draw. 170 N. Dearborn St. ⓒ **312/ 443-3800**. www.goodman-theatre.org. Tickets $30–$50 main stage, $10–$40 studio. Subway/El: Red Line to Washington/State or Lake/State; Brown or Orange line to Clark/Lake.

Noble Fool Theater   The newest addition to the downtown theater scene is this comedy-focused company, started in 1994 and featuring seasoned performers who've done time with Second City, Steppenwolf, and other well-known Chicago performing arts groups. The company recently moved into a new home at State and Randolph streets, and it has taken advantage of the extra space to offer an expanded, eclectic selection of entertainment. If you're looking for a fun show downtown, where you can relax and let loose, this is the place to go. The Main Stage features a full-length play, usually a comedy; the Studio hosts Noble Fool's signature show, *Flanagan's Wake,* an "interactive" Irish wake that encourages audience participation (call in advance for tickets because it does tend to sell out). Live music performances take place in the Cabaret (usually with no cover charge) and a regular improv show runs later in the evening; a recent offering was *The Baritones,* a dead-on takeoff of *The Sopranos.* 16 W. Randolph St. (at State St.) ⓒ **773/202-8843**. www.noblefool.com. Tickets $32–$36 main stage, $25–$29 studio stage. Subway/El: Brown Line to Randolph or Red Line to Washington.

OFF-LOOP THEATERS

Chicago's off-Loop theaters have produced a number of legendary comedic actors, including comic-turned-director Mike Nichols *(The Graduate, Postcards from the Edge, Primary Colors),* as well as fine dramatic actors and playwrights. David Mamet, one of America's greatest playwrights and now an acclaimed film director and screenwriter, grew up in Chicago's South Shore steel-mill neighborhood and honed his craft at the former St. Nicholas Players, which included actor William H. Macy *(Fargo, Boogie Nights, Pleasantville).*

The thespian soil here must be fertile. It's continually mined by Tinseltown and TV, which have lured away such talents as Macy, John Malkovich, Joan Allen, Dennis Franz, George Wendt, John and Joan Cusack, Aidan Quinn, Anne Heche, and Lili Taylor. But even as those actors get lured away by higher paychecks, there's always a whole new pool of talent waiting to take over. This constant renewal keeps the city's theatrical scene invigorated with new ideas and new energy. Many of the smaller Chicago theater companies place great emphasis on communal work: everyone takes part in putting on a production, from writing the script to building the sets. These companies perform in tiny, none-too-impressive venues, but their enthusiasm and commitment are inspiring. Who knows—the group you see performing in some storefront theater today could be the Steppenwolf of tomorrow.

Following is a small sampling of up-and-coming and established theater companies worth checking out.

About Face Theatre   About Face Theatre takes its mission seriously: to promote the creation of new works that examine gay and lesbian themes and experiences. While that often makes for a night of thought-provoking theater, the fare isn't always heavy with social-justice issues. One of the group's recent hits was a very campy musical version of *Xena: Warrior Princess.* In the Theatre Building Chicago, 1225 W. Belmont Ave. ✆ 773/784-8565. www.aboutfacetheatre.com. Tickets $18–$28. Subway/El: Red or Brown line to Belmont.

American Theater Company   With artistic director Brian Russell at the helm, talented individuals such as playwright Rick Cleveland in the ensemble, and a host of top directors and actors popping in for guest appearances, the American Theater Company (formerly American Blues Theatre) has become one of the most reliable off-Loop stages since it began in 1985. The company generally has focused on gritty American dramas (Mamet's *American Buffalo,* for instance, and works by Sam Shepherd and Thornton Wilder), but Russell has begun to introduce some comical, European, and even musical fare. Recent literary adaptations have included *Catch-22* and *Working,* based on the book by veteran Chicago writer Studs Terkel. American Theater also rents its converted warehouse space to several smaller companies, including the highly inventive Defiant Theatre. 1909 W. Byron St. (2 blocks south of Irving Park Rd. at Lincoln Ave.). ✆ 773/929-1031. www.atcweb.org. Tickets $25–$30. Subway/El: Brown Line to Irving Park.

Bailiwick Repertory Theatre   Bailiwick gets my vote as the most eclectic theater group in the city. Each year, the theater produces a main-stage series of classics and musicals, the Director's Festival of one-act plays by fresh local talents (in June), and gay- and lesbian-oriented shows during the Pride Performance series, which generally runs over 20 weeks from mid-May to early October. This is also one of the few companies to stage performances for deaf audiences, performing new spins on classics such as Thornton Wilder's *Our Town* with casts of hearing and hearing-impaired actors. The company's children's theater program produces an original musical for kids each spring. 1229 W. Belmont Ave. (at Racine Ave.). ✆ 773/883-1090. www.bailiwick.org. Tickets $20–$35. Subway/El: Red or Brown line to Belmont.

Briar Street Theatre *Kids*   The Briar Street Theatre has been turned into the "Blue Man Theater" since the fall of 1997. The avant-garde New York City performance phenomenon known as **Blue Man Group** has transformed the 625-seat theater, beginning with the lobby, which is now a jumble of tubes and wires and things approximating computer innards. The show—which mixes percussion, performance art, mime, and rock 'n' roll—has become an immensely popular permanent fixture on the Chicago theater scene (note to those with sensitive ears: It can also get pretty loud). The three strangely endearing performers, whose faces and heads are covered in latex and blue paint, know how to get the audience involved. Your first decision: Do you want the "splatter" or the "nonsplatter" seats? (The former necessitates the donning of a plastic sheet.) 3133 N. Halsted St. (at Briar St.). ℂ **773/348-4000.** Tickets $43–$53. Subway/El: Red or Brown line to Belmont.

Court Theatre *(Finds)* This 250-seat theater, affiliated with the University of Chicago, started out heavily steeped in Molière but has branched into other classics of French literature, Shakespeare, and equally highbrow stuff—with some Oscar Wilde and Noel Coward thrown in for fun. Court Theatre's actors are considered among the finest in the city, and with good reason; they turn classic texts into vibrant, energetic live theater. Every spring, Court schedules two plays in rotating repertoire, with the same cast performing in different shows on alternate nights (with both shows presented Sun.). It's a great way to glimpse the range of the talented Court acting troupe. 5535 S. Ellis Ave. (at 55th St.). ℂ **773/753-4472.** www.courttheatre.org. Tickets $30–$40. Bus: No. 6 (Jeffrey Express).

ETA Creative Arts Foundation Since 1971, this theater has been staging original or seldom-seen dramatic works by African-American writers from Chicago and beyond. Along with **Black Ensemble Theater** (which performs at the Uptown Center Hull House, 4520 N. Beacon St.; ℂ **773/769-4451**), this is one of the best. The company stages six plays a year in its 200-seat theater, including works geared toward children performed on Saturday afternoons. 7558 S. Chicago Ave. (at 76th St.). ℂ **773/752-3955.** www.etacreativearts.org. Tickets $25. Subway/El: Red Line to 69th St., transfer to bus no. 30.

Factory Theater This irreverent young troupe offers the quintessential low-budget Chicago theater experience. The group specializes in original works written by the ensemble, many of which are aimed at a young, nontheatrical crowd (you're encouraged to bring your own beer and drink it during their late-night shows). Their biggest hit (which they stage off and on throughout the year) is the raunchy trailer-park potboiler *White Trash Wedding and a Funeral;* it's hilarious, tacky fun, but not for those with delicate sensibilities. Lately, the Factory has been trying out serious dramatic works as well. But no matter what show you see, the razor-sharp timing, enthusiasm, and camaraderie are infectious. 731 W. Sheridan Rd. ℂ **312/409-3247.** Tickets $10–$15. Subway/El: Red Line to Sheridan.

Lookingglass Theatre Company ⭐ A rising star on the Chicago theatrical scene, Lookingglass has a style all its own, producing original shows and unusual literary adaptations in a highly physical and visually imaginative style. The company, founded more than a decade ago by graduates of Northwestern University (including *Friend* David Schwimmer), stages several shows each year. Recent ones included *Metamorphoses,* a sublime and humorous modern recasting of Ovid's myths that became a hit in New York; ensemble member Mary Zimmerman—who directed the show—has built a national reputation for her creative interpretations of famous literature (if she's directing a show while you're in town, don't miss it). Schwimmer himself has also been known to make appearances here, either as an actor or director. Lookingglass shows emphasize visual effects as much as they do acting, whether it's having performers wade through a giant shallow pool or take to the sky on trapezes. This year, the company celebrates the debut of its new theater in the Water Tower Pumping Station at Chicago and Michigan avenues, a tourist-friendly area that should raise the group's profile. 821 N. Michigan Ave. ℂ **312/337-0665.** www.lookingglasstheatre.org. Tickets $30–$50. Subway/El: Red Line to Chicago.

Neo-Futurists *(Finds)* A fixture on Chicago's late-night theater scene, the Neo-Futurists have been doing their hit *Too Much Light Makes the Baby Go Blind* since 1988 (it's now the longest-running show in Chicago). The setting isn't much (a cramped room above a funeral home), but the gimmick is irresistible: Every night the performers stage a new collection of "30 plays in 60 minutes." The "plays" vary from a 3-minute comedy sketch to a lightning-quick wordless tableau; the mood veers from laugh-out-loud silly to emotionally touching. The show starts at 11:30pm on weekends; you'd better get there about an hour ahead of time because seats are first-come, first-served—and the show does sell out. The late-night curtain attracts a younger crowd, although my 60-ish parents had a great time when I took them (unlike many improv comedy troupes, the Neo-Futurists don't rely on raunchy or gross-out humor). Admission is random: Theatergoers pay $5 plus the roll of a six-sided die. If you want to feel like you've experienced edgy, low-budget theater—but still want to be entertained—this is the place to go. 5153 N. Ashland Ave. (at Foster Ave.). ℂ 773/275-5255. www.neofuturists. org. Tickets $6–$11. Subway/El: Red Line to Berwyn.

Pegasus Players   It's worth seeking out this indefatigable champion of forgotten musical masterpieces. Performing in a rented college auditorium in the gritty North Side neighborhood of Uptown, Pegasus Players specializes in the kind of intellectually demanding fare that bigger mainstream theaters are afraid to risk. A production in the early 1990s of Duke Ellington's *Jump for Joy* was reason to do just that. And a few years ago, Pegasus scored a coup, convincing Stephen Sondheim to let the performers stage the U.S. premiere of his first musical, the little-known *Saturday Night.* Challenging musicals aren't the theater's only Herculean efforts. They've also mounted rarely produced dramatic works such as Robert Shenkkan's 1992 Pulitzer Prize–winning *The Kentucky Cycle,* a 6-hour nine-play marathon. O'Rourke Performing Arts Center, Truman College, 1145 W. Wilson Ave. ℂ 773/878-9761. www.pegasusplayers.org. Tickets $10–$25. Subway/El: Red Line to Wilson.

Redmoon Theater *Finds*   Redmoon Theater might well be the most intriguing and visionary theater company in Chicago. Founded in 1990, the company produces "spectacle theater" comprising masks, objects, and an international range of puppetry styles in indoor and outdoor venues around town—including, at least once a year lately, in Steppenwolf Theatre's studio space. Utterly hypnotic, highly acrobatic and visceral, and using minimal narration, their adaptations of Melville's *Moby Dick,* Mary Shelley's *Frankenstein,* Victor Hugo's *The Hunchback of Notre Dame,* and *Rachel's Love,* an original work based on Jewish folktales, were revelations that have earned the company an ardent and burgeoning following. If you're here in late October (and don't mind crowds), check out Redmoon's annual "All Hallows' Eve Ritual Celebration" in Logan Square—a combination of performance art and street theater that draws young trendy types from throughout the city. Various locations. ℂ 773/388-9031. www.redmoon.org. Ticket prices vary.

Roadworks Productions   One of Chicago's youngest—but already one of its most talented—theater companies, Roadworks attracted some national attention just a few short years after its founding in 1992. Praised for their strong ensemble work and deft touch with works about alienated youth, the performers beat out a slew of higher-profile competitors for the rights to a Midwest premiere of Eric Bogosian's *SubUrbia* in 1995 and have earned coveted spots in Steppenwolf Theatre's studio series. Roadworks aggressively seeks out Midwest and world premiere plays, making this company one to watch. 1144 W. Fulton Market St. ℂ 312/492-7150. www.roadworks.org. Tickets $16–$20. Subway/El: Green Line to Ashland.

Steppenwolf Theatre Company *(Overrated*   Once a pioneer of bare-bones guerilla theater, Steppenwolf has moved firmly into the mainstream, with a state-of-the-art theater and production budgets as big as any in town. The company has garnered many national awards and has also launched the careers of several highly respected and well-known actors, including John Malkovich, Gary Sinise, Joan Allen, John Mahoney (of *Frasier*), and Laurie Metcalf (of *Roseanne*). Famous for pioneering the edgy, so-called "rock 'n' roll," spleen-venting style of Chicago acting in the 1970s and 1980s—characterized by such incendiary tour de forces as Sam Shepard's *True West,* Lanford Wilson's *Balm in Gilead,* Lyle Kessler's *Orphans,* and an adaptation of John Steinbeck's *The Grapes of Wrath*— Steppenwolf lately has become a victim of its own success. No longer a scrappy storefront theater, it now stages world premieres by emerging playwrights, revivals of classics, and adaptations of well-known literary works. While the acting is always high caliber, shows at Steppenwolf can be hit or miss, and unlike the early days, you're certainly not guaranteed a thrilling theatrical experience.

Under artistic director Martha Lavey, Steppenwolf has drawn upon its star power—bringing back its big names to perform or direct from time to time (one of the founders, Terry Kinney, recently directed Gary Sinise in an adaptation of *One Flew Over the Cuckoo's Nest* that later moved to New York). But don't come here expecting to see Sinise or John Malkovich on stage; most of Steppenwolf's big names are too busy with their movie careers. Struggling storefront troupes sometimes perform at Steppenwolf's smaller studio theater, which stages more experimental fare. 1650 N. Halsted St. (at North Ave.). ✆ **312/335-1650.** www.steppenwolf. org. Tickets $35–$50 main stage, $25–$28 studio. If they're available, rush tickets for the main stage are sold at half price (studio tickets for $10) an hr. before a performance (call or stop by the box office). Subway/El: Red Line to North/Clybourn.

Theater on the Lake *(Value*   What a great way to see two of the city's signature strengths: a sublime skyline view from the water's edge and an evening of off-Loop Chicago theater. The Prairie School–style theater has hosted theatrical productions along the lake for half a century, but in recent years the park district has hit upon a perfect programming gimmick: Each week, a different independent theater company gets to strut their stuff. Performances run from June into August on Wednesday to Sunday evenings, and some shows do sell out, so it pays to reserve in advance. At intermission, you can walk out the theater's back door and look south to the city lights. If it's a cool night, it's a good idea to bring a sweater because the screened-in theater is open to the night air (allowing the

---

(Tips   **Theater for All**

Visitors with disabilities will find that some local theaters go the extra mile to make their performances accessible. Steppenwolf, Goodman, and Lookingglass theaters offer sign-language interpretation for deaf patrons and audio-described performances for visually impaired audiences. Bailiwick Repertory runs a regular series of plays featuring deaf actors. Victory Gardens Theater, which has a long-standing commitment to accessible theater, has special performances throughout the year that are customized for audiences with different disabilities. The theater even offers deaf patrons special glasses that project captions of dialogue onto the frame of the glasses.

noise of traffic on Lake Shore Dr. to intrude somewhat, too). Fullerton Ave. and Lake Shore Dr. © 312/742-7994. Tickets $12. Bus: No. 151 (Sheridan).

Trap Door Theatre   Trap Door is emblematic of the streetwise, no-holds-barred brand of off-Loop theater. A risk-taking, emotionally high-voltage company that has somehow stayed afloat despite performing in a converted garage hidden behind a trendy Bucktown restaurant, it concentrates on plays of a social or political bent. Many tend to be original works or decidedly noncommercial, provocative pieces by rarely produced cerebral artists. Be prepared to squirm and sweat: Theater doesn't get any more up close and personal than this. 1655 W. Cortland St. (1 block west of Ashland Ave.). © 773/384-0494. www.trapdoortheatre.com. Tickets $12–$15. Subway/El: Blue Line to Division.

Victory Gardens Theater *Finds*   Victory Gardens is one of the few pioneers of off-Loop theater still standing since the 1970s. The company was rewarded with a Tony Award for regional theater in 2001—a real coup for a theater of this relatively small size. What the Tony committee recognized was Victory Gardens' unswerving commitment to developing playwrights. The five or six productions presented each season are all new works, many of which have been developed through a series of Victory Gardens workshops. The plays tend to be very accessible stories about real people and real situations—nothing too experimental. Even though most shows don't feature nationally known actors, the casts are always first-rate, and the plays usually leave you with something to think about (or passionately discuss) on the way home. Victory Gardens sponsors free readings of new works, which are held twice a month on Sunday. 2257 N. Lincoln Ave. (at Belden Ave.). © 773/871-3000. www.victorygardens.org. Tickets $30–$35. Subway/El: Red or Brown line to Fullerton.

2 Comedy & Improv

In the mid-1970s, *Saturday Night Live* brought Chicago's unique brand of comedy to national attention. But even back then, John Belushi and Bill Murray were just the latest brood to hatch from the number-one incubator of Chicago-style humor, Second City. From Mike Nichols and Robert Klein to Mike Meyers and Tina Fey, two generations of American comics have honed their skills in Chicago before making their fortunes as film and TV stars. Chicago continues to nurture young comics, drawn to Chicago for the chance to hone their improvisational skills at Second City, the ImprovOlympic, and numerous other comedy and improv outlets.

ImprovOlympic *Finds*   ImprovOlympic was founded 20 years ago as a training ground for improv actors by the late, great, and inexplicably unsung Del Close, an improv pioneer who branched off from his more mainstream counterparts at Second City to pursue an unorthodox methodology. A colorful and legendary iconoclast (he was an outspoken advocate for the legalization of marijuana, among other crusades), Close developed a long-form improv technique known as "The Harold," which eschewed the traditional sketch format in favor of more conceptual comedy scenes (the audience suggests a theme for the evening, then a series of skits, monologues, and songs are built around it). The method has since been co-opted by Second City, whose vignette-blackout-vignette format had grown weary.

The ImprovOlympic offers a nightclub setting for a variety of unscripted nightly performances, from free-form shows to shows loosely based on concepts such as *Star Trek* or dating. Like all improv, you're gambling here: It could be a

An Escape from the Multiplex

Chicago has a fine selection of movie theaters—but even the so-called art houses show mostly the same films that you'd be able to catch back home (or eventually on cable). But three local movie houses cater to cinema buffs with truly original programming. The new **Gene Siskel Film Center,** 164 N. State St. (② **312/846-2600;** www.siskelfilmcenter. org; Subway/El: Red Line to Washington or Brown Line to Randolph), named after the well-known *Chicago Tribune* film critic who died in 1999, is part of the School of the Art Institute of Chicago. The center hosts an eclectic selection of film series in two theaters, including lectures and discussions with filmmakers. The Film Center often shows foreign films that are not released commercially in the United States.

The **Music Box Theatre,** 3733 N. Southport Ave. (② **773/871-6604;** www.musicboxtheatre.com; Subway/El: Brown Line to Southport), is a movie palace on a human scale. Opened in 1929, it was meant to re-create the feeling of an Italian courtyard; stars twinkle on the dark blue ceiling, and a faux-marble loggia and towers cover the walls. The Music Box books an eclectic selection of foreign and independent American films—everything from Polish filmmaker Krzysztof Kieslowski's epic *Decalogue* to a singalong version of *The Sound of Music.* (I saw the Vincent Price cult favorite *House of Wax,* complete with 3-D glasses, here.)

Facets Multi-Media, 1517 W. Fullerton Ave. (② **773/281-4114;** www. facets.org; Subway/El: Red or Brown line to Fullerton), a nonprofit group that screens independent film and video from around the world, is for the die-hard cinematic thrill-seeker. The group also hosts a Children's Film Festival (Oct–Nov) and the Chicago Latino Film Festival (Apr–May) and has an impressive collection of classic, hard-to-find films on video and DVD (which you can rent by mail).

big laugh, or the amateur performers could go down in flames. Monday is an off night for most other clubs in town, and ImprovOlympic takes advantage with a show called the Armando Diaz Experience, an all-star improv night that teams up some of the best improvisers in Chicago, from Second City and elsewhere. Besides Myers, successful alums include the late Chris Farley, Tim Meadows, Andy Dick, and Conan O'Brien's former *Late Night* sidekick, Andy Richter. 3541 N. Clark St. (at Addison St.). ② **773/880-0199.** www.improvolymp.com. Tickets $5–$12. Subway/ El: Red Line to Addison.

Second City For more than 40 years, Second City has been the top comedy club in Chicago and the most famous of its ilk in the country. Photos of its vast class of famous graduates line the lobby walls, from Elaine May to John Belushi to current *Saturday Night Live* cast members Tina Fey, Horatio Sanz, and Rachel Dratch.

Today's Second City is a veritable factory of improv, with shows on two stages (the storied main stage and the smaller Second City ETC) and a hugely popular training school. The main-stage ensembles do change frequently, and the shows can swing wildly back and forth on the hilarity meter. In recent years, the club has adopted the long-form improvisational program pioneered by Improv-Olympic (see above listing), which has brought much better reviews. Your best bet is to check the theater reviews in the *Reader,* a local free weekly, for an opinion on the current offering. To sample the Second City experience, catch the free postshow improv session (it gets going around 10:30pm); no ticket is necessary if you skip the main show (except Fri). 1616 N. Wells St. (in the Pipers Alley complex at North Ave.). 🕐 **312/337-3992** or 877/778-4707. www.secondcity.com. Tickets $8–$17. Subway/El: Brown Line to Sedgwick.

Zanie's Comedy Club   Just down the street from Second City in Old Town is Zanie's, one of the few traditional comedy clubs left in Chicago, which swarmed with them 30 years ago. Zanie's often draws its headliners straight off *The Late Show with David Letterman* and *The Tonight Show,* and it's a regular stop for nationally known comedians such as Jackie Mason and Richard Lewis. Stand-up routines are the usual fare, played to packed, appreciative houses. Inquire about smoke-free shows. You must be 21 or older to attend a show. 1548 N. Wells St. (between North Ave. and Schiller St.). 🕐 **312/337-4027.** Tickets $18 plus 2-drink minimum, more for big-name performers. Subway/El: Brown Line to Sedgwick.

3 The Music Scene

JAZZ
In the first great wave of black migration from the South just after World War I, jazz was transported from the Storyville section of New Orleans to Chicago. Jelly Roll Morton and Louis Armstrong made Chicago a jazz hotspot in the 1920s, and their spirit lives on in a whole new generation of musicians. Chicago jazz is known for its collaborative spirit and a certain degree of risk-taking—which you can experience at a number of convivial clubs.

Andy's Jazz Club   Casual and comfortable, Andy's, a full restaurant and bar, is popular with both the hard-core and the neophyte jazz enthusiast. It's the only place in town where you can hear jazz nearly all day long. To listen to the likes of Dr. Bop and the Headliners or clarinetist Chuck Hedges and his "swingtet," stop by for sets beginning at noon, 5pm, and 9pm on weekdays; Saturdays at 6pm and 9:30pm; or Sunday starting at 8pm. 11 E. Hubbard St. (between State St. and Wabash Ave.). 🕐 **312/642-6805.** Cover $4–$10. Subway/El: Red Line to Grand.

Back Room   One of the vestiges of the celebrated old Rush Street, the Back Room still packs a well-dressed crowd into this intimate candlelit spot tucked away at the back of a long gangway like a speakeasy. The tuxedoed doorman offers patrons a seat on the main floor or in the balcony overlooking the stage. Jazz quartets and trios perform four times a night. 1007 N. Rush St. (between Oak St. and Bellevue Place). 🕐 312/751-2433. Cover $8–$12, with a 2-drink minimum. Subway/El: Red Line to Chicago.

Cotton Club   This is an upscale jazz room on the Near South Side, named for the legendary Harlem nightclub. Friday and Saturday nights are the main times for jazz; other nights feature poetry readings, blues, and open-mike performances. A dance club adjoins the space. 1710 S. Michigan Ave. (between 16th and 18th sts.). 🕐 **312/341-0556.** Cover $10 (free Thurs before 8pm). Subway/El: Red Line to Cermak/Chinatown.

Green Dolphin Street ⭐   An old auto garage on the north branch of the Chicago River has been transformed Cinderella-like into a sexy, retro, 1940s-style nightclub and restaurant. The beautiful, well-appointed crowd shows up here to smoke stogies from the club's humidor, lap up martinis, and make the scene (there's also an expensive, fine-dining restaurant whose patrons can move on to jazz after dinner without paying the cover charge). Green Dolphin books jazz in all its permutations, from big band to Latin jazz. The club's main room is closed Monday and Tuesday. 2200 N. Ashland Ave. (at Webster Ave.). © 773/395-0066. www.jazzitup.com. Cover $10–$15. I recommend taking a cab from the Brown Line Armitage stop or the Red Line Fullerton stop (about a 10-min. ride).

Green Mill ⭐ (Finds)   In the heart of Uptown, the Green Mill is "Old Chicago" to the rafters. A popular watering hole during the 1920s and 1930s, when Al Capone was a regular and the headliners included Sophie Tucker—the Last of the Red Hot Mamas—and Al Jolson, it still retains its speakeasy flavor. On Sunday night, the Green Mill hosts the Uptown Poetry Slam, when poets vie for the open mike to roast and ridicule each other's work. Most nights, however, jazz is on the menu, beginning around 9pm and winding down just before closing at 4am (5am Sat). Regular performers include vocalist Kurt Elling, who performs standards and some of his own songs with a quartet, and chanteuse Patricia Barber (they're both worth seeing if they're playing while you're in town). The Green Mill is a Chicago treasure and not to be missed. Get there early to claim one of the plush velvet booths. 4802 N. Broadway (at Lawrence Ave.). © 773/878-5552. Cover $6–$15. Subway/El: Red Line to Lawrence.

Jazz Showcase (Kids)   Spanning more than 50 years and several locations, founder Joe Segal has become synonymous with jazz in Chicago. His son, Wayne, recently took over the business, but this latest venue in the River North restaurant and entertainment district is the spiffiest yet, a spacious and handsome room with sharp black-and-white photographs of jazz greats, many of whom have passed through Segal's clubs. There are two shows a night, and reservations are recommended for big-name headliners. Such well-regarded musicians as McCoy Tyner, Clark Terry, Maynard Ferguson, and Ahmad Jamal have made appearances in recent years. The Segals make an effort to cultivate new generations of jazz lovers, too: The club admits all ages (free for children under 12), has a nonsmoking policy, and offers a Sunday 4pm matinee show. The Segals's latest outpost is the new **Joe's Be-bop Cafe and Jazz Emporium** at Navy Pier, 600 E. Grand Ave. (© **312/595-5299**), a Southern-style barbecue restaurant with live music nightly. 59 W. Grand St. (at Clark St.). © 312/670-2473. www. jazzshowcase.com. Tickets $15–$20. Subway/El: Red Line to Grand.

Pops for Champagne (Finds)   A very civilized, elegant way to enjoy jazz, the Pops champagne bar is one of the prettiest rooms in the city, with fine murals, a vaulted ceiling, and a stage rising above the sunken bar. Live jazz—mostly small-combo piano jazz—is presented 7 nights a week, beginning at 8:30pm Sunday through Thursday, and 9pm on Friday and Saturday. Sundays and Mondays are free. While you're there, it's pretty much required that you sample one of the club's 100 varieties of bubbly. 2934 N. Sheffield Ave. (at Oakdale Ave.). © 773/472-1000. Cover $6–$12. Subway/El: Brown Line to Diversey.

Underground Wonder Bar   This intimate jazz club on the Near North Side only gets better as the night wears on (open until 4am, or 5am Sat). Look for jazz trios and R&B vocalists playing the quirky, compact, and, yep, below-street-level room. Co-owner Lonie Walker and her Big Bad Ass Company Band take the stage at 11pm on Friday and Saturday nights. Stick around until the wee hours, which is really when the fun begins—musicians stop by after gigs at other clubs to improvise a final set. Tex-Mex and other chow is served late. 10 E. Walton

Lincoln Park & Wrigleyville After Dark

American Theater Company **48**
Athenaeum Theatre **20**
Bailiwick Repertory Theatre **27**
Berlin **28**
B.L.U.E.S. **17**
Briar Street Theater **24**
The Closet **32**
Cocktail **35**
Corcoran's **6**
Cubby Bear **42**
The Duke of Perth **23**
Elbo Room **19**
Exedus II **38**
Factory Theater **49**
Gentry **31**
Ginger Man Tavern **46**
Glascott's Groggery **9**
Goose Island Brewing Company **8**
The Gramercy **15**
Green Dolphin Street **10**
Green Mill **51**
ImprovOlympic **44**
Intelligentsia **25**
Irish Oak **43**
John Barleycorn Memorial Pub **12**
Julius Meinl **41**
Lookingglass Theatre Company **21**
Kingston Mines **18**
Manhole **36**
Martyrs' **40**
Metro/Smart Bar **45**

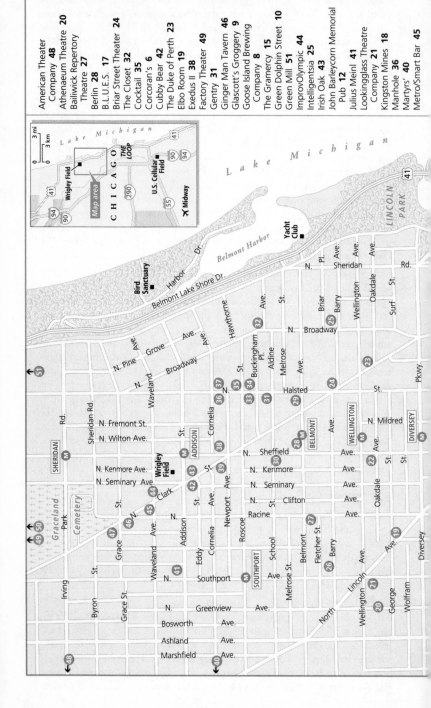

Neo-Futurists **50**
Old Town Ale House **4**
Pops for Champagne **22**
Red Lion Pub **16**
Roscoe's Tavern **33**
Schuba's Tavern **26**
Second City **5**
Sheffield's Beer and
  Wine Garden **30**
Sidetrack **34**
Spin **29**
Spoon **1**
Steppenwolf Theatre
  Company **7**
Theater on the Lake **14**
Uncommon Ground **47**
Victory Gardens
  Theater **13**
Voltaire **37**
Webster's Wine Bar **11**
Wild Hare and Singing
  Armadillo Frog
  Sanctuary **39**
Zanie's Comedy Club **3**
Zentra **2**

ⓜ Subway/El stop

0   0.25 mi
0   0.25 km

265

St. (at State St.). ℭ **312/266-7761.** www.undergroundwonderbar.com. Cover $5–$10. Subway/El: Red Line to Chicago.

Velvet Lounge *(Finds)* For 20 years, Fred Anderson has been running the Velvet Lounge, playing a mean tenor sax, and acting as a guiding force for Chicago's young improvisational musicians. His small, unpretentious haunt looks like it hasn't been updated—with the exception of the mics and recording equipment—in years, but the attraction here is the music, and its pull is strong 5 nights a week. The long-running jam each Sunday night attracts many of the city's best talents, and each Friday and Saturday night the place is packed until its 2am closing with old-school jazz lovers as well as North Side hipsters. International talents such as Hamid Drake, Ken Vandermark, Tatsu Aoki, Kent Kessler, and Jeff Parker perform frequently in different combinations. Fans pack the house, so arrive by 9pm if you want to sit. 2128½ S. Indiana Ave. ℭ **888/644-8007.** www.velvetlounge.net. Cover $5–$10. Subway/El: Red Line to Cermack/Chinatown.

BLUES

If Chicagoans were asked to pick one musical style to represent their city, most of us would start singing the blues. Thanks in part to the presence of the influential Chess Records, Chicago became a hub of blues activity after World War II, with musicians such as Muddy Waters, Howlin' Wolf, and Buddy Guy all recording and performing here. Chicago helped usher in the era of "electric blues"—where low-tech soulful singing melded with the rock sensibility of electric guitars. Blues-influenced rock musicians (the Rolling Stones and Led Zeppelin, for example) made Chicago a regular pilgrimage spot. Today, the blues has become yet another tourist attraction (especially for international visitors), but the quality and variety of blues acts in town is still impressive. Hard-core blues fans shouldn't miss the annual (free) Blues Fest, held along the lakefront in Grant Park in early June. See the "Chicago Calendar of Events" in chapter 3 for more on the festival.

Blue Chicago *(Kids)* Blue Chicago pays homage to female blues belters with a strong lineup of the best women vocalists around. The 1940s-style brick-walled room, decorated with original artwork of Chicago blues vignettes, is open Monday through Saturday, with music beginning at 9pm. Admission allows you to club-hop between this venue and a second location, open Tuesday through Sunday, down the street at 536 N. Clark St. Next door, at 534 N. Clark St., is the Blue Chicago Store, which sells blues-related clothing, merchandise, and artwork. From 8pm to midnight on Saturdays, the basement of the store becomes a venue geared to families, featuring the music of the Gloria Shannon Blues Band. The cover is $5 for adults and free for kids under 12. 736 N. Clark St. (between Chicago Ave. and Superior St.). ℭ **312/642-6261.** www.bluechicago.com. Cover $6–$8. Subway/El: Red or Brown line to Chicago.

B.L.U.E.S. On the Halsted strip, look for B.L.U.E.S.—the name says it all. This is a small joint for the serious blues aficionado—you won't miss a single move of the musicians standing on stage only yards away. Shows start at 9:30pm daily. 2519 N. Halsted St. (between Wrightwood and Fullerton aves.). ℭ **773/528-1012.** www.chicagobluesbar.com. Cover $5–$10. Subway/El: Red or Brown line to Fullerton.

Buddy Guy's Legends *(Finds)* A legend himself, the gifted guitarist runs one of the more popular and most comfortable clubs in town. Blues paraphernalia, from a Koko Taylor dress to a Muddy Waters tour jacket, decorates the walls of this club near the South Loop. You may catch Buddy on stage when he's in town. (Or, if you're lucky, one of his high-profile friends, such as Mick Jagger, will stop by for an impromptu jam session.) The kitchen serves good Louisiana-style soul food and barbecue. Buddy Guy's is planning a move 1 block north of the current location, so call first to check the address. 754 S. Wabash Ave. (between Balbo Dr. and 8th St.). ℭ 312/427-0333. www.buddyguys.com. Cover $10–$15. Subway/El: Red Line to Harrison.

Kingston Mines   Chicago's premier blues bar, Kingston Mines, is where musicians congregate after their own gigs to jam together and to socialize. Celebs have been known to drop by when they're in town shooting movies, but most nights the crowd includes a big contingent of conventioneers looking for a rockin' night on the town. But don't worry about the tourist factor—everyone's here to have a good time, and the energy is infectious. The show begins at 9:30pm daily, with two bands on two stages, and goes until 4am (5am Sat). The late-night kitchen serves up burgers and ribs. 2548 N. Halsted St. (between Wrightwood and Fullerton aves.). ℭ 773/477-4646. www.kingstonmines.com. Cover $12–$15. Subway/El: Red or Brown line to Fullerton.

New Checkerboard Lounge   One of the few surviving joints on the most famous street in blues history, the New Checkerboard Lounge is the real deal—from its battered linoleum floor to the long tables set perpendicular to the stage, to the raw, stripped-down music, which is very close to its Mississippi roots. There are four sets a night, beginning at 9:30pm. If this joint doesn't get your mojo workin', nothin' will. Now surrounded by a marginal neighborhood that has suffered the real blues for years, the club is best reached by car, not public transit. Park in the monitored lot across the street. 423 E. 43rd St. ℭ 773/624-3240. Cover $5–$20. Credit cards not accepted. Subway/El: Green Line to 43rd St., but I recommend a cab at night.

Reservation Blues   Blues singer Eddy "The Chief" Clearwater brings the blues to Wicker Park at his new club and restaurant. Clearwater, who plays up his Native American heritage as part of his stage persona, regularly performs in a headdress (a stained-glass portrait of the boss in his distinctive headgear fills the window facing Milwaukee Ave.). Music paraphernalia fills the place: Guitars and colorful boots hang above the bar, and photos of the Chief and his friends cover the brick walls. The kitchen serves up Southwestern food that's a cut above the usual bar fare (clearly, the restaurant was not an afterthought to the music). The live music starts at 9:30pm Wednesday through Sunday, with the Chief himself making regular appearances on stage. 1566 N. Milwaukee Ave. ℭ 773/645-5200. www.reservation-blues.com. Cover $5–$10. Subway/El: Blue Line to Damen.

Rosa's Lounge   Rosa's is strictly a neighborhood hangout, but it has live blues every night of the year and all the atmosphere required to fuel its heartfelt lamentations. Mama Rosa and her son, Tony Mangiullo, run a homey, lovable spot that, despite its somewhat-distant location off the tourist trail, is decidedly one of the best joints in town for spirited, authentic Chicago blues. Rosa's also sponsors a blues cruise on Lake Michigan every summer. The doors open at 8pm, and the show starts around 9:30pm Tuesday through Saturday. 3420 W. Armitage Ave. (at Kimball Ave.). ℭ 773/342-0452. www.rosaslounge.com. Cover $5–$12. Bus: No. 73 (Armitage).

ROCK (BASICALLY)

In the early 1990s, Chicago's burgeoning alternative rock scene, which produced such names as the Smashing Pumpkins, Liz Phair, Veruca Salt, Urge Overkill, and Material Issue, attracted the national spotlight. Although the city's moment of pop hipness quickly faded (as did most of the aforementioned bands), the live music scene has continued to thrive without all the hoopla. Most Chicago bands concentrate on keeping it real, happy to perform at small local clubs and not obsessing (at least openly) about getting a record contract. The city also is a regular stop for touring bands, from the big stadium acts to smaller up-and-coming bands. Scan the *Reader* or *New City* to see who's playing where.

The biggest rock acts tend to play at the local indoor stadiums: **United Center** (© 312/455-4500), home of the Bulls and Blackhawks, or **Allstate Arena** (© 847/635-6601), in Rosemont near O'Hare Airport. During the summer, you'll also find the big names at the outdoor **Tweeter Center** (© 708/614-1616), inconveniently located in the suburb of Tinley Park, about an hour outside the city (and cursed with pretty bad acoustics).

But you can catch other rock acts at local venues with a lot more character. The **Riviera Theatre,** 4746 N. Racine Ave. (© 773/275-6800), is a relic of the Uptown neighborhood's swinging days in the 1920s, 1930s, and 1940s. A former movie palace, it retains the original ornate ceiling, balcony, and lighting fixtures, but it has definitely gotten grimy with age (head upstairs if you want to avoid the crowd that crushes toward the stage during shows). The **Aragon Ballroom,** a few blocks away at 1106 W. Lawrence Ave. (© 773/561-9500; Subway/El: Red Line to Lawrence), was once an elegant big-band dance hall; the worn Moorish-castle decor and twinkling-star ceiling now give the place a seedy charm all its own. A former vaudeville house is now the **Vic Theater,** 3145 N. Sheffield Ave. (© 773/472-0366; Subway/El: Red or Brown line to Fullerton), a midsize venue that features up-and-coming acts (get there early to snag one of the lower balcony rows).

More sedate audiences love the **Park West,** 322 W. Armitage Ave. (© 773/929-5959; Subway/El: Brown Line to Armitage, or bus no. 22 [Clark St.]), both for its excellent sound system and its cabaret-style seating (no mosh pit here). I've caught excellent shows there with Sarah McLaughlin and Tori Amos, artists typical of the kinds of acts that thrive at the Park West. For tickets to most shows at all these venues, you're stuck going through the service-fee-grabbing **Ticketmaster** (© 312/559-1212).

Here are some bars and clubs that book live music most nights of the week:

Cubby Bear   Across from Wrigley Field, Cubby Bear is a showcase for new rock bands and an occasional offbeat act, and it draws a scrub-faced postcollegiate crowd. Concerts are staged on weekends and many Wednesday nights. Otherwise, there are always billiards, darts, and other distractions. 1059 W. Addison St. (at Clark St.). © 773/327-1662. www.cubbybear.com. Cover $6–$7 on band nights, more for special shows. Subway/El: Red Line to Addison.

Double Door *Finds*   This club has capitalized on the Wicker Park/Bucktown neighborhood's ascendance as a breeding ground for rock and alternative music. Owned by the proprietors of Metro (see below), the club has some of the better acoustics and sight lines in the city and attracts buzz bands and unknowns to its stage. When you need to escape the noise, there's a lounge-type area, the Dirt Room, with pool tables in the basement. Concerts are staged Tuesday through Sunday. 1572 N. Milwaukee Ave. (at North Ave.). © 773/489-3160. www.doubledoor.com. Tickets $5–$15. Subway/El: Blue Line to Damen.

Elbo Room *Value*   Step downstairs into this basement-level Lincoln Park music room for a lineup of nightly musical entertainment that's delightfully schizophrenic: rockabilly, hip-hop, soul, funk, and more. Acid jazz fave Sumo is a long-running draw on Sunday nights. 2871 N. Lincoln Ave. (at George St.). © 773/549-5549. www.elboroomchicago.com. Cover $5–$10. Subway/El: Brown Line to Diversey.

The Empty Bottle   This alternative rock club in the Ukrainian Village neighborhood is a haven for young arty scenesters drawn here for camaraderie, obscure bands, and cheap beer. Offerings are eclectic, with experimental jazz on Wednesday and other nights given over to a DJ's underground improvisations. A real treat is the annual Festival of Jazz and Improvised Music, held in the spring, which showcases an international assemblage of top avant-garde musicians. 1035 N. Western Ave. (between Division St. and Augusta Blvd.). ✆ 773/276-3600. www.emptybottle.com. Cover $5–$12. Subway/El: Blue Line to Western, then bus no. 49.

House of Blues   The largest in a national chain of music venues, the House of Blues could more appropriately be called the House of Pop. Although it is decorated with Mississippi Delta folk art, the bands that play here tend to be rock groups, '80s novelty acts, and the occasional hip-hop or reggae performer. This is a great place to see a show—concerts are held in a theater that recreates a gilded European opera house (minus the seats), and the sight lines are pretty good no matter where you stand. A restaurant also serves lunch and dinner with hometown blues accompaniment. The popular Sunday gospel brunch, offering a Southern-style buffet, brings a different Chicago gospel choir to the stage each week; the three weekly "services" often sell out, so get tickets in advance. 329 N. Dearborn St. (at Kinzie St.). ✆ 312/923-2000 for general information, 312/923-2020 for concert information. www.hob.com. Ticket prices vary depending on the act. Subway/El: Red Line to Grand.

Martyrs' *Finds*   Dedicated to the memories of such late great rock and blues performers as Jimi Hendrix and Janis Joplin (who are immortalized on the mural facing the stage), Martyrs' presents a variety of local bands and the occasional performance by national touring acts. On the first Thursday of the month, catch the popular Roots and Rockabilly Jamboree. The low tables, high ceiling, and huge windows make Martyrs' one of the best places to catch a rock 'n' roll show. 3855 N. Lincoln Ave. (between Berenice Ave. and Irving Park Rd.). ✆ 773/404-9494. www.martyrslive.com. Cover $5–$15. Subway/El: Brown Line to Addison.

Metro   Metro, located in an old auditorium, is Chicago's premier venue for live alternative/rock acts on the verge of breaking into the big time. There's not much in the way of atmosphere—it's basically a big black room with a stage—but the place has an impressive history. Everybody who is anybody has played here when they were starting out, from REM to Pearl Jam to such local heroes as the Smashing Pumpkins. Newer "alternative" bands that are getting attention from MTV and radio stations show up at Metro eventually. The subterranean Smart Bar—at the same location—is a dance club open 7 nights a week (you can get in for free if you've seen a concert that night at Metro). Some shows are all ages, but most require concertgoers to be 21 and older. Tickets are sold in person through the box office in the attached record shop, **Clubhouse** (sans service charges), or by phone through Ticketmaster. 3730 N. Clark St. (at Racine Ave.). ✆ 773/549-0203, or 312/559-1212 for Ticketmaster orders. www.metrochicago.com. Tickets $12–$20. Subway/El: Red Line to Sheridan.

Phyllis' Musical Inn   Typical of the neighborhood bars in Wicker Park, Phyllis' is a small, generally uncrowded club booking live rock music (sometimes jazz and blues) 4 to 5 nights a week. The bookers encourage musicians to perform original songs, so you won't find any Grateful Dead cover bands here. 1800 W. Division St. (at Wood St.). ✆ 773/486-9862. Cover $3–$5. Subway/El: Blue Line to Division.

COUNTRY, FOLK & ETHNIC MUSIC

The mix of cultures and ethnicities in Chicago's neighborhoods translates into a wealth of music clubs catering to all kinds of musical tastes, from mellow folk and melancholy Irish to suave salsa and spicy reggae. Chicago is also the place to hear the so-called insurgent country sound (country music meets rock and punk) pioneered by local indie record label Bloodshot Records and bands such as Wilco, Robbie Fulks, and the Waco Brothers.

Abbey Pub   Irish brogues abound at this barnlike gathering place for rock and folk acts from here and abroad. Besides Guinness and other Emerald Isle beers on tap, there's a full menu. 3420 W. Grace St. (at Elston Ave.). ☎ 773/478-4408. www. abbeypub.com. Cover $5–$20. I recommend a cab from the Blue Line Belmont or Addison stops (about a 10-min. cab ride).

Baby Doll Polka Club   Polka is alive and kicking in Chicago at the Baby Doll Polka Club, located across the street from the runways at Midway airport. Relive those golden memories of Lawrence Welk, and skip-step to the magic accordion of the house band, the Merry Makers. It's open daily, with live music on weekends only (the bands start at 9:30pm Sat and 6pm Sun—which is when the joint really hops). 6100 S. Central Ave. ☎ 773/582-9706. No cover. Subway/El: Orange Line to Midway Airport, then a 10-min. cab ride.

Exedus II   Like its flashier neighbor, the Wild Hare (see below), Exedus offers nightly reggae shows; the specialty here is Jamaican dancehall, performed live or by DJs. Although this small storefront tavern gets smoky and crowded, the music's good and the attitude of the international crowd is very laid back. In general, it's more authentic than the competition, which tends to draw more of the frat-party element. 3477 N. Clark St. (between Newport Ave. and Roscoe St.). ☎ 773/ 348-3998. Cover usually under $10. Subway/El: Red Line to Addison.

The Hideout *(Value)*   This friendly tavern's OLD STYLE BEER sign shines like a beacon, guiding roots music fans through the grimy industrial neighborhood that surrounds it. The owners' beer-can collection and some eclectic "celebrity" memorabilia are on display in the front room. In back, local musicians play country, rock, and bluesy tunes on a smallish stage backed by an impressive stuffed sailfish. It's no-frills all right. But the Hideout also books one of the best lineups of folk and "alt country" bands in the city, including the Blacks, the Pine Valley Cosmonauts, the Handsome Family, Jeff Tweedy (of Wilco), the Rachels, Devil in a Woodpile, and Kelly Hogan. 1354 W. Wabansia Ave. (between Elston Ave. and Throop St.). ☎ 773/227-4433. www.hideoutchicago.com. Cover usually $5–$10. Subway/El: Blue Line to Damen.

HotHouse *(Finds)*   This "Center for International Performance and Exhibition" schedules some of the most eclectic programming in the city, attracting well-known jazz and avant-garde musicians from around the world. When the heavy hitters aren't booked, you'll see anything from local musicians improvising on "invented instruments" to Afro-Cuban dance troupes to Japanese blues singers. 31 E. Balbo Dr. (at S. Wabash Ave.). ☎ 312/362-9707. www.hothouse.net. Cover $10–$25. Subway/El: Red Line to Harrison.

Old Town School of Folk Music *(Finds)*   Country, folk, bluegrass, Latin, Celtic—the Old Town School of Folk Music covers a spectrum of indigenous musical forms. The school is best known as a training center offering a slate of music classes, but it also hosts everyone from the legendary Pete Seeger to bluegrass phenom Alison Krauss. The school's home, in a former 1930s library, is the world's largest facility dedicated to the preservation and presentation of traditional and contemporary folk music. The Old Town School also houses an art gallery showcasing exhibitions of works by local, national, and international artists; a music store offering an exquisite selection of instruments, sheet music, and hard-to-find recordings; and a cafe. In midsummer, it sponsors the popular Folk and Roots outdoor music festival. The school maintains another retail store and a schedule of children's classes at its first location, 909 W. Armitage Ave. 4544 N. Lincoln Ave. (between Wilson and Montrose aves.). ℂ 773/728-6000. www.oldtown school.org. Tickets $10–$30. Subway/El: Blue Line to Western.

Schubas Tavern *(Finds)*   Country and folk singer-songwriters have found a home in this divine little concert hall located in a former Schlitz tavern. It's a friendly and intimate place, best experienced from one of the wooden booths ringing the room. There's music 7 nights a week, and Schubas occasionally hosts big-name performers such as John Hiatt and Marshall Crenshaw. You also find a bar up front and an attached restaurant, Harmony Grill, where you can grab a pretty good burger and fries after the show. 3159 N. Southport Ave. (at Belmont Ave.). ℂ 773/525-2508. www.schubas.com. Tickets $7–$20. Subway/El: Red or Brown line to Belmont.

Wild Hare and Singing Armadillo Frog Sanctuary   Number one on Chicago's reggae charts is the Wild Hare, in the shadow of Wrigley Field. Grab a Red Stripe and dance to bands from Jamaica and elsewhere, including Burning Spear, the Wailers, Shabba Ranks, and Yellowman. The atmosphere inside the bar—dark and slightly dingy—might have been transported from a side street in Montego Bay. 3530 N. Clark St. (between Addison and Roscoe sts.). ℂ 773/327-4273. www.wildharereggae.com. Cover usually $5–$12. Subway/El: Red Line to Addison.

CABARETS & PIANO BARS

The Baton Show Lounge   Catch the city's long-running revue of female impersonators at this River North lounge, which has been showcasing fabulous "gals" in outrageous getups for more than 30 years. Shows are held Wednesday through Sunday at 8:30pm, 10:30pm, and 12:30am. This is a very popular spot for bachelorette outings, so be prepared for some groups of rowdy women in your midst. 436 N. Clark St. (between Hubbard and Illinois sts.). ℂ 312/644-5269. Cover $10 plus 2-drink minimum. Subway/El: Red Line to Grand.

Coq d'Or   Whether you're huddled close around the piano or hanging back on the red Naugahyde banquettes, this old-time, clubby Chicago haunt in the historic Drake Hotel offers an intimate evening of song stylings. The Coq d'Or claims to be the second bar in Chicago to serve drinks after the repeal of Prohibition in 1933—and the place hasn't changed much since then. In the Drake Hotel, 140 E. Walton St. (at Michigan Ave.). ℂ 312/787-2200. No cover. Subway/El: Red Line to Chicago/State.

Davenport's Piano Bar & Cabaret *(Finds)*   The youthful hipster environs of Wicker Park isn't the first place you'd expect to find a tried-and-true piano bar and cabaret venue. But Davenport's is doing its best to revive a fading art form. Owner Bill Davenport and his partners have transformed a single-story storefront into an intimate, chic gem that provides a much-needed showcase for Chicago-bred talent, with a sprinkling of visiting performers from New York and LA. The piano bar in front is flashier than the subdued cabaret in back, featuring a singing waitstaff, blue-velvet banquettes, funky lighting fixtures, and a hand-painted mural-topped bar. The cabaret's sound equipment is first-rate. 1383 N. Milwaukee Ave. (just south of North Ave.). ℂ 773/278-1830. www.davenportspianobar. com. Cover $10–$25. Subway/El: Blue Line to Damen.

Jilly's   Named for Frank Sinatra's former manager, Jilly's has brought new life to Rush Street. Music and a lively buzz from the patrons spill into the street during warm weather, and piano stylists and trios play the dark room decorated with photos of the Rat Pack, Steve and Edie, and the like. Downstairs in the basement is the dance club Jilly's Retro, keeping the 1970s alive ($10 cover). This is the nightspot for wealthy Gold Coast residents, so dress to impress. 1007 N. Rush St. (at Oak St.). ℭ 312/664-1001. Subway/El: Red Line to Chicago.

Redhead Piano Bar   The Redhead attracts a well-heeled, sharp-dressed Gold Coast clientele, which tends to be older—at least in terms of the gents, who usually outnumber the ladies here. Yesteryear memorabilia, such as movie-star glamour shots, playbills, and old sheet music, covers the walls of this dimly lit spot. And the crowd teeming around the piano is a throwback as well. 16 W. Ontario St. ℭ 312/640-1000. No cover. Subway/El: Red Line to Grand.

Zebra Lounge *Finds*   The most wonderfully quirky piano bar in town, Zebra Lounge has a loyal following despite (or maybe because of) the campy decor. Just as you would expect, black-and-white stripes are the unifying decor theme at this dark, shoebox-size Gold Coast spot, furnished with black vinyl booths, a small mirrored bar, and zebra kitsch galore. As bar lore has it, the Zebra Lounge opened December 5, 1933—the day Prohibition ended. Since then, it has passed through numerous owners, but the name has remained the same, in tribute to a long-forgotten tavern in New York. For the past quarter century, it has been a raucous piano bar, attracting a multigenerational crowd of regulars. The scene is relatively mellow early in the evening, though it can get packed late into the night on weekends. 1220 N. State Pkwy. (between Division and Goethe sts.). ℭ 312/642-5140. No cover. Subway/El: Red Line to Clark/Division.

4 The Club Scene

Chicago is the hallowed ground where house music was hatched in the 1980s, so it's no surprise to find several dance clubs pounding away with a mostly under-30 crowd. A skeptical Midwestern sensibility has always reigned here, so the attitude and fashion required for a big dance club has limited appeal. But there are plenty of other clubs and bars with square footage given over to dancing. Some spots specialize in one brand of music, while others that offer an ever-changing mix of rhythms and beats that follow the latest DJ-driven trend. Given the fickle nature of club goers, some places listed below might have disappeared by the time you read this. But what's impressive about Chicago's club scene is the number of long-time survivors—clubs that have lasted more than a year or two and continue to draw loyal crowds.

Berlin   One of the more enduring dance floors in Chicago, Berlin is primarily gay during the week, but draws dance hounds of all stripes on weekends and for special theme nights (disco the last Wednesday of every month, and Prince the last Sunday of the month). It has a reputation for outrageousness and creativity, so this is prime ground for people-watching. The space isn't much—basically a square room with a bar along one side—but the no-frills dance floor is packed late into the evening. The owners are no dummies: The cover charge applies only on Friday and Saturday after midnight, which is about an hour earlier than you ought to show up. (For more, see below under "The Gay & Lesbian Scene.") 954 W. Belmont Ave. (at Sheffield Ave.). ℭ 773/348-4975. www.berlinchicago.com. Cover $5. Subway/El: Red or Brown line to Belmont.

Big Wig   Proprietor Miae Lim, the inventive hipster behind Wicker Park's late-night sushi hot spot Mirai Sushi, brought Chicago its own version of New York's Beauty Bar a couple of years ago. At the time, some thought she was nuts for transforming a former no-frills Polish bar along a then-seedy stretch of Division Street. They now think otherwise, because the area now lures fashionistas and other scenesters. Big Wig has an urban feel and attracts an eclectic mix of people—some come to dance, but many just want to hang and check out the scene. Lim's club features salon chairs for sofas, vintage plastic-bubble hair dryers as chandeliers, and mannequins in wildly colorful wigs. The dance floor downstairs is on the small side, but rarely gets too cramped. The tunes (spun by resident DJs and special guests) include acid jazz, hip-hop, house, and lounge music. 1551 W. Division St. ✆ 773/235-9100. www.bigwignightclub.net. Cover $5. Subway/El: Blue Line to Division.

Funky Buddha Lounge   Located a bit off the beaten path, west of the River North gallery district, this club blends in with its industrial surroundings—even the whimsical Buddha sculpture on the heavy steel front door is a rusted husk. Inside is a different scene altogether: low red lighting, seductive dens with black-leather and faux leopard-skin sofas, lots of candles, and antique light fixtures salvaged from an old church. The DJs are among the best in the city, flooding the nice-size dance floor with hip-hop to bhangra, funk to African, and soul to underground house. Recently, the club's original fan base of yuppies and after-dinner hipsters has been shaken as attractively as its signature martinis: hugely popular Thursday nights pack in the young, mostly white club kids, but Fridays and Saturdays feature a cool, eclectic crowd decked out in funky gear. 728 W. Grand Ave. ✆ 312/666-1695. www.funkybuddha.com. Cover $15–$20. Bus: No. 65 (Grand Ave.), but take a cab at night.

Harry's Velvet Room   Perhaps the coolest subterranean late-night scene in Chicago, this is the place to come when you want to party not-so-hearty with beautiful, upscale club-goers. Originally a posh cigar lounge located a few short blocks from its present home, the new Harry's has been retooled as a champagne, dessert, and wine destination, but the dimly lit, romantic aura that seduced scores of suave night crawlers remains intact. Warm earth tones flow throughout the space, from the plush leather booths, sofas, and chairs to the two bar areas; undulating ambient mellow grooves of dance and world beats throb in the background. Champagne and wine aren't the only libations on tap here: Harry's also boasts a wide range of martinis, bourbons, and single-malt liquors. 56 W. Illinois St. ✆ 312/527-5600. Cover: $10 on weekends, no cover weeknights. Subway/El: Red Line to Grand.

Le Passage   The Gold Coast's swankiest nightclub fits all the prerequisites for chic exclusivity, starting with the semihidden entrance at the end of a narrow (but well-lit) alleyway just steps from Oak Street's Prada and Barneys New York stores. You descend down a long flight of stairs into an environment filled with expensive, gilded furnishings and exquisite decor imported from France; to gain access you must first pass muster with the gatekeepers manning the velvet rope. The beautiful, the rich, and the designer-suited come here for the loungy aesthetic. The soundtrack mixes R&B, soul, hip-hop, house, funk, and acid jazz. Another highlight is the stellar French fusion menu. The place teems on Friday and Saturday nights, but Wednesday night caters to local fashion-industry folk, with occasional runway fashion shows. Stop by the Yow Bar—named for Yow Low, a legendary local bartender who was snagged from Trader Vic's—and hopefully you'll get Yow himself to spill some of his late-night tales. 1 Oak Place (between Rush and State sts). ✆ 312/255-0022. Cover $15–$20. Subway/El: Red Line to Chicago.

Mystique   Mix a dance club with a cocktail lounge, throw in a generous helping of humor, and what do you get? One of the city's most accessible
nightspots—figuratively and literally (its location near the Magnificent Mile
makes it a much closer stop for out-of-towners than many other clubs). Mystique fills a series of rooms on multiple levels, each with its own style and mood.
The Pillow Parlor is scattered with futons and pillows for lounging, and the
Martini Mischief Chalet attracts couples who snuggle by the cozy fireplace.
Upbeat dance tracks play in several different rooms, and you're encouraged to
get up on the cocktail tables to show your stuff. Women should be sure to stop
in the lavish ladies lounge, where a good-looking male bartender serves up
champagne. 157 W. Ontario St. (at LaSalle St.) ✆ 312/642-2582. Cover: $5–$10. Subway/El:
Red Line to Grand/State.

Red Dog   Another spot you have to reach by slipping down an alley, Red Dog
is a loft space overlooking the action in Wicker Park. The throbbing beats of
underground and industrial house attract serious clubgoers. As far as what to
wear, anything goes. Dress up, down, casual, or extreme—you'll see pretty much
everything here. The gay-themed Boom-Boom Room on Monday is hands-
down the most exotic night on the social calendar, with club kids, drag queens,
and platform dancers all bobbing to a house beat. Besides Monday, the club is
open Wednesdays and weekends. 1958 W. North Ave. (at Milwaukee Ave.). ✆ 773/278-
1009. Cover $6–$10. Subway/El: Blue Line to Damen.

Rednofive   Taking its name from the ubiquitous artificial dye used in food
products, rednofive is no fake, thanks to its sleek design and tight lineup of all-
star DJs spinning a sonic deluge of progressive and abstract house music. The
dark, underground feel attracts clubbers who are serious about their music; you
don't have to dress to impress, but don't show up in shorts and sneakers, either.
This club tends to attract a younger club crowd who want to dance and hang
out. The space isn't very large—there's a small lounge in front and a basic dance-
floor area surrounded by seating—but devoted dance fans pack the place on
weekends. 440 N. Halsted St. (at Hubbard St.). ✆ 312/733-6699. www.rednofive.com. Cover
$10–$20. Subway/El: Green Line to Clinton.

Sinibar   One of the most sensual spaces in the city belongs to Joe Russo's
Moroccan-style nightclub/restaurant/dessert lounge Sinibar in Wicker Park.
This is home turf for a diverse urban crowd; the overall look of the clientele is
hip without trying too hard. Despite an upscale vibe, this is a pocketbook-
friendly place, with no stiff cover charge and a reasonably priced French/Moroc-
can menu in the lush street-level bistro. There can be long lines, so getting there
a little early isn't a bad idea. There's dancing in the lounge downstairs, where
local DJs spin R&B, soul, house, hip-hop, and funk. But it's the overall exotic
vibe that keeps regulars coming back. 1540 N. Milwaukee Ave. (½ block south of Damen
Ave.). ✆ 773/278-7797. No cover. Subway/El: Blue Line to Damen.

Smart Bar   A long-established name on the dance circuit, Smart Bar, tucked
in the basement below the rock club Metro, spins the latest musical forms from
underground house to punk to ethereal and gothic. The scene starts late, and the
dancing denizens vary widely depending on which bands are playing upstairs
(concertgoers get free admission to the Smart Bar). A no-frills club that attracts
a diverse crowd, you never quite know what you're going to get here, and that's
part of the appeal. This is an established Chicago spot where clubbers can come
as they are, and you'll see a range of fashion. Smart Bar stays open until 5am on
weekends. No cover before 11pm during the week. 3730 N. Clark St. (at Racine Ave.).

© 773/549-4140. www.smartbarchicago.com. Cover $5–$15 (free with show at upstairs Metro). Subway/El: Red Line to Addison.

Transit   Carved out of a warehouse space beneath the elevated train tracks just west of the hip Randolph Street restaurant row, Transit is an excellent no-non-sense dance club that doesn't trick itself out under the auspices of any wacky theme. Its 10,000 square feet feature a sleek, boldly colored geometric interior with modern, minimalist furniture. The large dance-floor area, called the Oval, is surrounded by postindustrial metal staircases leading to a VIP room, the tiny Light Bar, and another VIP space named the Chandelier Room. The bone-rattling, state-of-the-art sound system and DJs—spinning progressive dance, remixed hip-hop, and R&B—don't disappoint the die-hard dance fans. Come wearing your best club attire. 1431 W. Lake St. *©* 312/491-8600. Cover $15–$20. Subway/El: Green Line to Ashland.

Vision   The spot now known as Vision has been through several name and decor changes over the years, but it keeps plugging away, taking advantage of a tourist-friendly location not far from Michigan Avenue. Stretching through four levels, Vision caters to the current nightclub trend of providing different envi-ronments on different levels. The dance floor—thumping with house, trance, progressive and hip-hop—fills the first floor; upper floors offer plenty of nooks and crannies for groups to sit and chat. The club's owners have ambitious plans to bring in internationally known DJs, so Vision may soon be setting some trends of its own. 640 N. Dearborn St. (at Ontario St.). *©* 312/266-1944. Cover $10–$20. Subway/El: Red Line to Grand/State.

White Star Lounge   Love it or hate it, White Star Lounge has become the see-and-be-seen spot for Chicago's beautiful people. Decorated Miami-modern style in cool tones of blue and silver, the scene is all about gathering on the sofas that surround the dance floor, or crushing against other thirsty souls around the bar. The music is designed to be accessible to the high-maintenance crowd, mostly Top-40 hip-hop and Euro dance hits. White Star does seem to attract a high percentage of attractive young women, although those ladies sometimes complain about a certain "cheesy" element among the slick male clientele. Fans say that White Star is the place to make the scene; detractors point out the superficial attitude and tiny dance floor. Judge for yourself, but don't forget to wear your best. 225 W. Ontario St. (at Wells St.) *©* 312/440-3223. Cover: $20 on weekends. Subway/El: Red Line to Grand/State.

Zentra   Club hoppers often make the Middle Eastern/Moroccan–flavored Zentra, which stays open into the wee hours, their last stop of the night. Plugged into a large four-room space, Zentra is riding the current trend wave of East meets West, with exotic Moroccan textiles, thick drapes, Indian silks, red lanterns and funky chrome fixtures, and even "Hookah Girls" proffering hits on hookah pipes packed with fruity tobacco blends. There are two floors, each catering to different sounds of both resident and guest DJs. Upstairs caters to those who want to dance to progressive dance and techno sounds, while downstairs has DJs spinning mostly house and hip-hop. Zentra attracts an eclectic mix of people who come to soak in exotic vibes, do some people-watching, and simply have fun dancing. In the summer, an outdoor deck lit by red lights puts a funky spin on the beer garden concept. There is no dress code, but feel free to dress up—you'll see a little bit of everything here. 923 W. Weed St. (just south of North Ave. at Clybourn Ave.). *©* 312/787-0400. Cover $15–$20. Subway/El: Red Line to North/Clybourn.

Tips Late-Night Bites

Chicago's not much of a late-night dining town; most restaurants shut down by 10 or 11pm, leaving night owls with the munchies out of luck. But if you know where to go, you can still get a decent meal past midnight. Here are a few spots that serve up real food until real late.

In the Loop, your best—and practically only—choice is **Miller's Pub** (p. 277), 134 S. Wabash Ave. (© **312/645-5377**), which offers hearty American comfort food until 2am daily. Many late-night visitors to this historic watering hole and restaurant are out-of-towners staying at neighboring hotels.

The acknowledged star of the late-night scene is the dark, moody **Iggy's** (p. 279), 700 N. Milwaukee Ave. (© **312/829-4449**). It's a bit off the beaten track (although an easy cab ride from nightspots in River North or Wicker Park), but the cool crowd descends here for pastas and breakfast items until 4am.

In River North, food is available until 4am at **Bar Louie** (p. 278), 226 W. Chicago Ave. (© **312/337-3313**). The menu is a good step above mozzarella sticks and other standard bar food: Focaccia sandwiches, vegetarian wraps, and salads are among the highlights.

After a night out, Wicker Park and Bucktown residents stop by **Northside Cafe** (p. 161), 1635 N. Damen Ave. (© **773/384-3555**), for sandwiches and salads served until 2am (3am Sat.). In nice weather, the front patio is the place to be for prime people-watching.

The bright, welcoming atmosphere at **Clarke's Pancake House,** 2441 N. Lincoln Ave. (© **773/472-3505**), is a dose of fresh air after an evening spent in dark Lincoln Park bars. Yes, there are pancakes on the menu, but plenty of other creative breakfast choices as well, including mixed skillets of veggies, meat, and potatoes. Clarke's is open 24 hours, if you need to satisfy a *really* late-night craving.

When the Lincoln Park bars shut down at 2am, the action moves to the **Wieners Circle,** 2622 N. Clark St. (© **773/477-7444**). This hot-dog stand is strictly no-frills: You shout your order across the drunken crowd and the only spots to sit are a few picnic tables out front. Open until 4am during the week and 6am on weekends, the Wieners Circle is the center of pre-dawn life in Lincoln Park—and I know people who swear that the greasy cheese-topped fries are the perfect hangover prevention.

5 The Bar & Cafe Scene

If you want to soak up the atmosphere of a neighborhood tavern or sports bar, it's best to venture beyond downtown into the surrounding neighborhoods. The Near North Side has a few entertainment zones that are saturated with bright, upscale neighborhood bars. But you'll also find numerous dives and no-frills "corner taps" in the blue-collar neighborhoods.

As for hotel nightlife, virtually every hotel in Chicago has a cocktail lounge or piano bar and, in some cases, more than one distinct environment where you can take an aperitif before dinner or watch an evening of entertainment. The piano bars at the Drake and in the Omni Ambassador East Hotel's Pump Room are standouts.

BARS
THE LOOP & VICINITY

The Berghoff   Women weren't admitted to the stand-up bar at The Berghoff—a Chicago institution with claim to the city's post-Prohibition liquor license no. 1—until they protested their way in the door in 1969. The only women's bathroom is in the dining room, but today Loop business types of both genders gather after work in the dark oak-paneled bar for one of The Berghoff's own drafts and a roast-beef sandwich. 17 W. Adams St. (between Dearborn and State sts.). (*) 312/427-3170. Subway/El: Red Line to Jackson.

Kitty O'Shea's   The Hilton Chicago is the unlikely home of an authentically appointed Irish pub, with no detail spared, from the carved mahogany bar to the Guinness pints expertly poured by the Irish native bartenders here on a work exchange. Irish duos and trios get the conventioneers—and even a few Irish guys talking about the latest soccer match—to do a jig on the small dance floor. There's also a menu featuring such traditional selections as shepherd's pie and lamb stew. 720 S. Michigan Ave. (between Balbo Dr. and 8th St.). (*) 312/294-6860. Subway/El: Red Line to Harrison/State.

Miller's Pub   A true Loop landmark, Miller's has been serving up after-work cocktails to downtown office workers for more than 50 years; it's one of the few places in the area that offers bar service until the early morning hours. There's a full dinner menu, too, in case you get the munchies. The walls are covered with autographed photos of movie stars and sports figures; while some might be unrecognizable to younger patrons, they testify to Miller's long-standing tradition of friendly hospitality. 134 S. Wabash Ave. (between Jackson Blvd. and Adams St.). (*) 312/645-5377. Subway/El: Red Line to Jackson.

Tantrum   Don't worry—you won't see folks pitching a fit at this stylish South Loop bar (the owners came up with the name after being pushed to the limit of their patience while trying to get their liquor license). The surrounding neighborhood hasn't quite caught up with Tantrum's cool vibe yet, but it's a good destination spot for anyone staying in a Loop hotel and searching for a casually cool cocktail lounge. The centerpiece of the spacious, airy main room is a long mahogany bar; modern touches include laser lighting and funky couches and chairs. Sip the signature Tantrum martini (Stoli orange mixed with orange juice) and enjoy a civilized conversation—the pleasantly diverse jukebox pumps out everything from smooth jazz to rap metal, but never at an ear-shattering volume, which is just how the hip, professional crowd likes it. 1023 S. State St. (at 11th St.). (*) 312/939-9160. Subway/El: Red Line to Roosevelt.

NEAR THE MAGNIFICENT MILE

Billy Goat Tavern *Value*   Tucked below the Wrigley Building is this storied Chicago hole-in-the-wall, a longtime hangout for newspaper reporters over the years, evidenced by the yellowed clippings and memorabilia papering the walls. But it's the "cheezeborger, cheezeborger" served at the grill that gave inspiration to the famous *Saturday Night Live* sketch. Despite all the press, the Goat has endured the hype without sacrificing a thing. 430 N. Michigan Ave. (*) 312/222-1525. Subway/El: Red Line to Grand/State.

Cru Café and Wine Bar *Finds* Located a couple blocks west of the Mag Mile, Cru draws both discriminating oenophiles and curious tourists with its sleek interior of gold-painted surfaces, a zebra-wood bar, and hip light fixtures—and with its 400-plus wine list. Comfortable and loungy, the cafe also serves a lunch, dinner, and late-night menu of seafood, soups and salads, quiche, caviars, sandwiches, and desserts. A 40-seat alfresco seating area is available in warm weather. 888 N. Wabash Ave. ✆ 312/337-4078. Subway/El: Red Line to Chicago.

Domaine Say goodbye to minimalism at this swanky new nightspot, a combination bar, restaurant, and homage to luxurious living. The decor here is sumptuous (floor-length velvet curtains, gold-framed paintings), which draws in a sophisticated crowd in their 30s and 40s. Reserve a table in advance if you want to sit anywhere other than the bar. The menu offers plates of hors d'oeuvres meant for sharing (although the prices are fairly high, ranging from $20 to $60). But most people come here to look, not to eat. Be prepared for a $10 cover charge on weekends. 1045 N. Rush St. ✆ 312/397-1045. Subway/El: Red Line to Chicago.

Signature Lounge The drinks here are pricey, but you're not surprised, are you? Anyway, here you can get a drink and a fabulous view for the price of a trip to the John Hancock tower's observatory, two floors below. It's open until 1am Sunday through Thursday and until 2am on the weekends. 96th floor of the John Hancock Center, 875 N. Michigan Ave. ✆ 312/787-7230. Subway/El: Red Line to Chicago.

RIVER NORTH & VICINITY

Bar Louie A slightly more upscale take on the neighborhood bar concept, Bar Louie has built its reputation on better-than-average bar food and a creative selection of beers and cocktails. Professionals gather here after work; their restaurant and club equivalents stop by between 1 and 3am. Bar Louie isn't doing anything revolutionary, but its friendly service and approachable atmosphere makes it a popular gathering place for people looking for a casual night out. In the past few years, Bar Louie outposts have also appeared in the West Loop (123 N. Halsted St.; ✆ 312/207-0500), Lincoln Park (1800 N. Lincoln Ave.; ✆ 312/337-9800), Lakeview (3545 N. Clark St.; ✆ 773/296-2500), and Bucktown (1704 N. Damen Ave.; ✆ 773/645-7500). 226 W. Chicago Ave. (between Franklin and Wells sts.). ✆ 312/337-3313. Subway/El: Red or Brown line to Chicago.

Brehon Pub Big front windows, a high tin ceiling, and a great antique back bar lend charm to this little neighborhood bar in (often) tourist-packed River North. Brehon regulars hang out weeknights after work and even at lunchtime, when the tavern serves up sandwiches and soup. In the 1970s, the *Sun-Times* newspaper set up this spot as a phony bar (appropriately named The Mirage) and used it in a "sting" operation to expose city corruption. 731 N. Wells St. (at Superior St.). ✆ 312/642-1071. Subway/El: Red or Brown line to Chicago.

Celtic Crossings Drop in on a Sunday evening for the bar's weekly traditional Irish jam session and you're sure to hear a bevy of brogues. There's no television in this quaint pub, just a decent jukebox stocked with Irish and American favorites, delicious pints of Guinness (the best in Chicago, claim many Irish expats), and a cozy fireplace. 751 N. Clark St. (between Superior St. and Chicago Ave.). ✆ 312/337-1005. Subway/El: Red or Brown line to Chicago.

Clark Street Ale House *Finds* A handsome, convivial tavern opened in 1995, and a popular after-work spot for white- and blue-collar types alike, Clark Street Ale House features a large open space filled with high tables and a long cherrywood bar along one wall. Better than the atmosphere are the 95 beers served here, a large majority of them from American microbreweries. The bar also offers a wide selection of scotches and cognacs. 742 N. Clark St. ✆ 312/642-9253. Subway/El: Red or Brown line to Chicago.

Fado   The crowds have abated somewhat since Fado opened a couple years back, but this sprawling, multilevel theme-park facsimile of an Irish pub still lures the masses most nights. Bursting with woodwork, stone, and double-barreled Guinness taps (all of it imported from the Emerald Isle), Fado has several themed rooms, each designed to evoke a particular Irish pub style—country cottage and Victorian Dublin, for instance. The victuals are above par for pub fare. Monday evenings feature Irish music sessions. 100 W. Grand Ave. ✆ 312/836-0066. Subway/El: Red Line to Grand.

Iggy's *Finds*   The unofficial dress code is anything black at this dark, velvet-draped late-night haven for terminally hip insomniacs. Perfectly situated on a desolate strip on the edge of downtown that gives it an extra edge of mystery, Iggy's serves food and drink long after most of the city's other bars have called it a night (4am most nights). On Sunday nights in the summer, movies are screened on the backyard patio. 700 N. Milwaukee Ave. (at Huron St.). ✆ 312/829-4449. Subway/El: Blue Line to Chicago.

Martini Ranch   Staying in a Magnificent Mile hotel and looking for a late-night libation? The Martini Ranch serves up 40 different versions of its namesake cocktail until 4am during the week, attracting bar and nightlife insiders (and a fair share of insomniacs). The Western theme is subtle (paintings of Roy Rogers and other cowpoke art) and the seating is minimal (come early to snag one of the four red booths). But fans swear by the chocolate martini, and the pop-rock soundtrack keeps the energy level high. If the crowded bar scene is too much, you can always chill out at the pool table in the back room or settle down at one of the tables in the heated beer garden. 311 W. Chicago Ave. (at Orleans St.). ✆ 312/335-9500. Subway/El: Red or Brown line to Chicago.

Narcisse   The cigar-and-martini virus has wrought this next-generation retro concept: a "champagne salon and caviar bar." Ivana Trump would feel right at home here among all the 1900-era imperial glamour: chandeliers, gilded walls, and yards of plush fabric. The glass tabletops are etched with labels of renowned champagne houses. The thick menu has pages and pages of champagnes (more than 50, with a few bottles topping $300), wine, martinis, and other mixed drinks. Besides about a dozen types of caviar, the kitchen serves French-Italian tapas and some tasty desserts. 710 N. Clark St. (between Superior and Huron sts.). ✆ 312/787-2675. Subway/El: Red or Brown line to Chicago.

Sugar   The latest see-and-be-seen spot bills itself as a "dessert bar," but it's the decor as much as the sweet treats that draws crowds. Lit in tones of orange and yellow, the overall mood is sophisticated yet fun; whimsical touches include beehive chandeliers hanging above the bar, and bar stools that look like hard candies. The desserts are delicious (although pricey), with clever literary-inspired names (MacDeth by Chocolate, Banana Karenina, and so forth). But most of the beautiful people here wouldn't be caught dead eating anything fattening; most simply sip martinis. There can be some attitude from the door staff on weekends; make a reservation so you can slip inside the velvet rope. 108 W. Kinzie St. (at Clark St.). ✆ 312/822-9999. Subway/El: Red Line to Grand or Brown Line to Merchandise Mart.

RUSH & DIVISION STREETS

Around Rush Street are what a bygone era called singles bars—although the only singles that tend to head here now are suburbanites, out-of-towners, and barely legal partiers (this is where we'd come to celebrate 21st birthdays when I was in college). Rush Street's glory days have long passed, but there are still a few vestiges of the old times. Division Street is filled with party-hearty spots that attract a loud, frat-party element. The bars lining Division Street include the **Alumni Club,** 15 W. Division St. (© 312/337-4349); **Shenanigan's House of Beer,** 16 W. Division St. (© 312/642-2344); **Butch McGuire's,** 20 W. Division St. (© 312/337-9080); the **Lodge,** 21 W. Division St. (© 312/642-4406); and **Mother's,** 26 W. Division St. (© 312/642-7251). Many of these bars offer special discounts for women, as loud pitchmen in front of each establishment will be happy to tell any attractive ladies who pass by.

OLD TOWN

The center of nightlife in Old Town is Wells Street, home to Second City and other comedy clubs, as well as a string of reliable restaurants and bars. You're not going to find many trendy spots in Old Town; the nightlife here is geared toward neighborhood pubs and bustling restaurants, filled mostly with a late-20s and 30-something crowd.

Corcoran's   Owned by the same family for about 30 years, this is one of Old Town's favorite local hangouts, and it makes a good stop before or after a show at Second City (right across the street). The cozy, wood-lined interior and hearty pub food (bangers and mash, shepherd's pie, fish and chips) will put you right at ease. In nice weather, check out the beer garden in back. 1615 N. Wells St. (at North Ave.). © **312/440-0885.** Subway/El: Brown Line to Sedgwick.

Old Town Ale House   This is one of Old Town's legendary saloons, a dingy neighborhood hangout since the late 1950s with a fading mural that captures the likenesses of a class of regulars from the early 1970s (John Belushi commandeered the pinball machines here during his days at the nearby Second City improv club). Put some quarters in the jukebox that's filled with an eclectic selection of crooner tunes, and just hang out. Open daily from noon to 4am (until 5am Sat). 219 W. North Ave. (at Wells St.). © **312/944-7020.** Subway/El: Brown Line to Sedgwick.

Spoon   The closest Old Town has to a trendy nightspot, this combination bar/restaurant pulls in an attractive, professional crowd on weekend evenings. The modern, loftlike space would be right at home in the River North neighborhood, but it's a novelty in tradition-bound Old Town. Weeknights are a little less frenzied, when locals are able to sip their Mucho Mango martinis in peace. 1240 N. Wells St. (at Division St.). © **312/642-5522.** Subway/El: Red Line to Clark/Division.

LINCOLN PARK

Lincoln Park, with its high concentration of apartment-dwelling singles, is one of the busiest nightlife destinations in Chicago. Since this is a residential neighborhood where prime real estate is at a premium, you won't find any warehouse-sized dance clubs here; most of the action is at pubs and bars. Concentrations of in-spots run along Armitage Avenue, Halsted Street, and Lincoln Avenue.

The Duke of Perth   This traditional Scottish pub serves one of the city's best selections of single-malt scotch plus baskets of fish and chips ($8.95 all-you-can-eat special on Wed and Fri). 2913 N. Clark St. (at Wellington Ave.). © **773/477-1741.** Subway/El: Brown Line to Diversey.

Glascott's Groggery   At the top of any self-respecting Lincoln Park yuppie's list of meeting places is Glascott's, an Irish pub that has been in the same family since it opened in 1937. You'll see groups of guys stopping in after their weekly basketball game, couples coming in after dinner to catch up with their friends, and singles hoping to hook up with old college buddies and meet new friends. 2158 N. Halsted St. (at Webster Ave.). (C) 773/281-1205. Subway/El: Brown Line to Armitage.

Goose Island Brewing Company *Finds*   The first brewpub in the city features its own Honker's Ale on tap, as well as several other beers produced here and at an off-site distillery. Ask for a tasting menu to try them all (you can sample three glasses for $5). Goose Island has the added benefit of a casual full-service restaurant with more than just bar food. A brewery tour is conducted on Sunday at 3pm (including a free sample). Goose Island recently added an outpost in Wrigleyville, 3535 N. Clark St. ((C) **773/832-9040**). 1800 N. Clybourn Ave. (at Sheffield Ave.). (C) 312/915-0071. Subway/El: Red Line to North/Clybourn.

The Gramercy   In a previous life, this space was occupied by the influential live-music club Lounge Ax, which reveled in its gritty, punky aesthetic. Now the ghosts of punks past have been exorcised with the building's recent transformation into the upscale Gramercy, an oasis of sophistication in a neighborhood of frat bars. The decor may appear snobby at first—an all-white interior with vinyl-covered booths and streams of water trickling down behind the bar. But the place is attitude-free: no dress code, no cover, and no obvious pickup lines being recited at the bar. This is a place where people come to talk—and where they can actually hear what their companions are saying. 2438 N. Lincoln Ave. (at Fullerton Ave.). (C) 773/477-8880. Subway/El: Red or Brown line to Fullerton.

John Barleycorn Memorial Pub   SE HABLA BEETHOVEN, states the legend beneath the sign of the landmark John Barleycorn Memorial Pub. In contrast to the frat-house craziness on much of the block, this is a tavern for highbrows, who are treated to a background of classical music, a continuous slide show of art masterpieces, and an extensive collection of model ships. The patio is nice in warm weather, and patrons can order a burger from the menu, too. A new location 3 blocks from Wrigley Field, at 3524 N. Clark St. ((C) **773/549-6000**), re-creates the art and classical music concept—except after Cubs games, when it becomes yet another sports bar. 658 W. Belden Ave. (at Lincoln Ave.). (C) **773/348-8899**. Subway/El: Red or Brown line to Fullerton.

Red Lion Pub *Finds*   An English pub in the heart of Lincoln Park, the Red Lion is a comfortable neighborhood place with a mix of old and young DePaul students, actors, and Anglophiles who feel right at home among the Union Jacks and photos of Winston Churchill. The British owner even claims the place is haunted. Old movies are screened on the TV during the day. 2446 N. Lincoln Ave. (between Fullerton and Wrightwood aves.). (C) 773/348-2695. Subway/El: Red or Brown line to Fullerton.

Webster's Wine Bar   The low-lit, sophisticated decor of Webster's in Lincoln Park is an alternative to the usual beer blast. The waitstaff can help you choose from a list of dozens of wines by the bottle or glass, or you can hone your taste buds with a flight of several wines. There's also a tapas-style menu for noshing. Step back into the library area to light up a cigar and recline on the couch. 1480 W. Webster Ave. (between Clybourn and Ashland aves.). (C) 773/868-0608. Subway/El: Red or Brown line to Fullerton.

WRIGLEYVILLE, LAKEVIEW & THE NORTH SIDE

Real estate in Wrigleyville and Lakeview is a tad less expensive than in Lincoln Park, so the nightlife scene here skews a little younger. You'll find a mostly post-collegiate crowd partying on Clark Street across from Wrigley Field (especially after games in the summer). But you'll also discover some more eclectic choices.

Chicago Brauhaus   Lincoln Square is the heart of Chicago's German community. Traditional delis and European shops (including a terrific old-fashioned apothecary stocked with homeopathic medicines and cosmetics) dot Lincoln Avenue from Wilson to Lawrence avenues. For a dose of Oktoberfest at any time of year, stop into the Brauhaus. German bands perform on weekends, when the older crowd puts the youngsters to shame on the dance floor. The Erdinger, Spaten, and BBK flow freely, and the kitchen serves up big plates of wurst, schnitzel, and sauerkraut. 4732 N. Lincoln Ave. (between Leland and Lawrence aves.). © 773/784-4444. Subway/El: Brown Line to Western.

Ginger Man Tavern   Ginger Man definitely plays against type on a row of predictable sports bars across the street from Wrigley Field. On game days, the earthy bar has been known to crank classical music in an attempt to calm drunken fans—or at least shoo them away. Pool tables (free on Sun) are always occupied by slightly bohemian neighborhood 20-somethings, who have more than 80 beers to choose from. 3740 N. Clark St. (at Racine Ave.). © 773/549-2050. Subway/El: Red Line to Addison.

Irish Oak *Finds*   Owned and staffed by folks from the Old Sod, this is one of the city's nicest Irish bars. The bar's handsome woodwork and collection of antiques give the tavern a mellow, laid-back feel. Irish bands perform once in a while on weekends. There are plenty of whiskeys, stouts, and ales to sip, and the kitchen offers shepherd's pie and other Irish fare. 3511 N. Clark St. (between Cornelia Ave. and Addison St.). © 773/935-6669. Subway/El: Red Line to Addison.

Sheffield's Beer and Wine Garden   A popular neighborhood gathering spot is Sheffield's, 1 block north of Belmont, on the corner of School Street. Its large beer garden, furnished with what has got to be the only outdoor pool table in the city, is the main attraction during the summer. The bar boasts a selection of more than 80 beers, including one featured "bad beer" of the month. Sheffield's can get jammed with a young, loud crowd, but the attitude is welcoming—there always seems to be room to squeeze in one more person. 3258 N. Sheffield Ave. (between Belmont Ave. and Roscoe St.). © 773/281-4989. Subway/El: Red or Brown line to Belmont.

WICKER PARK & BUCKTOWN

For an alternative scene, head over to Wicker Park and Bucktown, where slackers and some adventurous yuppies populate bars dotting the streets near the confluence of North, Damen, and Milwaukee avenues. Don't dress to impress if you want to blend in; a casually bohemian getup and low-key attitude are all you need to fit in.

Note: For a map of nightlife in the Wicker Park and Bucktown areas, please see the map "Dining & Nightlife in Wicker Park/Bucktown" on p. 157.

Betty's Blue Star Lounge   Wicker Park scene makers have made Betty's, an unpretentious, low-key neighborhood tavern just south of Wicker Park in Ukrainian Village, their latest late-night destination. Part local watering hole, part biker bar, it's your typical pool-table and darts joint earlier in the evening, but Thursday through Saturday the bar transforms into a jam-packed venue for local bands and DJs. The action is in the back room, equipped with a stellar sound system and lots of mirrors. 1600 W. Grand Ave. ℂ **312/243-8778**. Bus: No. 65 (Grand Ave.).

The Bucktown Pub *(Value)*   The owners' collection of groovy 1960s and 1970s rock 'n' roll posters and cartoon art is phenomenal. However, most Bucktown patrons are more interested in nursing their pints of imported and domestic microbrews than gawking at the walls. Other Wicker Park/Bucktown bars try to come off as gritty; this is the real thing, where attitude is firmly discouraged at the door. The psychedelic- and glam-rock–filled jukebox keeps toes tapping, and competition on the skittle-bowling machine can get quite fierce. Credit cards not accepted. 1658 W. Cortland St. (at Hermitage Ave.). No phone. Subway/El: Blue Line to Damen.

The California Clipper   Located a bit off the beaten path in Humboldt Park (just south of Wicker Park), the Clipper is well worth seeking out. For the past couple of years, this beautifully restored 1940s tavern, with its gorgeous Art Deco bar and red walls bathed in dim light, has been colonized on the weekends by the young and terminally restless. Friday and Saturday nights feature live music, mostly rockabilly and "country swing." 1002 N. California Ave. ℂ **773/384-2547**. www. californiaclipper.com. Subway/El: Blue Line to Damen.

Danny's Tavern   Located off the beaten Milwaukee/Damen path, Danny's has become the neighborhood hangout of choice for Bucktown's original angry young men and women, the ones who complain that an influx of yuppies is ruining the area. Just finding Danny's takes insider knowledge: the only sign out front flashes SCHLITZ in neon red. Inside, votive candles on the tables provide dim lighting; head to the back room to grab a seat on the leather couches and chairs. Once there, you can revel in the fact that you're hanging with the cool kids—just don't let them know you're a tourist. 1951 W. Dickens Ave. (at Damen Ave.). ℂ **773/489-6457**. Subway/El: Blue Line to Damen.

Get Me High Lounge *(Finds)*   If Wicker Park has a favorite late-night watering hole, it's likely this compact, atmospheric spot, owned by nightclub impresario and style-maker Dion Antic. Dimly lit with tealight candles hanging from the ceiling and humming with R&B music in the air, Get Me High has a devoted following, so get there early to claim one of the comfy couches in the back. 1758 N. Honore St. ℂ **773/252-4090**. Subway/El: Blue Line to Damen.

The Leopard Lounge   This cozy modern-retro bar has a cheesecake-and-spice ambience that would make Bettie Page proud. Vintage pinup-girl illustrations hang on the walls, and the lounge's seating is upholstered in (what else?) faux leopard skin. The snappily dressed crowd comes for the bartenders' quality cocktails. 1645 W. Cortland St. (between Ashland and Hermitage aves.). ℂ **773/862-7877**. Subway/El: Blue Line to Damen.

The Map Room *(Finds)*   Hundreds of travel books and guides line the shelves of this globe-trotter's tavern. Peruse that tome on Fuji or Antarctica while sipping a pint of one of the 20-odd draft beers available. The Map Room's equally impressive selection of bottled brews makes this place popular with not only the tattered-passport crew, but beer geeks as well. Tuesday nights are theme nights featuring the food, music, and spirits of a certain country, accompanied by a slide show and travel tales from a recent visitor. There's live music on Friday and Saturday nights. 1949 N. Hoyne Ave. (at Armitage Ave.). ℂ **773/252-7636**. Subway/El: Blue Line to Damen.

Marie's Riptide Lounge   Nothing here looks like it has been updated since the 1960s, and owners Shirley and Marie are long past retirement age. But their personal touch and the retro-cool of the place have made it a hip late-night stop on the nocturnal circuit. A jukebox stocked with campy oldies, a curious low-tech duck-hunting "video" game, and the occasional blast of black light make Marie's a hoot. The owners take great pains to decorate the interior of their little bar for each holiday season (the wintertime "snow-covered" bar is not to be missed.) 1745 W. Armitage Ave. (at Hermitage Ave.). ℂ 773/278-7317. Subway/El: Blue Line to Damen.

The Note   Located in the historic Flat Iron Building, The Note is a great after-hours bar with the right after-hours music: a jukebox exclusively devoted to blues and jazz. On weekends, this Wicker Park bar is unbelievably packed until closing time (4am; 5am Sat) with a cross-section of club crawlers who make this their last stop of the night. The Note has also assembled a pretty strong lineup of live jazz acts, from experimental free form to swing (with dance lessons). It's got pool tables, too. 1565 N. Milwaukee Ave. (at North Ave.). ℂ 773/489-0011. Live music cover $5–$7. Subway/El: Blue Line to Damen.

HYDE PARK

Jimmy's Woodlawn Tap (Value   One of the few places to hang in Hyde Park, Jimmy's survived neighborhood redevelopment in the 1960s that erased what was once a busy strip of bars. Namesake Jimmy, who worked behind the bar into his 80s, died in 1999, and the Woodlawn Tap almost went with him. But the bar holds a sentimental spot in many Hyde Parkers' hearts, and they came together to support the place even as it battled complicated city ordinances under new management. So even though Woodlawn Tap is the place's official name, it will remain forever "Jimmy's" to generations of U of C students. 1172 E. 55th St. (at Woodlawn Ave.). ℂ 773/643-5516. Bus: No. 6 (Jeffrey Express).

CAFES

Café Jumping Bean   A great little cafe in the heart of Pilsen, just southwest of the Loop, the Jumping Bean is ideal for watching the colorful ebb and flow of daily life in this vibrant Mexican-American neighborhood. It serves up the usual espresso drinks, muffins, and pastries, but it also offers decent salads, cheesecakes, natural vegetable and fruit juices, and—best of all—a tantalizing selection of *licuados,* a Mexican version of the American shake, which is made with milk, sugar, ice, and fresh fruit (try the mango). The artistic doings outside, characterized by colorful outdoor murals on building walls, spill over into the cafe, which features rotating exhibitions of paintings and hand-painted tables by local artists. The place even hosts live flamenco music and poetry readings in Spanish. Everyone is welcome, from families with little kids to the loft-dwelling artists who've lately infiltrated Pilsen. 1439 W. 18th St. (2 blocks east of Ashland Ave.). ℂ 312/455-0019. Subway/El: Blue Line to 18th St.

Intelligentsia   A down-to-earth San Francisco married couple has set up its own coffee-roasting operation here in the heart of Chicago's Lakeview neighborhood. Beans are roasted in a French roaster that dominates the cafe, and the owners also make their own herbal and black teas—served in a small pot with an hourglass that tells you when the tea is steeped. Warm drinks are served in handsome cups nearly too big to get your hands around, and tea sippers are furnished with their own pot and brew timer. Sit in the window or in one of the Adirondack chairs on the sidewalk and watch the world go by, or decamp to the homey seating area in the back. 3123 N. Broadway (between Belmont Ave. and Diversey Pkwy.). ℂ 773/348-8058. Subway/El: Red Line to Addison.

Julius Meinl   Austria's premier coffee roaster chose Chicago—and even more mysteriously, a location near Wrigley Field—for its first U.S. outpost. The result is a mix of Austrian style (upholstered banquettes, white marble tables, newspapers hanging on wicker frames) and American cheeriness (lots of natural light, smiling waitstaff, smoke-free air). The coffee and hot chocolate are excellent, served European-style on small silver platters with a glass of water on the side. But it's the desserts that keep the regulars coming back. Try the apple strudel or millennium torte (glazed with apricot jam and chocolate ganache) and for a moment you'll swear you're in Vienna. 3601 N. Southport Ave. (at Addison St.). ✆ 773/ 868-1857. Subway/El: Brown Line to Southport.

Third Coast   Just steps away from the raucous frat-boy atmosphere of Division Street is this laid-back, classic, independent coffeehouse. The below-ground space is a little shabby, but it attracts an eclectic mix of office workers, students, and neighborhood regulars. The full menu serves up food late, and the drinks run the gamut from lattes to cocktails. There's also often some kind of folk music on weekends. 1260 N. Dearborn St. (north of Division St.). ✆ 312/649-0730. Subway/ El: Red Line to Clark/Division.

Uncommon Ground   When you're looking for refuge from the riotous exuberance of Cubs game days and party nights in Wrigleyville, Uncommon Ground offers an oasis of civility. Not only that, but this two-room cafe commits what some might view as a coffeehouse heresy: Smoking is not allowed. Located just off busy Clark Street, the cafe has a soul-warming fireplace in winter (when the cafe's bowl—yes, bowl—of hot chocolate is a sight for cold eyes) and a spacious sidewalk operation in more temperate months (where smokes are permitted). Breakfast is served all day, plus there's a full lunch and dinner menu. Music figures strongly at the cafe; the late Jeff Buckley and ex-Bangle Susanna Hoffs are among those who've played the place. The cafe has even issued a CD compilation of favorite performers. Open until 11pm Sunday through Thursday, midnight Friday and Saturday. 1214 W. Grace St. (at Clark St.). ✆ 773/929-3680. Subway/El: Red Line to Addison.

6 The Gay & Lesbian Scene

Most of Chicago's gay bars are conveniently clustered on a stretch of North Halsted Street in Lakeview, making it easy to sample many of them in a breezy walk. While men's bars predominate, there are a few places in Chicago exclusively catering to lesbians, and a few gay bars get a mix of men and women. A couple of helpful free resources published each week are the entertainment guide *Nightlines* and the club rag *Gab*. The bars and clubs recommended below don't charge a cover unless otherwise noted.

In addition to the clubs below, **Red Dog** (p. 274), 1958 W. North Ave., at Milwaukee Ave. (✆ 773/278-1009), hosts the exotic gay-themed Boom-Boom Room on Mondays, when club kids, drag queens, platform dancers, and everybody else bobs to a house beat. Cover is $6 to $10.

Berlin   Step into this frenetic Lakeview danceteria, and you're immediately swept into the mood. The disco tunes pulse, the clubby crowd chatters, and the lighting bathes everyone in a cool reddish glow. Special nights are dedicated to disco, amateur drag, and 1980s new wave; male dancers perform some nights. Don't bother showing up before midnight; the club stays open until 4am Friday and 5am Saturday. 954 W. Belmont Ave. (east of Sheffield Ave.). ☏ **773/348-4975.** www. berlinchicago.com. Cover after midnight Fri–Sat $5. Subway/El: Red or Brown line to Belmont.

Big Chicks *Finds*   One of the more eclectic bars in the city, Big Chicks is a magnet for the artsy goateed set perhaps a bit weary of the bars on Halsted Street, some lesbians, a smattering of straights, and random locals from the surrounding rough-hewn neighborhood (the bar's motto is "Never a Cover, Never an Attitude"). They come for owner Michelle Fire's superb art collection (hung salon style from the bar walls to the bathrooms to the patio), the midnight shots, and the free buffet on Sunday afternoons. There is also dancing on weekends. 5024 N. Sheridan Rd. (between Argyle St. and Foster Ave.). ☏ **773/728-5511.** www.bigchicks. com. Subway/El: Red Line to Berwyn.

The Closet   The Closet is an unpretentious neighborhood spot with a loud and constant loop of music videos (and sports games, when it matters) that draws mostly lesbian regulars, although gay men and straights show up, too. The space itself is not much bigger than a closet, which makes it easy to get up close and personal with other partiers. There's also a small dance floor that's usually packed on weekends. Open until 4am every night, until 5am on Saturdays. 3325 N. Broadway (at Buckingham St.). ☏ **773/477-8533.** Subway/El: Red or Brown line to Belmont.

Cocktail   This corner spot, less frenzied than its neighbors, is more of a friendly hangout than a cruising scene; it's easy to converse and watch the passing parade from big picture windows. This is one of the few places on the street where men and women congregate. 3359 N. Halsted St. (at Roscoe St.). ☏ **773/477-1420.** Subway/El: Red or Brown line to Belmont.

Gentry   This gay cabaret in River North has been around since 1983, so expect to see plenty of regulars. The piano bar attracts plenty of out-of-town headliners, along with some quirky local favorites. There's also a Boys Town branch at 3320 N. Halsted St. (☏ **773/348-1053**). 440 N. State St. (between Illinois and Hubbard sts.). ☏ **312/836-0933.** Subway/El: Red Line to Grand.

GLEE Club at Crobar   On Sunday night, the sprawling nightclub hosts a long-running gay dance party that draws a young body-conscious crowd dancing to techno-pop and house. As for the dress code, almost anything goes. 1543 N. Kingsbury St. (south of North Ave.). ☏ **312/337-5001.** Subway/El: Red Line to North/Clybourn, then a 15-min. cab ride.

Roscoe's Tavern *Finds*   The picture windows onto Halsted make Roscoe's, a gay neighborhood bar in business since 1987, an especially welcoming place, with its large antiques-filled front bar, an outdoor patio, a pool table, and a large dance floor. The 20- and 30-something crowd is friendly and laid-back—except on weekends when the dance floor is hopping. The adjoining cafe serves sandwiches and salads. 3356 N. Halsted St. (at Roscoe St.). ☏ **773/281-3355.** Cover after 10pm Sat $4. Subway/El: Red or Brown line to Belmont.

Sidetrack *Finds*   If you make it to Roscoe's, you'll no doubt end up at Sidetrack. The popular bars are across the street from one another, and there's a constant flow of feet between the two. The windowless Sidetrack is a sleek video bar where TV monitors are never out of your field of vision, nor are the preppy professional patrons. A recent expansion made the place even more welcoming. Don't miss Show Tunes Night on Sundays and Mondays, when the whole place sings along to Broadway and MGM musical favorites. 3349 N. Halsted St. (at Roscoe St.). ☏ **773/477-9189.** Subway/El: Red or Brown line to Belmont.

Spin This dance club attracts one of Halsted Street's most eclectic crowds, a mix of pretty boys, nerds, tough guys, and the occasional drag queen. The video bar in front houses pool tables and plays a steady steam of dance-friendly music videos. The dance club, behind heavy drapes, thumps with house music. Spin keeps regulars coming back with daily theme parties, featuring everything from Friday-night shower contests to cheap drinks. 800 W. Belmont Ave. (at Halsted St.). ℂ 773/327-7711. Subway/El: Red or Brown line to Belmont.

Voltaire This restaurant/cabaret exudes a sophisticated vibe. Dinner is served in the Derby Room; there's also seating at the polished wood bar or at tables in the spotlighted cabaret room. Amy Armstrong sings show tunes on Monday nights; other evenings feature jazz, music videos, and vignettes performed by the singers/dancers of the Voltaire Troupe. 3441–3443 N. Halsted St. (between Roscoe St. and Cornelia Ave.). ℂ 773/281-9320. Subway/El: Red or Brown line to Belmont.

Appendix:
Chicago in Depth

1 History 101

By virtue of its location, Chicago became the great engine of America's westward expansion. The particular patch of land where Chicago now stands straddles a key point along an inland water route linking Canada, via Lake Erie, to New Orleans and the Gulf of Mexico by way of the Mississippi River.

The French, busy expanding their own territory in North America throughout the 17th and 18th centuries, were the first Europeans to survey the topography of the future Chicago. The French policy in North America was simple—to gradually settle the Mississippi Valley and the Northwest Territory (modern Michigan, Illinois, Wisconsin, and Minnesota). The policy relied on an alliance between religion and commerce: The French sought a monopoly over the fur trade with the Native American tribes, whose pacification and loyalty they attempted to ensure by converting them to Catholicism.

The team of Jacques Marquette, a Jesuit missionary, and Louis Joliet, an explorer, personified this policy to perfection. In 1673, the pair found a very short portage between two critically placed rivers, the Illinois and the Des Plaines. One was connected to the Mississippi, and the other, via the Chicago River, was connected to Lake Michigan and then onward to Montreal and Quebec.

Chicago owes its existence to this strategic 1½-mile portage trail that the Native Americans had blazed in their own water travels over centuries of moving throughout this territory.

Dateline

- **1673** French explorers Marquette and Joliet discover portage at Chicago linking the Great Lakes region with the Mississippi River valley.
- **1779** Afro-French-Canadian trapper Jean Baptiste Point du Sable establishes a trading post on the north bank of the Chicago River. A settlement follows 2 years later.
- **1794** Gen. "Mad" Anthony Wayne defeats the British in the Battle of Fallen Timbers; disputed Illinois Territory is finally ceded to the young American Republic by treaty a year later.
- **1803** Garrison of Fort Dearborn is established in Chicago, commanded by the grandfather of artist James McNeill Whistler.
- **1812** Incited by the British in the War of 1812, Potawatomi Indians destroy Fort Dearborn and slay its residents.
- **1816** Fort Dearborn is rebuilt.
- **1818** Illinois is admitted to the Union as the 21st state.
- **1833** Town of Chicago is officially incorporated, with little more than 300 residents.
- **1837** Chicago is incorporated as a city, with about 4,000 residents.
- **1847** *Chicago Tribune* begins publishing.
- **1848** The 96-mile Illinois and Michigan Canal is opened, linking the Great Lakes with the Mississippi River.
- **1850** Chicago's population is roughly 30,000.
- **1856** Chicago is chief railroad center in the United States.
- **1860** Republican National Convention in Chicago nominates Abraham Lincoln for the presidency.
- **1865** After Lincoln's assassination, his body lies in state at the Chicago Courthouse before burial in Springfield.

Marquette himself was on the most familiar terms with the Native Americans, who helped him make his way over the well-established paths of their ancestral lands. The Native Americans, of course, did not anticipate the European settlers' hunger for such prime real estate. Because the Chicago River provided a crucial link between the Great Lakes and the Mississippi River, the frontier city was destined to grow into the nation's great midcontinental hub of transportation and transshipment, facilitating travel and trade between the eastern settlements and the West.

FIRST SETTLEMENT

Over the next 100 years, the French used this waterway to spread their American empire from Canada to Mobile, Alabama. Yet the first recorded settlement in Chicago, a trading post built by a French Canadian of Haitian descent, Jean Baptiste Point du Sable, did not appear until 1781. By this time, the British already had conquered the territory, part of the spoils of 70 years of intermittent warfare that cost the French most of their North American holdings. After the American War of Independence, the Illinois Territory was wrested from British/Native American control in a campaign led by the Revolutionary War hero Gen. "Mad" Anthony Wayne, which ended with a treaty in 1795 ceding the land around the mouth of the Chicago River to the United States.

Between du Sable's day and 1833, when Chicago was officially founded, the land by the mouth of the Chicago River served as a military outpost that guarded the strategic passage and provided security for a few trappers and a trading post. The military base, Fort Dearborn, which stood on the south side of what is now the Michigan Avenue Bridge, was first garrisoned in 1803 under the command of Captain John Whistler, grandfather of the famous painter.

More than 125,000 mourners pay their respects.

- 1865 Chicago stockyards are founded.
- 1870 City's population numbers almost 300,000, making it perhaps the fastest-growing metropolis in history.
- 1871 Great Chicago Fire burns large sections of the city; rebuilding begins while the ashes are still warm.
- 1882 The 10-story Montauk Building, the world's first skyscraper, is erected.
- 1885 William Le Baron Jenney's nine-story Home Insurance Building, the world's first steel-frame skyscraper, is built.
- 1886 Dynamite bomb explodes during a political rally near Haymarket Square, causing a riot in which eight policemen and four civilians are killed, and almost 100 are wounded. Eight labor leaders and socialist-anarchists, demanding an 8-hour day, are later convicted in one of the country's most controversial trials. Four are eventually hanged.
- 1892 The city's first elevated train goes into operation.
- 1893 Completely recovered from the Great Fire, Chicago hosts its first World's Fair, the World's Columbian Exposition. The world's first Ferris wheel is a big draw.
- 1894 Led by Eugene V. Debs, members of the American Railway Union hold a massive strike against the Pullman Palace Car Company; President Grover Cleveland calls in federal troops after 2 months, ending the strike.
- 1900 The flow of the Chicago River is reversed to end the dumping of sewage into Lake Michigan.
- 1905 Wobblies, or Industrial Workers of the World (IWW), is founded in Chicago.
- 1905 Robert S. Abbott founds the *Chicago Defender,* which becomes the nation's premier African-American newspaper and later plays a major role in encouraging Southern blacks to move north during the "Great Migration" years.
- 1908 The Chicago Cubs win their second World Series. They haven't won one since!

continues

At first the settlement grew slowly, impeded by continued Native American efforts to drive the new Americans from the Illinois Territory. During the War of 1812, inhabitants abandoned Fort Dearborn, and many were slain during the evacuation. But before long, the trappers drifted back; by 1816, the military, too, had returned.

Conflict diminished after that, but even as a civil engineer plotted the building lots of the early town as late as 1830, periodic raids continued, ceasing only with the defeat of Chief Black Hawk in 1832. A year later, the settlement of 300-plus inhabitants was officially incorporated under the name Chicago, said to derive from a Native American word referring to the powerful odors of the abundant wild vegetation (most likely onions) in the marshlands surrounding the riverbanks.

COMMERCE & INDUSTRY

Land speculation began immediately, as Chicago was carved piecemeal and sold off to finance the Illinois and Michigan Canal that would eliminate the narrow land portage and fulfill the long-standing vision of connecting the two great waterways. Thus the domesticated East would be linked to the pioneer West, with Chicago at midpoint, directing the flow of commerce in both directions. Commercial activity was quick to follow: Within 2 to 3 years, local farmers in the outlying areas were producing a surplus. Chicago grew in size and wealth, shipping grain and livestock to the eastern markets and lumber to the treeless prairies of the West. Ironically, by the time the Illinois and Michigan Canal was completed in 1848, the railroad had arrived, and the water route that gave Chicago its raison d'être was rapidly becoming obsolete. Boxcars, not boats, grabbed the title of principal mode of transportation throughout the region. The combination of the railroad and the emergence of local

1917 The Chicago White Sox win the World Series. They haven't won one since!

1919 "Black Sox" bribery scandal perpetrated by eight Chicago White Sox players stuns baseball.

1920–33 During Prohibition, Chicago becomes a "wide-open town"; rival mobs battle violently throughout the city for control of distribution and sale of illegal alcohol.

1924 University of Chicago students Nathan Leopold and Richard Loeb murder 14-year-old Bobby Franks. They are defended by famed attorney Clarence Darrow and are found guilty, but spared the death penalty, in the "Trial of the Century."

1929 On St. Valentine's Day, Al Capone's gang murders seven members of rival George "Bugs" Moran's crew in a Clark Street garage.

1931 Al Capone finally goes to jail, not for bootlegging or murder, but for tax evasion.

1932 Franklin Delano Roosevelt is nominated for the presidency by the Democratic National Convention, held at Chicago Stadium (since demolished).

1933 Chicago Mayor Anton Cermak, on a political trip to Miami, is shot and killed during an attempt on president-elect FDR's life.

1933–34 Chicago hosts its second World's Fair, "A Century of Progress." The biggest attraction is fan dancer Sally Rand, who wears only two large ostrich feathers.

1934 Bank robber and "Public Enemy Number One" John Dillinger is gunned down by police outside the Biograph Theater.

1942 Scientists, led by Enrico Fermi, create the world's first nuclear chain reaction under Stagg Field at the University of Chicago.

1945 The Chicago Cubs make their last appearance in the World Series—and lose to Detroit.

1953 Chicago native Hugh Hefner starts publishing *Playboy* (the original Playboy Mansion was located in Chicago's Gold Coast neighborhood).

1955 Richard J. Daley begins term as mayor; he is widely regarded as the "last of the big-city bosses."

manufacturing, and, later, the Civil War, caused Chicago to grow wildly.

The most revolutionary product of the era sprang from the mind of Chicago inventor Cyrus McCormick, whose reaper filled in for the farmhands who now labored on the nation's battlefields. Local merchants not only thrived on the contraband trade in cotton, but also secured lucrative contracts from the federal government to provide the army with tents, uniforms, saddles, harnesses, lumber, bread, and meat. By 1870, Chicago's population had grown to 300,000, a thousand times greater than its original population, in the brief interval of 37 years since the city's incorporation.

THE GREAT FIRE

A year later, the city lay in ashes. The Great Chicago Fire of 1871 began somewhere on the southwest side of the city on October 8. Legend places its exact origin in the O'Leary shed on DeKoven Street, although most historians have since exonerated the long-blamed bovine that locals speculate started the blaze by kicking over a lantern. The fire jumped the river and continued northward through the night and the following day, when it was checked by the use of gunpowder on the South Side and rainfall to the north and west, just before spreading to the prairie. In its wake, the fire destroyed 18,000 buildings and left 90,000 homeless, taking a toll of 300 lives.

One thing that the fire could not destroy was Chicago's strategic location, and on that solid geographic footing, the city began to rebuild as soon as the rubble was cleared. By chance, Chicago's railroad infrastructure—factories, grain warehouses, and lumberyards—was also spared because it was located beyond the circle of fire on the southern periphery of the city. By 1873, the city's downtown business and financial district was up and running again, and 2

- 1959 Chicago White Sox make their last World Series appearance, losing to Los Angeles.
- 1960 John F. Kennedy and Richard Nixon hold the first televised presidential debate in WBBM-TV's studios.
- 1966 Civil rights leader Martin Luther King Jr. moves to Chicago to lead a fair housing campaign.
- 1968 After King's assassination, much of the West Side burns during heavy rioting. Anti–Vietnam War protests in conjunction with the Democratic National Convention end in police riot and a "shoot to kill" order by Mayor Richard J. Daley.
- 1969 Fred Hampton and Mark Clark are killed in a police raid on the West Side headquarters of the radical Black Panther party.
- 1974 The 1,454-foot Sears Tower is completed, becoming the tallest building in the world.
- 1976 Mayor Daley dies in office.
- 1979 Jane Byrne becomes the first woman elected mayor of Chicago.
- 1983 Harold Washington becomes the first African-American mayor of Chicago.
- 1986 The Chicago Bears win their only Super Bowl.
- 1987 Mayor Washington dies in office.
- 1989 Richard M. Daley, the son of the long-serving mayor, is elected mayor.
- 1992 A freight tunnel ruptures; the Loop is flooded underground by water from the Chicago River.
- 1994 Chicago hosts portions of soccer's World Cup, including the opening ceremonies.
- 1996 The city patches up its turbulent political history by hosting the Democratic National Convention, its first national political gathering in 3 decades. William Jefferson Clinton is nominated for a second term.
- 1999 Michael Jordan, arguably the best basketball player ever, retires (for the second time) after leading the Chicago Bulls to six NBA Championships in the previous 8 years.
- 2000 The Goodman Theatre opens its new $46 million theater complex in the Loop, completing the revitalization of a downtown theater district.

continues

decades later, Chicago had sufficiently recovered to host the 1893 World's Columbian Exposition commemorating the 400th anniversary of the discovery of America.

The Great Fire gave an unprecedented boost to the professional and artistic development of the nation's architects—drawn by the unlimited opportunities to build, they gravitated to the city in droves. And the city raised its own homegrown crop of architects. Chicago's deserved reputation as an American Athens, packed with monumental and decorative buildings, is a direct by-product of the disastrous fire that nearly brought the city to ruin.

2001 Chicago's second airport, Midway, opens a new $800 million terminal, attracting new airlines and giving travelers more options for Chicago flights.

2003 Millennium Park, Chicago's largest public works project in decades, rises at the north end of Grant Park. The centerpiece of the development is a modern, steel-sheathed band shell designed by famed architect Frank Gehry.

In the meantime, Chicago's population continued to grow as many immigrants forsook the uncultivated farmland of the prairie to join the city's labor pool. Chicago still shipped meat and agricultural commodities around the nation and the world, but the city itself was rapidly becoming a mighty industrial center in its own right, creating finished goods, particularly for the markets of the ever-expanding western settlements.

THE CRADLE OF TRADE UNIONISM

Chicago never seemed to outgrow its frontier rawness. Greed, profiteering, exploitation, and corruption were as critical to its growth as hard work, ingenuity, and civic pride. The spirit of reform arose most powerfully from the ranks of the working classes, whose lives were plagued by poverty and disease, despite the city's prosperity. When the sleeping giant of labor finally awakened in Chicago, it did so with a militancy and commitment that were to inspire the union movement throughout the nation.

By the 1890s, many of Chicago's workers were already organized into the American Federation of Labor. The Pullman Strike of 1894 united black and white railway workers for the first time in a common struggle for higher wages and workplace rights. The Industrial Workers of the World, or the Wobblies, which embraced for a time so many great voices of American labor—Eugene V. Debs, Big Bill Haywood, and Helen Gurley Flynn—was founded in Chicago in 1905.

AN AFRICAN-AMERICAN CAPITAL

The major change in Chicago in the 20th century, however, stems from the enormous growth of the city's African-American population. Coincident with the beginning of World War I, Chicago became the destination for thousands of blacks leaving Mississippi and other parts of the Deep South. Most settled on the South Side. With the exception of Hyde Park, which absorbed the black population into a successfully integrated, middle-class neighborhood, Chicago gained a reputation over the decades as the most segregated city in the United States. Today, although increased black representation in local politics and other institutions has eased some racial tensions, the city remains far more geographically segregated than most of its urban peers.

THE CHICAGO MACHINE

While Chicago was becoming a center of industry, transportation, and finance, and a beacon of labor reform, it was also becoming a powerhouse in national politics—again by virtue of its location. Between 1860 and 1968, Chicago was the site of 14 Republican and 10 Democratic presidential nominating conventions. (Some even point to the conventions as the source of Chicago's "Windy City" nickname, laying the blame on a politician who was full of hot air.) The first of the conventions gave the country one of its most admired leaders, Abraham Lincoln, while the 1968 convention was witness to the so-called Days of Rage, a police riot against demonstrators who had camped out in Grant Park to protest the Vietnam War. As TV cameras rolled, the demonstrators chanted, "The whole world is watching."

And it was; many politicos blame Mayor Richard J. Daley for Hubert Humphrey's defeat in the general election. (Maybe it was a wash; some also say that Daley stole the 1960 election for Kennedy.)

A few words about (the original) Mayor Daley: He did not invent the political machine, but he certainly perfected it. As Theodore White writes in *America in Search of Itself,* "Daley ran the machine with a tribal justice akin to the forest Gauls." Daley understood that as long as the leaders of every ethnic and special-interest group had their share of the spoils—the African Americans controlled the South Side, for example, and the Polish Americans kept their neighborhoods segregated—he could retain ultimate power. His reach extended well beyond Chicago's borders; he controlled members of Congress in Washington, and every 4 years he delivered a solid Democratic vote in the November elections. Since his death in 1976, the machine has never been the same. One election produced the city's first female mayor, Jane Byrne; another resulted in the city's first African-American mayor, Harold Washington. Neither was a novice at politics, but neither could hold the delicate balance of (often conflicting) groups that kept Daley in power for 20 years.

Today, Daley's son, Richard M., may have inherited his father's former office, but the estate did not include the Cook County machine. Mayor Richard M. Daley has abandoned his late father's power base of solid white working-class Bridgeport for the newly developed (some would say yuppie) Central Station neighborhood just south of the Loop. The middle-aged baby boomer appears to be finding himself, but many in the city still enjoy calling him—with more than a hint of condescension—"Richie."

The city has ongoing problems. With roughly 2.8 million people total, Chicago's black and white populations are almost equal in size—a rarity among today's urban areas—but the city's residential districts continue to be some of the most segregated in the country. Families are also trying to cope with the school system, which has been undergoing a major restructuring but whose outlook is still dismal. In 1995, the federal government seized control of the city's public housing, pledging to replace the dangerous high-rises with smaller complexes in mixed-income neighborhoods. It is a long-term goal, but authorities have been gradually tearing down the notorious apartment buildings of Cabrini Green, where then-Mayor Jane Byrne moved briefly to show her support for the crime-victimized residents.

2 The Politics of Clout

by Chris Serb

To understand Chicago, you must first take into account its two greatest passions: politics and sports. In this town, the two are often indistinguishable from each other. Forget Tammany Hall. More than any other city, Chicago has earned

Chicago & the Great Black Migration

From 1915 to 1960, hundreds of thousands of black Southerners poured into Chicago, trying to escape segregation and seeking economic freedom and opportunity. The so-called "Great Black Migration" radically transformed Chicago, both politically and culturally, from an Irish-run city of recent European immigrants into one in which no group had a majority and in which no politician—white or black—could ever take the black vote for granted. Unfortunately, the sudden change gave rise to many of the disparities that still plague the city, but it also promoted an environment in which many black men and women could rise from poverty to prominence.

From 1910 to 1920, Chicago's black population almost tripled, from 44,000 to 109,000; from 1920 to 1930, it more than doubled, to 234,000. The Great Depression slowed the migration to a crawl, with 278,000 blacks residing here in 1940. But the boom resumed when World War II revived the economy, causing the black population to skyrocket to 492,000 from 1940 to 1950. The postwar expansion and the decline of Southern sharecropping caused the black population to nearly double again, to 813,000, by 1960.

While jobs in the factories, steel mills, and stockyards paid much better than those in the cotton fields, Chicago was not the paradise that many blacks envisioned. Segregation was almost as bad here as it was down South, and most blacks were confined to a narrow "Black Belt" of overcrowded apartment buildings on the South Side. But the new migrants made the best of their situation, and for a time in the 1930s and 1940s, the Black Belt—dubbed "Bronzeville" or the "Black Metropolis" by the community's boosters—thrived as a cultural, musical, religious, and educational mecca, much as New York's Harlem did in the 1920s. As journalist and Great Migration historian Nicholas Lemann writes in *The Promised Land: The Great Black Migration and How It Changed America*, "Chicago was a city where a black person could be somebody."

Some of the Southern migrants who made names for themselves in Chicago included black separatist and Nation of Islam founder Elijah Muhammed; Robert S. Abbott, publisher of the powerful *Chicago Defender* newspaper, who launched a "Great Northern Drive" to bring blacks to the city in 1917; Ida B. Wells, the crusading journalist who headed an antilynching campaign; William Dawson, for many years the only black congressman; New Orleans–born jazz pioneers Jelly Roll Morton, King Oliver, and Louis Armstrong; *Native Son* author Richard

a reputation for machinations and shady dealings among its politicians. It has always been a city where "clout" rules. A place where any $40,000-a-year alderman can amass a million-dollar fortune by making a few key zoning changes. A place where a sewer worker's job is safe only if he delivers 200 registered Democrats to the polls each election day. A place where cops can pocket a couple hundred dollars a week by giving gamblers and prostitutes special "protection." A place where dead people regularly turn out to vote by the thousands.

Wright; John H. Johnson, publisher of *Ebony* and *Jet* magazines and one of Chicago's wealthiest residents; blues musicians Willie Dixon, Muddy Waters, and Howlin' Wolf; Thomas A. Dorsey, the "father of gospel music," and his greatest disciple, singer Mahalia Jackson; Robert Taylor, head of the Chicago Housing Authority, after whom the CHA's most notorious buildings are named; and Ralph Metcalfe, the Olympic gold-medalist sprinter who turned to politics once he got to Chicago, eventually succeeding Dawson in Congress.

When open housing legislation enabled blacks to live in any neighborhood, the flight of many Bronzeville residents to less crowded areas took a toll on the community. Through the 1950s, almost a third of the housing became vacant, and, by the 1960s, the great social experiment of urban renewal through wholesale land clearance and the creation of large tracts of public housing gutted this once-thriving neighborhood.

In recent years, however, community and civic leaders appear committed to restoring the neighborhood to a semblance of its former glory. Landmark status has been secured for several historic buildings in Bronzeville, including the Liberty Life/Supreme Insurance Company, 3501 S. King Dr., the first African American–owned insurance company in the northern United States, and the Eighth Regiment Armory, which, when completed in 1915, was the only armory in the United States controlled by an African-American regiment. The former home of the legendary Chess Records at 2120 S. Michigan Ave.—where Howlin' Wolf, Chuck Berry, and Bo Diddley gave birth to the blues and helped define rock 'n' roll—now houses a museum and music education center, **Blues Heaven Foundation** (✆ **312/808-1286**), set up by Willie Dixon's widow, Marie Dixon, with financial assistance from rock musician John Mellencamp. Along Dr. Martin Luther King Jr. Drive, between 24th and 35th streets, several public art installations now celebrate Bronzeville's heritage as well. The most poignant of them is sculptor Alison Saar's Great Northern Migration bronze monument, at King Drive and 26th Street, depicting a suitcase-toting African-American traveler standing atop a mound of worn shoe soles.

For tours of Bronzeville, contact the Chicago Office of Tourism's **Chicago Neighborhood Tours**, ✆ 312/742-1190; **Tour Black Chicago**, ✆ 312/332-2323; or the **Black Metropolis Convention and Tourism Council**, ✆ 773/548-2579.

"Chicago ain't ready for reform," once declared Alderman Paddy Bauler, a jolly, beer-drinking character who ran his ward office out of the back of a saloon during one of the city's more colorful political eras.

Bauler was speaking of the 1950s and 1960s, when Mayor Richard J. Daley's "Machine" Democrats had a stranglehold on the cops, the courts, the bribes, and, most important, the jobs. He could just as easily have been talking about 1999, when City Treasurer Miriam Santos was convicted of twisting businessmen's arms

Finds **Ethic Dining Near the Loop**

CHINATOWN

Chicago's Chinatown is about 20 blocks south of the Loop. The district is strung along two thoroughfares, Cermak Road and Wentworth Avenue as far south as 24th Place. Hailing a cab from the Loop is the easiest way to get here, but you can also drive and leave your car in the validated lot near the entrance to Chinatown or take the Orange Line of the El to the Cermak stop, a well-lit station on the edge of the Chinatown commercial district.

Chicago dining experts consistently praise affordable **Hong Min,** 221 W. Cermak Rd. (✆ **312/842-5026**), as one of the best Chinese restaurants in the city. The hot and sour soup gets raves, as do the noodle dishes and roast duck. If you can't decide what to get, opt for dim sum.

Penang, 2201 S. Wentworth Ave. (✆ **312/326-6888**), serves mostly Malaysian dishes, but some lean toward Indian and Chinese (they've even added a sushi bar, to complete the pan-Asian experience). Sink your teeth into the *kambing rendang* (lamb curry in 11 spices) or the barbecued stingray wrapped in a banana leaf.

The spacious, casually elegant **Phoenix,** 2131 S. Archer Ave. (✆ **312/328-0848**), has plenty of room for big tables of family or friends to enjoy the Cantonese (and some Szechwan) cuisine. A good sign: The place attracts lots of Chinatown locals. It's especially popular for dim sum brunch, so come early to avoid the wait.

The eclectic menu at **Saigon Vietnamese Restaurant,** 232 W. Cermak Rd. (✆ **312/808-1318**), doesn't include as many authentic Vietnamese dishes as one might want. The spring rolls are Vietnamese style, though, and go down nicely with a bottle of Chinese beer. A popular dish is shabu shabu, a kind of Japanese fondue in which you construct a soup: To a steaming bowl of hot broth, you add the shrimp, fish, and veggies.

In this mezzanine-level dining room of **Won Kow,** 2237 S. Wentworth Ave. (✆ **312/842-7500**), you can enjoy dim sum from 9am to 3pm daily. Most of the items cost between $1.50 and $2 an order. Other house specialties include Mongolian chicken and duck with seafood.

LITTLE ITALY

Convenient to most downtown locations, a few blocks' stretch of Taylor Street is home to a host of time-honored, traditional, hearty Italian restaurants. If you're staying in the Loop (an easy cab ride away), the area makes a good destination for dinner.

Regulars keep coming back for the straightforward Italian favorites livened up with some adventurous specials at **Francesca's on Taylor,** 1400 W. Taylor St. (✆ **312/829-2828**). I recommend the fish specials above the standard meat dishes. Other standouts include eggplant ravioli in a four-cheese sauce with a touch of tomato sauce and shaved parmigiano, as well as sautéed veal medallions with porcini mushrooms in cream sauce. (This is part of a local chain that includes the popular Mia Francesca, p. 154.)

Expect to wait well beyond the time of your reservation at **Rosebud on Taylor,** 1500 W. Taylor St. (✆ **312/942-1117**), but fear not—your hunger will be satisfied. Rosebud is known for enormous helpings of pasta, most of which lean toward heavy Italian-American favorites: deep-dish lasagna and fettuccine Alfredo that defines the word *rich*. But I highly recommend any of the pastas served with vodka sauce. A newer location is near the Mag Mile at 720 N. Rush St. (✆ **312/266-6444**).

Tuscany, 1014 W. Taylor St. (✆ **312/829-1990**), is one of the most reliable Italian restaurants on Taylor Street. In contrast to the city's more fashionable Italian spots, family-owned Tuscany has the comfortable feel of a neighborhood restaurant. The menu features large portions of Tuscan pastas, pizzas, veal, chicken, and a risotto of the day. Specialties include anything cooked on the wood-burning grill and Tuscan sausage dishes. A second location is across from Wrigley Field at 3700 N. Clark St. (✆ **773/404-7700**).

GREEKTOWN

A short cab ride across the south branch of the Chicago River will take you to the city's Greektown, a row of moderately priced and inexpensive Greek restaurants clustered on Halsted Street between Van Buren and Washington streets.

To be honest, there's not much here to distinguish one restaurant from the other: They're all standard Greek restaurants with similar looks and similar menus. That said, **Greek Islands,** 200 S. Halsted St. (✆ **312/782-9855**); **Santorini,** 800 W. Adams St., at Halsted Street (✆ **312/829-8820**); **Parthenon,** 314 S. Halsted St. (✆ **312/726-2407**); and **Costas,** 340 S. Halsted St. (✆ **312/263-0767**), are all good bets for gyros, Greek salads, shish kebabs, and the classic moussaka. On warm summer nights, opt for either **Athena,** 212 S. Halsted St. (✆ **312/655-0000**), which has a huge outdoor seating area, or **Pegasus,** 130 S. Halsted St. (✆ **312/226-3377**), with its rooftop patio serving drinks, appetizers, and desserts. Both have incredible views of the Loop's skyline. **Artopolis,** 306 S. Halsted St. (✆ **312/559-9000**), a recent addition to the neighborhood, is a casual option offering up tasty Greek and Mediterranean specialties, wood-oven pizzas, and wonderful breads and French pastries.

PILSEN

Just south of the Loop and convenient to McCormick Place and China-town, Pilsen is a colorful blend of Mexican culture, artists and bohemians, and pricey new residential developments. The area's nascent restaurant scene is showing signs of life, but, for now, the local fare is decidedly casual.

Nuevo Leon, 1515 W. 18th St. (✆ **312/421-1517**), is a popular Mexican restaurant, serving the standard offerings. Across the street, **Playa Azul,** 1514 W. 18th St. (✆ **312/421-2552**), serves authentic Mexican seafood dishes, favorites being the salads and soups.

On the more bohemian side, linger over coffee and eggs at **Bic's Hardware Café,** 1733 S. Halsted St. (✆ **312/850-2884**), or a salad, sandwich, or refreshing fruit milkshake *(liquado)* at the **Café Jumping Bean,** 1439 W. 18th St. (✆ **312/455-0019**).

for political "donations" from her City Hall office. (She was later retried on the same charges and exonerated, and she waltzed right back into her office, much to the chagrin of Mayor Richard M. Daley.)

Corruption was nothing new to the Windy City, even in Bauler's day. Turn-of-the-20th-century First Ward bosses Michael "Hinky Dink" Kenna and "Bath-house" John Coughlin put the organization in "organized" crime by collecting fees from the gambling and prostitution houses. During Prohibition, Mayor William "Big Bill" Thompson and his Republican Machine made a fortune in bribes from Al Capone and his bootleggers—and, in the process, Big Bill disillusioned the voters so much that the GOP hasn't won the mayor's office in the 70 years since then.

Until the 1970s, however, being on the take was not only profitable business, but it also was safe: Cops and precinct workers and lesser public servants might have done a little time in jail, but the big fish were never caught. U.S. Attorney Jim Thompson changed all that, winning convictions against Gov. Otto Kerner, who took a racetrack bribe; Alderman Paul Wigoda, who took payoffs in return for zoning changes; and the elder Daley's top lieutenant, Alderman Tom Keane, who found out where the city wanted to build parks or schools or housing projects, bought the land, and then sold it back to the city at inflated prices. By trying—and winning—so many high-profile cases, the Republican Thompson swept right into the governor's mansion and left the squeaky-clean U.S. Attorney's office and the FBI trying to match his record. So far, they've done a good job, winning convictions against almost 50 aldermen and key city officials in the past 25 years.

Large-scale corruption investigations include "Operation Silver Shovel," which nabbed six aldermen (including the once-saintly Lawrence Bloom) for taking bribes connected to an illegal construction-debris dumping site; "Operation Haunted Hall," which trapped several city officials paying friends and relatives full salaries for jobs that didn't exist; "Operation Incubator," which convicted 15 aldermen, city officials, and businessmen in a city-hall bribery sting; and, the granddaddy of them all, "Operation Greylord," where after hearing reports that defendants in Cook County courts were bribing judges, the FBI and local police officials set up phony robberies and drunk-driving cases, then secretly taped judges and other courthouse staff accepting payments to make the charges disappear. In all, more than 50 lawyers and 15 judges were sent to jail—and there was nobody they could pay to make those charges go away.

Other scandals, wrapping up only one or two politicians at a time, might have been smaller in scope but have had just as high a profile. Chicago-based Congressmen Dan Rostenkowski and Mel Reynolds did hard time, respectively, for skimming Congressional office funds and for having sex with a 15-year-old campaign worker. Mayor Daley's top lieutenant, Alderman Pat Huels, used his city position to drum up business for his security firm and was later forced to resign. Even "reform mayor" Harold Washington, an alleged ghost payroller himself during his early days in politics, once went to jail for repeatedly failing to file his income taxes.

The voters forgave Harold for his ethical lapses, although they almost didn't forgive him for the ethnical "lapse" of being black. White voters and aldermen and city workers were afraid that Washington would seize the clout that had always belonged to them and take the jobs, city contracts, and key political appointments that went with the clout. And, of course, that's what Harold did.

Race shouldn't have played much of an issue, though. Washington was just following a time-honored Chicago tradition. He was doing for the black community what Kenna and Coughlin and the original Daley had done for the Irish, what Fred Roti and Anthony Laurino had done for the Italians, what Jacob Arvey had done for the Jews, what Rostenkowski and Roman Pucinski did for the Poles. Harold simply stuck his hand out and recited the city's unofficial motto, *"Ubi est mea?"*—"Where is mine?" Paddy Bauler would've been proud.

Index

See also Accommodations and Restaurant indexes, below.

Frommer's®

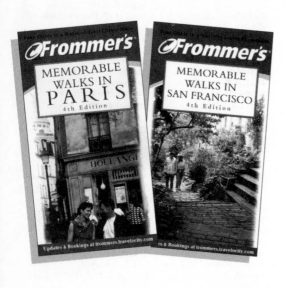

FROMMER'S® COMPLETE TRAVEL GUIDES

Alaska
Alaska Cruises & Ports of Call
Amsterdam
Argentina & Chile
Arizona
Atlanta
Australia
Austria
Bahamas
Barcelona, Madrid & Seville
Beijing
Belgium, Holland & Luxembourg
Bermuda
Boston
Brazil
British Columbia & the Canadian
  Rockies
Brussels & Bruges
Budapest & the Best of Hungary
California
Canada
Cancún, Cozumel & the Yucatán
Cape Cod, Nantucket & Martha's
  Vineyard
Caribbean
Caribbean Cruises & Ports of Call
Caribbean Ports of Call
Carolinas & Georgia
Chicago
China
Colorado
Costa Rica
Cuba
Denmark
Denver, Boulder & Colorado Springs
England
Europe
European Cruises & Ports of Call

Florida
France
Germany
Great Britain
Greece
Greek Islands
Hawaii
Hong Kong
Honolulu, Waikiki & Oahu
Ireland
Israel
Italy
Jamaica
Japan
Las Vegas
London
Los Angeles
Maryland & Delaware
Maui
Mexico
Montana & Wyoming
Montréal & Québec City
Munich & the Bavarian Alps
Nashville & Memphis
New England
New Mexico
New Orleans
New York City
New Zealand
Northern Italy
Norway
Nova Scotia, New Brunswick &
  Prince Edward Island
Oregon
Paris
Peru
Philadelphia & the Amish Country
Portugal

Prague & the Best of the Czech
  Republic
Provence & the Riviera
Puerto Rico
Rome
San Antonio & Austin
San Diego
San Francisco
Santa Fe, Taos & Albuquerque
Scandinavia
Scotland
Seattle & Portland
Shanghai
Sicily
Singapore & Malaysia
South Africa
South America
South Florida
South Pacific
Southeast Asia
Spain
Sweden
Switzerland
Texas
Thailand
Tokyo
Toronto
Tuscany & Umbria
USA
Utah
Vancouver & Victoria
Vermont, New Hampshire & Maine
Vienna & the Danube Valley
Virgin Islands
Virginia
Walt Disney World® & Orlando
Washington, D.C.
Washington State

FROMMER'S® DOLLAR-A-DAY GUIDES

Australia from $50 a Day
California from $70 a Day
England from $75 a Day
Europe from $70 a Day
Florida from $70 a Day
Hawaii from $80 a Day

Ireland from $60 a Day
Italy from $70 a Day
London from $85 a Day
New York from $90 a Day
Paris from $80 a Day

San Francisco from $70 a Day
Washington, D.C. from $80 a Day
Portable London from $85 a Day
Portable New York City from $90
  a Day

FROMMER'S® PORTABLE GUIDES

Acapulco, Ixtapa & Zihuatanejo
Amsterdam
Aruba
Australia's Great Barrier Reef
Bahamas
Berlin
Big Island of Hawaii
Boston
California Wine Country
Cancún
Cayman Islands
Charleston
Chicago
Disneyland®
Dublin
Florence

Frankfurt
Hong Kong
Houston
Las Vegas
Las Vegas for Non-Gamblers
London
Los Angeles
Los Cabos & Baja
Maine Coast
Maui
Miami
Nantucket & Martha's Vineyard
New Orleans
New York City
Paris
Phoenix & Scottsdale

Portland
Puerto Rico
Puerto Vallarta, Manzanillo &
  Guadalajara
Rio de Janeiro
San Diego
San Francisco
Savannah
Seattle
Sydney
Tampa & St. Petersburg
Vancouver
Venice
Virgin Islands
Washington, D.C.

FROMMER'S® NATIONAL PARK GUIDES

Banff & Jasper
Family Vacations in the National
  Parks

Grand Canyon
National Parks of the American West
Rocky Mountain

Yellowstone & Grand Teton
Yosemite & Sequoia/Kings Canyon
Zion & Bryce Canyon

FROMMER'S® MEMORABLE WALKS

Chicago
London

New York
Paris

San Francisco

FROMMER'S® WITH KIDS GUIDES

Chicago
Las Vegas
New York City

Ottawa
San Francisco
Toronto

Vancouver
Washington, D.C.

SUZY GERSHMAN'S BORN TO SHOP GUIDES

Born to Shop: France
Born to Shop: Hong Kong,
   Shanghai & Beijing

Born to Shop: Italy
Born to Shop: London

Born to Shop: New York
Born to Shop: Paris

FROMMER'S® IRREVERENT GUIDES

Amsterdam
Boston
Chicago
Las Vegas
London

Los Angeles
Manhattan
New Orleans
Paris
Rome

San Francisco
Seattle & Portland
Vancouver
Walt Disney World®
Washington, D.C.

FROMMER'S® BEST-LOVED DRIVING TOURS

Britain
California
Florida
France

Germany
Ireland
Italy
New England

Northern Italy
Scotland
Spain
Tuscany & Umbria

HANGING OUT™ GUIDES

Hanging Out in England
Hanging Out in Europe

Hanging Out in France
Hanging Out in Ireland

Hanging Out in Italy
Hanging Out in Spain

THE UNOFFICIAL GUIDES®

Bed & Breakfasts and Country
   Inns in:
   California
   Great Lakes States
   Mid-Atlantic
   New England
   Northwest
   Rockies
   Southeast
   Southwest
Best RV & Tent Campgrounds in:
   California & the West
   Florida & the Southeast
   Great Lakes States
   Mid-Atlantic
   Northeast
   Northwest & Central Plains

   Southwest & South Central
      Plains
   U.S.A.
Beyond Disney
Branson, Missouri
California with Kids
Central Italy
Chicago
Cruises
Disneyland®
Florida with Kids
Golf Vacations in the Eastern U.S.
Great Smoky & Blue Ridge Region
Inside Disney
Hawaii
Las Vegas
London
Maui

Mexio's Best Beach Resorts
Mid-Atlantic with Kids
Mini Las Vegas
Mini-Mickey
New England & New York with
   Kids
New Orleans
New York City
Paris
San Francisco
Skiing & Snowboarding in the West
Southeast with Kids
Walt Disney World®
Walt Disney World® for
   Grown-ups
Walt Disney World® with Kids
Washington, D.C.
World's Best Diving Vacations

SPECIAL-INTEREST TITLES

Frommer's Adventure Guide to Australia &
   New Zealand
Frommer's Adventure Guide to Central America
Frommer's Adventure Guide to India & Pakistan
Frommer's Adventure Guide to South America
Frommer's Adventure Guide to Southeast Asia
Frommer's Adventure Guide to Southern Africa
Frommer's Britain's Best Bed & Breakfasts and
   Country Inns
Frommer's Caribbean Hideaways
Frommer's Exploring America by RV
Frommer's Fly Safe, Fly Smart

Frommer's France's Best Bed & Breakfasts and
   Country Inns
Frommer's Gay & Lesbian Europe
Frommer's Italy's Best Bed & Breakfasts and
   Country Inns
Frommer's Road Atlas Britain
Frommer's Road Atlas Europe
Frommer's Road Atlas France
The New York Times' Guide to Unforgettable
   Weekends
Places Rated Almanac
Retirement Places Rated
Rome Past & Present

Booked aisle seat.

Reserved room with a view.

With a queen – no, make that a king-size bed.

th Travelocity, you can book your flights and hotels together, so
u can get even better deals than if you booked them separately.
u'll save time and money without compromising the quality of your
o. Choose your airline seat, search for alternate airports, pick your
tel room type, even choose the neighborhood you'd like to stay in.

Travelocity

**Visit www.travelocity.com
or call 1-888-TRAVELOCITY**

Fly.
Sleep.
Save.

Now you can book your flights and
hotels together, so you can get even better deals
than if you booked them separately.

Travelocity
**Visit www.travelocity.com
or call 1-888-TRAVELOCITY**